THE CONFLICT OF TRIBE AND STATE
IN IRAN AND AFGHANISTAN

The Conflict
of Tribe and State
in Iran and Afghanistan

Edited by

RICHARD TAPPER

CROOM HELM
London & Canberra
ST. MARTIN'S PRESS
New York

© 1983 R. Tapper
Croom Helm Ltd, Provident House, Burrell Row,
Beckenham, Kent BR3 1AT

British Library Cataloguing in Publication Data

The Conflict of tribe and state in Iran and
    Afghanistan.
    1. Iran––History
    2. Afghanistan––History
    I. Tapper, Richard
    955   DS295

    ISBN 0–7099–2440–2

Library of Congress Cataloging in Publication Data
Main entry under title:

The Conflict of tribe and state in Iran and Afghanistan.

    Based on papers from a conference held at the Scool
of Oriental and African Studies in London, July, 1979.
    Includes bibliographical references and index.
    1. Tribes and tribal system––Iran––Congresses.
2. Tribes and tribal system––Afghanistan––Congresses.
3. Iran––Social life and customs––Congresses. 4. Iran––
Politics and government––Congresses. 5. Afghanistan––
Social life and customs––Congresses. 6. Afghanistan––
Politics and government––Congresses. I. Tapper, Richard.
DS58.C66   1983   305.8'00955   83–3112
ISBN 0–312–16232–4 (St. Martin's)

Printed in Great Britain
by Billing & Son Ltd, Worcester

CONTENTS

Contents

Contents

Contents

Contents

LIST OF MAPS

LIST OF ABBREVIATIONS USED IN NOTES

AA - American Anthropologist
AE - American Ethnologist
Annales - Annales: Economies, Sociétés, Civilisations
AQ - Anthropological Quarterly
AUFS Reports - American Universities Field Staff
    Reports (Hanover, NH)
BSOAS - Bulletin of the School of Oriental and
    African Studies
EI - Encyclopedia of Islam
FO - Foreign Office Records, Public Record Office,
    London
IJMES - International Journal of Middle East Studies
IOL - India Office Library and Records, London
IS - Iranian Studies
JRAI - Journal of the Royal Anthropological Institute
JRCAS - Journal of the Royal Central Asian Society
JRGS - Journal of the Royal Geographical Society
LPS - L/P&S, Political and Secret Department, India
    Office Records
MEJ - Middle East Journal
MERIP Reports - Middle East Research and Information
    Project Reports
MIDCC - M. Bonine and N. Keddie (eds.), Modern Iran:
    The Dialectics of Continuity and Change (SUNY
    Press, Albany, 1981)
PPS - Equipe Ecologie et Anthropologie des Sociétés
    Pastorales (eds.), Pastoral Production and
    Society (Maison des Sciences de l'Homme, Paris/
    Cambridge University Press, 1979)
ZKORGO - Zapiski Kavkazskago Otdela Imperatorskago
    Russkago Geograficheskago Obshchestva

PREFACE

In 1978 and 1979, revolutions in Afghanistan and Iran marked a shift in the balance of power in South West Asia and the world. Since then, indeed, events in both countries have regularly dominated the media. Shaken by Khumeyni's overthrow of the Shah and the Soviet occupation of Afghanistan, the world has once more been made aware that tribalism is no anachronism in a struggle for political and cultural self-determination. In both countries there has been the sort of tribal resurgence that so often in the past accompanied political upheavals such as they are now experiencing.

The Shah of Iran, miscalculating the strength of opposition to the secularism, excesses and western orientation of his regime, fell, with a suddenness and completeness that confounded the predictions of almost all the experts, to a genuine popular revolution led by the remarkable Ayatullah Khumeyni. In Afghanistan, where a palace revolution in 1973 had replaced the 200-year-old Durrani monarchy with a Republic headed by the last King's cousin, the government was unable or unwilling to put into effect its programme of reform, but here too the socialist military coup in March 1978 came sooner than expected by most experts, who also failed to predict the scale of the subsequent Soviet military intervention at the end of 1979.

By 1980 both revolutions were in trouble. The Taraki and Amin governments had not merely failed to win popular support in Afghanistan but rather managed to alienate it, while the Soviet forces and their puppet Karmal seemed unlikely to be able, by any means short of genocide, to defeat the nationalist insurgency, widely supported in the country especially by Islamic and tribal elements. In Iran the fundamentalist leaders, though continuing to inspire

fanatical loyalties, no longer had the support of
all the disparate elements that once united behind
them. A major problem for the Islamic Republic was
the resistance on the part of regional, ethnic and
tribal minorities. Within the country, substantial
numbers of pastoral nomads settled over the last
decades have now resumed their former way of life,
and tribal leaders long used to exile in the West
have been welcomed back.

It has been difficult for observers, whether
interested laymen or supposed experts on the area,
to evaluate reports from the two countries. The
main obstacle has been lack of reliable information,
particularly on current events and aspirations in
the rural and tribal areas, and on the anthropological and historical background to the present crisis.
This volume is intended to go some way towards fulfilling the second of these needs. It is based on a
series of papers delivered at a conference held at
the School of Oriental and African Studies in London
in July 1979. The conference was in fact planned
as early as 1977, when the convenors (Richard Tapper
of SOAS and David Brooks of Durham) felt that in
view of the considerable amount of research that had
been done over the last two decades on the ethnography and history of the tribes of Iran and Afghanistan in the nineteenth and twentieth centuries, the
time was now ripe for stock-taking and generalisation, and an attempt at systematic comparison within
a historical perspective, both between Afghanistan
and Iran and also with other areas of the world.

By the time of the conference, the topic had
acquired added interest and contemporary relevance.
Most of the papers were circulated in advance, and
some useful and wide-ranging discussions took place.
Participants - anthropologists and historians of
many persuasions - came from various countries of
Europe and North America, but a major disappointment
was that the same political developments in Iran and
Afghanistan which made the conference so topical
also prevented the attendance of several scholars
from both countries who had been invited, though
there were valuable contributions to the conference
discussions from some of their compatriots resident
in Britain. Since then, the papers have been
revised to take account of the discussions, of the
central focus suggested by the editor, and of more
recent developments. A few papers presented at the
conference have been withdrawn, and their place
taken by others written since.

The main concern of the volume is not an analy-

sis of the causes and courses of the revolutions
themselves, nor of the sparse information available
on tribal involvement - though some of this is examined in several chapters. It is rather to provide
historical and anthropological perspectives necessary
to the eventual understanding of the events surrounding the revolutions. Nor does the volume offer a
single hypothesis or approach, but rather combines
different approaches to a single theme, explored in
a variety of contexts. It is maintained that, despite the spate of publications that have already
appeared purporting to explain the revolutions, complete and credible analyses will anyway have to await
further documentation of the motives and actions of a
rather wider spectrum of society in both countries
than has so far been represented. The volume, finally, pretends neither to a complete coverage of the
topics addressed, nor to complete representation of
experts on those topics - several well-known authorities are not included, though their works figure
prominently in the volume through citation and reference.

Thanks are particularly due to the Social
Science Research Council (UK), and to SOAS, for
jointly and generously sponsoring the conference on
which this book is based. The contributors to the
book owe much to the other participants in the conference, especially Asger Christensen, Klaus
Ferdinand, Alfred Janata, Nikki Keddie, Ann Lambton,
David Marsden, David Morgan, André Singer and Susan
Wright. The editor would like to acknowledge the
promptness with which the other contributors, in
spite of pressing commitments, responded to his communications, and to thank especially his fellow-
convenor David Brooks for help and advice in planning
and organising the conference. He is also grateful
to the following: to Michael Strange, Keith McLachlan,
Sarah Ladbury and Hugh Beattie for assistance during
and after the conference; to the Editorial Board of
the SOAS Bulletin for permission to republish chapter 7; and to Cambridge University Press for permission to make use of material to be published in
Volume 7 of the Cambridge History of Iran. Unpublished Crown Copyright material in Public Record Office
and the India Office Records reproduced in this book
appears by kind permission of the Controller of Her
Majesty's Stationery Office.

The book, finally, owes a great deal to the
help and encouragement of Ernest Gellner and Andrew
Strathern, who brought vital and stimulating non-
regional perspectives to the conference and have

Preface

written the two concluding chapters. Neither they
nor the other contributors saw the editor's
Introduction (the last chapter to be written) before
submitting their own final drafts. The editor is
responsible for the final condition of the book,
including the system of transliteration.

SOAS, London   Richard Tapper

A NOTE ON TRANSLITERATION AND USAGE

The system of transliteration used is a compromise
between the demands of consistency, convention, simplicity, literacy and closeness to spoken language.
There exists no one conventional system adequate for
both Iranian and Afghan Persian, let alone also for
Kurdish, Azarbayjani Turkish, Luri, Baluchi, and the
Pashto dialects represented here. For simplicity,
and since linguistic questions are not crucial in
this book, both hamzeh and ᶜayn and all diacritical
marks are omitted in the text; without them, linguistically expert readers will still easily recognise
names and terms; others will not miss them.
      The following system is employed: the letters
a, i, u, represent both long and short vowels in
Iranian Persian, supplemented by e, a long vowel in
some non-Persian names and words (as in Gardez, khel,
el), and by o, used as is conventional for the long
u in some Afghan Persian, Pashto and Kurdish words
(as in Dost, Pashto, kor, Simko). The letter a is
also used for the Pashto sound sometimes elsewhere
transliterated u (as in Pashto, mashar). The final
eh of Iranian Persian words is transliterated a in
many Afghan words (hamsaya, Painda, for example).
Among diphthongs, ai represents two distinct vowels,
separated in writing by ᶜayn or hamzeh; ay (pronounced as in English 'high'), ey (as in 'hey!'), and
oy (as in 'ahoy!') are diphthongs, as is ou (pronounced in Iran as in English 'home', in Afghanistan
as in 'house'). The glottal plosive q is transliterated k in some Afghan names (e.g. Kandahar). The
other consonants are more or less as in English,
with the following combinations: ch as in 'church',
sh as in 'sheep' (except in Ishaq, where the s and h
are separate), kh as Scottish ch, gh as Parisian r.
Some proper names (e.g. Herat, Tehran, Khyber) are
left as familiar in English.

In this volume, through no conviction but conforming with current usage, 'Iran' is used for the country sometimes known as 'Persia', and 'Iranian' for a citizen of Iran, with no ethnic connotations. 'Persian' is used for the language spoken as first or second tongue by most people in both Iran and Afghanistan; in both countries Persian is called farsi, though in Afghanistan it is known officially as dari. There are numerous dialects of spoken Persian in both countries, though the written language is virtually uniform. 'Persians' will be used for those Iranians for whom Persian is first language. 'Afghan' is used, as is conventional, for citizens of Afghanistan; local usage is different: for most people in Afghanistan and Pakistan 'Afghan' ('Oughan') denotes speakers of the Pashto (Pakhto, Pushtu, Pukhtu, etc.) language (often also called 'Afghani'), perhaps half the population of Afghanistan, who are here termed 'Pathans', 'Pashtuns' or 'Pakhtuns' (otherwise Pukhtun, Pushtun).

The plural s is used for larger linguistic/ethnic categories: Turks, Turkmens, Pathans (Pashtuns, etc), Kurds, Lurs, Baluches, Uzbeks, Aymaqs, Hazaras, Tajiks, Nuristanis; and for ruling dynasties; but not for other explicitly unified political groups or sub-divisions of any of the above.

No apologies are made for the use of terms such as 'Persian' (for the language or its speakers) or 'Pathan' (for speakers of Pashto). The misconceived pedantry that insists that English adopt some approximation to indigenous equivalents (Farsi, Dari, Pukhtun) ignores the fact that neither is English accustomed to do the same to French, German or any other more familiar languages or nationalities, nor does it insist that Iranians or Afghans (or anybody else) do the same for English.

THE CONTRIBUTORS

AKBAR S AHMED: formerly Political Agent in various
NWFP districts; ethnographic research among Mohmand
and others; author of Religion and Politics in Muslim
Society: Order and Conflict in Pakistan (Cambridge,
forthcoming), Pukhtun Economy and Society (Routledge,
1980) and other books on tribal society in Pakistan.

JON W ANDERSON: Alexander von Homboldt Research
Fellow, Südasien-Institut, Heidelberg; ethnographic
research among Ghilzai; author of forthcoming book,
Doing Pakhtu, on Ghilzai social organisation.

LOIS G BECK: Dept. of Anthropology, Washington
University (St Louis); ethnographic research on
Qashqai; co-editor of Women in the Muslim World
(Harvard, 1978), author of forthcoming book Tribe
and State: the Qashqai and Iran.

DAVID BROOKS: Dept. of Anthropology, University of
Durham; ethnographic and historical research on
Bakhtiari; author of forthcoming book on Bakhtiari
performative ritual.

MARTIN VAN BRUINESSEN: ethnographic and historical
research on Kurdistan; author of Agha, Shaikh and
State: on the Social Organization of Kurdistan
(Utrecht, 1978).

JEAN-PIERRE DIGARD: CNRS, Paris; ethnographic research on Bakhtiari; author of Techniques des nomades
baxtyâri d'Iran (Cambridge/Paris, 1981).

GENE R GARTHWAITE: Dept. of History, Dartmouth College;
historical research on Bakhtiari; author of Khans
and Shahs: a Documentary Analysis of the Bakhtiari
in Iran (Cambridge, 1983).

The Contributors

ERNEST GELLNER: Dept. of Philosophy, Logic and
Scientific Method, London School of Economics,
author of Saints of the Atlas (Weidenfeld and
Nicolson, 1969), Muslim Society (Cambridge, 1981)
and numerous other books on philosophy.

BERNT GLATZER: Representative in Pakistan of
Südasien-Institut, Heidelberg University; ethno-
graphic research in western Afghanistan; author of
Nomaden von Gharjistan (Steiner, 1977).

ROB HAGER: international lawyer, Washington, D.C.;
worked with UNDP in Afghanistan; research at SOAS
on Afghanistan and international law.

PHILIP CARL SALZMAN: Dept. of Anthropology, McGill
University; Chairman, IUAES Commission on Nomadic
Peoples; ethnographic research in Iranian Baluchistan; editor of When Nomads Settle (Bergin, 1980)
and other volumes on pastoral nomads.

ANDREW STRATHERN: Director, Institute of Papua New
Guinea Studies; also, Dept. of Anthropology, University College, London; author of The Rope of Moka
(Cambridge 1971) and other books on New Guinea
people.

NANCY TAPPER: Dept. of History and Philosophy of
Religion, Kings College, London; ethnography of
Shahsevan women, ethnography and history of Durrani
and others in northern Afghanistan; author of
articles on women, marriage, religion and ritual in
Middle Eastern Society.

RICHARD TAPPER: Dept. of Anthropology and Sociology,
SOAS, London; ethnography and history of Shahsevan
of Iran, and peoples (especially Durrani) of north-
central Afghanistan; author of Pasture and Politics
(Academic Press, 1979).

MALCOLM YAPP: Dept. of History, SOAS, London;
author of Strategies of British India (Oxford, 1980)
and other books and articles on Middle Eastern and
South Asian history.

THE CONFLICT OF TRIBE AND STATE
IN IRAN ADN AFGHANISTAN

Chapter 1
INTRODUCTION

Richard Tapper

The Scope of the Volume

The notion of 'tribe' is notoriously vague. For
some, 'tribes' are what anthropologists study, for
others a 'tribe' is a very specific form of economic
and political group. In fact the term has been used
in such a variety of ways in social anthropology, as
in other fields, that, as with 'race' in physical
anthropology, it has almost ceased to be of analytical or comparative value. The issues are conceptual,
terminological, and to some extent methodological.
Can we talk of 'tribal society' as a particular
stage of social evolution? Is 'tribal culture' an
identifiable complex? Are 'tribes' groups with particular features and functions? Are they found at
particular levels in a political structure? How far
can 'tribes' or 'tribal groups' be analysed in isolation from wider political, economic and cultural
contexts? Are 'tribes' the creation of states? Is
it useful to contrast 'tribal' with 'peasant'
society? Or 'tribalism' with 'feudalism', or with
'ethnicity'? Or 'tribe' with 'clan' or 'lineage' or
'state'? Is 'tribe' merely a state of mind?[1]
    Such questions are not merely academic. They
are live political issues in many countries of the
world, and in many cases, ignoring or sometimes
deliberately exploiting the ambiguities of the
notion of 'tribe', states adopt unfortunate and
often disastrous policies towards their 'tribal'
populations.
    The following chapters tackle some of these
questions as they affect two particular states, Iran
and Afghanistan, in whose provincial and national
history up to the present day 'tribes' and 'tribalism' have always played a prominent part. The
relation of tribe and state emerges as two clearly

1

Introduction

MAP 1:   *Sketch-map of Iran and Afghanistan, to show places mentioned in chapter 1, with approximate tribal locations in the nineteenth century*

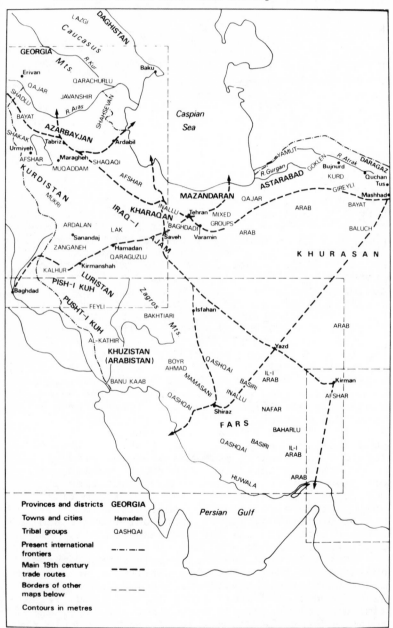

MAP 1, continued

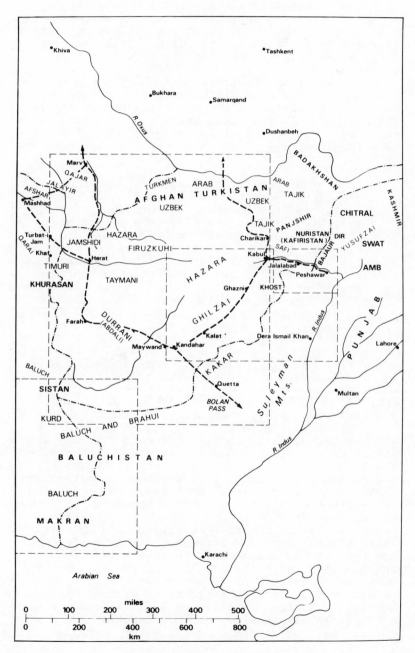

distinct but closely linked issues: the first is the
relation of specific tribal groups with specific
states as empirical political forces; the second is
more general, and shades into the classic oppositions
in the history of social philosophy, such as community and society, kinship and territory, status and
contract.

Tribal groups in Iran and Afghanistan are conventionally viewed as historically inveterate opponents of the state. They were notorious as makers
and breakers of dynasties, while both countries were
ruled by dynasties of tribal origins until the
twentieth century. Some years ago, Lambton observed
of Iran,

> Control of the tribal element has been and is
> one of the perennial problems of government ...
> All except the strongest governments have
> delegated responsibility in the tribal areas
> to the tribal chiefs. One aspect of Persian
> history is that of a struggle between the
> tribal element and the non-tribal element,
> a struggle which has continued in a modified
> form down to the present day. Various Persian
> dynasties have come to power on tribal support.
> In almost all cases the tribes have proved an
> unstable basis on which to build the future
> of the country.[2]

These remarks apply, though in very different ways,
to both Afghanistan and Iran, and in different ways
to the various tribal groups within each. They
apply of course to much of the Middle East, where
'tribes' have never, in historical times, been isolated groups of 'primitives', remote from contact
with states or their agents, but rather tribes and
states have created and maintained each other as a
single system, though one of inherent instability.
The reason for a comparative focus here on Iran and
Afghanistan is not merely that these two countries
are currently undergoing radical upheaval - nor that
the editor happens to have made a study of tribal
groups in both - but that historical and cultural
links between them and between their tribal groups
are broader and deeper than between either country
and any other of their neighbours. This is not to
deny the importance of links between tribal and
ethnic groups across the frontiers of Iran with
Turkey, Iraq, the Soviet Union and Pakistan, or of
Afghanistan with the Soviet Union, Pakistan and even
China, which are referred to in several chapters.

Nor is the historical period 1800-1980 chosen arbitrarily. By 1800, the Durranis and the Qajars, the last major tribal dynasties to rule each country, were in power, though shifts between the Sadozai and Barakzai branches of the Durranis were still to take place. Both dynasties survived until the twentieth century, at once because of and in spite of the Great Power rivalries which led to the end of independence and the apparent decline of tribalism in each country. The renewed, albeit changed importance of tribalism in the early 1980s needs no further comment at this stage. To have extended the historical baseline for the book back into the eighteenth century would have called for consideration of the rise of the Durranis and Qajars to power, and of their transformation from tribal chiefdoms into ruling dynasties. Although avoiding such important problems, subject perhaps for another book but beyond the scope of this one, several chapters do consider to what extent and in what senses the organisation and structure of the state in nineteenth century Afghanistan or Iran were permeated by the 'tribalism' of the ruling group.

The social, ecological, economic and other bases of the 'tribal problem' are considered in depth in this book, as is the role of the tribes and their leaders as actors and agents in the Great Game of Asia during the nineteenth and twentieth centuries. But if the states involved were preoccupied by a 'tribal problem', the tribes could be said to have had a perennial 'state problem'; none was ever, at least during recent centuries, totally unaffected by any state. Another major theme of this book is an assessment of this 'state problem', that is the role of states in creating, transforming, or destroying tribal institutions and structures.

In considering the degree to which the differential impact of states and their policies can explain the variety of economic, social, and political forms evident among the tribes of Iran and Afghanistan, contributors to this book insist on the necessity for a multi-causal explanation. Several chapters, accepting that there can be no example of a 'pure' tribal society in these countries, seek to elicit the essence of 'tribe' by distinguishing 'internal' and 'external' factors impinging on tribal society. This has led many contributors to the second, wider view of 'tribe-state' relations, not as an opposition of substantive social, economic and political structures so much as an opposition of tendencies, modes or models of organisation, not just

analytically distinct but consciously experienced as
a tension within the tribal groups discussed. It is
at this level that tribal forms and tribe-state
relations in Iran and Afghanistan seem to be most
fruitfully comparable with other parts of the world.

Any comparative study must begin, however, with
an attempt at definition, typology and classification, if only to establish what is be¹ng compared;
only then can the comparison produce explanation of
variation and generalisation. We begin here with an
inability to produce a substantive definition of our
subject - 'tribe' - which in Iran and Afghanistan
specifies little about system of production, scale,
culture or political structure. Historically, in
these countries, groups defined by a wide range of
different criteria have been called 'tribes'. Moreover, tribal groups commonly comprise several levels
of organisation, from camp to confederation. Again,
different criteria define membership of groups at
each level, and it is not agreed at which level the
term 'tribe' is appropriate. Definition is not
aided by indigenous terminology, which includes a
variety of words of Turco-Mongol and Arabic origins,
often used interchangeably and without precision in
the literature.[3]

Different writers - historians, anthropologists,
political agents, travellers; Europeans, Russians,
Iranians, Afghans - have, according to their previous experiences, their personalities and their
objectives, constructed, maintained and only occasionally confronted widely varying images of the
tribes they encountered in Afghanistan and Iran.[4]
The general view of tribal society among contemporary
writers of the nineteenth and early twentieth centuries opposed it to settled urban society, the
civilised Islamic ideal. While the city was the
source of government, order and productivity, the
tribes had a natural tendency to rebellion, rapine
and destruction, a tendency which might be related
to the starkness of their habitat and its remoteness
from the sources of civilisation, and also to the
under-employment inherent in their way of life. Such
a view has some justification, but it is superficial
and over-simplified.

Beyond this, conventional images of tribes in
the two countries differ. Afghan tribes are renowned as hardy, independent, warlike mountaineers,
farming barren fields and rigorous if not fanatical
in their devotion to Islam. The tribes of Iran by
contrast are supposedly pastoral nomads, organised
into strong centralised confederacies under powerful

and aristocratic chiefs, and notorious for their
ignorance of and indifference to Islam. There is
some truth in these stereotypes too, at least as a
basis for drawing a contrast between tribes in the
two countries, but they are nevertheless exaggerated,
and exceptions abound in each case.

A better understanding of the nature of tribal
political organisations, and of relations between
tribal and non-tribal society, must be sought in a
closer historical examination of the social and
economic basis of the tribal system. Unfortunately,
research on this topic has hardly begun. The sources
for it are mostly written from a distance by outsiders viewing the tribes with hostility or some
other bias. They mostly concern matters such as
taxation, military contingents, disturbances and
measures taken to quell them, and inaccurate lists
of major tribal groups, numbers and leaders. They
rarely deal specifically or in reliable detail with
the basic social and economic organisation of tribal
communities, and mention individual tribes only when
prominent in supporting or opposing the government,
when involved in inter-tribal disorders, or when
transported from one region to another. We still
have only the vaguest notions of tribal economies
in nineteenth and early twentieth century Afghanistan
and Iran: what the relations or production were and
how they have changed; who controlled land and how
access was acquired; what proportion of producers
controlled their own production, how many were
tenants or dependants of wealthier tribesmen or of
city-based merchants, and whether control of production was exercised directly or through taxation or
price-fixing. The sparse information in the sources
must be supplemented and interpreted by tentative
and possibly misleading extrapolations from more
recent ethnographic sources.

Some of the dangers are evident in the recent
interesting exchange in Iranian Studies between the
historians Helfgott and Reid. Helfgott, whose main
study has been of the rise of the Qajars, argues
that the Iranian state was composed of two or more
separate but linked 'socio-economic formations'.
Apparently extrapolating from the Basiri (Basseri)
of the modern era, he characterises Iranian tribes
as pastoral nomadic kinship-based chiefdoms that
form closed economic systems; such nomadic socio-
economic formations are distinct from but in constant
relation with the settled agricultural and urban
formations. Unfortunately he produces little evidence for his argument, overstresses the role of

pastoral nomadism, kinship and chiefship in Iranian tribal society, and underestimates the will and capacity of Iranian pastoral nomads to produce surplus. He is accused of theoreticism by Reid, whose own version of tribal organisation, to which he is led mainly by data on administration and the perspective of the state, is that its essence in Iran was the highly complex centralised oymaq system that flourished under the Safavids; oymaqs were neither simply pastoral nor based on kinship (though their sub-divisions may have been); they were 'states', but they were also 'tribes', says Reid, because their leadership was hereditary. Such groups, however, could not be called 'tribes' according to accepted criteria, but were rather 'confederacies', and they are not comparable with the nomadic tribal groups to which Helfgott is directing his argument; while on Reid's own admission the oymaq system disintegrated by the eighteenth century and hence was of no direct relevance to tribalism or pastoral nomadism in the period since.[5]

One fallacy that needs early correction is that tribes are essentially, if not generally, pastoral nomads. Numerous observers have noted how the geography and ecology of both countries favours pastoral nomadism. The terrain and climate make much of the land uncultivable under pre-industrial conditions, and suitable only for seasonal grazing; and as only a small proportion of such pastures can be used by village-based livestock, vast ranges of steppe and mountain are left to be exploited by nomads – mobile tent-dwellers. Such nomads until very recently numbered two to three millions in each country, and almost all were tribally organised. The difference was that, although most tribespeople in Iran were nomads, in Afghanistan most tribespeople were settled cultivators who had little or no leaning to pastoralism or nomadism.[6] In other words, as has been argued by Barth and others, tribalism is more necessary to nomadism than nomadism to tribalism.

Another area of misconception is that of tribal political structures. The allegiance of tribespeople to a set of comparable political groups and leaders is often assumed, especially in the literature on Iran. But this assumption is the product of a state viewpoint, according to which even the most autonomous inhabitants of the territory over which sovereignty is claimed should have representatives and identifiable patterns of organisation. The sources tend to record these as 'chiefs' and

'tribes', whereas such entities may not exist except
on paper. We are left wondering, for example, who
the Bakhtiari are: are they followers of the
Bakhtiari khans? or merely the khans themselves? or
the inhabitants of the territory known as Bakhtiari?
Are all those described as Bakhtiari conscious of
cultural or political unity? Tribal names found in
the sources - and used in the narrative below - imply
a uniformity of structure which (if it exists) may be
entirely due to administrative action, and may disguise fundamental disparities of culture and society.

If such problems are appreciated, it will clearly be impossible to attempt a precise terminology
that will not misrepresent the varied nature of the
tribal societies under consideration. But it may be
helpful to suggest some distinctions to bear in mind,
to be applied less to groups and individuals than to
the kinds of processes that affect them.

Tribe may be used loosely of a localised group
in which kinship is the dominant idiom of organisation, and whose members consider themselves culturally distinct (in terms of customs, dialect or
language, and origins); tribes are usually politically unified, though not necessarily under a central
leader, both features being commonly attributable
to interaction with states. Such tribes also form
parts of larger, usually regional, political structures of tribes of similar kinds; they do not
usually relate directly with the state, but only
through these intermediate structures.[7] The more
explicit term confederacy or confederation should be
used for a local group of tribes that is heterogeneous in terms of culture, presumed origins and perhaps
class composition, yet is politically unified,
usually under a central authority: examples include
the Khamseh and Qashqai (chapter 9), the Shahsevan
(chapter 14) and many Kurdish groups such as the
Shakak (chapter 13). It is useful further to distinguish confederacies, as groups of tribes united
primarily in relation to the state or extra-local
forces, from coalitions or clusters of tribes, more
ephemeral unions for the pursuit of specific local
rivalries, perhaps within a confederacy and probably
without central leadership.

It is better not to use the term 'tribe' for
major ethnic groups or nations, such as Afghans,
Pushtuns/Pathans, Kurds, Hazaras, Turkmens, Uzbeks,
Tajiks, Lurs, Arabs, Baluches, which are culturally
or linguistically distinct but not normally politically unified - though political and territorial
units bearing these names have existed in each case.[8]

A problem arises with some major subdivisions of
these ethnic groups, that are culturally and politically distinct and hence constitute 'tribes', yet
their own subdivisions, at perhaps more than one
level, may also fulfil the criteria of 'tribes': for
example, the Bakhtiari Lurs (chapters 10 to 12), or
the Durrani, Ghilzai, Wazir and other Pathans (chapters 3 to 7). My own inclination, in spite of their
relative cultural homogeneity, is to refer to these
groups, on the grounds of scale, as confederacies,
and to reserve the term tribe for their major components and those of the Qashqai, Shahsevan, Shakak,
Khamseh, etc. If we were to refer, as is sometimes
done, to all these ethnic groups, nations and major
confederacies as 'tribes', the problems of compara-
bility would have been even grosser, except in a discussion of state policies to minorities. The defin-
itions I have suggested aim to facilitate compara-
bility through establishing some equivalence of scale
and function among groups so designated by a single
term. There is evidence of named groups for whom
different terms (e.g. tribe, coalition, confederacy,
nation) would have been appropriate at different
points in their history.[9]
     It is also useful to distinguish tribe from
clan and lineage: a clan is a group of people, part
of a larger nation or ethnic group, who claim common
ancestry, though without necessarily being able to
trace it; a lineage is a localised and unified group
of people who can trace links of common ancestry; a
clan may thus comprise several lineages, while clans
and lineages at various levels may form a hierarchical, 'segmentary' nesting structure. Clan and lineage may be seen as the cultural or ideological dimension of tribes and their sections, when these are
politically-defined groups. When tribe is used to
denote a kinship-based group, then clan is its
synonym. An almost inevitable confusion arises from
the two rather different meanings of the adjective
'tribal': first, 'with the properties of a tribe'
(or clan) especially in the sense of kinship-based;
secondly, 'composed of tribes', which are not
necessarily related to each other by kinship. The
statement that a group or system is 'tribal' is
therefore ambiguous unless clarified by context.
     The state, finally, is a territorially-bounded
polity (see chapter 2) with a centralised government
and a monopoly of legitimate force, usually including
within its bounds different social classes and
ethnic/cultural groups. Some scholars have declared
modern concepts of the state to be inapplicable to

pre-modern Iran and Afghanistan, in terms of degree
of central control and the forms, functions and
ideology of government;[10] but for our purposes, the
existence of territorial frontiers (however vaguely
defined), a central government (however weak and
limited in its aims) and a heterogeneous population,
are enough to define the state. In these terms,
some confederacies constitute states, while some
states operate on the basis of tribal ties, or, in
the form of empires, recognise the autonomy of other
states and tribes within their territories.

Before proceeding to the historical survey
which is the necessary background to the chapters
that follow, it is appropriate to sketch some contrasts, in basic physical and cultural geography,
that have affected the tribal populations in the two
countries. Dominant physical features of Iran are
a central plateau and the surrounding mountain
ranges and steppes. The main centres of settlement
are located in or on the fringes of the plateau, the
mountains and steppes being occupied chiefly by
minority tribal groups, often Sunnis in a predominantly Shiite population: Kurds, Turkmens, Baluches
and Arabs. The centre of Afghanistan, on the other
hand, is a mountainous backbone, where several
minority tribal groups are found, including the
Shiite Hazaras and the people of Nuristan, formerly
Kafiristan. The majority Sunni population, including the dominant, tribally-organised Pathans, inhabit the surrounding steppes, plateaux and hills.

Persian was the language most understood in
nineteenth-century Iran and perhaps also in
Afghanistan, but the main tribal groups, as well as
the ruling dynasties, were not originally Persian-
speaking. In Iran the ruling Qajars and many other
tribal groups (Afshar, Qashqai, Turkmen, Shahsevan,
and other remnants of the Qizilbash confederacy of
the sixteenth and seventeenth centuries) spoke
Turki, while others spoke Iranian languages distinct
from Persian, such as Kurdish, Luri, Baluchi. The
Durrani rulers and the main tribal groups of
Afghanistan were Pashto-speakers, while significant
tribal elements spoke Turki, Baluchi and the Kafir
and Dardic languages of the north-east. But in both
countries the urban centres were dominated by Persian
language and civilisation, which often proved
stronger in the long run than invading tribal cultures. Here too, major differences are relevant:
for instance, Iran has always been more a city-
oriented society, Afghanistan more a confederation
of tribal groups. The Pathans who have dominated

11

Afghanistan have been able to preserve their territorial and political integrity since the eighteenth
century, far less affected by forced migrations than
many tribal groups in Iran.
   The dominant cleavage in Iranian society until
recently, between Turks (dominant but 'uncouth'
tribes, usually nomads) and Tats or Tajiks (subordinate but 'civilised' townsmen and peasants), is to
some extent paralleled in Afghanistan by a cleavage,
not between tribe and non-tribe, nor between nomad
and settled, but between Pathans (Afghans) and the
rest, whether urban, peasant or tribal. Pathans
tend to refer to the rest as 'Parsiwan' (or 'Farsi-
ban'), literally 'Persian-speakers'.

Iran and Afghanistan from 1700 to 1800

In the first half of the eighteenth century, the
histories of Iran and Afghanistan were intertwined.
In 1700 most of present-day Afghanistan was under at
least the nominal sovereignty of the Safavid rulers
of Iran based at Isfahan. Much of the Safavid
Empire, however, was de facto autonomous, even independent of the capital, and soon after 1700 many
tribal groups broke into rebellion, especially
Sunnis who predominated on the margins of the Empire.
Thus the Ghilzai Afghans made themselves independent
at Kandahar in 1709 and the Abdali followed by taking
control of Herat in 1715, while raids and incursions
by Baluches in the south-east, Uzbeks and Turkmens
in the north-east, and Lazgis and Kurds in the
north-west intensified.[11]
   The Safavid capital fell in 1722 to Mahmud
Ghilzai and his Afghan tribesmen; but Ghilzai rule
was shortlived, and in 1729, after gaining control
of most of the north-east, Tahmasp Quli Khan, an
Afshar tribesman from Khurasan, subdued the Abdali
at Herat and drove the Ghilzai from Isfahan, where
he restored nominal Safavid rule under a puppet
Shah. In the following years he recovered all the
territories that had been lost to the Afghans, and
to the Ottomans and Russians in the west and north-
west.
   Tahmasp Quli, or Nadir Shah as he became in
1736, was a military adventurer rather than a tribal
chief.[12] Several branches of the Afshar remained
opposed to him, and his following consisted of Turks,
Afghans, Kurds, and Lurs, whose basis for unity was
military discipline and a common interest in plunder.
Nadir himself had little time for civil administra-

tion. Although he established 'security' in the
country, his exactions, in the interest of his perpetual martial exploits, caused much of the settled
population to emigrate. Having deposed his Safavid
puppet, he broke away from the precedents of that
dynasty, establishing his capital at Mashhad in
Khurasan, and favouring Sunni tribal groups such as
Afghans and Turkmens. However he revived elements
of the tribal policy of his great Safavid predecessor Abbas I (1587-1639). Generally he governed the
tribes through their own leaders; in some cases he
appears to have nominated paramount chiefs. To
punish rebels and discourage the Ottomans during his
campaigns against them, he devastated the provinces
of the Caucasus, Azarbayjan, Iraq-i Ajam, and Fars.
Numerous tribes were transported from these areas,
from Kurdistan and Luristan and also from Herat and
Kandahar, to Khurasan, where they could be super-
vised, defend his metropolitan province and supply
pastoral produce and - most important - manpower
for his army. In the east, where his conquests
extended into the Mughal Empire beyond the Indus,
he did less to disrupt the tribal peoples; indeed he
paid tribute to the frontier tribes.
     Nadir was assassinated in 1747, and his empire
at once disintegrated under the rivalries of his
successors. The eastern half, and much of his
treasure, fell to his trusted Afghan general, Ahmad
Khan Abdali. The Abdali were the most important
Afghan tribal group, of whom the most powerful and
numerous element was the Barakzai tribe, led by
Hajji Jamal Khan of the Muhammadzai branch; Ahmad
Khan, of the less powerful but more aristocratic
Popalzai tribe (the Sadozai branch) was elected
leader by a _jirga_ assembly of Nadir's Afghan generals,
as something of a compromise. He later changed the
name Abdali to Durrani, supposedly after the title
he adopted - Durr-i Durran ('pearl of pearls'); and
his leadership among the tribal chiefs indeed remained that of _primus_ _inter_ _pares_.
     Ahmad Shah's realm was based at the Durrani
centre of Kandahar. Although he established a royal
court 'formed exactly on the model of Naudir Shauh's',
with a court ceremony conducted 'according to set
forms in the Toorkee language',[13] the government was
essentially tribal and feudalistic in that tribal
leaders were confirmed in their possession of lands
and the main offices of state were distributed among
the different tribes. The ruler moreover consulted
with a council of nine tribal chiefs. 'Thus the
Durrani kingdom more closely resembled a confedera-

tion of tribes and khanates than a centralised monarchy.'[14] To maintain his rule and consolidate his
monarchy, Ahmad Shah depended on the tribes. He was
able to keep their unity and support by means of the
revenue surplus gained in his campaigns into India,
through which he incorporated Punjab, Multan and
Kashmir into his empire. But, as Gregorian points
out, he failed to create a strong, independent urban
economy which could enable him to assert his authority over the tribes. In this major respect, the
early Durrani monarchy differed from that soon to be
established in Iran by the Qajars.

Ahmad Shah's son, Timur Shah, who succeeded him
in 1773, pursued similar policies. He moved the
capital to Kabul, a Tajik centre beyond the direct
influence of the Durrani chiefs, and added other
alliances to those he maintained with the powerful
Barakzai, but in the end failed to do more than his
father to make the monarchy independent of tribal
support. Indeed some Durrani even allied with their
rivals, the Ghilzai. Besides, the rising power of
the Sikhs in the Punjab, a consequent reduction in
state income from that quarter, and the increased
burden of taxation that had to be imposed on the
cities and the non-Pashtun population, weakened the
forces that the Shah needed to impose centralisation.
Timur Shah's son Zaman Shah (1793-1800) also failed
to achieve centralisation, conducted abortive campaigns against the Sikhs and faced threats from Iran
in the west. He tried to challenge the chiefs, but
ended only in breaking the Barakzai-Sadozai alliance.
In 1800 Painda Khan, son of Hajji Jamal Khan and
leader of the powerful Muhammadzai Barakzai, met his
death for plotting to remove Zaman Shah. As a consequence, Painda's son Fatih Khan removed Zaman Shah
and initiated the takeover of government by the
Muhammadzai leadership which had stood behind Sadozai
imperial rule since Ahmad Shah's election in 1747.
'Afghanistan thus entered the nineteenth century a
politically disunited, ethnically and religiously
heterogeneous, tribal-feudal state.'[15]

Nadir Shah's reign had left much of Iran, particularly the west, drastically depopulated. Many
groups escaped transportation, slaughter and the
ravages and requisitions of his campaigns by flight
beyond the frontiers or into mountain or desert fastnesses. After his death, various exiles began to
move back to their original homelands. In 1748 or
soon after, large numbers of tribespeople who had
been sent to Khurasan seized the opportunity to return home. Meanwhile, for two years his surviving

close relatives strove against each other for control
of Iran, before succumbing to the efforts of leaders
of various other tribes, particularly those returned
from exile. Azarbayjan was for some years occupied
by one of Nadir's Afghan generals, Azad Khan of the
Suleyman Khel Ghilzai, against the opposition of
most of the local tribes. In the central western
provinces, Lurs, Laks and Kurds came together in
their opposition to the Afghans, and were led first
by Ali Mardan Khan of the Bakhtiari Lurs, and then
by Karim Khan of the Zand Laks. Karim Khan won over
the Bakhtiari, beat off the Afghans, and set up his
base at Shiraz in Fars. In the north, Muhammad
Hasan Khan Qajar gained the support of the tribes of
Khurasan and command of the Caspian provinces, then
in 1757 campaigned in Azarbayjan and the Caucasus,
drove Azad Khan out, and proceeded the next year
against Karim Khan in the south. The Zand leader,
however, again won over his adversary's forces, and
Muhammad Hasan was killed early in 1759. Karim Khan
spent a few seasons in Azarbayjan reducing rebel
leaders of the Dunbuli, Shaqaqi and Shahsevan tribes,
and especially Fath Ali Khan Afshar, who controlled
Urmiyeh and Tabriz. He then established the comparative security and prosperity that lasted throughout
his domain, with few interruptions, until his death.
    While Ahmad Shah Abdali, Azad Ghilzai, Muhammad
Hasan Qajar, Ali Mardan Bakhtiari and Fath Ali
Afshar were tribal chiefs, Karim Khan, like Nadir
Shah, was not. He was more of a bandit by origin.
His own tribe, the Zand, amounted at most to a few
hundred families, and his following was composed of
a mixed collection of Lak, Lur, Kurd and Turk tribesmen. His final success in winning much of the western part of Nadir's empire was due less to tribal
loyalties or military conquests than to diplomacy
and luck.[16]
    Karim Khan was renowned for his peaceful and
equitable rule. He attracted back many of the
craftsmen and others who had fled the country during
the troubles of Nadir's reign and after. With the
tribes, he employed similar policies to his predecessors', though on a smaller scale: the more important tribes were governed through their chiefs; he
sent punitive expeditions against rebel groups, and
in one case carried out a wholesale transportation,
and he also brought groups to Fars to supplement his
standing army. He made no attempt to devastate or
colonise his frontier regions, which remained virtually independent of him. Khurasan served as a
buffer against Ahmad Shah Durrani, under whose

influence Nadir Shah's grandson Shahrukh reigned at
Mashhad. To the north-west the Ottomans and Russians
were no threat but rather were preoccupied with each
other. The Trans-Araxian districts were only nominally in Karim Khan's domains, while he managed to
claim the allegiance of the Azarbayjani chiefs by
taking hostages to Shiraz.

Karim Khan Zand's death in 1779 was followed by
a further period of dynastic struggles and the usual
accompanying insecurity and devastation in the
countryside. In the south, Zand chiefs fought for
the succession, while elsewhere local leaders pursued
their own ambitions. In Mazandaran and Astarabad,
the Qajar chief Aqa Muhammad (son of Muhammad Hasan)
carefully united the dissident elements of his
tribe, then he recruited support from the Turkmens
of the Atrak, reduced most of the chiefs of
Azarbayjan, and by 1794 had defeated the Zand in the
south. Next year, in the face of the Russian threat
in the Caucasus, he took swift measures to reassert
Iran's hegemony over Georgia and other Transcaucasian
areas, then in 1796 took Khurasan from the Afghan
puppet Shahrukh, having severely chastised the
Turkmen tribes, who had been allowed to move south
to the Gurgan plain in return for their aid to Aqa
Muhammad and his father but had not ceased their
marauding expeditions into Khurasan. During Aqa
Muhammad's brief reign (he died in 1797) order was
established in his domains through the terror of his
wrath and the might of his army, but the countryside
was laid waste in his continual campaigns. He
secured the allegiance of tribal leaders by keeping
members of their families in or near Tehran, the new
Qajar capital.

The Population of Afghanistan and Iran around 1800

The Kingdom of Kabul - the Sadozai Afghan Empire -
stretched to the Indus in the east and nominally
included Kashmir, Turkistan (south of the Oxus) and
much of Baluchistan, though not Badakhshan and
Kafiristan. The dominant Durrani (with their component tribes Nurzai, Ishaqzai, Alizai, Atsakzai (or
Achakzai), Barakzai, Popalzai, Alikozai) occupied
the south-western region from Herat to Farah,
Kandahar and Kalat-i Ghilzai. Between these last
two places they mingled with their rivals, the
Ghilzai (with their major tribes Suleyman Khel,
Hotaki, Kharoti, Andar, Taraki, Tokhi), whose lands
were mainly around Ghazni and as far as Kabul.

Durrani and Ghilzai territory included extensive
pastures and some irrigated farmlands, suited to
mixed farming; many of the tribesmen were pastoral
nomads, many were settled farmers, and substantial
numbers combined the two. South of the Durrani and
Ghilzai were the Kakar, while near Kabul were other
settled Pushtun groups: Wardak and Safi. The eastern Pakhtuns, mainly conducting irrigated farming,
included the Mohmand, Yusufzai and related tribes of
Peshawar and Swat and other valleys to the north.
In the mountains to the south were the 'highlanders',
later famous as the frontier tribes: Afridi, Orakzai
and Shinwari of the Khyber; south of them the Khatak
and Bangash, and the Jaji and Jadran of Khost;
towards Baluchistan, the Wazir and Mahsud. Almost
all these frontier highlanders conducted a marginal
agriculture, irrigated where possible (especially to
the north and round the Khyber area), but mostly
rain-fed. Beyond, in arid Makran and Sistan, in a
relation of partnership rather than allegiance to
Kabul, were the numerous but scattered Baluch and
Brahui tribes, mainly pastoral nomads.
   In the vicinity and hinterland of Herat, near
the disputed frontier with Iran, were the Persian-
speaking Chahar Aymaq tribes: Timuri (who were at
this time crossing in numbers to Iran near Turbat-i
Jam and Khaf), Jamshidi, Firuzkuhi, Taymani, Qala-i
Nou Hazaras, and many smaller groups, mixed farmers
and semi-nomads for the most part. To the north
and east, in Turkistan south of the Oxus, were the
lands occupied by various Turkmen groups and the
Uzbek tribes and khanates, only nominally in submission to Kabul; nomads included Turkmens, Uzbeks
and Arabs, while most Uzbeks and the non-tribal
Tajiks were settled in villages and towns. In the
high mountains of the centre of the realm, east of
the Aymaqs, were the Persian-speaking Shiite
Hazaras, still to a large degree autonomous, as were
the numerous unsubdued pagan tribes of Kafiristan in
the even higher mountains further to the east. The
rest of the population of the eastern areas near
Kabul and to the north were mostly non-tribal Tajiks,
though in Kabul itself there was also a substantial
group of Shiite Qizilbash, remnants of Nadir Shah's
tribal forces from Iran, mainly of Turkic origins.
   The total population of the Durrani realm must
have exceeded some 14 million, of which no more than
five million dwelt within the present frontiers of
Afghanistan. Half the population (as now) were
Pashto-speaking tribespeople. Most of the rest -
Hazaras, Kafirs, Aymaqs, Turkmens, Uzbeks, Baluches -

were also 'tribal' in organisation; only the Tajiks
were not - they are often considered by definition
to comprise   a residual category of all the 'non-
tribal' elements in the rural population.[17]
   The tribes of Iran were by 1800 already in a
state of extreme dispersal. Defined in broad terms,
the tribal population, predominating in the frontier
districts and in areas better suited to pastoralism
than cultivation, probably varied between one-and-a-
half and three million people during the nineteenth
century, forming at times a quarter or more of the
total population, but falling in this century to a
tenth or less.
   Starting in the north-west, the mountainous
provinces of Kurdistan, Azarbayjan and the southern
Caucasus, marked by higher rainfall and colder
winters than areas to the south-east, provide excellent grazing grounds but climatic conditions in
which pastoral nomadism is comparatively precarious.
Most tribal groups here practised cultivation and
tended to settle, or at least to spend the colder
season in villages. The frontiers of this region
were occupied by independent Sunni mountain tribes -
Lazgis and others to the north in Daghistan, and
Kurds in the west. There were also numerous Kurdish
tribes in the south: Zanganeh and Kalhur (partly
Shiite) near Kirmanshah on the main road between
Baghdad and Khurasan, and the Mukri towards Souj-
Bulagh and Maragheh. The Ardalan of Kurdistan proper
were under a Vali at Sanandaj. Elsewhere in the
region Kurds were mingled with Turks, tending to
become 'Turkicised' in language, religion, and some-
times culture. Muqaddam Turks dwelt at Maragheh,
and a large branch of the Afshar held Urmiyeh while
north of Lake Urmiyeh were Kurdish tribes such as
Shadlu near Ararat and the Turkicised Dunbuli at
Khoy. There were Bayat Turks at Maku, and a branch
of the Qajar in Erivan and Qarabagh, where Javanshir
Turks and Qarachurlu Kurds also lived. Mughan and
Ardabil were occupied by the Shahsevan, Qaradagh by
a variety of small Turkic and Kurdish groups, and
Sarab, Khalkhal and Mianeh by the Shaqaqi and other
Turkicised Kurds.
   Between the high central Zagros and the torrid
plains of Arabistan ranged the largest concentration
of nomadic tribes in Iran, numbering up to a million
people. Most of these were Lurs, and prominent
among them were the Bakhtiari, while at Khurramabad
the Vali of Luristan proper ruled over the Feyli and
an amorphous collection of other Lur tribes of the
Mamasani and the Kuhgiluyeh; in Arabistan lived the

Introduction

Banu Kaab, Al-Kathir and Mullai Arab tribes, many of
them Shiite.

In the province of Fars lived a heterogeneous
collection of nomad tribes. East of the Lurs and
ranging north and south of Shiraz were the Qashqai,
who had been dispersed after opposing Aqa Muhammad
Khan, some to the Bakhtiari and some to Mazandaran,
but were now reforming and included many groups from
the likewise dispersed Zand confederation. East of
them were the Il-i Arab, the Inallu, Nafar and
Baharlu Turks, and the Persian-speaking Basiri: these
five groups were to be united later as the Khamseh
confederacy. On the southern coast were Sunni Arabs
such as the Huwala.

In the arid south-east, various Baluch and
Brahui tribes remained more or less autonomous of
Iran, while nearer Kirman the largest tribe was
another branch of the Afshar. Numerous Arab groups,
and Qarai Turks, were scattered through the desert
zone of Sistan and southern Khurasan. Aymaqs from
Herat were also moving westwards into Iranian terri-
tory. North of Mashhad, Afshar Turks held Daragaz
and Tus, and towards Marv there were Qajar and
Jalayir Turks. In the mountain and plateau districts
to the west and north-west lived Gireyli and Bayat
Turks and substantial groups of Kurds introduced by
Shah Abbas I. The province of Astarabad near the
Caspian was occupied by the Sunni Turkmen tribes,
Yamut and Goklen, and further groups of Qajar and
Jalayir. Most of the 100,000 tribal families which
Nadir Shah was reported to have moved to Astarabad
and his metropolitan province of Khurasan had now
returned to their various homes in western and
north-western parts of Iran and to Herat and
Kandahar, though remnants were left among the longer
established groups.

Meanwhile Aqa Muhammad Khan had introduced
large numbers of Lurs, Laks, Turks and Kurds from
the west and south to his own metropolitan area,
stretching from Astarabad through Mazandaran (the
Qajar homeland) to Iraq-i Ajam. Major tribal groups
in the latter region were the Inallu and Baghdadi
Shahsevan, the latter near Kharaqan and Saveh; and
the Qaraguzlu Turks towards Hamadan.[18]

In several ways, the history and geography of
Iran and Afghanistan brought them into the nineteenth
century with similar political and cultural problems.
Most significant perhaps was a similarity of frontier problems. In 1800, both countries were bordered
on the north (in the Caucasus and Central Asia) by
semi-independent khanates, later replaced by the

19

expanding Russian Empire. On the west and south
Iran confronted the Ottoman Empire and later the
British; on the east and south Afghanistan faced the
Sikhs and was soon to face British India. In
Cottam's opinion,

> Although Iran and Afghanistan remained inde-
> pendent, at least to a degree, in the nine-
> teenth and early twentieth centuries when
> much of Asia and Africa was falling under
> foreign control, the freedom of these countries
> cannot be attributed to the courage and devo-
> tion of their inhabitants. Nor was their
> independence due to geographical obstructions,
> which by the nineteenth century were already
> beginning to lose their effectiveness. The
> reason for their continued independence was
> that Iran and Afghanistan occupied a geographi-
> cal belt at which the dynamics of Russian
> expansion and British expansion met. Neither
> Britain nor Russia could have gained and
> solidified control there without risking a
> major war.[19]

In such a situation, both countries were inevitably
major arenas for the Great Game, the conflict between
Russia and Britain in Asia; but both had, on their
frontiers, tribal populations which in fact played
prominent roles - often displaying both 'courage and
devotion' in that conflict.
    As stated earlier, certain scholars hold that
nineteenth-century Iran and Afghanistan cannot be
analysed in the same terms as modern states. Lambton
has put the issues thus:

> At the beginning of the Kādjār period the
> theoretical purpose of the state had been to
> secure the temporal framework within which the
> individual Muslim could live the good life
> according to the precepts of the sharīᶜa, from
> which it followed that the stability of the
> state and good government were bound up with
> right religion. The functions of government
> had been confined broadly to defence against
> external aggression and the maintenance of
> internal order. Political power had lain in
> the hands of the military classes, consisting
> primarily of the tribal leaders...By the end
> of the period Persia had become a modern terri-
> torial secular state, drawn into and affected
> by international politics.[20]

Introduction

These remarks also apply broadly to Afghanistan under the Durranis, and much of the history of Qajar Iran and Durrani Afghanistan concerns the very different processes and rates by which the ruling dynasties were transformed from tribal elites into constitutional monarchies, and their realms from near-theocratic empires into 'modern territorial secular states'.

Iran from 1800 to 1980

On Aqa Muhammad Shah Qajar's assassination in Qarabagh in 1797, there were further outbreaks of tribal dynastic ambitions in Azarbayjan, but Fath Ali Shah (1797-1834) established control of the realm and set about consolidating the state. He deliberately revived Safavid concepts of the absolute and irresponsible power of the sovereign. No warlord himself, he devoted his time rather to civil administration and court life, and to riding and hunting, the traditional tribal alternatives to warfare, and left the active generalship of his numerous campaigns to his heir Abbas Mirza.

A major threat to the stability of the state and peace in the countryside was the tribal system, which had both caused and thrived on the disorders of the previous century. The tribespeople were a valued source of revenue and irregular cavalry, but leaders of the larger tribes could withhold their dues, while in the more remote regions, particularly among Sunni and non-Turkic groups, virtual autonomy prevailed. Seeing the hereditary chiefs, and the fanatical devotion with which they were regarded in many cases, as a central feature of the tribal system, Fath Ali Shah determined to destroy or at least to limit their power. The policies he initiated to this end were continued by his successors.

Like previous rulers, Fath Ali kept the chiefs or their relatives near him as security for the good behaviour of their followers. At the same time, tribal leaders used to have their representatives at court, to keep them informed of matters concerning them. Also Fath Ali Shah created a wide network of marriage alliance linking his family with those of the important chiefs, and in addition he took advantage of the inability of the tribal leaders to unite and the endemic state of rivalry in the chiefly families and jealousy between different groups in a region. The principle of divide and rule was widely practised. When necessary, punitive expeditions were sent, a force recruited from one tribal group being

used to chastise another, often their traditional
enemies. Rebel chiefs were arrested, often by
deceit, and many were executed. The Qajar rulers,
further, appointed <u>ilkhanis</u> and <u>ilbegis</u> over the more
important tribal groups; though in fact they usually
had to nominate individuals acceptable to their
tribesmen, most often the hereditary chiefs. Recognised chiefs were expected to collect and pay the
taxes, to maintain order and to organise military
levies, which were due both to the Shah and often to
the provincial governor as well. Irregular tribal
levies continued to form the main body of the army,
though attempts were made to introduce more regular
disciplined troops.[21]
    Some of the tribes were broken up and others
relocated. The policy of forced migration to the
metropolitan area was continued under later rulers.
In the early 1800s, Morier observed that, apart from
the Arabs, whose chiefs were still feared, 'The
different tribes are now so much spread throughout
the provinces, that they have almost lost that union
which could render them formidable.'[22] In fact,
dynastic ambitions on the part of the tribes ceased
to be realistic with the advent in Iran of Great
Power rivalry, whereby the Qajar succession was
virtually guaranteed. This new factor also gradually
brought to an end the Qajars' own military endeavours
on the frontiers, and hence limited their ability to
provide the tribal militia with a legitimate source
of plunder. Thus, with the advance of the Russians
in the Caucasus, Iran's north-western frontiers
closed in. During the two Russian wars, ending in
the Treaties of Gulistan (1813) and Turkmanchay
(1828), a major preoccupation of the Shah was to
ensure the continued allegiance of tribes on both
sides of the Aras. Abbas Mirza succeeded in bringing various tribes south of the Aras and settling
them in Azarbayjan. Migrations across the frontier
in both directions appear to have continued after
1828, and also occurred extensively among the Kurds
on the Ottoman frontier.
    The north-eastern frontiers were a major problem
for the early Qajars. They carried on constant
military activity both in their attempts to regain
Herat and the western parts of Afghanistan, and
aginst the Turkmens and other slave-raiders, whose
expeditions depopulated Khurasan, penetrating at
times as far as the vicinity of Isfahan and seriously
disrupting the important trade of the north-east.
British protection of Afghanistan brought an end to
Iranian efforts in that direction in the 1850s, and

Russian victories in Turkistan later in the century
terminated raids from that quarter, but within Iran
the nomad sections of the Yamut Turkmens continued
to resist domination by the Qajars into the twentieth century.

Other tribal groups in Khurasan, the Kurds of
Quchan and Bujnurd, and the Arabs, Aymaqs and
Baluches towards the south and east of the province,
were more amenable to the authority of the government. The Baluch chiefs of Sistan and Baluchistan
had, under the earlier Qajars, evaded all but
trifling payments to the government, but they now
saw more of the tax officials, though they otherwise
maintained considerable autonomy until the 1920s
(see chapter 8). The Mamasani and Kuhgilu Lurs were
pacified by 1882, and authority was also extended
over the Arab tribes of the south-west during Nasir
al-Din Shah's reign (1848-96). The Validom of the
Ardalan Kurds was effectively taken over in the
1860s, and the Kurds of Kirmanshah were by 1907
administered by the Kalhur ilkhani. On the other
hand, the settled Lurs under the Vali of Pusht-i Kuh
were inaccessible enough to remain independent
throughout Qajar times, as were the nomad Lurs of
Pish-i Kuh and also most of the Kurds of western
Azarbayjan, the location of the abortive Kurdish
uprising under Sheykh Ubeydullah in 1880 (see chapter 13).

In the second half of the nineteenth century,
the power of many other tribal leaders was further
weakened. Some were replaced by local government
officials. Security in the country generally
improved, and raiding was suppressed. In many areas,
nomadic elements were settling in increasing numbers.
This tendency was strong, as always, in Azarbayjan,
where the only major tribes to remain nomadic were
the Shahsevan of Mishkin, who retained comparatively
temperate winter quarters in Mughan and were not yet
tempted to exchange their tents for more substantial
dwellings (see chapter 14). Settlement was also
widespread among groups recently introduced to the
north-central region, between Mazandaran and Iraq-i
Ajam.

Soon after 1900, Aubin held that ethnic and
tribal identities were losing their importance in a
general increase of national consciousness; the only
exceptions to this process of integration were the
small religious minorities, the larger tribes, and
those tribes which were remote from the centre or
could take refuge in the mountains, though none of
these could escape the royal power completely.[23]

In fact, this general impression of settlement
and 'detribalisation' was superficial and deceptive.
The conduct of the administration in some areas, so
far from undermining the tribal system, served
rather to accentuate its evils. For one thing, the
Iranian army had little to do in the latter part of
the nineteenth century; it was lacking in experience
and had deteriorated in quality since the introduction of 'disciplined' troops. The nomad tribes
remained the only effective militia, but they could
be relied on only when defending their own territory.
Tribal levies, which had been drawn from the families and retinues of the chiefs, were now unemployed
for long periods, and increasingly turned their
energies to banditry. At the same time, the main
emphasis of administration being on the collection
of revenue, in some areas the demands of officials,
including the appointed chiefs, were so oppressive,
extortionate, and arbitrary, that ordinary tribesmen
sought the security of joining the retinues of the
most effective of the local brigands. Meanwhile the
official chiefs themselves, whether through assimilation to the government bureaucracy or through
detention as hostages, became urbanised and estrang-
ed from the majority of tribesmen, and could no
longer exercise direct control over them.
        This was particularly the case in some frontier
areas of Kurdistan, Azarbayjan, Gurgan and Khurasan,
where the government of the later Qajars appeared to
foster both nomadism and tribalism. In the territories of the Kurds, Qaradaghis, Shahsevan and
Turkmens, where the nomads had continued for much of
the nineteenth century to cross the Ottoman or
Russian frontiers seasonally for grazing purposes,
a policy of maintaining a frontier strip of endemic
'tribal disorder' seems to have been tacitly revived
(from Safavid precedents) at the end of the century
as a defence against possible incursions. Local
authorities did little to curtail raiding activities
there, and indeed were sometimes said to be reaping
a share of the proceeds. When punitive expeditions
were sent, they frequently chastised not the real
culprits but some more accessible group. Often it
was only when the tribesmen raided across the frontier and the neighbouring power complained, that the
Iranian administration took measures, usually half-
hearted. In extreme cases, such as with the
Shahsevan of Ardabil and Mishkin in 1860, a programme
of enforced settlement was initiated, though without
permanent effect (see chapter 14).
        The tribes on the north-west and northern fron-

tiers, preoccupied with a near-anarchic situation of generalised brigandry, posed no major threat to security in the period before the First World War, except at a local level. Only rarely did any of them unite in groups of more than a few thousand warriors under a leader with ambitions on a national scale, on occasions such as the Kurdish revolt of 1880 already referred to, and the support given in 1909 to Muhammad Ali Shah against the Nationalists by the Turkmens and by the union of some Qaradaghi and Shahsevan tribes under Rahim Khan Chalabianlu. None of these lasted more than a few months. It was otherwise with the large and powerful tribal confederacies of the central and southern Zagros, the Bakhtiari, Qashqai and Khamseh, whose leading families were among the most influential in the country and, whether among their tribesmen or in Tehran, played an increasingly important part in political affairs of the later Qajar period.

The Bakhtiari tribes, numbering up to 50,000 families, mostly nomads, were the source of much trouble to the government, and were never wholly brought under control. Their chiefly families were constantly split by rivalries, a factor which the government was able to exploit. In the first half of the nineteenth century, the Bakhtiari chief Muhammad Taqi Khan carried out various measures beneficial to the tribes, but excited the jealousy of the governor of Isfahan and was arrested by deceit in 1841. Bakhtiari influence grew under Huseyn Quli Khan, who was appointed the first official ilkhani. After his assassination in 1882, his successors continued to dispute the leadership and the inheritance of the considerable landed property which he and his brothers had accumulated. With the discovery of oil in their territory, the main contenders for leadership were able to compose their differences and play a deciding role in the restoration of the Constitution in 1909, and they also dominated the government in the period immediately before the First World War (see chapters 10 to 12).

In Fars, the Qashqai confederacy emerged under Jani Khan early in the nineteenth century, and his successors as ilkhanis of the Qashqai rivalled the family of the merchant Hajji Ibrahim at Shiraz for influence in the province. This rivalry was exploited by the Qajar government to prevent an alliance (such as was nearly formed in 1831/2) which might threaten their own position. In 1861/2 the government created the Khamseh confederacy from the Il-i Arab, Inallu, Baharlu, Nafar and Basiri tribes, and placed it under the leadership of Hajji Ibrahim's grandson Mirza Ali Muhammad Khan, Qavam al-Mulk, to balance the Qashqai power in Fars. The Qashqai were stricken by the famine of the 1870s, their numbers falling from around 30,000 to under 15,000 families, many sections joining the Bakhtiari or the Khamseh, but they became powerful again under Ismail Khan, Soulat al-Douleh. During the Bakhtiari hegemony, which had the support of Qavam al-Mulk and the Khamseh tribes, Soulat al-Douleh made a pact with the Vali of Pusht-i Kuh and the Arab Sheykhs of Khuzistan, but this alliance came to nothing. The settlement of the Baharlu, Inallu and Nafar, initiated by the government, was largely complete before 1900; the Il-i Arab and Basiri tribes, and the majority of the Qashqai, continued to be nomads (see chapter 9).[24]

Government control over the tribes weakened, in frontier areas before the turn of the century, elsewhere during and after the Constitutional period (1906-11). In most tribal areas, the period from the 1890s to the 1920s was one of 'anarchy', known as khankhani or ashrarlikh. Some tribal chiefs managed to maintain a degree of local stability within the general turmoil, but other areas were simply battlegrounds for rival brigands, where raiding went unchecked, taxes were not collected, trade was disrupted, and farming peasants were forced to leave land and village to take refuge in town or among the brigand leaders' retinues. At the same time, measures had already been undertaken to establish the infrastructure necessary for the ultimate control of the tribes: a telegraph network was spreading, the roads were improving, and plans were made for railways. There were occasional government successes, as when a small but well-disciplined force under the Armenian Yeprem Khan and Sardar Bahadur Bakhtiari dealt piecemeal with the Qaradaghi and Shahsevan rebels in 1910, to show that at the end of the Qajar period, as at the beginning, it needed only a strong leader to subdue the tribes, which were as incapable as ever of uniting against determined military action.[25]

When Riza Khan came to power as Minister of War, one of his first steps to bring order to the country was to deal severely with the tribes. During a series of campaigns in 1921-5 he managed to defeat and largely disarm the major groups: Shahsevan, Bakhtiari and other Lurs, Qashqai, Turkmens. Later revolts among the Arabs of Khuzistan, the Kurds and the Qashqai were subdued. In most areas, pacifica-

tion and disarmament brought an abrupt end to banditry and armed inter-tribal hostilities, and established an unprecedented degree of security and
government control, maintained by strong garrisons
of troops and later the gendarmerie as a rural police
force.

The new security enabled long-abandoned lands
to be brought back under cultivation, and many
former peasants, who had taken refuge in towns or in
the tribal chiefs' retinues, now returned to their
villages. Both peasants and nomads were subject to
the new conscription laws, and men were forced to
wear 'western' forms of dress. In spite of the end
of banditry, the peasants continued to suffer as
ever from the exactions of landowners and government
officials. Riza Shah's plans for industrialisation
and modernisation included little provision for the
agriculture on which the economy of the country continued to depend. But the nomad tribesmen now often
recall the period as a golden age, compared with the
chaos that went before and the enforced settlement
that was to come after, though the army, Riza Shah's
new nobility, was greatly feared both by the tribesmen, among whom sheep-lifting was almost unknown for
a decade or more, and by the gendarmerie who, whenever an army officer was to visit, were sure to make
arrests among the tribesmen, to demonstrate their
vigilance. None the less, effective administration
of the tribes still depended on the co-operation of
their traditional leaders, and it was official policy to conciliate them as far as possible. Many
chiefs had been killed in battle or executed during
the pacification campaigns; others who proved recalcitrant were removed from the tribes; but most of
them, impressed with the strength of the new regime,
were willing to co-operate and to transfer to the
Pahlavi dynasty the allegiance which they had once
owed to the Qajars.

So far, Riza Shah's tribal policy had been only
a more effective and thorough version of those
attempted by the strongest of his predecessors, such
as Fath Ali Shah and Nasir al-Din Shah. However, in
his programme for unifying Iran and creating a modern, secular, Persian-speaking state, he saw in the
nomad tribes symbols of much that he was trying to
replace: alien cultures and languages, allegiance to
hereditary chiefs, a 'primitive' way of life, and a
mobility that made the tribes inaccessible to the
new legal system. Judging their organisation and
leadership to be a continuing political danger, and
their nomadism and autonomy to be anachronisms in a

modern state, Riza Shah eventually determined on the
more revolutionary step of destroying the tribal
system altogether. The nomads were to stop their
migrations, build houses, cultivate their pastures,
and submit to the same rural system of administration as other villagers.

The policy was implemented in the early 1930s.
It was not intended to put an end to the pastoral
economy: the settlers could entrust their flocks to
herdsmen with special permits to continue migration
to seasonal pastures where necessary. This was consistent with the semi-nomadic village-based pastoralism customary in various parts of the country and
also with the kind of dual economy already practised
by many tribal groups, where settled sections sent
their flocks to pasture with nomadic sections, providing the latter in return with agricultural produce
from the tribal villages. None the less, the
settlement policy has received considerable notoriety
as a brutal failure, though few details have yet
reached print concerning its effects on individual
tribal groups. Politically less than successful, it
was a social and economic disaster. There was little
increase in agricultural and a considerable drop in
pastoral production. The health of the former
nomads suffered in the unfamiliar sedentary life,
and few medical or educational facilities were
available to them. The pastoralists had not been
converted to cultivators; the tribesmen had learnt
no new attitudes, unless an increased contempt and
hatred for the peasant life they had now experienced
for themselves.[26] By the early 1940s, the tents
were brought back or rebuilt, the pastures were
reoccupied, and the chiefs resumed control, in some
cases even before Riza Shah's abdication, in
September 1941, following the British and Soviet
occupation of Iran to establish a supply route to
the Eastern Front.

During and after the occupation (1941-5) the
main tribal groups maintained a newly-regained
degree of autonomy under their chiefs. This was
particularly the case with the Kurds, whose leaders
with Soviet support established a short-lived
Republic at Mahabad in 1946. At the same time,
their neighbours the Shahsevan demonstrated their
loyalty to the Pahlavis (as they had almost unanim-
ously since their pacification in 1923) by helping
in the destruction of the Soviet-backed regime of
Azarbayjan. To the south the Bakhtiari, though not
politically united, were generally well-disposed to
the Pahlavis; the Qashqai on the other hand never

forgave the Pahlavis for the death of their chief
Soulat al-Douleh; more unified than other tribal
groups, they rebelled in 1946, successfully demanding
the removal of Communists from the Cabinet. Later
they demonstrated support for Dr Musaddiq between
1951 and 1953.

During the 1950s and the 1960s, after the downfall of Musaddiq, Muhammad Riza Shah resumed his
father's policy to the tribes, though more cautiously. The chiefs were deposed, chiefships were abolished, nomad settlement was encouraged and aided by
the instigation of irrigation projects in tribal
territories, and the Land Reform of the 1960s had
some success at least in undermining the economic
power of tribal chiefs. Resistance, such as the 1963
revolt of the Qashqai and Boyr Ahmad in Fars, was
ruthlessly suppressed. Often the very existence of
'tribes' and even 'nomads' was officially denied. In
a generally depressed agricultural sector, which
suffered heavily from discrimination in the increasingly centralised and industrialising state, pastoralism suffered most of all. Capitalist penetration,
rapid inflation, and government measures such as the
nationalisation of pastures and the strict control
of prices, especially of meat, ruined the economy of
nomad tribespeople by the later 1960s and 1970s.

So effective was this economic suppression that
by the mid-1970s the tribal political threat was
held to have disappeared; tribal cultures were now
'discovered', particularly by the Empress Farah, as
respectable objects of academic and touristic
interest. The growth of opposition to the regime
during the 1970s, however, though largely urban,
found strong echoes among some tribal groups. This
was mainly among Sunnis in border areas, and coincided with movements for autonomy among large ethnic
groups which straddled the frontiers: the Kurds, the
Arabs of the south-west, and the Baluches of the
south-east. Whatever the political colour of the
various movements, they demonstrated increasing
resentment of discrimination at both local and national levels and of the imposition of ethnic outsiders in positions of authority, and articulated
aspirations for some regional autonomy and the right
to cultural self-expression. Tribalism, as a basis
for the recruitment of support and the organisation
of resistance forces, appears to remain important at
least among Kurds and Baluches, much less so among
the Arabs.

Tribespeople as such played a very minor role
in 1978 in what was essentially an urban revolution.

Introduction

It was only as central control broke down in winter
1978-9 that some tribal groups began to take advantage of the situation, and only with the establishment of the Islamic Republic in spring 1979, and the
clarification of the nature of the new regime, that
a tribal resurgence became widespread around the
country.
   Reaction to the breakdown of control took
several, predictable forms: there were attacks on
government offices, and on army and gendarmerie
posts, with the apparent aims of seizing arms and
settling old scores; there was a reformation of old
tribal social and political groups, and the return
to power of former leaders; and there was a recovery
of pasture-lands that had been seized by government
and the ejection of city-based stockmen and merchants. Land has been a major factor in events since
the revolution, in tribal areas as elsewhere. Early
actions involving Kurds and Turkmens were apparently
associated with their seizure of lands which had
been removed from tribal possession under the
Pahlavis, while more recent owners received support
from agents of the new government. There was everywhere great competition and confusion over land,
with a general rejection of the results of the Shah's
Land Reforms.
   From early on the tribal groups were wary of,
and often hostile to, local representatives of the
revolution: the fanatical and insensitive pasdaran
guards, and the kumitehs - which usually represented
the continuing interests of landowners and merchants
under the Pahlavis. The consciousness of 'national
minorities', tribal or ethnic, was awakened and
inflamed by the government's attitude to them, early
shown in 1979 by Khumeyni's treatment of the Kurds
and Turkmens; later declarations of sympathy and
support for the minorities have not deceived them.
   There appears to have been little interest
among the tribes in the stated aims of the revolution. The only Islamic response of any scale has
been among Sunni groups, Kurds and Baluches, where
religious figures have led their followers in resistance to Shii/Persian domination. The left was generally distrusted, although some educated younger
tribespeople, students, professionals or former
soldiers, have tried to organise leftist activity
among their fellows. Among tribal groups, only the
Kurds and the Baluches again have political parties,
with connections across the frontiers; the Arab
resistance (for example as manifested in the London
Embassy siege in spring 1980) is not tribal in

character. Few people among the minorities want independence from Iran, but most appear to want local
autonomy and self-expression, control of their own
land, and at least much greater involvement in development projects instituted in their territory under
the Shah; these demands have in most cases been formulated and presented to the government, which has so
far shown little sign of granting any of them formally, though informally it has conceded control of
many tribal groups and sometimes whole districts to
tribal leaders. It has once more become respectable
and relevant to belong to a tribal group.

The revolution has had some beneficial economic
effects for the tribespeople, especially pastoral
nomads, who have not only regained their pastures
and returned to pastoralism on a large scale, but
have found much more favourable markets for their
produce. Like peasant cultivators, tribespeople may
have gained considerably from the cancellation of
interest payments on debts. The recovery of agriculture, on the other hand, has been slow, and is not
helped by the continuing political uncertainties.

During 1980 and 1981 attitudes seemed to have
hardened. The new regime's policy towards tribal and
other minorities is emerging as, if anything, harsher
in its discrimination and Persian chauvinism than
that of the Pahlavis. Though the tribal role, if any,
in the war with Iraq is not known to the present writer, there do appear to have been armed clashes between government forces and several tribal groups
other than the continuing conflict in Kurdistan.

Beck, who has written the most comprehensive
available accounts of the role of the tribes during
and following the revolution, notes that:

> The resurgence of tribalism, rather than being
> the 'survival' of an archaic form of organiza-
> tion, is instead a very contemporary response
> to current conditions of central weakness and
> to the center's attempts to establish political
> domination.[27]

Afghanistan from 1800 to 1980

By 1800 both Sadozai rule and Pushtun imperial pretensions were rapidly fading.[28] The first quarter
of the century was marked by intense rivalry between
the Sadozai Popalzai and Muhammadzai Barakzai
branches of the Durrani, and by considerable loss of
territory. Timur Shah's sons Zaman Shah (1793-1800),

Introduction

Shah Mahmud (1800-3, 1809-18) and Shah Shuja (1803-9)
alternated on the throne at Kabul, until the last was
forced into exile in India by the Muhammadzai, while
Shah Mahmud was driven off to Herat. In 1818 Fatih
Khan Muhammadzai was blinded and executed by his
protégé Shah Mahmud; this brought to an end Muhammadzai acceptance and support of Sadozai leadership of
the Pashtun tribal confederacy, which had now been
long cut off from its Indian revenues and relied on
the tribes for support. The Muhammadzai, who since
Hajji Jamal's time had been the most powerful tribal
faction in the empire, now formally took over control. Separate provinces (Peshawar, Kashmir,
Kandahar, Kabul) fell under the independant rule of
Fatih Khan's brothers, while Herat remained in
Sadozai hands under Shah Mahmud, who acknowledged
Qajar suzerainty until 1829.
     The youngest brother, Dost Muhammad, eventually
consolidated the Afghan provinces; but he began in
1826 with only Ghazni, Kabul, Charikar and Jalalabad
under his control, while Baluchistan and the eastern
territories of Kashmir, Multan and Peshawar were
lost to the Sikhs under Ranjit Singh, and the Uzbek
khanates of the north were autonomous of Kabul. Dost
Muhammad made up the loss of revenue from the east
by forcing non-Durrani tribes into payment of back-
taxes. He set about creating a Barakzai-led confederacy, using various strategies to gain the
support of the disparate groups. He appealed to
Muslim unity in the struggle against the Sikhs; he
won over the Shiite Qizilbash at Kabul and conquered
their co-sectarians in the Hazarajat, but prevented
them from uniting; he took wives from families of
religious leaders, wealthy merchants and tribal and
regional chiefs. At the same time he cultivated the
support of the frontier tribes such as Mohmand and
Yusufzai, and paid subsidies to the Khyber tribes,
continuing the practice of his predecessors since
Nadir Shah. Lack of funds prevented his completing
the political and economic integration of the
country by 1839, when the British, having previously
supported the deposed Sadozai Shah Shuja in an
attack on Kandahar, occupied Kabul in Shah Shuja's
name (see chapter 4). With the help of considerable
subsidies to tribal chiefs, the British remained in
Kabul and Kandahar for two years, until the Afghans
rallied under Dost Muhammad's son Akbar Khan to
eject the invaders.
     British policy towards the frontier tribes
since the 1830s, of dealing firmly by taking hostages,
imposing taxes and inflicting punishments, rather

than negotiating, served to sharpen tribal resentment of them and their representatives, so that any
Afghan ruler who openly had British support forfeit-
ed that of the tribes. On his return in 1843 from
exile in India, Dost Muhammad emerged from the first
Anglo-Afghan war with a new role as Defender of the
Faith against the infidel invaders, and as redeemer
of Afghanistan from an Empire whose power would seem
increasingly formidable with the passing years. But
after he unsuccessfully took the offensive against
the British in alliance with the Sikhs in 1848, the
Afghans gradually fell into dependence on the British
for their own defence.

For two decades from 1855 British policy towards
Afghanistan was formally one of non-intervention, or
'Masterly Inactivity'. Their main objective remained consolidation in India; as for the frontier
tribes, the Afghan Amir's authority over them should
not be recognised but they should be used as a buffer and dealt with by strategies of divide and rule.
By the agreements of 1855 and 1857, British support
in defence of the western frontier against Iran was
guaranteed, and the Afghans, receiving substantial
subsidies, remained quiet during the critical period
of the Indian mutiny, which started shortly after
the second treaty was signed. The expanding Russian
Empire was becoming a clear threat to the Afghans in
the north, as the British Empire was consolidating
its power to the east and south. These two
European Empires determined the environment in which
the Muhammadzai emirate in Afghanistan acquired
fixed territorial boundaries and evolved into a
state (see chapter 2).

During his second reign (1843-63) Dost Muhammad
succeeded with British assistance in reunifying the
Afghan realm. In the 1850s he took over the various
northern provinces and khanates, and Kandahar, while
just before his death he recaptured Herat, to which
Iran had abandoned claims, and thus completed the
consolidation of the present territory of Afghanistan.
The court at Kabul resembled a tribal council. The
non-Barakzai Durrani maintained their privileges
jealously, but the Amir challenged the non-Durrani,
especially the Ghilzai at Ghazni; and he claimed
sovereignty over the frontier tribes, though the
British still refused to recognise this.

After Dost Muhammad's death, civil war once
more ensued, until Sher Ali gained control in 1869.
He secured the co-operation of the tribes, on whom
he continued to depend. Meanwhile, as the Russians
advanced in Central Asia, advocates of 'Forward

Policy' gained ground in British Indian circles. By 1873 (without Afghan knowledge) the two Empires reached a territorial understanding that Afghanistan south of the Oxus would remain outside the Russian sphere of influence. Around the same time British arbitration settled the Sistan boundary with Iran, to Afghan disapproval.

While the British were thus defining his borders, Sher Ali was attempting to obtain subsidies from them, assurances of support against the Russians, and recognition of his son's succession in Kabul. Negotiations over this eventually broke down, whereupon Sher Ali turned to the Russians, and admitted a Russian envoy to Kabul while denying a similar privilege to the British. This was interpreted as a casus belli by the British, who invaded in late 1878. Sher Ali died while escaping towards Russia, and was replaced by his son Yaqub, who ruled in Kabul under British patronage until the September 1879 uprising, when for the second time Afghans slaughtered a British mission. After Yaqub's abdication, the British ruled directly in Kabul until August 1880, when they permitted Abd al-Rahman, Sher Ali's nephew and rival, who had spent the preceding decade in exile north of the Oxus, to accede to rule in Kabul under a settlement whose terms would govern Afghan-British relations for nearly 40 years. In return for subsidies, the Afghans yielded conduct of their foreign affairs to Britain.

While the British settlement with Abd al-Rahman was being negotiated, Sher Ali's son Sardar Ayub Khan advanced from Herat and defeated the British forces at the historic battle of Maywand. Assisted by Abd al-Rahman, General Roberts marched from Kabul and routed the Afghans, but even before Maywand the British had learnt for the second time that conquest of Afghanistan would be expensive and less likely than a friendly alliance to provide the defence they sought against the Russians. As Roberts wrote from Kabul on 29 May 1880, 'I feel sure that I am right when I say that the less the Afghans see of us, the less they will dislike us.'[29] Accordingly, although British troops had withstood the major attack by about 30,000 Afghan tribesmen on 23 December 1879 in their Sherpur cantonment, they left Kabul in August 1880 never to return. It would be another hundred years before foreign troops would again fight in Kabul.

Abd al-Rahman's consolidation of the modern state of Afghanistan and his relations with the tribes have been exhaustively and brilliantly dis-

cussed in two books by Hasan Kakar, and major aspects
of his tribal policy are described in chapter 7
below.[30] He gained British support in having his
borders defined in the north with Russia and in the
south and east with British India. With British aid,
again, he built an army with which he undertook military campaigns against groups that had retained
varying degrees of autonomy within his borders,
including invasions of Kafiristan, where he performed perhaps the last conversions to Islam by the
sword. He was the first Amir seriously to attempt
to break the power of the tribes, using a mixture of
force, alliance, reprisals, bribes, and intrigues.
His campaigns were perforce piecemeal, and he made
every use of traditional inter-tribal rivalries,
obtaining religious injunctions from the mullahs
whenever he could. He reduced many independent
tribes to order, broke some and scattered them
around the country, destroying their strongholds.
However, rebellions were continuous throughout his
reign - Kakar says there were more than 40 - and
many tribes retained their economic and hereditary
powers. The Amir failed to extend his authority
over the frontier tribes, in the face of their own
resistance as well as continuing British policy of
using them as a buffer.

The effect of the Durand Line, which was established in 1893 as the frontier between Afghanistan
and India (now Pakistan), was to divide the state
allegiance of many tribal groups, to create a 'no-
man's land' between effective Afghan and British
control (see chapter 5). It failed to result in
the imposition of authority, but rather strengthened
the tribes' political position in Afghanistan, whose
rulers from then on paid more heed to their wishes
in formulating domestic policy.

Abd al-Rahman's achievements in providing
Afghanistan with some of the forms and symbols of
statehood marked new ground in the transition from
the tribally-based Durrani Empire to the Muhammadzai
state of Afghanistan, but the Amir retained many of
the attributes of a tribal khan. He received subsidies from and maintained peace with the British; by
becoming adept in diplomacy with them, and keeping
relations cool and remote, he was able to avoid the
appearance of being a mere creature of his imperial
patrons. Another source of revenue was the fertile
non-Pashtun and largely non-tribal regions which
made up as much as half his domain and furnished
lucrative employment and landholdings for his supporters. Revenues from these sources provided a

surplus to be distributed in tribal fashion as subsidies as well as to finance the centralising institutions of the state.

Abd al-Rahman's son and successor Amir Habibullah
(1901-19) found the central government in a strong
position. At first he offered amnesty to many rebel
chiefs, and generally sought to co-operate with the
tribes rather than to coerce them. He established a
council of state for tribal affairs, and other
measures to allow the will of the tribal leaders to
be felt. But neither he nor his father succeeded in
freeing the Muhammadzai from dependence on the
support or at least the acquiescence of the tribes.

While Abd al-Rahman and Habibullah had been
content with the role of mediator between their
largely tribal polity and its powerful neighbours,
building a strong central army in the process,
Amanullah, who succeeded to rule in Kabul after his
father's assassination in 1919, was intent on per-
fecting the state order in Afghanistan as a means
for implementing social and economic reforms inspired
by the west. Where his predecessors viewed isolation from their neighbours as a measure of their own
independence, and cultivated a diplomatic style cal-
culated to preserve this, Amanullah sought to open
the doors to foreign influence as an instrument of
intentional social change, and fought the Third
Anglo-Afghan War (1919) to ensure that access would
not be impeded by the existing alliance with British
India. But the tribes who supported his rule in
Kabul found that British subsidies were not replaced,
while their tribal culture suffered an intrusion of
foreign ideas and values. Amanullah assembled a
national jirga to approve Afghanistan's first written
constitution. When he was obliged to amend this as
a result of the Khost tribal rebellion in 1924, he
received notice of the discontent with his policies
that would contribute to his overthrow.

Amanullah sought a revolution from above through
his comprehensive plans for change; his modernising
legislation was perceived as impinging on tribal and
religious jurisdiction, and he soon came under
attack from the tribes and religious leaders who
depended on the tribes for support. In a polity
where power was decentralised and the state primarily
an urban phenomenon, he erred in not taking better
account of tribal values and tribal politics in the
formulation and implementation of his programme.
His plan for an economically developing liberal
bourgeois state, while displaying real genius for
state-building formulas, neither reckoned with the

realities of tribal power, nor (perhaps his main
failure) provided the national army required for
quelling the predictable tribal rebellions. Where
Ataturk in Turkey and Riza Shah in Iran, contemporary rulers with similar programmes to his, came to
power by overthrowing previous long-established
tribal dynasties, Amanullah succeeded to power as a
tribal chieftain himself. His difficulties with the
tribes tended to focus on central cultural issues
raised by his reforms, such as the role of women,
but the source of his troubles seems to have been
his abandonment of the role of tribal leader, treat-
ing Afghanistan as the state he sought to build
rather than the tribal society that it was. He was
in 1929 finally deposed, significantly not by the
Pashtuns, who were temporarily content with preserving their independence from central government, but
by a Tajik bandit, who ruled briefly in Kabul as
Amir Habibullah II, otherwise known as Bacha Saqao,
before tribal forces led by Nadir Khan turned power
over to a family descended from a brother of Dost
Muhammad: the Musahiban.
    Nadir Shah (1929-33), who had successfully
dealt with a tribal revolt in 1910 and had led border tribes in successful campaigns against the
British during the Third Afghan War, was more adept
in the role of tribal chief than was Amanullah.
During his short reign he set in motion the policy,
which would continue under his son Zahir Shah (who
ruled 1933-73) and nephew Daud (Prime Minister 1953-
63, President 1973-8), of reintroducing much of
Amanullah's programme. Balancing the forms of the
modern state against the realities of tribal power
typified the whole Musahiban era. Nadir's legitimacy primarily rested on the support of those tribes
who placed him on the throne in Kabul, and on the
co-operation of the urban classes most interested in
the development of the secular state. In return for
their support, some of the frontier tribes secured
privileges such as exemption from taxation and conscription. As Nadir and his brothers Hashim and
Shah Mahmud slowly rebuilt the capacity of the central government to deal with the occasional tribal
rebellions, they also practised adroit tribal politics as a means to reattain the 'tenuous balance
between central government authority and tribal
power'.[31]
    With the impending British withdrawal from
India, the Afghans began looking elsewhere for
economic assistance. After the Second World War
they turned to the United States, who reluctantly

became involved, first privately in the Hilmand irrigation project, then in a government subsidy to meet its escalating costs. Meanwhile the Pakhtunistan issue emerged, a campaign to secure the independence of Pathan frontier territory from the new state of Pakistan. This resulted in the transfer of power in 1953 from the generation of Nadir's brothers to that of his son, the reigning Zahir Shah, whose first cousin and brother-in-law Sardar Muhammad Daud replaced Shah Mahmud as Prime Minister. Daud's first aim was to strengthen the armed forces, both to bolster the Afghan position on Pakhtunistan, and to aid control of domestic opposition. Compared to his uncles, who were experienced and adept at tribal diplomacy, Daud relied more on modern weapons and the power they gave him over the tribes. Failing to get military aid from the United States, Daud turned to the Soviet Union, which, through sales of military equipment and provision of training programmes and advisors in the armed forces, developed the influence, especially in the tank corps and the air force, that would grow and eventually surface as political power in 1978.[32]

Daud's Pakhtunistan policy was a largely unlamented failure, his authoritarian style of dealing with political dissent objectionable to modern liberals, and his relations with the Soviet Union ominous to all but the small pro-Soviet left. He did however leave power (in 1963) with the widespread respect of Afghans for his ability to maintain order, however repressively, and for his success in attracting subsidies and aid for public projects. There was a growth in real disposable income which also led to a growth in the urban classes, who were demanding greater political participation. One element of these, the left, had been working underground to develop the pro-Soviet Khalq and Parcham parties, which emerged as the main organised political groups in Zahir Shah's new constitutional democracy.

The decade of Zahir (1963-73) was dominated by his new Constitution of 1964, marking a shift of power from the monarch to the urban elite, together with an accommodation to traditional tribal and rural leadership in the elected parliament. Various reforms were instituted, the general thrust being in the direction of greater American involvement so as to redress the balance with Afghanistan's powerful neighbour. Development proceeded slowly, however, largely through administrative inefficiency and increased corruption, factors which were responsible

for the inexcusable failure to deliver relief food
supplies to stricken central and north-western areas
in the droughts and famine of 1970-2. But remote
rural areas were becoming politically integrated
with the centre, and Zahir had no major problems
with the tribes.

It was rather from the left that trouble came.
In the freer atmosphere of the Constitution, the
left's power of organisation, access to subsidies,
and influence in the armed forces, far outstripped
its representation and numerical strength in parliament or its political connections in government. It
was with left support that Daud was installed as
President in July 1973 after a nearly bloodless coup.
Pakhtunistan, and the aggressive posture of Bhutto
on the frontier, once again became the leading problem of foreign policy, while the Soviet Union
became the new Republic's major friend. Opposition
came from organised Islamic groups; most notable was
a substantial guerrilla operation in Panjshir in
1975.

Daud made sure, however, not to alienate the
religious leaders too far, and continued to project
himself to the tribes in terms of the legitimacy of
the Musahiban family. His accession to power was
more a palace coup than a revolution. Daud also
sought to reduce his precarious dependence on the
left and on the Soviet Union. He put the
Pakhtunistan issue on the shelf, and was in the
process of reaching settlement with Bhutto when the
latter was overthrown. Meanwhile post-Vietnam,
post-Watergate America gave no diplomatic priority
to Afghanistan and made little effort to counter
growing Soviet influence. Daud turned to the
American proxy in the region, the Shah of Iran,
who offered to share some of the post-1973 oil
wealth, and may have assisted Daud in his purges of
the left; but by 1976 the Shah was forced to cut
back expenditure, and Daud was disappointed. Economic and political conditions worsened, and by early
1978, when the revolutionary process was well under
way in Iran, Daud was isolated both internationally
and within the country. As he started to move on
his own against the left in response to a mass demonstration at the end of April 1978, the armed forces,
led by the Soviet-dominated tank corps and air
force, struck, ending nearly two-and-a-half centuries of Durrani rule.

The People's Democratic Party which formed the
new government was very small, almost entirely
urban-based, and fatally ignorant of affairs in the

countryside. The two factions of the party, which
combined in the revolution but later fell apart into
bitter conflict, were distinguished by ethnic and
class background, and by policy orientation. The
Khalqi faction, led nominally until summer 1979 by
Nur Muhammad Taraki but dominated by Hafizullah Amin
until the Soviet intervention, had strong support
among students, and drew members from among non-
Durrani Pashtuns. They were more radical, claimed
to be leading a 'proletarian' revolution, and instituted what they hoped would be popular measures such
as land reform, cancellation of rural debt, and
abolition of brideprice. The Parchami faction, whose
members were ousted in early purges but returned to
power under Karmal with Soviet support at the end of
1979, came largely from middle-class intellectual
Tajiks and Persian-speaking Pashtuns; less hasty in
their programme, they followed their Soviet mentors'
line in labelling the revolution 'national democratic'.

As in Iran, the role of the tribes as such in
the 1978 revolution was negligible. Some observers,
however, have interpreted it as a further episode in
the long-standing Durrani-Ghilzai conflict: Taraki
himself, and possibly Amin, as well as several members of their government, were Ghilzai by origin, a
factor which was used to canvas support in the
Ghilzai homeland between Kandahar and Ghazni. In
fact the revolution had considerable popular support
at the start, though it is hard to know how people
in the countryside viewed it, whether in ethnic,
class or other terms. Certainly over the previous
decade resentment of Musahiban domination had built
up and peasants and labourers in areas where Pashtun
landlords (and others) had proved oppressive were
becoming aware of their class interests.[33] Non-
Pashtuns resented the Musahibans as Pashtuns, while
other Pashtuns resented the fact that like many
other urban Durrani the Musahibans had become
Persianised. The Khalqis too were generally identified as Pashtun, though they included many non-
Pashtuns in the government and declared a policy of
self-expression for all national minorities.

The manner in which the Khalqis implemented
their reforms, the severity of their treatment of
opponents, and the growing Soviet presence, soon
alienated much of their support. Resistance grew,
both in town and countryside, and intensified in
response to Amin's brutalities in the latter half
of 1979. The resistance has been notorious from the
beginning for its lack of unity. The different

ethnic and tribal groups have had different aims,
and different class interests are also represented.
Thus most of the vocal groups familiar to the world's
press on the Pakistan frontier are more or less
reactionary, with an Islamic banner and a programme
that envisages abandonment of socialism and restoration of Pashtun control. Other frontier Pathans,
with their egalitarian and democratic traditions,
have proved ambivalent and sometimes accommodating
to the Kabul regime. Groups most active in resistance inside the country, especially Tajiks, Hazaras
and Uzbeks, have other ideas. Although Islamic
elements have received considerable support from
outside (from Pakistan and the Arab world, and particularly since the events of 1978-9 from Iran) there
has not been great interest inside the country in
the idea of an Islamic Republic, other than a general insistence on ridding Afghanistan of a regime
which is selling Islam to atheist Russians. The
Shiite Hazaras, who have had much success in liber-
ating their territory, have received support from
Iran but are not doctrinally committed to Khumeyni.
The Baluches and Brahuis of the south-west have
mostly gone to join their national liberation movements in Iran or Pakistan. The Tajik and Uzbek
population of the north, where much of Afghanistan's
industry has been located, are more progressive than
others, have long been anti-Pashtun, and many have
had bitter experience of life under the Soviets. One
of the most active and widely supported resistance
groups in 1980 was the United National Front, a
Chinese-favoured union of the independent left and
centre largely composed of Hazaras and other groups
operating in the northern half of the country: many
of them used to follow a Maoist line, but by 1980
they called themselves 'national democrats', though
non-aligned and of a very different character from
the Karmal regime. Their leader, Majid Kalakani, a
Tajik from the same village as Bacha Saqao, was
arrested in early 1980 and executed in June; he
became something of a nationalist martyr.[34]
     1980 and 1981 have seen the further promotion
of a Soviet-style 'nationalities' policy, designed
apparently both to undermine the unity of opposition
to the regime and to prepare the way for eventual
assimilation of non-Pashtun groups of the north with
the nationalities of Soviet Central Asia. Meanwhile
some of the most effective resistance operations
have taken place among non-tribal Tajiks, for
example in the Panjshir valley, while the Pashtuns,
the major tribal element, however successful in

pursuing their traditional guerrilla activity against the regime, have offered a far less effectively co-ordinated resistance, being frequently pre-occupied with their own internal (tribal) conflicts.

None the less, it is clear that whatever the political or religious platform of the different resistance groups, in the present crisis tribal and ethnic ties continue to provide most Afghans with their strongest loyalties and most effective mode of organisation.

The 'Tribal Problem' and the 'Problem of Tribe'

The foregoing narrative, following the main emphases in the sources, has summarised tribal political history largely from the state perspective, in terms of the way successive rulers have dealt with the 'tribal problem': how both to make use of and to control the tribal elements in the population. The use of the terms 'tribe' and 'tribal' has, however, concealed a wide diversity of social, economic, cultural and political forms. This diversity - almost as great within this region as anywhere in the world - precludes any substantive definition of 'tribe' as a particular kind of social group but raises more general theoretical issues associated with the 'problem of tribe' and the related problem of 'the origin of the state'.[35]

There are several major issues here. Are tribes precursors of the state in an evolutionary sequence or, as several writers have suggested, creatures of the state? How far are tribes defined in terms of their relations with states - and vice versa? What conditions bring about the combination of disparate elements, the development of hierarchical inequalities and the centralisation of government, in other words, the formation of confederacies or 'secondary states'? Does the state arise from social stratification or vice versa? How far are tribal systems necessarily segmentary, egalitarian, decentralised, autonomous, and hence opposed to the state as the source of inequality, central authority and government? Can we resolve the paradox presented by the perspective, perpetuated in the preceding account and in some of the following chapters, of the city as centre and the tribes as peripheral, while the political reality was often of the state and its dependant peasants and urban population dominated by tribal leaders? How far have tribal responses to the two recent revolutions been historically predictable as reactionary and anti-state?

Before such issues can be discussed further, the various forms of tribal organisation in the two countries should be summarised - at the risk, for the moment, of attributing a static nature to what were, throughout the period, changing and dynamic social systems.

Tribal Socio-Political Forms in Afghanistan. Afghan tribalism, which has remained a strong political force throughout the twentieth century, has not on the whole been based on pastoralism or nomadism, although the tribal groups that formed the Ghilzai and Abdali confederations and provided the basis for central, expanding leadership in the eighteenth century included large pastoral nomadic elements. Politically active ('troublesome') tribes were more often settled villagers or traders than pastoral nomads. Most nomads were tribal, but many more tribespeople were settled than nomadic. Nomads were indeed more vulnerable to oppression or attack than the warrior tribesmen of the hills with their strong forts.

There are two main dimensions of variation in socio-political forms among Afghan tribal groups: between different Pathan groups, and between Pathans and others. Of all tribal groups in Afghanistan and Iran, the Pathans had perhaps the most pervasive and explicit segmentary lineage ideology on the classic pattern, perpetuated not only in written genealogies but also in the territorial framework of tribal distribution. Since the time of Ahmad Shah (and earlier) the notion of the ethnic and cultural unity of all Pathans (in religion, genealogy, language, custom, especially features like Pashtunwali, jirga, seclusion) was familiar as a symbolic complex of great potential for political unity, but in spite of their centralisation in the monarchy the Pathan tribes were predominantly characterised by endemic inter-tribal hostilities and by diffuse political organisation, throwing up petty lords at most.

Among Pathans during the nineteenth century there were three main socio-political forms.[36] One involved marginal agriculture or pastoralism, practised in remote mountain valleys and producing little surplus; probably there was a regular short-fall, made up by trading or raiding or long-distance labour-migration; egalitarian, communal social forms flourished among independent tribal groups, fierce in their defence of territory but rarely persuaded

to campaign far away. Typical were North West
Frontier groups such as Afridi, Mohmand, Wazir
(chapters 3 to 5), often regarded as living closest
to the principles of Pakhtunwali. Another type,
equally remote from urban centres but inhabiting
more favoured, well-watered valleys where agriculture
was capable of producing a large surplus, exhibited
social stratification, usually with a leisured class
of martial Pakhtuns owning the land and dependant
groups working it; the best known example is the
Yusufzai of Swat.[37] A third, intermediate form was
found in areas that were more accessible to cities
and rulers, and where agriculture was reasonably
productive; here the influence of the state produced
a feudalistic, 'Asiatic' form of stratification,
involving a chiefly class with limited powers, a
broad mass of tribespeople, and a sizable substratum
of dependants. Many Durrani groups were of this
type (chapter 7).

Socio-economic differences between Pathans and
other tribal groups in Afghanistan were less significant than ethnic, cultural and political distinctions between them. Pathan relations with non-
Pathans are defined by rules proscribing intermarriage, by differences of language and sometimes
religion, and by economic exchanges that usually
mark the Pathans in superior status. Some non-Pathan
groups - Aymaqs, Hazaras and Uzbeks - had rather
more powerful chiefs than most Pathans. Within the
Durrani kingdom, where the pastures were dominated
by Pathan nomads, who could claim ethnic and political identity with the rulers, pastoral nomadism
could not be the refuge of subordinate political
groups that it was in Iran. Those that resisted
Pathan domination did so in mountain fastnesses
(the Hazarajat, Kafiristan/Nuristan) where they
practised a mixed agriculture similar to that of
some of their would-be rulers.

Pastoral nomadism in Afghanistan was an economic adaptation. More important than nomadism or
settlement as criteria for political or cultural
affiliations were ethnic and tribal identities.
Pastoral nomadism was not the basis for tribalism,
but tribal organisation, whatever its economic base,
has been an advantage for groups eager to maintain
their independence or to expand their frontiers.
Afghan rulers were more dependant on the main tribal
chiefs than were the Shahs of Iran, but neither
rulers nor chiefs kept close links with nomadic elements among their followers.

44

Introduction

<u>Tribal Socio-Political Forms in Iran</u>. In Iran, by
contrast, tribal organisation and nomadism may be
seen as political and cultural responses to a condition of alienation from and opposition to the state,
as much as economic or ecological adaptations. In
general, the city-based central authority in Iran
considered tribes and nomads synonymous as a major
focus of opposition. The Qajar rulers soon became
an urban elite, and other tribes grew alienated from
them, with no strong reason or means for identifying
themselves with the rulers culturally or otherwise.
In the late nineteenth century, the Qajar 'tribe'
was very small, a mere one or two thousand families;
perhaps aware of the inevitability of losing touch
with their original wider tribal support, the rulers
for some time continued a kind of migration to
summer quarters. The chiefs of the other major confederacies too, though establishing settled bases in
towns or cities, maintained nomadic households and
pretensions.
     Within nineteenth-century Iran, three main
socio-political formations among the nomad tribes
can be identified. Centralised, state-like nomad
confederacies developed in the southern Zagros area
(chapters 9 to 12) in conditions of comparatively
high population density, in close contact with
settled cultivators, in proximity to major cities
and trade routes, but at some distance from state
frontiers. In similar conditions in north-western
Iran, a number of confederacies were more fragmented
and ephemeral, but still unified (chapters 13 and
14); they differed from the southern Zagros groups
in being on or close to important frontiers, in
regions where a network of competing, semi-autonomous,
town-based khanates had flourished in the eighteenth
century. Thirdly, in the east were diffuse and
uncentralised tribal groups such as the Turkmens and
Baluches (chapter 8), some of which the Qajar government attempted to control through immigrant Kurdish
chiefs; these groups were near more open frontiers
and steppe areas, where population was scattered and
major cities were more remote; similar were some
groups in north-western Afghanistan (chapter 6).
     It is unclear how far the Iranian stereotype of
tribespeople as nomads had its roots in the culture
of settled Iranian society, in the self-image of
nomads/tribespeople themselves, or merely in the perceptions and writings of foreign visitors to the
country. There have certainly been shifts in perceptions and self-perceptions of the tribespeople/
nomads, particularly with the recent suppression of

both tribalism and nomadism in Iran.   There has
never been a simple correlation of the two, though
the usage of several ethnic/tribal names would suggest there were: in various parts of Iran, 'Kurd',
'Lur', 'Arab', 'Shahsevan', 'Baluch' are synonymous
with 'tent-dwelling pastoral nomad';[38] in such areas
settlement (the abandonment of pastoralism and
mobile tent-camps for cultivation and fixed dwellings) entailed loss of political mobility and probably independence and commonly led in other ways to
'detribalisation' unless in areas where the tribespeople could claim identity with the dominant ethnic
group or where they settled as kin-groups to cultivate their own land or that of their chief.   But
these same names (Kurd, Lur, etc.) are also used, in
other contexts, of and by tribal groups whose members are by no means all nomads or even pastoralists;
moreover, many Zagros groups (Bakhtiari, Boyr Ahmad,
Kuhgiluyeh, Mamasani) bear names referring to their
territory and not to nomadism.
    On the whole, however, the nomad/settled con-
ceptual distinction coincided with tribal/non-tribal;
at any one time substantial parts of many tribal
groups were settled or half-settled farmers, but the
economic basis of most tribally organised society in
Iran was pastoral nomadism or semi-nomadism.   Politically important tribal groups, at least until this
century, were almost all nomadic or semi-nomadic,
their importance related to their potential, when
united by a strong leader, for raising bodies of
cavalry.   Such armies, mobilised for campaigns away
from tribal territory, rarely exceeded a few thousand
men, but they were still the best organised and most
formidable in the country at the time.   On the other
hand, the militia that settled leaders could muster
numbered only in hundreds and were usually active
only locally.   Those local elements active as a
'problem' in national political affairs were however
by no means drawn exclusively from the nomads.   The
core of the military forces wielded by the larger
confederations comprised, first, warriors from leading families, who tended to form part of both settled and nomad society at once, and secondly, their
armed henchmen, recruited from the destitute and
refugees of both nomad and peasant origins.[39]
    The most tangible variations among tribal groups
in the two countries are in production systems and
political structures: the former ranging from pastoralism to intensive agriculture, long distance
trade, raiding or labour migration; the latter from
fragmentary and independent communities somewhat

resembling the bands of hunting and gathering peoples, to centralised chiefdoms involving hundreds of thousands of people, considerable differentiation of wealth and status, and many of the trappings of states.[40]

A major contrast, superficially at least, can be drawn between on the one hand nomadic tribal groups of western Iran, such as some Kurds, Shahsevan and many groups located in the Zagros area, and on the other the settled Pathan groups of eastern Afghanistan. The former have a long history of local tribal chiefdoms and confederacies, yet they never (in recent centuries) ventured far from home, let alone to found major dynasties in Iran, Anatolia or Arabia (exceptional are the Bakhtiari, with their dynastic efforts earlier this century). By contrast, the Pathans have on the whole avoided the formation of chiefdoms or centralised confederacies in their own territory, yet over the past centuries have sent a number of expeditions of conquest into Iran and India, and indeed founded states and dynasties there.[41]

One approach that attempts to explain the variation in tribal forms and the emergence of confederacies and central leadership, posits a single, ideal-type tribal system, whose features may include (apart from pastoral nomadism, which we have already had to reject) a simple division of labour, a segmentary lineage system, egalitarian ideals or organisation, and political autonomy. This sort of approach has a long-established pedigree in studies of Middle Eastern societies. Very similar are theories of a tribal (pastoral nomadic) mode of production or socio-economic formation.[42] There is little agreement, however, on which features are essential to the ideal type (or mode of production or socio-economic formation). Thus, among our contributors, following anthropological orthodoxy, Hager, Ahmed, Garthwaite and van Bruinessen have taken the segmentary lineage system as a minimal criterion to distinguish tribal from non-tribal society; yet the necessity for this very feature is explicitly questioned by Anderson, Glatzer, Salzman, Beck and Digard. In some cases, political autonomy and cultural distinctiveness are more significant features of so-called 'tribes'. As for egalitarianism, Glatzer, Ahmed and Garthwaite argue, whether from economic or logical a priori grounds, that it is inherent to tribalism and nomadism; while one of the earliest and best models of Pathan tribes includes a hierarchy of authority as a basic feature.[43]

Whatever the nature of the ideal type proposed, deviations from it are attributed to a series of differentiating variables, commonly grouped into internal (such as culture, demography, ecology, economy) and external (such as the role of the state, the proximity of frontiers, cities and trade routes). We should consider these factors in turn.

Internal Dynamics of Tribal Organisation. In terms of cultural factors, all the tribal peoples discussed here adhere at least nominally to Islam (whether Sunni or Shii), recognise individual rights to property, observe rules of patrilineal succession and inheritance, give primacy in political and social activities to males (especially to paternal kin), express preferences for marriage among kinsfolk, and value egalitarianism, individualism and independence. Differences in these values and in kinship, religious and other symbolic and cultural systems are of degree rather than kind, and can often be only subjectively assessed. For example, differences between Pathan and Kurdish political organisation might be attributed to Pathan aversion to authority and insistence on equality, as opposed to comparative acceptance of chiefship and stratification among Kurds; but such an explanation is too easy, and even if it were based on a valid assessment of cultural differences there are certainly further historical and sociological reasons for them and they must also be put in the context of ecological and economic differences.[44]

In the ecological, economic and demographic conditions in which pastoral nomadism is practised in Iran, these common cultural factors have (it has been argued) led, particularly at the level of households, camps and economic organisation, to certain basic similarities, namely the practice of allocating grazing rights to patrilineal descent groups, an expanding population, the ability to field large bodies of armed men, and a long-term tendency to encroachment on settled society or to settlement.[45] In pastoral systems, although animals are owned by individual families, grazing rights are usually held jointly by camps or groups of camps, guaranteed by their membership of a politically united tribal group or allocated to them by a leader. Some tribal cultivators operate a similar form of joint tenure, with periodic redistribution within the local community (Kurdistan) or between communities (some Pathans). If local communities thus have joint access to territory, a major potential cause

of internal conflict is absent. Most agricultural
groups, however, and some pastoralists (see chapters
6 and 14) recognise individual rights to territory,
which provide a cause of endemic conflict among
paternal kin within local communities. This is certainly at the basis of the tarburwali cousin-rivalry
among settled Pathans (chapter 5).[46]

At whatever level territory is held, rivalries
tend to develop between neighbouring holders, whether
brothers, cousins, camps, lineages or tribes. Particularly among settlers with individuated rights,
local-level rivalries over access to territory may
lead to pervasive factionalism, contradicting a segmentary ideology, and inhibiting unity in the face
of an outside threat. Nomads, with their tendency
to allocate territorial rights to larger groups, are
likely to co-operate politically on a larger scale
against outsiders; but even here, in the absence of
effective superior authority, relations between
autonomous political units within a region take on
the familiar chequer-board pattern: neighbours maintain relations of hostility on their boundaries, but
ally themselves with their neighbours' neighbours,
forming a larger pattern of two coalitions or blocs
throughout or even beyond the region. Such patterns
have been recorded at various levels, sometimes
several at once.[47]

Factional oppositions in a region mainly involve the leaders of the political units, and
subordinate leaders may upset a balanced relation by
defecting with their own followers to the other
side. Sometimes regional alignments of tribal groups
extend into urban society. Out of this tendency
arises the notorious reluctance of tribal groups to
combine on a regional, let alone a national basis
(see chapter 12); but ephemeral tribal combinations
were still the largest and most effective organised
political groups in nineteenth-century Iran and
Afghanistan.

When a strong leader seeks to control a whole
region, he usually gains support first from one bloc
alone and forms it into a coalition or confederacy
to overcome the other. Such tactics were employed
by the main conquerors of the period, by established
rulers in their tribal policies and by imperial
agents.

In some areas, especially among predominantly
segmentary Sunni groups such as Turkmens, Baluches,
Kurds and Pathans, factional rivalries among tribal
groups were mediated by locally-based religious
leaders: either Sayyids, sometimes from lineages

merged in the tribal system, or charismatic mullahs, or Sufi sheykhs or pirs. On occasion such religious leaders could move beyond their role of mediation and unite large groups into at least an ephemeral confederacy for specific politico-religious pur- poses.[48] It should be stressed that the ability to unite usually rested on the hope of material gain and the absence of material cause for conflict, as much as, if not more than, on any 'tribal' notions of common descent, or religious or other ideology of unity.

At the local level, effective leadership can be sustained as a non-productive role only if a surplus is produced, whether from a pastoral or agricultural economy, or from raiding, and whether traded or con- sumed within the tribal group. The ability to pro- duce surplus also attracts state attempts at control and extraction, but does not necessarily lead to meaningful inequalities in the form of leaders or a ruling elite: tribespeople may deliberately under- produce or suppress potential leaders in order to frustrate outside attempts at control. Large-scale political co-ordination and the control of conflict certainly call for leaders, but do not necessitate them.

'External' Variables: State Control. This discus- sion of 'internal' factors and processes in tribal organisation has treated them as systematically interconnected and to a degree culturally autonomous, that is, controlled by the perceptions and strate- gies of the tribespeople themselves. However, the main variables determining the emergence of central leadership and the political nature of individual tribal groups are generally agreed to be external, particularly the history, degree and kind of state control. Glatzer, Garthwaite and Gellner suggest that uncentralised, diffusely organised tribal groups are found either in the absence of state control or within a strong state. Garthwaite adds that tribes develop inequalities and form strongly centralised confederacies in order to confront the state, and are able to maintain such strength so long as the state bureaucracy is weak. Digard, accepting the importance of the state factor, draws attention to internal, evolutionary processes where- by such inequalities develop within a tribe, while van Bruinessen argues strongly that, in Kurdistan, tribes as political groups were the creation of the state and that when state influence was withdrawn there was a 'devolution' in scale and complexity of

tribal organisation. Yapp, more reluctant to gener-
alise than his fellow-historian Garthwaite, nevertheless suggests the principle that modern states
cannot tolerate diffusely organised, 'jellyfish'
tribes, but that in order to destroy them the state
must first provide them with a 'backbone' in the
form of chiefs. Indeed, many so-called tribes owe
their existence as political, even cultural units,
to the imposition of territorial limits and central
leadership by a state.[49] Many tribal groups lack
indigenous terms for chiefs and political groups,
using Turkish and Arabic terms presumably introduced
by the state.

At any time, state control extends over only
some of the tribal areas, and any one tribal area
comes under control only part of the time. Tribespeople commonly contrast 'tribal' with 'government'
periods in their history, while governments and
tribes refer to 'government' and 'tribal' areas. The
Pathans, for example, distinguish yaghistan from
hukumat (chapter 3), categories equivalent to the
Moroccan opposition bled es-siba/bled el-makhzen.[50]
These terms do not denote objective conditions, but
are cultural categories referring to perceptions of
particular places at particular times, for which I
shall use the term 'situation', whether 'government'
or 'tribal'.

In fact, rulers' notions of 'control' - and
indeed of 'tribe' - may be very different from the
perceptions of the tribespeople themselves. Also
relevant is Yapp's suggestion (chapter 4) that the
character of the state (or empire) itself determines
its attitude to tribal populations. He and other
contributors, moreover, stress that no state or
empire with which tribespeople have had to deal was
ever monolithic: it was represented at different
levels by individuals, each with political or cultural biases.

The nature of state control depends partly on
the strength of government and partly on the accessibility of the tribal group concerned, in terms of
both terrain, for example the proximity of mountain
or desert refuges, and distance from cities and
roads, the main organs of government. It also
depends on the will and attitude of both government
and tribes, their motives for seeking or avoiding
control.

One notion that has been extensively used in
anthropological studies of tribe-state relations is
that of 'encapsulation', a situation arising from a
variety of state policies whereby a degree of

cultural and political autonomy is allowed to tribal
groups located within the territorial boundaries of
the state. Policies towards encapsulated groups
range from nominal or geographical inclusion,
through 'indirect rule', to 'integration' which
breaks down the encapsulation.[51] Strictly speaking,
states do not recognise the existence or operation
of any semi-independent or autonomous polities within
their territorial frontiers, so that when states deal
with encapsulated tribes they are usually acting as
empires (see chapter 2): 'indirect rule', for instance, is the policy of an empire not of a state.
    In both Afghanistan and Iran up to the present
century, state attitudes to encapsulated tribes have
been ambivalent. Aspirants to power have relied on
tribal support, while established rulers cultivated
the tribes as sources of revenue, military levies,
and agricultural produce. But tribes were also
feared as disruptive elements, prone to raiding non-
tribal society, to damaging crops, to armed opposition to government, often to dynastic ambitions of
their own, though these, as well as the martial
ambitions of the rulers (and hence the spoils they
could offer their tribal supporters) were checked
by the commencement of the Great Game in the nineteenth century, when Russia and Britain interfered
to impose frontiers and keep them intact, to safeguard trade routes, as well as to keep dynasties in
power (chapters 2, 5, 7, 14).
    In Iran during Qajar times and Afghanistan
under the Durranis, a form of 'indirect rule' of
the tribes was usually attempted: the tribes were
allowed autonomy so long as they kept within certain
bounds of action defined by government.[52] Stronger
rulers would control the tribes by nominating
leaders, keeping chiefly members as hostages, establishing marriage alliances between chiefly and
royal families, executing dissidents, or fostering
dissension between rivals for leadership or between
neighbouring tribes. Following earlier precedents,
Fath Ali Shah in Iran and Amir Abd al-Rahman in
Afghanistan practised wholesale transportation and
relocation of tribal groups, a more drastic policy
which could achieve several results, not all
intended. Later rulers in Iran - Nasir al-Din Shah
and the Pahlavis - sought to assimilate the tribes
by integrating them into the rest of the population,
and attempted to break tribal power and extend state
control in the tribal areas by replacing hereditary
chiefs with local governors, developing disciplined
and non-tribal troops in the state army, improving

communications, and in some cases forcibly settling
nomadic elements (chapter 14). Far longer than the
Qajar Shahs, the Durrani Amirs of Afghanistan
remained paramount chiefs of a tribal confederacy on
the imperial pattern; Abd al-Rahman attempted to
establish a state in the modern sense, but only
Amanullah sought to break away completely from reliance on tribal support, with results fatal to his
reign. The Musahibans strove rather to extend state
control into tribal areas, while retaining their
role as chiefs (see chapter 2).

At various times, however, and almost continuously in several areas, government was unable to follow
even indirect methods of rule, and had to recognise
a 'tribal situation' in which its claims to the
allegiance of certain tribes were purely nominal
and territorial. Government might be able to mount
a predatory military expedition, with the aim of
collecting revenue. Tribes located on state frontiers might be encouraged by either side, by the
payment of open or secret 'subsidies', to remain
quiet as a buffer or to operate actively as 'wasps'.
This was particularly the case with the independent
tribes on Afghanistan's frontier with India/
Pakistan, whose relations with either state have
always been heavily influenced by the payment of
such subsidies (chapters 4 and 5).

In the present century, the fate of tribes in
Iran under the Pahlavis contrasts with the continued
dependence of the Durrani rulers of Afghanistan on
tribal support. As narrated earlier, by the 1970s
the Pahlavi regime had so effectively undermined the
economic base and political potential of the tribes
that it could increasingly direct public, academic
and touristic attention to tribal cultures as
picturesque and now harmless relics of a previous
age. This new attitude, undoubtedly influenced by
Western interest in the exotic, was partially
echoed in pre-revolutionary Afghanistan in regard
to the more colourful aspects of nomad and tribal
life, but here attitudes remained ambivalent in view
of the continuing importance of tribal affiliations
in many social and political contexts.

Tribal Attitudes and Strategies. State control is
clearly an important determinant of tribal political
organisation; but it is not simply an 'external'
force; its impact depends on how it is 'internalised'
by the tribespeople, and how they react to it.
Tribespeople normally have a number of choices.

When a government is serious about administering

tribal groups within its frontiers, these can react
by submission or resistance, that is, they can seek
a 'government' or a 'tribal' situation. Voluntary
submission is usually conditional, government continuing to tolerate tribal patterns of organisation
and ruling indirectly through chiefs responsible to
them. If the state is intent on unconditional submission and the more drastic measures of total
destruction of the tribal structure and integration
of people into the wider population, resistance is
likely and can take various forms. Tribespeople may
organise for military confrontation as a confederacy.
Another strategy is to avoid engagement, for example
by refusing to recognise any leader, indigenous or
imposed, and by maintaining a diffuse form of organisation - Yapp's 'jellyfish tribes' (chapter 4), and
Gellner's 'divide that ye be not ruled'; in some
cases the avoidance strategy even leads to the
abandonment of 'tribal' forms of organisation such
as segmentary lineages (chapter 6); or tribespeople
may choose flight rather than fight.[53] All such
avoidance strategies, whose most successful practi-
tioners have managed not to attract government attention at all, are more feasible in frontier, desert
and mountain locations, and in marginal conditions
where surplus is not produced and strong indigenous
leadership is unlikely, but they commonly go together
with an institutional inability to unite in extremis
to resist determined military aggression.
     The strategies of particular tribal groups may
alternate over time between acceptance of indirect
rule, military resistance, and avoidance, depending
on variations in the abilities and ambitions of both
their own leaders and government. The most successful tribal groups are probably those that maintain
a set of alternative institutions (for example,
leadership roles, institutionalised councils, segmentary lineages) and ideologies (both egalitarian
and materialist) by which they can adapt to conditions of autonomy as well as to the different
aggressive policies of states - of different states
or the same state at different times (cf. chapter
8). Tribesmen are often reported (e.g. chapters 6
and 12) to refer wistfully to an earlier 'golden age'
when supposedly there were 'real khans we could
willingly have followed, not like the charlatans of
today'; this could be interpreted as evidence of
alternative ideologies, an acceptance of the idea of
leadership under certain conditions.[54]
     In no case can tribal groups avoid some accom-
modation of their behaviour and organisation, either

in conformity with the aims and perceptions of one
state or another, or in opposition to the state so
as to maintain a degree of autonomy on their own
terms. In many cases, egalitarian ideals conflict
with a situation of real inequality due to interaction with the state.[55] On the other hand, the
coincidence of democratic ideals with the achievement of social forms approximating them, as in
tribal groups such as Wazir and Mohmand, is not
evidence of a 'pure', 'untouched' condition of tribal society, unaffected by any state or empire
(chapter 5), but rather the privileged and precarious result of 'encapsulation' in Bailey's sense,
and is possible only in certain frontier conditions
and as a direct reflection of relations with states.
That is, in my view, the social structure of the
North West Frontier tribes in the twentieth century
is a historical result of their ideological if not
military confrontations with states.

Types of Leadership. Tribal and government situations give rise to contrasting types of tribal
leadership, which may be termed the 'brigand' and
the 'chief'. In tribal situations there are opportunities for successful brigands to collect followers
and challenge states or their appointed agents.
Where tribespeople accept government authority,
however, there is usually a difficulty of communication, especially where there are disputes between
tribal nomads and settled peasants, and both sides
need an intermediary such as a hereditary chief,
with the resources both to represent his tribal
constituents and to deal on equal terms with government agents. Quite different abilities and strategies seem called for by the two types of leader.
The contrast corresponds to that drawn by Bailey
between the 'hirelings' and the 'faithful', bound
to their leaders by transactional and moral ties
respectively.[56]
     Actual leaders combine elements of the two
types. A brigand commonly begins with moral authority over a core of his fellow-tribespeople, though
the allegiance of other followers depends on his
ensuring a continuous flow of booty, and his
authority over them is strictly limited to this
transaction. Then, unless he has the abilities of
a Nadir Shah, he reaches the limits of his expansion,
and to retain his wider leadership he must extend
his moral authority by establishing a hereditary
dynasty or by acquiring recognition by a more powerful ruler as the legitimate, official leader of his

followers.

A chief, on the other hand, has to prove himself more able to command than his kinsmen; then, however strong the moral and symbolic authority of the chiefship, he has to maintain his personal position not only by performing the specific functions of chiefship, but by rewarding his followers, if not with booty, at least with lavish entertainment and hospitality; otherwise they may abandon him and support a rival, even the chief of another tribe. A chief with government support can maintain his position more easily than a brigand can widen his authority. A chief has duties to both government and followers, and his position is close to that of a feudal lord. Typically he collects tax and military levies, and maintains order for the government, while for his followers he conducts external political relations, adjudicates disputes, and (for nomads) allocates pastures and co-ordinates migrations.

These various 'functions' and 'duties' of chiefship, which followers may not accept as necessary, even where they consent to them, are all likely to provide the leaders with additional sources of wealth and power. Among some nomads, for example, the right to allocate pastures, particularly when recognised by government, was a major base of a chief's continuing power over his tribal followers. In addition, apart from various customary dues, he took for himself a large proportion of the tax he collected, and was given land grants for his services by some rulers. With this wealth, supplemented by private lands and flocks, a chief can not only display conspicuous hospitality and generosity to his followers and others, he can also support a large retinue of servants and henchmen to coerce opponents.

Although actual leaders combine elements of both brigand and chief, indigenous categories of leadership to some extent correspond to the two ideal types. The prototype khan in most tribal societies comes close to the brigand: khans are self-made men who achieve their position through personality, not age or genealogical position, though these may help; they create unity out of difference, or restore a previous unity; they are patrons, acting on behalf of trusting clients, but use their own initiative in action, risking their followers' disapproval; they speak to government as representatives rather than delegates. Anderson analyses (chapter 3) the problems of a Ghilzai

Introduction

leader who has gained power through leading a faction
but must legitimise it by 'tying the knot' of a
lineage group. The similar problems faced by the
Kurdish leader Simko are described by van Bruinessen
(chapter 13).
    A khan who achieves, or relies on, recognition
by the state, becomes something else - a chief - for
which there are other indigenous categories: the
Turkish beg, or ilbegi, the Kurdish agha, elsewhere
the katkhuda, malik, kalantar, sometimes sardar. By
contrast with khans, these are appointed by government or its agents among the tribespeople. An
extension of the chief is the 'paramount chief':
sardar or ilkhani, leader of a large tribal group,
recognised almost as a 'feudal lord' by the state.
    Other categories of leader include the 'elder'
or 'grey-beard' (mashar, spin-zhirey, sar-khel,
mastair, rish-safid, rispi, aq-saqal, etc.), a respected spokesman for a small lineage group or community. The elder is usually qualified on grounds
of age and seniority, and his political function is
likely to be impersonal, as a delegate not a representative. Elders do not bring unity to a group,
they emerge from unity.

Leaders, Cities, Trade and Frontiers. There was
always a close and necessary relation between tribal
leadership and cities. The first aim of a politically ambitious 'brigand' was the capture of a city;
a hereditary chief, on the other hand, would find
himself in a city, either as a hostage or on official
business, and he too inevitably made a base there.
When any leader came to town, he brought some of his
immediate followers and they would settle as his
servants or henchmen. Then there developed the well-
known paradox that a tribal dynasty needed a settled
urban base, but once established there it was corrupted by the luxuries of city life and sooner or
later drew away from most of its original tribal
support.
    The distance of a tribal group from cities,
frontiers and trade routes affected the ease with
which it could be controlled by government, and also
the ease with which in tribal times a leader could
acquire a source of wealth and security and a base
for expansion. Not only were remoter tribes comparatively free from interference, but it was more
difficult for a leader to persuade people to leave
home and join an expedition to capture a distant
city. Ambitious leaders needed both urban bases and
tribal support, and no ruler could rely on just one

of these elements. Each of the ruling tribal dynasties after the Safavids (Ghilzai, Afshar, Durrani,
Zand, Qajar) had a different metropolis, though each
conqueror first captured that of his predecessor
before moving to safer, neutral ground, which was
then diluted with forcibly transported elements.

In Afghanistan the Durrani dynasty was first
set in the tribal centre Kandahar but later moved to
Kabul, a comparatively neutral centre. Rulers then
had to make a choice between installing tribal
chiefs as official governors of their local towns,
thereby recognising their autonomy, or sending their
own state officials as governors with the difficult
task of conciliating and controlling the local
tribes. Control of trade routes was also a central
factor in the importance of the tribes on the
Afghan-Indian frontier, especially those in the
vicinity of Kabul and Peshawar, though for other
reasons the frontier tribes did not produce chiefs
who used either the trade routes or the cities as
springboards, unlike the various ambitious and
competing khans of nineteenth-century Afghan
Turkistan.

In Iran, Isfahan, Shiraz and Tehran were important in the rise of tribal dynasties other than the
rulers. The Bakhtiari khans grew in influence in
Safavid times as leaders of the tribal group closest
to the capital Isfahan, occupying at the same time
comparatively inaccessible territory. Tehran too,
the Qajar capital, was close enough for the
Bakhtiari chiefs to occupy in 1909. Meanwhile the
rise of the Qashqai khans in the late eighteenth
century was probably connected with the location of
the Zand capital at Shiraz, though they were always
vulnerable in that their migration routes passed
close to the city. In the nineteenth century,
Bakhtiari, Qashqai and Khamseh chiefs gained power
from their ability to control the increasingly
important trade crossing their lands. Later these
chiefs acquired further influence from their relations with the British. Many smaller cities were
left in the control of local tribal chiefs for all
or part of the period. Although no other confederacies developed central leadership on the scale of
the Bakhtiari and the Qashqai, some groups such as
the Shahsevan, Kurds, Turkmens and Baluches became
of as much concern as the former to the Qajar
government, mainly because of their widespread
raiding activities and disruption of the main trading routes. Baluches raided widely in the south-
east, while Turkmen forays, particularly on the

Tehran-Mashhad road, made both cultivation and trade
perilous in north-eastern Iran throughout the Qajar
period.

Many tribal groups have had a historical, if
intermittent role as guardians of state frontiers,
though in less secure times they may have served as
buffers, in effect to prevent too close definition
of a disputed frontier. This role was transformed
in the nineteenth century, when the states of the
region had their frontiers defined by the Great
Powers, and when communications began to improve.
Frontier tribes became increasingly a source of dispute between neighbouring states, and even more
preoccupied with their own role and situation. A
frontier location was a mixed blessing for any tribal
group: cross-frontier raiding and the attention of
governments could be a limited source of wealth or
local power for leaders, but their homelands were
now vulnerable and an insecure base for further
expansion. It was otherwise with groups further
away (such as the major Zagros confederacies), whose
interest for government, and whose vulnerability,
came from other sources: trade routes, proximity to
cities, location and accessibility of pastures and
migration routes.

Although the material is not yet available for
a systematic comparison to be made, location and
history of settlement clearly influence tribes-
peoples' perceptions of time and space, of descent
and territory, of tribe and state. Tribal groups
(such as Shahsevan) relatively recently located on
a frontier will have very different notions from
those (such as Kurds) whose lands have long straddled state frontiers, and these will all differ
again from groups (such as Bakhtiari, Qashqai,
Durrani, Ghilzai) located for centuries well inland.
Frontier tribes, for example, are more likely to
internalise the notion of territory (see chapter
14). Such matters require much further research.

Kurds and Pathans Contrasted. The contrast noted
earlier, between centralised groups in the Zagros
and north-west Iran and the 'republican' frontier
Pathans, could be rephrased as a question: why did
the latter never develop the chiefdoms of the
former, even on the limited scale of the Shahsevan
or the Kurds? Some assessment can now be made of
the relevant ecological and historical variables.
First must be that some at least of the frontier
tribes, such as the Wazir (chapter 5) but perhaps
not those of the Khyber (chapter 4), were too poor

economically to produce surplus necessary either to
support a class of leaders or to attract revenue-
seeking administrators; they were also too inaccessible. This poverty, and the individuated system of
land tenure, rather encouraged local rivalries, emi-
gration in search of employment, and expeditions in
search of plunder. Frontier tribes resisted control
by the competing Safavid and Mughal empires: using
'jellyfish' tactics, they refused to recognise
chiefs. In the eighteenth century, the tribes participated in the Afghan empire to the extent of giving
their support in return for subsidies and recognition of their autonomy. In the nineteenth century
the British, alternating between inactivity and
forward policy, sought control, whether through conquest or subsidy, in order to keep the frontier
quiet and the trade routes open, but the tribes, who
had not accepted even fellow-Pashtuns as rulers,
had no intention of recognising the hegemony of outsiders. By the twentieth century, egalitarianism
and independence of authority had been historically
validated long enough to have become central elements in the Pakhtunwali ideology dominant on the
frontier.

The Kurds, on the other hand, have a long history of at least nominal subordination to surrounding
states: Ottoman, Safavid and Qajar rulers insisted
on a measure of administrative control over the
tribes, however indirect, using emirates and chiefships to this end. Many emirates took the form of
vassal (or 'secondary') states, with established
hierarchies of wealth and authority, and notions of
tribal autonomy, democracy and egalitarianism were
not strongly rooted in Kurdish self-consciousness.
Among Pathans, the Abdali/Durrani most resemble the
Kurds in history and structure. They too had a
history of chiefship and involvement with empires
such as the Safavids before forming their own.
Features of Kurdish society picked out by van
Bruinessen are also characteristic of the Durrani:
a mixed ethnic milieu; a sharp division between a
tribal (Durrani) military land-owning aristocracy
with a pastoral nomadic base, and a non-tribal
(Parsiwan) peasantry; a segmentary organisation of
society based on a descent ideology. This resemblance fades somewhat after the eighteenth-century
emergence of the Durrani ruling dynasty and tribal
state in Afghanistan, and the abolition of the
Kurdish emirates by the Ottoman and Qajar governments in the early nineteenth century.

Among Zagros groups, the Bakhtiari display some

marked (if subtle) similarities to Pathan groups
such as the Ghilzai and the frontier tribes: all inhabit inaccessible mountains, in which there is
comparative local ethnic homogeneity, with tribespeople combining pastoral nomadism and settled
agriculture; the Bakhtiari relate to Isfahan and
Tehran as urban centres just as the Pathan tribes do
to Peshawar, Kandahar and Kabul; the nomads, whether
Bakhtiari or frontier powindahs, avoided the attention of authority, organising under local headman
only for defence on migration. The Bakhtiari chiefship of later Qajar times may be explained away, in
this perspective, by their wealth and their relations with government; the ordinary tribespeople
came to hate chiefs (chapter 12) in a way that is
not reported, for example, of Kurds or Qashqai, but
resembles the attitudes of Ghilzai and frontier
Pathans. The tarburwali of the latter (chapter 5)
echoes the Bakhtiari 'enemy within' (chapter 12).

Some Models of Change in Tribal Society. The tribal
groups under consideration show evidence of processes of both evolutionary and cyclical or alternating
change. Political evolution in scale and complexity,
from a tribal polity into a state or state-like confederacy, involving processes of unification of
disparate groups, centralisation of authority, and
stratification, has occurred in cases ranging from
the major confederacies such as Bakhtiari, Khamseh,
Qashqai and Durrani, to local chiefdoms such as the
Yarahmadzai Baluch. The reverse process is also
seen, however, in Kurdistan, with the dissolution of
the emirates in the nineteenth century and their
consequent 'devolution' or 'retribalisation' into
more diffuse organisation and simpler groups; and
also among the Shahsevan, whose unified confederacy,
formed in the eighteenth century by the state, broke
up in the nineteenth into independent tribes and
rival coalitions.[57] On the other hand, in terms of
a shift from society organised on kinship/descent
principles to one based on territorial allegiance
and control of the means of production, the Shahsevan
could be said to have 'evolved' in the nineteenth
century; but in these terms too, 'devolution' is
possible: abandonment of territorial principles in
favour of segmentary lineage ideology and 'jellyfish'
tactics can be an adaptive move by a tribal group
resisting state control.
    None of these cases of apparent evolution or
devolution however can be interpreted as clear-cut
evidence in support of any particular theory of

'tribe' or 'state' formation; in all cases, the role
of the state and tribal reactions to state policies
are the central factors in change. Clearly tribe
and state form a single system, whose dynamics are
the concern of other theories and models. Thus,
cyclical processes are evident in the history of
tribal dynasties in Afghanistan and Iran, which at
both national and local levels appear to pass
through four phases of development. In the expansion
phase, a leader recruits followers from different
groups, rewarding them usually with booty from successful banditry. Those tribesmen most likely to
leave home on raiding expeditions with the hope of
booty are the otherwise unemployed: men from families
wealthy enough to employ others to work their property (land or flocks), and men who have lost their
own property and are unwilling to work that of
others. The leader uses this support to gain control
of a city and its surrounding region, including
dependant non-tribespeople. Eventually the expansion ceases and the establishment phase begins,
whereby the leader settles in the city and takes
over the administrative machinery, with the aim of
collecting revenue and controlling the tribes, who
are now frustrated in their drive for booty. In due
course the dynasty becomes used to urban life and
enters a phase of decay. The tribes, now alienated
from the dynasty, refuse support, rebel in favour
of other leaders, take over outlying regions and
begin to converge on the city, which is now helpless
without their support. In the final, replacement
phase, one tribe or coalition under a strong leader
invades the city and a new cycle begins.

This cycle is similar to the model developed by
Ibn Khaldun with reference to early Islamic history,
largely on the basis of his observations in north-
west Africa.[58] He laid down a variety of rules
defining relations between cities and tribes, and
the nature and importance of the 'solidarity' that
characterises tribes and their original attachment
to the leader. The duration of a dynasty, before it
was replaced by another conqueror from the periphery,
he put at three generations.

The different Durrani dynastic branches appear
to show just such a pattern. The Sadozai rulers
lasted about sixty years, passing three generations
from Ahmad Shah to his grandsons in the early 1800s.
They were replaced by the Barakzai, who provided
three different family dynasties in succession: first
came a cycle of three rulers, lasting over fifty
years from Dost Mohammad (who came, however, not from

the periphery but rather from the centre of a highly
disunited tribal polity) to his grandson Yaqub.
Next, Yaqub's cousin, Abd al-Rahman, came from
Turkistan, largely with the support of non-Pashtuns;
after another three generations and fifty years,
Amanullah lost the throne to a Tajik bandit. The
final Barakzai family, the Musahiban, won the throne
with the aid of Wazir frontier tribesmen, and they
too lasted three rulers (though only two generations)
and fifty years, to be replaced in 1978 by a new
regime led by non-Durrani intellectuals educated
beyond the frontier, It must be remembered that
Ibn Khaldun's three generations would have lasted
120 years, so the brevity of the four Durrani cycles
(little more than 50 years each) must be attributed
at least in part to constant external interference
in dynastic rivalries and the succession, especially
by the British in India.

The far longer duration of the Qajar dynasty
in Iran in a single line of succession - seven Shahs,
but conforming in time (125 years) to Ibn Khaldun's
prediction - may by contrast be attributed to the
fact that succession was for long guaranteed by the
Great Powers. Moreover, by the late nineteenth century, when the cyclical model would predict a revolt
from the periphery, political and economic pressures from Russia and Britain were becoming intense,
while their support of the dynasty was confirmed;
but at the same time, a tribal resurgence was indeed
occurring in outlying areas in the form of escalating brigandry and frontier troubles which hastened
the end of the dynasty, though eventual replacement
came from a non-tribal periphery. The Pahlavi
regime - which saw the completion of the transformation of Iran from eighteenth-century tribal empire,
through nineteenth-century 'Asiatic'/feudalistic
state, to twentieth-century nation-state - lasted
little more than the 50 years of the Durrani cycles,
and involved only two rulers, but encompassed
immeasurably greater changes in society than any
other cycle. Rapid growth of oil wealth and massive
industrialisation and urbanisation produced a large
middle class committed to the regime but also a
large, alienated intelligentsia and proletariat. The
revolution that eventually overthrew the Pahlavis
was led by a mullah from beyond the frontier, but
supported by intellectuals and proletariat from
within the geographical centre.

Bases of Tribal Solidarity. Ibn Khaldun's 'solidarity' ('group feeling', asabiya) is a moral sentiment

arising from common descent and ethnic and cultural
similarity. Such a sentiment would seem to have
played a minor part in the rise of ruling dynasties
in eighteenth and nineteenth-century Iran, which all
came to power with the support of coalitions of disparate ethnic elements held together for the most
part by non-tribal, transactional bonds such as
military discipline and a desire for plunder. But a
major source of solidarity, and basis for leadership, is religious in character. The Shiite tribes
of Iran had a history of following Sufi leaders with
aspirations to the throne, the most prominent example
being the establishment of the Safavid dynasty
around 1500. The religious fellowship that united
the Qizilbash tribes under the Safavids had its
legacy under their successors: both Nadir Afshar and
Karim Zand used Safavid puppet Shahs to help legitimise their authority, while the Qajars attempted
to revive Safavid notions of absolute and near-
divine sovereignty. None the less, the tribal
forces that brought the Ghilzai, Afshar, Zand and
Qajar rulers to power in Iran in the eighteenth
century were heterogeneous, and all except the Zand
included substantial Sunni elements. Ahmad Shah
Durrani, on the other hand, was himself a Sufi, and
had some success with appeals to elements of Pashtun
self-consciousness, including common descent and
Sunni Islam. From 1800 onwards, differences widen
between Afghanistan and Iran and between Sunni and
Shii tribal groups.

The Shiite ulama in Iran, who were commonly in
dormant or active opposition to the Shahs, particularly when they acted autocratically, have led or
participated in a series of confrontations that cul-
minated in the events of 1978. Sunni leaders in
Afghanistan, however, supported the Durrani rulers
as defenders of the faith, opposing individual rulers
only when they appeared to be endangering that faith.
Throughout the period, it was Shiite tribal groups
that had the most developed chiefship: in Qajar Iran
the major Shiite groups under their powerful leaders
supported the dynasty, though they sometimes rebelled
against individual members in the name of their
political rivals. In Afghanistan the Shiite minority
consisted mainly of the tribal Hazara, who preferred
to play down their religious status and rely on
secular forms of political leadership and organisation. Among Sunni tribal groups, apart from the
Durrani dynasty itself, political leadership was
poorly developed, ranging from the petty chiefdoms
of Kurds, Baluches and Aymaqs, to the independent

Turkmen and Pathan tribes who in the absence of
strong (or any) chiefship were often willing to rise
at the call of a religious leader against a given
ruler. There is an apparent paradox: Sunni groups,
whether in Iran or Afghanistan, have been politically
less centralised and have responded more readily to
religious appeals to rise against the state, although
in religious theory they should be more tolerant of
temporal leadership and the state than Shiites, among
whom in fact chiefship and support for the state
have been more prominent.
     Populations on a local level are more likely to
be united by moral sentiments, especially within
regions that are of comparative ethnic homogeneity,
such as Azarbayjan, Kurdistan, Luristan, Baluchistan,
the Hazarajat, and the central Pathan highlands. But
this does not mean that people of such regions are
necessarily all tribally organised, let alone likely
to form large tribal confederations. Actually, the
history of tribal transportations meant that many
other areas such as Fars, Kirman, Khurasan, Herat,
Kabul and Turkistan, and the region between Hamadan,
Tehran and Mazandaran, were ethnically quite mixed,
and anyway the major confederacies, some of which
came from these regions, were of composite origins.
None the less, tribal groups in a locality are
capable of developing 'solidarity' over time, even
when of different origins and languages. When such
groups occupy neighbouring territories and give
their allegiances to a common chiefly dynasty,
although this political union may have begun fortuit-
ously as a result of forced migration, or with quite
material objectives, it may well, after a few generations, develop cultural symbols of common identity,
and disparate origins may then be discounted as
politically irrelevant. Even an ideology of common
descent may be constructed out of political-
territorial unity. At the same time, descent can as
well be the source of dissent as of consent, of
factionalism as of unity: where common descent also
brings neighbouring rights to property, factions and
blocs (see above) are likely to emerge; similarly,
differing descent may be the basis of an 'ethnic'
stratification, of landowners as against non-
landowners.[59]

Tribe and State as States of Mind. The cyclical
model elaborated above throws some light on relations between tribes and states as empirical groups
in eighteenth to twentieth-century Iran and
Afghanistan. The model is, however, based essentially

on 'ideal-type' notions of both tribe and state,
and these should be examined further, particularly
in terms of their nature as conceptually opposed
tendencies, modes or models of organisation, not
just analytically distinct but consciously articulated as cultural categories within the groups discussed.

As bases of identity and political allegiance
and behaviour, 'tribe' gives primacy to ties of
kinship and patrilineal descent, while 'state'
insists on the loyalty of all persons dwelling within a defined territory, whatever else their relation
to each other. 'Tribe' stresses personal, moral
and ascriptive factors in status, while 'state' is
impersonal and recognises contract, transaction and
achievement. The division of labour in the 'tribal'
model is 'natural'; in the 'state' model it is
complex. The 'tribal' mode is socially homogeneous,
egalitarian and segmentary, the state is heterogeneous, egalitarian and hierarchical. 'Tribe' is within the individual, 'state' external to him.

The opposition between these two models, their
confrontation with each other and with social
reality, creates a tension, a dialectic with varying resolutions. Thus, whether because of ecological limitations, state pressures or inherent
contradictions, the 'pure' tribe is an empirical
impossibility. Most groups that have been termed
tribes have some form of segmentary ideology as the
basis for political loyalties, but all use other
principles too, to guide action and association at
different levels of organisation. All tribal
groups discussed here have a territorial dimension,
though they tend to ascribe common descent to all
those who, by whatever means, have acquired rights
in their territory.[60] But there are some 'tribes',
especially in Iran, that do not even pretend to an
ideology of common descent, organising as explicitly
political local groups with a common leadership; in
these terms, they are proto- or mini-states within
larger, empire-like states. The strength of
egalitarian ideals varies widely, as does the extent
of inequality in practice; even the most 'egalitarian' tribal groups (as described for example in
chapters 3 to 6 and 8) display some inequalities
of wealth (however narrow) and leadership roles
(however lacking in authority). Conflict over
material interests, between rivals or between rich
and poor, is endemic to all tribal groups; and
'anti-segmentary', territorially-based blocs and
factions are regular tribal phenomena.

The 'pure' state is similarly impossible.
Citizenship (that is, in pre-modern Iran and
Afghanistan, subjection to the ruler) is acquired
through a mixture of territoriality and descent.
Every state must boost its legitimacy, claim the
moral allegiance of its citizens, by promoting elements of a common national culture and way of life.
The most powerful symbols in a nationalist ideology
are shared religion and a concept of mother/father-
land, but insofar as the ideology stresses common
descent or origins (real or fictive, plausible or
otherwise) it resembles a tribal one. Some states
go so far as to deny the existence of any internal
ethnic differentiation, but most have to recognise
'minorities', which may be 'tribal' in culture or
organisation though today they are often termed
'ethnic' or 'regional' groups or 'nationalities'.[61]
   In other words, there is 'state' within every
tribe, and 'tribe' within every state; state is
partly defined in terms of tribe, tribe in terms of
state. Most empirical tribes and states are various
forms of hybrid, such as tribal states, confederacies or chiefdoms. A confederacy is a union for
political purposes, sometimes an alliance of groups
on the basis of imputed common descent, usually with
a central leadership (e.g. Bakhtiari, Durrani), but
sometimes without (e.g. Yamut Turkmen, and see
chapter 4), though some would deny the term confederacy to such an uncentralised alliance, naming it
a coalition. Other confederacies are more heterogeneous in composition, unified under a leader either
by state action (e.g. Shahsevan, Khamseh) or elect-
ively as an indigenous response to state or other
external pressure (e.g. Qashqai, Shakak Kurds).
Centralised tribal unions, territorially based and
stratified under a ruling elite, are states in form,
though dependant, vassal or 'secondary'. They may
be 'tribal' only in the sense of being composed of
tribes.
   'Tribal states' may be of two forms. Some
modern states have promoted a 'tribal' nationalist
ideology, claiming common descent or origins for all
citizens and denying or eliminating differences.
Others, controlled by one 'tribal' (descent-based)
elite, may make no attempt to disguise cultural
differences under a national ideology, rather reser-
ving privileges and power for the dominant tribal
group. To this extent, Durrani and Qajar states
were 'tribal', and in this respect empires rather
than states, strictly speaking.
   How are 'tribe' and 'state' articulated by

tribespeople? Both modes exist as opposed cultural
categories within the experience of individuals, as
well as in the structure of systems. This experience, and the tensions it brings, are the concern
of several chapters, in which the categories appear
in various forms. Hager (chapter 2) shows how the
distinction between tribe and state as ideal-type
polities is grounded in 'fundamentally different
bases for exercising legal jurisdiction', namely
personal and territorial spheres of validity.
Anderson (chapter 3) discusses the dialectic involving the oppositions khan and khel, qoum and gund, as
paired sets of concepts articulating contrasted
realms of Ghilzai experience. Ahmed (chapter 5)
counterposes nang (honour) and qalang (rent, taxation) as 'key features' of contrasted models dominating two distinct categories of Pakhtun society -
though he maintains that the former represents tribal
purity and the latter its inevitable corruption by
the state. Salzman (chapter 8) shows why and how a
chiefly hierarchy and a segmentary lineage system
coexist as 'organisational alternatives' within a
Baluch tribal political structure. Beck (chapter 9)
quotes with approval Helfgott's discussion of the
'constant dynamic in Iranian history' between two
distinct 'socio-economic formations' (sc. the 'tribal' and the 'state'). Garthwaite (chapter 10)
contrasts 'tribe' and 'confederation' as heuristic
models differentiated primarily by function and
operating at different though overlapping levels of
Bakhtiari political organisation, while Digard
(chapter 11) prefers to see them as different but
complementary processes (sc. incorporation by descent, and political transaction) of formation of the
same groups, operating at all levels.

In these cases, 'tribe' and 'state' can be seen
not just as empirical groups, nor merely as analytical distinctions, but as representations of explicit cultural categories articulating opposed modes
of organisation. They are terms for models used
both for explaining social organisation and as
guides for practical action in crises and disputes.

These distinctions closely parallel similar
oppositions reported from many other contexts. One
of the best known in anthropology is the gumsa-
gumlao system of the Kachin of Highland Burma.
Leach analysed three 'types' of community as part
of a single system: the egalitarian gumlao, the
hierarchical Shan kingdom, and the intermediate and
unstable gumsa chiefdom. These types were ideal
patterns, set out for Kachin in ritual and myth, but

by means of ambiguous symbols allowing alternative interpretations, which individuals could exploit. The whole system was full of inconsistencies, and Leach showed evidence that individual communities in the long term oscillated between the extremes, each of which was inherently structurally unstable.[62]

This analysis has been criticised on various grounds. Friedman, for example, has recently and influentially attempted a major revaluation, showing how, in his terms,

> What appears as oscillation is but part of a multilinear development generated by a specific structure of social reproduction, and the evolution of 'Asiatic' states as well as devolution towards more permanently 'egalit-arian' big-men societies both result from the underlying properties of a single tribal system...The dynamic of the Kachin system might be envisaged as an evolution towards increasing hierarchy and state-formation which comes into contradiction with its own material constraints of reproduction but which, by means of gumlao revolts, succeeds in re-establishing the conditions for a renewed evolution.[63]

Such a Marxian approach may bear fruit if applied to tribal history and society and state-tribe relations in Afghanistan and Iran. Recent papers by writers such as Digard and Helfgott apply similar hypo-theses, though a good deal more primary research needs to be done before adequate materials will be available to substantiate them.

Leach's model of oscillation, derived from Pareto's discussion of the alternating dominance of 'lions' and 'foxes', has often been compared with Ibn Khaldun's theory of the circulation of tribal elites, in reference to North Africa, and its development by Montagne and later Gellner, in terms of relations between siba (peripheral, dissident, segmentary and egalitarian tribes) and makhzen (areas administered by the state).[64] This model also has recently been subject to debate. A too literal application of terms such as 'segmentary' and 'egalitarian' to North African places and people has been criticised as part of a general reconsideration of classical anthropological seg-mentary theory. These terms, the critics insist, as well as siba and makhzen, are not descriptive but cultural categories, idioms which are inadequate to

explain the fluid and complex workings of actual
tribal societies, let alone the relations of tribe
and state; account must be taken of the formation of
'anti-segmentary' communities at certain levels of
organisation, of the patterns of bloc alliances
among them, and of increasing centralisation involving hierarchical relations of patronage.[65]

I would argue that varying articulations of all
three processes - segmentarity, community and bloc
formation, and centralisation/patronage - produce
the transformations of tribal society that are
observed. The major variable is the influence of
the state, both as an external force and as an idea
in opposition to the idea of tribe. The essence of
the latter is indeed kinship and egalitarianism (the
basis of a segmentary lineage system), while that
of the former is territoriality (the basis of communities and opposed blocs) and central authority
(the basis of patronage). It is in these terms
that we can understand both variation in actual
tribal forms and changes that have occurred, whether
we adopt a cyclical (oscillation) model of change or
acknowledge the apparently irreversible (evolutionary) changes that have now taken place in the transition from tribe to state.

The most purely segmentary tribal groups are,
as argued earlier, not those completely independent
of state influence, but rather those in a position,
and with the motivation, to maximise their segmentarity practically and ideologically in opposition
to either a real state or the idea of state. Dif-
fuseness of organisation, where segmentarity is
also weakly developed, occurs either in tribal
groups beyond the influence of states (real or
ideal), or as a strategy by a weak tribal group to
resist encroaching state control. When state control strengthens, state principles (territoriality,
hierarchy of authority) grow in influence, and so
then do the roles of factionalism and patronage.
Finally, as an 'alternative ideology', or 'social
structure in reserve', segmentarity persists in many
modern tribal societies in spite of bearing little
relation to political groups and behaviour.

New Frontiers, New Oppositions. In concluding this
introduction, rather than attempting either to construct a theory of the revolutions or to summarise
each chapter and its argument, I merely offer a few
speculative observations on the continued relevance
of a cyclical model and on the relation between the
tribe-state opposition and that of empire and revo-

lution.
   The essential elements in the cyclical model,
it will be recalled, were the foundation of a dynasty
in the centre by a conqueror with support from the
periphery; settlement in the centre; loss of support
from the periphery; and replacement thence by
another conqueror within (in Ibn Khaldun's version)
three generations. I have suggested that such a
cyclical pattern can be discerned in tribe-state
relations in Iran and Afghanistan at both local and
state levels during recent centuries, subject to
some modification by external political and economic
pressures, especially from the Imperial Powers since
the nineteenth century. I also implied that the
Khalq-Parcham revolution in Afghanistan and the rise
of Khumeyni in Iran can also be seen as continuing
the pattern, if our notions of 'frontier' and 'periphery' are transformed somewhat.
   We have already seen how frontiers are a key
element in the confrontation between tribe and
state, whether as empirical groups or as conceptual
categories. Frontiers need not be territorial. In
order to maintain an ideology of independence when
threatened by confrontation with the state and other
outsiders, a tribal group must erect a cultural
frontier; some achieve this by means of a spatial
frontier, through avoidance; others maintain a social
frontier, using middlemen and chiefs. Some sacrifice of freedom, whether of movement or of choice,
allows the maintenance of an ideology of independence of action.
   Such frontiers are in the mind. Perhaps all
frontiers should be seen as cultural categories.
The conception of city as central and tribes as
peripheral frontier groups is, after all, the bias
of the state. Evidence presented here supports
arguments from elsewhere suggesting that for tribespeople it is the state that is peripheral; the
frontier, the cultural 'mirror' in which they perceive and sometimes experience the contrary to tribal values (see chapter 3), is located in the city.
   In both countries, though more pronounced in
Iran, we can see the emergence of this other frontier, which is neither geographically peripheral
nor strictly tribal in nature. As territorial frontiers were better defined during the last century,
and geographically peripheral tribal groups came
under more direct central control than ever before,
the new frontier has been emerging within the centre
among people alienated from the ruling elite either
by ideology (often of external inspiration) or by

Introduction

deprivation of control of means of production. The
new frontier is located spatially, if anywhere, in
the factories, slums and prisons. In the early days,
for example with the rise of urban mobs under the
Qajars, the new frontiersmen had no common interests
and made no common cause with the still powerful
tribes on the geographical periphery; but it is
interesting that more recently, with tribes, urban
proletariat and intellectuals forming alliances in
opposition to oppressive governments, the legendary
endurance and struggle of the tribes have inspired
the efforts of the rest.[66]
     So tribe and state, centre and periphery, are
not geographically distinct but exist within each
other; this should be predictable from the fate of
other dichotomous formulations that have been examined in recent years, such as Great and Little
Traditions, mosque and shrine religion. For example,
the city has been shown to be not only the centre of
the Great Tradition and of formal, doctrinal religion, but also the location of flourishing Little
Traditions and shrine cults. Simple dichotomies
are attractive and ideologically very powerful; but
they lead to confusion among actors and those inter-
preting their actions; they are of little use as
sociological models unless interpreted as actors'
conceptual categories. As such they tend to merge
with each other, and also with other slippery
conceptual dichotomies: worker/bourgeois, illiterate/
literate, primitive/civilised, dar al-Harb/dar
al-Islam, nomad/peasant, pastoral/agricultural...
     Recent events in Iran and Afghanistan are
constantly discussed in terms of the opposed ideologies involved, particularly with the changed
meaning given to 'revolution' by that in Iran, and
the realisation of an Islamic political ideology
opposed to both socialism and capitalism. Both
revolutions were against regimes seen as Western-
oriented (the Shah's and Daud's), and against Western imperialism generally; but while the Khalq-
Parcham revolution was wholly socialist and Soviet-
oriented, the movement against the Shah was primarily
under an Islamic banner, rejecting both Eastern and
Western materialism and imperialism. Since the
revolutions, there have been complications in both
cases. In Iran, the union of socialist elements
which aided (they would say, brought about) the revolution, has since been rejected by the religious
fundamentalist rulers; Khumeyni's opponents now
include a variety of bourgeois monarchists, regional-
tribal minorities, socialist elements, and Muslim

72

moderates. The Khalq-Parcham regime in Afghanistan
attempted at first to discount three main ingredients
of Afghanistan's national ideology: Islam, independence of foreigners, and tribal loyalties; each of
these then became key symbols of the resistance,
which here too includes a variety of elements: bourgeois and tribal monarchists, Islamic fundamental-
ists, and pro-Chinese socialists.

So the revolutions of 1978-9 (and other not so
recent events) call for understanding in terms of a
further conceptual dichotomy: empire and revolution.
I suggest that these opposed ideal types are related
to, if not derived from, the tribe/state dichotomy
with which we are concerned. Hager (chapter 2) discusses Hans Kelsen's four 'spheres of validity' of
legal norms, namely the personal, territorial,
material (i.e. subject matter) and temporal. As
bases for exercising legal jurisdiction, these correspond to the following ideal-type polities respectively: tribe, state, empire, and I suggest, revolution.

To elaborate: tribe (ethnic group) is a polity
in which personal identity and kinship ties are
basic to membership, and social reproduction
(through marriage ties) is the underlying concern of
interaction. State overrides tribal or ethnic affiliations and claims political authority over all
occupants of a defined territory. Empire accepts -
or ignores - the personal ties of tribespeople and
the political allegiances of territorially-defined
states, in its concern with the exploitation of
economic resources and the channelling of material
wealth to the centre. A revolution, particularly
one with a millenial ideology and totalitarian
methods (which includes the founding of both the
fascist Third Reich and the communist Soviet Union,
and of both the Democratic Republic of Afghanistan
and the Islamic Republic of Iran), demands total
personal commitment, claims universal relevance
beyond territorial frontiers, and denies established
relations of production and exchange; it promises
a morally better system and focuses on a temporal
event (the Revolution) in which a complete break is
made with the past and a glorious future is
inaugurated.

We have seen how tribe and state as ideal types
are in a relation of opposition and contradiction. I
suggest that empire and revolution are in a similar
relation. Empires are this-worldly and materialistic,
intent on expansion, while revolutions are other-
worldly and moralistic, particularly in the case of

millenial movements, classic expressions of opposition to imperialism. Revolution may take place
within a given state, but the avowed enemy is not
that state itself but the international system said
to be supporting that state - Western capitalism or
international socialism, both forms of imperialism.

In each case of opposition, various resolutions
are possible; that is, each type of polity has two
main empirical options for dealing with its opponent,
involving the adoption of organisational features of
either its opponent or one of the other types of
polity. These options may be summarised as follows:

First, a tribe wishing to confront a given
state can either transform itself into a centralised,
state-like confederacy, or take a revolutionary path
after a religious leader. A state intent on controlling tribal groups can either appeal to nationalist (sc. 'tribal') ideals, or adopt an imperial
policy of indirect rule. An empire, finding that
blatant economic exploitation of subject peoples
leads inevitably to revolutionary tendencies, may
appeal to universalistic (i.e. 'revolutionary')
moral ideals (freedom, progress, human dignity,
collective good...), or may follow a 'tribal' strategy: either by appeal to a common cultural heritage
or historical experience (as in the Commonwealth
today), or by adopting a diffuse segmentary form of
organisation: in the modern age of revolutions, the
functions of empire are no longer overtly performed
by formal political entities such as governments,
but by quasi-autonomous, multi-national corporations,
economic empires that are less vulnerable to revolution in any given state. A revolution, finally, in
its attack on imperialism, may adopt an 'imperialist'
policy of infiltration and subversion of the production process, picturing in its ideology a highly
materialist millenium, whether as 'cargo' or as
paradise, as reward for support; when the millenium
does not arrive and harsh economic realities must be
faced, the revolution can define itself territorially
and organise as a state, whether theocratic or totalitarian.

Such a model is clearly incomplete and simplis-
tic, but it has the virtue of depicting, and relating
to each other, many of the different forms of polity
that have operated in recent Iranian and Afghan his-
tóry.

I end this discussion with a plea for the reconsideration of the image of tribalism in the modern
world. The record of tribal societies should speak
for them: they have been less savage than historical

states and empires, less 'clannish' than many ruling
elites; neither the evils that the twentieth century
has ameliorated (such as ignorance and disease), nor
the evils that it has brought (such as overpopulation, alienation, ecological disaster and
mass destruction) can be attributed to tribalism.
In many cases, such as the Pathans, Kurds, Baluches
and Turkmens, states and empires have not only
created tribes as political groups, but they have
then prevented them from developing their own political identities as nation-states. Tribalism has
its faults and limitations, but its provision of
social security and its long-term survival value
should recommend it as no anachronism in the last
decades of the twentieth century.

NOTES

1. For earlier discussions of the 'problem of tribe',
see: M. Sahlins, *Tribesmen* (Prentice-Hall, Englewood Cliffs,
1968); J. Helm (ed.), *Essays on the Problem of Tribe* (American
Ethnological Society, 1968), esp. papers by M. Fried and E.
Colson; M.H. Fried, *The Notion of Tribe* (Cummings, Menlo Park,
1975); M. Godelier, 'Le concept de tribu: crise d'un concept
ou crise des fondements empiriques de l'anthropologie?'
Diogène, 81 (1973), pp. 3-28; E. Marx, 'The tribe as a unit
of subsistence: nomadic pastoralism in the Middle East', *AA*,
79 (1977), pp. 343-63.
2. A.K.S. Lambton, *Islamic Society in Persia* (School of
Oriental and African Studies, London, 1954), p. 6.
3. A.K.S. Lambton, 'Īlāt', *EI*, 2nd ed., 3, pp. 1095-6.
4. In chapter 4, Yapp clearly shows the mistaken stereotypes with which British Indian agents approached the Pathans,
while chapters 2, 7 and 14 include discussions of Russian attitudes to the tribes they encountered in their drive through
Central Asia.
5. L. Helfgott, 'Tribalism as a socioeconomic formation
in Iranian history', *IS*, 10 (1977), pp. 36-61; id., 'The structural foundations of the national minority problem in revolutionary Iran', *IS*, 13 (1980), pp. 195-214; J.J. Reid, 'The
Qajar Uymaq in the Safavid period, 1500-1722', *IS*, 11 (1978),
pp. 117-43; id., 'Comments on "Tribalism as a socioeconomic
formation"', *IS*, 12 (1979), pp. 275-81.
6. This is discussed further below. Potentially misleading conflations of pastoral nomadism with tribalism are
particularly common among writers on Iran, e.g. Helfgott,
'Tribalism'; F. Halliday, *Iran: Dictatorship and Development*
(Penguin, Harmondsworth, 1979), pp. 11-12, 214; J.-P. Digard,
'Les nomades et l'état central en Iran: quelques enseignements

d'un long passé d'"hostilité réglementée"', *Peuples Mediterran-*
éens/Mediterranean Peoples, 7 (1979), p. 45; N. Keddie, most
recently in her Introduction to *MIDCC.* E. Marx's recent proposal (in 'The tribe ...', p. 358) to define the Middle Eastern
tribe as 'a subsistence unit ... a social aggregate of pastoral
nomads who jointly exploit an area providing subsistence over
numerous seasons', cannot apply to Iran or Afghanistan.
   7. See the useful summary discussion of pastoral nomadic
tribal chiefdoms in Sahlins, *Tribesmen,* pp. 32-9.
   8. Afghanistan, Turkmenistan, Uzbekistan and Tajikistan
are recognised states; Kurdistan, Luristan, Arabistan and
Baluchistan are sometime provinces of states; Pakhtunistan is
a territory disputed between states; while unlike all these,
only the Hazarajat, a region with no political definition,
coincides roughly with an ethnic distribution.
   9. The authors of the three chapters on the Bakhtiari
disagree on what to call this group: a 'confederation' (chapter 10), a 'tribe' (chapter 11), or a 'failed state' (chapter
12). Clearly in the context of Afghanistan and Iran the
'problem of tribe', and problems of definition and analysis of
substantive tribal groups and their relations with the state,
are quite different from those in the nations of Africa, see
P. Gutkind (ed.), *The Passing of Tribal Man in Africa* (Brill,
Leiden, 1970).
   10. See e.g. N. Keddie, 'The Iranian power structure
and social change 1800-1969: an overview', *IJMES,* 2 (1971),
p. 4; other writers, such as V. Gregorian, *The Emergence of*
Modern Afghanistan (Stanford University Press, 1969), talk of
any unified and centralised policy as a state.
   11. Passages concerning Iran in this and the two subsequent sections are derived largely from my 'The tribes in eighteenth and nineteenth-century Iran', forthcoming in P. Avery
and G. Hambly (eds.), *The Afshars, Zands and Qajars,* vol. 7
of The Cambridge History of Iran (Cambridge University Press),
where full references and more detailed instances can be found.
   12. A.K.S. Lambton, 'The tribal resurgence and the
decline of the bureaucracy in eighteenth-century Persia', in T.
Naff and R. Owen (eds.), *Studies in Eighteenth-Century Islamic*
History (Southern Illinois University Press, Carbondale, 1977),
pp. 108-29.
   13. M. Elphinstone, *An Account of the Kingdom of Caubul*
(London, 1815), vol. 2, pp. 252-3.
   14. Gregorian, *Emergence,* p. 48.
   15. Ibid., p. 51.
   16. See J.R. Perry, *Karim Khan Zand* (University of
Chicago Press, 1979).
   17. The best source on the distribution of tribal and
ethnic groups in Afghanistan in 1800 is Elphinstone, *Account,*
whose description of their social organisation too has yet to
be surpassed.

18. On the distribution of tribal groups in Iran in 1800, see Lambton, 'Ilat', and my 'The tribes'; the best sources are A. Dupré, *Voyage en Perse, etc.* (Paris, 1819), vol. 2, pp. 452 f.; P. Amedée Joubert, *Voyage en Arménie et en Perse, etc.* (Paris, 1821), pp. 250 f.; J. Morier, 'Some account of the Íliyáts, or wandering tribes of Persia, obtained in the years 1814 and 1815', *JRGS*, 7 (1837), pp. 230-42.

19. R. Cottam, *Nationalism in Iran* (University of Pittsburgh Press, 1964), p. 158.

20. A.K.S. Lambton, 'Kadjar', *EI*, 2nd ed., 4, p. 399.

21. Compare the policies of Mackeson on the Indian Frontier (chapter 4), also those of Amir Abd al-Rahman (chapter 7).

22. Morier, 'Some account', p. 236.

23. E. Aubin, *La Perse d'Aujourd'hui* (Colin, Paris, 1908), pp. 177-8.

24. See also P. Oberling, *The Qashqā'i Nomads of Fārs* (Mouton, The Hague, 1974).

25. On the Qaradaghi and Shahsevan tribal union and its fate, see my 'Raiding, reaction and rivalry: the Shahsevan tribes in the Constitutional period', forthcoming in M. Bayat (ed.), *The Constitutional Revolution in Iran;* for tribal distributions around 1920, see H. Arfa, *Under Five Shahs* (Murray, London, 1964), pp. 439-46.

26. On the effects of Riza Shah's settlement policy, see my 'The Shahsavan of Azarbaijan ...', unpublished PhD thesis, University of London, 1972, pp. 676-82. Quantitative data on economic and social effects in any tribal group are totally lacking.

27. L. Beck, 'Revolutionary Iran and its tribal peoples', *MERIP Reports*, 87 (May 1980), p. 18. For further relevant background information on recent events in Iran, see other articles in *MERIP Reports* 86, 87 and 88 (all of 1980); *MIDCC;* F. Kazemi (ed), *Iranian Revolution in Perspective,* special issue of *IS,* 13 (1980).

28. This account of Afghan history and the relation of the rulers to the tribes draws heavily on a manuscript by Rob Hager, to whom I am much indebted; I remain responsible for any errors in this version.

29. J. Dacosta, *A Scientific Frontier; or, the Danger of a Russian Invasion of India* (W.H. Allen, London, 1891), p. 10.

30. H. Kakar, *Afghanistan: a Study in Internal Political Developments 1880-1896* (Punjab Educational Press, Lahore/Kabul, 1971); id., *Government and Society in Afghanistan: The Reign of Amir Abd al-Rahman Khan* (University of Texas Press, Austin, 1979).

31. L. Poullada, *Reform and Rebellion in Afghanistan 1919-1929* (Cornell University Press, Ithaca, 1973), p. 212.

32. Cf. L. Poullada, 'Afghanistan and the United States: the crucial years', *MEJ*, 35 (1981), pp. 178-90.

33. On this issue see my 'Ethnicity and class: dimensions of inter-group conflict in Afghanistan', forthcoming in N. Shahrani and R. Canfield (eds.), *Revolutions and Rebellions in Afghanistan.*

34. See D. Khalid, 'Afghanistan's struggle for national liberation', *Internationales Asienforum,* 11 (1980), pp. 197-228. Other useful sources of background information on recent events in Afghanistan are: L. Dupree, *AUFS Reports* (S. Asia Series), 1979, nos. 32, 44, 45, and 1980, nos. 23, 27, 28, 29, 37; *MERIP Reports,* 89 (1980); and newsletters of national groups supporting the Afghan resistance, e.g. the Swiss *Afghanistan Info.*

35. See note 1 above. On the 'origin of the state', see F. Engels, *The Origin of the Family, Private Property and the State* (International, New York, 1972 (1891)); R. Lowie, *The Origin of the State* (Harcourt, Brace and World, New York, 1927); M.H. Fried, *The Evolution of Political Society* (Random House, New York, 1967); L. Krader, *The Formation of the State* (Prentice Hall, Englewood Cliffs, 1968); E.R. Service, *Origins of the State and Civilization* (Norton, New York, 1975); R. Cohen and E.R. Service (eds.), *Origins of the State* (ISHI, Philadelphia, 1978); H.J.M. Claessen and P. Skalnik (eds.), *The Early States* (Mouton, The Hague, 1978); id., *The Study of the State* (Mouton, The Hague, 1981). For a classic study of states and tribes in one region (East Africa) see L. Mair, *Primitive Government* (Penguin, Harmondsworth, 1962); for discussion of the problem in a Middle Eastern context, see E. Gellner, 'Flux and reflux in the faith of men', in his *Muslim Society* (Cambridge University Press, 1981).

36. Elphinstone, *Account,* Books 3 and 4; for a summary of the similar formulation by I.M. Reisner, *Razvitie feodalizma i obrazovanie gosudarstva u Afgantsev* (Akad. Nauk, Moscow, 1954), see Gregorian, *Emergence,* pp. 42-3.

37. F. Barth, *Political Leadership among Swat Pathans* (Athlone, London, 1959).

38. Cf. B.J. Spooner, 'Politics, kinship and ecology in south-east Persia', *Ethnology,* 8 (1969), pp. 149-50.

39. Contrary to Gellner's observation on Moroccan tribes ('Flux and reflux', p. 20) Iranian tribes had a low Military Participation Ratio (Andreski's phrase), dependant on the supply of surplus, tribute and booty.

40. It should be noted that several tribal groups in Iran and Afghanistan not discussed explicitly in this volume have been recently studied by anthropologists and historians; many of the published accounts are referred to below.

41. For previous comparisons of 'dissident' tribal groups such as Berbers, Kurds and Pathans, see for example C.S. Coon, *Caravan; the Story of the Middle East* (Holt, Rinehart and Winston, New York, revised ed., 1958), chapter 16; J.D. Seddon, 'Introduction' to R. Montagne, *The Berbers,* tr. J.D. Seddon (Cass, London, 1972), pp. xxxiv-vii.

42. Helfgott, 'Tribalism'; J.-P. Digard, 'Histoire et anthropologie des sociétés nomades: le cas d'une tribu d'Iran',

Introduction

Annales, 28, 6 (1973), pp. 1423-35. Helfgott seems to equate 'socioeconomic formation' with 'mode of production', on the grounds that for Marx the former is characterised by the latter; while Digard appears to follow Althusser and Terray in analysing any social formation as comprising two or more modes of production.

    43. Elphinstone, *Account,* vol. 1, pp. 215 f.; see also R. Loeffler, 'Tribal order and the state: the political organization of Boir Ahmad', *IS,* 11 (1978), pp. 145-71, who considers that for some tribes of Iran the political system is 'intrinsically centralized'.

    44. Cf. F. Barth, 'Ethnic processes on the Pathan-Baluch boundary', in G. Redard (ed.), *Indo-Iranica* (Wiesbaden, 1964).

    45. See my 'The tribes ...'; variation in camp and household size and structure may be related to the differential impact of these cultural factors, see my *Pasture and Politics: Economics, Conflict and Ritual among Shahsevan nomads of north-western Iran* (Academic Press, London/New York, 1979), chapter 8.

    46. See also A.S. Ahmed, *Pukhtun Economy and Society* (Routledge and Kegan Paul, London, 1980); on tribal forms of land tenure, see F. Barth, *Models of Social Organization,* Occasional Paper no. 23 (Royal Anthropological Institute, London, 1966), chapter 3; on individuated grazing rights among nomads, see my 'Individuated grazing rights and social organization ...' *PPS,* pp. 95-114.

    47. Opposed blocs are pervasive among Swat Pathans, see Barth, *Political Leadership,* also his 'Segmentary opposition and the theory of games', *JRAI,* 89 (1959), pp. 5-21. Blocs have also been recorded among Shahsevan camps, see my *Pasture and Politics;* among Caucasian and East Azarbayjani khanates in the eighteenth and early-nineteenth centuries, see my 'Shahsavan of Azarbaijan', chapters 7 and 8; among Yamut Turkmen tribes, see W. Irons, *The Yomut Turkmen,* Anthropological Papers no. 58, Museum of Anthropology (University of Michigan, Ann Arbor, 1975). Institutionalised local rivalries, which often relate to such bloc oppositions, include the pervasive Heydari/Nimati factionalism in Iran, see H. Mirjafari, 'The Haydarī-Ni^cmatī conflicts in Iran', *IS,* 12 (1979), pp. 135-62; see also the divisions of the Qajar tribe into upper and lower branches, the Kurds into Left and Right, the Bakhtiari into Chahar and Haft Lang, various Pathan groups into Zirak and Panjpay, Spin and Tor, Gar and Samil ...

    48. See chapters 3 and 13; also Irons, *The Yomut Turkmen;* Gellner, *Muslim Society.*

    49. Similar points are made by D. Eickelman, *The Middle East: an Anthropological Approach* (Prentice Hall, Englewood Cliffs, 1981), pp. 87 f. On tribes created by states, see R. Cohen, 'Introduction', in Cohen and Service, *Origins,* p. 16; Colson and Fried, papers in Helm, *Essays;* R. Cohen and J. Middleton (eds.), *From Tribe to Nation in Africa* (Chandler,

Scranton, PA, 1970), p. 27.

50. See Barth, *Political Leadership*, p. 133; Montagne, *The Berbers*; E. Gellner, *Saints of the Atlas* (Weidenfeld and Nicholson, London, 1969); Coon, *Caravan*.

51. F.G. Bailey, *Stratagems and Spoils* (Blackwell, Oxford, 1969). On chiefs as middlemen, see F. Barth, *Nomads of South Persia* (Allen and Unwin, London, 1961). For application of Bailey's and Barth's insights, see my 'Shahsavan of Azarbaijan'; R. Loeffler, 'The representative mediator and the new peasant', *AA*, 73 (1971), pp. 1077-91; G.R. Fazel, 'The encapsulation of nomadic societies in Iran', in C. Nelson (ed.) *The Desert and the Sown* (Institute of International Studies, University of California, Berkeley, 1973); P.C. Salzman, 'Continuity and change in Baluchi tribal leadership', *IJMES,* 4 (1973), pp. 428-39; id., 'Tribal chiefs as middlemen: the politics of encapsulation', *AQ,* 47 (1974), pp. 203-10.

52. On Qajar tribal policies, see A.K.S. Lambton, 'Persian society under the Qajars', *JRCAS*, 48 (1961), pp. 123-39.

53. Gellner, *Saints*; W. Irons, 'Nomadism as a political adaptation', *AE*, 1 (1974), pp. 635-58; D. Bates, 'The role of the state in peasant-nomad mutualism', *AQ,* 44 (1971), pp.109-31; cf. non-tribal nomads in Iran, such as Sangsari or the Komachi, D. Bradburd, 'Size and success: Komachi adaptation to a changing Iran', in *MIDCC,* pp.123-37; see also T. Barfield, *The Central Asian Arabs of Afghanistan* (University of Texas Press, Austin, 1981).

54. Cf. E. Gellner, 'Doctor and Saint', in his *Muslim Society;* P.C. Salzman, 'Does complementary opposition exist?', *AA,* 80 (1978), pp. 53-70; id., 'Ideology and change in tribal society', *Man (NS)*, 13 (1978), pp. 618-37; Bailey, *Stratagems,* pp. 15-16. For examples of shifts in tribal political organisation or leadership resulting from transformations of the state, see also chapters 6, 13 and 14 below.

55. Cf. J. Black, 'Tyranny as a strategy for survival: Luri facts versus an anthropological mystique', *Man (NS),* 7 (1972), pp. 614-34.

56. Bailey, *Stratagems,* chapter 3.

57. On the Kurds see chapter 13 below. In *Agha, Shaikh and State* (PhD thesis, Utrecht, 1978), pp. 288 f., 246, Martin van Bruinessen discusses two confederacies that survived. F. Barth considered detribalisation in Kurdistan to be irreversible, *Principles of Social Organization in Southern Kurdistan* (Jørgensen, Oslo, 1953), p. 135; just as A.S. Ahmed holds that the movement from *nang* to *qalang* forms of Pathan society is unidirectional, *Millenium and Charisma among Pathans* (Routledge and Kegan Paul, London, 1976), p. 81. On the Shahsevan, see chapter 14 below, and the Appendix to my 'The tribes ...'. Cf. the fate of the Qizilbash confederacies such as Shamlu and Afshar in seventeenth and eighteenth-century Iran, and of the Ghilzai in Afghanistan after their defeat by the Durrani in the eighteenth century.

Introduction

58.   Ibn Khaldun, *The Muqaddima,* tr. F. Rosenthal
(Routledge and Kegan Paul, London, 1967). The literature on
Ibn Khaldun is vast, see A. al-Azmeh, *Ibn Khaldun in Modern
Scholarship: a Study in Orientalism* (Third World Centre,
London, 1981); for applications to Iranian history, see e.g.
C. Issawi, *The Economic History of Iran 1800-1914* (University
of Chicago Press, 1971), p. 4 f.; B. Spooner, 'Politics, kin-
ship and ecology'; Tapper, 'The Shahsavan of Azarbaijan'.
59.   For example in Fars, where tribes of the Khamseh and
Qashqai confederacies have lived for some centuries, the
former are known as 'Arab' and the latter as 'Turk', even
though they are both of highly varied languages and origins.
The Pathans too are regarded as ethnically one, though every
tribe includes elements of disparate origins, sometimes
Persian- or Turkish-speaking. The same is true of the Shahsevan and many other tribal groups. In contrast, various
groups more recently transplanted to Khurasan and the vicinity
of Tehran by Nadir Shah or the early Qajars, have remained for
the most part ethnically and politically distinct.
60.   On the territorial basis of Middle Eastern descent
groups, see F. Barth, 'Descent and marriage reconsidered', in
J. Goody (ed.), *The Character of Kinship* (Cambridge University
Press, 1973); for local communities and corporate groups, see
my 'The organization of nomadic communities among pastoral
societies of the Middle East', in *PPS*, pp. 43-65.
61.   Commentators on recent events in Iran, such as
Halliday, *Iran,* and Helfgott, 'Structural foundations', distinguish Azarbayjanis, Kurds, Baluches, Arabs and Turkmens as
'national minorities' with aspirations for autonomy, from
'tribal' groups such as Bakhtiari, Qashqai and others.
62.   E.R. Leach, *Political Systems of Highland Burma*
(Athlone, London, 1954).
63.   J. Friedman, 'Tribes, states and transformations',
in M. Bloch (ed.), *Marxist Analyses and Social Anthropology*
(London, Malaby, 1975), pp. 161, 186; in a supplementary note
to a new reprint of *Political Systems,* Leach accuses Friedman,
with some justice, of 'ignoring the facts on the ground altogether'.
64.   V. Pareto, *The Mind and Society,* ed. A. Livingston
(Dover, New York, 1963); Montagne, *The Berbers:* Gellner,
Saints; cf. O. Lattimore, *Inner Asian Frontiers of China*
(American Geographical Society, New York, 1940).
65.   See, for example, C. Geertz, H. Geertz, and L. Rosen,
Meaning and Order in Moroccan Society (Cambridge University
Press, 1979), pp. 106, 264, 377; M. Meeker, *Literature and
Violence in North Arabia* (Cambridge University Press, 1979),
pp. 11 f., 220; Eickelman, *The Middle East,* esp. p. 104; E.
Peters, 'Some structural aspects of the feud among the camel-
herding Bedouin of Cyrenaica', *Africa,* 32 (1967), pp. 261-82;
for Gellner's response to some of these critics of segmentary
theory and its application, see his *Muslim Society,* and also

chapter 15 below.

   66. The classic documentary film *Grass,* by M. Cooper and
E. Schoedsack (1924), depicting the struggle of Bakhtiari nomads
against the elements, apparently had a cult following in recent
years among dissident Iranian youth, see H. Naficy, 'Non-
fiction documentaries on Iran', *IS*, 12 (1979), p. 223; similarly, the reputation of the North West Frontier Pathans for
resistance to the British has been an inspiration for all
those fighting for the withdrawal of the Soviet invaders of
Afghanistan.

Chapter 2
STATE, TRIBE AND EMPIRE IN AFGHAN INTER-POLITY RELATIONS

Rob Hager

A Model of State, Tribe and Empire as Types of Legal Order

For at least a millenium, the Pashto-speaking people have preserved their independence and flourished through a tribal political organisation in their homeland straddling the present Afghanistan-Pakistan international border. The tribal organisation of these people - more commonly called Afghans to the west, Pathans to the east, and Pushtuns/Pakhtuns on both sides of this border - today provides them not merely with a distinct cultural or ethnic identity, but, especially for those in the central homeland nearest the border, with a form of polity alternative to that of the state. Tribal institutions and norms, just as those of a state, can and do perform the political tasks of interest mediation, dispute resolution, and military organisation. In a changing political environment the Pashtun tribes have preserved their own forms of organisation and even today remain independent, more or less, of the states within whose boundaries they now reside. Their political independence is expressed through the autonomous enforcement of the tribal legal order - the Pashtunwali. Inter-polity relations between these tribes and neighbouring governments have been structurally characterised by their fundamentally different kinds of legal orders, based respectively on the Pashtunwali and central state institutions and ideologies.

The distinction between tribe, based on descent, and state, based on control of territory, associated with the thought of Morgan and Maine,[1] is not merely descriptive but has a conceptual grounding in the fundamentally different bases for exercising legal jurisdiction in these two ideal-type polities. Hans

Kelsen analyses the jurisdictional bases of legal
norms in his statement of the principles of international law, which relies upon four 'spheres of
validity' of legal norms: the personal, the territorial, the material (i.e. subject matter) and the
temporal. These are ontological categories.[2] Human
behaviour that can be subjected to norms is identified with a person at a place in time. For Kelsen
the determination of the spheres of validity of
national legal orders is the essential function of
international law, which 'renders it possible for
the states to be considered as coexistent side by
side as equal subjects'. Kelsen made clear the
relationship of the state to his classification of
jurisdictional spheres: 'Those normative orders that
are designated as states are characterised precisely
by the fact that their territorial spheres of validity are limited'.[3] This understanding is basic to
the international law that provides a normative
referent for relations between actors in the modern
state system. De Visscher observes that 'historically the territorial home of the state is the
foundation of the political and legal order born in
the sixteenth century and definitively consecrated
in Europe by the Treaties of Westphalia'.[4]
     The post-Westphalian system admitted as parti-
cipants in the new international legal order only
those polities which exercised exclusive legal
jurisdiction over a fixed territory. The alternative
kinds of polities which are conceptually excluded
from this paradigm are suggested by two other of
Kelsen's ontological categories or legal 'spheres of
validity'. These alternative polities exercise
legal jurisdiction either over a defined group of
persons and are characterised by the fact that their
personal spheres of validity are limited, or over
only certain kinds of human behaviour and are characterised by the fact that their material spheres of
validity are limited.
     The tribe or ethnic group exercises its legal
jurisdiction on the basis of personality, and therefore corresponds to the first of these alternative
polities. A consideration of boundary concepts
reveals the radical difference between the ideal-type
tribe and the state as defined above. As Fredrik
Barth has written, it is 'the ethnic boundary that
defines the group', and the ethnic or tribal boundary
demarcates a change in normative order, the 'differences in criteria for judgment of value and performance'. Tribal or ethnic boundaries are not drawn on
the ground, but rather separate groups of persons

who identify with different 'basic value orientations, the standards of morality and excellence by which performance is judged ... Belonging ... implies a claim to be judged and to judge oneself by those standards that are relevant to that identity'. Pashtun tribes were Barth's specific reference in making these observations, and many others have confirmed the importance of adherence to the Pashtunwali in the group-consciousness of the Pashtuns.[5]

As Kelsen points out, it is the task of international law to delimit the jurisdictional reach of the 'specifically juristic unit' that is the state, so that state units may coexist with independence and equality.[6] Barth describes the kind of inter-ethnic law that would apply to relations among diverse tribal or ethnic groups. Interaction among such groups 'both requires and generates a congruence of codes and values' and implies a 'structuring of interaction which allows for the persistence of cultural differences'. Barth argues that such relations require a 'systematic set of rules governing inter-ethnic social encounters', which would include 'a set of prescriptions governing situations of contact ... and a set of proscriptions on social situations preventing inter-ethnic interaction in other sectors, and thus insulating parts of the cultures from confrontation and modification'.

According to Barth, then, a tribally-organised ethnic group will generate a normative order to govern its relations with another such group so as to permit them both to coexist with independence and, presumably, equality. However, unlike the normative order that governs relations among states, this 'inter-ethnic' normative order governs primarily social relations among persons. The objective of this normative order is to permit interaction through 'agreement on codes and values ... relevant to the social situations in which they interact',[7] while permitting members of the diverse groups to preserve their self-identifying adherence to their own distinct values and norms, such as are expressed in the Pashtunwali. Inter-polity relations among tribally-organised peoples are made through personal and individual accommodations between diverse normative orders at the ethnic boundary, rather than between the formal and specialised institutions of the state. The state, which is defined by its capacity to enforce its domestic normative order through monopolising the exercise of force within its borders, must also monopolise conduct of relations outside its borders. By contrast, the external relat-

ions of a tribally-organised polity, which is defined
by the adherence of its members to the tribal normative order, are - like that personal adherence to
the internal order - personal relations which challenge and reinforce the distinctiveness and unity of
the normatively-defined tribal group.

So, the ideal-type bribe and state polities not
only rest their internal normative orders on ontolo-
gically diverse jurisdictional bases - personal and
territorial - but the different boundary concepts
resulting therefrom give rise to radically different
styles for the normative conduct of external relations: that expressed through international law on
the one hand, and a kind of inter-tribal law on the
other. 'Law' is a generic term to describe a normative order in dialectical relation to power. Each
of these normative orders, state and tribe, internal
and external, satisfies Hoebel's conventional cross-
disciplinary definition of law: 'A social norm is
legal if its neglect or infraction is regularly met,
in threat or in fact, by the application of physical
force by an individual or group possessing the
socially recognised privilege of so acting'. This
definition is more fully satisfactory if 'physical
force' is taken to include various kinds of depri-
vations, and 'regularly' is given a liberal interpretation to include weak legal orders. Law is
characterised not only by the use of force justified
through appeal to a rule, but also by the stylised
form of argumentation employed in determining and
applying the rule. A common vocabulary of argument
is the dominant feature of a horizontal legal order
such as international law.[8]

The structure for normative relations between
the ideal-type tribe and state is thus determined by
these discongruities between their legal orders.
First, power in the state is monopolised by a central
government, while in tribes such as the Pashtuns it
may typically remain distributed among persons who
adhere to the tribal law or may occasionally be consolidated within various levels of latent tribal
hierarchy. Among Pashtuns, hierarchical organisation
seldom surpasses the minimal lineage grouping of the
extended family. Second, the state legal order articulates vertically and exclusively over a fixed
territory while the tribal legal order provides the
framework for horizontal relations and consolidation
of power among persons for whom the legal order
provides a shared identity.[9] Third, the style of
legal argument in the state is authoritative, ultimately linked to a legitimated hierarchical source

such as legislative enactments, administrative regulations, appellate court decisions, judicial and
administrative rulings, while in the tribe the style
of argument is never far removed from the individual's own social power and ability to communicate
and personify tribal norms. Structure is also normative.[10] Because of their structural uniformity
states share a common normative basis for a recipro-
cative international law. The fundamental principles
of this law may be thus reciprocally expressed by
states: you respect my sovereignty (exclusive jurisdiction over claimed territory) and I will recognise
yours; I will defend that which is subject to my
jurisdiction by force and in return I will be responsible for any infringements on yours by that which is
under my power.[11] Such reciprocal statements, however, are not available where the underlying normative diversity inherent in interpolity relations is
further compounded by structural discongruities as
in relations between state and tribe. The structure
of the tribe violates the constitutive or structural
state norm 'consecrated' at Westphalia, just as the
structure of the state leaves little room for the
personal commitments that constitute the tribe.
Accommodation across this normative gap defining the
boundary between tribe and state involves structural
change and unstable attachment to normative refer-
ents.
      The third alternative form of polity derived
from Kelsen's ontological classification describes
one form this accommodation might take. The delimi-
tation of the material 'sphere of validity', or the
articulation of legal jurisdiction on the basis of
the subject matter of norms, but without regard to
territorial or personal limitations, describes a
universal legal and political order that may be
identified with the jurisdictional assertions of
historical empires. Although tribes have provided
the dominant class in historical empires such as
those of Islam, the Mongols or the Afghan Durranis,
the basis of jurisdiction for imperial norms is not,
as it is in the ideal-type tribe, personality.
Similarly, though states have provided the dominant
metropolitan base for empires such as the Roman,
the overseas European empires, and the imperialism
of the modern superpowers, empires are not characterised, as is the ideal-type state, by the enforcement of exclusive jurisdiction over territory. The
empire does not enforce its own comprehensive normative order over defined persons or territory to the
exclusion of all other normative orders; it is

rather characterised by an exercise of dominance over subordinate polities which preserve their own diverse and partially autonomous normative orders based on either territorial (state) or personal (tribe) jurisdictions.

Imperialism, in the sense of the relationship between a ruling power and the peoples under its control, 'is not complete without an imperial creed held by its governing class'. It is such a creed that legitimates the infringement by the empire of the sovereignty of lesser political bodies. This infringement is 'of the essence' of imperialism, and takes the form of appropriation of power or influence over the jurisdiction to tax, conscript, enact public policy, keep the peace, enforce the criminal law, enforce civil arrangements, settle civil disputes or dominate any other function of the internal or external legal order, generally with the minimal objectives of controlling the exercise of military force and the flow of commerce. As with tribal or state legal orders, the maintenance of the imperial order involves a dialectic between norm and power, or as Lichtheim calls it, 'of being and consciousness'.[12] Niebuhr has written: 'Since authority in nation and empire is always compounded of prestige and force, and since prestige always depends upon an ideological framework, it is inevitable that a dominant community should acquire for its prestige whatever ideological framework is most serviceable for its pretensions'.[13] The empire conserves and legitimates its power to exercise jurisdiction over certain sovereign matters of subordinate political entities by means of its imperial idea or system of ideas: its ideology. The more heterogeneous the empire the more abstract and universal must be the imperial ideology. Unlimited by territorial or personal boundaries, the boundary of empire is the line that divides the reach of its jurisdiction over subordinate polities from the partially autonomous internal normative orders of those polities.

Unlike the territorial boundary of the state and the 'ethnic' or personal boundary of the tribe, which can be determined by relatively fixed and determinable rules, the ideological boundary of the ideal-type empire is a standard describing a changeable and elusive jurisdiction for the empire.[14] The imperial idea on the one hand may be little more than a prestigious symbol legitimising some exercise by the imperial regime of military, fiscal and monetary powers sufficient to keep the peace and facilitate commerce among its subordinate polities. For

example, it has been written that at the end of the
eighteenth century 'a policy calling itself imperial
could still evoke the image of an internationalism,
albeit hierarchical, which served to maintain peace
among nations'.[15] At the other end of the spectrum,
as the imperial idea is elaborated into a detailed
and comprehensive normative order, the empire may
approach the exclusive territorial sovereignty of
the ideal-type state. What the empire seeks to uni-
versalise, the state particularises. The ideal-type
empire is accordingly not defined within a single
fixed category, but is rather a range of political
accommodations from the near-state to a nearly
'horizontal' international system. The locus of any
empire on this spectrum depends upon whether the
power emerging from its dialectic of 'being and consciousness' is turned outward to aggregate new
groups to the empire, or inward to pulverise the old
groups under a more comprehensive normative order.
    For the ideal-type empire, unlike the state and
tribe, there is no discontinuity between the internal and external legal order. The external relations of the tribe and state are conducted in accordance with a discrete set of norms designed to
preserve the independence and autonomy of the diverse legal orders of each tribe or state entity.
Imperial relations involve an extension abroad of
the same ideology which underlies the power of the
ruling elite or metropolitan centre of the empire.
The fortunes of the imperial ideology at the periphery of the empire react back upon and affect its
integrating strength at the centre.
    No ideology is inherently 'imperial'. The same
ideology that legitimates imperial assertions of
jurisdiction can also form part of the legitimising
concepts of a state. In the nation-state however,
these ideas will also combine with more particular
'nationalistic' ideas derived from the dominant
national culture. The basic concept of a normative
unity within the national culture justifies the
exclusive jurisdiction of the state over the 'nation'
in the manner of a tribe, while imperial-type ideas
justify the extension of the state's jurisdiction to
other groups that are not part of the dominant
national group. What distinguishes the state, particularly the heterogeneous state, from the empire,
is a fundamentally different normative approach to
the border, or external relations. While the state
accepts a horizontal external order which isolates
various and diverse legal orders within discrete
territorial units, the empire seeks to apply its own

internal normative order in its external relations.
While the international law of the state system
provides a procedural framework for defining the
jurisdiction or 'sphere of validity' of the state's
internal normative order, the normative contents of
the empire's external relations are substantive
values which it seeks to impose over a part of the
jurisdiction of diverse subordinate polities.

In the context of the contemporary state
system, 'the object of imperialist policies is control of other states in forms which leave their
statehood and formal independence more or less
intact, but which in fact add their territories and
resources to those of the imperialist Power'.[16] The
contemporary empires are also states, whose imperial
character is revealed in their boundary concepts.
The United States' imperial ideology is well revealed in the writings of the leading American international legal scholar, Myers McDougal, who has
greatly influenced post-World War Two thinking on
international law from his teaching post at Yale.
McDougal frankly states his view that 'It has long
been demonstrated that "territorial" notions of
jurisdiction are largely outmoded'. In place of
these 'notions' which constitute the basis of the
state system, McDougal advocates an 'integrative
universalism'. As he states, 'Our overriding aim is
to clarify and aid in the implementation of a universal order of human dignity'. That this new kind
of international law involves substantive policies,
and not just a framework for horizontal relations
among states, is clear:

> By an international law of human dignity I
> mean the processes of authoritative decision
> of a world public order in which values are shaped
> and shared more by persuasion than coercion, and
> which seeks to promote the greatest product-
> ion and widest possible sharing without
> discriminations irrelevant to merit, of all
> values among all human beings.

McDougal defines 'values' as security, wealth, respect, enlightenment, well-being, rectitude and
affection.[17]

This crucial though not entirely precise definition of the chief American school of international
law does make clear that its objective is not to
preserve the internal legal orders of territorial
states, but rather to promote the 'greatest production' of values, according to some unarticulated

order of priorities, and their 'widest possible
sharing' according to some unarticulated order of
merit. McDougal's 'international law of human dignity' may be seen as an attempt to erect a respectable intellectual edifice for the American imperial
idea of the 'free world' formulated in the context
of the post-war rivalry between the superpowers;
but it provides the vaguest of standards for applying substantive values in international relations
and has been criticised as subjective and as unusable
'by any one lower than the angels'.[18] Whatever the
quality of his intellectual achievement, McDougal
presents a theory of international law that is
clearly imperial and in express conflict with existing international law of the horizontal state
system.
     The leading Soviet exponent of international
law similarly, although in a less sweeping manner,
rejects the basic structure of the existing state
system. The authoritative treatise by Tunkin, who
has served as legal adviser to the Soviet government, states:

>   The social consequences of the operation of
>   socialist international legal principles
>   differ completely from the consequences of
>   the operation of norms of general inter-
>   national law ... They aim at strengthening
>   and developing relations of the fraternal
>   commonwealth of socialist countries, at
>   ensuring the construction of socialism and
>   communism, and at protecting the gains of
>   socialism from the infringement of forces
>   hostile to socialism.

The standard applied here is socialism. The chief
ambiguity in the 'international legal principles
which comprise the unified system of principles of
socialist internationalism' is the definition of
socialism. This is important both for determining
membership in the 'fraternal commonwealth' and for
applying duties to 'strengthen friendship' and to
'render assistance', as were performed by the USSR
in Hungary in 1956, Czechoslovakia in 1968, and now
in Afghanistan in 1979-80. Tunkin's statement
makes it quite clear that within the socialist
'commonwealth' at least, the purpose of the legal
order is not to preserve the autonomy of the legal
orders of the various component states but rather
to promote the substantive aims of constructing and
preserving the gains of socialism.[19]

It would be futile to jump into a political thicket by attempting to discuss whether McDougal's 'human dignity' or Tunkin's 'socialist internationalism' provides the more precise and manageable concept for governing relations between a dominant power and subordinate political entities. The point is that both of these theories of 'international law' are examples of imperial ideas which articulate and legitimate assertions of jurisdiction on the basis of subject matter - here concerning 'human dignity' or 'socialism' - rather than on the basis of territory or personality. Substantive, albeit vague, concepts are foremost; protection of the borders of independent polities, within which to work out internal legal orders through self-determination, is secondary in these imperial ideologies. McDougal illustrates the kind of partial self-determination contemplated by these imperial orders when he states that his 'International law of human dignity' would 'balance self-determination with capacity for, and acceptance of, responsibility and seek an organisation of government in territorial units large enough to discharge responsibility'.[20] While McDougal would hold all countries responsible to a vaguely defined standard of 'human dignity', Tunkin would hold only those countries within the 'fraternal commonwealth' responsible to a standard of socialism. In either case, the imperial border is defined by a mutable concept which serves to delimit the material jurisdiction of subordinate polities and accordingly conforms to the ideal-type empire by asserting jurisdiction on the basis of subject matter rather than either territory or personality.

Because empires do not recognise territorial or personality boundaries to their power and ideology, relations between them are inherently competitive. The essential character of the ideal-type empire being unilateral encroachment on the jurisdiction of other polities in a relationship of inequality and domination, means that empires do not have available a common normative order for maintenance of stable boundaries between them on the basis of equality and independence, as do states and tribes. Empires of the 'international' type compete for the allegiance of polities outside their spheres of influence, or through the subversion of polities within the competitor's sphere. As the threat of subversion requires deepening of jurisdiction toward the state pattern, and as empires become geographically proximate, they may resort to state-type territorial boundaries to divide their respective

spheres. For example, boundaries drawn by the
British and Russian empires in the second half of
the nineteenth century delimited the territory of
the state of Afghanistan.

Tribal and Imperial Orders in Afghanistan

Afghanistan's geographical position at the crossroads
between India, Iran and Central Asia has provided
it with a long history of imperial competition and
conquest, from Achaemenid, Bactrian, Kushan,
Sasanid, Umayad and Abbasid, to Ghaznavid, Mongol,
Timurid, Safavid and Mughal. Some of these empires
brought their religions, and in Afghanistan
Zoroastrian met Buddhist and Hindu met Moslem.
Caught between competing empires, Pashtuns commonly
fought or intrigued with both sides, even when the
opponent was a Pashtun regime. Pashtun tribesmen
fought with Timur against the Pashtun-supported
Delhi Sultanate, they fought with Babur when the
Mughals overthrew the Lodi Afghan rulers of Delhi,
they fought with Nadir Shar Afshar when he defeated
the Ghilzai Afghan rulers of Isfahan and Kandahar
in the early eighteenth century, and were caught up
in the Safavid-Mughal competition for Kandahar in
the sixteenth and seventeenth centuries. The environment in which the tribes developed their own
political institutions was thus dominated by empires
and imperial competition of various colours long
before the classic nineteenth-century confrontation
between the Russian and British empires in the
'Great Game' - for which Afghanistan and the Pashtun
tribes were the main arena.
    The relations between Pashtun tribes and var-
ious empires that attempted to extend influence over
them reveal some of the patterns of relations
between those two different types of polities. Two
patterns which stand out are, first, imperial alliances with factions or particular tribes used to
control other factions or tribes, and second, the
recruitment of tribesmen into imperial armies. The
second pattern was not only a way to divert the
fighting strength of the tribes and secure some
loyalty to the imperial standard, but was also a
means of transferring wealth to the tribal area
through soldiers' remittances. Direct subsidies to
tribal leaders or factions was another common tool
of imperial diplomacy, used for example by the
Mughals, particularly with the tribes that guarded
the passes into India.

One way in which the imperial ideology may be introduced is through an epochal change like the conversion of the Pashtuns to Islam. Pashtuns now identify their own tribal law with Islam, and would acknowledge no difference between the two, though it may still be questioned how far Islam has displaced Pashtunwali in the internal legal order of the tribes.[21] Islam rather provides symbols through which the Pashtuns may express their own unity in transcendental terms as well as a framework for relating to non-tribal and non-Pashtun peoples and governments. The use of Islam by a strong government, to legitimate the encroachment of the imperial boundary more deeply into the internal Pashtun legal order, has always remained more potential than real with the tribes in the easily defended terrain north-west of the Suleyman Range.

Not every empire arrives flying the banner of religious conversion. The expansion of Islam, with its theologically accessible and politically egalitarian content, brought a unique experience to the peoples it touched, not easily comparable to other imperial ideologies. The more common means by which empires impose their ideology upon the normative orders of subordinate tribes, is by co-opting tribal leaders into representing imperial interests and promoting that ideology. Imperial order is an inherently hierarchical order. The empire seeks to impose such an order upon its subordinate tribes and to conduct relations through this familiar structure. The Pashtun tribal institutions provide a consensual decision-making structure for representation of progressively more inclusive groupings of lineage and faction. Implicit in this structure is potential for communicating command as well as consensus. However, attempts to turn institutions like the malik and jirga from democratic uses to imperial purposes of hierarchical control have not always been successful.[22] These institutions do not seem to afford means for acquiring power of hierarchical command, but rather provide a context through which personal power consolidated through other means may be exercised.

Among Pashtuns, as for other Central Asian tribal groups, power of leadership is acquired through the process of becoming a khan,[23] which is a non-institutional status or descriptive title for those who achieve positions of influence in tribal politics. Anderson shows how this status is achieved through distribution of patronage, turning economic surplus into political capital, and broker-

age among tribesmen and more especially between the
tribe and the metropolitan society and government
with which it has relations. The khan performs for
the tribe the public service of representing and
mediating between groups so as to build more inclusive unities within the tribe. Representation and
mediation with the metropolitan society serve to
maintain tribal unity in the face of an intrusive
external polity. In the person of the khan, the
imperial quest for hierarchy articulates with the
tribal need for unity when faced with an encroaching
empire.[24]
     The empire is also able to supply resources
essential to the making of a khan - wealth for
patronage and connections for brokerage. The khan's
role of broker with the empire can be adorned with
imperial titles and honours which add to his prestige and charisma within the tribe; at the same time
he becomes adept in manipulating the metropolitan
culture.[25] While the khan who mediates relations
with the empire from a subordinate, subsidised position adopts and integrates in his person some part
of the imperial ideology as a necessary vesture of
his office, he cannot be seen to be a creature of
the empire without losing legitimacy within his
tribal constituency. The dilemma inherent in the
mediator's role becomes more tolerable to the extent
that the empire and its ideology can be domesticated
and legitimated within the tribal normative order.
In return for the resources needed to perform his
role as patron and broker, the khan places his
charisma and his mastery of metaphor and meaning
within the tribe in the service of the imperial ideology. It is perhaps no coincidence that the greatest Pashtun poet, Khushhal Khan Khatak, was also
chief of the tribe most closely allied with the
Mughals. Similarly Ahmad Khan Abdali (later
Durrani), scion of the closest Afghan allies of the
Iranians and himself Nadir Shah Afshar's principal
Afghan commander and, according to tradition, designated successor, was also a poet.[26] The khan's
ability to integrate the personal qualities of a
tribal leader with fluency in the imperial ideology,
defines his position at the boundary between tribe
and empire, a highly fluid articulation between
distinct normative orders and political structures.
Factional divisions along the fault lines of tribal
lineage and alliance may result from the khan's
failure to retain both tribal legitimacy and imperial favour. While such factions undermine the
tribal unity required to face the external threat

at full strength, and provide an opening for the
empire to impose its jurisdictional boundary more
intrusively upon tribal institutions, for example
by assuming the task of dispute settlement between
factions,[27] they also deny hierarchical order. Relations between tribe and empire are thus built on
paradox. The empire requires tribal unity through
the mechanism of tribal leadership in order to
create the hierarchy required for indirect rule and
to promote its legitimating ideology; yet it also
exploits tribal fission as a means of maintaining
its control over the tribe. The tribe, bound up in
the same paradox, needs unity to oppose an encroaching empire effectively; however, the process of
building up unity may involve legitimation of the
empire and 'ultimately precludes action' by the
tribe.[28]

Tribe and empire are structurally complementary,
just as the state and tribe are structurally dis-
congruous. The career of empire is aggregation of
tribal and state units to its imperial order and
ideology, while the tribe obtains from empire the
means to build up its own internal order and unity
against the centrifugal forces that lineage and
faction bring to a polity based on personal jurisdiction. Where, as has commonly been the case with
Pashtuns, an equivalence of power subsists between
the tribe and empire, the complementarity of their
relations may be worked out within a framework of
normative argument. While the empire may be excluded from the language of kinship, and tribesmen
from the circle of meaning defining the imperial
elite, both the imperial ideology and a tribal normative order like Pashtunwali provide fields where
argument may be joined. Success in forging a common
language for relations from these separate normative
materials will depend upon the universality and
adaptability of the imperial ideology as well as
the quality and resilience of the tribal order. The
tribesmen become fluent in the imperial ideology as
the empire learns to turn the tribal order to its
own ends.

For the Pashtun tribes Islam has long provided
an additional resource for relations with the Muslim
empires they have confronted. Undoubtedly Islam has
facilitated the stability of relations between tribe
and empire throughout this region. Even in the
absence of Islam, however, the dialectic between
imperial ideology and tribal order provided a normative basis for relations, for example, with the
British in India. This process can be illustrated

by the comments of a British officer who worked with
the Mahsuds in the 1920s. He writes that the typical Pashtun is

> no less difficult to deal with on planes
> other than that of force than he is to conquer
> in the field. First, there are the same
> qualities which make him formidable as a
> fighter - his ingenuity and his persistence,
> backed by amazing plausibility in argument,
> such as would excite the envy of an Athenian
> demagogue.

This compliment, which echoes those of others who
have studied or experienced Afghan diplomatic skills
from the fifteenth-century Suri Sultanate of Delhi
down to the present, evidences the ability of the
tribesmen to adapt their normative referent to that
of their adversary. At the same time, Howell himself illustrates the attitude arising from successful imperial accommodation to the tribesmen, when
he confesses, with the appropriate measure of ambiguity, that he is 'not at all sure that with reser-
vations I do not subscribe to their plea' of superiority for the tribal normative order, which he
states as follows: 'A civilization has no other end
than to produce a fine type of man. Judged by this
standard the social system in which the Mahsud has
been evolved must be allowed to surpass all
others'.[29]

Systems of Inter-Polity Relations

By this mutual accommodation between their separate
spheres of jurisdiction, the ideal-type tribe and
empire are able to construct an ad hoc normative
order for their bilateral relations that can be
contrasted with the international legal order between states. The fundamental distinction between
the two kinds of inter-polity normative orders is
that the imperial order is unequal, hierarchical or
vertical, while the inter-state order is theoreti-
cally horizontal, based on the equality of its
subject states, and reciprocal. The ideal-type
empire maintains a balance of force among its subordinate polities sufficient to overpower any one
of them if necessary to enforce its rule. The tribe
maintains its autonomy within this unequal order by
making it expensive for the empire to enforce its
rule against the opposition of the tribe, but has no

reciprocal right or capacity, short of conquest, to impose its norm over the empire. By contrast, in the inter-state order every principle that may justify the exercise of force by one state may be reciprocally enforced against that state on an equal basis by every other state. The accommodation between the normative orders of empire and tribe contrasts with reciprocal respect for the normative autonomy of states within territorial spheres whose boundaries are defined by accommodation. The egalitarian, fissile, and consensual order of the tribe seems to require a hierarchical external order for its completion and unity. The state by contrast requires a hierarchical, unified, and exclusive internal order to maintain its identity as an equal participant in a horizontal state system of international legal order.[30]

These two contrasting structures of ideal-type international legal orders provide models for the dominant systems of inter-polity relations in historical times. The empire-tribe structure corresponds to systems most prevalent before the seventeenth-century Westphalian beginnings of the now universal state system. Nevertheless, it still retains relevance as a model, alternative to the contemporary state system, for the normative conduct of international relations, such as in proposals for the 'globalization of natural resources from state to humanity as a whole', which reduce the importance of territory for the state in favour of a personality-based form of polity.[31] In both the empire-tribe and inter-state structures of relations, boundaries are prior to the normative order. In the absence of a constitutional settlement defining the respective material spheres of tribal and imperial norms or allocation of territory among states, failure of the inter-polity normative order is linked to change of structure: the empire metamorphosing to the state form by pushing back autonomous tribal jurisdiction - substituting direct for indirect rule - and the state behaving as empire by abandoning reciprocal respect for the exclusive territorial jurisdiction of states in favour of the unilateral imposition of a substantive ideology in its foreign relations.

This model of ideal-type polities, and of typical structures of relations among them, begins from the premise that any independent polity of whatever form exists by virtue of its effectiveness in ordering the lives of those subject to its norms. Lacking a single universal and exclusive normative order, a polity may subject human behaviour to norms only within the territorial, personal and material 'spheres of validity' to which its jurisdiction reaches. Jurisdiction may reach to whatever the polity is able to coerce by force, or it may be de-limited by principle or norm, thus permitting a stable and consensual division of its jurisdiction from that of other polities. Force and norm are not simply opposite means for determining juris-diction. As Michel Foucault has written, using 'knowledge' in a normative sense, 'Power is not caught in the alternative: force or ideology. In fact every point in the exercise of power is at the same time a site where knowledge is formed. And conversely every established piece of knowledge permits and assures the exercise of power.'[32] Force and ideology are dialectically related as much in the definition of the jurisdiction of norms as in the enforcement of the norms themselves. The norma-tive definition of jurisdiction on personal, terri-torial or material bases forms part of the legiti-mating ideology of the polity, while it also consti-tutes the structure of relations with other polities. Since the alternative bases of jurisdiction are ontological elements of behaviour, they provide an enduring model for typing any normative order and for identifying structural characteristics of rela-tions between types.

From the perspective of legal science, the selection from among the three jurisdictional bases for enforcement of norms may be considered arbitrary. Through whatever structure, in the end norm is applied to behaviour. From the perspective of the polity, however, 'Hobbesian abhorrence'[33] of tribal society by 'civilised' metropolitan society is reciprocated in the disdain the tribe expresses for the transactional relations of the metropolis, com-pared to the personal and kinship relations of the tribe. These normative judgments reflect divergent attitudes towards dealing at different levels of political integration with values such as hierarchy, equality, order and freedom. In addition to iden-tifying these normative qualities, it is also possible tentatively to postulate some adaptive material qualities of these three jurisdictional bases of norms. The state may correspond to a political economy where intensive utilisation of land or natural resources is the key factor in the production of wealth or military power. In the tribal form of polity, people, rather than territor-ial resources, may be the crucial factor for prod-uction and war. Empires perhaps flourish where exchange (i.e. commerce and transaction of goods and knowledge), rather than either people or resources, becomes the principal determinant for the acquisition of wealth, which alone or combined with some factor of military technology permits consolidation of a decisive balance of power over subordinate territorial or person-based polities.

The political types and structures which have been outlined here are conceptual models that neither conform to nor necessarily even appear in reality. Real characteristics typical of these political and juristic models may identify a political unit with one of the three conceptual types, although every polity will have elements of more than one type. For example, the Pashtun normative order, which is discussed here as an example of the tribal type, also has distinctive territorial features bound up with its tribal norms at both the individual and the group levels.[34] Robert Lowie clarified this relationship of territory to the tribe in his discussion of Henry Maine's view that 'sharply separated two principles of uniting individuals for governmental purposes - the blood tie and the territorial tie'. After comparing several tribal societies, Lowie concludes 'that the blood tie is frequently the overshadowing element in the governmental activities of primitive peoples. Yet, though it often dwarfs the territorial factor, it never succeeds in eliminating it'.[35] Ideology, territory and personal factors conjoin to formulate the legitimacy of any polity. By isolating the dominant factor, one may identify types such as the tribe or state. In some polities no single factor dominates, but rather various permutations of these factors yield hybrid types and ambiguous boundaries. The closer that interrelating polities approximate to the stable and coherent boundaries of a discrete type, the more predictably and unambiguously may their external relations be conducted within the normative order of a compatible inter-polity structure.

Multiple Polities and Structural Change in Afghanistan

Imperial Rivalries in Afghanistan since 1800. Empires, tribes and the state have all been important actors in the politics of Afghanistan during the nineteenth and twentieth centuries. As much as any area in the world, Afghanistan has been characterised by conflicts and tensions among all three types of polity.

The model of ideal types outlined above may be
employed to sort out the separate factors and to
understand the dynamics of their interaction both in
the historical era beginning around 1800 as well as
in the contemporary period of intense change.

Since the breakdown of the tribally-based
Sadozai empire in the first quarter of the nineteenth
century, and the gradual consolidation by Dost
Muhammad of the central Pashtun areas and Turkistan
within a Muhammadzai emirate, Afghanistan has been
the scene of nearly continuous imperial rivalry.
The emirate was a minimal khanly state uniting city
and tribe, where according to one Amir, 'every
official and every chief has his own laws'. The
rivalry between the Russian and British Empires in
the 'Great Game' determined the environment in which
the Muhammadzai emirate acquired fixed territorial
boundaries within which it began to assert a more
comprehensive state-type jurisdiction, 'putting it
into the form of a kingdom'.[36] Both empires realised
that 'advance through Afghanistan means hard fighting with Afghans by whomever it is undertaken'.[37]
On their side, the Afghans realised that they were
not equal to preserving complete independence from
both European empires by force. This mutual recognition of the power balance set the stage for
establishing normatively-based relations, turning
on the Afghans' desire for autonomy and subsidies
on the one hand, and the ideologies and interests of
their neighbouring empires on the other.

The imperial ideologies of the two European
empires were qualified by their ambiguous character
as states subject to the rule of international law
in Europe while sustaining imperial expansion abroad.
Britain partially avoided this paradox in India by
inheriting its acquisitions from an English Company
which had consolidated power as one contestant in
the political free-for-all of the late Mughal Empire.
By the time the myth of Mughal legitimacy gave way
to a concept of the British Empire, with Victoria
as Empress of India, the problem could be presented
in the state-like terms of finding the proper 'frontier' for India. Turning between state and imperial
approaches to boundaries, this issue became 'an
obsession of British diplomacy and public opinion'.[38]
The first approach accepted a limitation of jurisdiction within a fixed border, originally assayed
at the Indus, within which would be pursued state-
like objectives such as 'to reconcile the people of
India to the ruler of the day, to give them the best
Government in our power, to improve the conditions

of the country which need immense development,
rather than pursue a policy which, reckless of the
consequence, was all and all for advance'.[39] This
policy became dominant after the disastrous First
Anglo-Afghan War, when it acquired the label
'Masterly Inactivity'.

'Forward Policy' was the term applied to various
more expansive and intrusive approaches to India's
western borders.[40]   Although it went through
several formulations in different contexts, the
Forward Policy, in an era of geopoliticians, generally crystallised around the concept of a 'Scientific
Frontier', that is, the most defensible boundary for
India. The Scientific Frontier theory involved
securing control of passes such as the Khyber and
Bolan, as well as a capacity to defend the northern
approaches to the Hindu Kush as a first line of
defence. The British public and the Indian Treasury
would not long support military campaigns in pursuit
of these strategic goals, particularly when carried
out against what was perceived as an independent
state, Afghanistan, which had proved its capacity
for resistance. Realities of tribal resistance on
the one hand, and political compromise between
imperial and state boundary conceptions on the other,
gave rise to a complex boundary policy, sometimes
known as the 'Threefold Frontier'.[41] The first
frontier was the state or 'administrative border'
within which the laws of British India were enforced.
Beyond this to the 'political border' was the North
West Frontier, encompassing the important mountain
passes and occupied by tribes who were self-governing
in their internal affairs but over whom British India
exercised a fluctuating and uncertain degree of
influence. Adjoining the political boundary was the
'protectorate' of Afghanistan, bound to British
India by treaties and serving as a buffer with the
neighbouring Russian Empire north of the approaches
to the Hindu Kush. As one British official described this relationship:

> Afghanistan occupies the almost unique position
> of being an absolutely independent kingdom and
> at the same time a protected state...Afghan
> independence is so far absolute that we have
> no British European resident at the Court of
> Kabul, and it is only by grace of a very
> special favour that any European visitor is
> permitted access to the capital at all.[42]

The compromise contained sufficient ambiguity to

reflect a territorial view of boundaries while at
the same time leaving more space than could be
digested for imperial adventure by those who might
advocate such unabashedly imperial sentiments as
these: 'In the interests ... of peace ... of commerce ... of moral and material improvement ...
interference in Afghanistan has now become a duty'.[43]
Such vague and romantic imperial ideas were never
entirely excluded from the debate over the
Afghanistan question, but they were rarely politically palatable, except perhaps in the Disraeli
years, 1874-80.

Makers of Russian frontier policy, by comparison, did not need to satisfy a divided public opinion.
Nor were they in need of a policy that was basically
defensive in design. In the latter half of the
nineteenth century the Russian Empire was actively
moving its imperial boundary through Asia towards
Afghanistan. The British saw behind Russia's
advance two geopolitical objectives: first, realisation of Peter the Great's wish for a Russian port
on the southern seas, and second, control of the
overland 'gateway to India' through Afghanistan, in
furtherance of the Napoleonic strategy of an overland attack on Britain's rich Asian possession. At
that time there was no oil industry, though
Turkistan north and south of the navigable Amu
Darya was (and long had been) a populous and wealthy
producer of agricultural commodities and handicrafts.
Whatever its geopolitical objectives, the Russian
Empire was able, in a way which the British Empire
probably was not, clearly and frankly to express
the idea which informed and justified its expansion.

In 1864 Prince Gorchakov, the Russian Imperial
Chancellor, explained the imperial idea intended to
justify Russia's expansion into Central Asia, in an
official memorandum circulated to its European
embassies. The Gorchakov memorandum relies on a
state-like perception of relations between 'civilised states' and 'wandering tribes possessing no
fixed social organisation', stating that 'the interests of security on the frontier, and of commercial
relations, compel the more civilised state to exercise a certain ascendancy over neighbours whose
turbulence and nomad instincts render them difficult
to live with'. Gorchakov likens the Russian 'dilemma' to that of other state-empires, the United
States, France, Britain and Holland, observing that
either 'it must allow an anarchy to become chronic
which paralyses all security and all progress ... or
on the other hand it must enter on a career of con-

quest and annexation such as gave England her Indian Empire'. Favouring neither of these alternatives, Gorchakov presents the boundary concept that would justify the further expansion of empire in Central Asia while appearing to accord the respect to state boundaries upon which the European system rested. Gorchakov's concept distinguishes 'nomad tribes' who make 'the worst neighbours possible' from the 'agricultural and commercial populations, wedded to the soil, [who] given a more highly developed social organisation, afford for us a basis for friendly relations which may become all that can be wished. Our frontier line then should include the first, and stop at the boundaries of the second.' The Russian Empire would therefore absorb areas and peoples lacking 'a social organisation and a government which directs and represents it', but not those who, possessing some semblance of these attributes of a state polity, accept 'that peaceful and commercial relations with her are more profitable than disorder, pillage, reprisals and chronic warfare.'

Accordingly the imperial boundary would extend to wherever it might meet a government able to impose order on a population 'wedded to the soil' and also willing to maintain commercial relations with the Russians. The Gorchakov memorandum expressly states the premise lying behind this test, the idea of 'civilisation': 'The progress of civilisation has no more efficacious ally than commercial relations. These require in all countries order and stability as conditions essential to their growth.' The Russian imperial border was not one dividing two cultures but one which articulated the jurisdiction of the empire with another polity sharing the common 'ally' of commercial relations and, implicitly, the power to make further Russian expansion expensive. Concepts such as 'order' and 'civilisation' are highly subjective, and Gorchakov forewarned the Central Asian emirates, who were the momentary beneficiaries of his analysis, that 'in spite of their low civilisation and nebulous political development, we hope that regular relations may one day in our common interest replace the chronic disorders which have hitherto hampered their progress'.[44] The traditional emirates, which were once vigorous centres of much different civilisations, would not in time meet the standards of the European commercial empire then entering upon the early stages of the industrial revolution. In 1865 Tashkent was taken, in 1868 Samarkand was absorbed, while Bokhara became a 'subsidiary ally', and in 1869 negotiations

were opened in St Petersburg with the civilised,
ordered, and commercial state with which the Russian
Empire would ultimately define the limits of their
Central Asian territory: Great Britain. By 1873,
the Russians and British Empires, without the knowledge of the Afghans, reached a territorial understanding that Afghanistan, south of the Amu Darya,
would remain outside the Russian sphere of influence.
At this stage there began a contest, not for territorial conquest, but for diplomatic influence within
the new state whose boundaries were taking shape.
After this contest gave rise to the Second Anglo-
Afghan War (1878-80), it was resolved by the understanding that Afghanistan would conduct its foreign
relations only through the British, while the
Afghans proceeded to deny both empires influence or
even access to its internal affairs.
    The subsidies acquired as an outcome of this
rivalry between imperial powers assisted Afghan
rulers, especially Abd al-Rahman (1880-1901) and his
son Habibullah (1901-19), to achieve the central
power required for unity within the country. This
pattern of relations survived in the Soviet-American
rivalry for influence in Afghanistan which began in
the 1940s.[45] The new rivalry was a continuation of
the old by other means. Subsidies were received
from both sides this time, which meant the preservation of autonomy in foreign relations. But the
new and substantial subsidies - over $1.5 billion by
the 1970s - were accompanied by numerous advisers
and other foreigners, which compromised the internal
autonomy and even isolation that the earlier
arrangement had deliberately safeguarded.

Tribalism and the Durrani State. It was under Abd
al-Rahman that the state boundaries of Afghanistan
were finally drawn and, with an assured annual subsidy from the British of £120,000 (later raised to
£180,000), some significant steps were taken towards
creating a state polity, by building up the military
power of the central government, extending control
over internal minorities, co-opting the powers of
the clergy, and keeping the peace. These developments manifested themselves in greater central control over and expanded reach of the legal system.[46]
The fragility of Abd al-Rahman's creation, and its
dependence on retaining military superiority over
the tribes, was revealed when his grandson
Amanullah (1919-29), having lost the British subsidy
upon independence and weakened his army, was overthrown as a result of tribal rebellions. The next

Durrani King, Nadir Shah, was the nominee of the
tribesmen who put him in power. Amanullah had represented a growing new class of government employees,
intellectuals and other urban elements which would
expand greatly under Nadir Shah's nephew, Prime
Minister Daud (1953-63), when foreign subsidies -
under the rubric of development and - were stepped up
markedly. With Soviet assistance, Daud was able to
built up an army, about double the size maintained
by Abd al-Rahman, which was equipped with tanks, jets,
and other modern material. This growth of the
economic and military power of the central government
and of the urban classes provided the state institutions with an expanded power base and a new level of
influence over regional and tribal elements.

In the period of Zahir Shah's direct rule (1963-
73), under his liberal constitution regional and
tribal elements were given a new vehicle for opposing the central government through their control of
the elected parliament. During this period, when
Zahir attempted to preserve his rule more by political than military means, there were no more than
minor challenges from tribal elements. The state's
finances remained primarily dependent upon foreign
subsidies and foreign trade taxes.[47] The principal
form of exactions from the countryside were, as
ever, not direct taxes but rather official corruption,[48] which had the effect of making government
employees as responsive to the wishes of local
leaders as to the directives of the state. Corruption also affected the legal system, which was
dominated by the religious elite who retained a good
measure of the autonomy recovered after the fall of
Amanullah. In some areas tribal autonomy left the
state-appointed qazi courts largely idle. Even
where courts were utilised, the overwhelming bulk
of the law applicable to life outside the cities was
not state-made but rather the uncodified principles
of the sharia which gave the religious elites an
open field for interpretation of the law and performance of their time-honoured function of mediation
between tribe and state. It was little more than a
year before the end of Muhammadzai rule that comprehensive civil and criminal codes were enacted.

Not only was the state's jurisdiction poised
against regional and tribal autonomy, but the state
was itself dependent on the tribes for its own
legitimacy. The Afghan tribes had provided the
basis of power for government ever since the
Sadozai empire of Ahmad Shah. Hajji Jamal Khan of
the Muhammadzai branch of the Barakzai Durranis, the

most powerful of the tribal leaders, had been instrumental in electing Ahmad Shah Sadozai to be first king of the Afghans in 1747.[49] His grandson Fatih Khan was powerful wazir and king-maker to the last Sadozais, while Fatih Khan's youngest brother Dost Muhammad established the Muhammadzai dynasty and Muhammadzai legitimacy, by ejecting the Sadozais and defeating the last pretender (and British protégé) Shah Shuja, as well as by consolidating the central provinces of the much reduced former empire and successfully defending them against the British in the First Anglo-Afghan War (1839-43). When Amanullah exhausted this legitimacy nearly a century later, he was replaced by a descendant of another brother of Fatih Khan - that is, another Muhammadzai. This Muhammadzai legitimacy, which stretched with remarkable continuity from the eighteenth century down to the socialist coup of 1978, reflected a tribal settlement of national leadership. Legitimacy did not follow any rule of primogeniture but rather, in accordance with Pashtun custom, fell on the most able and acceptable member of the chiefly lineage. Daud, who established the Republic in 1973, was the last Muhammadzai ruler and the last beneficiary of this tribal legitimacy.

Over the half-century since Nadir Shah was placed on the throne, with the gradual growth of government and the urban classes, and with the penetration into rural areas of modernising technology, from roads and radios to tractors, tribes and tribal organisation have undoubtedly weakened.[50] The urban and intellectual classes meanwhile have supplemented the legitimacy of a tribally-based government with the idea of constitutional government, whether of the monarchical or the republican variety. These ideas had a considerable pedigree, with the first constitution coming in 1923, followed by Nadir's constitution in 1931, and the most democratic constitution of Zahir in 1964. Constitutionalism has remained an important symbol of legitimacy for the republican governments. Daud enacted a constitution in 1977; Hafizullah Amin, immediately upon coming to power, appointed a constitutional drafting committee which included legal officials who had served under Daud and Zahir Shah; Babrak Karmal stated at his first press conference that he would be adopting a constitution, and by April 1980 he had a set of 'Basic Principles' (<u>usul-i asasi</u>, i.e. 'constitution') ratified by the Revolutionary Council.[51]

<u>Tribalism facing Soviet Empire</u>. State legality,
through the formal enactment, repeal and amendment
of written laws, as a corollary of constitutionalism,
has also provided a remarkable continuity to the
state's statute book. Those who took power after
the 'Saur Revolution' of 27 April 1978, while maintaining the symbols of state legitimacy through
constitution-making and formal legislation, cut the
knot of tribal legitimacy that Daud had preserved
as the leading Muhammadzai. Not only were the coup
leaders Taraki and Amin by origin Ghilzai, the
tribal group that had been traditional rivals of
the historically dominant Durrani tribes represented
by the Muhammadzais, but they were also ideologically and, perhaps most important, personally alienated from tribalism as such. The Parcham and Khalq
parties had a nearly exclusively urban base and an
ideology which rejected tribal organisation as back-
ward or 'feudal'. Their alienation from tribal
values is perhaps best symbolised in Babrak Karmal's
formal disinheritance by his father. Since communism is considered by Afghans to be inconsistent
with Islam, attempts were made, especially by
Taraki, to avoid the word 'communism' and instead to
speak in terms of socialism. However, Khalq and
Parcham (united in 1977 as the People's Democratic
Party of Afghanistan, PDPA) were perceived as pro-
Soviet communist parties, a perception given plausibility in both word and deed by their leaders.
Amin, for example, gave speeches laden with references to Lenin that read like Marxist-Leninist
tracts, and broadcast comments such as that the
'hammer and sickle have got together in making a
proletarian dictatorship ... in Afghanistan'.[52]
This perceived hostility to Islam, aggravated by
active and nearly unanimous opposition to the regime
by religious leaders such as the Mujadadis and the
Geylanis, severs the second traditional thread for
relations between the tribes and the central government.

The PDPA government is sensitive to these two
causes of disaffection by the tribes. Consequently,
especially under Taraki and now under Babrak Karmal,
it has paid lip-service to both Islam and tribal
values. This has recently been elevated to party
doctrine in the 'Thesis of the PDPA Central
Committee for the Second Anniversary' announced on
17 April 1980.[53] Paragraph 11 of this Thesis
explains the PDPA government's central policy of
limiting land ownership as 'just and right from the
point of view of social justice and the sacred

religion of Islam'. It goes on to declare in paragraph 14 the 'full freedom and rights of Moslems',
and to attack 'imperialism ... under the name of
Islam'. At no time had the PDPA been content to
abandon Islam to the rebels, and Taraki had even
gone so far as to declare jihad against the rebels
just as they had against him. Paragraph 13 of the
Thesis is directed at the Pashtun tribes in recognition of their 'special role in defence'. It
states that the Party and government both 'deeply
respect their customs, traditions and way of life'
and calls for a 'revitalisation' of the tribes and
for the 'democratic observance' of their customs
and traditions. Statements of this kind indicate
that the PDPA is acutely aware of the problem of
its own legitimacy with the tribes, though they must
ring hollow when announced by a government that has
called to its support against the tribes almost
twice as many foreign troops as Shah Shuja brought
with him during the First Anglo-Afghan War, and has
wrought unprecedented destruction in the tribal
areas.[54]

Soviet troops in Afghanistan, at the time of
writing, apparently far outnumber those of the PDPA
itself, which, according to reports, are being
depleted by defections and desertions, besides the
attrition of war. The PDPA government is increasingly dependent on these foreign troops for its
survival. Moreover, Soviet advisers also exercise
control over civilian ministries. Although there
may still be room for cavil, there is every appearance that those tribes who are fighting against the
Karmal/PDPA government are in direct conflict not
only with an imperial ideology but also with the
prodigious military force of the empire that stands
behind that ideology. Short of genocide, this
empire will need eventually either to withdraw or
to reach some settlement with the tribes. The failure of its PDPA allies to substitute a new tribal
legitimacy for the historic settlement by which the
Muhammadzais held power, and the problem of perceived hostility to Islam, do not of themselves
preclude an accommodation between tribe and empire.
The British were no more Muslim or Pashtun than the
Soviets are, but they were able, by a combination
of the occasional show of force in punitive expeditions, subsidies, and tribal politics conducted
through political agents, to preserve a tolerable
modus vivendi with the tribes on their side of the
Durand line for nearly a century. The report of a
Pravda correspondent concerning 'successful negotia-

tions with representatives of some tribes' may indicate that initial steps towards political accommodation with the tribes are being taken.[55]
    No new settlement could be reached, however,
without some test of forces in the pattern typical
of the periodic 'oscillations of power between the
tribes and the central government'. The PDPA at the
time of the coup had at most about 10,000 members,
roughly comparable to a smaller border tribe such as
the Shinwari, and it is estimated that no more than
3,000 troops were actually engaged in fighting on
both sides during the two-day coup. The PDPA forces
were soon complemented by 3,000 Soviet military
advisers and perhaps as many civilian advisers, but
the level of organisational and military power displayed in the coup was not proof that the PDPA would
be able to govern the country.[56] A tribal rebellion
started in Nuristan, one of the least accessible
regions of Afghanistan, and soon spread to neighbouring Pashtun tribes and other parts of the
country, eventually forcing the PDPA to call in substantial reinforcements of Soviet troops. Having
virtually defeated the PDPA troops, the tribes began
in the winter and spring of 1980 to measure swords
directly with the augmented forces of empire.
    The opposition to the PDPA was not restricted
to the tribes. The March 1979 uprising in Herat,
and the June demonstration in Kabul, showed that
there was also opposition among urban classes. The
numerous Islamic organisations in opposition, some
active since the time of Daud, also indicate a base
for organisation alternative to, but not necessarily
separate from that of the tribes. After the introduction of Soviet reinforcements tipped the balance
between indigenous and foreign support for the PDPA,
the spread of popular urban opposition in Kabul and
Kandahar recalled the Kabul uprisings against the
British during the First and Second Anglo-Afghan
Wars. The techniques - shouting Allahu Akbar from
the rooftops as a political rallying cry, strikes in
the bazaar, and mass demonstrations - were more akin
to those that had been used to bring down the Shah
in Iran. While such political action in the cities
may demoralise elements of the PDPA government's
armed forces, as it did the Shah's, so long as
Soviet forces remain stationed in the cities this
kind of opposition will not alone succeed in overthrowing the PDPA regime. The military conflict
will remain a protracted war of evasion in the
countryside until the balance of military power itself shifts, if ever, or an accommodation is made

between tribe and empire.

The ease with which both Zahir and Daud were overthrown demonstrated the exhaustion of the remarkably tenacious Muhammadzai legitimacy, thus marking a new epoch in Afghanistan. The tribal power that had traditionally underpinned central government in Afghanistan needed to accommodate a politicised military that, since the time when Amanullah's armed forces rapidly disintegrated in the face of tribal revolt, had become aligned with the modernising urban classes. It was perhaps inevitable in this context that a new political settlement, integrating both what remained of tribal power and the new urban classes, would involve some test of military strength. That the forces of the PDPA government have been able to maintain any integrity at all, after two years of fighting the tribes, is a further demonstration of the weakening of tribal ties and the increased strength of the urban classes who are contesting tribal influence in the state.

Even before the Soviet Union introduced forces as strong as any that have operated in Afghanistan in recent times, the state trod a tenuous path between the tribes on the one hand and empires on the other. Its finances were overwhelmingly dependent on foreign relations, both commercial and political. Its legal system was in the hands of quasi-autonomous religious elites who mediated between central and regional power, just as its bureaucracy was typified by middlemen serving the highest bidder. The army did not have a monopoly of force, but was adequate for suppressing limited revolts confined by political means to isolated localities and tribes. The Afghan state had many attributes of the tribal khan, maintaining peace among autonomous groups through its role as patron and broker.

The challenge to the tribes posed by the collapse of the tribal-based 'khanly' state is, on the most immediate level, military. A new state apparatus might defeat and break up the tribes, imposing state-made laws, taxes and an efficient bureaucracy throughout the country, while establishing for the first time a thoroughly state-like jurisdiction based on the non-tribal urban classes. So long as this strategy is backed by the comparatively unlimited military strength of the Soviet Union, the challenge is serious indeed. Before concluding that the challenge is insuperable, it is necessary to assess some of the strategic assets of the tribes

such as were described as follows by a British
officer who fought them just 100 years ago:

> Attacking the Afghan tribes is like making
> sword thrusts into water. You meet with no
> resistance but you also do no injury ... Each
> separate tribe is, as it were an independent
> centre of life, which requires a separate
> and special operation for its extinction ...
> The only way in which we could hope to enforce
> our authority throughout Afghanistan would be
> by a simultaneous occupation of the entire
> country.[57]

Conventional wisdom about occupying a country with
the size and rugged terrain of Afghanistan suggests
that as many as one million troops would be needed
to suppress mobile, well-equipped, and determined
guerrilla resistance. The Pashtuns were known by
the British as 'perhaps the best skirmishers and
the best natural shots in the world' and 'the
country they inhabit [as] the most difficult on the
face of the globe'. The British respect for the
Pashtun guerrilla fighter continued as long as they
were in India. A 1946 memorandum summarised the
British experience, concluding that the Pashtun
tribesman is 'on his own ground probably the finest
minor tactician in the world', and estimating that
on the Indian side of the Durand line the 'tribes
could probably muster nearly 500,000 rifles'.[58]
It is impossible to translate these assessments
by the British into predictions about the current
struggle by the tribes against a Soviet army equipped with a new generation of counter-insurgent
technology. However, the imponderables of the new
technology, its effectiveness in terrain like
Afghanistan, and the effectiveness of defensive
weapons and tactics in neutralising the advantage
it affords to material wealth over people, are
perhaps all best resolved in Mao's dictum: 'Weapons
are an important factor in war but not the decisive
one; it is man and not material that counts'. As
much as Afghanistan may be a testing ground for
weaponry, the struggle between tribe and empire is
also a test of the now rusty machinery of tribal
military organisation. Mao also said 'unorganised
guerrilla warfare cannot contribute to victory'.
The capacity of the tribal political order to organise the tribes will be an important factor in the
struggle. The crucial importance of the sanctuaries
in tribal areas on the Pakistan side of the Durand

line, and the participation of tribes living there in the Afghan jihad, will eventually challenge the Pashtuns to co-operate as a whole nation.[59]
     The tribes, and perhaps even the Pashtuns, no longer have the same dominance in Afghanistan that they once had. The political integration required for organising the resistance to empire now goes beyond the tribes to non-tribal and non-Pashtun groups, such as Badakhshani, Nuristani, Hazara, who have organised primarily under the banner of Islam. Here Islam performs its traditional role of trans-cending the tribal order, and in this sense the continuing capacity of Islam for political integra-tion is being tested along with the tribal institu-tions. Faced with outside opposition, Islam could provide the ideology for a new legitimacy in Afghanistan, as it has in Iran. The reaction of Afghanistan's Islamic neighbours and other Islamic nations to its struggle suggests potential for a new unity in the Islamic world that would move modern Islam another step beyond ideology towards broader political relations. As the Islamic Conference becomes a forum for political action and a conduit of military assistance to the Afghans, the imperial potential of Islam begins a tentative revival after lying dormant for centuries. Khumeyni, the man who perhaps best symbolises that revival, has said 'today Islam is confronting the super-powers', and Bani-Sadr has referred to the Russians' 'worry over the Islamic revolution in Iran and fear of its effect on the Islamic republics inside the Soviet Union itself'.[60] The credibility of an Islamic threat to the superpowers is being tested in Afghanistan, where the Pashtun tribes are again, as so often in their history, the focus of conflict between empires.
     In the present conflict, factors typical of the tribe-empire structure of relations are likely to be important. Because the Soviet Union clearly has significant military advantage over the tribes, the tribal strategy must be two-fold: first to make it prohibitively expensive for the empire to main-tain the level of force required to rule the tribes, and second to seek alliance with other groups within the empire. For the latter strategy, Islam provides a convenient bond. As for finances, increased smuggling across the unsettled frontiers and the decline of western development aid have cut into the state's regular sources. The most import-ant exploitable resource, natural gas piped directly from the northern fields into the Soviet Union, is

vulnerable to sabotage. The expensive technology
of counter-insurgency - helicopters, tanks and
jets - are vulnerable imports not to be foraged from
the countryside. By comparison, Afghans are not
only free of dependence on a capital-intensive standard of living and fighting, but positively value
the rugged mobile existence shared by guerrillas and
nomads. As tribal resistance empties the imperial
war chest, the Soviet Union may discover the economies the British introduced by paying subsidies to
the tribes. Abd al-Rahman settled for an annual
subsidy from the British which amounted to about
one-tenth the cost of keeping Shah Shuja on the
throne during the First War, and less than one per
cent of the total cost of the Second War.

As a matter of economy, the empire may need to
learn about tribal politics,[61] as the British did
with measurable skill. The particular ruthlessness
with which the Soviet military is wielding its
power against civilians seemed aimed at rapid pacification, but could rebound badly in a protracted
conflict with tribesmen, for whom the blood feud is
a cultural imperative. On the other hand, the
tribes may need to put forward leaders fluent in the
imperial ideology and capable of forging a Bani-Sadr
style of progressive, democratic and non-aligned or
revolutionary Islam, that would co-opt the ideology
of the pro-Soviet left, and establish a normative
basis for relations in a language familiar to the
empire, while preserving the autonomy of which the
tribes are proverbially jealous. This would be an
extraordinary achievement in a culture as traditional
as the Afghan. But as a perceptive observer,
Muhammad Iqbal, wrote: 'The Afghan conservatism is
a miracle; it is adamantine yet fully sensitive to
and assimilative of new cultural forces'.[62] Their
recent admission to the 'socialist commonwealth' may
confront the Afghans with the greatest challenge to
their capacity for assimilation since their conversion to Islam.

NOTES

    1. See M. Godelier, *Perspectives in Marxist Anthropology*
(Cambridge University Press, 1977), pp. 72-4; R. Lowie, *The
Origin of the State* (Russell and Russell, New York, 1962), p.
51.
    2. Cf. H. Post, 'Classification of the rules of inter-
national law according to spheres of validity', *Netherlands
Yearbook of International Law*, 7 (1976), pp. 157-95.

3. H. Kelsen, *Principles of International Law* (Holt, Rinehart, Winston, New York, 2nd ed., 1966), pp. 306-7.

4. C. de Visscher, *Theory and Reality in International Law*, tr. P. Corbett (Princeton University Press, 1968), p. 204; see also J. Brierly, *The Law of Nations* (Clarendon, Oxford, 6th ed., 1963), p. 162.

5. F. Barth, 'Introduction', in *Ethnic Groups and Boundaries* (Allen and Unwin, London, 1969), pp. 14-15; cf. Ahmed, chapter 5 below.

6. Kelsen, *Principles*, p. 183.

7. Barth, 'Introduction', p. 16.

8. E. Hoebel, *The Law of Primitive Man* (Harvard University Press, Cambridge, Mass., 1954), p. 28; A. D'Amato, *The Concept of Custom in International Law* (Cornell University Press, Ithaca, 1971), p. 266.

9. For the vertical-horizontal metaphor, see R. Falk, 'International jurisdiction: horizontal and vertical conceptions of legal order', *Temple Law Quarterly*, 32 (1959), pp. 295-320.

10. E.g., J. Blondel, *Thinking Politically* (Penguin, Harmondsworth, 1976) p. 59.

11. Cf. G. Schwarzenberger, 'The fundamental principles of international law', *Recueil des Cours*, 87, 1 (1956), pp. 195-385.

12. G. Lichtheim, *Imperialism* (Penguin, London, 1971), pp. 10, 12, 15, 31.

13. R. Niebuhr, *The Structure of Nations and Empires* (Scribners, New York, 1959), p. 242.

14. For discussion of the rule-standard distinction, see D. Kennedy, 'Form and substance in private law adjudication', *Harvard Law Review*, 89 (1976), pp. 1685-1778.

15. G. Arrighi, *Geometry of Imperialism: The Limits of Hobson's Paradigm*, tr. P. Camiller (New Left Books, London, 1978), p. 39.

16. G. Schwarzenberger, *Power Politics: A Study of World Society* (Stevens and Jones, London, 3rd ed., 1964), p. 110.

17. M. McDougal, *Studies in World Public Order* (Yale University Press, New Haven, 1960), pp. 969, 990, 16, 987, 32-6.

18. O. Schachter, Book Review, *American Journal of International Law*, 72 (1978), p. 161. P. Allott, 'Language, method and the nature of international law', *British Yearbook of International Law*, 45 (1971), pp. 79-135.

19. G. Tunkin, *Theory of International Law*, tr. W. Butler (Allen & Unwin, London, 1974), pp. 435-40.

20. McDougal, *Studies*, p. 1010.

21. E.g., J. Spain, *The Pathan Borderland* (Mouton, The Hague, 1963), p. 72.

22. E.g., E. Howell, *Mizh: a Monograph on Government's Relations with the Mahsud Tribe* (Government of India Press,

Simla, 1931), IOL: R/12/199, pp. 6, 50.
23. See e.g. M.N. Shahrani, *The Kirghiz and Wakhi of Afghanistan: Adaptation to Closed Frontiers* (University of Washington Press, Seattle, 1979), pp. 164-6.
24. See chapter 3 below.
25. See L. Lockhart, *The Fall of the Safavi Dynasty and the Afghan Occupation of Persia* (Cambridge University Press, 1958), pp. 85-7, 95-6, for Abdali and Ghilzai leaders under the Safavids.
26. G. Singh, *Ahmad Shah Durrani, Father of Modern Afghanistan* (Asia Publ. House, Bombay, 1959), p. 19.
27. See chapter 4 below.
28. See chapter 3 below.
29. Howell, *Mizh*, p. 48 and Preface; cf. A. Pandey, *The First Afghan Empire in India, 1451-1526 A.D.* (Bookland, Calcutta, 1956), pp. 87-9; R. Newell, 'Foreign Relations', in L. Dupree and L. Albert (eds.), *Afghanistan in the 1970s* (Praeger, New York, 1974), p. 76.
30. The comparison between these two kinds of orders is made explicit in M. Barkun, *Law without Sanctions: Order in Primitive Societies and the World Community* (Yale University Press, New Haven), 1968.
31. D. Ronen, *Quest for Self-Determination* (Yale University Press, New Haven, 1979), p. 119; cf. J. Herz, 'The rise and demise of the territorial state', *World Politics,* 9 (1957), pp. 473-93; de Visscher, *Theory,* p. 405.
32. M. Foucault, *Power, Truth and Strategy*, ed. M. Morris and P. Patton (Feral, Sydney, 1979), p. 59.
33. A term borrowed from R. Tapper, 'Nomadism in modern Afghanistan: asset or anachronism?' in Dupree and Albert, *Afghanistan,* p. 136.
34. One writer states, 'The Pathan's very "citizenship" in the tribe rests on his right to a *daftar* or share in the land', Spain, p. 81; another observed, 'Hill Pathans organize themselves within segmentary lineage groups corresponding to known territorial boundaries', A.S. Ahmed, *Millenium and Charisma among Pathans* (Routledge & Kegan Paul, London, 1976), p. 74. The Mangals and Jajis long and hotly contested a territorial boundary dispute, and Barth, *Ethnic groups,* p. 126, remarks on the 'exclusive territorialism' of the Pathans.
35. Lowie, *Origin*, pp. 51, 73.
36. Abdur Rahman, *The Life of Abdur Rahman, Amir of Afghanistan,* ed. S.M. Khan (Murray, London, 1900), vol. 2, pp. 200, 176-7.
37. G. Curzon, *Persia and the Persian Question* (Longmans, Green, London, 1892), vol. 1, p. 236.
38. Schwarzenberger, *Power Politics,* p. 48.
39. J. Lawrence, quoted in M. Khan, *Anglo-Afghan Relations 1798-1898: a Chapter in the Great Game in Central Asia* (Universal Book Agency, Peshawar, c. 1963), p. 239.

40. See e.g. R. Bruce, *The Forward Policy and its Results* (Longmans, Green, London, 1900).

41. G. Curzon, *Frontiers* (Clarendon, Oxford, 1907), p. 4; also A. Embree, 'Frontiers into Boundaries: from the traditional to the modern state', in R. Fox (ed.), *Realm and Region in Traditional India* (Vikas, New Delhi, 1977), pp. 255-80.

42. T. Holdich, *Political Frontiers and Boundary Making* (MacMillan, London, 1916), p. 110.

43. H. Rawlinson, quoted in A. Bilgrami, *Afghanistan and British India 1793-1907: a Study in Foreign Relations* (Sterling, New Delhi, 1972), p. 138.

44. W. Fraser-Tytler, *Afghanistan* (Oxford University Press, 3rd ed., 1967), pp. 333-6.

45. See generally, N. Kamrany, *Peaceful Competition in Afghanistan* (Communication Service Corp., Washington, 1969).

46. See S.M. Khan, *Constitution and Laws of Afghanistan* (Murray, London, 1900) who, p. 118, calls Abd al-Rahman the 'Justinian of Afghanistan'.

47. M. Fry, *The Afghan Economy: Money, Finance, and the Critical Constraints to Economic Development* (Brill, Leiden, 1974), pp. 214, 186.

48. M.H. Kakar, 'The fall of the Afghan Monarchy in 1973', *IJMES*, 9 (1978), pp. 205-6.

49. Singh, *Ahmad Shah*, p. 26.

50. See e.g. J. Anderson, 'There are no *Khans* any more', *MEJ*, 32 (1978), pp. 167-83.

51. *Kabul Times,* 2 Oct. 1979; *Summary of World Broadcasts (SWB)* (BBC, Reading), FE/6312/C3; *SWB*, FE/6401/C2/1-6.

52. *SWB*, FE/6295/C/2, 12 Dec. 1979; see e.g. H. Amin, 'Text of speech', *Afghanistan Quarterly,* 32, 1 (1979), pp. 1-35.

53. *SWB*, FE/6403/C/1-7.

54. E.g. *Christian Science Monitor,* Internat. Ed., 7 Apr. 1980.

55. *SWB*, SU/6368/C/4; cf. accusation of Russians buying tribal support, *International Herald Tribune,* 31 Dec. 1979; F. Boyd & G. Gretton (eds.), *Report on World Affairs,* 1 Oct. - 31 Dec. 1979.

56. L. Poullada, *Reform and Rebellion in Afghanistan, 1919-1929* (Cornell University Press, Ithaca, 1973), pp. 33, 160; F. Halliday, 'Revolution in Afghanistan', *New Left Review*, 112 (1979), p. 40; L. Dupree, 'Red Flag over the Hindu Kush, Part II: the accidental coup, or Taraki in blunderland', *AUFS Reports* (S. Asia series), 1979, no. 45, p. 13.

57. J. Dacosta, *A Scientific Frontier, or the Danger of a Russian Invasion of India* (W.H. Allen, London, 1891), p. 125.

58. Liddell Hart, 'Foreword', p. xiv, in Mao Tse Tung and Che Guevara, *Guerrilla Warfare* (Cassell, London, 1962); C. Callwell, *Small Wars: their Principles and Practice* (War Office, London, 3rd ed., 1906), p. 320; N. Mansergh (ed.),

The Transfer of Power, 1942-1947 (HMSO, London, 1977), vol. 7, p. 31.

59.   Mao Tse Tung, *On the Protracted War* (Foreign Language Press, Peking, 1954), p. 56; Mao and Guevara, *Guerrilla Warfare* p. 34; *SWB*, FE/6319/C2.

60.   *SWB*, ME/6316/A/6, 8 Jan. 1980; *SWB*, ME/6342/A/4.

61.   See D. Chaffetz, 'Afghanistan in turmoil', *International Affairs,* 56 (1980), p. 33, alleging a present 'Soviet myopia'.

62.   M. Iqbal, 'Foreword', p. viii, in L. Ahmad and M. Aziz, *Afghanistan: A Brief Survey* (Kabul, 1934).

Chapter 3
KHAN AND KHEL: DIALECTICS OF PAKHTUN TRIBALISM

Jon W. Anderson

Introduction[1]

Understanding the relation of tribe and state in Afghanistan depends on first grasping the dynamics of tribe. This is not to suggest that tribe is historically or logically prior to the state: by all available evidence, Pakhtun tribes share with other similar formations throughout the Near East a history of development in settings where metropolitan states figure prominently, and the present configuration of Pakhtun tribes emerges from their contribution to the collapse of the Safavid and Moghul empires in the eighteenth century. Nor does it mean that tribe explains state, as a continuation of tribalism by other means, as has been claimed in the case of Afghanistan.[2] But the two are organically connected in some subtle ways beyond their particular institutional junctures. To expose this connection, which is the actual empirical context of tribe-state relations, I will outline the nature of Pakhtun tribalism with particular reference to nontribal - even, in a sense to be explained, antitribal - formations.

The Problem of Pakhtun Tribalism

In the standard histories by Caroe and Gregorian, as well as in derivative interpretations by Frazer-Tytler and Dupree[3] 'tribes' enter as abstractions refracted through the prism of state-oriented political analyses, and then often negatively with respect to other subjects, most particularly 'national' development. Perceiving the political 'state' to be weak by comparison with western counterparts,

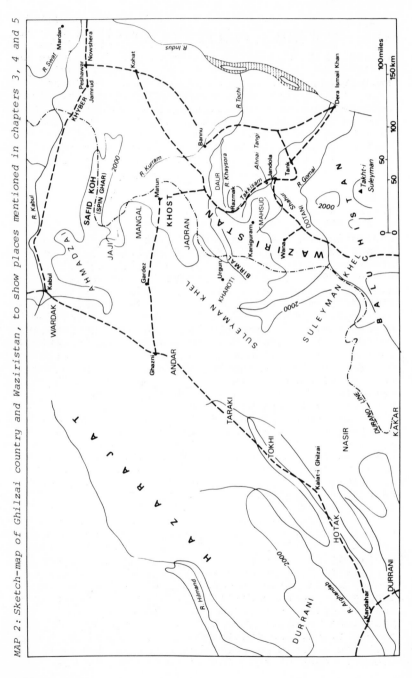

MAP 2: Sketch-map of Ghilzai country and Waziristan, to show places mentioned in chapters 3, 4 and 5

such approaches conceive of 'the tribes' monolithi-
cally as constituting a separate, competing political
system, out of which, paradoxically, emerged the
monarchy which lasted for over two hundred years up
to 1973 as a kind of tribal empire. Alternatively,
and especially from south and east of the Durand
Line, 'the tribes' are understood in terms of independence from and rebellion against government. Each
reading is valid, although in too limited a sense to
exclude or include the other. Each proceeds from a
partial description, to which is fitted extra information about 'tribe' and 'state' that is rooted in
the imperial settings of the previous century. It
is in the shadow of the Frontier that 'the tribal
problem' takes shape, including what is conceived to
be problematic about tribes generally and for these
states in particular.[4] In that context, political
analyses of limiting factors produce the paradox of
states created by tribes and tribes created (or at
least sanctioned) by states, which is as artificial,
and as enduring, as the line separating them and,
like that line, the creature of imposed frames of
reference.

Historically, of course, these views are two
of many perspectives of a kaleidoscope of encounters,
collapsed into schematisations from which no factor-
ing analysis will extract a description of anything
other than its own terms, and the adequacy of which
depends on matching the terms of the case. The
actual terms of the case can be found only in
Pakhtun views of their relations with 'the state',
including what they stipulate 'the state' to be.
A methodology appropriate to all (and only) the
facts must take account of the prime fact that
Pakhtuns do not oppose 'tribe' and 'state' typolo-
gically as <u>sui generis</u> or autonomous institutions.
They do not see them as equivalent in that respect,
as competitors in contest for the same ground.
Indeed as far as they are concerned, it is 'state'
and not 'tribe' which occupies the periphery of
things, and it is to the state that <u>all</u> the characteristics of the peripheral attach, most especially
dissipation.

Pakhtun tribesmen look out upon a world where
the order of 'tribe', emerging out of that of the
family, is seen to dissipate or unravel into congeries of social, political, economic and other
relations which to them typify contingency. There,
as congeries, the 'state' is found as a thing of
parts on a field of parts having no necessary relations to each other. That field, where others

are encountered in activity-defined roles rather than as whole persons, is not a different order of reality or merely another context. Tribesmen move easily through non-tribal settings, some quite close to home, without adopting different techniques or personalities; hence, the puzzling continuities of family and politics, in states resembling family businesses, and in families displaying all the characteristics of conspiracies except the choice whether to join. Rather, that field is something more akin to the swirling void, or the wild primeval state, out of which 'tribe' is realised as a kind of domestication. The 'state' as such is not opposed to 'tribe', but is a manifestation of the realm of contingent relations into which 'tribe' itself threatens to collapse, quite literally to turn feral, in failure not so much of effort as of the will to keep its synthesis intact. Both absolutely in time and space and relatively in all social relations, 'tribe' emerges from the maelstrom only to dissolve back into it at some point of organisational failure that is a symptom of its own problematic, inconclusive, ambivalent character.

The terms of this understanding which are near to Pakhtun experience are sufficiently far from anthropological terms to seem metaphysical. Indeed, they are virtually eschatological to Pakhtuns, some of whom see 'tribe' as the this-worldy counterpart of creation itself. But that should not stand in the way of recognising several crucial facts about their terms. The first and most immediate is that those terms are the everyday coin of their dealings with life, including the various apparatus and other manifestations of 'the state'. In that coin, the processes out of which 'tribe' emerges are reversed or undone in the realm of 'state', which, put most comprehensively, is an inversion of that of 'tribe'. That is, as objects (immediate) 'tribe' and 'state' are comprehended within the same frame of reference, as moments of a dialectic articulating the universe of Pakhtun experience. In that dialectic, 'tribe' for Pakhtuns is at once a prime datum and an expression, both a definer and something to be defined, made definitive or actualised in social formations.

It is from activities in respect to these efforts at definition that we gain access to what is actually (in action) going on, both in motives for action and in meanings of events. Similarities between the Pakhtun view just sketched and those formulated from the viewpoint of the state (such as

Caroe's and Dupree's, not to mention Ibn Khaldun's)
are striking and evocative of the elusiveness which
observers seem to find characteristic of Pakhtuns.
Tribes seem to be there and not to be there, and
tribesmen seem at once just out of reach and too
close for comfort. As elsewhere in the Near East,[5]
tribes disappear only to reappear unpredictably. To
speak of dormant or reserved tribalism[6] only re-
states the mystery, for there is something here more
significant than an alternative, complementary viewpoint on the same thing. Tribal formations have the
dual significance of being at once given and made, a
collapsing of the normative into the experiential
from which their own (propositional) terms can be
retrieved; and the point of access is the organisation of those terms, for that organisation is what
is phenomenally present.

My purpose here is, first, to set Pakhtun
tribalism in the context of the meanings it has for
Ghilzai Pakhtuns in eastern Afghanistan and, second,
to do so in a fashion that indicates how that tribalism is set in relation to other contexts. To that
end, I begin with an analysis of Ghilzai social
epistemology and present the terms in which they
conceive of social formations, then examine their
application in the interplay between leadership
(khans) and lineage (khel) processes. It is in
this interplay that the embodiment - or, more properly speaking, the enactment - of 'tribe' continually emerges from a dialectic which links the
interplay of khan and khel to larger dialectics in
the society and, because of the range of formations
those dialectics connect, makes that interplay an
exemplary 'text' for Pakhtun understanding of those
dialectics. This is not to claim that one social
form is prior to, the model for, or the context of
the other, but only that the realm of tribe and the
realm of state are understood within the same frame,
and that tribalism is, for Pakhtun, a key text of
the problem or subject articulating that frame.

The Terms of Pakhtun Tribalism in Ghilzai Country

The terms in which Pakhtuns explain tribalism have
to be understood as propositions making concrete an
otherwise inchoate understanding of the world.
Pakhtuns expend considerable effort on just such
exegesis of events and situations, not as idle
philosophising, although many otherwise idle hours
are so spent, but as a serious enterprise in which

they are constantly engaged, in the recognition that
tribe, for them, does not exist in isolation. It has
beginnings and ends which they seek to grasp, maintain, and manoeuvre both with and within. For these
activities, Ghilzai understand what 'tribe' is, by
contrast to what it is not, primarily through three
cognate distinctions - qoum : gund, atrap : shahr,
yaghistan : hukumat. These terms are a portion of
a larger set, and articulate particular domains of
reference in which they take shape in characteristic
- and characteristically fugitive - ways. They are
not ideal types and do not describe types of Pakhtun
society, but rather frame tendencies inherent in all
Pakhtun social formations. As propositions, they
articulate a thematic tension which is the motif of
Pakhtuns social organisation by predicating a range
of objective relations which is both open-ended and
logically closed. These are not all the terms that
Pakhtuns use, and not all Pakhtuns do use these
particular terms, which are current in the northern
portion of Ghilzai country where they articulate one
sample of Pakhtun experience.

Ghilzai are a group of patrilineally related,
territorially contiguous, named tribes, whose homeland (wtan) is that portion of the total Pakhtun
country lying south of the Kabul River, between the
Spin Ghar and Takht-i Suleyman ranges on the east
and the Hazarajat on the west down to the vicinity
of Kandahar. Ghilzai rose to prominence in the
eighteenth century when they overthrew the Safavid
empire, but were subsequently eclipsed by Durrani
Pashtuns from the Irano-Baluch borderlands who
established the Afghan kingdom. Pakhtuns, or
Pashtuns, call themselves Afghan and are so called
by others, although the name has been appropriated
by the state of Afghanistan for its citizens. In
that context, Ghilzai were suppressed by Durrani
monarchs and diverted into conquering their non-
Pakhtun neighbours in their capacities as Pakhtuns
and as ghazis ('warriors for Islam') against the
heretics (Shii Hazara) in the Hazarajat and the
kafirs (unbelievers) north of the Kabul River in
what is now Nuristan. That the term 'Ghilzai' has
mostly historical significance today, is testimony to
Durrani success in diverting the consciousness of
these tribesmen to greater (ethnic) and lesser
(local) identities. They know they are Ghilzai in
contrast with the Durrani to the south and with
numerous small tribes in the mountains to the east;
and they know that this identity is genealogical,
although few concern themselves with its details.

124

Dialectics of Pakhtun Tribalism

But the identity is defunct, since the largest desig-
nations which are normally named unprompted are the
seven major Ghilzai tribes. From south to north,
these are Hotak, Tokhi, Nasir, Taraki, Kharoti, Andar
(including Sohak), and Suleyman Khel plus its numerous offshoots, including Ahmadzai who are accounted
a separate tribe.[7] Each tribe is continuously seg-
mented in localised patrilineages (khel), identified
by forefathers whose patrilineal descendants constitute a qoum. This latter term applies to any level
of inclusion above the household (kor) and collapses
kinship and ethnicity into a single category of common patrilineal descent in contrast to all other
relations.
    Ghilzai do not see 'tribe' in relation to
'state' but locate each as aspects of opposed, dialectically related realms which take temporal and
transient shape in a continuous play of integration
and disintegration. What they put in opposition are
the activity and seats of government (hukumat, where
governing takes place) to the lands of freedom or
unrestraint (yaghistan), as points on a plane.
Yaghistan is where no man is above another, in contrast to hukumat where there are governors and
governed. In Ghilzai usage, these terms make substantial a basic contrast between on the one hand
the encompassment of one person by another in a particular relationship, as the ruled by a ruler in
hukumat, and on the other their equality by virtue
of shared identity, maximally by reference to a
common ancestor. The distinction is basic and has
wide ramifications: it opposes the specific nature
of place, time, action and inequality in situated
relationships, to the general and infinite nature
of equality as identity in reference to an absent
(past) third term in which the two equals were once
joined. These various features are, so to speak,
taken apart and variously recombined in cognate distinctions, between identity with another and differentiation from another, through which Ghilzai play
out their social organisation.
    In terms of location and occupation, the dis-
tinction is recapitulated in a more common one
between atrap and shahr. Atrap is the 'countryside',
from the Arabic for 'directions' (atraf). It conveys in Pakhto a notion of room in all directions,
lack of differentiation, or continuity, in contrast
to the dimensionality, confinement, and partial
identities of the 'city' (shahr), where the whole
man comes apart into specifically located, component
roles. Atrap is the tribal domain in contrast to

125

the domain of the city, where equality in the
Pakhtun sense of 'no difference' dissolves in the
face of diversely originated persons engaged in
diverse, and all partial, ways. Atrapi, literally
'country people', is the common objective designation
for 'tribesmen' in general (qoumi is the inclusive
'fellow-tribesman') and frequently is used figura-
tively to evoke the straightforward or ingenuous
'whole man' in contrast to clever (chalak, 'dissimu-
lative', 'tricky'), anonymous, urban (shahri) ways
and people. 'City' stands as the antithesis of
'tribe', as the provenance of social relations proceeding on the basis of what differentiates, as
opposed to those proceeding on the basis of mutuality. Tribalism, as the engagement of the whole man,
gives way in such contexts to situationally defined
encounters with others of diverse origin, mostly
over divisions of labour (or exchange) which are
necessarily unequal and antagonistic for want of
any prior shared identity short of the universe of
humanity. The city is the place of strange persons
in familiar roles. Moreover, it is located in time
and space, while atrap is timeless space. The city
is a conjunction of diversities in contrast to a
uniform field, contingency in contrast to necessity,
and randomised individuality in contrast to the part
which replicates the whole.

The replication of the whole in every part is
the key abstract feature of qoum, which refers to
any, all, and only categories of common patrilineal
descent. The term (borrowed from Arabic) in Pakhto
usage predicates homogeneous unity, virtually common
substance, continuously subdivided through time into
replicas of itself. By contrast, gund ('faction')
is a composite whole of diversely originated and
complementary parts of persons playing these parts
or roles. Qoum stipulates an original unity or
primordial integrity in the image of a common
father; it wholly encompasses one's very being in
the world, while gund are articulated situationally
out of temporary differences. Qoum represents a
total identity, the indivisible part of one's inheritance, such as the unity of brothers, and gund a
coalition of partial and fleeting engagement with
complementary others. Qoum stipulates that there
is, in a Pakhto phrase, 'no difference' between
persons, while gund proceeds by magnifying differences as the focus of relationship. Thus, tribalism
(qoumi, qoumwali) is understood, abstractly and
essentially, as the antithesis of factionalism
(gundi), each emerging in opposition to the other,

as wholes equal to any sum of their parts versus
wholes both more or less than any part.
    These are very nearly the most comprehensive,
widely resonating, and morally loaded distinctions
that Ghilzai normally make. They make them epistem-
ologically, however, in the form of metaphors for
relating the particular to the general, the instant
to the principle. Together, they can be understood
as contrasts between replicate wholes and complementary wholes or between original homogeneity and
initial heterogeneity marked by the presence or
absence of a comprehensive encompassment of self and
other by a third term not merely including self and
other but formally identical to each. The contrasts
are dialectical, for the tension which these distinctions express is present in all social formations.
It confers on them a dual character and a tendency
to resolve in either direction so that the conduct
of social relations takes on the character of a
contest between making unity the grounds for action
and bringing unity out of diversity or specificity
in time and space. Put positively, the oppositions
state as the fundamental problem, or subject, of
Pakhtun social life a tension between acting on
unity and turning a situated activity into an enduring unity. When tribesmen approach the bazaar, for
example, there is a tendency to try to turn situated
and partial engagements of buying and selling into
trading partnerships by discounting bargaining in
favour of, literally, 'favour' (khidmat, 'grace')
which broadens the context of the relationship. At
the same time, this makes a deal problematic to the
extent that one wishes to narrow the relationship to
the deal itself; and dealing with the hukumat in the
persons of officials turns this problem into the
relationship itself, in the form either of ritualised
wagering with real, often mortal, stakes or of extended serious talk about unserious topics. In a
sense that would not seem paradoxical to Pakhtuns,
unity ultimately precludes action, while action
denies unity. To be ruled is to become an extension
of the ruler, which can be avoided only by not being
ruled at all. Irresolvable in its own terms, this
tension is, thus, merely relocated in manipulations
which reveal to Pakhtuns the motivation of social
relations as proceeding either from an a priori identity, and thus making action problematic, or from a
priori disparity, and thus tending to dissipate in
the disintegration of the actors themselves.
    Put abstractly into ontological terms,[8] the
distinction is hard to grasp, and Pakhtuns normally

put it metaphorically in more concrete terms as arguments about definition. They metaphorise these
terms across various domains that are, in that
fashion, linked to an underlying reality as aspects
of a subject which is at once given to them and
which they seek to fathom in locutions such as
atrapi for 'tribesmen'. The particular distinctions
Ghilzai make overlap with others such as that between
nang ('fighting') and qalang ('taxation'), reified
by Ahmed into types of Frontier Pakhtun society, or
the parallel distinction noted by Barth between bar
('upper', remote) and kuz ('lower', toward the government centre) in Swat, or Elphinstone's report
of hearsay that remoter tribes were more 'republican'
than those he encountered directly. They find
echoes in observers' distinctions such as Mayne's
between Pathan as 'settled' and Pakhtun as 'independent'.[9] Across all such distinctions, there is a
continuous communication in the form of multiple
residences, marriage and other exchange networks,
including share-cropping and grants of asylum which
converge in clientage relations, in alternations
between rebellion and quiescence on the part of particular groups, and in daily individual switching
between 'rough' (dzgh) and 'polite' (hajah) interaction as well as between 'tribal' and metropolitan
settings. These distinctions are objectifications
predicating an otherwise unknown subject in order
to organise the significance of the particular or
fleeting as an instance of the general, essential,
or eternal. Adding them together, so to speak, re-
constructs that frame of reference from which
Pakhtuns proceed and, by reversing the process,
reveals the problem of Pakhtun social thinking or
consciousness to turn on the relative priority
accorded to incorporation or transaction, mutuality
or complementarity, equality or hierarchy as the
grounds for relationship. Such terms define each
other as inversions in an unfolding dialectic for
the reading of which the master metaphor or exemplary 'text' is found in tribal formation itself.
In the problems of realising the abstract 'tribe'
(qoum) for organisational purposes as a specific
lineage (khel), and in connecting these to other
social formations, Ghilzai quite literally encounter
the terms of their own existence.

Dialectics of Khel

Ghilzai are distributed in patrilineages which are

more or less acephalous and segmentary; that is,
some segment in institutionalised fashion and feature
leadership that amounts to an office, while among
others both leadership and groupings depend on personal achievements and largely charismatic qualities.
Uniting the specific forms of any particular place,
continuously segmenting social fields tend to replicate a single format of localised patrilineages,
which join qoum, the encompassing political frame,
to kor (household), the only institutionally indivisible group, in a series of nested groupings defined
by, or as the descendants of, successively remoter
'fathers'. Any individual household is thus located
within widening circles of paternal cousins, from
its local component lineage through intermediate
groupings to the named tribes and, through parallel
relations between tribal ancestors, to all other
Pakhtuns through their putative common ancestor,
Qays, called Abd al-Rashid by the Prophet, from whom
he received Islam. This nominal claim to 'companionship' with the Prophet obliterates any pre-Islamic
past for Pakhtuns and makes their existence co-
terminous with ordered time as well as wholly within
the realm of Islam. Segmentation is indeterminate
and more potential than actual in terms of the emergence of distinct groups, for larger groupings than
the household are not in any organisational sense
corporate. By variably projecting the institutional
nature of the household onto categorical social
fields defined by descent, Ghilzai, and indeed all
Pakhtuns/Pashtuns, are ideally and ideologically
related through an emergent system of localised,
ramifying patrilineages called, variously, khel or
*-zai (as in Ghilzai, from ziy 'sons'), which locate
qoum in space and time.
     The scheme comprehensively maps genealogical
and territorial space as aspects of the same thing
(wtan, the patrimonial 'homeland') through patrilineal inheritance of land by males only. Daughters' claims on their patrimony are discharged with
their marriages. Each local settlement consists of
one or more khels, composing the patrilineal descendants of a 'father', five or six generations removed,
after whom the whole group and its place are named.
In-married wives and contractual clients (hamsaya,
'neighbours', who share another's 'shadow') are
nominally identified with the proprietors as residing
in and living off the place of the owners, thus
'placed' there by an inclusive relationship. That
is, their identities are subsumed under those of
their sponsors in one of the archetypes of hierarchy

where one dimension is made to characterise the whole relationship. Such minimal khels in turn group into more inclusive ones, nominally identified by the linking ancestor but not terminologically distinguished as types, which compose the major segments of the tribe. The named tribes are the largest territorial divisions of the total Pakhtun/Pashtun country, which thus as a whole and in each of its parts continuously subdivides down to the parcels of individual holders.

From a Ghilzai point of view, khels represent the division of what was once a unitary proprietorship of the linking ancestor. They speak of all lineages as having 'grown' through time from a founding father, and imagine khel to represent the residual unity of his descendants. In the normal course of events, partition proceeds outwards from more to less intensively utilised space. Brothers normally separate their domestic quarters after marriage or when becoming fathers in their own right. After their father's death, they divide first the production (still sharing the land) and then the land itself, beginning with the nearer and more intensively utilised and proceeding over time to the further and less intensively utilised. The process may be accomplished all at once but more often continues into subsequent generations, as less intensively used lands, or those better exploited jointly, such as those used for intermittent dry farming or for grazing, are maintained as a species of commons. While lineages do 'grow' in this fashion from a single household, cases where the actual histories of khels can be retrieved suggest that they also 'grow' backwards by regrouping relatives in the present in terms of a shared ancestor in the past, particularly in instances of colonisation on new lands.[10] Similarly, when land is sold, and small parcels often are, a first option to purchase lies with the nearest collateral agnates who, Ghilzai say, would otherwise stand to inherit it. The sharia doctrine of haqq-i shaff (the right or interest of the neighbour in one's real estate) is interpreted by Ghilzai to apply first to those who have divided what previously was whole.

Particular segments may decline and merge with adjacent ones, or grow and divide, simply by refocusing on another ancestor, for khels are not at any level corporate with respect to land tenure. Real property is owned by individuals, inheriting from former proprietors, each constituting with his own household an independent economic unit separately

endowed with the same types of resources as any
other. Each contains the same package of water,
plotted fields, dry lands, pasture, and waste. While
neighbouring proprietors may jointly exploit resources which cannot easily be divided or whose use is
intermittent, they do so severally as individuals
laying claim on the basis of partitioned holdings in
an ecologically unified package. At inheritance,
unitary holdings are divided into new units with all
the component resources, replicating the former
unity rather than separating its components. Mediating between kor and qoum, rather than as corporate
groups, khels are thus frames for association where
such rights are exercised as fractions of putative
former unities. They maintain a continuous replication of part and whole, upon which rests the volatile or fleeting character of specific formations
within an overall stability of format.

Structurally speaking, greater and lesser groupings are analogues of each other, rather like the
branches of a tree, which is in fact a metaphor
Ghilzai employ to talk about them. They emphasise
this continuity by speaking of the tribe as a family
writ large and of the family as the kernel or small-
est version of a tribe; and they apply to any grouping from minimal to maximal lineage the general term
qoum, whose associated territory is a patrimonial
homeland or wtan. This likening of tribe and
family is, however, partial and conceptual. The
continuity marked by khel between kor and qoum is a
dialectical one, which resolves the temporal hierarchy of the household, where all members are exten-
sions of the social personality of the father, into
the timeless equality of tribal brotherhood by the
abstraction of the father into a linking ancestor.
Ghilzai are quite clear about this conception, describing larger groupings as faded or abstracted
versions of the smaller, such that more distant
ancestors, denoting more people, correspondingly
connote less (i.e., something abstracted) about their
relations. This continuity gives to Pakhtun politics their familiar familial cast and to families an
equally familiar political complexion;[11] it is, of
course, quite ambivalent, even contradictory, resting
on a tension of conflicting solidarities - those of
hierarchy and equality, or complementarity and
mutuality - which only take shape over time and then
only to dissolve over unresolved contradictions.
Ambivalent intermediate forms, khels simultaneously
mark the failure of the vital to endure and the want
of vitality in the only thing that does. But as

constructions they mark attempts to anchor the vital in the abstraction of its life-giving property.

Khels are shot through with this ambivalence and, consequently, tend to dissolve as frames for action. No clear evidence exists of tribes actually coalescing into large-scale corporate bodies for joint action, even defensively, even for defence of territory. In fact, there is no thing at stake in khel. Khels are not significant functionally so much as structurally; and that significance is personal in the deepest sense of defining who - indeed, what - one is absolutely, one's very integrity as whole rather than as determined by situated roles.

Put as an organisational problem, the solidarity of all such groupings is indeterminate by reason of the dual character underlying their part-whole continuity, and has to be achieved or argued ad hoc; and when it is achieved, it is by realising approximations of the internal hierarchy of the household on a larger scale. But any such realisation which collapses the duality by breaking the continuity of whole and part, fixing hierarchy in its own terms, marks the dissolution into gund (faction) of what was realised, as brotherhood, in qoum. This can occur at any level, down to and including that of the individual who dissolves into his component roles, just as khels made to play a substantive role either dissolve or, which is the same thing, turn into gund. Without qoum, solidarity can only take the form of a purposive alliance, which is to say a contract. Specific to a particular situation or to particular components of one's identity, such contracted relations cannot engage the whole man, what he is in the world, and thus have no compelling reality apart from personal volition or compulsion (by another) itself. Transitions from smaller, more family-like groupings to larger, more shifting social fields, which is always a relative distinction, turn on the figures who mediate their relations. Smaller and larger social fields intersect as conversions of the resources and potentials of one sphere into those of another; and these conversions are drawn together in complex fashion by khans, who are neither merely 'first among equals' not quite 'feudal lords' but are, in a Ghilzai idiom, both creatures and creators of khel and, for that, equally as transient.

Dialectics of Pakhtun Tribalism

Khan as Patron: the Dual Logic of Leadership

Khan is a protean word. It may be given as part of
a personal name, and it attaches almost automatically
as a title of address to the names of older men of
substance and procreative or political success.
Among some Pakhtuns, notably the Durrani around
Kandahar, it designates any landowner, however small
the holding. Ghilzai reserve the term for more sin-
gular individuals; and everywhere it conveys a
notion of deploying others in one's own enterprise,
or identifying one's enterprise with that of a collectivity. Most narrowly, it signals a man whose
authority runs beyond his own household and beyond
the general run of householders thereabouts.
    In Ghilzai thinking, the prototypical form of
command over others is exercised by mashar, or heads
of households. The mashar owns the land, commands
those who work on and subsist from it, represents
them to others as an integral unit that is an extension of his person, and generally derives their
identities from his own in a metaphor of 'fatherhood'.
Sons, for example, have no independent economic or
political identities apart from their father during
his lifetime; their wives are acquired as his
daughters-in-law and, in a telling Ghilzai idiom,
'become agnates' (qoumi shwi); while, at a further
remove, clients (hamsaya) are attached to the fringes
of a household as part of its enterprise under the
mashar in a fashion similar to sons deriving their
identities from the father. Somewhat wishfully and
often wistfully, Ghilzai idealise this relationship
to speak of the leading figures in larger social
fields as mashars, but the likeness evoked is a partial one. No khan has quite the power in a khel
that mashars exercise in their smaller realms. A
khel is not his creation in an ontogenetic sense. He
neither owns the land nor commands its members, and
there is no right of succession; but a khan can bind
together the members of a khel by standing, like a
mashar, at crucial organisational intersections where
their residual unity can be put into action.
    Not all khans are leaders in the most positive
sense, and not all leaders are khans, for khanship
represents an on-going achievement rather than a
clear-cut or structurally given position. Neither
elected nor appointed, khans are defined more by the
nature of their following than by their own leadership. The khanly field of endeavour is found between
the total tribe and the constituent sovereign households, in the field of medial segmentation where the

smaller can be put together into larger arrangements, and where portions of larger groupings can be detached. In a sense, minimal segments present too small and undifferentiated a social field for khanly leadership, and the maximal segments encompass too much play for a single coherent game. So it is in the intermediate range that khanly leadership finds its arena, where khans endeavour to mediate or connect the more abstract qoum to the more concrete groupings by bringing various of them together. Theirs is a sisyphean task of joining abstract potentials to down-to-earth realities. Constrained on the one hand by the limited scale of effective organisation (essentially that of the <u>kor</u>) and, on the other hand, by the limited corporateness of larger social fields, the actual leadership exercised by khans is as temporal and as ambiguous as the ephemeral realisations of tribal structure that are their actual subjects. Many individuals compete for influence on grounds of wealth, wisdom, piety, political and economic connections, oratorical and other abilities; but Ghilzai assert that khans, properly so called, are distinguished as those who 'feed the people' and 'tie the knot of the tribe'. More than merely means and ends, these phrases point to the actions (feeding, tying) and to the predications (<u>the</u> people, <u>the</u> knot, <u>the</u> tribe) combined in khanly as opposed to other leadership.

'Feeding people' covers all conversions of personal wealth into social relations through hospitality, occasional gifts and favours, providing employment, and other less clear-cut patronage. Construed as 'helping' persons more or less unable, temporarily or permanently, to sustain an autonomous existence, such patronage focuses miscellaneous needs of a recipient upon a benefactor who, through various subsidies from his own possessions, weaves about himself a network of dependency relations. These relations are systematically graded.

The archetypal expression of solidarity among all Pakhtuns, commensality, is made to cover these relations. Sharing a meal is the symbol and expression of equality, and the degree to which one is fed by another is a rough but public measure of alliance to the host. The least pervasive dependence is incurred by guests, whose 'subsidy' is as temporary and small as a meal, although it is morally loaded and hence the basis, potentially, for much more. To have 'eaten another's salt' makes any subsequent transgression against him doubly odious, and to share food (which is always sacrificed and eaten 'in

the name of God') terminates enmity. To be a guest
is, among Ghilzai, the most direct and, momentarily,
the most complete expression of being 'fed' by
another. But it is also as brief as it is perfect,
and guests who do not pass on quickly come to find
that perfection converted into total incorporation.
The guest who stays is the archetype client (hamsaya,
'shade-sharer').

At the other extreme, the most inclusive relationship, short of those within a household, is that
of master and servants, who are in effect made marg-
inally part of his household. Servants expand a
household's personnel, and their subordination is
total as an extension of the master-patron's identity. This relationship lacks the egalitarian gloss
of hospitality in that servants are without the
independence to reciprocate in kind. Servants are
the extreme case of employees who, in return for
their entire livelihood, expend their undivided
labour and loyalty for their employer as part of his
enterprise.

Guests and servants mark the limits of clientage relations, but neither hospitality nor service
are by themselves adequate bases for politically
significant patronage. The one is too brief and
the other too inclusive, and both are too hierarchical and domestic. More commonly political in a
purposeful and convertible sense are relations with
share-croppers and with companions. Their subsidies
take the form of a patron's investment in the
client's own enterprise rather than incorporation of
a client within the patron's. Such relations lack
the total surrender of independence implicit in
guests and employees. Characteristically, these
relations are discretionary and partial on both
sides, and they are intermittent for companions or
temporary for share-croppers. In practice, the
statuses of companion (malgarey) and of share-cropper
(bazgar, but more commonly the neutral Persian term
for 'villager', dehqan) tend to merge together, as
otherwise independent tribesmen with limited personal holdings enter into varied share-cropping or
other arrangements with persons having more lands
than they can farm or want to farm themselves. Many
'tenants' are just this sort of small farmers seeking to supplement their own marginal enterprises,
just as many owner-operators often put their land
in pawn (grou) and end up giving to a creditor the
share of production appropriate to the owner of the
land in a manner little different from that of landless tenants. Quite complex layered arrangements

can result, as individuals, farming their own land,
some or all of which may be pawned, or land obtained
through grou, seek supplementary share-cropping contracts to make ends meet. All cases of such strategies, separately or together, occur when a man finds
that the costs of pursuing the lifestyle of an independent tribesman exceed what he earns from his
heritage. Tenant and companion relations are thus
in Ghilzai estimations transitional between complete
independence and total dependence. Instead of being
fed directly, they are financed in their own enterprises by a patron who thereby makes something more
of his own.

The important difference between share-cropping
and companionship is that the former is an explicitly
contractual relationship with fixed, usually annual,
terms and conditions, while companions enjoy a more
generalised reciprocity of indeterminate term and
implied conditions. Companionship is continuously
'negotiated', while tenancy is, essentially, negotiated once for a term; and tenancy is a more partial
relationship with fewer dimensions than companionship, which is broader and more inclusive, more
nearly involving the whole man. Tenants thus tend
to merge with outright employees, as workers for
someone else, but companions merge with guests, as
the recipients of unreckoned favour, which Ghilzai
liken to khidmat ('grace' or 'service' especially to
God) and see as fulfilling the duty of Muslims to
pay zakat (the obligatory dedication of personal
wealth to community purposes). The distinction is
more of intent than of content. Patrons may prefer
the less ambiguous relations with servants and tenants, emphasising that the enterprise is the patron's
own. Or they may prefer the image of 'helping'
others to maintain their own enterprises, even to
the extent of lending or granting the use of lands,
animals, and equipment. The choice comes down to
which of two sides of the relationship is sought and
can be secured.

Companionship is the type of relation that
politically ambitious patrons seek to create and
focus on themselves. Transitional between the more
specific relations with guests and employees, it is
the one which, being voluntary on both sides, is
most consistent with the conventional image of khanly status. Companions are usually, but not always,
kinsmen distant enough to have no interest in each
others' estates but near enough to have an interest
in each other. Malgarey accompany a khan and provide
the retinue that testifies to his importance. The

more obviously a person is incorporated dependently
into another's enterprise, the greater his political
disability. Companions are instead fellow-tribesmen
and co-proprietors who, although formally equal to
their patron, just lack the wherewithal to realise
that equality in tangible self-sufficiency. By
'feeding' such persons, literally as dinner-guests
but more importantly in the figurative sense of sub-
sidising their enterprises, the khanly patron binds
companions to him voluntarily in myriad subtle but
crucial ways. Less transient than with guests, and
less total than with employees, the relationship is
also less truly voluntary and affective than the
'natural' social compact that khans seek to realise.
Companionship is a formalised and special case of
patronage-based leadership that is consistent, if
only partially so, with the autarchic and egalitarian
emphases in relationships measured against an ideal-
isation of undifferentiating reciprocity that amounts
to giving and getting the same thing. In such a
framework, khans emerge as social creditors rather
than as lords.

Nearly all Ghilzai participate to some degree
at some time in these transactions, as givers as
well as receivers. Even the poorest tribesmen can
have a guest, so long as he has something of his own
to share. Public life takes on the character of
competitive jockeying for relative eminence against
a background of egalitarianism. Khanly patronage is
distinguished in the first instance by combining the
entire range of guest, companion, tenant, and servant relations into a coherent whole. Those who
would be khan thus surround their households with
servants, and their enterprises with tenants and
other employees. They variously supplement the
enterprises of companions and, as magnets of hospitality, are open to reaching everyone else within
their orbits, to feed some people all the time and
nearly all people at some time. Ghilzai describe
the idealised career of a khan as beginning with
attracting many guests through force of character or
some special ability. The accumulation of responsibilities requires employment of servants and tenants
to support the emerging enterprise; some of the
relationships solidify into companionships that provide the core around which free allegiances cluster.

The integration of these piecemeal relations
into a coherent whole depends on the outstanding
qualities of the man at the centre, but this is not
really a whole of a 'tribal' (qoumi, qoumwali) sort
until it does not have to be continuously created.

Charisma alone is not enough to make a khan of the patron seeking to make his presence felt publicly beyond his own household. To the extent that a following is but a miscellany of diverse dependants, the patron is not a khan in the fullest sense but merely 'big' (qaland or stur 'massive'), and his following is a mere faction (gund). The 'heavy' (drund) quality which makes a patron incontestably a khan comes from turning patronage to the collective use of a particular constituency that has a sui generis character, and from doing it in terms definitive of that character, such that the 'knot' of the 'tribe' is 'tied'. These predications are important for understanding how khan and khel interact, not simply as chief and lineage or as leader and follower, but in a more complex fashion as mutual contingencies in an emerging dialectic between charisma and legitimacy.

'Tying the Knot of the Tribe'

In a sense that is quite real to Ghilzai, a khan is a self-financed public servant, expending his own wealth for the aggregate good of a community which, if he is to constitute a 'genuine' (rasti, 'correct', or 'right[handed]') khan, is made from a genealogically identifiable portion of the Pakhtun population. The normative quality which makes this more than just a personal following, although it is surely that, transcends mere economics, no matter how subtly made into social relations. To emphasise that a khan is rasti is to invoke the symbolic load of the right hand, which conveys blessed food to the body, in contrast to the left (chap, khin) hand which conveys away waste. Ghilzai say that (mere) man's work is a parody of creation and formless - literally, that it is shit - and explicitly make the point about khans' constructions. It is in turning their knowledge and ability to get things done to the service of a 'natural' or given (even God-given) community of kinsmen, that khans 'tie the knot of the tribe', as a kind of public works.

In this capacity, a khan has no more power to order than he has to tax. Khans do not even actively adjudicate but prefer to leave that vexation to experts in tribal law (narkhi), while confining their own efforts to reconciliation of differences rather than to adjudication. Khans, instead, distinguish themselves from the mass of men by endeavouring to realise an abstracted integrity. They direct their

activities into subsidy rather than command, operating by influence, sounding public opinion, articulating common interests, and persuading on the basis of
skills effectively and convincingly deployed. In
joining patronage and respect, with all of the ambiguities of service and influence, to a framework of
qoum relations, khans actuate the tribe as a public
work. The 'knot' of the 'tribe' is comprehensive
and exclusive; anything less is mere factionalist
pandering to fleeting and partial interests that
divide rather than unite men. The crucial 'tying',
which for Ghilzai distinguishes genuine (rasti as
opposed to sarchapa, 'upside-down' or, literally,
'inverted' from chap, 'left') khans from persons of
specialised competence, is not only between tribesmen, but between the tribe and those outside it.

No right of incumbency or of succession insti-
tutionalises a khanship, although as a public utility
and as an avidly sought prize a particular khanship
tends to outlast its incumbent. Some, however,
approximate hereditary chieftainships. Two Ghilzai
groups are alleged to have such khan khels ('leading
lineages'), the Hotak in the Arghandab valley above
Kandahar and the Jabar Khel Ahmadzai in the Kabul
valley.[12] But that distinction is denied to them
by other Ghilzai and seems more plausibly an historical expression of the leading roles played by Hotak
against Safavid Persia and the Durrani in the eighteenth century and by the Jabar Khel against British
traverse of the Kabul valley in the nineteenth century. A contemporary example of institutionalised
khanship is found in the Kharoti Ghilzai,[13] whose
homeland is wedged in the hills between the large
and aggressive Suleyman Khel Ghilzai and the Wazir
tribes. Kharoti explain their khanship as necessitated by intertribal relations, and it conveys little
more authority - in some respects less - than more
achieved khanships in other, more flexible settings.
Kharoti are relatively few, and this institutionalisation for inter-group dealings has counterparts
among the small tribes of the neighbouring Khost
valley, just to the north-east of Kharoti, where, in
addition, specific endowments of reserved plots
(da khano pati), are attached to the office, separate from the private property of the incumbent, to
be used for supporting the public expenditures of
these tribes.[14] Other Ghilzai reckon these tribes
to be more successful in joining the categorical
qoum with the institutional character of the kor,
although they also suggest that, because these tribes
are reacting to larger neighbours, they are on that

139

account somewhat pathetic.

　　More significantly, these small Khost tribes
are arranged into two composite regional factions,
Spingund and Torgund, involving them and small
neighbouring groups in the hills around them. This
is reminiscent of a tendency in Ghilzai tribes to
separate into two major segments around two maximal
(loy) khans, and of Barth's account of how Yusufzai
Pakhtuns in Swat concentrate their oppositions into
two dispersed blocs (dala).[15] People of Khost allege
that Spin (white) and Tor (black) alignments are
permanent and without genealogical significance,
saying that the links are forged 'historically' or
that they were insinuated by the British to divide
the tribes. In more than a formal sense, these are
all versions of the same thing, 'voluntary' associations with respect to agnation commencing beyond the
reach of qoumi unity under one 'father'. And it is
at this juncture that khans achieve the full significance of their relation to khel as, in Ghilzai
parlance, creating each other. Each is, in a sense,
the salvation of the other at the point where chaos
is reached. Equally, each is the destruction of the
other when the match is not achieved.

　　The structural significance of khans lies in
their articulating the constituent family units of
tribal society into more or less coherent (replica-
tive) social fields in a fashion that connects those
fields to wider spheres of relations with the metropolitan society as well as with other tribes.
Village maliks are, by comparison, merely the government's termini of official communication with the
citizenry. It is largely through khans that Pakhtun
tribes as such articulate with the government and the
metropolitan society. While each tribesman has some
connections in the metropolitan commercial and official spheres, khans are disposed to develop special
competence to reach the pertinent points bearing on
the lives of tribesmen jointly and severally. The
'state', even in its limited manifestation of the
national government, is not all of a piece; and the
various pieces which would tax, conscript, deliver
education and health services, count persons and
land, regulate traffic and, most especially, those
agencies devoted to 'national' development, all
impinge in different ways, at different times, and
to different degrees on individual tribesmen. To
the extent that khans stand in the way of these
piecemeal approaches, or gather them up, they serve
to secure 'the tribe' itself on a larger ground.
They do this by standing at the intersection of the

tribal and external spheres, controlling or seeking
to control or being selected (by both sides) to control the flow from one to the other, by brokering
their resources to each other. Khans seek out this
brokering role to add to their arsenal of favours,
and are sought out in turn by those who find them
conveniently sophisticated in both shahri and atrapi
ways, indeed more sophisticated than many townsmen
and tribesmen themselves.

Thus, to their activities within the tribe,
khans add mediation between complementary social
fields. No little of a khan's power with respect to
his competitors (both other khans and those who would
broaden their talents), as well as to his supporters,
inheres in what might be summarised as his Kabul
Connection; this lends credibility to frequent complaints by the disgruntled against specific khans,
that they are 'made' by the government. This had a
special plausibility when that government was a regime associated with tribal support and identified
itself with the Pakhtun/Pashtun interest, pursued
policies of mollification, and appointed local officials often less vigorous than the khans themselves.
The histories of many khanships at some point intersect with some form of government sponsorship, usually in the form of royal favour, either from
Amanullah for supporting the 1919 war against
British India which secured Afghanistan's de jure
independence, or from Nadir Shah for supporting the
restoration after a Tajik bandit had seized the
throne a decade later. But a comparison of the
authority and influence of the more blatant creatures of Kabul with those of the more resolutely
'tribal' khans suggests that outside sponsorship is
less decisive in creating a khan than in confirming
one. Certainly, outside sponsorship alone is not
enough; and the system does not, on that account,
warrant interpretation as 'feudal', for khans are
not the king's men. But it is equally certain that
some of the insecurity of khanly position derives
from potential outside intervention in local competitions for influence.[16] Being 'made by the government', therefore, refers narrowly to interference in
successions and more broadly to any sort of enabling
favour from Kabul such as, for example, grants of
land or, more recently, favouritism in dispensing
development aid.

Dialectics of Pakhtun Tribalism

From Ground to Figure: Qoum into Gund, Atrap into Shahr

Still, relations between tribe and state go beyond
mere complementarity into a dialectic on many levels,
for two reasons. First, the 'state' is not one
thing but many things. Minimally, it is many organs
of government that, in bureaucratic fashion, specialise in dealing with limited ranges of matters. So
the tribesman confronts a thing of parts, which are
often in competition and, in the case of the former
monarchy, not all pulling together. While the state,
in the form of the national government in the larger
context of Afghanistan as a multi-ethnic nation, was
largely identified with Pakhtun/Pashtun interests
and their expansion,[17] that was not always nor often
perceived to be the case in the Ghilzai homelands.
Many were forcibly relocated, and most found strang-
ers settled in their midst in a manner hardly to
their interests or liking. Even the more positive
'development' projects in Ghilzai country, and the
multiplication of subgovernorships (woluswali) which
(in the form of parliamentary boroughs) increased
Ghilzai representation, were often perceived to have
the more insidious design of dividing loyalties, as
they did not coincide with local tribal boundaries.
     Second, and more important, it is not the gov-
ernment alone which Ghilzai oppose to qoum, but the
metropolitan society of which government partakes
and which exemplifies primordial heterogeneity in
contrast to the encompassing uniformity of qoum, the
partial man in contrast to the whole man, situated
and fleeting interests jostling each other in contrast to common interests given in eternity and
symbolised by the connection of ancestry itself.
Ghilzai see the metropolis as inverting the social
form of qoum by proceeding from a priori diversity.
Shahr is the place of gund at the lowest level, of
rulers and ruled, in divisions of labour that are
necessarily unequal. It is almost as if tribesmen
were paraphrasing Ibn Khaldun, but in reverse, which,
in a round-about way, suggests how this frame of
reference is unitary and why tribesmen can identify
with the state as their agent or as their sponsor,
but not with the city.
     The transition from kor to qoum - from the
hierarchy of the household as an activity system to
the equality of the tribe as a state of being - that
is effected in khel by the domestication of khans
into public servants, is reversed in the transition
from qoum as the ground on which social formations

take shape to qoum as a figure on a larger ground.
In such a situation, as one of many diversely-
originated players with no necessary connection to
the others, qoum is self-negating. It is encountered as unique with respect to that which falls outside
its purview and, thereby, as a factional (gund)
formation. So, as much as hukumat and shahr set the
context for tribalism, 'tribes' set the context for
organising the extra-tribal as anti-tribal, for
locating government and city as factionalising anti-
theses of <u>social</u> order as it is conceived by Pakhtuns
when they characterise their point of departure as
the conjunction of differences.

Such a situation seems to have emerged in Swat,
suggesting that it is not the physical 'city' that
shahr represents but cosmopolitanism as the antithesis of tribalism. Barth described a situation in
Swat where Pakhtuns secured by conquest the land
that is the ground on which tribal competitions are
played out. The autochthonous population was dis-
possessed, but not displaced, as seems to have happened in parts of Ghilzai country where there is
evidence of Pakhtun expansion.[18] Drawing non-
Pakhtuns into those competitions as clients - effectively converting the economic dependencies of a
<u>jajmani</u>-like system into political capital - con-
duces to a 'game' of every-man-a-khan. That is,
drawing in outsiders of diverse origins degrades the
Pakhtun game into a kind of civil war which, with
every man's hand against his brother, is the Pakhtun
approximation of Hell and the negative side of shahr.
Living in less favoured circumstances, Ghilzai immediately recognise the <u>dala</u> (bloc system) of Swat as
gundi (factionalism), contrast it to qoumwali (tribalism), and can point to examples of each within
their own orbit. It cannot be surprising that an
outcome of such situations should be the political
emergence of religious figures. For, in a situation
of primordial diversity, those speaking for Islam,
the largest unity within creation itself, speak over
the head of 'tribe' and find an audience when tribalism is mere gundi. Ghilzai point to border villages
as the ones with the most, and most obstreperous,
mullahs, where <u>akhundzada</u> (descendants of a divine)
have plausible claim to precedence within fields of
mixed, and often refugee, ancestries.

It is not, however, the mere presence of outsiders that urbanises Pakhtun contexts, but the capacities in which they affect Pakhtuns. Poignantly
aware of the threat posed by mullahs and hereditary
religious figures, whether quieter sayyids or more

active pirs. Ghilzai often endeavour assiduously to
keep them out of tribal affairs for just this reason.
Similarly, while some non-Pakhtun tenants, tradesmen
and craft specialists are found in Ghilzai country,
nowhere outside the bazaar towns do they approach
the 80 per cent of the population that Barth reported in Swat.[19] In the Ghilzai atrap, a backwoods
compared to Swat and the 'settled districts' along
the Indus, such persons are contained either by
pressuring fellow-tribesmen into full responsibility
for their clients (or into avoiding taking too many),
or by making certain indispensable specialists the
joint clients of a body of co-proprietors. Mullahs
and barbers, who provide essential services that
cannot be obtained elsewhere, are thus the only
specialists in most Ghilzai communities; and they
are supported jointly by its members as their collective clients (hamsaya). Nearly all other specialists are sought on an individual basis in the bazaars
of Kabul, Ghazni, Gardez, Kandahar, and in some of
the larger, usually non-Pakhtun settlements and
government stations, where merchants and craftsmen
are brought under official sponsorship as government
clients. The shahr comes deep into the countryside
in the form of every stranger who overstays his
welcome.

Conclusion

To recognise that 'tribe' and 'state' interpenetrate
is still only half an analysis, for it is the nature
of that interpenetration which is decisive. Tribesmen confront not a monolithic state but a thing of
parts on a field of parts, each engaging only part
of him. He confronts specific officials who, with
diverse other urban-based specialists in trades and
services, including religious services, are not
interested in the whole tribesman but are charged
with or wish to address themselves to - indeed, to
define him in terms of - only certain of his capacities. So all such relations are hierarchical and
emerge as a contest between the importuning and the
recalcitrant, roles which are experienced by both
tribesman and official. With each official interested in some roles of all tribesmen but never in
all the roles of any tribesman, every tribesman's
experience is unique, but all experiences are of a
piece as partial. So the 'state', whether in its
limited institutional forms or more broadly as an
aspect of shahr, takes shape as a confrontation in

the context of a unified scheme which dialectically
relates that which distinguishes individuals so that
they complement each other and that which unites
them as parts of the same thing. And the experience
takes shape as various resolutions of an opposition
between joined action and joint existence in constructing social relations.

Much as khan and khel mutually realise each
other, so do tribe and state, although in an opposite, negative fashion. Each contextualises the
other, but such contexts are not fixed, for the
process is joined on all levels, from the resolution
of fatherhood into brotherhood to the dissolution of
brotherhood into hierarchies that are purely situational and without the inner necessity of an encompassing frame. The process is without termination
and is manifest in all social relations as a tension
between formations predicating diversity and those
predicating total continuity of all the parts with
the whole, of which tribe(qoum)itself is the primary
manifestation. It needs to be emphasised that in
this tribalism, and perhaps in others, the 'segmentary organisation' is a phenomenon more profoundly
logical, even ontological, than sociological.   It
is not just an economic or political phenomenon but
rather an organiser of these, and better understood
as the active subject than as a passive or constituted object. That is to say, the relationship between such a system and what it organises is not
necessary but contingent, and has to be established
descriptively as a description of predicates for,
among the actors themselves, it amounts to a continuous argument whose continuity is literally their
own.

The point is important beyond the epistemologi-
cal status of the subject. There is in the ethnographic literature on the Near East in general, and
on South West Asia in particular, a tendency to
confound the properties of tribalism with those of
pastoral nomadism, to make an equation of tribe with
nomad and presume that all nomads are tribally-
ordered, which is not the case in Afghanistan,[20] or
that all tribes are nomadic, which is not even the
case in Iran (vide the Kurds). Their frequent coincidence, especially in Iran, leads to a misunder-
standing of the tensions between pastoralists and
farmers, or those between nomads and administrators,
as comprehending those between tribesman and metropolitan. But even this is not the case in Afghanistan. Ghilzai and other Pakhtun tribes are for the
most part settled and specialise in wheat farming.

In addition, even nomadic Pakhtun often nomadise
from landed bases, and they usually migrate to pastures they own.[21] A number of specific, substantive
confusions result from failing to make clear that
tribalism and nomadism are not the same thing, in
fact not even the same phenomenon; but all of these
turn more generally on a methodological confusion
inherent in searches for external causes of tribal
formations as adaptations, under the presumption
that what they are adaptations to consists in something (else) more stable than tribal formations
themselves. This is, again, emphatically not the
empirical case with Pakhtuns, where 'the state' or
states they confront are no less evanescent than
their tribalism, and not only no less emergent but,
as argued here, emergent from the same social onto-
logy.
    Moreover, there is a continuity between these
cultivating tribesmen and their nomadic cousins in
all respects save their balances of herding to cultivating; and together they constitute the main body
of the citizenry of Afghanistan. That 'state' has
taken their ethonym for itself and has its historical
roots in their ascendancy over certain of their
neighbours, while it is circumscribed by the ascendancy of others of their neighbours over some of them.
It is in their interests as much as in anyone's,
and more than for most, that the government of
Afghanistan exists and functions. This leads to
another easy misinterpretation, that the state is a
creature of Pakhtun - or rather of Muhammadzai
Durrani Pashtun - tribalism. It is partially such a
creature, historically and politically, but it is
not merely that. While it secures some Pakhtun
interests and facilitates some Pakhtun expansion, it
hinders others. And from the time of the first
Afghan monarch, that state has sought to break up
tribes. The state has a life of its own and the
'nation' a constituency of its own; and Afghan nationalists are not necessarily Pakhtun chauvinists or
vice versa. There is a body of persons committed to
the government by employment, circumstance, and
sympathy with its goals. Others would grasp the
apparatus of the state for their own, individual
ends. Many of these persons are tribesmen as well,
especially in the officers' corps and the higher
civil service, which have been largely Pakhtun/
Pashtun preserves. Much tribalist support for, or
acquiescence to, the state rests on the very mundane
fact that it provides in these agencies a system of
indoor relief for supernumerary tribesmen, and indeed

realisation of this by many non-Pakhtun is one of
the more important aspects of this state. But the
state becomes an instrument for pressing the interests of Pakhtun/Pashtun or of some of them, only
within a context recognised as one of primordial
diversity, where the point of departure is fundamentally atomistic. Conceptually opposed to tribalism,
the 'state' is in part a tool of tribalism only
when that tribalism is itself partial.

Not unexpectedly, considerable confusion and
ambiguity obtain on the ground in 'tribe-and-state'
relations in Afghanistan. A kind of word-game
ensues over identifications with the tribe, with the
state, with both and often, especially in the case
of non-Pakhtun/Pashtun minorities, with neither.
Some persons manage these shifts of reference easily;
others, especially the more successful khans who
survive the contradictory pulls of tribal and national associations,[22] trade on the contradictions
and flourish in the ambiguities that allow them to
play more than one game at a time, which, to Ghilzai,
is the bravura performance. Others manage less
easily, finding themselves forced to choose between
being nationalists and being tribesmen, between
loyalty or rebellion (but to which cause?), between
upward or outward mobility. These are not impossible choices: people have to make them all the
time. But they are difficult, and making them all
the time can be profoundly demoralising. Ethics
that become too situational to live by, or too
abstract to live with, first become more aesthetic
than ethical, and then mere idioms that are both
corrupted as forms and bankrupt as morals. It is
likely that just such sneaking realisations underlie
some of the mixed feelings harboured by many Near
Easterners toward both tribe and state in their
various manifestations - which one observer has
characterised as a paradoxical ethos of insecurity
that finds peril in refuge.[23]

That, plus the fervour of exclusive enthusiasms
as well as the completeness with which they reverse,
rests in turn on the subjective, hence definitive,
fact that these forms do not function, and cannot be
explained, economically or politically, but as profoundly thoroughgoing coimplicates of a logical,
even ontological, scheme. It is not as specialists
or as outsiders that Ghilzai tribesmen confront 'the
state', either specifically as government and its
agents or more generally as metropolitan social
forms; not do they confront one another as disjunc-
tive systems. That engagement takes place on many

147

levels, linked in a fashion which, hidden from our constructions on what 'tribe' and 'state' are, makes their relationship problematic. That problematic (subject-object relationship) is, for Ghilzai, quite different from what it is for others, and for this reason an understanding of its terms and predicates is essential for a comprehension not only of what that relationship is but of what, in fact, is being related.

NOTES

1. This chapter utilises fieldwork conducted in Afghanistan between November 1971 and January 1974 with the support of U.S. National Science Foundation grant no. GS-30275. For comments on earlier drafts of this argument, I am grateful to Fredrik Barth, Andrew Strathern and Malcolm Yapp.

2. L. Dupree, *Afghanistan* (Princeton University Press, 1973).

3. O. Caroe, *The Pathans 550 B.C. - A.D. 1957* (MacMillan, London, 1958); V. Gregorian, *The Emergence of Modern Afghanistan* (Stanford University Press, 1969); W.K. Fraser-Tytler, *Afghanistan* (Oxford University Press, 3rd ed., 1967); Dupree, *Afghanistan*.

4. I have in mind not so much the Anglo-Afghan contests of the century prior to 1947 as two contexts which frame our knowledge of them. The first is the intellectual setting of utilitarianism, brilliantly described by E. Stokes, *The English Utilitarians in India* (Oxford University Press, 1959), which feeds subtly into British interpretations of political history. The second, and perhaps the more profound for being more inchoate, is the Scottish background of so many frontier writers, beginning with M. Elphinstone, *An Account of the Kingdom of Caubul, etc.* (London, 1815), whose work was the source of much subsequently and whose intuitive grasp of the ambivalence of tribal leaders may owe much to his eighteenth-century Scottish upbringing.

5. E.g. A. Cohen, *Arab Border-Villages in Israel* (Manchester University Press, 1965); F.I. Khuri, *From Village to Suburb: Order and Change in Greater Beirut* (University of Chicago Press, 1976).

6. E.g. P.C. Salzman, 'Ideology and change in Middle Eastern tribal societies', *Man (NS)*, 13 (1978), pp. 618-37.

7. See J.W. Anderson, 'There are no *Khans* anymore', *MEJ*, 32 (1978), pp. 167-83.

8. A more extended discussion of the ontologic of this construct in the setting of interpersonal relations is in my 'Social structure and the veil', *Anthropos*, 77 (1982), pp. 397-420.

9. A.S. Ahmed, *Millenium and Charisma among Pathans* (Routledge and Kegan Paul, London, 1976); F. Barth, *Political Leadership among Swat Pathans* (Athlone, London, 1959); Elphinstone, *Account;* P. Mayne, *The Narrow Smile* (Allen and Unwin, London, 1955).

10. J.W. Anderson, 'Tribe and community among Ghilzai Pashtun', *Anthropos,* 70 (1975), pp. 588, 593.

11. Dupree, *Afghanistan,* pp. 181-92 *et passim.*

12. *Gazetteer of Afghanistan, Part IV, Kabul* (General Staff of India, Simla, 1910), pp. 148, 509.

13. *Gazetteer,* p. 286.

14. Cf. W. Steul, 'Eigentumsprobleme innerhalb Paschtunischen Gemeinschaft', Heidelberg, Südasien-Institut (mimeo); H.J. Wald, *Landnutzung und Siedlung der Paschtunen im Becken von Khost* (Hain, Opladen, 1969); H.C. Wylly, *From the Black Mountain to Waziristan* (MacMillan, London, 1912).

15. Barth, *Leadership.*

16. While H. Kakar, *Afghanistan: a Study in Internal Political Developments 1880-1896* (Punjab Educational Press, Lahore/Kabul, 1971), indicates that this seemed particularly the case in past struggles over national integration, his sources were documents and intelligence collected by British political agents. Contemporary evidence is not so categorical.

17. Cf. K. Ferdinand, 'Nomadic expansion and commerce in central Afghanistan', *Folk,* 4 (1962), pp. 123-59; Kakar, *Afghanistan;* N. Tapper, chapter 7 below; J.W. Anderson and R.F. Strand (eds.), *Ethnic Processes and Intergroup Relations in Contemporary Afghanistan,* Occasional Paper no. 15 of the Afghanistan Council (Asia Society, New York, 1978).

18. Barth, *Leadership:* D. Balland, 'Vieux sédentaires Tadjik et immigrants Pachtoun dans le sillon de Ghazni (Afghanistan oriental)', *Bull. Assoc. de Géographes Francais,* 51 (1974), pp. 171-80.

19. Barth, *Leadership,* p. 30.

20. Cf. T. Barfield, 'The impact of Pashtun immigration on nomadic pastoralism in Northeast Afghanistan', in Anderson and Strand, *Ethnic Processes,* pp. 26-34.

21. Ferdinand, 'Nomadic expansion'; id., 'Nomadism in Afghanistan', in L. Foldes (ed.), *Viehwirtschaft und Hirtenkultur* (Akademiai Kiado, Budapest, 1969).

22. Cf. Anderson, 'There are no Khans'.

23. J. Gulick, *The Middle East: An Anthropological Perspective* (Goodyear, Pacific Palisades, 1976).

Chapter 4
TRIBES AND STATES IN THE KHYBER, 1838-42

Malcolm Yapp

Introduction

Commonly, in the historical experience of the last
two hundred years, it has not been the model
relationship of tribe and state which has been most
familiar, but that of a plurality of tribes and
states. For that bundle of social, economic and
political relationships, to which we give the name
'tribe', has declined (at least in numerical significance) under the pressures of a modernising world
and has survived most successfully in those remote
and difficult regions which often form the frontiers
of states and where international borders and the
burgeoning international system have offered possibilities of manoeuvre which have been exploited by
tribes in their efforts to resist the encroachments
of governments. Such a region provides the setting
for this paper.

The Khyber Pass is one of the many passes which
facilitate communication through the range of mountains which separate the Indian sub-continent from
Afghanistan. Its celebrity is due to the circumstance that it presented the fewest physical obsta-
cles to direct communication between Peshawar and
Jalalabad. For merchants employing laden animals
this physical superiority was of less consequence
than the human difficulties represented by the tribes
which controlled the Pass, and such merchants often
preferred other, physically more difficult, but more
peaceable routes. But for governments, using armies
which required wheeled transport, there was no easy
alternative to the Khyber and, willy-nilly, they
were drawn into a close and uncomfortable relationship with the tribal peoples.

Where the series of passes known as the Khyber
begins and ends is and was a matter for dispute.

For the purposes of this chapter, I have chosen a
narrow definition - from Jamrud to Landi Khana, a
distance, depending on the route chosen, of no more
than 25 miles.[1] In effect this decision reduces the
number of tribal confederations to be considered to
three: the Afridi, the Shinwari, and the Orakzai,
although as will be seen the matter cannot be sim-
plified so easily, for these confederations were
themselves involved in relations with others which,
though they had no direct contact with the Khyber,
were able to exercise an important indirect influence
upon the Pass.[2]

These confederations belonged to the group of
Pashto-speaking tribal peoples known to the British
as Pathans, although they used the term 'Afghan' to
describe themselves. The main features of their
political, social and economic organisation were
similar. It will be convenient here to describe the
Afridi and reserve an account of the Orakzai and the
Shinwari until later.

The Afridi inhabited the spurs which formed the
northern and eastern flanks of the Safid Koh range.
They were semi-nomadic. Their summer residences
were in the high valleys of the Bara, Bajgal and
Tirah; in winter most of the men dwelled in earthen
caves cut into the hillsides of the lower Bara and
Bazar valleys and Khyber itself and in the plains of
Bagiara and Kajurai. They, or mainly their women-
folk, raised grain crops, especially rice, and they
maintained herds of cattle and flocks of sheep and
goats. Apart from a few grass ropes and nets they
had almost no manufactures and sought these in their
principal market, Peshawar, offering rice in exchange. Their commercial links with Peshawar and
their presence in winter in Kajurai made them more
accessible to state influence than might otherwise
have been the case, and also gave importance to the
chiefs or Arbabs of the Khalil Pathans, who were
settled in the Peshawar valley near the foothills
and through whose lands the mountain Pathans passed
on their way to market. The Khalil Arbabs became
important intermediaries between the state and the
Afridi.

Structurally the Afridi were divided into eight
tribes: the Kuki, Sipah, Kamar, Kambar, Malikdin,
Zakha, Aka and Adam Khels. Of these the Adam Khel,
whose lands lay along the Kohat Pass, were of no
concern to the British in the period under review,
although to the government at Lahore they were of
considerable importance, and Lahore government policy
towards the Afridi was framed chiefly with the Adam

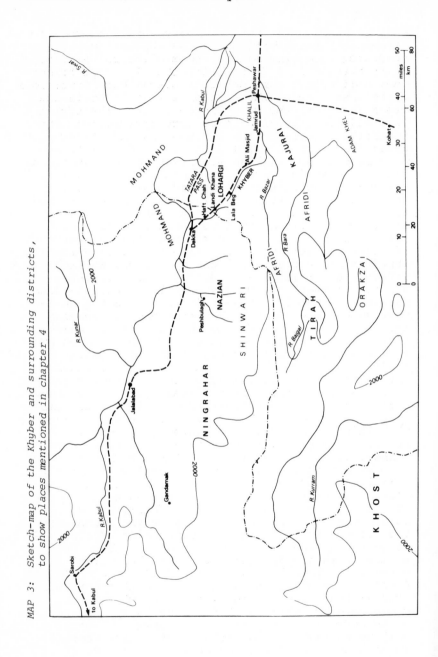

MAP 3: Sketch-map of the Khyber and surrounding districts,
to show places mentioned in chapter 4

Khel in mind, a circumstance which produced conflict
between Lahore and Britain. The Aka Khel may also
be disregarded because they controlled no territory
in Khyber itself. It was with the first six tribes
that British transactions took place; each controlled
a short section of Khyber from east to west in the
order in which they were listed above. The Afridi
were all Sunni Muslims; they were divided into the
two factions of Gar (Kuki, Kambar and Adam) and
Samal (Sipah, Kamar, Malikdin, Zakha and Aka).

Each of the tribes was divided into a number of
clans. It is unnecessary to list these clans in
detail, but it will be useful to mention those of
the Zakha Khel, as the inter-clan rivalries of that
tribe were to play some part in the events which
are to be described. Different authorities list
varying numbers of Zakha Khel clans, but the account
of Bellew, which is usually accepted, gives eight:
the Shan, Zaodin (Ziya al-Din), Paendah, Khasrozai
(Khasrogi), Mohib, Nasir al-Din, Bari and Pakhey
Khels. Of these the Pakhey was the principal clan
and included in its subdivisions the two men who
were recognised as chiefs of the whole Zakha Khel
tribe, Allah Dad and Fayztalab. It will be evident
however that their status did not enable the chiefs
to command obedience from other clans. Amongst the
Afridi, as among other confederations, important
decisions were usually made by elders who met in
councils, or jirgas. Such jirgas might be held at
various levels of organisation. Religious leaders
also played some part in the formation of decisions.

This chapter also considers only a limited
period, that of the first Anglo-Afghan War, when
three states were involved in the area: the restored
Sadozai monarchy of Shah Shuja al-Mulk, in whose
territories the Khyber was nominally included; the
Sikh state of Lahore, wherein lay Peshawar; and the
East India Company's government of British India,
whose presence was accounted for by the circumstance
that it was the principal upholder of the Sadozai
monarchy. My main concern is, indeed, with the
British part in these affairs, and the central character is Frederick Mackeson (1807-53), the Political
Agent at Peshawar, who was in charge of the Khyber
from 1839-42. For Britons this was their first
close experience of the Pathan tribes and of the
North West Frontier region. In the years to come
Britons and Pathans were to become deeply involved
in each other's affairs and the British concept of
tribe was to receive a new and permanent colouring
as a result of the experience.

153

British Images of 'Tribe'

There is neither time nor space to explore here the
evolution of the image which the word 'tribe' con-
jured up in British minds at the beginning of the
nineteenth century. Neither in its Biblical nor in
its classical usage did the term have the derogatory
significance which it subsequently acquired. It was
only with the sixteenth-century expansion of Europe
into the Americas and Africa that the association of
tribes with a more primitive order of mankind began,
and only in the Enlightenment of the eighteenth century that this was formalised into that concept of
progress which set tribal peoples outside the pale
of civil society. It was then supposed that the
natural course of human development was a progression
to higher levels of social, economic and political
organisation, which could be equated with civilisation; and that those peoples who remained grouped in
tribes represented an earlier, lower form of life,
left behind by the march of history and destined to
be redeemed and refashioned by the intervention of
superior forces. The epithet most commonly found in
association with the word 'tribe' was 'savage'. To
this judgement the Evangelical revival of the early
nineteenth century added a religious authority.
     The early experience of the Britons in India,
in their dealings with such tribal peoples as those
of Chota Nagpur and the Bhils of Khandesh, did
nothing to alter that view. The Bhils, who were
incorporated into British territory in 1818, were
described as hunters, plunderers and cattle stealers,
who lived off the toils of the cultivators of the
plains (and in doing so deprived the Company of valuable revenues). They were considered to be of low
intelligence and poor physical development and to be
given to superstition and alcoholic excess - in
short, degraded beings, lacking any sense of right
and wrong and altogether reduced to the level of
animals.
     The mixture of coercion and conciliation which
the British employed against the Bhils came to be
the accepted policy of British India for dealing
with tribal peoples. On the one hand, it involved
punitive military operations to impress the tribes
with the superiority of British power and the inescapable retribution which would follow breaches of
its rules; and, on the other hand, it embraced the
offer of pensions and jobs - in particular, employment in the police and in irregular military units.
Such units as the Bhil Light Infantry Corps both

served as cheap, coercive instruments for use against recalcitrant tribesmen, and also functioned as civilising agents, by teaching habits of obedience and discipline, and by inculcating an understanding of a system of authority based on contract and independent of ascriptive tribal authority. At a later stage were added the encouragement of settled agriculture and the provision of schools as further civilising agents, although it was recognised that civil society owed more to the sword than to the plough or the pen. Throughout this programme of moral redemption, an essential feature was seen to be the constant, guiding hand of a British officer, who was to be in close, personal contact with the tribal peoples, winning their respect and trust, and who was not to be trammelled by the burden of regulations thought more suitable for advanced communities.

The success of this policy in converting treacherous savages into worthy citizens was subsequently claimed to be one of the major achievements of British rule in India. In its final form the British view of tribes was stood on its head and there developed the cult of the redeemed savage or laundered tribe, a neo-Rousseauesque view in which the tribesman, purged of those base practices which he had developed in the past, was to be insulated by British officers from contact with the corruption of Indian civil society and kept in a state of perfect childhood innocence.[3]

From the beginning Britons in the Khyber found it difficult to make this image of tribal peoples and this notion of how to deal with them fit into what they observed. True, the Pathans were believed to possess many of the characteristics attributed to other tribal peoples: they were perceived to be thieves and murderers, to be treacherous and unprincipled, having, as Bellew put it, sunk to the lowest grade of civilisation, bordering upon the savage.[4] And yet there were features of their life which did not fit the accepted picture: their physical appearance was striking and their independent way of life strongly impressed Britons who found distasteful the submissiveness to authority which seemingly characterised the people of Bengal. So Elphinstone made the point that, whereas to the Briton who came to the Pathan country from Europe the tribes appeared as savages, given over to anarchy, to the Briton who came from India they possessed more admirable qualities.[5] And, of course, the Pathans possessed one other attribute which distinguished them from other tribal peoples: they had firearms and could use them

155

efficiently. In the Khyber the technological gap
that prevailed elsewhere was almost closed.

The Khyber between Afghan and Sikh States

Before considering British management of the Khyber
during the First Anglo-Afghan War, it will be useful
to consider the relations of the Kabul and Lahore
governments with the area. To the Sadozai monarchy
in Afghanistan (1747-1818) the Khyber was not a
border territory but a line of internal communications. The richest part of the Durrani Empire lay
east of the Khyber, and year after year the Afghan
armies marched through the Khyber to concentrate at
Peshawar for a new campaign. To obtain regular,
easy passage through the Pass, the Durrani paid
allowances to the tribes but also employed other
devices to ensure their support. The Sadozai could
appeal to a common religion, they could offer employment on lucrative campaigns, they could provide rent-
free lands in areas in which the Pathans were subject
to closer scrutiny, and they could form marriage
alliances with the tribes. Indeed, for the Sadozai
the Khyber provided a refuge in time of need, and
they were not excluded from Tirah itself. The situation changed when the Durrani monarchy became
engulfed in civil war and eventually collapsed in
1818. After that date the Sadozai ruled in Herat
alone, the Durrani lands east of the Indus were lost,
and the remaining territories were divided among
various Barakzai rulers. The Khyber ceased to be an
important route for government communications and
merchants found other routes. The Pass then became
a boundary between the possessions of the Barakzai
of Jalalabad and Kabul on the one side and those of
the Barakzai of Peshawar on the other. Allowances
for transit were no longer paid to the tribes. Nevertheless, the Barakzai retained, in their situation
as border managers, some of the advantages previously
enjoyed by the Sadozai rulers, notably in their
ability to manipulate religious and tribal links, as
it were, from the inside; for example, the Barakzai
not infrequently passed their summers in Tirah.[6]
    The situation was considerably altered by the
advent of the state of Lahore under the rule of
Ranjit Singh. From 1818 onwards there were repeated
Sikh interventions in the area west of the Indus.
From 1823 the Barakzai of Peshawar paid tribute to
the Sikhs. In consequence the Barakzai ability to
manipulate religious appeals was diminished, and

from 1827 until 1831 opposition to the Sikhs in the
Pathan lands was led by the puritanical religious
leader Sayyid Ahmad of Bareilly, whose followers
came from India but who also attracted considerable
tribal support. Sayyid Ahmad included in his attacks
the Barakzai of Peshawar, whom he accused of sacrifi-
cing Islam by serving the Sikhs. But in the end his
activities caused resentment among his Yusufzai followers, who deserted his cause, and in 1831 he was
killed in battle against the Sikhs.[7] Thereafter a
change took place in Sikh policy in the regions west
of the Indus; tributary rulers were increasingly
replaced by direct rule from Lahore. In 1834 it
was the turn of Peshawar: Sultan Muhammad Khan, the
Barakzai ruler was replaced by a Sikh governor, Hari
Singh Nalwa, who began to pursue an aggressive policy
against the tribes, even threatening an advance on
Jalalabad or Kabul.[8]
    With the elimination of the Barakzai of Peshawar,
the Khyber became a frontier area interposed between
the territories of the Barakzai ruler of Kabul, Dost
Muhammad, and those of the Sikhs. Whether Dost
Muhammad's concern was to protect his territories
against a possible Sikh invasion, or whether he
hoped to gain control of Peshawar, or whether, as
seems most likely, he was merely responding to the
importunities of the many Afghan refugees from
Peshawar who crowded into Kabul and to whom he was
obliged to pay pensions, is uncertain. At all
events, he made three attempts which could be interpreted as efforts to alter the situation in Peshawar.
In 1835 dissension among the Barakzai forced him to
retire from the Khyber before any engagement took
place; in 1836 his army was again assembled for no
result; and in 1837 a clash with Sikh forces took
place at Jamrud, at the eastern end of the Khyber,
in which Hari Singh was killed. Probably Dost
Muhammad had not intended that any battle should
take place - indeed one story has it that the Afghan
commander was obliged to fight in consequence of an
Afridi threat that if he did not do so they would
go over to the Sikhs.[9]
    In the result Dost Muhammad acquired new
entanglements. He built a new fort at Ali Masjid in
the narrowest part of the Khyber and placed a permanent garrison in it, and he was forced to pay
allowances to the Khyber tribes, who at first resented the presence of his troops but subsequently
acquiesced in the situation. The allowances were
not generous and even after Jamrud amounted to no
more than £2,000 a year. But with his troops, these

modest payments, and his ability to use tribal and
religious appeals and to present himself as the protector of the Khyberis against the Sikhs, Dost
Muhammad was able, for ordinary purposes, to acquire
a satisfactory degree of influence in the area.

Following the battle of Jamrud there was also
a change in Sikh policy: the belligerent methods of
Hari Singh were abandoned, at least for the time
being, and the policy of Lahore assumed a more defensive aspect. A mixture of threats and conciliatory gestures were offered to Dost Muhammad to try
to induce him to abandon his greater pretensions and
to make peace, and orders were issued to win over
the Khyber tribes. Under the new arrangements a
more generous role was accorded to the Peshawar
Barakzai, who had continued to live on the rent-free
lands, but who were now employed more extensively as
managers of the frontier under the Sikhs, or, to be
more precise, under the so-called Jammu faction
which had great influence in the Lahore government
and which possessed extensive lands in the area. The
Sikhs also employed as intermediaries the Khalil
Arbabs mentioned above.

The British in Kabul: Mackeson Appointed to the Khyber

It was at this point that, for reasons which do not
concern us, the East India Company resolved to replace the Barakzai rulers of Kabul and Kandahar with
the Sadozai Shah Shuja al-Mulk and to extend a
species of protectorate over Afghanistan.[10] The
legal instrument of this adventure was a Tripartite
Treaty between the Company, Shah Shuja and the Sikhs,
which was in turn founded upon an earlier agreement
made between Shah Shuja and the Sikhs. By the
treaty the Sikhs apparently secured recognition of
their claims in the frontier areas, although these
subsequently became a matter of dispute between
Britain and Lahore, and there eventually developed
a strong movement among British officers who were
concerned with the restored Sadozai monarchy to
exclude the Sikhs from the regions west of the Indus
and to attach these regions to Afghanistan.

At the risk of confusing the issues by moving
ahead too rapidly, it may be worth pointing out here
that an important aspect of the differences that
arose between the two states of Britain and Lahore
concerned their attitudes to the tribes. To the
British the Khyber tribes appeared as subjects of

Afghanistan and as groups to be conciliated because
of the need for the use of their territory for communications between India and Afghanistan. To the
Sikhs the tribes appeared as a border problem, either
to be propitiated through the agency of their
Barakzai or Khalil subjects, or to be coerced by
various devices employed by the ruthless Italian
Governor of Peshawar, General Avitabile. Avitabile
asserted that the Peshawar valley was his business
and that Britain's concern was with the Pass alone.
But the Afridi themselves were not to be divided in
this manner; they had economic links with Peshawar
and some of the Kuki Khel even lived outside the
Pass in the Peshawar plain. Accordingly, when
Avitabile harassed them with demands for revenue and
introduced one of those reverse blockades which were
to become so characteristic a feature of British
frontier management, the Afridi threatened to close
the Pass to Britain unless Avitabile desisted; and
the British were obliged to put pressure on the
Lahore government to comply with their demands. In
the process Mackeson enunciated the extraordinary
doctrine that Avitabile had no right to take any
measures against Shah Shuja's subjects, but that
Shuja was not responsible for crimes committed by
his own subjects, on the grounds that they paid no
revenue and gave little allegiance.[11] For the
Afridi, agreement not to commit crimes within the
Pass was matched by Mackeson's agreement not to
interfere with their conduct elsewhere. The British
also strongly objected to the activities of the
Peshawar Barakzai, who operated within a tribal
framework and were consequently accused of giving
refuge and aid to the enemies of the Shah. British
and Sikhs commonly found themselves supporting rival
factions within tribes.

In the relationship between tribe and state it
is a common experience that the state finds democratic forms an inconvenience and wishes to create
a more authoritarian form of tribal government which
will enable it to fix responsibility for the behaviour of the tribe upon some individual. But this
observation should not be generalised into a law
governing the relations between tribe and state. It
is true that the British in their operations in the
Khyber between 1839 and 1842 sought hierarchical
structures, but it is not the case that the Afghan
and Sikh states desired to promote similar developments. Whether a state seeks to control a tribe by
creating a more authoritarian structure, or whether
it prefers to proceed by fostering disintegration or

co-operation, or whether it prefers to work through
fine manipulation, depends upon its purposes (defensive or aggressive), its power and resources, and,
it will be argued later, its self-image.

As part of the operations to set Shuja on his
throne, a diversionary movement in the Khyber was
planned in 1838. The main British forces were to
march via the Bolan Pass and Kandahar, a route chosen
in order to minimise the role of the Sikhs in the
business, it being thought that their presence would
be damaging to the reputation of Shuja in the eyes of
Afghans.[12] To prepare the diversionary movement,
Shuja's eldest son, Muhammad Timur, was sent to
Peshawar with instructions to conciliate the Khyber
tribes. A British agent, Dr. P.B. Lord, was also
sent there with £5,000 to distribute in bribes and
many proclamations. 'I'm sick of seeing them', he
wrote,

> You'd laugh if you heard my man directing a
> party of Khyberees gathering in an old Masjeed
> to read the Proclamation. They spent two days
> over it discussing every paragraph and the end
> was that they could not decide whether the
> Firingees were about to give the country to
> Shah Sooja or Runjeet Singh.[13]

What the Khyber tribes thought of Lord would be
equally interesting. His largesse acquired many
supporters for Shuja but, according to another
British observer, they were all men without influence.[14] They did not include the most powerful man
in the Khyber, Khan Bahadur Khan, _malik_ (chief) of
the Malikdin Khel Afridi.

When Lord's superior, Claude Wade, arrived to
take charge he decided to test the worth of Lord's
bought men by asking them to take the fort of Ali
Masjid. They refused and he discharged most of
them.[15] Wade, who for many years had been the leading British agent on the frontier, had hoped for the
leading role in the Afghan expedition, and was very
disappointed to be placed in charge of a diversionary operation. He constantly pressed for the Khyber
operations to be given greater importance but was
refused by his government.[16] It was important to
him, therefore, to achieve some notable success in
the Khyber, and he was decidedly aggrieved when,
despite all the payments made, despite the successes
of British arms elsewhere, and despite all the promises given by the Khyberis, the Malikdin Khel and
the Kuki Khel under their chief Abd al-Rahman opposed

the British advance with arms. In July 1839 Wade
and his forces, supported by the Sikhs, were obliged
to force their way through the Pass.[17]
     The military success and the retreat of Dost
Muhammad's forces brought some improvement in the
situation. The maliks of the Zakha Khel and some of
the Shinwari accepted payment for protecting the
Pass. But Wade was still obliged to place troops
under British command in Ali Masjid, and other Afridi
remained unreconciled and soon began to harass con-
voys passing through the Khyber. Wade blamed everyone for his misfortunes - the Sikhs for failing to
co-operate, Shuja for not exerting himself to win
the support of the Afridi and Shinwari maliks whom
Wade took to Kabul to meet their new ruler, and, by
implication, his own government for not supporting
him adequately. But most of all he blamed the Khyber
maliks, and on his return through the Khyber he made
no effort to meet them. Instead he advocated a
tough policy. No payments should be made, the existing chiefs should be overthrown and replaced by
Shuja's own supporters, and the tribes taught a severe lesson by British military power. The Pass
should be guarded by troops under British control;
there could be no reliance on the Khyberis to keep
it open.[18]
     Britain, however, had no intention of embarking
upon so drastic and expensive a policy as Wade reco-
mmended. Wade was blamed for having missed the
opportunity to conciliate the Khyber tribes, and a
new man was put in charge of relations with them.
This was Wade's former assistant, Frederick Mackeson,
who had already been involved in the abortive negotiations which preceded Wade's advance in July 1839.
     Mackeson was thirty-two when he was appointed
to the charge of the Khyber, a former Bengal Native
Infantry Officer who had transferred to political
duties some five years previously and had served
since then mainly on the Indus. After 1849 he was
to acquire a significant reputation for his frontier
wisdom when he became Commissioner for Peshawar; he
learned his trade between 1839 and 1842.[19]
     Mackeson was appointed to take charge of the
Khyber in October 1839 by William Macnaghten, the
British Envoy with Shah Shuja. Mackeson and
Macnaghten held discussions at Kabul before his
instructions were issued.[20] Mackeson was advised to
adopt the method tried successfully (it was said) in
India and the Bolan, of 'conciliating and enlisting
the wild tribes whose occupation was formerly
plunder'. He was to disband the inefficient levies

recruited by Wade at Peshawar and replace them by a new corps of Khyber levies recruited from the tribes of the Pass. It was thought that members of the Kuki Khel, who had already been enlisted, would make an excellent nucleus, but other Afridi Khels should also be employed, as well as Shinwari and Orakzai. The new corps should have the duty of guarding the Pass and should have uniforms, traditional weapons and elementary drill and discipline when possible. Its European officers would be drawn from those presently in Wade's levies. In short, Mackeson was to apply the Bhil formula to the Pathans.

Before Mackeson could make a start on these longer-term projects, he had to reach some agreement with the Khyber tribes, who had now burst into violent action against the British. In late October a series of incidents took place. The Malikdin Khel attacked Ali Masjid on the 24th, and on the 27th they over-ran a post garrisoned by Muslim auxiliaries employed by the Sikhs, killed 400 of them, and closed the Pass. Although Sikh forces re-opened the Pass on 30 October there were continued attacks on supply columns. On 10 November a body of troops which had escorted supplies to Ali Masjid was attacked while returning·through the Pass, and Mackeson lost all his personal baggage, an unfortunate introduction to his new empire. The Malikdin Khel were the most active in these attacks, but other tribes also contributed, and when the commandant of Ali Masjid, Captain J. Ferris, called on the supposedly friendly Zakha Khel for help, he received none.[21]

Mackeson was forced to buy peace expensively. It has been mentioned that Dost Muhammad's payments after Jamrud rose to about £2,000 per annum. Wade had offered £4,000 but the maliks had refused this offer. Now, after lengthy negotiation, Mackeson was forced to pay £8,000. The maliks of the Malikdin and Kuki Khels were now given the same sum (approximately £1,600) as the Zakha Khel maliks and those Shinwari who immediately bordered the Pass. A further £1,600 was allotted to all other tribes. Khan Bahadur Khan also received a personal allowance of £200.[22] Still the tribes were not satisfied, and the whole history of the next three years may be written in terms of a constant effort by the Khyberis to increase their allowances. At the beginning of January 1840 a further sum of £800 was added to the allowances of Khan Bahadur Khan and Abd al-Rahman Khan of the Kuki Khel. Mackeson proposed to take it out of the shares of the others, but Macnaghten told him to pay it as an extra sum.[23] But there were

still others to be satisfied, as we shall see when
we consider the role of the Orakzai and the Shinwari.
   At this stage, however, it may be convenient
to describe the general organisation and duties of
Mackeson's office.[24] In general Mackeson acted as
intermediary between the British, Sikh and Afghan
governments and the Khyber tribes. His poor official relations with the Sikh Government in Peshawar
have already been mentioned; Mackeson was one of the
strongest advocates of the exclusion of the Sikhs
from the region. In his relations with the Government which he nominally served, that of Shah Shuja,
he was assisted by an agent sent by the Shah, Abd
al-Rahim Khan Malazai, and he was also able to call
upon the services of a similar agent who worked with
the Political Agent in Jalalabad. He made frequent
use of these agents in negotiations with the Khyber
tribes. Mackeson also used the Khalil Arbabs, although he says little about them in his despatches
and he may have been uncertain about their allegiance
because of their close connection with the Sikhs.
Mackeson also employed other individuals with the
tribes. It is, however, impossible to determine
what influence these various agents had upon British
policy and it seems likely that Mackeson made his
own decisions based upon information received from
several local sources.
   Mackeson himself described his duties as follows. First, to issue passports to travellers
between India and Afghanistan. Second, to be the
medium for dealings between the Afghan tribes and
the Sikh authorities in Peshawar, and to collect
information about Sikh activities west of the Indus.
Third, and this is the part which principally concerns this chapter, to superintend the Khyber,
Orakzai, Afridi, Mohmand, Shinwari and Bajauri tribes
and possibly others, and to look after the Khyber
Pass. In effect this meant maintaining relations
with all the tribes living in an area sixty miles
square. Mackeson was also responsible for the collection of tolls in the Khyber and the maintenance
of posts there (at Ali Masjid, Jamrud, Haft Chah and
Landi Khana) and for the construction of roads and
wells. Road construction had been begun by workers
recruited by Wade and this work was continued under
Mackeson. In direct charge of the work was
Mackeson's cousin, Philip Mackeson, and it was the
civilian Philip, and not Frederick, who was responsible for what came to be known as Mackeson's road,
which provided a shorter gun road of seven miles
from the eastern mouth of the Pass to Ali Masjid,

avoiding the length route which followed the bed of
the stream as it swung southwards.

Mackeson had an officiating assistant, Lieutenant Caulfield, who went to Kabul on sick leave in
July 1840, leaving his duties to be assumed by the
surgeon, Dr Reid. In December Mackeson got a
replacement in the person of the well-known Captain
Colin Mackenzie, but Mackenzie too went off to Kabul
on sick leave and was caught up in the rising there
in November 1841. Reid again took over as assistant,
and a new surgeon, Dr Richie, was appointed. In
December 1841 Mackeson received another eminent
assistant in the person of Henry Lawrence. The
strain on Mackeson himself, however, was very great,
and his health suffered badly. He repeatedly asked
for a transfer to a colder climate and hoped to get
the post of Political Agent in the Kohistan of Kabul,
but Macnaghten would not release him, believing him
to be indispensable at Peshawar.[25]

Mackeson's Policies for Controlling the Tribes

In pursuance of his instructions, Mackeson formed
two military units, the Jezailchi Regiment and the
Khyber Rangers. The former, commanded by Captain
Joseph Ferris and with its headquarters first at
Dakka and subsequently at Peshbulaq, supplied garrisons for Ali Masjid and other posts in the Pass and
bodies of troops for escort duties through the
Pass.[26] Its strength was nominally 1,000, it was
armed in traditional fashion, and military law was
not introduced, disputes being settled by councils
of Pathan officers. Ferris commented that the
Pathan officers were not very good. It was not
recruited from the Afridi and Shinwari who inhabited
the Pass, but from other Pathan tribes: Laghmani,
Bajauri and, especially, Yusufzai.

Afridi were recruited into the other military
unit, the Khyber Rangers, which, despite its name,
did not operate in the Khyber proper but was stationed further west at Gandamak and was used for
escort and guard duties along the stretch of territory around Jalalabad.[27] The size and organisation
of the Khyber Rangers was similar to that of the
Jezailchis although the number of NCOs was much
higher. It was recruited from Orakzai, Wazir,
Mohmand and Shinwari, but mainly from Afridi, who
supplied well over half of the recruits. The
Malikdin and Kambar Khels provided the greatest number of these. The greatest problem was to keep

recruits, since most deserted or took their discharge
after only a few months.[28] The commander, Captain
H.P. Burn, was disgusted with his command. He concluded one report with the words 'Such are the men,
without exaggeration, I have the satisfaction to
command. I have no confidence in them and shall
have none as long as they continue the most dishbeart-
ening system of quitting the regiment after a few
months' service.'[29] Neither he nor his adjutant,
Lieut. Hillersden, spoke Pashto and they could communicate with their men only through interpreters.
Macnaghten, however, was not disheartened by this
dismal catalogue: the Rangers, he argued, were quite
useful for local duties and their poor service record was better than that of the Bhils at a similar
stage. He even took comfort from the high turnover
in men because it meant, he thought, the wider dis-
semination of notions of British power, justice and
liberality.[30]

Macnaghten's thinking, however, was evidently
on a time scale which was not to be realised. When
the major uprising against British power in Afghanistan broke out in the autumn of 1841, many of the
Rangers deserted to the enemy and the British commander in the area, General Robert Sale, abandoned
the remainder of the force because he thought it too
unreliable. The Afridi made their way back to the
Khyber region where they were numbered among those
most hostile to British influence. The Jezailchis
held together rather better, mainly because of the
hostility on the part of the Shinwari and Afridi
towards the Yusufzai, which prevented the latter
deserting.

In the context of British policy towards tribes,
however, the most interesting feature concerns the
ethnic composition and areas of service of the two
corps. It is evident that the notion of using tribesmen against their fellow-tribesmen was thought to
be altogether too risky; Pathans would be enlisted
but they would be used in other areas - in this way
there was a marked departure from the Bhil formula.

From the beginning Mackeson had to deal with a
series of robberies in and around the Pass. The
theory of the allowance system had been that if property was stolen in the Pass the maliks would
recover it, or its value would be deducted from their
allowances. What he discovered was that the maliks
had little power over their tribesmen and that the
tribesmen received little or no benefit from the
allowances paid to their chiefs. In January 1840 a
British soldier was murdered and the property he was

guarding was stolen by some Zakha Khel. The maliks
did their best to help and some of the property was
recovered, but Mackeson was dissatisfied and felt
that the murder should be marked by some punishment.
He did not demand the surrender of the plunderers
but he urged the chiefs to punish them, using other
clans of the Zakha Khel against the offending Nasir
al-Din Khel. But the Zakha Khel maliks protested
that they had no power over the Nasir al-Din Khel,
and the latter complained that they received nothing
from the Zakha Khel maliks.[31] Mackeson thought the
situation most unsatisfactory, as it struck at the
basic assumption of the allowance system, viz. that
the maliks should restrain their tribesmen. 'So
convinced am I of the necessity of an example in the
present instance that nothing but a sense of the
difficulty of success would induce me to refrain
from coercive measures, should the maliks unfortunately fail in obtaining redress for us.'[32] British
progress in reclaiming the Afridi would be very slow,
he argued, if they did not feel that we had the
power to punish them. It is clear from this passage that the frustrations of his position were
already pushing Mackeson into the desire for coercion
to which Wade had so quickly succumbed. It says
much for Mackeson's patience and sense of realism
that he kept this desire under control.

Mackeson wanted some other device to supplement
the allowance system. One possibility was to collect hostages from the Pathans and to keep them at
Peshawar. There was no question of executing them
as Avitabile would have done, but Mackeson thought
that the chance that they might be sent to India
would restrain their relatives and fellow-tribesmen.
But at this time Mackeson did not feel strong enough
to demand hostages; the Afridi might refuse and he
would be unable to do anything about it.

Another possibility was a variant of coercion.
Britain should take control of the Pass and of the
approaches to the Bara valley (in which dwelled many
of the Afridi) and also occupy Bazar. He thought
this would put Britain in a position to demand the
restoration of property and the delivery of hostages,
threatening the destruction of crops and houses and
the ending of allowances.[33]

Yet another possibility was to exploit inter-
tribal divisions. There was here a contradiction in
Mackeson's policy. Local factions sought to involve
him in feuds but he invariably refused, saying these
were no concern of his providing the Pass did not
become the scene of inter-tribal fighting. But it

would become very difficult for him to maintain this position if he fostered feuds; there was no way in which he could ensure that fighting was confined to Tirah.

A partial solution was found with the help of the Shah's agents. It was to construct a tribal league (the Maymana League) to coerce the offending Nasir al-Din Khel. This was a difficult process, for Khan Bahadur Khan of the Malikdin Khel was not anxious to take action against the Nasir al-Din Khel because he was in the habit of employing them in the prosecution of his feuds with the Kuki Khel. The Zakha Khel maliks also presented some problems because of the enmity that existed between them. But eventually the League was put together, and the Nasir al-Din were surrounded and their escape routes cut off. They agreed to surrender two men (Mackeson said they were probably just slaves and he would soon release them).[34] The episode proved expensive, as Mackeson was obliged to pay secret bribes worth £300 to the maliks. The Maymana League was kept in being for the future. Mackeson arranged to transfer £360 of the allowances hitherto paid to the Zakha Khel maliks to the Nasir al-Din and Shan Khels and to make the League the agency of the payment. Mackeson shortly called upon the League again when the Zakha Khel continued plundering. Khan Bahadur Khan then proposed to send '54 aged and principal persons' drawn from various khels to be quartered on the offending clan until they disgorged.[35] The Zakha Khel agreed but the maliks now asked if they could assume responsibility for the Nasir al-Din and Shan Khels and if the allowances could be paid through them. Mackeson therefore had had some success in his objectives of creating a form of collective organisation to reinforce the power of the maliks and also of inducing the maliks to assume greater responsibility and hence help to develop the chain of authority which the British thought necessary.

Petty thefts in the Khyber continued and in the winter of 1840-1 became more frequent. Mackeson still urged that the value of the stolen property should be deducted from the stipends paid to the maliks. This proceeding led to some dissatisfaction on the part of the maliks who complained that in many cases they were not informed of the robberies until it was too late to take any action to recover the property. So Mackeson tried a new device. He appointed an agent to reside at Ali Masjid and invited the maliks each to send a representative to

reside there. In this way, robberies could be
reported and investigated immediately and there was
a better chance of recovering the property. The new
system began operating in early February 1841 and
had some success; in May and June 1841 seventy robberies were reported and in most cases all the
property was restored. The cases in which robbery
was not recovered were mainly night robberies and to
this problem Mackeson next turned his attention. The
Afridi maliks denied responsibility for robberies
that took place in the Pass at night or for those
which took place at a distance from the high road at
any time. They also tried to disown responsibility
for 'single thefts', claiming that these were the
work of the caravan men (mainly Shinwari) and not
of the Afridi. On some of these points compromises
were arranged: the Afridi were relieved of responsibility for night robberies but not for 'single
thefts'.36

By patience and by the use of several devices
in combination Mackeson had some success in improv-
ing the conditions of ordinary travel through the
Pass. But he was not satisfied with this situation.
He recognised that such arrangements, although use-
ful, were no answer to the needs of Britain. The
British position in Afghanistan demanded that the
Pass be available for use at all times and not sub-
ject to closure or interruption by the Afridi.
Mackeson explored other ways of controlling the
Afridi. His main effort was a sustained attempt to
enlist the Orakzai as a controlling group.

Orakzai and Afridi

The Orakzai are a Pashto-speaking group which claims
to be Pathan but which is not included in the Pathan
genealogies. Living north-west of Kohat, they had
no territory which directly abutted the Khyber but
they shared with the Afridi the same upland valleys,
including Tirah. Their economy was similar to that
of the Afridi. Ninety per cent were Sunni and ten
per cent Shii, and they were roughly equally divided
between Gar and Samal. The Orakzai confederation
was divided into four main tribes: Daulatzai,
Ismailzai, Lashkarzai and Hamsaya. The names of the
tribes suggest the arbitrary nature of these divisions. The tribes were each divided into clans.
From the British records it is not easy to identify
which tribes and clans were involved in the events
of the period. Those clans which are mentioned

belong to the Lashkarzai and Hamsaya but the British
also pensioned Shii religious figures suggesting that
they sought influence among the Daulatzai clans.
One would suggest tentatively that the British were
more uncertain about the distribution of power among
the Orakzai than in other Pathan groups, and that
they tended to over-rate the power of chiefs and
other leaders to command obedience.

As early as the end of 1839 Mackeson had begun
to contemplate using the Orakzai to control the
Afridi.[37] The Orakzai themselves were anxious to
obtain a share of the allowances paid to the Afridi
for guarding the Khyber. The Afridi malik, Khan
Bahadur Khan, refused this Orakzai request, arguing
that the Afridi had sole control of the Khyber and
that Alam Khan, the Orakzai chief, had failed to aid
the Afridi in resisting the British in July 1839.
In January 1840 Khan Bahadur Khan suggested that if
the Orakzai were willing to join the Afridi in opposition to the British the two confederations could
recover Ali Masjid. Just as Mackeson hoped to exploit the divisions between the two confederations,
so Khan Bahadur Khan hoped to heal them in order to
present a united front against the British that would
greatly increase the bargaining strength of the
Pathans and enable them to extract a much higher
price for the use of the Khyber.[38] When Mackeson met
Alam Khan in March 1840 at the mouth of the Khyber
to try to strike a bargain with him, the Afridi became alarmed and proposed to pay the Orakzai chief
something themselves. But Mackeson had the greater
financial resources and agreed to pay the Orakzai
£1,200 a year.[39]

Mackeson realised that the Orakzai themselves
could not keep order in the Pass, because their
lands were separated from it. But he believed they
could bring the Afridi under control by attacking
them in Tirah and by winning over a party among the
Afridi and by taking Afridi hostages. Mackeson did
not see this as an immediate course of action;
rather he wished to have the Orakzai card held in
reserve for use in negotiations with the Afridi or
to be used in an emergency.[40] He continued to cultivate the Orakzai in the months that followed. In
May 1840 he entertained Alam Khan and other chiefs
and three hundred of their followers in Peshawar.[41]

Mackeson was not able to control the course of
events that he had set in train. When Alam returned
to Orakzai country he met certain of the Orakzai
jirgas. The jirgas demanded that he should lead
them in war against the Afridi.[42] Mackeson certainly

did not want a war at this time and he used his influence with Alam's son, Muhammad Zaman Khan, who
was the principal direct beneficiary of the financial
arrangements made between Britain and the Orakzai,
to persuade his father to oppose war.[43]   Alam informed Mackeson that he had kept the peace at the price
of alienating some of the Orakzai divisions and that
he had been forced to pay out money in bribes, which
he asked Mackeson to refund through an increase in
his allowances to the £1,500 that had been promised
to him. The episode suggests that Mackeson may have
been the victim of a plot by Alam to improve his own
allowances. Mackeson had however been seriously
worried and had forbidden the Afridi to go to Tirah
until the Orakzai were pacified. In their turn the
Afridi were extremely suspicious of Mackeson's role
in these affairs and it was rumoured among them
that, far from striving for peace, Mackeson had
actually paid Alam £200 to incite trouble, Khan
Bahadur Khan again began to hint at an Afridi-
Orakzai alliance and wrote to Mackeson a touching,
if unconvincing, letter about the loyalty of the
Afridi and the untrustworthiness of the Orakzai.
     Mackeson was learning quickly, and he observed
with interest the tactics employed by the two confederacies. Instead of building up their own strength in preparation for the likely clash between
them, they concentrated on reducing the strength of
their opponents by exploiting factional divisions.
In each of the Afridi khels there were powerful
rivals to the existing maliks and these men were
possible allies of the Orakzai; similarly, there
were Orakzai divisions which could be exploited by
the Afridi. Numbers, Mackeson observed later, counted for little in tribal warfare, because no numerical superiority could take a fort. The strongly
built little forts that dotted the Pathan country
were impregnable against attack with the weapons
possessed by tribesmen, although artillery would
tumble them like ninepins. The essential ingredient
of tribal warfare, remarked Mackeson, was money.
Money, he wrote, enabled a tribe to buy the support
of one section of the enemy and to force the others
to submit to terms.
     It is a pity that Mackeson did not elaborate
his remarks on this subject. Plainly he was not
saying that money enabled a tribe to buy support in
numbers since he had already argued that numbers had
no military significance. He must have been implying that disunity within a tribe was the major cause
of weakness. But why should disunity affect a man

shut up in his own fort with a good supply of food and ammunition? The answer must lie in the nature of intra-tribal relationships, the power of the jirga, and the premium placed upon unanimity. Mackeson does not allow us to penetrate his thinking on these matters, but his emphasis upon money was characteristic. He came to think that money was the answer to everything in dealings with the Pathans, who, he thought, were motivated principally by cupidity. This view was subsequently echoed frequently by Britons who dealt with Pathans, and was expressed in many comments on their character, including the common observation that they would gladly and cheaply sell their wives (if their wives did not sell themselves first). The shortcomings of this characterisation are obvious, if understandable in the officials of a wealthy state which dealt with the tribes principally by means of bribes and stipends.

The Orakzai card was beginning to resemble the nuclear deterrent in our own day: in reserve it was an invaluable way of putting pressure on the Afridi, but if it had to be played the game was lost, Mackeson thought, because an Afridi-Orakzai war would mean the closure of the Pass, higher allowances all round, and might even result in an Afridi-Orakzai alliance against Britain. It might indeed have seemed better to discard the card altogether, but Mackeson continued to defend it on the grounds that he had nothing better and that Britain had so little power in the Khyber that there was not much to lose. 'The little control we ever obtained in the pass was obtained by force,' he wrote in August 1840. 'Our control is now merely nominal and the Afreedees watch our measures to increase it with the greatest jealousy.'[44]

In the summer of 1841 the Afridi-Orakzai problem surfaced again. On 6 July, Mackeson reported that the Afridi proposed to make another effort to heal their internal divisions and to make a united approach to the Orakzai with the object of getting rid of Alam Khan Orakzai and forming an alliance with the Orakzai to demand more pay from the British.[45] If they failed to win over the Orakzai they would try to neutralise them by causing civil war in the Orakzai confederation. There was at this time considerable discontent with Alam Khan among the Orakzai because of his failure to share his allowances with his tribesmen. The disaffected Orakzai approached Khan Bahadur Khan, but the Malikdin malik refused to deal with any but the whole of the Orakzai confederation, clearly hoping to thrust upon them the onus of solving their internal problems and wishing to avoid becoming involved in a civil war which could be exploited by the British.[46]

Khan Bahadur Khan had been the outstanding Afridi leader throughout this period and had steadily outmanoeuvred Mackeson, working always towards the construction of a united Afridi front and of an Afridi-Orakzai alliance. Just at this point, however, he was taken ill and retired to his summer residence where he died in October 1841. Mackeson's comment is interesting. 'This old man's influence kept the Afridis united together. They will hereafter be less formidable as enemies but as friends, in the absence of any directing head to whom the different maliks look up, it will be much more difficult to keep on terms with them.'[47] In short it suited the British better to have a strong leader to deal with, even if he were hostile, than to have to deal with the traditional, decentralised tribal structure.

Just before his death Khan Bahadur Khan's policy was temporarily successful. It was carried out by his eldest son, Allah Dad Khan, who was sent by him with other Afridi maliks to meet the Orakzai in Tirah. At first matters went badly and in August 1841 clashes took place.[48] The Orakzai launched simultaneous attacks on various Afridi khels but had no real success. The total losses were about thirty killed and wounded. The Afridi immediately countered by buying off the Mashti Khel, a Hamsaya Orakzai clan which belonged to the Samal group and therefore were usually inclined to favour the Afridi. This move broke up the Orakzai unity.[49] Alam Khan prepared to punish the Mashti Khel, but the Afridi quickly produced peace overtures through the ulama in Tirah, and the Orakzai forced Alam to agree. The two confederations drew up a petition to Shah Shuja asking for allowances for the Orakzai, 'for without doubt on the pay that has already been granted and received it is impossible that the tribes of the Orakzais and the Afridis should subsist'.[50] The petition also contained an admission of the Orakzai claim to half the stipends of Khyber. Since the Afridi had no intention of accepting any reduction in their own allowances, this virtually amounted to a demand that the British should double the amount they paid for passage through the Khyber.

Mackeson's policy had rebounded on him and what he had feared had come to pass: a possible 30,000 fighting men were united in demanding money from

Britain. But he would not pay more, and still hoped
to break up the alliance, especially since its main
architect, Khan Bahadur Khan, was dead. Mackeson
still hoped to use Alam as the weak point of the
alliance. A condition of the Afridi-Orakzai agreement was that Alam would break his connection with
the British, but Mackeson was sure he would not
sacrifice his own allowances. Mackeson proposed to
force Alam to choose by demanding that he should
send his son, Zaman, to Peshawar, being confident
that the Afridi would withdraw from the agreement
when Alam agreed. Alam did agree, but before the
matter could develop further it was engulfed in the
consequences of the Afghan uprising of November 1841.

The Shinwari

At the western end of the Khyber were the Shinwari,
a Pathan confederation divided into four tribes: the
Ali Sher Khel, the Sipay, the Manduzai and the Sangu
Khel. The Ali Sher Khel, who inhabited the valley
of Lohargi, controlled the section of the pass between Lala Beg and Haft Chah (and therefore going
beyond Landi Khana) and allowances for them were
fixed in 1839.[51] The Ali Sher Khel might have been
easy to control, because they were the principal
carriers of goods between Peshawar and other markets
on the route to Kabul, and they came down to the
Peshawar valley in great numbers at all seasons.
But, of course, the application of economic sanctions
against them was in the hands of the Lahore state
through its governor of Peshawar, and not in those
of Mackeson, so this weapon, which was employed
effectively in subsequent years, was not available
to the British in 1838-42. The Manduzai were the
weakest of the Shinwari tribes and actually paid
revenue to the government, an almost unheard-of
phenomenon in the Pathan area. The Sipay lived
further west, beyond the Pass, in Ningrahar, and
they received allowances, though they were not content with what they received. But the most powerful
of the Shinwari tribes, the Sangu Khel, which inhabited the valleys of Saroli and Nazian on the northern slopes of the Safid Koh beyond Peshbulaq (which
lay south of the Khyber) received very little.
     The Sangu Khel had five clans. Of these the
Tsalur Plar and the Taus lived in Saroli, the Gadu
and Korma lived in Nazian, and the small Ghani Khel
lived at Peshbulaq itself. It was the Ghani Khel
maliks who were recognised as nominal chiefs of the

whole of the Sangu Khel, and the British and Shuja
each gave small pensions to Muhammad Gul Khan and
his sons, Mir Afghan and Sayyid Gul. But the Ghani
Khel maliks were intermediaries between the state
(in its various forms) and the Sangu Khel, rather
than chiefs in any commonly accepted sense. They
had no power to give any command to the Sangu Khel
clans and, because of their easily accessible position at Peshbulaq, were unable to resist the demands
of the state. Under Brakzai rule in Afghanistan the
Ghani Khel maliks had functioned as negotiators; for
the Sangu they were a window on an outside world
which was disliked but indispensable; for the governors of Jalalabad they were a point of contact with
a group of intractable tribal subjects. The British
failed to appreciate their position at first and
apparently believed that by pensioning the Ghani
maliks they were restraining the Sangu Khel. They
were rapidly disillusioned when the Sangu Khel began
attacking caravans.

Mackeson first decided that the Sangu action
reflected a general Shinwari discontent with the
allowances they received, and he suggested that the
Sangu attacks might have been instigated by the
Ningrahar Shinwari in the hope of gaining allowances
equal to those of the Afridi. The Ningrahar maliks
claimed that half of the Khyber belonged to them;
they were clearly advocates of the largest definition
of the Pass.[52] Mackeson's answer was to fine the
Lohargi Shinwari, who agreed to bring in the maliks
of the Sangu Khel and to persuade them to surrender
hostages. This, Mackeson pointed out, would be of
little use, for it was now clear to him that the
Sangu maliks had no power at all over their own
tribe. The Sangu Khel made their own comment on the
proposal by attacking the Shinwari posts in Khyber,
killing a number of Shinwari of the Ningrahar and
Lohargi clans.

The Ningrahar and Lohargi Shinwari now admitted
that they could not keep open the Pass without the
co-operation of the Sangu Khel and they offered part
of their own allowances. The Sangu Khel maliks
offered to receive nothing for themselves but to pay
all their allowances to their tribesmen.[53] Still the
Sangu refused, and Mackeson was persuaded to agree to
a further increase in allowances. He also tried the
Maymana League. The maliks agreed to seek redress
from the Sangu Khel or, if this failed, to aid
Britain in coercive action.[54] The Lohargi maliks
also offered to help. Mackeson was now able to come
to an agreement with the Sangu Khel. On 22 June 1840

a deputation of 200 of the Sangu came in, bearing
with them twelve hostages. They agreed to become
responsible for guarding the Khyber between Landi
Khana and Haft Chah in return for £600 p.a. The
Lohargi Shinwari continued to receive their allowances of £840 p.a.[55]

Mackeson was now ready to take a hard line with
the Ningrahar Shinwari and stop their allowances.
Without the support of the Sangu Khel they were
powerless to hurt Britain, and as their villages were
in the plain and close to the road they could be
coerced by Britain if necessary. He ignored their
claim to half the Khyber stipends, and in August
1840 the Ningrahar Shinwari gave up their opposition
and came into Peshawar and asked that their allowances should be restored, to which Mackeson agreed.[56]
On 20 June 1840, at the conclusion of the arrangements with the Shinwari and the Orakzai, Mackeson
reported that the arrangements for the security of
the Pass by paying all parties who had claims were
completed. In all, Mackeson was paying out rather
more than £10,000 a year in allowances.

Trouble with the Sangu Khel recurred at the end
of 1840 when they attacked some nomadic Ghilzai of
the Tagar tribe. The full circumstances of this
episode did not emerge for some time. At first
Mackeson believed that the Sangu Khel had attacked
the Ghilzai on Mohmand land out of a desire for
plunder and a wish to prosecute a feud with the
Mohmand.[57] Later it appeared that the land was disputed, that the Sangu claim was at least as good as
that of the Mohmand, and that in the past the
Ghilzai had paid rent to the Sangu Khel for grazing.
It eventually began to seem possible that the
Ghilzai had seen the opportunity for free grazing
and that the Mohmand had hoped to embroil the Sangu
Khel with the British. If this were their intention, they were eminently successful.

When the Ghilzai complained to Shuja's officials, Afghan troops were sent and quartered on the
accessible Sangu lands. The Sangu protested to the
British that they had kept their word not to molest
travellers on the high road, but claimed the right
to prosecute their feuds elsewhere. Seven of their
hostages with Mackeson in Peshawar escaped, leaving
the nominal chiefs, who had little power. Mackeson
stopped the Sangu allowances but continued to pay
the Shinwari guards who remained at their posts in
the Pass. His approach was conciliatory but his
superior, Macnaghten, was anxious that an example
should be made of the Sangu Khel.[58] Macnaghten

wrongly believed that they were weak in fighting
strength, had no allies, were readily accessible to
military force and could easily be coerced by a
tribal force. They were plunderers, he declared,
and should be made an example of; talk of feuds was
irrelevant.

Mackeson attempted to deflect Macnaghten. Coercion was not the answer, he argued; the Sangu Khel,
he conceded (wrongly), were dependent on plunder but

> I rather look to a gradual improvement in the
> state of society arising from a better as well
> as a more vigorous government than to the
> effect of any sudden exercise of severity. The
> rude state of these men cannot be understood
> until it has been witnessed, they are little
> raised above the savage and their motives of
> action are to us unaccountable.[59]

Besides, he pointed out, Britain lacked the means
of coercion. The Sangu had twice the fighting
strength that Macnaghten believed them to have and
their principal stronghold, the Nazian valley, was
not easily accessible. Any expedition against them
would have to include European troops and artillery.

Mackeson first tried a pacific approach to the
Sangu Khel through their nominal malik, Mir Afghan,
asking for the return of the hostages and the plunder. While waiting for an answer he conducted a
personal reconnaissance of the area, finding a position from which he could peer into the Nazian valley
itself. He decided it was inaccessible to artillery
and he laid plans to block exits from the valley.[60]

On 15 February 1841 the Sangu replied, offering
to return the hostages but not the plunder, which
they argued was rightfully theirs, as in 1840
Mackeson had agreed that he would not interfere in
feuds with other tribes and the Ghilzai had been
using their pastures without payment. Mackeson
countered by reasserting that this was not a feud
and that the Ghilzai had been on Mohmand, not Sangu
lands. He then went on to put forward a radical
proposal which, if accepted, would have changed the
whole concept of crime and retribution that existed
among the tribes. He asked the Sangu to send a
jirga to meet representatives of the Mohmand and
Ghilzai, and to agree to stop feuds and to recognise
a breach of the peace as a crime against the state,
deserving of punishment. But he was now warming
towards the idea of an expedition. He dismissed the
argument that the Sangu Khel were dependent on

plunder. 'They will find the means of subsistence without plunder when they have been coerced and made an example of', he wrote.[61] His radical project failed. The Mohmands accepted his proposal for settling feuds but the Sangu rejected it; they would send no jirga and their feuds were their own business.[62]

Mackeson now accepted the need for coercion and prepared for the expedition. As it happened the troops were at hand: a relief brigade on its way to Kabul was then at Jalalabad. Indeed the existence of the means of coercion, ready to hand for the first time since the end of 1839, must have influenced the decision to attack the Sangu. Ever since 1839 there had been talk among British officers of making an example of some tribe or other in the area, and there is strong suspicion that the quarrel with the Sangu at this time provided the excuse that was needed. Certainly this helps to explain Macnaghten's precipitate recommendation of violent retribution; as Envoy to Shah Shuja he felt the need to uphold the authority of the Shah, and the action against the Sangu served an Afghan purpose more than it did a British need, for there had been no disruption of communications. The presence of the troops was also the factor which brought Mackeson to support coercion.

A substantial force commanded by Brigadier Shelton was quickly assembled. It included a European infantry regiment, two regiments of sepoy[63] infantry and one of the Shah's, and artillery. It left Jalalabad on 21 February and arrived at Peshbulaq on the 23rd. Shortly after dawn the following day, the troops entered the pass leading to the Nazian valley, and by 1.00 p.m. Shelton was in control of most of the valley. On the days that followed, the troops completed the conquest of the valley and penetrated the valleys that ran off it.[64] Mackeson had hoped that peace could be arranged once the troops had penetrated the valley, and indeed the Sangu sent in a jirga composed of the most influential men in the tribe. But while negotiations were in progress, fighting continued, and a British officer, Captain Douglas, was killed. After that, Mackeson commented, there was no hope of peace because the British troops wanted revenge. The revenge was comprehensive. Casualties were not great; the Sangu lost 30-40 killed and 30 prisoners were taken, but the majority of the tribe escaped into the hills, Mackeson not having been able to complete his arrangements to block the exit routes. But the forts, houses and cultivation in the valleys were destroyed. Shelton blew up no less than 140 forts.

Both Mackeson and Shelton were surprised at the extent and richness of the cultivation, and the size of the population that it supported. Such surprise was to be a feature of British dealings with the Pathans. The British could never quite rid themselves of an image of hungry mountaineers drawn irresistibly towards the wealth of the cultivated plains. Such a description might have fitted many Scottish Highland clans, and perhaps fitted the Wazir, but it did not fit the tribes in the Khyber region, and the British surprise at the sight of Sangu wealth was to be duplicated many years later when they penetrated the Swat valley and Tirah. But they did their best to destroy the wealth of the Sangu; what the troops did not destroy was stolen by irregular tribal auxiliaries and camp followers who accompanied the force.

Mackeson's verdict was that the tribes had been taught a lesson. Experience of tribal warfare had led the Pathans to believe their forts were impregnable, and as the British troops marched into the Nazian valley men stood on top of the forts shouting opposition and firing their matchlocks in perfect confidence, Mackeson thought, that they could not be successfully assailed. They were quite paralysed, he commented, by disciplined, rapid fire. The affair would have a powerful effect upon all neighbouring tribes. 'I am much surprised if hereafter in this part of the country we find any of the tribes keeping to their forts against us.'[65]

Mackeson made various military dispositions to control the area, and began negotiations with the Sangu maliks, who were still available to act as intermediaries. Agreement was eventually reached by which the Sangu paid the Ghilzai £600 compensation for the stolen sheep and delivered ten hostages. In addition Mackeson agreed to entertain two influential Sangu leaders, Khan Mir and Khan Gul. He offered to pay the Sangu allowances (which he now agreed to resume) through these men, but, interestingly, the Sangu said they would prefer to receive these through the nominal malik, Mir Afghan of the Ghani Khel branch of the Sangu, as before. The Sangu seemingly maintained a distinction between their real leaders and those whom they preferred to act as intermediaries with the state. The Sangu renewed their engagements with Shuja and once more manned their posts in Khyber.[66]

By this time Mackeson had come to believe that

the Sangu's original complaints about Mohmand and
Ghilzai encroachment on their lands had much justice,
and he warned the Mohmand and Ghilzai chiefs against
such practices in the future. The Mohmand complained
that no boundaries had ever been drawn. They agreed
to abide by the arbitration of Mackeson, who there-
upon drew a line on a map bisecting the disputed
area. Both parties then agreed to live in peace.
After all, Mackeson had succeeded in advancing the
position of the state against that of the tribes,
and had apparently passed from the role of enforcer
to that of arbitrator.

The British Lose Control of the Khyber

Mackeson's laboriously constructed Khyber system
collapsed rapidly in November 1841. In October disturbances took place amongst the Ghilzai tribes
between Kabul and Jalalabad. Communications between
the two cities were severed. At the beginning of
November an uprising took place in Kabul which eventually led to the evacuation of the British garrison
on 6 January 1842 and its complete destruction during
the next few days. The first repercussions of these
events were felt in the Khyber on 13 November when
Ferris's headquarters at Peshbulaq were attacked.
Ferris withdrew the garrisons of the posts at Landi
Khana and Haft Chah, and on 16 November evacuated
Peshbulaq and returned to Peshawar via the Tatara
Pass, losing all his baggage and the government
treasure. When Ferris withdrew his posts the trouble
spread to the Khyber, and from the Shinwari to the
Afridi. On 16 November Zakha Khel tribesmen, acting
without the agreement of their chiefs, attacked the
fort of Ali Masjid, which was defended by Philip
Mackeson and 150 poorly armed Yusufzai. The Zakha
Khel were soon joined by other Afridi.[67]
    Confronted by this situation Mackeson tried
desperately to keep some control over the Pass, passage through which would be required either for the
retreat of the British forces in Afghanistan or for
the march of relieving forces from India. His problems were not with the maliks, who continued to
assure Mackeson of their loyalty and who agreed, in
return for substantial bribes, to allow him to send
supplies to Ali Masjid (although no troops) and to
turn a blind eye to his use of the Tatara and
Abkhana roads to send supplies, money and even
troops to Jalalabad. The problem was presented by
the tribesmen, over whom the maliks had no control.

179

'Their mullahs are preaching against us and the popular feeling is too strong for the maliks to oppose
or restrain', Mackeson wrote on 28 November.[68] The
maliks, he wrote, cared nothing for religion, or
Kabul, or anything but money, but with the tribesmen
the matter was different.

In late December, when news of the reverses
suffered by the Kabul garrison began to reach the
Khyber, there was fresh excitement. From 22 December
the maliks held almost daily jirgas at which the
question of whether to go to war with the British was
discussed. The maliks, influenced by further bribes
from Mackeson, succeeded in preventing any decision
for war, but the jirgas continued, and at the beginning of January the Afridi were joined in council by
the Orakzai.[69] On 9 January Mackeson reported that
the tribes were still undecided and were choosing
new maliks. But the news from Kabul had plainly
tipped the balance against the British. On January
10 the maliks warned Philip Mackeson to look to his
own safety, and from 10 to 15 January Ali Masjid was
repeatedly attacked. The Yusufzai garrison was becoming disaffected and it was plain that it could
not hold out much longer. Agreement had now been
reached with the Sikhs to support the British advance from Peshawar which took place on the night of
15-16 January. The Afridi refused a free passage to
the troops, saying that it would be against their
religion; Mackeson commented that they could not
have gone against the religious feeling in their
tribes.[70]

The British advance was botched: the troops got
through to Ali Masjid but lost nearly all the supplies they were carrying up and found themselves
freezing in the open on half rations. The situation
became serious when another relieving force from
Peshawar was repulsed at the mouth of the Pass on
the night of 18-19 January, after the Sikh force
which was to have accompanied it had mutinied.
Mackeson was now desperate: he offered Alam Khan
Orakzai £2,000 to create a diversion in Tirah and
take over the Khyber, and he instructed his deputy,
Henry Lawrence, to support rivals of the Afridi
maliks now in power.[71] It was to no avail and on
24-25 January Mackeson was obliged to evacuate Ali
Masjid and return to Peshawar. The British had now
completely lost control of the Khyber.[72]

During the next ten weeks Mackeson sought to
recover some influence by negotiation, while the
Afridi negotiated both with the British and with
representatives of the Barakzai leader of the Kabul

rising, Muhammad Akbar. From the British the Afridi sought to discover whether they intended merely to relieve Jalalabad and retire, or whether they intended to try to recover their position in Afghanistan. From Akbar they demanded money and refused for a long time to admit his troops to the Pass or to sell them fodder. Curiously enough, throughout this period the Afridi continued to deal with the Sikhs on the familiar basis, despite Mackeson's efforts to induce the Sikhs to treat the Afridi as enemies. Mackeson continued to try and create a rival party among the Afridi maliks which would be favourable to the British, and paid a large sum to Alam Khan to create a diversion. But the Orakzai came to an agreement with the Afridi and the rival party among the latter asked for £30,000 to provide a passage for British troops. Mackeson agreed to pay £5,000 and in the meantime advanced £400 in expenses to enable the pro-British chiefs to purchase support. He also entertained 1,000 Afridi at Peshawar and Jamrud and collected many hostages. The Afridi responded with criticisms of the chiefs who had declared themselves to be British supporters, and a split took place in the Kuki Khel between Abd al-Rahman, who was pro-British, and a rival, Nasir Khan, who had formerly been an officer in Ferris's Jezailchis and who was connected by marriage with Allah Dad Khan of the Malikdin Khel.[73]

Thus the continuation of tribal rivalries prevented the Afridi assuming a united front, despite the call of religion. But at the end of March their divisions were largely healed through outside intervention. Muhammad Akbar sent down from his camp outside Jalalabad a body of some 200 horse and 500 foot with two small guns to co-operate with the Khyberis in resisting the advance of any British force. This body provided the nucleus of the strong resistance which the Afridi mounted on 5 April 1842, when the British finally decided to force the Pass. Almost to the last Mackeson continued to negotiate with his so-called supporters and he advanced £2,500 of the promised payment. But on the day before the British set off, the pro-British Afridi confessed that they were unable to fulfil their part of the bargain, claiming that the advent of Akbar's force had turned the scales against them.[74]

The British force overcame the resistance of an estimated 10,000 tribesmen, broke into the Pass, and retook Ali Masjid on 6 April. They were supported by a Sikh advance to Ali Masjid by another route. Thereafter the British commander, General Pollock,

moved forward cautiously because of the necessity of
securing his communications. The pro-British chiefs
now returned to the fold, including Alam Khan
Orakzai, Allah Dad Khan Zakha Khel and Abd al-Rahman
Khan Kuki Khel. Unfortunately, two sons of influential supporters of Allah Dad were accidentally
killed by sepoys. Mackeson paid compensation and
endeavoured to hush the incident up, but Allah Dad's
influence in his own khel was seriously weakened.[75]
Some Shinwari maliks also came in to make their
peace with the British.

Mackeson hoped that the pro-British chiefs
would be able to take on responsibility for keeping
the Pass open, but he was disappointed. Pollock
reported that 'Fanaticism and contempt for us [are]
so great that chiefs, though willing to come to
terms, cannot get tribes to agree.'[76] Eventually
Mackeson made some arrangements with the chiefs, but
he had no confidence in them and most of the Pass
was garrisoned by Sikh troops (east of Ali Masjid)
and by British-controlled forces at Ali Masjid and
other positions west of it.[77] From June 1842 onwards
the Pass was subject to attacks by hostile Afridi,
but the arrangements sufficed until the British
forces had completed their work and were finally
withdrawn from Afghanistan through the Khyber in
early November. It need hardly be said that the
rearguard suffered attacks and losses in the Pass,
but the British had done with the Khyber, and in
the same month the various irregular forces that had
held the Pass were finally disbanded.

Conclusion

The three states involved in the Khyber during the
period studied looked on the tribes in different
ways. To the Afghan government the Khyberis were
subjects in a peculiar but not unfamiliar category:
they paid no revenue to the government and the
government paid no attention to them and accepted no
responsibility for their behaviour.

To the British the Khyberis bore a dual aspect.
On the one hand they were subjects of a government
which was visibly supported by Britain and which
therefore had to behave, to some extent, in a manner
approved by Britain; in short it must accept some
responsibility for its subjects and demand some
standards of behaviour from them - hence Macnaghten's
insistence upon upholding the authority of Shuja's
government in the case of the Sangu Khel, a position

which readily led to exploitation both by subordinate officials of Shuja's government and by other tribes.

On the other hand the British saw the Khyberis as people who had the capacity to obstruct a vital line of communication. The obvious solution to this problem was to sweep the Khyberis out of the way and establish British control of the Khyber through overwhelming force. But this mode of action was too expensive and would have involved a long-term commitment which was no part of British policy.

Accordingly Britain settled for a more modest approach to the problem: to try and get what she wanted by tribal management. This policy had some limited success but it failed conspicuously to provide the degree of control required. It failed for two reasons. First, the British suffered from serious disadvantages in the management of the tribes: they did not sufficiently understand the social, economic and political structure of the tribes, and certain resources that were open to an Afghan government were closed to them - the use of marriage ties and of religion, and the ability to use hostages in the manner in which they were meant to be used, or abused. The greater financial resources at the disposal of the British did not compensate for these deficiencies; their Pathan military units failed to achieve their purpose; and the word of a British officer was not sufficient. The Bhil formula for tribal management was simply not good enough for the Pathans.

Second, the British could not be content to play so humble a role as that imposed by the exigencies of tribal management: such a status did not fit their notion of how a government should behave. Governments, they thought, should govern, especially in Asia; and subjects should obey. If they did not obey, prestige demanded that they should be punished. Hence there was in Wade and Mackeson a leaning towards a drastic, military solution to the problem - a demonstration of inevitable and invincible British power; and a movement towards the imposition of a British view of how rulers and subjects should behave towards one another. It might have been thought that a state would have welcomed the anarchical political system of the Pathans as affording opportunities for manoeuvre. For the British this was not so: manoeuvre was a _pis aller_; the preferred mode of dealing with the tribes was through a hierarchical structure of authority which the British were anxious to identify or even to create. Also the British found the tribal attitude to crime and

punishment unacceptable and endeavoured to replace
it with systems more familiar to them; the Maymana
League and the Ali Masjid jirga were attempts to
limit tribal discretion and to impose some larger
authority; Mackeson's proposal to the Sangu Khel for
the abolition of feuds took the process much further.

For the third government, that of the Sikhs,
the matter was simpler: the Afridi were a border
problem, a people who raided the Peshawar plain. The
Sikhs experienced neither the need to uphold their
prestige, which later drove the British into frequent punitive expeditions, nor the scruples that
subsequently kept the British from more indiscriminate
vengeance. They practised under Avitabile a simple
policy of deterrence - execute some Afridi to encourage the others to desist from raids, and impose
economic sanctions upon them - and combined this
policy with that of tribal management through Afghan
intermediaries, notably through the Barakzai of
Peshawar and the Khalil Arbabs. Unfortunately for
the Sikhs they had to work with the British, who
disapproved of their methods and did not sympathise
with their objectives. The British gradually reduced the deterrent power of the Sikhs, deprived them
of their Barakzai agents, objected to their other
Afghan intermediaries who were rivals of British
protégés, and finally dragged the Sikhs unwillingly
into the Khyber itself.

Contemplating the behaviour of the three states
in the Khyber, one may suggest the hypothesis that
in relations of states with tribes it is the character of the states themselves that provides a major
determinant of the possible limits of their dealings with tribes. If this hypothesis has any value
it implies some change in the preoccupation of anthropologists. Anthropologists have concentrated
their attention primarily on the tribe itself and
on its political, economic and social structure; and
have sought the reasons for the changing fortunes of
tribes primarily within this framework. The state
has been assumed to be a Weberian, impersonal,
bureaucratic and military machine which makes its
standard demands on the tribes for taxes and recruits.

But there are at least as many models of states
as there are of tribes and the structure of the
state is no less complex. In the period with which
we have been concerned, the British state was represented by several layers of authority ranging from
the Cabinet in London, through the Board of Control
and the East India Company Courts of Directors and

Proprietors to the Supreme Government in Calcutta, and thence through the Envoy in Kabul to the Political Agent in Peshawar. And this list takes no account of the rival layers of authority that impinged upon the Khyber, such as the Political Agent at Ludhiana who was responsible for the conduct of relations with the Sikhs, or the Political Agent at Jalalabad whose bailiwick included Ningrahar, and all the various military officers of the British and East India Company armies with their separate command structures.

It should not be supposed that these various agencies functioned harmoniously; British policy was the outcome of innumerable disputes and compromises. Throughout the period there were major differences between the Envoy in Kabul and the Political Agent in Ludhiana concerning what policy should be pursued towards the Sikhs; and there were disputes between Envoy and generals concerning the use of troops. And this picture of conflicting authority still ignores the factor of personality. Those who held office remained individuals; their characters continued to shape their recommendations. Mackeson was not the finely-honed drill at the business end of a vast, well-oiled machine, but a man seeking to survive and prosper in a jungle of warring factions. His recommendations were framed not merely in relation to the situation as he perceived it, but also in relation to their likely reception by Macnaghten, Clerk, Pollock and other individuals within the state system. Mackeson was an intelligent, able and ambitious man, who lacked any personal influence which might be exerted on his behalf and who was obliged to make his way through his own efforts. He identified himself too closely with the policy of extending British influence in Afghanistan, was correctly suspected of misrepresenting the situation in the Khyber in 1842 in order to justify a decision to reconquer Kabul, and paid the price of his commitment when the Afghan policy found disfavour with the next Governor-General, Lord Ellenborough. In short, Mackeson was compelled to represent the situation in the Khyber not just as it was but also as one faction within the state hoped it would be.

States, it would seem, have a variety of characters from which they choose that which they wish to exhibit at any time. In the case of the British Indian state there was a peculiar ambivalence deriving from the conflict between the character which it wished to exhibit to the people of India and that which it chose to display to the people of England.

To the first it wished to appear as a state of iron will, inexorable determination and limitless power; to the second it tried to show itself a state of justice, benevolence, reason and Christian principle. The consequent amalgam came to be known by its friends as imperial and by its enemies as hypocrisy. To the Khyberis it must have seemed pure mystery.

And what of the tribes themselves? Plainly the heavily decentralised system of government within the tribes, and the bitterness of their rivalries, made it difficult for them to bargain effectively with the states concerned, or to exploit the possibilities inherent in the differences in approach of the three states and the ambiguities of British policies. Khan Bahadur Khan seemingly had some perception of the situation and attempted to forge some tribal unity but, although he had some success, he and his successors were not able to hold the tribes together. For the maliks there were gains to be made in strengthening their position within the tribal system by exploiting the chances presented by the British identification of them as the people with whom they should deal. No doubt the extra cash income derived from the British enabled the maliks to increase their power over their tribes to some degree, but how limited this power remained was well-demonstrated in the autumn of 1841 when the tribesmen broke away from their maliks and selected new leaders. Religion, it seemed, was still the one factor which could briefly overcome tribal divisions and, when skilfully exploited by the tribal religious leaders and by the Barakzai of Jalalabad, give a greater direction and unity to tribal policy than any other factor. But in the end the divided character of Pathan tribal organisation defeated the efforts both of the British to subdue the tribes and of the maliks, religious leaders and Barakzai to manipulate them. Like the jellyfish, the absence of a backbone to be broken was the greatest defence of the tribes against the waves of state power which beat upon them.

To destroy a tribe a state must first create it. Such appears to be the conclusion to which this chapter leads. Of course, like many paradoxes, the statement conceals a double meaning. Translated into anthropologists' jargon it would read: to destroy a segmentary lineage system a state must first convert it into a chiefly polity. And in this form the statement brings us back to the question that was raised earlier concerning the natures of states and of their objectives in their dealings with tribes. It was then suggested that what might be a suitable comment on the British state's attitude to tribes would not do for other states. But the British attitude more closely represents that of the modern state and its concept of itself in relation to its citizens and to other states.

The period with which we have been concerned was too short a time span in which to observe the full development of British policy towards the Pathans, but even in that brief period the desire to create an hierarchical structure of authority in the tribe is perceptible. Two modes were employed: to create chiefs and to work through the jirga. The second mode, which was used extensively in later years, appears to offer a compromise through which the tribe may retain its acephalous character and the state may secure the influence it desires, but the jirga system would not bear the weight of authority placed upon it and would not serve the purposes of the British. So long as the tribe is placed on an innocuous frontier the acephalous system may pass, but a modern state cannot tolerate jellyfish tribes in its midst or on those frontiers that are affected by the operation of the international state system. Jellyfish tribes challenge the modern state's concept of proper organisation, menace its prestige, and threaten its security. They may be destroyed, preserved in cocoons as curiosities, or converted into something different. A hierarchical system is something different; with that a state can live.

NOTES

1. There are many descriptions of the Khyber. One contemporary with the period considered in this chapter is R. Leech, Memo 1 Oct. 1837, India Office Records, Encl. to Secret Letters (ESL) Vol. 48, Encl. No. 30 of dispatch No. 1 of 8 Feb. 1838. (Since the notes on which this chapter is based were taken, this series has been included in the series entitled Letters Political and Secret and renumbered; there is no difficulty however in finding the corresponding volume numbers, so I have not troubled to change my references.) A convenient description of the Khyber is that in the article KHAIBAR in C.M. Macgregor (comp.), *Central Asia Part I. The North West Frontier of British India* (Calcutta, 1873). Macgregor included the more open area at the western end of the Khyber, giving an approximate length of 33 miles. I rejected this definition partly on physical grounds but also because it would have involved a consideration of British

policy towards the Mohmand and introduced a number of complications so as to extend the chapter beyond all reason. It will
be noted that the definition employed here places the Pass
wholly in modern Pakistan. At the time with which the chapter
is concerned the Pass was wholly within Afghanistan; ownership
changed in consequence of the Second Anglo-Afghan War of 1878-
80, when the Khyber was annexed to British India. One would
have thought that by no stretch of the imagination could the
Khyber be placed in Afghanistan between Jalalabad and Kabul,
but that feat was recently accomplished by at least one newspaper correspondent.

2.   In this chapter the term 'confederation' is used to
signify units such as Afridi, Orakzai and Shinwari; 'tribe'
for the main subdivisions of these units; and 'clan' for the
primary subsections of these subdivisions. The term *'khel'* is
used indigenously for all divisions below that of the confederation.

3.   See Sir F.J. Goldsmid, *James Outram*, (Smith, Elder,
London, 1881), vol. 1, pp. 51-115; Sir J. Malcolm, *Report on
the Province of Malwa* (Calcutta, 1927), pp. 395-6; Sir J. Kaye,
The Administration of the East India Company (Bentley, London,
1853), pp. 463-92; W.W. Hunter, *The Indian Empire* (Trübner,
London, 1882), pp. 86-8.

4.   H.W. Bellew, *The Races of Afghanistan* (Thacker,
London, Calcutta, 1908), p. 82. Similar views were expressed
by Macgregor, *Central Asia*; W. Moorcroft and G. Trebeck,
Travels in the Himalayan Provinces, etc. (London, 1838), vol.
2, p. 348; and A. Burnes, *Travels to Bukhara, etc.* (London,
1834), vol. 1, p. 113.

5.   M. Elphinstone, *An Account of the Kingdom of Caubul*
(London, 1838), vol. 1, pp. 197-9. Similar views expressed by
J. Wood, *A Journey to the Source of the Oxus* (Murray, London,
1872), p. 99.

6.   C. Masson, *Narrative of Various Travels, etc.* (London,
1842), vol. 1, p. 162.

7.   On Sayyid Ahmad see Qeyamuddin Ahmad, *The Wahabi
Movement in India* (Mukhopadhyay, Calcutta, 1966), containing
a useful survey of the sources.

8.   Report by A. Burnes on the Political Power of the
Sikhs West of the Indus, 8 Sept. 1837, ESL 48, No. 45 of No. 4
of 21 Feb. 1838.

9.   Masson, *Narrative*, vol. 3, pp. 328-411; J. Harlan,
A Memoir of India and Afghanistan (Philadelphia, 1842), pp.
162-4; N.K. Sinha, *Ranjit Singh* (University of Calcutta, 1933),
pp. 94-100; Mohan Lal, *Life of Dost Muhammad Khan* (London,
1846), vol. 1, pp. 172-83; Mackeson to Wade, 24 Oct. 1837,
ESL 68, No. 71 of No. 1 of 8 Feb. 1838; Masson to Wade, 31 Mar.
1837, ESL 47, No. 20 of No. 22 of 27 Dec. 1837; Masson to Wade,
17 Apr. 1837, No. 26; Wade to Macnaghten, 25 June 1837, No.
28; Masson to Wade, 7 May 1837, No. 39, and 18 and 19 May 1837,
No. 43.

10. On the origins and course of the First Anglo-Afghan War see: J. Kaye, *History of the War in Afghanistan* (London, 1858); H.M. Durand, *The First Afghan War* (London, 1879); J.A. Norris, *The First Afghan War* (Cambridge University Press, 1967); M.E. Yapp, *Strategies of British India* (Clarendon, Oxford, 1980).

11. Mackeson to Macnaghten, 3 May 1842, ESL 69, No. 23 of No. 72 of 6 July 1840.

12. See Yapp, *Strategies*.

13. Lord to Wade (pte), 14 Dec. 1838, ESL 58, No. 18 of 11 July 1839 (PC).

14. Masson, Statement, IOL, EM 642 f. 126.

15. Shahamat Ali, *Sikhs and Afghans* (London, 1849), p. 292.

16. Colvin to Wade (pte), 22 Nov. 1838, Br.Lib. Add.Ms. 37694 f. 127.

17. The best account of these operations is in W. Barr, *Journal of a March, etc.* (London, 1844).

18. Wade to Macnaghten, 28 Oct. 1839, Wade to Maddock, 28 Oct. 1839, ESL 67, No. 223 of No. 28 of 13 Apr. 1840.

19. Mackeson was held in high esteem by all who had deal-ings with him. See for example the comments of George Clerk, with whom he had serious policy differences: Clerk to Maddock, 3 Jan. 1843, ESL 91, No. 47 of No. 6 of 20 Jan. 1843.

20. Macnaghten to Mackeson, 12 Oct. 1839, ESL 66, No. 43 of No. 9 of 10 Feb. 1840.

21. There is an account of these disturbances in H. Havelock, *Narrative of the War in Afghanistan* (London, 1840), vol. 2, pp. 192-226.

22. Mackeson to Macnaghten, 7 Dec. 1839, ESL 64, No. 3 of No. 9 of 13 Jan. 1840.

23. Same to same, 3 Jan. 1840, ESL 69, No. 44 of No. 67 of 16 June 1840.

24. Same to same, 8 July 1840, ESL 70, No. 123 of No. 85 of 10 Aug. 1840.

25. Macnaghten to Maddock, 7 Dec. 1840, ESL 74, No. 70 of No. 4 of 21 Jan. 1841.

26. Same to same, 8 Apr. 1841 and enclosures, ESL 78, No. 54 of No. 58 of 8 July 1941.

27. Capt. H. Burn to Macgregor, 5 Jan. 1840, ESL 66, No. 14 of No. 23 of 16 Mar. 1840.

28. Brigadier J. Anquetil, Report and enclosures, 20 Apr. 1841, ESL 78, No. 47 of No. 58 of 8 July 1841.

29. Burn to C. Troup, 18 May 1841, ibid.

30. G. Lawrence to Anquetil, 22 May 1841, ibid.

31. Mackeson to Macnaghten, 21 Mar. 1840, ESL 69, No. 7 of No. 64 of 8 June 1840.

32. Same to same, 21 Jan. 1840, ibid.

33. Same to same, 3 Mar. 1840, ESL 69, No. 19 of No. 68 of 22 June 1840.

34. Same to same, 28 Mar. 1840, ESL 69, No. 25 of No. 64 of 8 June 1840.

35. Peshawar Akhbar, 27 Mar. 1840, ESL 68, No. 38 of
No. 44 of 8 May 1840.
36. Mackeson to Macnaghten, 6 July 1841, ESL 80, No. 44
of No. 79 of 20 Sept. 1841.
37. Same to same, 17 Jan. 1840, ESL 66, No. 22 of No. 23
of 16 Mar. 1840.
38. Same to same, 21 Jan. 1840, 13 Apr. 1840, 18 Apr.
1840, ESL 70, No. 2 of No. 82 of 10 Aug. 1840.
39. Same to same, 7 Mar. 1840, ESL 69, No. 18 of No. 68
of 22 June 1840.
40. Same to same, 5 May 1840, ESL 69, No. 21 of No. 72
of 6 July 1840.
41. Ibid.
42. Peshawar Intelligence, 31 July - 3 Aug. 1840, ESL 71.
43. Mackeson to Macnaghten, 12 Aug. 1840, ESL 72, No. 56
of No. 124 of 16 Nov. 1840.
44. Ibid.
45. Same to same, 6 July 1841, ESL 80, No. 44 of No. 79
of 20 Sept. 1841.
46. Same to same, 5 Aug. 1841, ESL 80, No. 45A of No. 79
of 20 Sept. 1841.
47. Mackeson to Clerk 17 Oct. 1841, ESL 80, No. 20 of
No. 96 of 20 Nov. 1841. Khan Bahadur Khan had a status which
went beyond the Afridi arena. He had resided at court before
1818 and Shuja had married one of his daughters.
48. Mackeson to Macnaghten, 28 July 1841, ESL 80, No. 40
of No. 88 of 21 Oct. 1841.
49. It is interesting to note that the Shii religious
leader, Sayyid Madad Gul, who was influential in the Gar
faction, who had been sympathetic to the British cause, and
whose son was to receive a British pension, and who therefore
might have been expected to support Alam, remained neutral in
the dispute.
50. Mackeson to Macnaghten, 6 Oct. 1841, ESL 80, No. 13
of No. 96 of 20 Nov. 1841. This claim should not be taken
seriously; neither the Afridi nor the Orakzai were dependent
upon the subsidies for subsistence.
51. Same to same, 9 Jan. 1840, ESL 66, No. 18 of No. 23
of 16 Mar. 1840.
52. Same to same, 6 June 1840, ESL 70, No. 43 of No. 85
of 10 Aug. 1840.
53. Same to same, 4 June, 1840, ibid.
54. Same to same, 20 June 1840, ibid., No. 91.
55. Same to same, 22 June 1940, ibid.
56. Same to same, 18 Aug. 1840, ESL 71, No. 39 of No. 112
of 16 Oct. 1840.
57. Same to same, 8 Jan. 1841, ESL 75, No. 30 of No. 19
of 21 Mar. 1841.
58. Macnaghten to Mackeson, 13 Jan. 1841, ESL 75, No. 30
of No. 19 of 21 Mar. 1841.

59. Mackeson to Macnaghten, 27 Jan. 1841, ESL 75, No. 32 of No. 19 of 21 Mar. 1841.

60. Same to same, 14 Feb. 1841, ESL 75, No. 33A of No. 19 of 21 Mar. 1841.

61. Same to same, 15 Feb. 1841, ibid.

62. Same to same, 17 Feb. 1841, ibid.

63. Shelton to Macnaghten, 19 Feb. 1841, ibid.

64. Details of expedition in Shelton to K. Elphinstone, 24 Feb. 1841, 15 Feb. 1841, 28 Feb. 1841, ibid. Nos. 33B and 33C; and Shelton to Macnaghten, 14 Mar. 1841, ESL 75, No. 52 of No. 34 of 22 Apr. 1841.

65. Mackeson to Macnaghten, 1 Mar. 1841, ESL 75, No. 43 of No. 34 of 22 Apr. 1841.

66. Same to same, 22 Mar. 1841, ESL 76, No. 22 of No. 37 of 12 May 1841.

67. Same to same, 20 Nov. 1841, ESL 81, No. 47 of No. 109 of 22 Dec. 1841; Ferris to G. Lawrence, 22 Nov. 1841, ESL 81, No. 64 of No. 109 of 22 Dec. 1841.

68. Mackeson to Maddock, 28 Nov. 1841, ESL 81, No. 55 of No. 109 of 22 Dec. 1841.

69. Mackeson to Clerk, 24 Dec. 1841, 25 Dec. 1841, 26 Dec. 1841, 2 Jan. 1842, ESL 82, Nos. 10, 11 and 16 of No. 9 of 22 Jan. 1842.

70. Mackeson to G. Pollock, 10 Mar. 1842, ESL 85, No. 9 of No. 3 of 21 Apr. 1842.

71. Mackeson to H. Lawrence, 20 Jan. 1842, 21 Jan. 1842, ESL 83, No. 55 of No. 16 of 19 Feb. 1842.

72. Mackeson to Maddock, 27 Jan. 1842, ESL 83, No. 78 of No. 16 of 19 Feb. 1842.

73. Macnaghten to Pollock, 10 Mar. 1842, ESL 85, No. 9 of No. 3 of 21 Apr. 1842.

74. Mackeson to Pollock, n.d., ca. 2 Apr. 1842, ESL 85, No. 15 of No. 3 of 21 Apr. 1842.

75. Same to same, 17 Apr. 1842, ESL 86, No. 7 of No. 14 of 17 May 1842.

76. Pollock to Maddock, n.d. Apr. 1842, ESL 85, Agra Letter 23 Apr. 1842.

77. Mackeson to Pollock, 6 May 1842, ESL 86, No. 17 of No. 15 of 8 June 1842.

Chapter 5
TRIBES AND STATES IN WAZIRISTAN

Akbar S. Ahmed

Introduction: Buffer Zones and the Great Game

The aim of this chapter is to examine certain underlying principles in the complex relationship between
tribes and states on the frontier between Afghanistan
and Pakistan (or before 1947, British India). The
relationship is not of war or peace, black or white,
but rather shades of grey, and reflects the continuing socio-political dynamics of a situation peculiar
to the region. The chapter will attempt to explain in
a historical perspective the continued relevance of
the relation between tribes and states in the region;
to assess the effects of the state and its policies
on tribal economics, culture and political organisation, using concepts such as 'encapsulation';[1] to
identify what elements of tribal culture (in the
broadest sense) can be interpreted as reflecting
attitudes to or interaction with the state as a
source of political, cultural or religious authority
and orthodoxy; and to show how differing social
systems, although juxtaposed or connected, manage to
coexist and maintain their separate identities and
structures within larger administrative frameworks.
I shall examine these problems of tribe and state in
my role as an anthropologist working in the Tribal
Areas of the North West Frontier Province (NWFP) of
Pakistan, with special reference to Waziristan, the
area I have recently held in my charge as Political
Agent.
    A major question that emerges, is why the
Tribal Areas were loosely incorporated but not quite
absorbed, encapsulated but not integrated, into the
British Indian structure, and left undisturbed by
contrast with the creation elsewhere of 'feudal'
estates and even small quasi-autonomous dependant
states such as Swat. The answer is not to be sought

merely in the context of the administrative frameworks and military manoeuvres of states, but rather
in the nature of the expansionist aims, policies and
strategies which led to the Great Game, that is the
competition between Russia and Britain in Central
and Southern Asia, particularly in relation to the
intervening state of Afghanistan.

For the British, the Game was an extension of
the Public School ethos of upper-middle-class
Victorian England. It involved worthy players,
referees, rules and limits. It was cast in the
mock-heroic mould and posture of Empire, with associated concepts of 'honour' and 'glory', and with a
dash of intrigue and danger in the service of 'Queen
and Country'. The mystique of the Game and its participants was increased by the creation of the NWFP
in 1901 by Lord Curzon, the champion of Empire, and
by the literary productions of Kipling, its minstrel;
and the nature of the Game provided some of the most
evocative and popular writing of Empire, specially
exemplified in works such as Kim.[2]

But the players were not only mighty empires;
the Game took place, in fact, on three levels: at
the level of competition between the Empires; at
the level of relations between either of the imperial
powers and the intervening buffer state, Afghanistan;
and at the level where the empires tried to influence, control and use the individual tribal groups
that occupied the low production zones along the
central mountain regions dividing the states and
empires from each other. Such tribes, matching
heavy artillery and eventually air bombardment with
dated but deadly .303 rifles, could stop and destroy
entire battalions sent by the imperial powers. The
best plays in the game involved moving pawns on the
board without actually having either to escalate the
Game into a full-scale war or to commit any important pieces. On the Central Asian board, however,
pawns often moved of their own volition - and sometimes it seemed more expedient to lose a king than a
pawn.

The tribes did not see themselves as playing
either the British, or the Russian, or the Afghan
game; they were simply playing their own game. It
may not have been on the same scale as the Great
Game, with major campaigns, air action, large-scale
expenditure and organisation and sophisticated
logistics, but it was certainly played with the bril-
liance of born tacticians, and enabled them to remain
independent at a crucial period in one of the most
important regions of Asia. A Mahsud malik (headman)

summed up the essence of the Game to me succinctly:
'We are like men with two jealous wives - both pulling us in different directions; sometimes we prefer
one, sometimes the other.' Such a statement would
indubitably have angered the Colonial Secretary at
Delhi, who would have assumed he was calling the
cards.

A series of policies towards the trans-Indus
areas, including the NWFP, that emanated from Delhi
over the last century, reflected conflicting minds
and changing circumstances. The 'Masterly Inactivity'
of mid-century was followed by a greater show of
interest through 'Conciliatory Intervention' and led
to the tougher 'Close Border Policy' and finally the
aggressive 'Forward Policy'.[3] While Afghanistan
came to be treated as the buffer between the two
Empires, the British found it convenient also to
keep a buffer zone between them and Afghanistan. A
somewhat unusual situation developed. Buffer zones,
shatter zones, scorched-earth policies and the like
are common in the history of empires but not so common in the case of vigorous, aggressive and expanding empires such as the British in the last century.
After deliberations at the highest level, the border
was left purposely independent, in a defined zone, a
no-man's land, officially designated the Tribal
Areas, and the tribes were allowed to play their own
'little game' and to maintain a large degree of cultural and political autonomy, escaping integration
into the larger framework of Empire.

The establishment of the Durand Line in 1893
added a further dimension to the problem, and further
underlined the independence of the border tribes.

> The tribes between the administrative border
> and the Durand Line were a buffer to a buffer,
> and the Line had none of the rigidity of other
> international frontiers. The countries on
> either side of it had each to realize that any
> attempt to enlarge their influence with the
> tribes must excite the suspicions of the other.
> It was the usual British compromise, but there
> was no other acceptable solution and, consider-
> ing the complexity of the problem, it worked
> very well.[4]

However, the pious hope of international harmony
contained in the Durand agreement - 'The Government
of India will at no time exercise interference in
the territories lying beyond this Line on the side
of Afghanistan, and his Highness the Amir will at no

time exercise interference in the territories lying beyond this Line on the side of India'[5] - was rarely respected, and the Treaty was constantly broken on both sides.

The British relationship with Kabul was a function of politics in the Tribal Areas. It is seldom realised how close Kabul is to the Tribal Areas: some 50 miles from the border of the Kurram Agency, less than a day's journey by truck and bus. The situation in the Tribal Areas was also important for British strategy in the Great Game with Russia, the competition for influence in Afghanistan. In this, the British had the advantage over the Russians in the very nature of Pakhtun tribal organisation and the peculiar form of administration that was imposed among the tribes; for example, a tribal raid into Afghanistan could always officially be discouraged, disowned, or denounced by the British, when in fact a Political Agent might well be financing or even directing it.[6]

Although it is accepted that 'The border tribes have always played an important role in determining who was to hold power in Afghanistan',[7] the Tribal Areas were a mixed asset to the British, and kept them anxious and alert. On balance, however, they could always use the tribes to cause trouble for Kabul across the Durand Line.

Culture and Society in the Tribal Areas

It is important to distinguish the peoples of the Tribal Areas from those of the Settled Areas of the NWFP. From the late 1890s, when the British incorporated the tribes that lived along the Durand Line into what they called the Tribal Agencies or the Tribal Areas, no civil, criminal or judicial procedure codes were applied to them. This was agreed to in written treaties signed by jirgas, councils of elders representing the tribes, and by the state. For instance, a man who committed homicide in broad daylight and in front of witnesses in the Tribal Areas would not be tried according to laws prevalent in the rest of British India (including the Settled Areas) but according to Pakhtunwali,[8] the customary and traditional Code of the Pakhtuns, as interpreted by the jirga; a man even today can shoot his wife or cousin with impunity according to Pakhtunwali, and still remain outside the laws that prevail in the rest of Pakistan. This fundamental difference between the Tribal and Settled Areas has wide ramifica-

tions in the social and political organisation of
the peoples concerned. The Tribal Areas present an
exceptional, perhaps unique example of a no-man's
land that has existed almost until today - and has
been called 'the last free place on earth'.[9]
    In previous studies, I have suggested that for
heuristic purposes Pakhtun peoples of the NWFP may
be generally divided into two categories of society,
dominated by two distinct models: one is a system of
acephalous, segmentary, egalitarian groups associated with low-production zones, the other a system of
ranked groups with super- and subordinate social
positions, associated with irrigated lands. The key
feature of the former category of society is nang
(honour), as qalang (taxes and rents) is of the
latter. For convenience I shall refer to tribes or
tribesmen as nang or qalang, according to which model
dominates their society.[10]
    It is important to stress that nang tribesmen,
unlike tribesmen elsewhere in South Asia who have
been subjected and incorporated into the larger
state, do not suffer a sense of economic suppression
and cultural humiliation. In the NWFP Tribal Areas,
for historical and geographical reasons, the tribesmen has always emerged as one who has held his own
against any larger state system, whether Mughal,
Sikh or British. What is more important in sociological terms, he is acutely aware of his independence
and the factors responsible for it; he is inclined
to play upon his own reputation for courage and
honour to emphasise his ethnic uniqueness on the
Subcontinent. The 'man-to-man' attitude of the
Pakhtun tribesman has led to a certain romanticisa-[11]
tion and mystification of his character and history.
    The history of the nang tribes of the Tribal
Areas tells of their accompanying successful armies
to India but being unable to establish empires. On
their own ground, they have resisted Mughals, Sikhs
and British, three of the most powerful empires of
South Asia, but they have not been able to organise
dynasties of their own. The contrast to the qalang
tribes, who have invaded India and provided Delhi
with at least six Pakhtun dynasties, reflects the
general discipline, organisation and pyramidal authority structure of the qalang system.[12]
    The reasons why the nang tribes did not esta-
blish themselves politically or militarily on the
larger stage of India around Delhi or Bengal over
the last centuries, lie in part in the structure and
organisation of the tribes, and in the economic and
ecological limitations on such adventures. Military

movements among the nang tribes are not, for instance, patterned on Ibn Khaldun's model of cyclical emergence of tribal elites, like the Berbers who come down from the hills fresh with 'tribal solidarity' (asabiya) to settle and start new dynasties only to degenerate over three generations and become vulnerable to conquest by fresher tribal stock.[13] During military encounters in the Tribal Areas, the aim is neither to occupy nor to settle remote lands. The establishment of a dynasty is discounted by the pervasive cultural principle of jealousy and rivalry between paternal cousins (tarburwali). A typical clash, invariably as a climax to tarburwali, is a short raid, usually at sunrise or sunset, culminating in the capture of the village or booty like cattle. The glory of participation in an encounter, not the setting up of a dynasty or the lengthy involvement with administration that it implies, is the motivating factor. For example, all the major raids from the Tribal Areas over the last hundred years, whether to Kabul or to Kashmir, have been characterised by their blitzkrieg nature, by their swift irresistible penetration and by the rapid inevitable disintegration of the war party (lashkar). Often the Pakhtun warrior will simply pack up and leave after a hard day's fighting, without co-ordination with or command from the lashkar.

The individualistic approach of the Frontier tribesmen to battle, and indeed to life, was familiar to British officers serving in the NWFP. For example, in the late 1930s, Colonel Pettigrew, in the course of a patrol to cover an engineer road reconnaissance, found himself on the site of an encounter between Mahsud and British forces in the campaign of 1920. On the top of a hill whose capture by the British was officially said to have been due to surprise, he met an ancient Mahsud. He asked him if he had been in the fighting.

> 'Of course, that is my house over there.'
> 'Then tell me, why didn't you fight hard to hold the ridge?' He shrugged his shoulders, hands palm upwards, a smile showing through his thick, untidy beard. 'It was freezing. There had been snow, and we were hungry and cold, so we went away.'[14]

This independent and highly democratic attitude to tribal war, characteristic of tribesmen in the nang category, is I suggest a direct reflection of tribal organisation.

There are some further significant aspects of
warfare as a relationship between tribe and state in
this region. First, tribal war is 'seasonal': it is
invariably linked with the pattern of crops and cultivation. Engagements tend to be fought before or
after the harvest and many a leader has discovered
to his dismay that his followers have melted away at
the climax of a battle if the current crop has to
be harvested.[15] Secondly, tribal warfare is short
and quick. The nature of their mountainous terrain
and their tribal organisation enable the tribesmen,
ideally, to harass an invading state army of superior logistical and economic power, and to hit back
in incessant guerrilla raids, but the logistic problems prevent them from sustaining a movement for
any length of time, especially outside their territory. British soldiers who fought the Mahsud
observed, like Pettigrew, that 'the Mahsud likes his
victories to be quick. He has no stomach or patience
for long drawn out affairs'.[16] The short-term
aspect of tribal warfare is also related to the inherent structural democracy of tribal organisation.
The people who inhabit the areas on both sides of
the Durand line are organised in segmentary societies that are acephalous and egalitarian in the
extreme, and by definition it is difficult for them
to accept the leadership of one man over any period
of time. I have shown elsewhere how in extraordinary times of crisis, particularly involving
concepts of religious war (jihad), religious leaders
have successfully united tribes against the British.
This has always proved to be a short-term social and
military unit, and once the fighting is over the
tribal groups tend to disperse, leadership reverts
to the level of maliks, and society to what has been
termed 'ordered anarchy'.[17]
     Two fundamental features of nang Pakhtun tribal
structure are crucial to an anthropological understanding of these aspects of tribal warfare. These
are agnatic rivalry (tarburwali) and an intense
egalitarian ethos. Both features are connected, in
a fashion which makes it difficult to sustain any
tribal movements for long or under the leadership of
one man. Although there have been successful forays
and even swift victories over neighbouring states
and established armies, the very nature of their
organisation prevents tribes from consummating victory or setting up an independent administration of
their own. Too often, like the old Mahsud who spoke
to Pettigrew, the tribesmen will fight a good day's
fight and leave for home without orders or co-

ordination within the larger context of the battle.
These two tribal features, tarburwali and tribal
democracy, are key factors determining success or
failure in relationships between the tribe and the
state within this region.

In terms of the historical relationship between
tribe and state, the former has been the constant,
the latter the unstable factor. Empires have risen
and fallen over the centuries, while tribal society
has to a large degree maintained its political
boundaries and safeguarded its social and cultural
traditions. Incorporation into the British Empire
made little impact on the tribes in the Tribal Areas,
who continued in their intransigence and persistent
defiance of central authority. The spirit of tribal
independence was never checked by the British, however savage the measures they took.[18] Although the
British were manipulating the tribes to their own
purposes in embarrassing Afghanistan, their turbulence and democracy made them a dangerous weapon,
unsafe to handle.

The Treaties that were signed at the earliest
period of contact between nang tribes like the Wazir
and the imperial state, were fundamentally different
in nature, content and tone from those involving
qalang leaders representing emergent, quasi-
autonomous states such as Swat. The British signed
treaties with the Wali of Swat, the Mehtar of
Chitral, the Nawabs of Amb and Dir, subsequently
ratified by the Government of Pakistan,[19] clearly
specifying terms and conditions, rights and duties
of the Rulers. All important matters such as defence, external affairs, religious matters, would be
the direct concern of the Central Government. By
contrast, treaties with the nang tribes do not
reflect the confrontation of a superior power with a
subjugated or defeated people. Indeed, there are
underlying and not very subtle notes that make the
treaties worth less than the paper they were written
on. For example, promises to 'behave' and forgo
raiding were entirely conditional on the regular
payment of allowances.

Thus of 5 April 1902 an agreement with a jirga
representing the Mahsud stipulated that the tribe
'will be of good conduct and commit no offences in
areas occupied by Government, that is to say districts like Bannu, Dera Ismail Khan, the Sherani
country, or Wana or the Tochi, or roads like the
Gomal or other trade routes'. The area where
'offences' could be committed is immense and left
undefined. The British promised to pay the tribe

Rs.54,000, to be distributed according to <u>nikat</u> (hereditary right), one third each to the <u>three</u> Mahsud clans, Alizai, Bahlolzai, and Shamankhel. The promises of good conduct were made 'in consideration of these allowances'.[20] In political terms, such treaties were intended to prevent the tribes from raiding into British India, an intention so often frustrated as almost to deprive them of legal stature.

Treaties with the nang tribes quite specifically stipulate that the tribesmen would be allowed to administer their own territory and organise their social and economic life just as they had in the past according to custom and tradition. They would, however, in a rather ambiguous and not clearly defined manner, accept the fact that they now belonged to a larger entity called British India, though the clause that they formed part of a 'special area' within that entity was clearly underlined. Pax Britannica in the Tribal Areas was to extend to the main roads and a hundred yards either side of it, and no more. The state, that is the most powerful empire at the turn of the century, thus for various historical and strategic reasons, tolerated a buffer zone stretching from Bajaur to South Waziristan Agency, almost entirely inhabited by what I have described as nang tribes. This situation in itself contributed to the continuation of the Great Game, and added a dimension to its complexity.

Waziristan and the Wazir Tribes

Waziristan is divided into two Agencies, North and South Waziristan, and probably falls into a special category as the most turbulent area on the Sub-continent, even within the special category of the Tribal Areas, as testified by the literature in which solutions to the problem are offered.[21] About half the Wazir tribes are located in Afghanistan (Birmal and Matun) and half in Pakistan (North and South Waziristan Agencies). These tribes seldom recognise the existence of the international border as a legal reality, and movement between the two countries among related clans is unrestricted. Movement for trade or raid from either side is facilitated by the fact that surveillance of the border is practically impossible. In the summer of 1979, with a large company of Wazir maliks, I became the first Political Agent to visit Birmal right up to the Durand Line. The impact of this visit was momentous.

Wazir fighting near Kabul with the Mujahidin, religious resistance against the Soviet-backed regime, took time off to write to congratulate me - showing their awareness that their last sanctuary had finally been penetrated.

This was the only area on the entire Subcontinent to be at one stage directly administered by the Central High Command of the Indian Army. Up to 31 March 1924 it was considered to be an 'action service area', and political authority was vested in the force commander, advised of course by political officers. The numbers of civil and military officers killed in Waziristan must be some sort of an imperial record: five of the 35 Political Agents (heads of Administration) from 1895 to 1947 died violently on duty there. By 1923, 17 crack British battalions were posted in Waziristan, as well as para-military forces, the South Waziristan Scouts (for South Waziristan) and the Tochi Scouts (for North Waziristan) - about 2,000 men in each corps. During the 1930s, there were 28 battalions in Waziristan - more troops than on the rest of the Sub-continent. Such unusually large numbers were necessary to 'hold' Waziristan and its tribes, who were in constant rebellion and a formidable force on their own ground. The 1919-21 campaign, following the Third Anglo-Afghan War, saw the heaviest fighting the British ever experienced on the Frontier, and in the Ahnai Tangi battle the Mahsud Wazir inflicted over 2,000 casualties on the British forces.[22]

North and South Waziristan Agencies, totalling about 5,000 square miles of highly inhospitable mountainous country, broken by ravines and valleys almost inaccessible through lack of roads, have rarely been penetrated by outside armies. According to the latest census data, based on rough 'estimates', the population is about 550,000, of which about 250,000 are Mahsud (entirely in South Waziristan) and about 200,000 Wazir; the remaining 100,000 are Daur and other smaller tribes such as Suleyman Khel and Dotani.[23]

The Wazir and Mahsud, the two major tribal groups, are cousins, descended from Karlanri, a son of the Pakhtun apical ancestor Qays Abd al-Rashid. Both Wazir and Mahsud trace their descent through some 13 to 14 generations to Wazir, who is said to have lived in the sixteenth century. It is only recently that Mahsud have adopted an independent identity, dropping the appellation Wazir from their names: until a few decades ago they were commonly known as 'Mahsud Wazir'.

The political organisation of both tribes may
be summarised as acephalous, egalitarian and segmentary. They approximate closely to the nang category
of Pakhtun society. Wazir and Mahsud society is
'democratic' and all major decisions are made through
the jirga, where each household head, elder (mashar)
or headman (malik) speaks his mind openly and may,
if he wishes to disagree with the final verdict,
even refuse to go along with the communal decision.
The malik's status and strength in society depend on
two factors: his individual reputation for leadership qualities, especially wisdom and courage, and
the number of guns he can muster in his support,
usually those of close paternal relatives. Rarely
do such headmen tower above the tribal section or
sub-section in leadership. The possibility of accu-
mulating wealth and thereby armed henchmen is mini-
mised by the restricted economic base.

Land holdings are small and population scattered. In any case, the nature of the rain-fed (barani)
land, and the system of inheritance, do not permit
accumulation of large holdings and therefore do not
provide the means for any one man to emerge with
significant economic or political power over his
fellow-men.

In what way was Waziristan different, and the
tribes living there more difficult to administer
than others in the Tribal Areas, such as the Afridi
and Mohmand, themselves famous for their martial
qualities? Various answers may be suggested. First,
Waziristan is the only area which borders not only
Afghanistan but also the Province of Baluchistan,
both of which provide ideal escape routes after
raids. Secondly, the tribes are well-armed. In
1924, 'according to the latest return the armament
of the tribes of Waziristan, apart from other weapons, comprises 10,880 bolt action weapons of .303
bore, of which 6,850 are said to be in Mahsud
hands'.[24] Moreover, they know how to use their
weapons. Generals who have commanded troops against
him 'place the Mahsud highest as a fighter'[25] in the
Tribal Areas. Thirdly, this is physically the
largest area, and South Waziristan the largest Agency
in the Tribal Areas, and contains possibly the most
difficult terrain in the entire region. Fourthly,
·Waziristan has no fertile valleys that might attract
an invader to shed blood in an attempt at conquest.
Finally, it was remote in terms of distance, whether
by road or rail, from centres of British military
concentration such as the cantonments at Peshawar,
Kohat, Mardan or Nowshera. Waziristan is not on the

main routes into India such as the Khyber, and hence
no Alexander, Timur or Babur have had to cross or
attempt to settle it.

The Wazir Tribes between Afghanistan and British India

In 1849 the British conquered the trans-Indus
Districts from the Sikhs and occupied Peshawar. They
soon came to realise the special relationship between
the Frontier tribes and the Afghan Government: 'The
sentiments and tendencies of such characters are
naturally antagonistic to our rule, and they can
only resort to Kabul for encouragement to persist
in them.'[26]
    It was only after the famous attack on Tank
(the winter headquarters of South Waziristan) by the
Mahsud in 1860, that Neville Chamberlain was ordered
to lead a field force, composed entirely of British
Indian troops, into Waziristan. He advanced to
Jandola and the Takkizam, and returned down the
Khaysora to Bannu, having marched for 16 days through
country no foreigner had ever seen or dared to enter
before. His force consisted of three squadrons of
cavalry, 13 mountain guns, and nine infantry battalions. There were in addition some 1600 tribal
levies under their maliks and khans. It was the
most formidable fighting machine ever assembled in
the area, and the first time in history that an
army had marched into Waziristan. Considerable
damage was done to the Mahsud, but no formal surrender was achieved.[27]
    Fearing the aims of the British in their terri-
tory, the Mahsud had sent urgent deputations to
Kabul appealing for help, on the grounds that the
British were annexing their territory. The memory
of the First Afghan War had still not faded in
Afghanistan, however, and the country was in no immediate mood for further military adventures.
    Afghan-British interests in Waziristan continued
over the century with varying fortunes. The Afghan
Government came to cultivate leaders from Waziristan
assiduously, and after the Third Anglo-Afghan War in
1919 treated them with an extra show of respect: 'On
their arrival at the capital [Kabul] the Maliks were
received by the Amir in person with every mark of
honour and conducted to a sarai [guest-house] which
had been reserved specially for their use.' Marks
of honour were bestowed on the Waziristan tribes to
enlist and confirm their sympathy:

> Subsequently the Amir issued rewards and pre-
> sented medals to the Maliks. The latter was
> similar to those issued to his own troops for
> the recent operations against the British. Of
> the officers who had deserted from the militias
> each received a special award of Rs.300 and the
> sepoys Rs.100.[28]

As late as 1920 Wana (summer headquarters of South
Waziristan) was occupied by a small Afghan contingent, though a few months later a British force of
two infantry brigades advanced from Jandola through
the Shahur Tangi and retook the settlement; it was
then decided to occupy Wana permanently, and the
road through the Shahur Tangi to Wana was also constructed.[29]

A few years later the Afghan strategy began to
pay off, and their influence among the Wazir and
Mahsud tribesmen increased; two corps of Wazir militia with headquarters at Matun and Urgun were formed
with a nominal strength of 1200. Recruiting was
opened in July 1924, and by the end of August 400
had enlisted. Some of these Wazir and a larger number of the Mahsud militia distinguished themselves
in the fighting on the Turkistan frontier in the
northern provinces of Afghanistan, for which services
they received generous rewards.[30]

But the Indian Political Department and its
officers who manned the Tribal Areas still had a
trick or two up their sleeves and their opportunity
came when King Amanullah was deposed in 1929. It
was not difficult for an imaginative Political Agent
to suggest to the Waziristan tribes that there was
booty to be had in Kabul, and honour and glory
awaited them if they were to slip across the border
for a few days of adventure. In 1929 Mahsud and
Wazir crossed the border to Khost and joined Nadir
Khan in autumn at Matun. Caroe reminds us, in his
chapter on Waziristan, that 'This lashkar formed the
spear-head of Nadir's advance; it was they who took
Kabul for him and made it possible for a Durrani
dynasty to be restored. They were in fact the King-
makers of the day.'[31] Since then they have never
ceased to remind the rulers of Kabul of their chief
share in that conquest.

As payment to Wazir and Mahsud tribesmen, Nadir
Khan, faced with an empty treasury, was forced to
allow them to loot his own capital. These tribesmen
returned home by the end of the year with a great
amount of loot, rifles and ammunition. Shortly
after, an insurrection almost in the suburbs of

Kabul among the followers of the dead Bacha Saqao forced Nadir Khan once again to call the Pakhtun tribes to his support. This time he was able to get them home without having to let them loot Kabul in recompense. Within a few years the same tribesmen were denouncing Nadir Khan and arguing that they had supported him only for the purpose of restoring Amanullah, the rightful King. The Waziristan tribes, aware that 'King-makers can as easily be King-breakers',[32] felt ready for yet another exercise in King-making and gathering of booty in addition. In 1933 they invested Matun in Khost and it was only with great difficulty that the Afghan army, led by Hashim Khan, the King's brother, repelled them, otherwise they might well have repeated the story of 1929.

The tribes were always a two-edged weapon. It was not long before other powers, attempting to fish in the troubled waters of the Tribal Areas, took advantage of the situation. In the later 1930s a young Syrian from the revered Jilani/Geylani family, popularly called the Shami Pir, was installed at Kaniguram in the heart of Waziristan, whence it was rumoured he would lead an opposition army, though whether against the British or to Kabul was not precisely clear. With the warclouds gathering in Europe the British could ill afford another Waziristan adventure. Wazir and Mahsud tribal lashkars began to collect, and the British could have found a rapidly growing insurrection in their own backyard had not some quick-witted Political Agent once again acted swiftly. The Shami Pir was persuaded to fly out of Waziristan, apparently the richer, it is estimated, by £20,000 in gold sovereigns. These lessons were not lost on Kabul. What £20,000 could stop, a similar or smaller sum could start. Afghan subsidies to the Pakhtun tribes, especially on the British side of the Durand Line, were stepped up, and khilats (robes of honour) were liberally distributed to visiting maliks in royal audiences in Kabul.

The final example of tribe-state interaction in Waziristan had the 1947 Partition of India as a backdrop. In 1947 the tribes showed that they had not lost their capacity for swift and brilliant strategic military movement against larger state systems and superior and established armies. Spontaneously and voluntarily, they moved in large numbers to the Muslim state of Kashmir, which was disputed between India and Pakistan and in a state of turmoil. Almost alone the Pakhtun lashkar swept aside the regular troops and came within an ace of conquering Kashmir.

They scattered battalions of Dogras, the crack
Kashmir regulars, and by 30 October were at Pattan,
18 miles from Srinagar. Sikh battalions of the
regular Indian army were flown in and reached the
Srinagar air-strip barely in time to deny it to the
tribesmen and allow troops to pour in from India.
It was only with the massive intervention of the
regular troops and their superior logistics, with
heavy armaments moved in by an all-out air-lift from
Delhi, that the situation was saved for the Indians.
Otherwise the tribesmen would have captured one of
the most important areas of the Sub-continent and
altered its subsequent destiny and history. Over
the next thirty years India and Pakistan were to
engage in three wars over Kashmir.

Although the main battle for Kashmir was fought
in the Vale, the raiders erupted into all parts of
the State. The distance from home, always an important factor in determining the length of their involvement, must be kept in mind. Srinagar is 290 miles
from Fort Jamrud at the entrance to the Khyber; it
is almost twice that distance from Razmak, in the
heart of Waziristan. It is interesting to conject-
ure how the classic syndrome of Waziri war tactics
would have affected their performance if the engagement had been protracted.

It is important to point out that Pakhtun
tribes on both sides of the Durand Line saw the
Kashmir adventure as a straightforward jihad, and
that many Wazir tribesmen from the remote Birmal
areas joined the lashkars, ethnic solidarity cutting
across the Durand Line. There is nostalgia even
today in the Tribal Areas regarding the Kashmir
episode, and maliks describe it thus: 'It was the
best time of my life. We went along singing and
holding our rifles. Nothing was able to stand before us.'[33] Section elders speaking on behalf of
jirgas meeting political officers in the Tribal
Areas even today invariably begin with: 'Sahib, we
have sacrificed everything for Pakistan. We fought
in Kashmir and lost kin and property. We have shed
blood for Islam and Pakistan. We have a right to
make demands.'

Spain's comment on the Kashmir jihad is particularly relevant in the context of the argument of
this chapter. 'Little attention has been paid to
this, and in it lies a key to the character of the
tribes and a demonstration of the limitations and
potentialities of their power'[34] - the 'limitations'
being the jealousies inspired by agnatic rivalries
in the tribal organisation, and the 'potentialities'

the formidable fighting prowess fired by a fierce
sense of independence.

Conclusion

The Mahsud maliks confronted, assessed and rejected
Western civilisation as represented by the British
Empire, and requested their Resident, Sir Evelyn
Howell, to 'let us be men like our fathers before
us'.[35] In the end perhaps one may well agree with
the comment on the political administration of
Waziristan made by a senior British official after
he read Howell's little classic, Mizh: 'What a
record of futility it all is!'[36] The ethnic, political and administrative problem of the Tribal Areas
remained as far from solution in 1947 as it had been
for a hundred years.
      The creation of the state of Pakistan in 1947
changed many things in the relationship between tribe
and state. The obvious rallying point for the tribes,
their rationale for raid and invasion, that is the
religious motive, was abruptly removed. After 1947,
to the south and east of the Durand Line it could no
longer be argued that incursions and kidnappings
were not directed against the Muslim local population but against the non-Muslim rulers of the land.
The Wazir and Mahsud did come down in large numbers
in 1947, but it was to take over the shops and bazaars left behind by the Hindus. Today Tank is
almost entirely occupied by Mahsud, who own a thriving transport business, from lands around the town,
and are gradually acquiring the ways of the Settled
Districts. The Wazir have moved to the settled
District headquarters of Bannu (from North Waziristan) and Dera Ismail Khan (from South Waziristan).
Both tribes still jealously maintain the independence
of their houses and lands in the Tribal Areas, and
are not prepared to lift the veil that still hangs
over their lives there. The forms of tribal administration and the patterns and rituals of tribal life
in the Tribal Areas still continue largely as if
nothing had changed.
      None the less, rapid changes are afoot, with
far-reaching social and economic implications. Today
there is a Mahsud Political Agent in the Tribal
Areas, a Mahsud General in the Pakistan army, and a
Mahsud Development Commissioner in charge of a
Province. Apart from these senior officials, thousands of other Wazir and Mahsud serve in various
Departments of the State of Pakistan. Service it-

self implies changes in life-style, changes in attitudes, and eventually changes in culture and tradition. Perhaps the social and geographical boundary between tribe and state will in the future be no longer as sharp as it was in the past, and therefore less strongly upheld, and the next generation may even see the final absorption of the tribes, their customs and traditions, into the states on both sides of the border.

When I ask Wazir and Mahsud whether they are 'men like their fathers before them' in the most profound sense, they invariably reply in the negative. 'No. We are now soft. We have become businessmen. We own shops in Tank and Dera Ismail Khan. We run transport buses. We cultivate lands in Districts (Bannu and Dera Ismail Khan) and we have given up the ways of our fathers.' Change is in the air. Schools, roads and services are bringing fundamental changes in cultural and social attitudes.

The tribes had been 'played with' by the states, but they had also 'played off' the states against each other; they managed to remain to a great extent unadministered and culturally intact. The relation of the tribes generally, and the Waziristan tribesmen in particular, to their adjacent nation-states, changed with the rather abrupt end of a round in the Great Game in 1947 when the British left the Sub-continent. The immediate consequences are that the tribesman in Pakistan sets the pace for integration in his relationship to the larger state, whether for economic development or political absorption as in the 1970s, but in an increasingly cordial relationship. Secondly, he finds his role in the old Great Game was radically changed by the departure of one player in 1947. The balance now appears palpably uneven. In addition, although their tribal structure is still largely intact in the Tribal Areas, economic developments, large-scale migration to the Gulf States, education, the acquisition of land in the Settled Areas, and involvement in administration and business in the rest of the country, will most certainly have affected tribal organisation and the martial spirit and attitudes of the tribesman. The last military adventure on any scale involving the Waziristan tribes was over 30 years ago, that is, a full generation. Whether the new generation is capable of emulating the independent spirit and martial qualities of their forefathers, or whether they consider that model worth shedding blood for, are questions that only history can answer. Even if the tribes wished to, perhaps they

could no longer fully play the Great Game with their
old élan and confidence. Tribes in Asia appear to
grow weaker in direct proportion as the states grow
stronger.[37]

NOTES

1. See F.G. Bailey, *Stratagems and Spoils* (Blackwell,
Oxford, 1969).
2. A.S. Ahmed, 'An aspect of the colonial encounter
in the NWFP', *Asian Affairs*, 9,3 (1978); id., 'The colonial
encounter on the NWFP: myth and mystification', in *Journal of
the Anthropological Society of Oxford*, 9, 3 (1978).
3. R.I. Bruce, *The Forward Policy and its Results*
(Longmans, London, 1900).
4. J.G. Elliott, *The Frontier 1839-1947: the story of
the North-West Frontier of India* (Cassell, London, 1968), p.53.
5. Point 2 of the Durand Agreement, signed in Kabul by
Amir Abd al-Rahman on 12 November 1893.
6. For instance, see the role of the political officers
as described by O. Caroe, *The Pathans, 550 BC - AD 1957*
(Macmillan, London, 1958); and E. Howell, *Mizh: a Monograph on
Government's Relations with the Mahsud Tribe* (Government of
India Press, Simla, 1931; reprinted with a foreword by A.S.
Ahmed, Oxford University Press, Karachi, 1979). Both Caroe
and Howell were political officers of note. For a topical
comment on political administration and the Great Game, in
which Caroe pays the highest possible compliment to the writer
as a Political Agent, see his review of the reprint of *Mizh,
Asian Affairs*, 11, 1 (1980).
7. J. Spain, *The Pathan Borderland* (Mouton, The Hague,
1963).
8. Generally defined as *melmastia* (hospitality), *badal*
(revenge), *nang* (honour) and *tora* (bravery). See Caroe, *The
Pathans;* Spain, *Borderland;* F. Barth, 'Pathan identity and its
maintenance', in F. Barth (ed.), *Ethnic Groups and Boundaries*
(Allen and Unwin, London, 1969); A.S. Ahmed, *Millenium and
Charisma among Pathans: a critical essay in Social Anthropology*
(Routledge and Kegan Paul, London, 1976); id., *Social and
Economic Change in the Tribal Areas* (Oxford University Press,
Karachi, 1977); id., *Pukhtun Economy and Society: Traditional
Structure and Economic Development in a Tribal Society*
(Routledge and Kegan Paul, London, 1980).
9. B. Moynahan, 'The Free Frontier: warriors of the
Khyber Pass', *Sunday Times Magazine,* 21 March 1976. See Ahmed,
works listed in note 8 above.
10. Ahmed, *Millenium,* etc.
11. See note 2.
12. The Yusufzais of Rampur, who ruled Rampur State,
trace their ancestry to Yusuf, the eponymous ancestor of the

qalang Yusufzai, and have a highly developed ethnic sensibility, see M. Elphinstone, *An Account of the Kingdom of Caubul* (London, 1815).

13. See E. Gellner, *Saints of the Atlas* (Weidenfeld & Nicolson, London, 1969).

14. H.R.C. Pettigrew, *Frontier Scouts* (published private-ly, 1965); as quoted in Elliott, *The Frontier,* p. 258.

15. See Ahmed, *Pukhtun Economy and Society,* p. 72.

16. Pettigrew, *Frontier Scouts,* p. 7.

17. See E. Evans-Pritchard, *The Nuer* (Clarendon, Oxford, 1940), p. 181.

18. See, for example, Spain, *The Pathan Borderland,* p. 187, for a compilation of records of 'offences' by Frontier tribes on British India from 1920-38.

19. Instruments of Accession between the Governor-General of, and on behalf of, Pakistan and the Rulers of Chitral (the Mehtar - dated 19 March 1953), Swat (the Wali - dated 17 Feb. 1954) and Amb (Nawab - dated 29 Apr. 1953), Government of Pakistan (Confidential).

20. Howell, *Mizh* (reprint), pp. 108-9.

21. See: Caroe, *The Pathans;* C.C.S. Curtis, *Monograph on Mahsud Tribes* (Government of North-West Frontier Province, 1947); Elliott, *The Frontier;* E. Howell, *Waziristan Border Administration Report for 1924-25* (Government of India Report (Confidential), 1925); id., *Mizh;* H.H. Johnson, *Mahsud Notes* (Government of India (Confidential), 1934); id., *Notes on Wana* (Government of India (Confidential), 1934); F.W. Johnston, *Notes on Wana* (Government of India (Confidential), 1903); J. Masters, *Bugles and a Tiger* (Four Square, London, 1965); Pettigrew, *Frontier Scouts;* Spain, *The Pathan Borderland.*

22. Elliott, *The Frontier,* pp. 261f.; Howell, *Mizh.*

23. Government of Pakistan, 1972 Census Report.

24. Howell, *Waziristan...1924-25,* p. 16. See also A. Keppel, *Gun-running on the Indian North-West Frontier* (Murray, London, 1911).

25. A. Skeen, *Passing it on: short talks on tribal fighting on the North-Western Frontier of India* (Aldershot, 1943; reprinted by Nisa Traders, Quetta, 1978), p. 2.

26. Letter no.120-P, dated 8 October 1881, written by Major Macauly, Deputy Commissioner, Dera Ismail Khan, proceed-ings 21 July 1882, nos.8-20, quoted in p.2 of Howell, *Wazir-istan...1924-25.*

27. Elliott, *The Frontier,* pp.225-35.

28. General Staff, *Operations in Waziristan* (Army Head-quarters, Calcultta, 1924), p. 84.

29. Elliott, *The Frontier,* p.261f.

30. General Staff, *Military Report on Waziristan* (Cal-cutta, 1935).

31. Caroe, *The Pathans,* p. 407.

32. ibid.

33. Spain, *The Pathan Borderland ,* p. 310; see also I.

Stephens, *Pakistan* (Benn, London, 1963).

    34. Spain, *The Pathan Borderland*, p. 206.

    35. Howell, *Mizh*, Preface.

    36. Howell, *Mizh* (reprint), p. 95.

    37. Ahmed, *Social and Economic Change*; also Foreword to Howell, *Mizh*.

Chapter 6
POLITICAL ORGANISATION OF PASHTUN NOMADS AND THE STATE

Bernt Glatzer

Afghan Nomads and Tribes[1]

The ruling elite of Afghanistan up to 1978 was ethnically, and to a certain extent even genealogically, closely related to those Pashtun tribes to which the bulk of Afghan nomads belong. Thus one might expect that the Afghan state had taken over at least some of the political functions of the nomads and therefore altered their political organisation to the extent that they no longer needed their own decision-making institutions or political leaders.

An examination of written reports on Afghan nomads of different areas from different times, beginning with Elphinstone and ending with current anthropological accounts, reveals the seemingly simple pattern that the closer the nomad-state relations the more likely hierarchisation takes place among the nomad groups concerned, that is, the more powerful the nomad leaders that appear. As Elphinstone noted in the early nineteenth century, 'tribes most under the king's influence are the most obedient to their Khaun'.[2]

The relationship between state and nomad society is well described and analysed for Iran.[3] Yet these analyses are not easily applicable to Afghanistan where, unlike Iran, most of the nomads belong to the politically and numerically dominant ethnic group of the country, and are not considered ethnic or tribal minorities.

More than 80 per cent of Afghan nomads are estimated to be Pashtun, but within each Pashtun tribe they form a numerical minority. Even among those tribes which are most famous for being 'nomadic', like the Ghilzai or the Durrani tribes such as Nurzai, Ishaqzai, Barakzai or Atsakzai, the majority at least in the present century, are sedentary

farmers and I doubt if they were ever purely nomadic.
Thus, when considering the organisational abilities
of the Ghilzai who held the throne of Isfahan for a
brief period in the early eighteenth century, and
nearly established an Afghan state, one has to remember that they were not nomadic. The same is true of
the Durrani who shortly after did succeed in establishing an Afghan state. Not only on the state
level did the Afghan nomads play a peripheral role,
but also on the level of their own tribes. As
Richard Tapper has stated, 'Afghan tribalism...has
not on the whole been based on pastoralism or
nomadism...Politically active ('troublesome') tribes
were more often settled villagers or traders than
pastoral nomads.'[4]
The question now arises as to whether Afghan
nomads may be considered social entities at all. My
contention is that they can, if properly placed in
the economic and social framework of their wider
society.
Pastoral nomads are professional specialists in
arid areas where for ecological reasons agriculture
and animal husbandry need spatial separation. This
economic specialisation results not only in spatial
separation of the pastoralists from the agriculturalists but also in a differentiation in life-styles
and forms of social organisation on the local level.
In addition to spatial mobility, nomadism as I
observed it in north-west and west Afghanistan
requires a great ability for frequently establishing
new social ties and resolving old ones. Camps and
herding units re-group more than once a year, thus
forming extremely ephemeral local groups with corresponding social and political institutions.
In this respect one has to consider nomad
groups as particular social and political entities
sharply distinct from sedentary groups, without
neglecting the fact that pastoral nomadism in
Afghanistan (as elsewhere) is only part of the local
rural economy. On a wider social level Afghan nomads
are well integrated into a complex social system
that includes peasants, traders, artisans, nomads
and others. Furthermore, there always was an exchange of individuals between these occupational
groups. Barth could have had Pashtun nomads in mind
when he wrote, 'nomad and villager can...be regarded
merely as specialized occupational groups within a
single economic system'.[5]
From my knowledge of them I would say that the
political organisation of nomads in Afghanistan
tends to be egalitarian unless either the nomads are

MAP 4:   *Sketch-map of western parts of Afghanistan, to show
places mentioned in chapters 6 and 7*

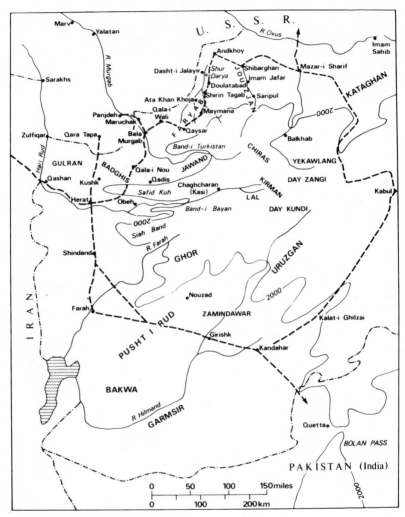

forced to react to political pressure from neighbours
or the state, or the state itself imposes institutions of power and authority on the nomads or strengthens existing political positions such as the khan
or the malik, whose functions were previously more
representative than authoritative.

Imposing new or strengthening existing authority
roles seems to be a traditional strategy employed by
oriental states in ruling their nomads. Only if
government administration develops as efficiently as
it did in Iran in the last decades can the state
transform this indirect rule into direct rule and
make its nomads 'acephalous' again.

In order to support these general statements,
especially those concerning the egalitarian tendencies of Pashtun nomads, I wish to present some facts
drawn from my observations and from the literature
consulted.

Nomads of Western Afghanistan

In 1970 I spent seven months among Durrani Pashtuns
in Ghor and Badghis in north-western Afghanistan.[6]
From 1975 to 1977 the biologist Michael Casimir and
I conducted a detailed field study on economy,
ecology, social organisation and socialisation among
other Durrani Pashtun nomads and villagers in Farah
in western Afghanistan.

The nomad group I studied in 1970 was composed
of members of the Atsakzai, Ishaqzai and Nurzai
tribes of the Durrani (or Abdali) branch of Pashtuns.
Attached to this group were a few households of
Pashtunized Timuri. Their winter area is the fertile
loess steppe of the Jawand district of Badghis. In
summer the nomads cross the Safid Kuh range (called
Paropamisus in older maps) to the south, and migrate
into the northern parts of the province of Ghor. The
whole area lies between the upper courses of the
rivers Murghab and Hari Rud. Their winter area in
Jawand is characterised by an undulating plain covered with a rich grass pasture, and criss-crossed by
canyons sometimes about 2,000 feet deep. The value
of this steppe for nomadic pasture is limited by the
lack of water: every drop has to be carried up from
the bottom of the canyons by pack animals. The
flocks cannot move too far away from the canyons,
because every other day, in order to drink, they have
to climb down the dangerous paths which the nomads
have cut into the sheer cliff-walls of the canyons.
Temperature is a second factor limiting animal

husbandry in Jawand. It ranges from a mean annual
minimum of -18°C to a mean annual maximum of 42.5°.[7]
The nomads can winter there only by protecting their
sheep and goats in the numerous small rock caves so
characteristic of the area. The most suitable caves
are owned privately by individual households. The
number of existing caves limits the number of animals
that can be pastured there in winter.

On the loess plains of Jawand dry farming is
possible, and about half the nomads raise wheat,
barley and melons. No nomad household, however, is
able to satisfy its own need for agricultural produce, and all of them have to buy cereals from settled farmers, for which they use cash obtained by
selling animals in the main livestock market of
central Afghanistan, at Chaghcharan in Ghor. There
is no co-ordination among the nomads over market
relations. Every household decides by itself when
to go to market and what to sell and buy.[8]

Most of the settled farmers in the area are
Persian-speaking Firuzkuhi Aymaq. In the winter
area of Jawand there is no competition for land
between Pashtun nomads and Firuzkuhi because the
latter cultivate irrigated fields in the canyons and
dry fields near the afore-mentioned Safid Kuh mountain range, where precipitation is higher but regular
watering-places for the nomads' animals are far away.

Although the pasture-lands are owned by neither
individuals nor groups, access to pasture in Jawand
is not free. Normally a household acquires pasture
rights either through spending several consecutive
winters, or by purchasing agricultural land in a
place. These rights are held by individuals and are
not conferred by virtue of membership in a certain
group. Newcomers can be granted pasture rights only
by individuals or groups of individuals who already
have them, and an individual can grant these rights
only if there are no objections from other members
of his camp. The granting of pasture rights also
includes protection for the newcomer and help in
finding caves for his animals in winter.

A nomad who seeks prominence in the political
arena tries to gather such newcomers around himself
in order to build up a clientele. But if a danger
arises that too many newcomers might overstock the
pastures, the rest of the nomads have an effective
means of controlling the immigration of new households, by simply blocking the narrow and steep paths
in the canyon walls.

These client relations are short-lived, usually
because the clients quickly establish new social

relations with as many other households as possible.
For example, by creating bonds of friendship through
frequent visits and invitations, by co-operation in
herding and other economic activities, and finally
by marital ties, the client can become independent
of his patron.

There are other opportunities for ambitious
persons to gain power, but before I describe them,
more background information is necessary. In their
summer area in northern Ghor, their ecology and
relations with the settled population, that is with
the Firuzkuhi Aymaq, are quite different from in the
winter area. During summer the nomads camp around
wells or along small rivers. Wells and river banks
are privately owned, either by the Firuzkuhi or by
wealthy nomads. The animals are grazed on the high
plateaux covered by shrubs of Artemisia and thorn
bushes. Although these plateaux are not private
property, access to them is effectively controlled
by the Firuzkuhi villagers and their chiefs. Only
those nomads who own wells or land there can graze
their animals without asking permission from the
Firuzkuhi, and have also a limited right to bring
clients with them. In this area, settled people and
nomads compete on pasture land, because the villagers
also engage in animal husbandry, especially goats
and cattle. The only way for the nomads to spend
their summers in Ghor is to establish peaceful relations with the Firuzkuhi. Since pasture rights are
never held by nomad groups, neither in Jawand nor in
Ghor, each household has to look for pasture individually. Thus, in the summer area of Ghor a nomadic
household has two alternative strategies available.
First, if it is wealthy enough it buys a well or a
field along a river bank, including the associated
pasture rights. However, since nomads dislike camping alone, the head of such a household has to ask
others to join him. Unless they are very close kinsmen (father, brothers, sons) he has to win the agreement of the Firuzkuhi who live nearest that place.
The normal procedure for winning this approval is to
establish personal friendship with the chief of the
Firuzkuhi group, and to pay some rent (alafchar).
The second alternative is simply to become the client
of another nomad who owns such pasture rights.[9]

A nomad seeking political prominence by collecting clients in this way will be only a seasonal khan,
a 'summer khan', if he cannot find other ties to
bind the clients to him. During the rest of the
year, these summer relations are unimportant. For
eight to nine months of the year the nomads live in

Jawand, therefore in order to understand better their
egalitarian political organisation let us have a
closer look at economic and social activities there.

The economic basis is breeding fat-tailed sheep;
in addition the nomads also raise goats, making up
about ten per cent of the flocks, and camels and
horses for transport. Further, as stated above, some
nomads also engage in dry-farming. As among all
nomads, animals are individually owned, and as among
most nomads, several households form herding units
in order to build up herds of optimum size: that is,
the maximum number of animals which can be herded by
the minimum number of shepherds; also, the grazing
and social behaviour of sheep and goats depend on the
size of the herds.[10] My informants considered the
optimum size to be 500-600 sheep and goats. The
average household in Jawand owned only 120 head,
therefore the average herding unit consisted of four
to five households. In fact I observed herding units
ranging from two to ten participants.

A household's wealth in animals changes frequently, the major factors being natural growth and
losses, selling, buying, and bridewealth transactions. Change in household wealth also causes changes
in the herding units. These changes, and the yearly
search for individual pasture rights in summer,
force the herding units to reorganise at least twice
a year. Normally several herding units form one
camp, the size of which depends mainly on the quality
of the surrounding pasture. Camps are as unstable
as their constituent herding units. Other reasons
for the instability of local groups are quarrels
between individuals and disagreements on political
matters.

Among the Pashtun nomads in the province of
Farah, we were able to document the comparable instability of local groups. In the winter of 1975-6
we started fieldwork there in a camp with 11 households. After two months the camp split up, with
some households joining other camps, others taking
on newcomers. Thus, during the 18 months of our
stay we found the initial 11 households in twelve
different camps in various combinations with others.
When we finally left them our 11 households were
living in four different camps, together with 15
other households.

It should be noted that animal husbandry among
the western Pashtuns is rather labour-intensive. The
amount of labour a household can perform sets an
upper limit for the accumulation of animal property.
Here, ten sheep and goats per adult household member

is the minimum a household needs to continue nomadic
life, while about 50 sheep per adult household member is the maximum for the household's labour capacity.
   As Barth reported for the Basiri in southern
Iran, nomads whose flocks fall below the minimum
tend to become landless peasants, while nomads at
the upper limit of wealth prefer to invest their
surplus in land and then leave nomadism for land-
lordship.[11]   In fact, in some areas of the Murghab
valley (between the Jawand river and Kham Gerdak)
and in the Shindand region of Farah province,
former nomads have purchased land, quit nomadism,
and now employ impoverished nomads as tenants or
seasonal workers. Thus, variation of wealth among
those who remain nomads is limited, and so therefore is the use that the politically ambitious can
make of economic resources for gaining power among
the nomads.

The Role of Kinship and Descent

Households are independent units, and may be said to
be the only stable social units in the society.
Although it seems paradoxical, this fact requires
from the nomad not only individual decision-making
but also an unusual ability to make social contacts,
for he must be continually ready to make social ties
with new and different partners in order to ensure
his survival. This does not mean that kinship relations are irrelevant for camp formation. Patrilineal, matrilateral and affinal relations facilitate
access to a camp, and the choice of partners. I
often observed in the nomads' discussions before the
regrouping of herding units and camps, that next to
economic factors, affinal and matrilateral relations
between households were as important as agnatic
relations.
   After economics and close kinship, there is a
third principle of social organisation: the tribal
or clan system, based on a national genealogy.
While this tribal or clan system permeates the
thinking of the Pashtun nomads, it plays the least
important role in their social group formation.
Nevertheless, it requires description and analysis,
because people themselves consider it important,
even if the anthropologist can hardly observe its
social relevance.
   Pashtuns believe they are patrilineal descendants of one common ancestor, yet his name is not

remembered by all. Most genealogies name him Qays
Abd al-Rashid, with the surname Pathan or Pashtun.
In some parts of Afghanistan he is known as Khaled
Baba, or Daru Nika,[12] or other names. He is supposed to have had three or four sons, who in their turn
had several sons, grandsons, and so forth. The
direct patrilineal descendants of Qays formed the
lineage of the founders of the various Pashtun sections, clans and sub-clans. The genealogy within the
sub-clans is generally unknown. At least in western
Afghanistan, only a few Pashtuns claim to be able to
trace their personal pedigree back to the clan ancestor. In general, however, the clan and sub-clan
ancestors or founders can be linked by a continuous
genealogy to all other clan founders and to the common ancestor of the Pashtuns, thus forming a lineage
of their own, i.e. a lineage of the clan ancestors.

Since Pashtuns live dispersed over a vast territory, traditions have diverged during the centuries,
especially when for political reasons in some areas
certain genealogies were manipulated, or when for
demographic reasons clans were subdivided or joined
with others, and when these alterations were not
accepted or not known by all Pashtuns. My informants were well aware of this; one Atsakzai in Jawand
related the following story.

> Once the Barakzai were only a sub-clan of the
> Atsakzai, since Barak was a son of Atsak. When
> Ahmad Shah Baba, a member of a small clan
> (Popalzai), came to power, he felt threatened
> by the large and powerful clan of Atsakzai,
> and therefore he divided up the Atsakzai into
> the Barakzai and the rest of the Atsakzai,
> simply declaring that Barak was not a son but
> a brother of Atsak.[13]

In spite of the impossibility in principle of
drawing a generally accepted genealogy of all
Pashtuns, some authors have tried it, and some even
with relative success, such as Khwaja Nimatullah
al-Harawi in the early seventeenth century,[14] or the
author of the Afghan _Tazkirat al-Muluk_ of the later
eighteenth century.[15]

The genealogical clan system is not the social
system of the Pashtun nomads, nor is it merely an
ideology. The majority of Pashtuns are settled, and
there is no valid evidence that they have ever been
nomads to a larger extent than they have been recently. Therefore, this genealogical clan system is a
pattern of settled people and was developed among

peasants, not nomads. Accordingly it would be misleading to explain this model of social categorisa-
tion by anything which has to do with nomadism. Nor
would I explain it as a 'social structure in
reserve'.[16]

But what do the Pashtun nomads do with this
model, inherited or adopted from their settled ancestors or neighbours? They can hardly use it for
territorial divisions and political groupings, but
they do use it for maintaining social relationships
with the settled society, and for stressing their
membership in the Pashtun nation. No one could
doubt the Pashtunwali (being a good Pashtun) of a
nomad, no matter how far away from Pashtun settlements, if he can trace his descent in a renowned
Pashtun tribe and if he can link himself genealogically to Qays Abd al-Rashid or Baba Khaled.

In theory, Pashtun nomads can also use their
clan model for recruiting raiding parties or groups
united for aggression and mutual defence, as Sahlins
has suggested for segmentary lineage systems in
general.[17] Yet empirically I could find no cases
among Pashtun nomads in western Afghanistan where
such groups were based on the patrilineal descent
system. Instead, I found them invariably formed on
the basis of local neighbourhood, common economic
interests and close consanguineal and affinal kinship.

One is tempted to ask whether the clan model or
'segmentary lineage system' of these nomads is in a
late developmental stage as described by Sahlins:
'the segmentary lineage system is self-liquidating.
It is advantageous in intertribal competition, but
having emerged victorious it has no longer raison
d'etre'.[18] This situation might be held to exist
among the settled Pashtuns of western Afghanistan,
who conquered the area more than two centuries ago
and now use the most fertile agricultural lands
there without serious competition from the outside.
But the nomads in western Afghanistan still have to
defend their pasture both against intrusion by other
nomads and against non-Pashtun settled people, mainly
in the summer areas of central Afghanistan. Here
Sahlins' inter-tribal competition is still alive.

In short, all Pashtun nomads belong to tribes,
clans and lineages, but at least those I observed
in the west - and I doubt if it is fundamentally
different elsewhere - are organised socially not on
the basis of a segmentary lineage or clan system,
but on other bases such as common economic interests
and close affinal and cognatic kinship bonds. If we

221

find camps where members of a certain tribe are
numerically dominant, this is not because they are
tribally organised, but rather because there is a
tendency for brothers and cousins to camp together,
that is cousins of all categories, who, given a
preference for lineage endogamy, tend to belong to
the same clan. If they camp together it is not
because they belong to the same tribe or clan, but
simply because they are brothers or cousins.

Political Organisation and Leadership

Since segmentary lineage organisation in the strict
sense does not exist, and since the social and political organisation of the western Pashtun nomads
does not extend beyond narrowly delimited groups, I
want first to consider the political organisation at
this level.

All group decisions which concern more than one
household are reached by discussions in open councils
(majlis - called 'jirga' by the eastern Pashtuns).
All men concerned take part in the council and each
participant has the right to speak. Since decisions
are not reached by majority vote, each household can
be represented by as many members as it likes, and
even women are allowed to speak. Discussions continue until counter-arguments are no longer raised, or
until it becomes evident to everyone that a consensus is impossible, at least for that meeting. When
differences of opinion persist and factions form,
mediators appear and try to reconcile the differences. If they fail, the herding unit or camp usually breaks up and the households form new groups.
There are no chairmen or discussion leaders, and
opinion leaders or mediators are influential not by
virtue of office, birth or wealth, but because of
personal qualities such as experience, age, and
eloquence. Persons having such qualities are known
as spin-zhiri ('white-beards').

Despite the fact that decisions are reached in
councils, there are some political roles. Thus,
when a herding unit regroups, it chooses a spokesman
(sar-khel), who is generally the head of the household richest in livestock, since one of his responsibilities is to give hospitality to visitors to the
herding unit. His chief task is to represent the
herding unit in its outside dealings; for example,
with hired shepherds or with other herding units.
If the joint herd becomes too small, he is responsible for building it up by bringing in new house-

holds along with their animals. No power to make
decisions is delegated to him. He represents and is
dependent upon the consensus of the herding unit.
     Another political role is that of the <u>malik;</u>
this is a traditional institution in Pashtun
society,[19] and is at present anchored in the state
administration. The office of malik carries no
power or authority, neither in its traditional nor
in its state-approved form. The task of the malik
is to represent his group or clientele in its relations with the outside, especially with the state.
In this role, he is dependent on the group that he
represents. In addition, the state entrusts him
with the task of presenting regulations and pronouncements to his clients. His clientele is not restricted to members of a single herding unit or camp,
but is composed of members of different villages or
camps. The number of clients a malik has can vary
from five to 70 persons. These clienteles are more
stable than herding units or camps, but a malik must
always be aware that his clients may choose another
man in his stead. The head of each household is
free to choose whichever man in his winter region he
prefers as his malik, or to offer himself as a candidate.
     The British colonial officer J.A. Robinson
accurately characterised the malik as follows:

> Powindah [i.e. Pashtun nomad] maliks wield
> much less power than do the maliks of the tri-
> bal territory of the Frontier; in fact it is
> only during the actual migration, when fighting
> is imminent, or when they are required by their
> tribe or section to make representations to
> government officials that they seem to have
> any power at all. Even then the course they
> are to follow is decided upon by the jirga...
> When maliks are powerful, it is because they
> possess strength of character, wealth, numerous
> relations, influence with Government and, last
> of all, birth. The Powindah is far more impa-
> tient of control not only by Government but by
> his own maliks...While he is proud to have
> king or malik, yet nothing in the world is so
> important than that they should not exercise
> any arbitrary power over him.[20]

Even a hundred years earlier, Elphinstone was aware
of the egalitarian aspect of the <u>malik</u> when he wrote
that 'the elected Mulliks...are obliged, in their
turn, to obtain the consent of their divisions'.[21]

The khan is a politically more important office.
Although one person can be <u>malik</u> and <u>khan</u> at the
same time, the offices should be clearly separated.
The word <u>khan</u> has a wide range of meanings in Pashto,
corresponding perhaps to those of the German word
'<u>Herr</u>'. 'Khan' placed after a person's name is the
polite form of address for every grown man, for
example, 'Yusuf Khan'. Khan alone means a powerful,
politically influential person. The khan is not an
institutional political office. To be a khan is
rather a quality that, in principle, any man can
acquire. In a group there can be several khans,
one, or even none.

A man distinguishes himself as khan through his
ability to attract followers, mainly by offering
them economic advantages, as mentioned previously.
At present in Jawand, a man becomes khan usually in
the following way: When a nomad's livestock holding
reaches a certain size, profits can no longer be
used to increase the herds but must be reinvested in
a different way, since the number of livestock a
household can take care of is limited. These profits
are therefore used to buy farm land, which is then
rented to landless and herdless families. While
these khans emerge from the nomadic sector, they
have their power base in the agricultural sector,
and although they try, they are hardly able to
extend their power over the nomads.

The relationship between khan and client is
dyadic, generally short-lived, and can be dissolved
by either side at any time. Therefore, the clientele of a khan changes continually, and his position
of power needs continuous reaffirmation. Khanship
is not a hereditary office.

The existence of khans does not contradict the
egalitarian basis of nomadic political organisation.
The egalitarian organisation is not now supported by
egalitarian ideology; on the contrary, my informants
clearly expressed a desire for the 'good old days'.
They believe that in those days khans had strong
authority and guaranteed the glory and prosperity of
the clan, and every Pashtun happily obeyed them. If
there were such khans today, they say, they would
readily follow them. Yet it seems to me very unlikely that such powerful nomad khans ever existed
in the past.

One of the reasons why there are no such khans
is that there are too many men who aspire to become
khan and thus effectively block each other's political ascent. In principle everyone would subordinate
himself to a great khan, but never to his neighbour

or anyone he knows too well, or one against whom he
has struggled for political power. In addition, the
nomads' system of production and relations with
their sedentary neighbours and the state are not
structured in a way that requires strong leaders.
   The egalitarian political organisation of
Pashtun nomads is not a recent phenomenon, but was
recorded also last century by European observers.
For example,

> The shepherds [i.e. nomads] are also in a
> great measure emancipated, even from the
> control of their internal government ...

> Among the [nomadic] eastern Ghiljies ... the
> power of the chief is not considerable enough
> to form a tie to keep the clan together, and
> they are broken into little societies ...
> which are quite independent in all internal
> transactions.

> The shepherds [i.e. nomads] near Cunchoghye ...
> have much leisure, no restraint, no government,
> and yet no crimes.

> The [nomadic] Naussers ... live almost entirely
> free from the restraint of government, while
> the temporary appointment of a Chelwashtee
> [i.e. temporary war leader] is sufficient to
> provide for the order and safety of their
> marches ... When the people are collected into
> camps, they are governed by their own Mooshirs
> [i.e. informal elders], without any reference
> to the Khaun, and when they are scattered over
> the country, they subsist without any govern-
> ment at all.[22]

Or as Broadfoot reported on nomadic Ghilzai Pashtuns
in eastern Afghanistan:

> the natural head of each family is implicitly
> obeyed; the oldest by descent of these heads
> of families is usually, not always, the malik
> of the khel, with a power but little obeyed...
> the head of the senior khel is chief of the
> tribe, and the King often grants him the title
> of khan. He dares not collect any income from
> his tribe, but lives on the produce of his own
> lands ... Among the eastern tribes ... he uses
> his influence to head plundering expeditions
> ... His seniority in birth makes the Afghans

> pay him the respect of an elder brother but
> nothing more. If his character is disliked,
> he has not even that; the lowest of his tribe
> eat, drink, and smoke with him. In urgent
> danger the khan is often set aside and a
> 'Toelwashtee' or leader is chosen, and while
> the danger lasts is pretty well obeyed.[23]

Hughes-Buller observes of the nomadic Atsakzai that
'as usual in Afghanistan, [they] appear to have no
recognized chief among themselves'. He also points
out how the Afghan government was altering this
egalitarian system:

> it was usual in Afghan times [when the Atsakzai
> area was governed by the Amir of Kabul] to
> appoint one of a particular family ... to
> supervise the tribe on the part of the govern-
> ment and probably to be responsible that their
> notoriously predatory propensities were kept
> within moderate bounds.[24]

Nomads and the State

An analysis of the political organisation of Pashtun
nomads must obviously take into account the fact
that these nomads are part of a larger ethnic unit -
the Pashtuns. Except perhaps under Ahmad Shah
Durrani (1747-73), who succeeded in unifying a significant part of them, the Pashtuns have never, so
far as we know, had an all-encompassing central
political organisation. Ahmad Shah however was following egalitarian Pashtun tradition, as he was only
a primus inter pares ('durr-i durran' or 'pearl
among pearls'), and could hold the loyalty of his
followers only by his continuous success in war.[25]
Not until the end of the nineteenth century did some
Pashtuns found a stable state, and even then only
under strong outside pressure.

To my knowledge, nomads were never actively
involved in the formation of the state. Amir Abd
al-Rahman granted the nomads new large pasture areas
during the 1880s in order to hold together the new
state and to secure it. Despite these attempts, even
today most nomads are not fully integrated into the
state. Abd al-Rahman and his successors were forced
to recognise that the nomads not only were not integrated into the state but also, for ecological and
economic reasons, were not able to fulfil their
abscribed function as a boundary cordon. Therefore,

attempts were made to settle them and to establish
hierarchical and state-dependent political positions
and offices. The settlement succeeded only in part,
and institutionalised authorities developed only
among the settled population.[26]
    The nomads' specialised production system is an
important part of the national economy of Afghanistan,
and the ruling elite, especially the royal family,
was closely related to the Pashtun nomads by the
tribal system. Despite this, the nomads remained
a quasi-foreign matter in the administrative body of
the state, with their own independent and egalitarian political decision-making institutions. The
state administration of Afghanistan was still developing at the time of my fieldwork, and did not
cover all parts of the population. The nomads tend
to reside in thinly-populated steppe and mountain
regions, where the influence of the state authorities is weakest. In Jawand, state influence is
limited to the irrigated river valleys, while the
steppes and high plateaux where most nomads live
are out of reach of the administration.
    The function of the state in shielding the
nomads from outside aggression should not be under-
estimated; but it is only in this regard that the
nomads can be considered a part of the state. One
might think that, if not directly, then at least indirectly, the state's protective function would
affect the political organisation of the nomads, and
one might also suppose that in former times, when
the state did not exist in this form, the nomads had
political offices with military functions that are
not now necessary. But in fact there is no historical evidence that such institutions ever existed.
It appears that even in earlier centuries, for military purposes they had only ad hoc leaders with
limited powers.[27]
    Even the loose organisation of the nomads of
Jawand is sufficient to form such ad hoc military
groups. Local groups based on joint herding contracts and common pasturing, as in Jawand, are
effective enough to organise defence, as I was able
to observe in several cases. Neither a political
hierarchy, nor regrouping along the lines of the
clan and lineage system, are needed. The fact that
today the state has made northern Afghanistan secure
has in my opinion contributed little to changing the
nomads' political organisation, but simply enables
them to use that herding range. Even before the
establishment of a central state administration,
most European observers labelled them 'republican'

or even 'democratic' (see citations above).

Nomad groups that were most subject to the influence either of the Afghan state or of the British
colonial administration, tended to form central
institutions of authority on their own. Frequently
the state or colonial authorities directly or indirectly created or strengthened the development of
the nomads' political institutions in order to facilitate control over them; or the nomads themselves
created such institutions in order to be able to
react to the state's interference. The older
European literature clearly documents this.[28]
Robinson, for example, gives numerous documents of
the British-Indian administration in which the principle of 'indirect rule' is to be extended to include even those Pashtun nomads that only seasonally
came within reach of the administration. The nomads
were required to present go-betweens in order to
make communication possible with the local officials.
They could easily respond to such demands, because
they possessed an appropriate traditional institution, namely the malik. Traditionally the maliks
had no authority of their own, and it was the colonial administration which gave it to them, for
example by making them sign contracts by which they
became acknowledged leaders, by granting them the
right to collect taxes, by paying them allowances,
and so forth. In 1926 the British authorities at
Dera Ismail Khan forced the maliks of the most
important nomad groups that wintered in their area
to sign a treaty which made them formal leaders with
political authority and gave them powers and responsibilities they never had before.

> We, the undersigned Sulaiman Khel, Nasar,
> Dautani, Niazi, and Aka Khel tribal maliks,
> accept the following terms on our own behalf
> and on behalf of our respective tribes:
> 1. No men of our tribe will commit any offence
> either against any other Powindahs [i.e.
> Pashtun nomads] or British subjects.
> 2. If any man of our tribes does commit any
> offence, we the maliks, and our tribes will be
> responsible to pay Rs.3,000 as fine and
> 'harjana' to Government (cost of the property
> looted will be in addition).
> 3. In case of any offence as in No.2, if the
> Deputy Commissioner wishes to imprison any
> responsible malik, we will have no objection.
> 4. We will not harbour any accused or deserter
> in our kirris [camps] but, on the other hand,

> will hand him over to the Government.
> 5. We will return looted cattle of this year
> within five days and will also pay decrees in
> arrears within five days. If we fail to do
> so, we will pay Rs.3,000 as fine to Government
> (in addition to the value of the looted pro-
> perty).
> Followed by signatures of 37 maliks and of
> C.E. Bruce, Lt.-Col., Deputy Commissioner.[29]

In 1930-31, the disarmament of all immigrating
nomads was announced in the 'Rules for Powindah
Migration' of the district of Dera Ismail Khan; only
the maliks were allowed to keep private weapons.
According to the same regulations the maliks were
granted a personal passport in which the officially
approved camps, routes, and times for migrations
were stated. These regulations made it impossible
for the common nomads freely to appoint or dismiss
their maliks. Also the traditional jurisdiction
became meaningless, because the maliks were held
personally responsible for offences against the
laws, and received the means to enforce these laws
with their own weapons, by asking for police support, or by denouncing offenders to the administration.[30]

Reports on the movement of Pashtun nomads to
northern Afghanistan at the end of the nineteenth
century mention a number of nomad khans who organised the migration; but, as Nancy Tapper points out,
these khans were army generals who had served before
in the army of Amir Abd al-Rahman and who were personally entrusted by the Amir with the Pashtunisa-
tion of the north. Nevertheless, these official
khans did not succeed in institutionalising their
office among the nomads. Amir Habibullah also
failed in 1903 to establish a hierarchical administration among the nomads.[31]

Examples of nomads building up their own institutions of leadership as a reaction to the surrounding state are not so explicitly observable in
Afghanistan as in Iran, at least not in the present
or the last century. The relatively large influence
some nomad khans exercise in Paktia seems to derive
from the particular need of the Paktia nomads to
defend their interests against the Afghan state,
for many eastern Afghan nomads lost their winter
pastures when the Pakistani border was closed after
1961, and they then had to seek new pasture areas
within Afghanistan, partly by force, partly with the
state's help.[32]

In other areas of Afghanistan, for example in
Jawand, nomads have little reason for negotiating
with the state through co-ordinated and united
action under overall leaders. In Jawand, interaction between nomads and the state is irregular.
The steppes are not under the state's administration.
At least until 1970, the time of my fieldwork, the
state did not try to administer these nomads, either
by direct or by indirect rule. The nomads did not
feel threatened by the state, but they are quite
aware that the state guarantees the security of
their area, without expecting anything from them in
return such as taxes or military service.

Where nomads live closer to government centres,
as for example the group Casimir and I studied near
Shindand in the province of Farah, there is a noticeable tendency for the administration to succeed in
extending its influence over them; thus it distri-
butes identity cards among them, intervenes in conflicts over grazing rights, tries to control the
smuggling of animals into Iran, and most important,
drafts young men for military service. This increased influence reaches the nomads through the
maliks. These maliks become so busy with administrative affairs that they have to reside permanently
near the government centres; alternatively the nomads
choose sedentary maliks already living there. As a
consequence, nomad clients tend to lose control of
their maliks when they become quasi-permanent officials.

The egalitarian organisation of Pashtun nomads
cannot be explained by nomadism alone, since nomad
Pashtuns are only part of a mainly sedentary ethnic
group, and sedentary Pashtuns show very similar
egalitarian tendencies. Nevertheless, I hope I have
made clear why their nomadic pastoral economy does
not provide a basis for hierarchisation, and why
only external factors, such as a state administration, can force the nomads to alter their political
systems.

NOTES

1. Field research among Pashtun nomads in Jawand and
Shindand was generously supported by the Südasieninstitut der
Universität Heidelberg (1970) and by the Deutsche Forschungs-
gemeinschaft (1970, 1971, 1975-7).

I would like to thank Ursel Siebert for thoughtful
suggestions and criticisms of an earlier version of this paper.
I am also grateful to Roger J. Bel for proof reading and for

his valuable comments.

2. M. Elphinstone, *An Account of the Kingdom of Caubul* (London, 1815), vol. 1, p. 217.

3. See various chapters in this volume.

4. See chapter 1, above.

5. F. Barth, 'Nomadism in the mountain and plateau areas of South West Asia', in *Problems of the Arid Zone,* Arid Zone Research, No. 18 (UNESCO, Paris, 1962), p. 345.

6. The results of this fieldwork are published in Bernt Glatzer, *Nomaden von Gharjistan: Aspekte der wirtschaftlichen, sozialen und politischen Organisation nomadischer Durrani-Paschtunen in Nordwestafghanistan,* Beitr.z.Südasienforschung 22 (Steiner, Wiesbaden, 1977).

7. *Kabul Times Annual* (Kabul Times Agency, 1970). The data are from Maymana, the nearest place to Jawand for which climatic data are available; the means are reckoned over eight years from 1961-9.

8. On the livestock markets and itinerant bazaars of central Afghanistan, see K. Ferdinand, 'Nomad expansion and commerce in Central Afghanistan: a sketch of some modern trends', *Folk,* 4 (1962), pp. 123-59.

9. For more details see Glatzer, *Nomaden,* p. 87f.

10. See W.W. Swidler, 'Some demographic factors regulating the formation of flocks and camps among the Brahui of Baluchistan', *Journal of Asian and African Studies,* 7 (1972), pp.69-75.

11. F. Barth, *Nomads of South Persia* (Universitetsforlaget, Oslo, 1961).

12. Khaled Baba: pers. comm. by Muh.Sabir Khan of Kabul University; Daru Nika: information from an Atsakzai nomad from Shindand - other informants in that area had no idea of his name.

13. Elphinstone, *Account,* vol. 2, p. 98, reported a similar story.

14. Nimatullah ... al-Harawi, *Tarikh-i Khan Jahani va makhzan-i Afghani,* ed. S.M. Imamuddin, 2 vols, Publications 4 and 10 (Asiatic Society of Pakistan, Dacca, 1960-2).

15. The *Tazkirat al-Muluk* is a history of the royal house of Sadozai of Ahmad Shah Durrani and his followers. The preface (*muqaddima*), containing a genealogy of the Durrani Pashtuns, was translated by Raverty in the Introduction to H.G. Raverty, *A Grammar of the Puk'hto, Pus'hto, or Language of the Afghans* (Longmans, London, 1860).

16. P.C. Salzman, 'Ideology and change in Middle Eastern tribal societies', *Man (NS),* 13 (1978), pp. 618-37.

17. M. Sahlins, 'The segmentary lineage: an organization of predatory expansion', *AA,* 63 (1961), pp. 322-43.

18. ibid, p. 342.

19. Cf. Elphinstone, *Account.*

20. J.A. Robinson, *Notes on Nomad Tribes of Eastern Afghanistan* (New Delhi, 1935, IOL:LPS/20, B 300), p. 8.

21. Elphinstone, *Account*, vol.1, p. 234.

22. ibid, vol.1, p. 304; vol.2, pp. 152, 170-1, 179.

23. J.S. Broadfoot, 'Reports on parts of the Ghilzai country and on some of the tribes in the neighbourhood of Ghazni', *JRGS, Supp. Papers*, 1, 3 (1886), p. 359.

24. R. Hughes-Buller, *Baluchistan District Gazetteer Series, V, Quetta-Pishin District, Text* (Ajmer, 1907), p. 72.

25. Cf. Mir Munshi Sultan Mahomed Khan (ed.), *The Life of Abdur Rahman, Amir of Afghanistan* (Murray, London, 1900), vol.2, p. 216; O. Caroe, *The Pathans 550 B.C. - A.D. 1957* (London, Macmillan, 1958), p. 255.

26. Cf. N. Tapper, chapter 7 below. The first to speak of a 'cordon of Pushtu-speaking races' in this context was C.E. Yate, *Khurasan and Sistan* (Blackwood, Edinburgh and London, 1900), p. 23.

27. The organisation of warfare, raids and defence among Pashtun nomads is described by Elphinstone, *Account*, vol.2, pp. 175-77; Broadfoot, 'Reports', p. 359; G. Oliver, cited in *Census of India 1911, VIII North-West Frontier Province* (Government Press, Peshawar, 1912), vol.1, p. 46; Yate, *Khurasan*, p. 11; Ferdinand, 'Nomad expansion', p. 154; see also Glatzer, *Nomaden*, pp. 196-203.

28. E.g. Elphinstone, *Account*, vol.1, p. 217; Broadfoot, 'Reports', p. 359; I.M. Reisner, *Razvitie feodalizma i obrazovanie gosudarstva u Afgantsev* (Akad.Nauk, Moscow, 1954), p. 225.

29. Robinson, *Notes*, p. 195.

30. ibid., p. 191.

31. See chapter 7 below.

32. See A. Janata, *Nomadismus*: Grundlagen und Empfehlungen für eine Perspektivplanung zum Regionalen Entwicklungsvorhaben Paktia/Afghanistan. Im Auftrag der Bundesstelle für Entwicklungshilfe für den B'minister f. wirtsch. Zus'Arbeit (W. Germany), vol.7, 5 (1972).

Chapter 7
ABD AL-RAHMAN'S NORTH-WEST FRONTIER: THE PASHTUN COLONISATION OF AFGHAN TURKISTAN

Nancy Tapper

The aim of this chapter is to give an account of the considerations that led Amir Abd al-Rahman Khan (1880-1901) to encourage Pashtun migration to northern Afghanistan, the difficulties met in the execution of this policy, and the reasons for its final success. As a case study, this account illustrates a type of policy frequently employed by Afghan and Iranian rulers towards their tribal populations; it also throws light on some of the domestic problems that faced the Iron Amir and demonstrates a new aspect of his role in the 'Great Game' between Russia and Britain.[1]

Several thousand families of Pashto-speaking pastoral nomads or semi-nomads have their homes today in the frontier provinces of north-western Afghanistan. Many of the groups living in Jouzjan and Faryab date their advent in the region to the reign of Abd al-Rahman and remember that the Amir asked their fathers and grandfathers to migrate from their ancestral lands in Farah and Kandahar to the north, where they were to establish security, defend the frontier against Russian expansion, and moreover promote their own and the nation's prosperity by exploiting vacant but fertile territory.[2]

Amir Abd al-Rahman's North-West Frontier

North-western Afghanistan is generally acknowledged to be among the richest agricultural areas of the country, yet at the beginning of Abd al-Rahman's reign great stretches of fertile land there lay unused. Much of the more mountainous interior was cultivated by Turkic-speaking Uzbeks and Persian-speaking Aymaqs, Arabs and Tajiks, and earlier in the century Uzbek, Turkmen, Arab and Aymaq pastoral-

ists had occupied the frontier districts; in the
early 1880s, however, the latter had few settled or
nomadic inhabitants. The local communities had been
weakened and depopulated by a long series of inter-
necine wars before Afghan rule was established, by
cholera epidemics and famine (especially in 1871-3),
but perhaps most drastically by the Turkmen raids
that were continuous throughout much of the nineteenth century - Salur, Sariq and Teke coming from
the west, and Qara Arsari from the Oxus.

Badghis and Gulran, the northern frontier districts of Herat province, were for many years
virtually deserted, but Maitland's enthusiastic description suggested that this condition could easily
be remedied:

> Badghis is a country of beautiful grassy downs,
> sloping gently to the northward. The soil of
> the valleys, and also of the high ground when
> near the hills, is exceedingly fertile and pro-
> duces excellent crops of wheat and barley
> without irrigation. The grass in spring and
> early summer is magnificent, standing several
> feet high in the bottoms, sweet and good as
> English meadow grass and, like it, filled with
> wild flowers.[3]

Likewise the once-populous settlements north and west
of Maymana were abandoned by 1880, having

> gradually succumbed to the attacks of the
> Turkomans one after another, in many cases
> being absolutely destroyed, the people - men,
> women, and children - all being carried off
> into slavery, and the result is that no one
> has dared to go out to those places ever since.
> Not only has the population of these outer
> districts been carried off bodily, but even
> that in the more settled districts along the
> high road has suffered in proportion.[4]

To the north-east of Maymana, in the plains of
Afghan Turkistan, there was a similar dearth of population, both in the cities and in the countryside,
in which, according to Yate, 'the supply of water
was far in excess of present requirements, and cultivators were the only things wanting',[5] while Peacocke
observed that 'Granted only a sufficient population,
a very few years would suffice to develop the plains
of Afghan Turkistan into a granary that would quite
eclipse that supposed to be afforded by the Herat

Valley.'[6] Amir Abd al-Rahman determined to repopu-
late these wastelands, and in this he largely succeeded.

Clearly a primary imperative of his policy
regarding these lands was that their economic potential be realised, so as to increase the wealth and
revenue of the country. Political considerations,
however, were even more important: Russian moves in
Central Asia, more or less openly threatening Afghanistan, were to cause the Amir great anxiety throughout his reign, and even before the north-western
border was clearly delineated he had decided to
fortify the marches and to settle a trustworthy
population there, both to protect the interior from
Russian advances and to ensure that his own territorial claims would be recognised. To these ends he
applied to the Indian Government for maps and other
information concerning the frontiers of his realm as
they had been defined in the Agreement of 1872-3,
and he requested that they should be properly demar-
cated. In 1883, finding revenues insufficient to
allow him to continue with the fortification and
settlement of the north-western regions, he called
on the Viceroy to provide funds for these purposes;
in the same year an annual subsidy of twelve lacs of
rupees was arranged, enabling the Amir to proceed
with measures for the protection of his frontier.
Among the measures already in train was the attempt
described below to establish sections of the Herat
tribes as border guards. It was when this attempt
proved unsuccessful that he first introduced large
numbers of Pashtuns to the north-west, and since that
time their numbers have steadily increased.

The First Attempt to Colonise the North-West Frontier

The Russian advance across Transcaspia had been
watched with anxiety in Afghanistan. In early 1882
the Russians were heard to be encouraging agriculture and settling nomads as cultivators near Marv and
Sarakhs. The Amir was moved to action, and in the
spring of that year the Governor of Herat was ordered to direct his attention to the northern regions
of his province, where lay the most vulnerable and
least clearly defined sections of the Afghan frontier. Forts were to be repaired and garrisons established, and the Governor began to arrange for the
settlement of loyal and warlike populations near by.
These provisions were initially directed against the
Turkmens who were in retreat from the Russians and

moving southward from Marv, Sarakhs, and Yalatan;
only later were they seen as measures against the
Russian advance itself.

Two of the Aymaq tribes of Herat, the Jamshidi
and the Qala-i Nou Hazara, were considered by Abd
al-Rahman as potential settlers and both were anxious
to win the assignment. Eventually in January 1883
priority was definitely given to the Jamshidi, who
were not only former occupants of the lands in question but were also considered the more loyal of the
two groups. Under the Jamshidi leader Yalangtush
Khan, Jamshidi and Sariq Turkmen of Panjdeh began to
settle; by June, the programme of colonisation seemed
to be making progress in its aims of 'improving the
country', freeing the border areas from the continuing threat of Teke and Qara Turkmen raids, and
securing the region against possible Russian encroachment. Meanwhile, the other Herat tribes were
all eager to gain access to the now relatively
secure lands in Badghis and along the Murghab, and
their intrigues forced the Herat officials to admit
Firuzkuhi and Qala-i Nou Hazara to participation in
the settlement scheme alongside the Jamshidi and the
Sariq. Funds for the scheme soon ran short, however,
and the grain and forage supplies in the area were
used up; moreover, attempts to collect high revenues
from the Sariq alienated their support. Disputes
arose among the various tribal leaders in Badghis,
including Tajo Khan Ishaqzai, the Pashtun commander
of the military escort sent by the Government. The
resultant confusion, which continued throughout 1883
and 1884, put the project in jeopardy. None the
less, by the beginning of 1885 some 1,000 to 2,000
families of Jamshidi, Hazara, Firuzkuhi and Sariq
had successfully established themselves in the vicinity of Bala Murghab.

The fact that the frontier was still undefined
at this time set the stage for an important episode
in the 'Great Game'. There was great fear in
England that the Afghan claims to and presence at
Panjdeh would lead to open fighting with the approa-
ching Russians under General Komarov and become a
casus belli between Russia and England. The Viceroy's
direction of Afghan foreign affairs did not guarantee
automatic British support against foreign aggression,
but with British concern to prevent any Russian intervention in Afghanistan and especially a Russian
advance on Herat, the possibility of a major crisis
became real. As tension increased on the frontier
in the early months of 1885, Colonel Ridgeway of the
Afghan Boundary Commission advised the withdrawal of

the new settlers to the interior, where they could
more easily be supported in case of a Russian attack.
Nothing was done, however, and the Panjdeh crisis in
late March proved a severe and perhaps unfair test
of the settlers' capacity for defending their country, for most of them, like the Afghan and British
troops on the frontier at the time, were thrown into
disorder by the Russian move, and they retreated
southwards with their families. The Jamshidi and
Sariq remained, but belief in their loyalty too was
shaken. It seemed likely that all the Herat tribes
might eventually succumb to Russian influence and
intrigue.
        The Amir declared that the Sariq, whose only
worry was the safety of their property, were un-
trustworthy; moreover, with the Russians using ethnological arguments to justify their territorial
claims, the Sariq presence on both sides of the frontier complicated the boundary settlement and endangered its permanence. Yalangtush Khan Jamshidi,
though praised by A.C. Yate for his behaviour during
the Panjdeh affair,[7] was removed from his chiefship,
accused, probably unjustly, of having carried on
seditious correspondence with the Russians from the
time of their occupation of Marv in 1884. With
other members of his family he was taken prisoner to
Kabul. The Amir is reported to have said later that
it was 'a mistake to trust any but Afghans with the
charge of the Chahar Aimaks'.[8] The removal of this
popular leader aggravated the later problems in settling the frontier areas and almost certainly provoked Aymaq collaboration with the Russians; fear of
Aymaq treachery was a continuing theme throughout
Abd al-Rahman's reign.
        In June C.E. Yate sent in a memorandum on
Badghis in which he stated that, in spite of their
prior right, the Amir would be wise to remove the
Jamshidi from the border and replace them with
Ghilzai Pashtuns unlikely to submit to Russian influence, and in July Colonel Ridgeway requested that
the Amir be informed of such a recommendation. The
Ghilzai concerned were those inhabiting the Dara-i
Bum and Upper Murghab valleys, whom Yate wrongly
claimed to be recent arrivals from Kalat-i Ghilzai;
some undoubtedly were, but most were related to the
Tokhi, Hotaki and other Ghilzai, both nomads and
cultivators, whose ancestors had been removed by
Nadir Shah Afshar from their homeland in Kalat to
the Obeh region east of Herat. The inhabitants of
Qadis were later included in the plan, as were some
Achakzai Durrani of Pusht-i Rud, whose summer quart-

ers were in the hills north-east of Herat.

By the autumn of 1885 Abd al-Rahman had determined that the Sariq Turkmens and Jamshidi who had
remained in the Bala Murghab region should be removed from the frontier, and should be replaced by
Pashtuns on whose loyalty he could depend. This
measure, which was to be put into effect in the following spring, coincided with the maturation of the
Amir's plans for colonising the Turkistan waste-
lands.

Abd al-Rahman's 'Waste-Lands' Policy

In August 1885 the Amir was quoted as saying:

> There was an extensive plain in Turkistan which
> was lying waste. I had a great mind to make it
> a cultivated and inhabited place. I devised a
> plan to root out from Afghanistan the enmity
> of cousinship and domestic quarrels, which are
> mixed up in the nature of this people. So I
> gave takavi [advances] and road expenses to
> such people, and sent them to that direction.
> Up to this time, 18,000 families have settled
> there.[9]

To consolidate his rule in Afghanistan, throughout his reign Amir Abd al-Rahman employed the practice of removing political dissidents to parts of
the country far from their homes. Several thousand
such exiles - though it is unlikely to have been as
many as 18,000 families - had already reached the
north of the country by 1885; most of them were
Pashtuns though very few were nomads. (Before his
accession there were few Pashtuns in Afghan Turkistan
apart from a colony of some 3,000 families of Ghilzai
cultivators settled near Mazar-i Sharif.) Certainly
as early as 1882 the Amir was aware of the various
advantages that could come of such a practice: if he
helped the exiles to begin cultivation in their new
homes, while confiscating their former lands and
including them among the Government holdings, not
only did he benefit the country by increasing both
internal security and the area of land under cultivation, but he also gained two new sources of much-
needed revenue, both the confiscated and the newly-
exploited lands. In the early years of his reign he
gave growing important to the idea of opening up
these unused lands, but it was only in 1885 that he
announced a new and rather different policy, of

encouraging voluntary migrations to the north. Tax
concessions, road expenses, and provisions for grain
and agricultural implements were among the various
incentives used to attract prospective migrants;
often sanctions of a more compelling nature were
added. That there were sometimes also political
motives to this new policy is evident from the Amir's
remarks quoted above, but the policy differed significantly from that of political exile, for the voluntary migrants were not necessarily regarded as
politically dangerous in their former homes.

While exile to Turkistan for specifically political reasons did not cease, during the rest of Abd
al-Rahman's reign voluntary migration there was a
continuing and important theme. The Amir wanted the
migrants, largely but not exclusively Pashtuns, to
engage 'in the cultivation of waste lands in Turkistan, in the hopes of strengthening Turkistan in
case of war by the admixture of Afghan races'.[10]
Another consideration was the overpopulation felt to
exist in Kabul and other parts of the south-east.
Thus, a grain shortage in late 1885 convinced the
Amir that Kabul province was not sufficiently productive to support its population, and he persuaded
many Kabulis and others to migrate north; in October
it was reported that:

> About 3,000 families have emigrated from Deh
> Afghanan, and about 5,000 families from the
> Ghilzai country to take up their residence in
> Turkistan. Sardar Muhammad Ishak Khan
> [Governor of Turkistan] is giving them crown
> lands for cultivation. Of these emigrants the
> most respectable and strongest Afghans are sent
> to reside in Maimena. The Amir grants 2 lbs
> of flour to each emigrant daily, and one mule
> for every seven emigrants for their carriage
> free of charge; people go most willingly on
> account of the scarcity in Kabul.[11]

Maitland, travelling between Aq Ribat and Sayghan in
November 1885, met a 'constant stream of people
migrating from the country about Kabul to Afghan
Turkistan' and noted that they were motivated by
food shortages as well as the Amir's encouragement
in hopes of leavening 'the Usbak population of Turkistan with people on whose support he can rely in
case of foreign invasion and from whom also the
Turkistan troops can be recruited'.[12]
Such reports are numerous from late 1885 onwards, and by early 1886 the number of new settlers

in the area stretching from Maymana to Badakhshan, but particularly in the eastern parts, may well have exceeded the 18,000 families claimed by the Amir in the previous August. Most of the migrants were already experienced farmers and were instructed to continue cultivation in their new lands, which they did with much success. Thus, in the summer of 1886 Yate observed near Balkh that 'A certain portion of the waste land has been taken up by Afghan immigrants from Kabul, who seem to be rapidly extending their gardens and orchards and to be good cultivators.'[13]

The Amir did not at first consider fostering pastoralism in Afghan Turkistan. Practised on a large scale, it would entail the absence of settlers from the frontier for several months of the year, frustrating a main aim of his policy - the establishment of a settled population to defend the border regions. Indeed, at the inception of his policy of encouraging voluntary migration, he does not seem to have appreciated the degree to which pastoralism and cultivation were economically complementary and both necessary if the waste-lands were to be exploited with maximum benefit. He lacked sympathy with the nomadic way of life and moreover was unaware of the difficulties entailed by his insistence that nomad immigrants to the north should settle and start cultivation. In late 1886, however, he began to realise the advantages of restocking the extensive northern grazing lands from Bala Murghab to Badakhshan, and by 1890 was talking of this as a new way of increasing the wealth of the country and the Government revenues. In fact, both the abortive attempt to settle the Herat tribes on the Badghis frontier, and the more successful colonisation of the area from 1886 onwards by Pashtun tribes, were having the effect of opening up the grazing-lands for the nomads.

The Second Attempt

In the winter of 1885-6, the region of Bala Murghab and Qala-i Wali was still occupied by Jamshidi and Sariq Turkmens; the Governor of Herat was awaiting the spring before replacing them, according to instructions, with local Ghilzai. The Amir, however, apparently now intended a more comprehensive colonisation of the region, involving a wholesale northwards migration of his own tribesmen - Durrani. The Durrani lands were south of Herat city but even at this time many Pusht-i Rud Durrani nomads (especially

Ishaqzai and Nurzai) entered Ghor, the easternmost district of the province, in the summer; some of these went as far as the Band-i Bayan near Kasi (modern Chaghcharan) for pasturage, a few (the Achakzai already mentioned) crossed into Badghis, while the rest, content with the abundant grazing in the valleys of Taymani country, remained there from May to September. Nomads from the south and west had been using the pastures in Ghor for generations, but they were now expanding steadily northwards, and in the mid-1880s the numbers of these summer immigrants (estimated at some 14,000 families) were said already to equal those of the local Taymani population, and to be increasing yearly. This tendency probably contributed to a significant degree to the eventual success of Abd al-Rahman's plans to locate Pashtuns on the north-western frontier. The Durrani tribes most strongly represented among the groups that eventually became established in the north-west were the Ishaqzai and the Nurzai; their homelands lay within the former province of Farah, where the nomadic portions of each tribe probably numbered some 5,000 families, based particularly in the large sub-province of Pusht-i Rud, in the districts of Zamindawar, Nouzad, Girishk and Garmsir.

Early in 1886 orders were issued to the Governors of Kandahar, Farah, and Herat, to collect Pashtuns and invite them to migrate to the frontier areas of Herat. To judge from the later confusion, the orders were not sufficiently specific on two important points: whether the migrants should be landowners in their present homes or not; and whether they should be pastoralists or cultivators by occupation. It would appear that the orders were aimed at landless pastoral nomads, but in the event failed to reach any substantial number of these. At any rate, the incentives offered indicate the Amir's intention that whatever the migrants' former condition, in their new homeland they should receive land and cultivate it.

In March, the Governor of Herat invited Pashtuns from Pusht-i Rud to come and settle in Badghis at Maruchak and Qala-i Wali, while the Governor of Kandahar published a proclamation from the Amir to the following effect: the Amir had for seven years been planning to improve the condition of members of his own tribe by sending them to colonise the lands of Murghab and Badghis, which had been devastated by the Turkmens. The area in question, he said, were both fertile and well-watered by the Murghab river, and offered highly desirable dwelling-places for

both pastoralists and cultivators. He bade the
nomads of Pusht-i Rud, in their own interest, move
up there and settle down; the Government would pay
all road and baggage expenses and would provide
advances (taqawi) for bullocks and seed; the advances
were to be paid back after three years, and from the
fourth year onwards taxes would be collected at the
rate of one-quarter from irrigated and one-tenth
from dry-farmed land. The nomads should consider
the offer, and if agreeable should apply to their
respective local authorities for the road expenses,
set out for their destinations, and begin to farm.[14]
    There was no response, however, and the
Governor of Kandahar called the Durrani leaders to
explain to him their objections to the Amir's offer.
They professed their loyalty to the Amir, but considered it folly that they, who had villages and
lands of their own, should leave their homes for new
areas. This was reported to the Amir; he was annoy-
ed with the Durrani lack of enthusiasm for a project
which he had considered in their own interest. Early
in April he gave orders that one family from each of
the 12,000 ploughlands (qulba) in Kandahar district
should be compelled to migrate north: they would
receive road expenses and bullocks for cultivation,
but should be supported financially by the families
left behind. The Amir specifically summoned Tajo
Khan of Nouzad, the Ishaqzai chief who had commanded
the sowars escorting the first colonisation attempt
three years earlier, and called on him to take
people of his own tribe northwards, expecting that
people of other tribes would follow. The Governors
of Kandahar and Farah were instructed to give him
every assistance. He returned from Kabul to Pusht-i
Rud, where he set about collecting people for the
migration north.
    Meanwhile, in Badghis, the planned replacement
of the Sariq and Jamshidi by the Ghilzai was duly
effected in May. Most of the Sariq went north to
Panjdeh, while the Jamshidi were moved to Kushk and
Obeh. C.E. Yate witnessed the scene on the Murghab
as the Jamshidi crossed the bridge from the eastern
to the western bank, where some 1,000 to 2,000
families of Ghilzai were waiting to take their
place. He remarked on the contentment with which
the new situation was accepted by both groups, particularly the Ghilzai, who affirmed 'that they would
never allow a single Russian to cross the frontier'.[15] According to the Saraj al-tawarikh, the
newcomers were '2,400 families from the people of
Farah, Isfazar, Pusht-i Rud, and the Herat plain,

who were in Badghis'; of these, 500 Farah households were now settled by the Governor of Herat in the Qashan district and the rest in Murghab.16 Such places of origin seem to imply that these groups were Durrani, not Ghilzai. The account does not fit exactly with Yate's observations; possibly it refers to the 1,000 Durrani families who arrived from Farah some months later. In June, however, some 300 families of Achakzai Durrani from Pusht-i Rud, who had reached their customary summer quarters not far to the south of Bala Murghab, were invited, at the Amir's orders, to settle in Qala-i Wali.

While these newcomers were settling in, the next wave of immigrants, Durrani from Farah and Kandahar, was slow in getting under way. During May and June, with the aid of a body of Government sowars, Tajo Khan collected a large number of nomad families from Pusht-i Rud and forced them to begin the march northwards. Many of the leading nomads in the party objected to Tajo Khan's authority, and some of them went to Kabul to appeal before the Amir, protesting that they had been forced to abandon their own lands, while his orders had specified that only the landless should migrate. They received a firman confirming that those with land in the south should not leave it, so the chiefs rejoined their families, who had by now passed through Farah into the mountains east of Herat, and set off home for Pusht-i Rud. After encounters with the authorities of Herat and Farah, some of them were sent back north, others were allowed to remain in their homeland.

The rest of the Pusht-i Rud migrants proceeded in early September to Herat, and were directed to settle in Firuzkuhi country in eastern Badghis. According to the Saraj al-tawarikh, only 1,363 families left Pushti-Rud with Tajo Khan; in late October, however, General Ghous al-Din Khan reported to the Commander-in-Chief at Herat that 5,000 families (25,000-30,000 souls), all of the Ishaqzai tribe, had arrived in the north-west, though this report was later shown to be inaccurate. In November Tajo Khan himself declared that 2,600 families (19,000-20,000 souls) had arrived and said that more would come the following year. Meanwhile a separate group from Farah, about 1,000 families (5,000 souls) of nomads of the Barakzai, Ishaqzai, Nurzai and 'Farsi' tribes, had also reached Herat in September, and were in their turn sent to Qaratapa and Gulran.

It seems that the arrival of these immigrants, probably amounting to some 4,000 families, and the

Amir's directives as to accommodating them and supplying them with grain, threw Herat into confusion -
for the harvest had failed that year and the population was already in a state of distress. Soon after
their arrival, the nomads were said to be without
money and in need of grain and advances to enable
them to cultivate. The next month, the Jamshidi at
Kushk and the Hazara of Qala-i Nou began to complain
of the requisitions being made on them, and of the
fact that they had been forced to build shelters
for the newcomers. Meanwhile the Russians too were
disturbed by the influx of Pashtuns into the frontier districts: they were said to have strengthened
their garrisons at Marv and Sarakhs. There was general apprehension on both sides that clashes would
occur between the Pashtuns and the Turkmens, and
accordingly some attempt was made to preserve a
vacant strip of land along the frontier.

At the end of October, since Tajo Khan's party
had not yet settled down, General Ghous al-Din was
deputed from Herat to visit Qala-i Nou and assign
quarters to them in the Murghab region. Wheat supplies were issued from Government granaries in
Herat, Farah and Ghorat, but the nomads themselves,
in spite of their claims to be destitute, managed to
buy all the wheat available in the Maymana district.
All the newcomers were said to be unhappy and in
great fear of the coming cold season - one report
stated that they had even left their flocks behind
in Pusht-i Rud.

The Amir clearly intended the nomads to become
self-sufficient economically, by growing their own
grain in the future. This was essential in order to
avoid further drains on Government resources and
increased hostility on the part of the local inhabitants. It is not clear, however, whether he
expected the nomads themselves to become settled
cultivators, or to engage labourers or tenants to
work for them, or to adopt a semi-nomadic existence.
In November, when he was brought a map of the frontier between Maymana and Herat, showing the lands
which had been allotted to the newcomers, he is
said to have observed that a million pastoral families would be needed to populate the waste-lands of
Badghis.

At the end of 1886 it became known that while
the Farah groups settled around Gulran had duly
begun cultivation, the settlers near Bala Murghab
had not and were becoming restless and insubordinate.
Tajo Khan himself complained to the Amir that the
Firuzkuhi were threatening to rob his followers of

244

their flocks and camels. In January 1887, General
Ghous al-Din, having completed the task of assigning
lands and villages to the settlers, was given direct
administrative control of the Jamshidi of Kushk, the
Hazara of Qala-i Nou, the Firuzkuhi, and the Pashtun
nomads. According to Ghulam Rasul Khan Akhundzada
of Ata Khan Khoja near Maymana (interviewed in 1971),
his great-grandfather Qazi Jan Muhammad of the
Babakzai Ishaqzai was appointed qazi to the newcomers, while Tajo Khan Khanikhel Ishaqzai was
hakim, assisted by Mir Afzal Khan, chief of the
Nurzai, as naib.
        Although the success of the new settlement
scheme was far from assured, the Amir was now determined on prosecuting his new policy for strengthening the north-western frontier. Already in June
1886 he was quoted as saying, 'It is proper that as
the King is an Afghan, his tribesmen the Afghans
should guard the frontiers';[17] now, in March 1887,
replying to the Viceroy of India who had expressed
himself worried by the Amir's policy of sending
Afghans (i.e. Pashtuns) near the frontier and thus
possibly giving the Russians an excuse for intervention, he wrote:

> I want to see the Herat frontiers manned and
> furnished not only with the regular troops but
> also with my own tribesmen, the Durranis.
> During this year alone I have had 8,000 fami-
> lies removed from the country on the other
> side of the Helmund.[18]

The Amir was soon to be disappointed. A few days
later he heard more reliable information on the composition of the migrant groups settled in western
Badghis; there were only 3,000 families (some
20,000 souls), of which only about 500 families were
actually Durrani of the Ishaqzai, Nurzai, and
Achakzai tribes; the rest were a motley assortment
of Opra,[19] Parsiwan, and Ghilzai, who had eagerly
joined the migration, having no lands of their own
in the south. The Amir was upset, and ordered that
the nomads should pay for the 6,000 kharwar of wheat
they were about to be given, but being now well supplied with the grain they had bought themselves in
Maymana they were able to ignore the Government
issue.
        None the less, the spring of 1887 was a disas-
ter for the settlers; through lack of rain the
pastures failed, and the animals died in large numbers. Then, on their way south to their traditional

summer quarters in the Siah Band range, the Ishaqzai
and other Pusht-i Rud nomads were robbed of thousands of animals by the Firuzkuhi Aymaqs. Tajo Khan
wrote to the Amir to inform him of these hardships;
he complained that there was no sweet water in
Badghis other than that from the Murghab river, that
the pastures, however, excellent, were inadequate
for more than a few hundred families, that the camels
suffered terribly from the flies and mosquitoes, and
that the nomads found life there impossible. The
area should be colonised by sedentary agriculturalists, who could more easily defend their few animals
from summer insects and winter cold. Tajo Khan's
complaints were largely justified, but the Amir replied scathingly that if the nomads could not protect
their flocks from a few wretched Firuzkuhi, how
could they possibly be expected to guard the frontier against the Russians? Let them go, he added,
wherever they want, and find themselves a place
where their animals will no longer be troubled by
flies, nor themselves by fleas.[20]
    The nomads did not wait for this answer, and
having reached the mountains in July, many of them
moved on south towards Pusht-i Rud, and were apparently already there by August. The Amir is reported
to have passed the following scornful comments,
which may also have reflected his current disappointment with the lack of Durrani support during the
Ghilzai rebellion:

> With regard to the Ishakzai Maldars who
> returned from Badghis-i Herat to Pusht-i
> Rud-i Helmand the effect [of] their return
> is of no consequence. His intention, he says,
> was that the Durranis should become the ruling
> race, and accordingly he offered them a chance
> of displaying their valour by holding against
> the enemy the frontiers of Afghanistan; but
> as they have chosen to decline this honourable
> post, it is their own affair.[21]

Those that did return north at the end of the summer
abandoned Badghis and moved towards Maymana and
Turkistan proper.
    Meanwhile in Bala Murghab the Achakzai and
Ghilzai of Herat had successfully irrigated some
lands, and were more content with their situation.
On the other hand, the failure of the spring pastures, accompanied by total ruin of the grain crops
through drought and locusts, had by autumn rendered
desparate the situation of the Farah groups settled

at Gulran and Qaratapa, and in spite of their more
auspicious beginnings they too began to return to
their old homes.

The second attempt to colonise the north-west
frontier ended, like the first, in failure, due this
time to lack of preparation by the local authorities
for receiving the newcomers, to the hostility of the
Aymaqs, and above all to natural disasters. It
could also be argued that the nature of executive
action under Abd al-Rahman made the failure of such
a policy likely. There was extreme centralisation
of the Government at Kabul. Communication with provincial officials was poor; and it would seem they
were rarely kept informed of policies indirectly
affecting their areas or, more importantly, of later
ad hoc decisions made by the Amir in response to
petitions or reports from perhaps only one part of
the area concerned. As the latter often contradicted the initial directives, yet were not widely
publicised, there was considerable scope for individuals to manipulate the administration to their own
ends. In short, discrepancies in administrative
interpretation and implementation were rarely anticipated and were often dealt with in a piecemeal
and hence ambiguous fashion. None the less, perhaps
the Amir's greatest strength was his perseverance;
in this particular case he did not abandon his new
policy, and indeed it did not take much to encourage
new waves of Pashtun nomads, who soon came up to
live in the north-west in larger numbers than before.

The Establishment of the Nomads in the North-West

Amir Abd al-Rahman's initial orders were that some
12,000 families from Pusht-i Rud and Farah should be
sent to the Herat frontier; as we have seen, no more
than 4,000 families had arrived in 1886, though Tajo
Khan himself promised that more would come the following year. In fact it seems that 1887 saw no new
migrations from south to north, only the retreat of
many of the nomads to their original homelands. It
is not clear which groups these were - Tajo Khan
Ishaqzai and Mir Afzal Khan Nurzai, both of whom did
return south, may have left the bulk of their followers in the north. Those who remained certainly
included Achakzai and many of the Ghilzai and others
who apparently had no land elsewhere. Whatever the
situation after Tajo Khan's first expedition, nomads
living today in the north-west say that their ancestors were brought there by Tajo Khan Ishaqzai, but

they do speak of a second migration as having occurred a year or two after the first.

A second organised migration may have taken place during the year 1888. At the beginning of that year Tajo Khan was still speaking of his people's unlucky attempt to move north and the difficulties they had experienced, but in January it was reported that the Governor of Kandahar had again been asked by Abd al-Rahman to send about 12,000 families of Ghilzai and others from Pusht-i Rud to the Murghab area, and in the spring the Amir ordered the Governor of Herat to encourage the cultivation of waste-land in the province and authorised him to grant taqawi advances to suitable persons. None the less, no large groups of nomads, comparable to those of 1886, were reported arriving on the frontiers at this time and the few who had arrived in Badghis, Murghab, and Maymana by the autumn of 1888 took no part in the troubles which then disrupted the neighbouring province of Turkistan.

In the months of August and September 1888, the Governor of Turkistan, the Amir's cousin Sardar Muhammad Ishaq Khan, made a bid to establish the independence of Turkistan under his own control and had himself proclaimed Amir. Abd al-Rahman moved quickly to suppress this rebellion, and its failure caused the hitherto semi-autonomous provinces of Turkistan and Maymana to be fully integrated under Abd. al-Rahman's rule. This whole episode had, however, surprisingly little effect on either the Pashtun nomads on the north-west frontier or the Amir's immigration policies generally. While Ishaq sought support from the Ghilzai prisoners and exiles in Turkistan whom he freed and used to contact their tribesmen in the south-east, there is no record of similar approaches to the nomads; such contact was possibly prevented by Maymana's position as a province independent of Ishaq Khan. Of the nomads during the rising we hear only that those on the Murghab, 'apprehending danger from the Usbegs took refuge in intrenchments',[22] though during the disorder following Ishaq Khan's flight to Russia at the end of September, the nomads raided as far north as Doulatabad and Andkhoy.

The Amir was generally pleased with the loyalty of the people of Herat province, while he came round to the view that the Uzbeks of Turkistan, who had been among Ishaq Khan's most important supporters, were innocent and the Ghilzai, Kabulis, and other emigrants from eastern Afghanistan had been the source of trouble. He carried out harsh reprisals

on all the inhabitants of Turkistan, executing or
exiling the worst offenders; the eastern immigrants,
ordered to return to their former homes, did so in
large numbers. Despite this unsatisfactory end to
one aspect of his waste-lands policy the Amir was
undaunted, and particularly during his stay in Turkistan (from late 1888 until the summer of 1890) he
made great efforts again to encourage settlement
there: 'The Amir is trying to induce families from
all parts of Afghanistan to emigrate to Turkistan
and settle there to replace those who have fled
across the Oxus or been deported. Liberal terms are
being promised to those who will go.'23 Firmans
were sent to the various Governors directing them to
explain to the people,

> You people are poor and servants of His High-
> ness the Amir. Some of you should willingly
> go to Turkistan and reside there. Government
> will supply you with funds to enable you to go.
> When you reach Turkistan, Government will furn-
> ish you with implements for agricultural
> purposes gratis, and an advance of money for
> the same purpose and Government lands to build
> your houses on. His Highness requires 30,000
> families to be there. He will take care of
> them in every way.24

However, it was in the settlement of the north-
eastern parts of the country that these measures had
their greatest effect. In the north-west, it is
probable that many of the nomads who in 1887 fled
back to Pusht-i Rud and Farah were now of their own
accord beginning to return in a piecemeal fashion to
the borderlands. Various factors would have persuaded them to do this: oppression in their homeland,
the continuing and loudly proclaimed interest of the
Amir in opening up the north-west, and the fact that
they had already been assigned places in the frontier
regions; besides, in the summer quarters they would
have renewed contacts with their fellow-tribesmen
who had remained in the north, and would have heard
from them that the natural disasters of 1886-7 were
exceptional. Indeed, many nomads arriving in the
north now declared the potential wealth of the pastures there compared with those in their homeland,
and were delighted to have been introduced to them.
Moreover, the newcomers were attracted by the proximity of markets in Russian territory, especially
that at Panjdeh, and they were quick to begin trading in grain, livestock, and pastoral produce; in

this they were indirectly encouraged by taxes and transit dues on trade within Afghanistan. Measures taken by the Amir to prohibit such trade and redirect it to internal markets or to create Government monopolies in such goods seem to have had only temporary effect.

It is certain that a voluntary migration of nomads to the north was soon under way. For instance, in the summer of 1890 some of the Kandaharis settled at Bala Murghab appeared before the Amir and pleased him greatly when they told him that they were some 8,000 families and that their numbers were increasing daily. Yate also attests to this trend: in 1893 he heard how Nurzai who had emigrated from Bakwa in Pusht-i Rud to the western parts of Badghis found the area a paradise for grazing, and how the nomads from Nouzad and Zamindawar by then living on the eastern side of Badghis travelled back and forth between there and their former homelands, serving as an important line of communication. Noting that every year the colonisation of the frontier was increasing, Yate declared Abd al-Rahman's policy of peopling it with Pashtuns an excellent one.[25]

Tajo Khan himself appears to have remained as hakim of the nomads in Pusht-i Rud, where he and Mir Afzal Khan Nurzai were involved in the years 1888-90 in almost continuous dispute with the Government over the taxation of their followers. In late 1889 various groups of Pusht-i Rud nomads, numbering 400 families, went to see the Amir in Turkistan to complain of Tajo Khan's behaviour. The settlement of their grievances was entrusted to the Governor of Kandahar, though with little success. Further complaints led, at the end of 1889, to the dismissal of Tajo Khan from the post of hakim. Meanwhile it seems reasonable to suppose that many of the complainants remained in Turkistan, probably at the instance of Abd al-Rahman himself.

Some of Tajo Khan's followers had already in 1887 or 1888 moved eastwards to winter in the region of Maymana and Turkistan proper. Others followed them some years later: for instance in 1895 numbers of Achakzai nomads in Badghis moved towards Maymana, where they hoped to benefit from General Ghous al-Din's more favourable administration. Again, in 1896, difficulties with local officials in Badghis determined many of the Pusht-i Rud nomads there to move further east. However, large numbers of both Ghilzai and Durrani continued to occupy Badghis and Gulran. Others of Tajo Khan's followers dispersed to more distant quarters, Pashto-speaking Baluch

groups, for example, going as far as Imam Sahib on
the Oxus, though some of these later returned to the
Sar-i Pul region. Later, some of the southern
nomads who had fellow-tribesmen already in Turkistan
came directly through the central mountains to join
them: this process was continuing in 1970.
    The areas initially involved in General Ghous
al-Din's distribution of lands and villages among
the immigrants in 1886 were those extending between
Zulfiqar on the Iranian border and Qadis, though the
regions west of Maymana may also have been included.
Most of the Pashtun nomads inhabiting the northern
parts of the present-day Faryab province, such as
the Shur Darya and Shirin Tagab valleys, say they
arrived in those places at General Ghous al-Din's
direction, though this may not have occurred until
the 1890s, when the General was based in Maymana.
Pashtuns now living in the Shur Darya valley, in Ata
Khan Khoja and Dasht-i Jalayir, say these were
waste-lands (jangal), and indeed Yate observed of
the Qaysar/Shur Darya valley in 1886:

> Formerly it was well inhabited, and there were
> large settlements of both Arab and Ersari
> nomads, who grazed their flocks in the chul
> to the west: these, though, were gradually
> reduced by [Sariq] Turkoman raids, and in 1877
> the last two Usbeg villages at Ata Khan Khojeh
> and Jalaiar were attacked and plundered, and
> since then the land has lain waste.[26]

Possibly lands distant from the frontier were also
distributed at this time. Some Ishaqzai and Baluch
groups living now in the districts of Shibarghan and
Sar-i Pul say their ancestors settled there immediately after their arrival from Nouzad with Tajo
Khan. Indeed they say these districts too had been
largely vacant and unused, and that Tajo Khan himself took possession of lands near Sar-i Pul for a
time.
    Whatever the status of those parts of the
newly-settled regions away from the frontier, by
1903, and probably many years earlier, they were
certainly occupied by groups associated with Tajo
Khan's migration. According to a letter from the
Governor of Balkh to Amir Habibullah, dated 28 June
1903, Tajo Khan's sons Kamal Khan and Aqa Muhammad
Khan had submitted for the Amir's information material 'regarding the settlement of the Durrani sheep-
and cattle-owners' residing in different places in
Turkistan. The Amir directed the Governor to make

appropriate arrangements for them, and suggested that they should not live in small groups but in compact settlements of 1,000 houses, and that these settlements should be specific distances from each other. Meanwhile he sent two separate firmans to the nomads 'of the Nurzai and Ishakzai tribesmen, inhabiting Sar-i-pul, &c., in the district of Turkestan'. A census was to be taken and the nomads were to elect a khan. All these proposals seem to have been designed to create an efficient military organisation, and it was further arranged that the nomads buy arms for themselves. In the spring of 1904 Kamal Khan and his brother were called to Kabul on this business.[27]

A report of 1907 by the Kabul news-writer who accompanied Amir Habibullah on his journey from Herat to Mazar-i Sharif, enumerates the Pashtun tribes which he observed living at that time in the north and north-west of Afghanistan. Altogether, there were 11,000 families of Durrani, comprising 1,100 Alizai in Maymana, and 9,900 Ishaqzai, of whom 2,000 lived in Badghis, 900 in Maymana, 7,000 in Sar-i Pul; while there were 9,200 families of non-Durrani Pashtuns: 3,400 of them living in the Maymana and Andkhoy regions, and 5,800 in the vicinity of Sar-i Pul and Shibarghan. The numbers are almost certainly greatly exaggerated, but several important groups - notably Nurzai - escaped observation. Contrary to Abd al-Rahman's fears concerning the excessive proportion of Opras in the first migration 20 years earlier, by 1907 the majority of the Pashtun colonists appeared to be of the royal tribe - Durrani; this preponderance has continued in those areas until the present.

There was one final factor, not the least important, which contributed to the Pashtun movements into Turkistan. This was the opening up of the Hazarajat as summer pasturages for the nomads.

The Hazara Revolt and Consequences of its Suppression

Because of their support of Ishaq Khan's rebellion the Amir began in the autumn of 1888 to remove the Sheykh Ali Hazaras from their commanding position on the main road from Kabul to the north, and scattered them in colonies throughout Afghanistan. On his way north in December the Amir was reported as saying that he would not punish the Sheykh Ali Hazaras,

> But I will not allow them to live in the
> country. I am quite wearied of the behaviour
> of these people. They should take with them
> their families and household property and go
> out of the country, and I will populate their
> country with Afghans.[28]

Thus the area was opened to settlement, as had been
other parts of the eastern Hazarajat during the same
period; before this, Pashtun encroachment in the
Hazarajat had been minimal. It was only with the
end of the Hazara war that the Ghilzai began to penetrate deep into the Hazarajat from the east and
nomads from both south-west and north-west Afghanistan extended their summer quarters into the country
of the Day Zangi and Day Kundi Hazaras.

The Hazaras rebelled against efforts on the
part of the Amir to extend government control in the
Hazarajat, their mountainous homeland in central
Afghanistan. The rising began in Uruzgan in the
spring of 1891 and was soon transformed into a vic-
ious religious war between the Shiite Hazaras and
the Sunni majority in Afghanistan. The rebellion
was suppressed in September 1893. The southern
Durrani were slow to take part in the Hazara campaigns, believing that the Amir intended to weaken
and impoverish them through service and requisitions.
Likewise the nomads in Badghis refused to send troops
against the Hazaras in Uruzgan. Among others Tajo
Khan Ishaqzai was in 1892 enjoined by firman to
support the war, and shortly afterwards his son
Kamal Khan, recently dismissed for oppression from
his post as Governor of Balkhab, was appointed to
disarm the Hazaras. His zeal proved excessive, however, and in 1893 he found himself a political prisoner in Kabul. Seyf Akhundzada Ishaqzai (ancestor
of the leading Pashtun family in Jouzjan in 1970)
was similarly involved in the campaigns and his descendants' present control of lands in the Hazarajat
almost certainly dates from this period. Indeed,
from the time of the Hazara war and the slightly
earlier revolt in west-central Afghanistan of the
Firuzkuhi Aymaqs, the summer quarters of the nomads
wintering in Jouzjan, Faryab and Badghis have extended from Kasi, Lal and Kirman in the south to the
Band-i Turkistan range in the north.

The Amir had hoped to establish permanent year-
round settlements in the Hazarajat. Tribal levies
and the nomads who had provided him with transport
for the campaigns were offered land, and the Durrani
of Kandahar and various Ghilzai groups were asked to

send many thousands of families to settle there.
Many nomads were encouraged to seek summer grazing
in the Hazarajat but, principally because of the
extreme winter cold, very few permanent settlements
would seem to have been established. The more immediate effect of the Amir's policy was to open up
central Afghanistan to travel and trade, and over a
number of years certain trading practices developed
which enabled the Pashtuns to dominate the local
inhabitants and assured them control of farmland and
grazing in some areas.[29]

Early Leaders of the North-Western Nomads

Tajo Khan, already prominent in the early 1880s,
remained an important figure among the nomads for
many years. His influence on the national scene is
indicated by the fact that two of his daughters and
a grand-daughter were married to royal princes.
However, after his return to Nouzad in 1887, though
he retained nominal chiefship of the frontier nomads
as their hakim, his actual role grew less important
to them, and he seems to have remained aloof from
affairs in the north-west. Thus, when he was dismissed from his post as hakim of the Pusht-i Rud
nomads at the end of 1889, it was because of his
activities in the south. This event cannot have
caused more than a temporary decline in his influence in Pusht-i Rud, though the post of hakim seems
to have been transferred to Mir Afzal Khan Nurzai.
Tajo Khan died at the end of 1892, and Mir Afzal
Khan a few months later; chiefship of the Ishaqzai
tribe and general authority over the Pusht-i Rud
nomads were given to Tajo Khan's two sons, Kamal
Khan and Jamal Khan, who in spite of various conflicts with the Government maintained their leadership during the rest of Abd al-Rahman's reign.
    The manner in which the northern nomads were
administered during Amir Habibullah's reign (1901-
19) is somewhat obscure. For some time there was
apparently a hierarchy involving a hakim of all the
nomads of Kataghan, Turkistan, Herat and Pusht-i Rud,
a sarrishtadar of the nomads of Turkistan itself,
and the tahsildar subordinate to the latter. In
January 1908, Tajo Khan's son Jamal Khan was appointed to the post of hakim; he probably had little
direct contact with the nomads, though he was officially expected to

    look after the welfare of his subjects and

enquire into their grievances against the
local Hakims. He will also make enquiries as
to the amount of money realized from them as
fines in recent years, and whether it was
credited to the State treasury, or not.[30]

Jamal Khan's brother Kamal Khan was chief of the
Pusht-i Rud nomads, and like him resided at Dara
Mian in Nouzad in winter and at Puza Lich near Kasi
in summer.
    Meanwhile new leaders emerged in the north.
Ghulam Rasul Khan Nazarzai Ishaqzai, whose father
Seyf Akhundzada had been involved in the first northward migration under Tajo Khan, was recognised chief
khan of the Turkistan nomads and appointed their
sarrishtadar early in Habibullah's reign. In 1906-7,
however, there were complaints about Ghulam Rasul
Khan's activities as sarrishtadar, possibly instigated by his tahsildar, Nik Muhammad Khan of Khanikhel,
a relative of Jamal Khan. Amir Habibullah appointed
a Muhammadzai as sarrishtadar of the Turkistan nomads in place of Ghulam Rasul Khan, a move strenuously
opposed by the latter. The Amir himself soon made a
tour of the provinces (1907), during which he visited Ghulam Rasul Khan at Ziarat Hazrat Imam (now
known as Imam Jafar) in Sar-i Pul. The new sarrishtadar was suspended and replaced by another Muhammadzai, Khuday Dad Khan, who retained the post until the
end of 1909. Ghulam Rasul Khan accompanied the Amir
back to Kabul, having been told that he was to be
provided with arms to safeguard the people living on
the border of Turkistan; but he was detained in the
capital for over a year while his former conduct was
investigated. Eventually petitions sent by the
Sar-i Pul Ishaqzai appealing for the return of their
Khan, and other support which he acquired in Kabul,
secured his release. By the autumn of 1910 Ghulam
Rasul Khan had regained the Amir's favour, and he
and Tajo Khan's son Kamal Khan were appointed to
guard the boundary between Russia and Turkistan,
having been supplied with some 3,000 fire-arms for
that purpose. In 1914 we learn that Ghulam Rasul
Khan, who already had the responsibility for the
collection of grazing taxes in Turkistan, was granted the monopoly of collecting tolls at the Turkistan
border.
    Tajo Khan's sons continued for a while to be
recognised as leaders of all the Ishaqzai, but eventually lost contact with and influence over those
branches of the tribe settled in Turkistan, devoting
themselves exclusively to affairs in Herat and

Pusht-i Rud; some of Tajo Khan's family were important in Gulran in the 1970s. Ghulam Rasul Khan and
his seven brothers severed their ties with the south
and consolidated their position of dominance in the
Sar-i Pul region, especially after the Saqawi rebellion of 1929.[31]

Conclusion

The successful colonisation of north-western Afghanistan by Pashtun nomads was due to various factors;
only some of these were recognised or controlled by
Amir Abd al-Rahman, but without the impetus provided by his policies the eventual large-scale movement
would never have taken place. Three related considerations prompted the Amir's policy of encouraging
Pashtun migration to the north-west: Russian moves
in Central Asia, the ethnic diversity and hostility
of the population of the Afghan borderlands, and the
economic potential of the vacant lands there.
    Abd al-Rahman had spent his youth near Mazar-i
Sharif, and considered Afghan Turkistan and Herat to
be integral parts of any Afghan nation. This view
conformed with later British and Russian concern to
maintain Afghanistan as a buffer-state. Alternative
frontiers would have endangered Afghan geographical
integrity, and would have been unacceptable to any
Afghan leader. However, many groups in the population of these regions identified with culturally
similar communities over the frontier to the north
and west, and all of them were at best uncommitted
to Afghan hegemony. After the Panjdeh débâcle, the
Amir no longer trusted even the more loyal of these
groups; he decided that only Pashtuns could be
relied on in the borderlands. The dearth of population there facilitated his policy, and the unoccupied
but fertile lands provided him with the incentive
needed for encouraging Pashtun colonisation. This
decision to infuse the area with Pashtun settlers
was a novel and seemingly astute solution to the
problem of controlling Turkistan and the north-west
and integrating them into the Afghan state, but the
Amir appears not to have appreciated the scale of
the plan, and he took little account of the social
and administrative difficulties entailed in its
implementation.
    Though Abd al-Rahman rarely hesitated to use
force if other methods proved inadequate, in this
case he was constrained by events in other parts of
the country. Even during more pacific times a suc-

cession of local risings provided continuous employment for all the troops at the Amir's disposal; no
sooner was one revolt quelled than the troops concerned had to be diverted to meet some other emergency. During the period when the colonisation
policy was being carried out, the Ghilzai rebellion,
the rising of Ishaq Khan, and the Hazara war fully
occupied the Amir's available forces. Of course, if
the migration had been completely forcible, this
would have alienated the loyalty of the colonists
to the Amir's regime, and defeated the main purpose
of his policy. But this consideration probably
counted for little with the Amir, and although he
offered considerable incentives, he did deploy what
force was available to 'encourage' the migration.
Much of his domestic policy was pursued by such
carrot and stick methods.

Given the immense Government effort that would
have been required to ensure success, the colonisation plan might well have failed but for the inherent attractions that north-western Afghanistan
offered to the newcomers. Above all, cultivable
lands were abundant, and winter and spring pastures
were superior to those in the south-west; besides,
the central mountains were now conveniently opened
to the Pashtun nomads for use as summer pasturage.
On arrival in the north-west the nomads were able
to continue their pastoral way of life, which became
increasingly profitable on the inclusion of karakul
sheep in their flocks. Few of them had any inclination towards agriculture at first, and although
their winter tent-villages often stood on arable
land, this in most cases lay uncultivated for several decades. Only the leading nomads were quick to
settle and establish claims to extensive areas of
farmland as well as pasturage. As large landowners
they entered the elite of rural society and gained
ascendancy in that area. The Pashtuns brought with
them ideas of their ethnic superiority which were
reinforced by Government support and by the grant
of both formal and informal privileges over the
other ethnic groups. With these political and economic advantages, the Pashtun khans were from the
beginning able to assert and maintain their dominance in the north-west. However, they were able to
unite their Pashtun following for political purposes
only on exceptional occasions, when the Pashtuns as
a group were threatened - the most significant being
the Saqawi period of 1929. At this time only the
Hazaras stood by them when the Uzbeks, Tajiks, and
Aymaqs of Turkistan rose in support of the Tajik

leader Bacha Saqao, who had seized the throne at
Kabul. With the rout of the local population in
Turkistan following the restoration of the Durrani
monarchy by Nadir Shah, even more lands came under
Pashtun control in Turkistan and the north-west.
Around this time, the rank and file nomads began to
realise that they could survive the summer heat of
the plains (which they had doubted before) and that
farmland could be an important and secure economic
resource. A trend towards a dual economy, based on
both cultivation and pastoralism, was initiated.
     In the provinces of Jouzjan and Faryab, the
Pashtuns continued in the 1970s to dominate the
other ethnic groups politically, even though numerically they did not exceed some 25 per cent of the
local population. Far less than half of the Pashtuns continued to practise an exclusively pastoral
nomadic way of life. A significant number were
wholly oriented towards settled agriculture, while
possibly the greatest proportion were semi-sedentary,
having winter villages and farmlands which half the
members of the group remained to supervise during
the summer months, the rest accompanying the flocks
to the steppes and mountains during the spring and
summer. It would appear that the lands available in
the area for cultivation and pastoralism were
already overexploited by present techniques; but it
may be said that in the 80 or so years since the
nomads' advent in north-western Afghanistan they
had, as a result of their personal economic ambitions, come near achieving the goals established by
Abd al-Rahman.[32]

NOTES

     1. This chapter is a slightly revised version of my
'The advent of Pashtun *maldars* in north-western Afghanistan',
BSOAS, 36, 1 (1973), pp. 55-79. The original article, where
full references are given, was based primarily on the diaries
and news-letters of the British news-writers in Afghanistan,
found in the series LPS/7 in the India Office Library, London.
These records must be used with caution, but can often be
checked against the major Afghan source for the period, Mullah
Fayz Muhammad Hazara, *Saraj al-Tawarikh,* vol. 3 (Kabul, 1333/
1914-5). The contemporary sources were sometimes supplemented
by oral traditions collected by Richard Tapper and myself
during the course of field research in northern Afghanistan
in 1970-2 as part of a Social Science Research Council project.
In addition, H. Kakar's book *Afghanistan* (Punjab Educational
Press, Lahore 1971), the only substantial study of Abd al-

Rahman's domestic policies, was of considerable use. My thanks are due to Hasan Kakar, Habib Pashtunzoy, Musa Pashtun-Marufi, Adrian Mayer and Malcolm Yapp for comments on early drafts of the article; I am especially indebted to Richard Tapper for supplying material from the *Saraj al-Tawarikh*.

2. There has been no historical account of the proces-ses and policies that led to the large-scale northward migra-tion, other than a cursory discussion by R.D. McChesney in 'The economic reforms of Amir Abdul Rahman Khan', *Afghanistan*, 21, 3 (1968), pp. 19-20; his account of the migration was based on a single source, Fayz Muhammad, *Saraj*. Pashtuns in the north-west were mentioned briefly in the following: J. Humlum, *La géographie de l'Afghanistan* (Gyldendal, Copenhague, 1959); H.F. Schurmann, *The Mongols of Afghanistan* (Mouton, The Hague, 1962); S.I. Bruk, *Karta narodov peredney Azii* (Akad. Nauk, Moscow, 1960); however, the major Soviet ethno-graphy, N.A. Kislyakov and A.I. Pershits, *Narody peredney Azii* (Akad. Nauk, Moscow, 1957), omits all reference to them. Since the publication of my original article, further accounts of Pashtuns in the north-west have appeared: first, a brief geographical survey of Badghis by X. de Planhol, 'Sur la frontière turkmène de l'Afghanistan', *Revue géographique de l'Est*, 13, 1-2 (1973), pp. 1-16; secondly, ethnographic accounts by B. Glatzer (based on field research in 1970), *Nomaden von Gharjistan* (Steiner, Wiesbaden, 1977) and see chapter 6 above; and B. Tavakolian (based on field research in 1977), see esp. 'Research Report: Sheikhanzai pastoral nomads of Northwest Afghanistan', *Newsletter of Commission on Nomadic Peoples*, 4 (Sept. 1979), pp. 9-16. Meanwhile, Hasan Kakar has published an even more substantial historical study of Afghan-istan during Abd al-Rahman's reign, in which he gives an account of the colonisation of north-west Afghanistan that essentially agrees with mine, see his *Government and Society in Afghanistan* (University of Texas Press, Austin, 1979), pp. 131-5. His comments (pp. 243f.) on the sources we have both used are particularly enlightening.

I refer to these migrants as 'nomads', but it must be born in mind that in their own self-consciousness their nomad-ic migrations are subsidiary in importance to their identity as Pashtun tribesmen and as pastoralists (*maldar*).

3. *Gazetteer of Afghanistan, Part III, Herat* (Calcutta, 4th ed. 1910), p. 14.

4. C.E. Yate, *Northern Afghanistan* (Blackwoods, Edinburgh and London, 1888), pp. 134-5.

5. ibid., p. 254.

6. *Gazetteer of Afghanistan, Part II, Afghan Turkestan* (Calcutta, 4th ed., 1907), p. iv.

7. A.C. Yate, *England and Russia face to face in Asia: travels with the Afghan Boundary Commission* (Blackwoods, Edinburgh and London, 1887), p. 329.

Pashtun Colonisation of Turkistan

8. Anon., *Biographical Accounts of Chiefs, Sardars, and Others of Afghanistan* (Calcutta, 1888), p. 228.

9. 'Kabul news-letter' (KNL), 29 Aug. 1885, LPS/7/45, 759.

10. 'Peshawar confidential diary' (PCD), 28 Nov. 1885, LPS/7/45, 1640.

11. PCD, 24 Oct. 1885, LPS/7/45, 1252. Certain tax concessions were also promised, see KNL, 29 Dec. 1885, LPS/7/46, 999.

12. Maitland to Ridgeway, 28 Jan. 1886, LPS/7/46, 1483.

13. C.E. Yate, *Northern Afghanistan*, p. 254.

14. Fayz Muhammad, *Saraj* p. 511; 'Memorandum of trans-frontier intelligence' (MTFI), March 1886, LPS/7/46, 1427. The latter contains a translation of much of the Amir's proclamation as it was read during Friday prayers in the mosques; there is no indication that the message was ever directly transmitted to the pastoral nomads at whom it was aimed.

15. C.E. Yate, *Northern Afghanistan*, p. 218.

16. Fayz Muhammad, *Saraj* p. 495.

17. KNL, 29 June 1886, LPS/7/47, 901.

18. Abd al-Rahman to Dufferin, 15 Mar. 1887, LPS/7/49, 1302.

19. For taxation and other purposes, two tribal divisions were recognised by government: Durrani and Opra. The latter was a residual category including 'Parsiwans', Ghilzai, and Hazara among others. Today in northern Afghanistan the term Opra is used by the Durrani, though they may not include Ghilzai within the category. The term is synonymous with the more common 'Parsiwan', which includes (a) all Pashto-speaking groups lacking the *-zai* suffix in their name, both those such as Baluch whose diverse origins are recognised, and those such as Maliki, Khalili, Baburi, etc., whose origins are obscure and who are said by Durrani to speak Persian rather than Pashto among themselves; (b) peoples who speak Persian as their first language, such as Aymaqs, Tajiks and Hazaras. Uzbeks and other Turkic-speakers are often classed as Parsiwan, but not usually Opra, by the Durrani.

20. Fayz Muhammad, *Saraj* p. 567.

21. 'Kandahar news-letter', 16 Aug. 1887, LPS/7/51, 259. The Ghilzai rebellion in 1886 and 1887 was essentially a reaction to the harsh taxation imposed on the Ghilzai. To suppress it, the Amir tried, as he did in the face of most disturbances, to exploit ethnic or tribal rivalries, to divide and rule. It is in this case somewhat ironic that a ruler who came to power with Ghilzai support (the Amir's own tribesmen, the Durrani, having sided with his rival Sardar Ayub Khan in 1880-1) was forced in late 1886 to seek Durrani help. The failure of Pashtun migration to the north-west was connected to other aspects of the Amir's policy towards the Durrani: in September 1886 the Barakzai Durrani, who had previously enjoyed land-grants (*jagir*) free of taxation, learned that they

260

would no longer be exempted from these or other dues. Though
the Barakzai were inclined to consider this simply a further
means devised by the Amir for oppressing and ruining the
Durrani of Kandahar, officials claimed it was a punishment for
those Durrani who had refused to go to Badghis when ordered to
do so. In January 1887 Abd al-Rahman reversed his decision
about the Barakzai jagirs to gain their support against the
Ghilzai.

    22. 'Herat news-letter', 20 Aug. 1888, LPS/7/55, 492.

    23. MTFI, Apr. 1890, LPS/7/60, 13.

    24. KNL, 16 Apr. 1890, LPS/7/60, 155.

    25. C.E. Yate, 'Notes on the fortifications and troops
of Herat and on Badghis and northern Afghanistan', 25 May
1893, LPS/7/70, 1790ff.

    26. C.E. Yate, *Northern Afghanistan*, p. 231-2.

    27. 'Memorandum handed to Mr Dobbs by H.H. Amir on 27th
July 1904', LPS/7/169, 1733.

    28. KNL (from Camp Dahanah-i Ghori), 4 Dec. 1888, LPS/7/
55, 1389.

    29. See K. Ferdinand's most illuminating discussion of
the various debt relations between Pashtuns and Hazaras,
'Nomad expansion and commerce in central Afghanistan', *Folk*,
4 (1962), pp. 140, 149. However, he implies a helplessness on
the part of the Hazaras and Aymaqs in the face of Pashtun
expansion which is perhaps misleading; certainly the Aymaqs
of Chiras and elsewhere in the north have a local reputation
for fearless resistance to Pashtun oppression, and the
Yakawlang, Day Kundi and Day Zangi Hazaras are famous among
the Pashtuns of Turkistan for their ability to unite
for common political or economic ends in the Hazarajat. Cf.
R. Tapper, 'Ethnicity and class: dimensions of inter-group
conflict in Afghanistan', forthcoming in N. Shahrani and R.
Canfield (eds), *Revolutions and Rebellions in Afghanistan*.

    30. 'Kabul Diary', 22 Jan. 1908, LPS/7/212, 436; Fakir
Saiyid Iftikhar-ud-din, 'Report on the tour in Afghanistan of
His Majesty Amir Habib-ulla Khan G.C.B., G.C.M.G., 1907',
Simla, 1908, LPS/7/225, 319, p. xi.

    31. See R. Tapper, 'Ethnicity and class'.

    32. See further, R. Tapper and N. Tapper, Report on
Project No. HR 1141/1, 'The role of nomads in a region of
northern Afghanistan', Social Science Research Council, London
1972; N. Tapper, 'Marriage and social organization among
Durrani Pashtuns in northern Afghanistan', unpublished PhD
thesis, University of London, 1979; and works by R. Tapper,
Glatzer, Tavakolian, referred to above.

Chapter 8
WHY TRIBES HAVE CHIEFS: A CASE FROM BALUCHISTAN

Philip Carl Salzman

Heuristics

Tribal political structures are influenced, condit-
ioned and determined by both internal, local factors
and external, supra-local factors. It is misleading to single out a priori, as is sometimes
done, one or the other sphere as of primary importance, for this means either ignoring major influences or bringing them in through the back door by
taking them as given.
    Internal forms, inherent tendencies, and local
system parameters are major influences in the formation and operation of tribal political systems:
such factors as tribal values, cognitive frameworks,
and cultural commitments, as mode, means and relations of production, and as environment, adaptation
and eco-system must be examined and taken into
account, but internal and local causes cannot be
assumed a priori to be the decisive determinants.
    Similarly, external ties, foreign relations,
and extraneous pressures are major influences in the
formation and operation of tribal political systems:
such factors as high religions, literary traditions,
and formalised cultural transmission, as state pressures, government preferences, and national administration manoeuvres, and as inter-tribal alliances,
rivalries and conflicts, must be examined and taken
into account, but external and supra-local causes
cannot be assumed a priori to be the decisive determinants.
    Accounting for tribal political structures, and
for the tribal political systems of which they are
the skeletons, requires consideration of all elements which inhabit and constrain, and those which
encourage and facilitate, the development and maintenance of the particular forms under examination.

Any particular political form results from the
interplay of various factors, each pushing in its
own direction, and thus can be seen as a compromise
consequence of the multiplicity of factors.

To take this interplay of factors into account
requires an analysis placing each major characteristic of the political system under consideration on
a scale of greater and lesser value, so that each
factor can be seen as working towards one or another
value on the scale, and the place of the existing
characteristic as a result of all the factors at
work. In this way, the influence of both positive
and negative factors can be scrutinised, and the
impact on the structure of a change in one or another factor understood.

In specifying these factors, and examining the
part they play, elements both internal to tribal
life and external to it must be considered as positive and negative factors. Culture, economy, and
adaptation, and high culture, state pressures, and
inter-tribal relations are all likely to be of some
importance, and at least several will be major
factors.

But what, exactly, is the phenomenon to be
understood, the pattern to be explained, the 'dependent variable'? What are the constituents of
'tribal political structures' and how do they vary?
'Political structures' I take to be arrangements
for handling questions of leadership, decision-
making, conflict and the like. ('Tribes', for the
purposes of this discussion, need not be defined
analytically; customary usage will suffice.)

In considering variation among tribal political
structures, there are six dimensions that can provide a basis for initial exploration: First there
is the <u>scale</u> of the unit. What is the size of the
population for which the particular political structure exists? In comparing political systems, similarity in form of structure - whether segmentary
lineage system, chiefdom, or other - is not enough
to indicate similarity of political system; a polity
of 100 families is significantly different from a
polity of 10,000 families. Conditions underlying
differences of scale, and consequences from differences in scale, need to be examined. Second, there
is the degree of <u>contingency</u> in the political structure. To what extent does the political system work
in an ongoing fashion, and to what extent is it in-
operative in some circumstances and operative in
others? In some cases maximal political units are
activated only very occasionally, while in other

cases they and their political structures are operative at all times; contingent and ongoing polities,
even if of the same scale and structure, are substantially different from one another. Third, there
is the extent of centralisation. To what degree are
decisions made on behalf of the collectivity, and to
what degree by constituent parts, such as sub-groups
and individuals? Fourth, there is the presence or
absence of specialised political offices. Are there
roles specified in terms of political authority?
Even when there is a degree of centralisation, decisions can be based upon different structures, from
general assemblies, to councils, to officials. It
is important to note the conditions under which political offices, as opposed to assemblies, are found,
are the consequences of different degrees of specialisation in political roles. Fifth, there is the
scope of authority. To what areas of life does political authority extend; what are the spheres within
which decisions are made by means of the political
structure? Similar political structures can vary in
the scope of their intervention in spheres of tribal
life, from highly restricted to widely applicable.
Sixth, there is the basis of enforcement. To what
extent, and by what means, can decisions made in the
political system be enforced; what is the basis of
acceptance and conformity in the polity? Different
political systems rely on different combinations of
motivations - intrinsic, internalised, and extrinsic
(positive and negative sanctions); these various
patterns require different bases and have different
consequences.
    These analytic dimensions provide conceptual
tools for acting upon the assumption that political
systems vary from society to society and from tribe
to tribe (as long as tribes are not defined as those
groupings with a particular type of political
system). More specifically, to say that two tribes
have segmentary political systems, or that two
others have chiefs, is hardly to say that the tribes
in each set have similar political structures except
in terms of structural form. After all, the role of
chief varies markedly from group to group: there are
chiefs and CHIEFS, and no doubt Chiefs and chiefs.
And the role and importance of lineages varies
between tribes: there are lineages and LINEAGES; and
so on.
    Furthermore, we have been warned about charac-
terising whole societies in terms of particular
structural forms. It is misleading to do so because
particular forms can have different scope and con-

MAP 5:   *Sketch-map of Iranian Baluchistan, to show places mentioned in chapter 8*

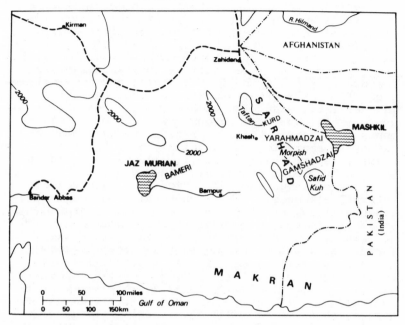

tent, and can live with a variety of institutional neighbours, any set of which can influence the total effect.

So it is rather important to pin down as precisely as possible the nature of the political system, and the range of variations between tribal political systems, before looking to explanation. But once this is done, one can turn attention to the complex of factors, both positive and negative, of which the political structure, or one or more characteristics of it, is the consequence. Why is it that one tribe consists of 500 souls and another of 50,000 souls? Why is it that pasture is centrally allocated in one tribe and entirely open in another? Why can one chief collect substantial taxes while another cannot? Why can a council of elders in one tribe enforce judicial decisions whereas in another tribe resolutions of conflict must be voluntarily accepted by all parties? Why are some tribes larger, more centralised, more structurally stable, more specialised in role development, or more interventionist, than others?

In attempting to answer such questions, it will be necessary to look at factors both within and without the tribe, both internal and external to it, both local and supra-local. Taking the full range of factors into account might be facilitated by a regional perspective. This approach, rather than taking the tribe as the most exclusive unit of analysis, focuses upon the wider region, and examines the place of the tribe in the region and the influence of other regional sub-groups upon the tribe. The heuristic assertion underlying the regional approach is that local groups not only make adjustments to others within the region but that many of the group characteristics which can be taken as primary features arise specifically as a result of inter-group relations within the region.

At the same time, attention must be given to internal elements, such as cultural commitments, organisational patterns, and demographic parameters, which are forces and constraints in their own right. How much of an independent force these internal factors are, and to what extent external factors are able to influence patterns of tribal life, are central questions to be explored. Probably the questions cannot be answered at a general level, but can be dealt with only through specification of the circumstances under which a particular factor, or complex of factors, is influential to one extent or another.

In any case, the determination of the importance of various factors requires, at the present state of knowledge, further exploration of case material, which will provide more grist for the theoretical mill and will bring closer the day when more systematic and detailed comparative analysis is possible.

The Yarahmadzai Political Structure, 1850-1935

The Yarahmadzai (Shah Nawazi) Baluch of south-eastern Iran[1] have what might be called a rather unlikely political structure: it is rather difficult to describe and explain, and presents something of a puzzle to the anthropologist. At the most abstract level, it might be characterised as a segmentary lineage system with a chief on top. Now both of these institutions - segmentary lineage systems and chiefs - are familiar presences in the Middle Eastern tribal scene; so what is the cause of the difficulty, the puzzle? The awkwardness of the Yar-

ahmadzai political system for the anthropological
observer is not so much in the separate parts of the
system, but rather their juxtaposition, their combination as parts of a system. Chiefs and segmentary lineage systems do not, should not, fit very
well together.

It is all very well to say that the Yarahmadzai
political structure is 'a segmentary lineage system
with a chief on top'. But the thing about segmentary
lineage systems is that they have no tops, and thus
there is no top for a chief to be on. So where is
the chief, or, to put it another way, how can there
be a chief in a system with no top? For we mean by
'chief' the office of highest political authority in
the group, and so there must be a hierarchy of authority at the top of which the chief may reside. But
by 'segmentary lineage system' we mean a set of
equal lineages allied relatively and contingently
for political action, decisions being made by assemblies and councils, with no offices and no hierarchy
of authority, and thus no top. Chiefs and segmentary lineage systems would seem to be incompatible,
both logically and practically; a chiefdom is hierarchical, centralised, and based upon stable relations among its constituent groups, whereas a segmentary lineage system is egalitarian, decentralised,
and based upon variable and contingent relations
among its constituent groups.

Given, then, that the Yarahmadzai political
system is made up of incompatible elements, how does
it work? Two patterns can be discerned: One is an
allocation of spheres, a division of activities between the two contradictory political frameworks,
such that one kind of circumstance elicits response
in terms of one framework, i.e. the segmentary lineage system, and another kind of circumstance elicits response in terms of another framework, i.e.
the chiefship. The second pattern, although it is
tempting to call it an anti-pattern, is the repeated
trespassing of one system upon the other, thus
making the operation of each system skewed, as it
were, by the influence of the other. Here the in-
compatibility of the two organisational frameworks
manifests itself in claims and counter-claims,
interactions reflecting the cross-purposes of the
actors, and a good deal of plain, old-fashioned confusion and inefficiency.

Let us now approach the Yarahmadzai political
structure through a more detailed examination of the
chiefship. In general, the Yarahmadzai chief
(sardar in Baluchi, the local language) is weak in

267

comparison to many other tribal chiefs in Iran, although more or less typical for independent tribes in Iranian Baluchistan (such as the Ismailzai/Shah Bakhsh and the Gamshadzai of the Sarhad, and the Bameri of the Jaz Murian). The authority of the Sardar is quite limited and his power severely constrained; he is much more a leader than a ruler, his tribesmen much more followers than subjects.

Perhaps, before exploring the details of the position of the Sardar, it is appropriate to allude to the underlying questions of this investigation: Why do the Yarahmadzai have a chief? Why, having a chiefship, is not the chief stronger? What are the elements underlying the existence of the chiefship and its particular role in the political system? It is to these questions that the discussion is ultimately directed, and to which we shall turn after an account of the sardarship in terms of the six dimensions of tribal political structure: scale, contingency, centralisation, specialised offices, scope of authority, and enforcement.

Scale. In the approximately 200 years of its development, the Yarahmadzai tribe has grown from a handful of individuals to a population of several thousand souls. Estimates vary, but perhaps the safest figure for the present is 5,000; this is certainly the correct order of magnitude: many more than hundreds, and considerably less than 10,000. Of course, in previous decades, the population was substantially smaller, and the farther one goes back, the smaller the tribal population was. Now the purpose of this elementary and imprecise exercise in demography is to establish the constituency of the Yarahmadzai chief, the number of individuals for whom the Sardar is chief. The tribe today, as a maximal political unit, is a relatively small one compared with others in Iran, and at the turn of the century was at best half its present size. So the Yarahmadzai Sardars led a small tribe: the warriors numbered in the hundreds and the tribal economy was that of households numbering in the hundreds. From the demographic perspective, the Sardar was not especially powerful, having a relatively modest following.

Contingency. The Yarahmadzai tribe is now an ongoing maximal political entity, a permanent focus of ultimate political loyalty, a framework of ties and obligations which remains relevant whatever the political issue and the level of sub-groups involved.

Why Tribes have Chiefs

This fact is both manifested in and affected by the
office of Sardar, which stands for the tribe as a
whole. The tribal level of political organisation
does not lie inactive until being brought into life
by certain political events and structural configur-
ations; on the contrary, the tribe is an ongoing
entity at all times, and tribal membership is a relevant fact for all tribesmen at all times.

    However, this is not to say that the tribe as a
polity comes even close to monopolising political
status within the tribe. Lower-level units maintain
substantial political rights, duties and responsibilities. The most important of these are protection
of life and property, manifested in self-help and
collective responsibility, which is organised in
terms of patrilineages of structural equivalence
which are activated contingently. Control of certain
resources, such as wells, also lies with minor lineage groups. Thus, within the ongoing tribal framework, sub-units of various levels are contingently
activated and de-activated and reactivated in response to conflicts over life, injury and property.
The individual tribesman finds himself not infrequently acting as a member of a lineage of greater
or lesser depth (depending on the structural distance
of the adversary) in regard to matters of the grav-
est importance, matters that are clearly political,
in a fashion that is clearly political. The degree
of contingency within the tribe must therefore be
seen to be significant.

    The coexistence of the non-contingent tribe
with a series of contingent political sub-groups can
be seen not only as a parameter of the efficacy of
the tribal units, but also as a potential threat to
the unity of the tribe and thus its existence as an
ongoing entity. The balance is maintained, and the
tribal unit reinforced, by a division of spheres
between the tribe and its sub-groups. While the
lineages have the right and obligation to defend
members and property through self-help, to take
revenge and demand compensation according to the
laws of blood feud, the tribe as a whole has the
right and obligation to press for peace, to encourage settlement, and to compensate the injured. This
division of rights is seen most dramatically in the
formation of adversary groups according to the rules
of structural equivalence, and the contrary structuring of compensation after peace-making, in which
all minimal lineages of the tribe other than the
offended one, no matter whether close to the offending or offended minimal lineages, contribute to the

compensation of the latter. That is to say, in the settlement compensation, all minimal lineages act as members of the tribe as a whole in redressing the grievance of the offended lineage. Thus, in spite of the contingent sub-groups and the heavy political content of their rights and responsibilities, the tribe as a whole maintains its presence and influence, never disappearing, hovering always in the background, asserting its presence in ongoing and decisive ways.

In sum, the tribe as a unit, although far from monopolising the political rights and responsibilities of tribal life, is able to maintain a continuing influential presence. Tribal affiliation and tribal claims continue to be in the minds of the tribesmen, even when they are acting as members of sub-groups, even when the claims of sub-groups take first priority. That this is the case is largely the result of the office of chief, for the Sardar is the living symbol of the tribe as a whole and is the active advocate of tribal claims, reminding, encouraging, threatening, pleading, manipulating, and agitating on behalf of the tribe in the name of the tribe as a whole. Make no mistake, the tribe as a political unit is greatly weakened by the contingent political sub-groups within it, for these groups carry rights and responsibilities which are thus outside the control of the tribe, and because the sub-groups therefore present a continual threat to the unity of the tribe. Limited in power, competing for loyalty with its constituent sub-groups, threatened by schism and disunity, the tribe as a political unit none the less exists continually, and continually influences the course of events.

Centralisation. The Yarahmadzai tribe is highly decentralised. As indicated above, defence and vengeance rest with the lineages that make up the larger tribal entity. And while the tribe has peace-making as a legitimate area of application, such processes are far from limited to the tribe; bilateral peace-making between lineages is built into the rules of blood feud and is available at any level subject only to the will of the parties involved. Access to pasture and natural water sources within tribal territory is a birthright and not subject to any central allocation or control. Livestock and cultivation are owned, controlled, and disposed of by individuals and small families. Dwellings and household equipment are owned and controlled by individuals and their families. Weapons are acquired and owned

by individuals. Movement out of and back to the
tribal territory is a matter of individual discretion. Movement within the tribal territory is based
upon the discretionary decision of herding camps and
individual families. Religious observance is guided
by mullahs living among and supported by the tribesmen. There is no internal aspect of tribal life
which is centrally controlled; the Sardar has virtually no hold over the resources or activities of
the tribesmen, nor is there much in the way of co-
ordination or guidance, and what little there is -
as in regard to peace-making - is voluntary on the
part of the tribesmen.

What centralisation there is among the Yarahmadzai can be seen primarily in external relations, in
foreign affairs. External groups wishing access to
tribal territory, such as tinkers or herders from
other tribes, must receive sanction from the Sardar.
More important are other groups of political weight,
such as neighbouring tribes and representatives of
the government. Here the Sardar represents the
tribe and acts on its behalf. Negotiations with
outsiders over such weighty matters as war and
peace, control of disputed resources, and political
alliance and affiliation, are conducted through the
Sardar. However, the term 'through' is used advi-
sedly, for the Sardar represents the tribesmen, he
does not and cannot dictate to them; he leads rather
than rules them. A leader whose followers refuse to
follow is no longer a leader, and so, even in this
area which is especially the realm of the chief, he
must be highly sensitive to public opinion, to the
preferences of and constraints upon his tribesmen.

Office. Beyond that of the Sardar, there is only
one other political office in the tribal structure,
the leader (mastair) of the minimal lineage. Now
'mastair' is a general concept of political precedence, and in any group of tribesmen - a family, a
group of children, a maximal lineage - there is a
ranking in terms of this precedence. But in most
cases the status of mastair is informal. Only in
the case of the minimal lineage headman is the
recognition formal, the formality residing in the
explicit acknowledgement given by the Sardar. As the
leader of a small constituent sub-group of the
tribe, the mastair looks first and foremost to his
lineage, and only secondarily to the Sardar as leader of the tribe. He is not an agent of the Sardar
without a constituency of his own; on the contrary,
he holds his office largely by virtue of support

from his lineage.

Among the Yarahmadzai, then, there is one
political office, the chiefship, which represents
the tribe as a whole. There is a second office, the
minimal lineage headmanship, which provides a link
between the smaller, cohesive groups of kinsmen and
the chief. There are no offices at the tribal level
for agents of the Sardar. Nor are there offices
representing the higher level of lineage organisation which draw together larger agglomerations of
tribesmen. Thus the Sardar has no proto-bureaucracy
at his command, no functionaries whom he controls.
Nor has he a lengthy chain of command, no line of
officials based upon larger groupings which could
conceivably carry out directives and provide political support. In consequence, the Sardar has no
political apparatus on which to depend, and so must
rely upon general support from the tribesmen at
large in a context of independent lineage groupings
and fluid public opinion.

Of course, the relative structural solitude of
the Sardar and the fluidity of his political base,
while defining the limitations of his role, do not
nullify the importance of his office. The continuity and influence that the sardarship provides for
the tribal level of organisation clearly mark off
the political system of the Yarahmadzai from those
based solely upon segmentary lineage systems or
other wholly decentralised structures without offices at the maximal level of organisation.

Authority. The authority of the Yarahmadzai Sardar
is severely limited. As the leader of independent
tribesmen, the Sardar stands for and represents the
tribe, but is largely the servant of the tribe. Most
areas of tribal life are in the hands of lower-level
groups or individuals, as discussed above, which
leaves little of policy or administration in the
hands of the Sardar. Decisions pertaining to the
tribe at large are based, as is the case at every
level of organisation, on discussion, consultation,
debate, assessment and reassessment, and compromise.
One would not be far wrong to characterise the internal role of the Sardar as that of animateur, giving
life to, actuating, propelling the tribe as a political unit through providing an example for, encouraging, bullying, inspiring, and threatening his
tribesmen. But as with any animateur, the Sardar
ultimately depends on the decisions and actions of
his tribesmen, for without them voluntarily behind
him, he is little more than a figure-head, an empty

symbol. In setting tribal policy - usually done in
terms of specific cases rather than through abstract
general pronouncements - and making decisions, the
Sardar must to a large extent be crystallising and
enunciating public sentiment and opinion, for to
deviate too far from his tribesmen would undermine
his support and his position. There is no advantage
for the Sardar in taking positions which arouse
resentment among his followers, which will prove
difficult or impossible to implement, and which will
in the end undercut his limited authority.

Enforcement. The restricted nature of the Sardar's
authority is clearly manifested in the virtual absence of means for sanctioning. Generally speaking,
the Sardar is unable to enforce policies, decisions,
and jural dispositions. There is no police arm
available to the Sardar, no mechanism for bringing
physical coercion to bear upon the tribesmen. Not
that he has any such authority: capital punishment,
corporal punishment, or incarceration are not acts
that would be legitimate for him. In any case, the
means of coercion are distributed throughout the
tribe, and the organisation of coercion is a decentralised tribe-wide system, the segmentary lineage
system. The Sardar, as every other tribesman, is,
in regard to matters of physical coercion, caught up
in the lineage system; coercive action by the Sardar
and members of his lineage, at whatever level of
segmentation, would simply activate the structurally
equivalent opposing lineage. Physical force is not
a means available to the Sardar for governance of
the tribe.
     Nor is the Sardar able to sanction by offering
or withholding material resources. Little of the
collective tribal resources is under his control.
And, given the notoriously volatile nature of wealth
in livestock and the highly restricted possibilities
of cultivation in the tribal environment, the Sardar
hardly has the private economic means to use material resources as a major means of supporting his
position. The Sardar is not an economic patron; he
is not able to support his tribal followers and thus
place them in the position of clients. The Sardar
is not in a position to use economic resources for
sanctioning power.
     However, the Sardar does perform services for
the tribesmen, and these are valuable and valued.
Perhaps the most common service is acting as an
intermediary (wasta) between individual tribesmen,
between groups of tribesmen, between the tribe and

other tribes, and between the tribe and government
authorities. These services can be offered or with-
held, and by such means tribesmen can be sanctioned,
positively or negatively, at the discretion of the
Sardar. Now while tribesmen can be so sanctioned,
the Sardar's latitude of manoeuvre is not so great
as might seem at first glance. In fact, the incumbent of the sardarship fulfils his role and maintains his status by means of performing these services for his tribesmen; there is little more to the
role of peacetime Sardar than providing such services. And providing these services to assert his
office, the Sardar is not in a position - beyond
limited selectivity in application - to grant or
withhold them at will, to use them as sanctions to
pressure or punish his tribesmen. In short, the
Sardar cannot impose his will upon tribesmen by means
of force or by manipulating transactions.

To sum up, the sardarship is a weak political
office. The Sardar leads a small tribe, the unity
of which is to a degree undercut by politically
strong sub-groups of a contingent nature which operate more or less independently of the tribal level
of organisation. Few important areas of tribal life
fall under the central control of the Sardar, who
has no political apparatus to assist him and few
sanctions at his disposal. Far from being an oriental despot, a powerful ruler, or even a well-placed
patron, the Sardar is a leader of independent tribesmen, a symbol and representative of the tribe and
the tribesmen, and an animateur for the tribe as a
maximal political entity.

Explaining the Yarahmadzai Chiefship

In accounting for the nature of the Yarahmadzai sardarship and its particular characteristics, we must
take into account a complex of factors, some influ-
encing in one direction, some in another, this factor supporting a particular type of structure, that
factor undercutting the same type of structure, such
that the Yarahmadzai political structure can be seen
as the consequence of conflicting currents.

Let us begin with the factors that inhibit
political hierarchy, offices, and centralisation of
decision-making, control, and enforcement. Three
types of factors are of major importance here: ecological adaptation, technology and social demography.

In general, the adaptation of the Yarahmadzai -
which might be characterised as 'multi-resource

nomadism' - militates against hierarchical political
structures. The environment of northern Baluchistan
is harsh and erratic, with high aridity and highly
variable precipitation. Both the small-stock pastoralism and the limited-rainfall grain cultivation
are subject to great fluctuations of success and
failure. The supplementary date-palm cultivation,
hunting and gathering and predatory raiding are more
dependable but more restricted in importance.
     The tribal adaptation has a number of conse-
quences which have important implications for the
political system. First, the volatility of the
primary forms of production inhibits the accumulation of wealth in the hands of individuals and small
groups. At the same time, the available alternative
forms of accumulation (perhaps most important as
modes of compensation for local failures), especially
predatory, are open to all members of the tribe, and
would likely favour those less well off. Thus differentiation in terms of material wealth, which
would support a hierarchical structure, is not a
significant characteristic of the tribal economy.
Second, the high level of mobility, the ability to
move spatially, guarantees that the tribesmen are
not a 'captive' constituency. They and their families move frequently in the course of the annual
round. The primary capital resources, livestock,
are highly mobile. The technology of household
living, storage, and consumption, is attuned to nomadism: the dwellings are tents and the household
equipment is portable. Each household has transport
animals, usually camels, or access to them. Thus
the tribesmen have easy access to strategies of retreat and escape from internal despotism or external
threat. A Sardar who oppressed, exploited, or even
seriously irritated his tribesmen would find his
constituency disappearing into the mountains or over
the horizon. Third, the availability of natural
resources, especially pasture and water, is extremely erratic and unpredictable, both in time and space.
This fact, together with the sparseness of the resources whenever and wherever they occur, make
decentralised decision-making about exploitation of
natural resources virtually mandatory. Thus co-
ordination of population movement and of resource
exploitation, which could be an important function
of a central authority, is not possible here. Fourth,
the low population density resulting from the factors already mentioned means that the tribesmen are
spread over great distances, which makes it difficult
to contact and keep in touch with them. This further

makes co-ordination and control difficult. In addition, the low density means that tribesmen seldom
feel crowded or need externally controlled organisation or co-ordination.

Further technological factors support the considerations presented above. First, the means of
communication and transportation are primitive;
animal transport and face-to-face communications
are most common and more or less the limits. Second,
the means of physical coercion (weaponry) are primitive, limited to small fire-arms at best, and are
equally distributed throughout the tribe. That a
small group could establish political control through
superior fire-power, or enhance their power through
a monopoly of weaponry, is inconceivable in the
tribal context. Third, technological means for developing agriculture, especially through the use of
irrigation, are not available on a significant scale,
such that they could provide an economic basis for
political differentiation and an anchor for a non-
mobile sector of the population which would be less
independent. The absence of such a development
deprives the Sardar of control over a body of dependent agricultural workers and of patronage that could
have made independent pastoral producers more dependent.

Finally, the social and political demography of
the region inhibits a tight political control by the
Sardar. Retreat and escape are possible for tribesmen because of two factors. First, the region is far
from crowded. The Yarahmadzai are not pressed in on
every side by other populations crowded in their own
territories and loathe to sustain any intruders. On
the contrary, there are more or less unoccupied areas
which could support new groups in the austere style
to which they had become accustomed. Second, the
surrounding tribes (especially the Gamshadzai and
Ismailzai, which are similar in most respects to the
Yarahmadzai) and other groupings are not unwelcoming.
There are no serious linguistic, religious, or ethnic
barriers. In some cases, there is a history of collaboration, of affinal ties, and even of common descent. These factors contribute to the voluntary
nature of participation in the tribal polity, and
work against a mandatory, compulsory presence within
the tribe, and thus place constraints on the ability
of the Sardar to control his tribesmen.

The adaptation, economy, technology, and demography of the Yarahmadzai tribesmen are conducive to
autonomy of the household and the minimal lineage.
They tend to make very difficult any concentration

of the means of production, or coercion, or administration, thus removing the support that any such
concentration would provide for political differentiation and hierarchy, for control and centralisation.
    What, then, is the basis of the political dif-
ferentiation and hierarchy in the tribe, as manifested in the office of Sardar? The functional answer is
that it is based on the provision of an essential
service: mediation between the tribe and external
powers. The structural answer is that a population
which is intimately and immediately engaged with a
powerful external presence, but which does not throw
up a political organisation that can compete with the
external presence on a more or less comparable level,
will become dependent on that external force or be
absorbed by it, the only alternative being retreat
and escape. Thus tribes with politically powerful
neighbours take three forms: the subordinate, the politically evolved, and the no-longer-present. The Yarahmadzai, with its chief and ongoing level of tribal
organisation, is an example of the second type of
tribe, a tribe which has evolved politically in response to engagement with a politically more highly-
organised neighbour.
    The Yarahmadzai tribe did not come into being in
a political vacuum. On the contrary, from its beginning, the tribe was located, if not in, at least on
the borders of, a territory that was occupied by a
highly-organised system of formidable economic and
political power. This quasi-feudal proto-state was
organised and controlled by the Kurds, who supplied
the political and military elite, and the hakom,
ruler, of the complex polity.[2]
    The Kurds were originally sent to the Sarhad of
Baluchistan by Shah Abbas the Great as part of his
policy of weakening dangerous tribes by removing them
from their local territories, by splitting them up,
and by sending them to distant areas occupied by diverse, and thus not solidary, populations. As with
certain other groups, he was able to make the Kurds
his agents, acting on his behalf, by sending them to
an unsettled (but not unoccupied) outlying area with
a mandate to establish order in the name of the crown.
    In the Sarhad, the Kurds established themselves
at the location of the only substantial natural water-
source in the region, on the slopes of the Kuh-i
Taftan, and at the central, strategic location on the
plains, at Khash, which was an area of good but not
readily accessible water and of good soil. They gained control over the small, dispersed, and socially
fragmented populations of the region, some of which

were primarily settled cultivators on the mountain slopes, and others of which were locally-organised small-stock pastoralists, and all of which, as told by the Kurds, were pagan rather than Muslim. The Kurds established a tribute (rayat) system, in which they regularly received a substantial portion, in kind, from the producers, who were labelled rayati. Other groups, mainly nomads, became part-time retainers providing additional political and military support, in return for a portion of the spoils: these retainers were called topangchini.

This type of system - the hakomate, ruled by a hakom with support from his kin group, the hakomzat, based in fortified agricultural centres while extending throughout a region, provided for primarily by dependent agricultural populations and in a more limited fashion by pastoral producers, supported by quasi-military subordinates, usually nomads - is common in Iranian Baluchistan, especially the regions south of the Sarhad. But it is rare in the Sarhad, a region with less accessible water and with a climate unsuitable for date-palm cultivation. The Sarhad is occupied, for the most part, by nomadic tribes having multi-resource economies; it is only in the Taftan/Khash region that a hakomate developed, under the Kurds.

The Kurdish hakomate was well established as the embryonic Yarahmadzai moved from the Safid Kuh in the south-east to the Morpish mountain range on the south-eastern border of the hakomate. There they settled, increasing over the years and expanding in a relatively unoccupied area toward the east and the Mashkel drainage basin, and at the same time towards the west and highland plains area of the Kurdish hakomate. Initially, as reported by the Kurds but stoutly denied by contemporary Yarahmadzai, the latter were topangchini, fighters, for the Kurds, having a subordinate political status but maintaining considerable autonomy and independence. In all probability, the Yarahmadzai did recognise the political ascendancy of the Kurds, acknowledging it symbolically when necessary and co-operating with them when convenient and desirable. The Yarahmadzai, unlike the nomadic groups of the hakomates in southern Baluchistan, never recognised the hakom as a leader to whom they had allegiance. Instead, it seems, the Yarahmadzai threw up their own political leader, the Sardar, and crystallised their unity at a maximal, tribal level of political organisation.

Now although the Kurds maintained a loyalty to the Iranian crown, governed as agents of the crown,

and received some encouragement and support from the
crown, officials of the government and their monetary
and military resources were far from the hakomate, in
distant Bampur to the south or even more distant Kirman to the west. In practice, the Kurdish hakomate
was for the most part on its own, although it could
draw for support upon alliances with other hakomates.
Thus, as the Yarahmadzai tribe grew larger, more
powerful, and more ambitious, the Kurds faced a serious challenge. In the event, the Yarahmadzai tribe
expanded at the expense of the Kurds and their de-
pendents. This engagement between the Kurds and the
Yarahmadzai took place in fits and starts, over several generations during the nineteenth and early
twentieth centuries. During the course of the on-
again, off-again conflict, interspersed with periods
of settlement and peace-making, considerable blood
was spilled, and at one point the Kurds were driven
out of the Sarhad altogether. The final disposition,
at the time of arrival of the Iranian government in
1928-35, was that the Yarahmadzai had taken control
of the plains and the Kurds had re-formed in the
Taftan range, and that the Yarahmadzai tribe was the
major political power in the region.

During this conflict, the Yarahmadzai Sardars had
been war-leaders and peace-negotiators, strategists
and mediators, meeting the Kurdish hakoms as independent political leaders. Here we can see positive
feedback at work in political development: the Yarahmadzai could challenge the Kurds because of (among
other things) their tribal political structure, with
its leadership and coherence at the maximal level,
and at the same time the tribal political structure
was reinforced and enhanced by the engagement with the
Kurds, in which the value and importance of the
sardarship and tribal unity was demonstrated.[3]

In sum, the centrifugal influences upon the Yarahmadzai political system, balanced by the centripetal
influence of political engagement with highly organised external powers, have resulted in the particular
form of Yarahmadzai political structure, the restricted chiefship ingeniously fitted to a modified segmentary lineage system. That the lineage system is a
major structure, that the chiefship is highly limited,
and that the tribe is as egalitarian and decentralised as it is, are largely the effects of these centrifugal factors. That there is a chiefship and continuing maximal level of organisation, that the tribal
political system is as hierarchical and centralised
as it is, are largely effects of that centripetal factor.

Before returning to general considerations, a

word remains to be said about the multiformity of the
Yarahmadzai political system, about the fact that the
system contains two more or less separate, almost contradictory, structures, that is, the chiefship and the
segmentary lineage system. Now we have taken this
juxtaposition, this combination of two seemingly incompatible structures, as anomalous, as peculiar, as
difficult to explain. But we have attempted to explain
it, both in terms of the factors and influences that
gave rise to each, and in terms of the ways each is
fitted to the other, how the two structures have ac-
commodated so as to coexist. However, the sense of
anomaly remains, because there is in our analytic
models an implicit assumption of perfect integration,
of structural purity, of institutional consistency.

And yet, it does not really make much sense to
expect a society to be all of a piece.[4] This is especially true if we regard society as, in some substantial measure, a set of social arrangements for
dealing with needs, for coping with problems, for
adapting to circumstances and external forces.[5] Circumstances and problems are not all of the same type
and cannot all be addressed by the same response, nor
are the needs constant over time, but rather there is
one thing and then another quite different. With these
considerations in mind, we might consider multiformity, as in the case of the Yarahmadzai political
structure, as a set of organisational alternatives
which can be brought to bear alternately as different
types of problems and circumstances come up, such
that a particular situation can be responded to by
means of the most appropriate organisational form of
those available. In the Yarahmadzai case, situations
most effectively dealt with by a decentralised response can be attacked through the segmentary lineage
system, whereas situations most usefully dealt with
by means of co-ordination can be responded to through
the chiefship. Thus multiformity is not necessarily
a reflection of malintegration, but is more likely a
prudent maintenance of organisational alternatives in
response to the variety of circumstances with which
the tribesmen must deal.

Since 1935 and the more effective encapsulation
of the Yarahmadzai tribe within the Iranian state, the
balance between the tribal political hierarchy and
the segmentary lineage system has shifted, with the
hierarchy and the chiefship coming to have relatively
more weight and the lineage system somewhat less.
With encapsulation, the Sardar became the reluctant
bottom man in the national government hierarchy, presenting demands of the government to his tribesmen,

and being responsible to government for the actions
of his tribesmen. The Sardar, from being an independent leader of free tribesmen, became a middleman, the
two-way channel of information and goods, the resolver
(or obfuscator) of differences between the tribe and
government representatives, and the advocate of the
tribe to the government.[6]
    The Sardar took this new role under threat of
military sanction, but also in response to financial
benefits. These levers have had serious consequences
not only for the parameters within which the Sardar
operates, but also for the relationship between him and
the tribesmen. One consequence is that the chief has
limited but significant external politico-military
support, independent of the intentions and wishes of
the tribesmen. A second is that the chief has external sources of economic goods and services, which can
be used both to bolster his own economic position and
also as patronage to influence his tribesmen. So there
has been a shift in the relationship, with the Sardar
somewhat less of a leader and somewhat more of a patron, and the tribesmen somewhat less independent followers and somewhat more dependent clients. Economic
and political differentiation and centralisation thus
increase, and the egalitarian, decentralised lineage
system less frequently and less effectively provides
the means for dealing with political and economic
concerns. The tribal political system remains multiform, but is now weighted more heavily than before
towards hierarchy.

Conclusion

Tribal political systems are a consequence of multi-
directional and sometimes contradictory influences
stemming from internal forms, inherent tendencies, and
local system parameters, on the one hand, and extraneous pressures, foreign influences, and external ties,
on the other hand. The structural forms resulting
from these influences are compromises of all the varying tendencies; sometimes these compromises can be
built into a unitary structure, but sometimes they
are of a multiform nature.
    The internal factors - adaptation, economy, tech-
nology, demography - that influenced the Yarahmadzai
political system towards egalitarian, decentralised,
contingent structures, would, with other characteristics than obtain among them, have influences in
other directions. Richer and more dependable natural
resources would provide a better basis for an extrac-
table surplus and for control and co-ordination. An

economy based more upon market exchange, especially
with external populations, would be more susceptible
to control and co-ordination. More stable means of
production would be more conducive to accumulation of
wealth and economic differentiation. Higher population density, both internally and externally, would
make the tribesmen more accessible. A less nomadic
technology of production would also make the producers more accessible, and a military technology less
available to the population at large would facilitate
concentration of the means of coercion. Differentiation and concentration of the means of production,
coercion, or administration would favour increased
political differentiation, hierarchy, centralisation
and organisational diffusion. Internal factors with
values in the other direction, such as even lower
population density, or an economy based more upon marginal resources, or the like, would influence the
political system more strongly towards egalitarianism,
decentralisation, and structural contingency.

The external factors among the Yarahmadzai - especially political engagement with a more highly organised external power - that influenced their political system towards hierarchical, centralised structures and institutions, particularly the chiefship,
would, with other characteristics than among the
Yarahmadzai, have influences in other directions. External relations limited to decentralised tribal
groups would probably not support the development of hierarchical, centralised structures.[7] External relations
based upon extensive economic exchange with other,
especially sedentary populations, would require
liaison and co-ordination, and would support institutionalised offices and structures. Engagement with an
even stronger external power would, if the tribe were
to remain independent, require greater mobilisation
of human and economic resources, and thus an even
higher level of organisation. Encapsulation within a
powerful state (as happened to the Yarahmadzai after
1935, the point at which they became the Shah Nawazi)
can lead to a more hierarchical, centralised, and
crystallised structure as a result of a state policy
of indirect rule and the consequent access of the
tribal political hierarchy to the resources (administrative, economic and military) of the state.

In sum, we shall have more hope of understanding
why tribes have chiefs:

- if we carefully delineate the various substantive
  aspects of tribal political systems and conceptual-
  ise them as structural and functional variables;

- if we do not underemphasise the multiplicity of the
  factors, not all pressing in the same direction,
  that influence tribal political systems;
- if we do not underestimate the importance of factors intrinsic to non-political aspects of tribal
  life, and at the same time do not underestimate the
  importance of factors extrinsic to tribal life, especially those pressures that arise from engagement
  with other populations;
- if we recognise that societies are not perfectly
  integrated or structurally pure, that there is often
  a multiformity, with two or more structural forms
  maintained as organisational alternatives, each of
  which may be activated in response to particular
  types of challenges; and
- if we concentrate upon the specification of those
  conditions, of the complex patterns of sometimes
  contradictory forces, under which one or another
  type of tribal political system develops and is
  maintained.

NOTES

1. P.C. Salzman, 'Movement and resource extraction among
pastoral nomads: the case of the Shah Nawazi Baluch'. *AQ*, 44
(1971), pp. 185-97; id., 'Adaptation and political organization in Iranian Baluchistan', *Ethnology*, 10 (1971), pp. 433-44;
id., 'Adaptation and change among the Yarahmadzai Baluch',
unpublished PhD thesis, University of Chicago, 1972; id.,
'Multi-resource nomadism in Iranian Baluchistan', in W. Irons
and N. Dyson-Hudson (eds.), *Perspectives on Nomadism* (Brill,
Leiden, 1972), pp. 60-8.

2. B.J. Spooner, 'Politics, kinship and ecology in
southeast Persia', *Ethnology*, 8 (1969), pp. 139-52; J.F. Bestor,
'The Kurds of Iranian Baluchistan: a regional elite', unpublished MA thesis, McGill University, 1979.

3. Cf. R. Cohen and E. Service (eds.), *Origins of the
State* (ISHI, Philadelphia, 1978).

4. P.C. Salzman, 'Introduction: processes of sedentarization as adaptation and response', in P.C. Salzman (ed.),
*When Nomads Settle: Processes of Sedentarization as Adapta-
tion and Response* (Praeger/Bergin, New York, 1980), pp. 1-19.

5. P.C. Salzman, 'Ideology and change in Middle Eastern
tribal societies', *Man (NS)*, 13 (1978), pp. 618-37.

6. P.C. Salzman, 'Continuity and change in Baluchi tribal leadership', *IJMES*, 4 (1973), pp. 428-39; id. 'Tribal
chiefs as middlemen: the politics of encapsulation in the
Middle East', *AQ*, 47 (1974), pp. 203-10.

7. Cf. M.D. Sahlins, 'The segmentary lineage: an organization of predatory expansion', *AA*, 63 (1961), pp. 322-43.

Chapter 9
IRAN AND THE QASHQAI TRIBAL CONFEDERACY

Lois Beck

Introduction[1]

This chapter is directed toward understanding the
dialectical processes involved in the contact between pastoral nomadic tribes and state-organised
societies. In recent discussions in anthropology and
history, the existence of socio-political units is
sometimes explained in terms of external and more
powerful forces. This is a welcome change of perspective from previous holistic and functionalist
orientations, but it is incomplete. Knowing what
the external powers are and how they impinge on
pastoral nomadic populations does not adequately explain why some populations develop hierarchical
political institutions and form confederacies while
others do not. It does not explain why, among
tribes under the rule of a single state, confederacies emerge in one area and not another, nor why
the life spans of different confederacies within a
state do not coincide. Knowing the nature of the
external stimulus does not explain how political
hierarchies emerge, nor can it predict where the
core leadership will emerge. Finally, it does not
explain the relative effectiveness of tribal leaders
and their confederacies.
Internal factors also contribute in important
ways to the emergence of hierarchical political
institutions, and it is an understanding of the
dynamic interaction between external and internal
factors that best explains political development.
Also, the setting in which the interaction occurs
introduces factors that mediate between the population and external powers. For example, the context
in which a trade route is opened, a commercial enterprise is developed, or a foreign power is involved
may restructure the interaction between a population

and an external power to the point that institutionalised political structures develop within the population. The following factors are relevant in the
development of political hierarchies and confederacies among nomadic pastoralists: ecological setting,
geographical and strategic location, resource base,
economic production and exchange, socio-economic
stratification, trade (regional, national, international), trade routes, capitalist penetration,
foreign involvement, proximity of cities, competing
groups and classes, warfare, ties with instituional-
ised religion, and minority (or ethnic) status. They
can change in importance through time, and each is
dynamically connected with others.
    In the case of the Qashqai, the factors of
urban proximity, trade routes, and foreign involvement were closely connected, and explanations for
the historically early emergence of the confederacy
as a major political power in south-west Iran, and
for its longevity, include involvement with the
Iranian state and all the factors mentioned above.
The Qashqai case is unusual in these respects, but
its examination can illuminate tribe-state relations
elsewhere and inform the development and testing
of hypotheses. The complexity of the Qashqai case
invalidates any single-cause explanation for tribal
and confederacy development. Those who seek explanations for political hierarchies in single features
such as population growth, resource scarcity,
capitalist penetration or 'state' pressure, may be
encouraged by the discussion of the Qashqai case to
look again at historical and ethnographic materials
for indications of additional, interacting features.
    Recent hypotheses concerning political develop-
ment among pastoral nomads focus on their interactions with states, state-organised societies, and
external stimuli. Irons suggests that

> among pastoral nomadic societies, hierarchical
> political institutions are generated only by
> external political relations with state
> societies, and never develop purely as a result
> of the internal dynamics of such societies ...
> in the absence of relatively intensive politi-
> cal interaction with sedentary society, pastor-
> al nomads will be organized into small autono-
> mous groups, or segmentary lineage systems.
> Chiefly office with real authority will be
> generated only by interaction with sedentary
> state-organized society.[2]

285

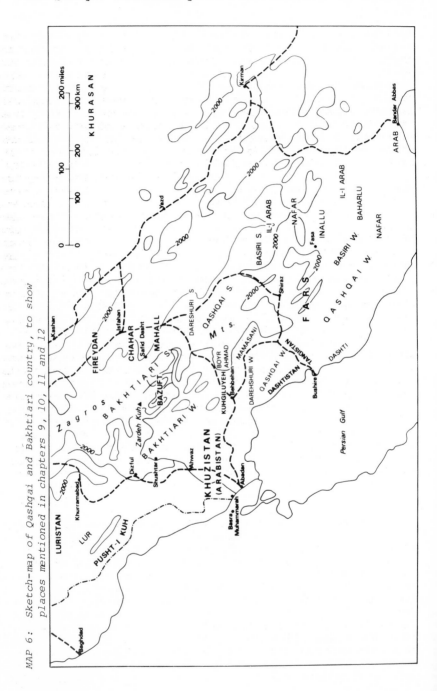

MAP 6: Sketch-map of Qashqai and Bakhtiari country, to show places mentioned in chapters 9, 10, 11 and 12

But since all pastoral nomadic societies interact politically with sedentary state-organised societies, the 'internal dynamics' of the former cannot be seen apart from their contacts with the latter. Also, a determination of the time when interaction between the two societies becomes 'intense' is problematic. Tapper explains two ideal types of tribal leaders - 'brigands' and 'chiefs' - in terms of the relative weakness or strength of the central government, while Garthwaite suggests that 'the potential for tribal confederation is directly proportional to the strength of an external stimulus',[3] a hypothesis which is general and broadly applicable.

In order to enhance the utility of hypotheses concerning tribe-state relations and the formation of tribal confederacies, the dynamic, dialectical processes involved in the interactions must be considered. Helfgott's discussion of the 'constant dynamic in Iranian history involving the structured relations between two distinct socioeconomic formations - one characterized by the natural division of labor and kinship relations and the other characterized by a more complex division of labor and class rule'[4] is relevant in this regard. Hypotheses should also recognise complexities within the socio-political unit and the external powers. Therefore, it is hypothesised that the more complex and multi-faceted a pastoral nomadic population's interactions are with external political powers, the greater the potential for hierarchical political institutions and the formation of a tribal confederacy. Finally, an adequate explanation of the interaction between pastoral nomadic societies and state-organised societies is not possible without an understanding of the historical, ecological and socio-political context.

Background

From earliest historical evidence, the various groups affiliated as 'Qashqai' were not of homogeneous origin. The dominant political elements were Turkic, derived from western Oghuz/Ghuzz groups. One reference places some Qashqai south of Isfahan in 1415, and Fasai mentioned the involvement of Farsi-Madan (later a major Qashqai tribe) in a revolt against Shah Abbas in 1590. The main development of the Qashqai confederacy appears to have begun in the seventeenth century. However, no detailed historical data on the Qashqai exist until the eighteenth

century. Some Qashqai were sent to Khurasan from
Fars by Nadir Shah Afshar in the 1730s, but their
organisation with others in Fars previous to that
time is not known. Once further into the eighteenth
century, there is substantial evidence for Qashqai
activity.[5]

The key role in tribe-state relations in the
Qashqai case was that of the ilkhani or paramount
leader. In his history of the Qashqai, Oberling
uses the ilkhani title for Jani Aqa (early 1700s)
and for subsequent paramount tribal leaders, while
Garrod states that the first ilkhani was appointed
by Karim Khan Zand (1747-79). Lambton notes the
appointment during Karim Khan's reign of a Qashqai
khan as ilbegi (chief) of all Turkic tribes in Fars,
which may have been the precursor of the ilkhani
appointment. Fasai claims that Jani Khan was the
first Qashqai to possess the ilkhani title, which
was bestowed by government, he says, in 1818/19.
Whether earlier khans were regarded as ilkhani by
their subjects or formally appointed by the state
before 1818 is not yet documented. However, Malik
Mansur Khan, a current Qashqai leader, says that his
ancestors were first made ilbegi mamlakat-i Fars by
the state, then ilkhani mamlakat-i Fars, and finally
ilkhani Qashqai. Muhammad Huseyn Khan Qashqai says
that Jani Khan was ilkhani mamlakat-i Fars and
Muhammad Quli his son the first ilkhani Qashqai.[6]

It is clear that Qashqai leaders were a major
political force in the region well before the 1818
date given by Fasai. Centralised tribal leadership
was present by the time of Jani Aqa in the early
1700s, and paramount leadership has remained in one
lineage to the present day. Many tribal groups and
individuals brought by Karim Khan Zand to Fars to
serve as his standing army remained behind after the
Zand collapse and contributed to Qashqai strength
and organisation. The proximity of the Zand capital,
Shiraz, and the nature of Karim Khan's rule, undoubtedly contributed greatly to the centralisation of
the Qashqai.[7] Bestowal of the ilkhani title by the
state, whenever it occurred, appears to be the recognition of a position already in existence rather
than the 'creation' of it. This is not to say, however, that centralised leadership did not always
serve in a mediatory capacity with regard to external political powers, particularly the Iranian
state.

The Qashqai are distinguished from other tribal
and nomadic pastoral populations in south-west Iran
by their political allegiances and affiliations.

Many of the Turks, Lurs, Kurds, Arabs, Persians and gypsies who sought resources in Qashqai territory aligned themselves with Qashqai leaders and over time assumed Qashqai identity. The primary basis of this identity was political allegiance to leaders and affiliation to tribal groups (subtribes, tribes, confederacy). In the twentieth century, the major Qashqai tribes were Amaleh, Darehshuri, Kashkuli-Buzurg, Shish-Buluki, and Farsi-Madan. Others were Qarachahi, Kashkuli Kuchik, Safi-Khani, Namadi, Igdir, Jafarbeglu, Rahimi, Bollu, and Gallehzan. Identity also came with residence in Qashqai territory and the assumption of associated rights and duties of control and defence. Qashqai identity implied various cultural features such as Turkic speech, dress and custom, but these were not uniformly adopted by tribal members, and cultural variation among Qashqai still exists today. It is not uncommon to find Qashqai speaking Luri or Kurdish. The identifying labels 'Qashqai' and 'Turk' (which in Fars are virtually synonymous) are associated with these political affiliations.

The Ruling Family

The nature of the lineage and family of the paramount leaders helps to explain Qashqai political power and continuity. Leadership remained within a single lineage for a longer period than in any other tribal group or confederacy in Iran, comparable in longevity to some of Iran's urban-based elite families. Also, Qashqai khans and supporters have had close cultural and personal ties, which contrasts with the situation in some other major tribes and confederacies in Iran. For example, Bakhtiari khans were said to be despised by much of their affiliated populations,[8] while the Qashqai ruling family had the support of their tribal followers and considerable charismatic influence over them.

The contemporary leaders of the Qashqai confederacy trace descent from Amir Ghazi Shahilu (reputed relative of Shah Ismail (1501-24) who established Shii Islam as the state religion) and from his descendant six generations later, Jani Aqa, who is considered the founder of the confederacy.[9] The fact that paramount leadership has never left the Shahilu patrilineage, the inability of other Qashqai political forces to take over leadership of the confederacy after the leaders' exile in 1954-6, and the speed with which the latter resumed leadership on

their return from exile in 1979, are evidence of the
charismatic notions held about the lineage and its
leadership.[10]
    The Shahilu lineage did not derive from one of
the Qashqai tribes, nor is it today a segment of one.
It has been a separate socio-political unit since at
least the time of Jani Aqa. The paramount leaders
were therefore not structurally or socially constrained by kinship ties to one particular tribal
group. However, since groups were affiliated directly to the ruling lineage, the attachments could be
tenuous, for the rulers ran the risk of losing
supporters if their actions or demands were unacceptable.
    Marriage restrictions have helped to maintain
the exclusiveness of the Shahilu lineage. Outsiders
have rarely been allowed to marry women of the family, and the lineage's small size has meant that
finding marriage partners within the family for both
sexes has been difficult. But through the generations, the family has created alliances in carefully-
chosen sectors of Iranian politics. Men of the ruling family married within the lineage or with collateral kin, or they married with a few select khan
families of component Qashqai tribes, with other
tribal elites such as the Bakhtiari khans, and with
city-based elite. Women of the ruling family did
not have this range of possible marriage partners,
since more control was exercised over their marriages.
Some never married, and the reason often given was
that suitable men of comparable or higher status did
not exist. However, marriage would deprive these
women of much of their power within and outside the
family, and so some chose to remain unmarried.
    Another key to understanding the strength and
longevity of the confederacy is in the paramount
leaders' consistent identification, in the twentieth
century and possibly earlier, with Qashqai culture
and life-style, certain aspects of which they helped
to form. In tribal territory and often in cities,
the leaders wore distinctive Qashqai hats (in two
styles). They rarely dressed like Iran's upper-class
political elite, nor did they identify with the latter, despite superficial similarities. They established tent-camps, perfected hunting and riding
skills, worked personally on their properties, and
were available - whether in tent-camps or urban residences - to any tribesperson who came to them. They
delighted in wedding celebrations, in which central
elements of the Qashqai cultural system were expressed. Women of the ruling family often wore Qashqai

women's dress and participated in camp life and
wedding ceremonies. Both men and women set themselves apart, when possible, from Persians, whom
they privately ridiculed. They associated Persian
culture with corruption, dishonesty, deceit, and
disingenuous politeness, traits which have given
them difficulty in the past.

The khans' use of the cultural system was a
prime reason for the loyalty and allegiance of the
Qashqai population. In contrast with the Bakhtiari
case, cultural connections between Qashqai khans and
commoners were strong and overt. Their relationships were generally respectful and sometimes emo-
tional. There was pride for both in being Qashqai,
and each acknowledged the importance of the other in
history. Especially in the period of nation-state-
building in twentieth-century Iran, the disadvantages
of being a national minority were lessened by the
khans' powerful national position.

The identification of both khans and commoners
with the Qashqai cultural system was closely connected with the politics of Qashqai-state relations.
It was strongly asserted when the state was weak,
while in periods of state strength there was more
assimilation to the national culture.

The Setting

The context in which the Qashqai confederacy developed contains many features that help explain its
particular character. The setting was especially
favourable for the political forms that emerged.
It is noteworthy that the tribal groups immediately
to the north-west and south-east of the Qashqai,
residing in quite different settings, had different
political institutions. Aspects of the context that
were particularly significant in the Qashqai case
are: ecology, strategic location (urban proximity,
trade routes, distance from national borders, distance from national centre), isolated and protected
seasonal pastures, migration routes, geographical
distribution, and the role of the Persian majority.

The Qashqai occupy territory that is ecologically varied and rich in resources. It is not a
marginal desert region with greatly fluctuating
pastoral resources. Population density in and near
tribal territory, given the severe climate and lack
of water and natural fuels, are suitable only for
seasonal occupancy, others are permanently occupied.
De Planhol notes that nomadic pastoralism in the

relatively lush Zagros Mountains is unexpected since
the physical environment seems to favour a settled
agricultural way of life.[11] Competitors have included other pastoralists (tribal and non-tribal),
agriculturalists, village and urban settlers, and
collectors of natural resources. A key factor of
political development in this area, therefore, is
the ecological setting; the area's history has involved a struggle for access and control. It is
suggested that centralised political institutions
were essential for any population's sustained control and use of this land.[12] Tribal and confederacy
organisation allowed Qashqai households to produce
at maximum levels with relative freedom from predatory incursions and to extract the resources and
surpluses of others, which augmented household economies (especially in times of poor pastoral conditions or government harassment) and contributed to
the overall, long-term political strength of the
population.[13] The state's interest in the Qashqai
is partly explained by its desire for the economic
surplus generated by the population. Finally, the
ecological setting contributed to socio-economic
stratification and the emergence and maintenance of
a wealthy ruling class.

The Qashqai are also strategically located.
Shiraz, the major city in south-west Iran, is located between their winter and summer pastures, south
and north of the city, and most Qashqai must migrate
past it twice annually. Shiraz was a magnet for
Qashqai political and economic affairs. Top tribal
leaders had residences and extensive contacts in the
city which, combined with their tribal backing and
their wealth, made them major figures in local politics. Tribal and urban politics often overlapped.
Some Qashqai khans were able to use their position
in the region as a basis for national prominence.
Much economic activity in Shiraz was geared towards,
and supported by, the economic production of its
hinterland, an important part of which was Qashqai
territory. Qashqai economies were tied with this
market centre and were therefore integrated into
regional, national and international economic systems. Important trade and travel routes linked
Shiraz and its hinterland with national and international markets. It was especially the link between
the Persian Gulf and south Iran (via Bushire and
Bandar Abbas) that drew the attention of the state
and foreign powers, and figured directly in the struggles among these powers and regional ones (local
government, tribes, merchants). Had Qashqai terri-

tory not bisected or abutted the three principal
routes (to Bushire, Bandar Abbas and Isfahan) a
very different tribal history would have been recorded.[14]

Qashqai territory did not touch or overlap with
Iran's state frontiers. The state never used them
to defend its borders, except in the eighteenth century when some Qashqai were taken to Khurasan, and
they were free from pressures which might be applied
by neighbouring states and by fellow-tribespeople
across frontiers. Other tribal groups do have members across frontiers, which may contribute to their
lack of commitment to the state and may encourage
efforts at unification that threaten the state. Borders provide escape routes for tribes that resist
state pressure, as in the Turkmen case.[15] Tribes
situated on borders may benefit from outside military support, but they can also suffer in numbers
and wealth because of ensuing conflicts. Border
tribes are often victims of competitions between
other forces.[16] Leaders of such border tribes can
use the presence of two states, often competing, but
they are also more vulnerable to internal political
rivals, who can play to the interests of the rival
states.[17] It is suggested that distance from borders was conducive to tribal autonomy in the long
run, and the absence of competition over the Qashqai
between bordering states helped the Shahilu lineage
to retain leadership over a long period.

Distance from the capital is another strategic
feature. As noted above, Qashqai proximity to the
Zand capital at Shiraz was an important factor in
the early development of the confederacy. With the
fall of the Zand dynasty in the 1790s, the central
government moved to Tehran, where it has remained.
This allowed the confederacy, after the important
formative years under the Zands, a high degree of
autonomy from state control and interference. Tribal
proximity to the capital can bring influence in
national affairs, but it can also sever tribal leaders from their tribal base; both occurred in the
Bakhtiari case. Except for a brief period during
the Constitutional era (1905-11), the Qashqai were
not viewed by the state as a military threat to the
capital. Before Riza Shah, Qashqai leaders did not
pursue national leadership as persistently as did
Bakhtiari leaders; most Qashqai leaders preferred to
use their Tehran connections to serve their class
and tribal interests in Fars. During and following
the Riza Shah period, they attempted to strengthen
their position with regard to the state, and a few

did seek national leadership, but the Qashqai masses
were too distant from the national capital to be
much involved. (They were, however, affected when
the state brought punishments against them because
of their leaders' actions.)

Another feature of the Qashqai context is the
relatively isolated nature of the winter and summer
pastures, which were largely inaccessible to external forces, while their mountains were easily defensible. Before the advent of Riza Shah's improved
roads and mechanised army, a state force could only
with difficulty attack the Qashqai or threaten their
lands. Even in the modern age of aircraft, paved
roads and tanks, military forces can do limited
damage to the dispersed, mobile Qashqai population.
No major military adventures were undertaken in
their territory at their expense, with the important
exception of aerial bombing of migrating groups, and
no other tribal confederacy seriously threatened
their occupancy of land.[18] In the 1960s, some Qashqai who were fugitives from Pahlavi justice successfully hid in mountain strongholds under Qashqai
protection. The Islamic Republic has been unable to
impose its authority over Qashqai territory during
its first two years.[19]

The isolated, easily protected nature of Qashqai pastures contrasts with the nature of their migration routes. These have been their Achilles'
heel, and they are also a factor behind the development of hierarchical tribal leadership. Qashqai
pastoralism depended, for ecological reasons, on the
seasonal movement of herds between widely separated
pastures; nomadism was not a political adaptation in
the Qashqai case.[20] Migration routes took them past
Shiraz and through heavily settled, non-tribal agricultural areas. External powers capable of blocking
migration routes threatened their economic survival.
Regional, national and foreign armies have attempted,
sometimes successfully, to keep some Qashqai from
travelling between winter and summer pastures. As
recently as 1971, the gendarmerie prohibited their
migrations until the celebration of the 2,500 years
of the monarchy had concluded, on the grounds that
the movement of tribal people by Persepolis and
Shiraz would be a security risk to the government
as well as to the important international guests.
While the Shah celebrated, nomads suffered and many
animals died, trapped in the cold and barren summer
pastures. The Qashqai were also vulnerable to raids
and attacks by non-Qashqai populations during their
migrations between seasonal pastures.

Until the imposition of gendarmerie control in the mid-1960s, Qashqai khans and headmen played important roles in co-ordinating movements of population during political crises, and the ilkhani often ceremonially announced the commencement of the spring migration to leaders of the major tribes. However, the role of Qashqai leaders in the general co-ordination of migrations has been exaggerated, partly following Barth's reports on the neighbouring Basiri.[21] Except under conditions of political instability, the Qashqai were relatively free to migrate when and where they chose, uncontrolled by leaders, especially after the migration had begun. Dozens of major routes and hundreds of minor ones existed, and migrating groups were independently able quickly to alter their paths if harassment, congestion, or poor conditions were reported to lie ahead.

The geographical distribution of the large Qashqai population in vast, widely-separated seasonal pastures has always caused problems for state administration. While some of Iran's major tribes reside and migrate within single provinces and can be administratively contained, the Qashqai are found in significant numbers in five areas (the present provinces of Fars, Isfahan, Kuhgiluyeh-Boyr Ahmad, Khuzistan, the Gulf coast) and fall under different provincial governments. Many reside in two or more provinces during the year. The government's administration of the Qashqai was almost always indirect, even during most periods of strong state rule, and government policy, being relayed through tribal mediators and state officials, was often vague and unimplemented.

A final element in the Qashqai setting is their minority status in relation to the dominant Persian population of the region and nation. Tribal leadership and the organisation of the confederacy protected and co-ordinated Qashqai activities and served as political and military counter-forces to intrusions and to Persian control of nearby centres of power and wealth - the state apparatus, the bazaars, and the religious institutions. Although of diverse ethnic and tribal origins, the Qashqai express their common identity as 'Turks', affirming group solidarity and creating boundaries between them and members of the surrounding society, who are Persians ('Tajik') or Lurs (often called 'Tajik' by the Qashqai). As noted above, Qashqai leaders shared this cultural identity and used its associated symbols and institutions to support their leadership.

The Qashqai Confederacy

Pressures from Outside

The nature and impact of external political powers
on the Qashqai must now be examined. It is suggested that the more complex and multifaceted a pastoral
nomadic population's interactions with external
political powers, the greater the potential for
development of hierarchical political institutions
and formation of a tribal confederacy. Why external
political powers were interested in the Qashqai, and
how the tribal population and its leaders responded,
must be considered. It is not just an issue of
'response', however, for Qashqai leaders were often
in a position to initiate interaction. They cannot
be seen as passive victims of external forces.
     External political powers include the central
government, provincial government, foreign powers,
other tribes and confederacies, and institutionalised
religion. Another external stimulus consists of
economic forces. Although two or more powers occasionally combined forces to deal with the Qashqai,
their respective interests did not necessarily coincide. In fact, much of the colour in the history of
south-west Iran derives from the opposing interests
and resulting conflicts between and among these
powers. The relationships of tribal, provincial,
national and international politics through time, as
outlined in Oberling's The Qashqa'i Nomads of Fars,
for example, are extremely complex. Discussion of
each kind of external power has as its necessary
backdrop the contextual conditions outlined above.
     The central government is the most important
and continuous of the external powers. The literature often but ambiguously uses 'state' and 'central
government' interchangeably.) Part of the central
government's interest in the Qashqai would apply to
any population occupying the rich southern Zagros:
taxes and revenues, military service, law and order
(especially near settled areas and trade routes),
loyalty and obedience. But mostly its interest was
drawn by the fact that the Qashqai, numerous,
tribally-organised, armed, mobile, and sometimes
politically independent, resisted imposition of
government control (taxation, conscription, loyalty)
and interfered with central administration. From
the time that historical materials first mention
them and perhaps earlier, they were seen as a threat
by central authorities. Some governments were not
in a position to discipline or control the Qashqai,
who were then autonomous. Others worked through,
rather than against, Qashqai leaders in order to

facilitate their administration. Still other governments intrigued and battled against them, sometimes quite effectively.

Relations between the central government and the Qashqai follow a general pattern of indirect but locationally close rule under Karim Khan Zand in the latter part of the eighteenth century, direct decentralised rule under the Qajars in the nineteenth century, direct centralised rule under the Pahlavis between the 1920s and 1978, and, up to at least January 1981, weak disintegrated authority under the Islamic Republic of Iran.

Under the Safavids, the Qashqai tribes appear to have grown by an amalgamation process through the exercise of tribal leadership.[22] According to tribal legend, some of them fought for Safavid rulers, and some leaders were given government titles and privileges. Ismail Khan and Hasan Khan, sons of Jani Aqa, accompanied Nadir Shah on his conquest of India in 1738 but were later mutilated by him and exiled to Khurasan. Karim Khan Zand allowed Ismail Khan to return to Fars, and the two men had a close personal relationship. Karim Khan, 'surrounded by friendly tribesmen',[23] appointed a Qashqai ilkhani or ilbegi.[24] Ismail Khan's son, Jani Khan, supported Karim Khan's Zand successors, and Aqa Muhammad Khan, the first Qajar ruler, took revenge on the Qashqai. The Qajar period was characterised by varying tribe-state relations, largely due to the often conflicting involvement of other external powers and the different abilities and interests of successive Qajar rulers. The Qajars sought to rule the Qashqai indirectly by instituting the office of paramount leader. The Pahlavis worked to destroy tribal power, and tribe-state relations entered a new era. The Khumeyni regime has as yet been unable to establish its authority in the Qashqai areas.

During each of these periods, paramount Qashqai leaders dealt directly with state rulers - a major characteristic of Qashqai relations with central authorities through history. Local officials were often ignored by both sides, and they suspected, often correctly, that politicking was occurring behind their backs. Relations between khans and rulers ran the gamut of intermarriage and parliament service to imprisonment and execution, sometimes in the same individuals. In attempts to exercise greater control, rulers occasionally exiled Qashqai families to distant locations, kept tribal leaders and/or relatives as court hostages, and arranged marriage alliances with court families.

Five aspects of central-government power need elaboration. First, from at least Qajar times, the central government's confirmation/appointment of the paramount Qashqai khan as ilkhani made him a government official responsible for handling tribal as well as non-tribal affairs, such as tax collection, conscription and order. While the formal appointment almost always coincided with internal recognition of a paramount leader, the powers and privileges that accompanied the title were considerable, and ilkhanis were able to enhance their already strong positions. On several occasions, the central government - often under pressure from other powers - deposed a tribally-favoured ilkhani and named a rival, intending to create an internal tribal crisis. However, tribal members usually refused allegiance, and the government was stuck with a leader who could not perform effectively.

Second, the taxes to be derived from the Qashqai and from tribes and villages under their control were considerable. In the 1830s the governors of Fars and Kirman literally chased the Qashqai from one province to the other and back again, supposedly for the privilege of having them on their tax rolls.[25] From the time of the establishment of the ilkhani, and perhaps before, his lieutenant, who held the title of ilbegi, had the task of collecting taxes from tribal members. The ilbegi kept a portion for his immediate supporters (the Amaleh), who were exempt from taxes, and on occasion passed part to the central government authorities. The central government was therefore interested in amicable relations with the ilbegi and other members of the ruling family.

Third, formal arrangements between Qashqai leaders and central authorities specified that levies would be produced for the shahs' armies. In the years of the Qashqai regiment, and when the khans had command of forces, national service brought the Qashqai leadership arms, ammunition, booty, legitimate military action against competitors, and general tribal strength.

Fourth, the central government at different periods entrusted to Qashqai leaders the task of securing the countryside. Their territory was often considered an autonomous administrative region - Vilayat-i Qashqai - and the ilkhani held responsible for it. The ilkhani and members of the ruling family were assigned various local governorships and the duty of bringing order to neighbouring tribes and areas, which added to their power and wealth. The

loci of government concern were the rich agricultural areas of Fars (from which the government could
then safely secure taxes and conscripts) and the
trade routes to Bushire, Bandar Abbas and Isfahan
(from which the government could profit by its
foreign and mercantile connections). There was much
for Qashqai leaders to gain in these ventures, and
largely as a result, much of Fars was in the hands
of, or connected with, the Qashqai.[26]
   Fifth, the central government rarely reached
the Qashqai masses directly, and when it did, contact was through agents and officers who were assigned duties but assumed additional, more profitable
ones at their own initiative. One of the main roles
of the leaders was handling such government officials
and protecting tribespeople from their predatory
incursions. Individuals and groups affiliated themselves to Qashqai leaders in order to escape the
harassments and extortions of officials. Non-Qashqai
agriculturalists in and near Qashqai territory,
tending their own or Qashqai fields, also sought
protection in this way; they were called rayat-i
Qashqai. Those who fell under Qashqai protection
had advantages in this regard that others did not,
and the leaders in turn gained agricultural surpluses, clients, and territories.
   National government was sometimes directly
opposed to provincial government - the second external power - which was not always organised to serve
national interests, such as in tax collection and
military activity. The Qashqai were often used in
power struggles between the two governments, and
Qashqai leaders, in their own interests, actively
promoted their connections with each. As a check on
provincial autonomy, the central government installed its own power figures in the south, such as
relatives of the monarch. The Governor-General of
Fars was a state appointee, but local interests,
such as mercantile families, foreign powers and
Qashqai leaders, could influence, even determine,
the appointment. (No Qashqai was ever Governor-
General.) The Governor-General occasionally con-
firmed/appointed the ilkhani on behalf of the state.
The central government was sometimes unable to control its provincial governors, who were then able to
act in their own interests. Both the Qashqai and
the British took advantage of central-government
weakness in this area. The Governor-General of Fars
and the ilkhani were frequently considered the two
top political figures in the south. A third powerful local figure, who also had important national

connections, was the Qavam al-Mulk, head of a wealthy
Shiraz merchant-landowner family. Through the nineteenth and early twentieth century, this family's
interests and those of the Qashqai ruling family
were opposed. However, their opposition was stimulated by the British, who used the Qavam (and his
Khamseh confederacy troops - see below) to fight the
Qashqai. During this period Qashqai political history was partly an expression of the varying relations
between the ilkhani, the Governor-General of Fars,
and the Qavam al-Mulk. In summary, provincial government was a mix of national and local politics.
Qashqai leaders, who were directly involved at both
levels, were used by and contributed to the various
conflicting interests.

Foreign powers - particularly the British and
to a lesser degree the Germans and Americans - form
the third category of external power. The Russians,
who were the major power in northern Iran in the
nineteenth and first half of the twentieth century,
had little direct impact on the southern Zagros
tribes, while the British played major roles in
local politics and in Qashqai history. From the
early eighteenth century to the mid-twentieth, and
especially during the Constitutional revolution and
the two World Wars, British diplomatic and commercial affairs intruded into the political and economic life of the province. While pursuing their own
interests, the British claimed that they were acting
on behalf of the Iranian government, whose apparent
inability to bring order to southern Iran they found
increasingly frustrating.

The first clashes between the British and the
Qashqai were recorded in 1850-60, when Qashqai
troops assisted in the defence of south Iran during
the Anglo-Persian war, and the British encouraged
the Iranian government to punish a few Qashqai for
the destruction of telegraph wire near Shiraz.[27]
The concern of the British with the Qashqai originally focused on what they believed to be Qashqai
disruption of their trade. In 1861-2, partly
because of British pressure on the government, the
Khamseh tribal confederacy was created, under the
leadership of the Qavam al-Mulk, to provide a balance of power in the south. The Qavam's family had
similar commercial interests to the British, who
used and financed this confederacy's leaders and
forces for their own ends. When the British threatened to create their own local army, the central
government, apparently lacking other options, entrusted the maintenance of safety on the roads and

stability in the province to the Qashqai ilkhani.
When the British could still not find safe passage
for their commerce, they pressured the government to
support the establishment of a Swedish-officered
gendarmerie, and provided additional money to the
Qavam al-Mulk for road safety and for attacks on the
Qashqai.[28]

At the beginning of World War I, the British
were mainly concerned with the safety of the Khuzistan oil fields. The German General Staff sent
Wilhelm Wassmuss, a former German Consul in Bushire,
to provoke tribal uprisings against the British and
their allied Khamseh tribes. Wassmuss dealt directly with the Qashqai ilkhani and helped to organise
Qashqai forces. Regional politics during these
years were an expression of the British-German struggle. In 1916, dissatisfied with the Qavam's performance of what they thought had been lavishly paid
for, the British financed and officered their own
military force, the South Persia Rifles, which added
another military power to the area. (A third foreign military force in the region at the time was a
cavalry regiment brought from India to strengthen
the British consular guard in Shiraz.) In 1916-18
Sir Percy Sykes and the Qashqai ilkhani arranged
peaceful relations; the British even formally recognised the latter's title. (This is the only reported occasion of ilkhani entitlement by a foreign
power.) But peace was ended when the Qavam used the
South Persia Rifles against the Qashqai; this was
'as much a Qawāmi invasion as a British one'.[29] The
British resumed efforts to create dissidence among
the Qashqai khans by offering money and arms to
those who would side with them against the ilkhani.
Sykes successfully pressed for the dismissal of the
ilkhani, but this was not accepted by the affiliated
tribes and he was shortly thereafter reinstated.

The British and Germans exploited and, to a
great extent, even created local politics in south-
west Iran in what they felt were their own national
interests. The Qashqai lost much and gained little
in their foreign affiliations during World War I.
One of the reasons Riza Shah came down so heavily on
Iran's pastoral nomadic tribes was his fear of tribal and foreign collusion against his new nation, a
fear well justified by events prior to his reign.
The foreign presence directly contributed, therefore, to Riza Shah's oppressions of the tribes.

During World War II, connections between the
Qashqai and the Germans were re-established, largely
to counter renewed British involvement with the

Qavam and the Khamseh tribes. Two of the ilkhani's
brothers resided in Germany, and one of them served
with the German army in Russia. The Germans sent
agents to the ilkhani camp. The British played a
part in the 1943 treaty negotiation between the
Qashqai and the central government, and they were [30]
apparently involved in the 1946 'tribal uprising'.

The United States became deeply involved in
Iran after World War II. The greatest blow to the
Qashqai came with the ousting (through United States
intrigue) of Prime Minister Muhammad Musaddiq, who
had been supported by Qashqai leaders, and with the
resulting exile of the ilkhani and his brothers in
1954-6. Although United States policy stressed
Iran's national armed forces, concern over oil and
the Soviet presence prompted suggestions for programmes for 'the tribes', some of which were implemented: incorporation of tribesmen in the army,
settlement schemes, and health and education programmes. The Qashqai received another major setback
under the United States-encouraged land reforms of
1962-72. Qashqai lands were nationalised, as well
as deeded to and encroached upon by non-Qashqai, and
Qashqai khans were removed from office. Without
their leadership, most Qashqai were extremely vulnerable to external pressures.[31]

Foreign powers have had major impact on southern Iran. They have never, except for brief forays
by the South Persia Rifles, invaded Qashqai territory, but their manoeuvres and intrigues against one
another and with and against national and local governments, other tribes, and some dissident Qashqai
groups, were major influences in the course of Qashqai political history.

The fourth category of external power consists
of other tribes and confederacies. The history of
inter-tribal relations in south-west Iran has yet to
be written, but ethnographic and historical evidence
demonstrates that this aspect of tribe-state relations was also important. The southern Zagros contains many tribally-organised populations which
compete over supporters, land, resources, and links
with external powers. The Qashqai were particularly
successful in these matters. The cultural diversity
within the confederacy is partial evidence for
inter-tribal mobility. It seems reasonable to attribute changes of affiliation and allegiance among
tribal groups and leaders to popular perceptions of
political effectiveness. Inter-tribal alliances
were largely provoked or necessitated by pressures
from external powers. A chequerboard model of inter-

tribal relations[32] may be appropriate for some specific historical events, but it does not represent
the complexity of ties through time nor the many
changes in alignment, and it does not explain the
differential impact of other external powers.
      One inter-tribal relationship that appears
fairly consistent from 1861 to World War II was that
between the Qashqai and the Khamseh confederacies.
The Khamseh was created specifically to foment conflict in the area, and it was used by British and
local mercantile interests against the Qashqai.
Before this, the tribes of what became the Khamseh
had been loosely affiliated with the Qashqai. The
ending of British support, and the state's removal
of both indigenous and externally-imposed leaders,
signalled the effective end of these tribes as political forces.
      The major tribes to the north-west, the Boyr
Ahmad and the Mamasani (both Kuhgiluyeh Lur tribes),
were on occasion allied with the Qashqai, particularly in hostile action against government troops,
the British, and the Qavam's Khamseh troops. But on
other occasions, the government used the Qashqai to
fight against the Lurs, and at least three governors
appointed from the Qashqai ruling family were given
responsibility for establishing order in the Kuhgiluyeh.[33] The Lur tribes never had the centralised
political organisation of the Qashqai or the Bakhtiari, largely, I suggest, because of the nature of
their location. They were not as strategically
located in terms of urban areas, trade routes, and
(in the twentieth century) oil fields, and as a
result foreign powers and state authorities were not
so interested in manipulating or controlling them.
A centralised, co-ordinating, mediatory leadership
was not needed and did not emerge.[34] However, the
Qashqai khans viewed the Lur tribes as potential
political allies, and intermarriages between the
khan families attest to the complex political relations between them. Many - perhaps even a majority
- of the Qashqai are Lur in origin, which indicates,
among other things, the extent to which the Qashqai
political system attracted and retained populations
in the region.
      North of the Qashqai summer pastures are the
Bakhtiari, who are also Lurs. Their shared border
is not long, and Qashqai commoners had less contact
with Bakhtiari than with Lurs. Partly because of
the ties of the Bakhtiari with the central government and the British, the paramount khans of the
two tribal groups were frequently at odds. On occa-

sion they supported dissident movements in each
other's confederacies. They were never effectively
allied. Hostility between the leaders of the Bakhtiari and the Arab tribes of Khuzistan, fostered by
British manipulations, led to a formal (but unprod-
uctive) alliance among Arab, Qashqai, and Lur
(Pusht-i Kuh) tribal leaders in 1910. The Bakhtiari khan Sardar Asad, from a position of national
leadership, pressured the government to replace the
existing Qashqai ilkhani with another, but the intended result did not materialise. Bakhtiari and
Qashqai tribespeople have periodically moved into
one another's territories. The Qashqai tribe of
Darehshuri particularly, whose summer pastures connect with Bakhtiari lands, used the threat of flight
to the protection of Bakhtiari khans as a weapon
against pressure from the ilkhani and as an assurance of autonomy.

The Tangistani, Dashtistani, and Dashti tribes
of the Persian Gulf coast, to the west of the Qashqai, were frequently allied with them in efforts
to fight the British and to control and exploit the
trade routes to the Gulf. Finally, there were many
other, smaller tribes in Fars that joined forces
with Qashqai leaders on various political occasions.

The fifth category of external power is that of
institutionalised religion. The Qashqai are Shii
Muslims. On a number of occasions, including the
Constitutional era, Qashqai khans were in direct
contact with ulama from Shiraz and Najaf (in Iraq)
concerning national and regional politics. They
shared a hatred of foreign interference. In 1918
Qashqai troops were allied with ulama-inspired
Shirazis in fighting the British, and in 1946 there
were meetings of tribal and religious leaders in
protest against government policy and foreign involvement; one meeting was convened by the ilkhani.[35]
In 1978 Nasir Khan Qashqai, the exiled ilkhani, paid
a personal visit to the Ayatullah Khumeyni in France
but, while they remained in contact during the early
months of the revolutionary government, they later
fell out.[36] In general, ties of the Qashqai khans
with the ulama were politically expedient. They had
little use for organised religion in the conduct of
internal and most external affairs. They did not
rely on persons of religious eminence as advisors or
mediators, and they were not devout, practising
Muslims.

The final category of external power is that of
economic forces. Economic matters have not been
neglected in the foregoing discussion, but additional

factors remain to the considered. Local and wider
economic interests were directly connected with regional politics; political figures were wealthy and
controlled a major part of the means of production.
   Qashqai land was very productive for pastoralism and cultivation, and there was competition for
control of access, use and profit. The khans, as
allocators of usufruct rights, gained economically
from the proceeds of production, and they and other
wealthy Qashqai had close ties with the market and
were among the regional elite. Urban merchants and
middlemen competed for their business and provided
additional opportunities for wealth through contracts
in animal husbandry and agriculture and in the production of wool, carpets, and opium. Capitalist
penetration of the Qashqai economy was facilitated
by the khans' activities and directly enhanced their
wealth, power and prestige. This, in turn, aided
their competition in political arenas.
   National and international economic forces per-
vaded the region. The production of wool, carpets,
opium and gum tragacanth was stimulated by foreign
commercial interests. The significance of trade
routes through Qashqai territory has been noted; by
selling 'protection' to commercial transport, by
collecting road taxes, and by raiding, some Qashqai
(and others) used the routes for economic advantage.
   Exclusive and relatively secure use of pastureland facilitated the production and market relations
of the Qashqai masses, who could more easily compete
in the regional system because of the supportive
tribal system. [37]
   Membership in the tribal system facilitated the
many economic activities of both wealthy and less
wealthy Qashqai and connected them with wider economic and political forces.

Internal Tribal Dynamics

Discussion of 'the Qashqai' as a political force
ought more properly to read, 'the Qashqai khans',
for they were the power brokers who dealt directly
with other powers in the region. Much 'Qashqai
history' is therefore a history of the Qashqai
khans. [38] It is clear, however, that the khans could
not have been the political figures they were without the political hierarchy or the support of the
Qashqai tribespeople. An account of internal tribal
dynamics is therefore essential to the discussion of
the formation and operation of the confederacy. How

the tribal population was organised, and how it articulated with the political hierarchy, should be
seen in the context of the particular setting and
the external pressures, both of which called for
centralised hierarchical leadership. Allegiance to
Qashqai leaders and membership in the tribal confederacy had advantages for the Qashqai, and facilitated their interactions with external powers.

The Qashqai were organised into a series of
socio-political groups, each of which had one or
more leaders. The lowest level of socio-political
organisation was the household, whose head represented it in most domains beyond the encampment. The
encampment was a flexible, temporary association of
households; the oldest, most respected men made some
decisions that concerned the unit, but households
had considerable independence. The pasture group, a
collection of camps in a geographically defined area,
was also a flexible arrangement of tents and camps.
A sub-tribe (tireh), consisting of one or more pasture groups in winter and summer pastures, was a
political group defined largely by kinship ties and
by attachment to a headman (kadkhuda). A tribe
(taifeh) was a collection of sub-tribes and was
headed by a family of khans, one of whom often had
the title of kalantar and role of liaison with the
ilkhani. The khan families (khavanin) comprised a
small, distinct socio-economic class with dynastic,
aristocratic characteristics. Finally, the confederacy (il) was a collection of five large and a
number of small tribes and was headed by a man of
the ruling family, often entitled ilkhani. The
chain of political authority was from household head
to elder, headman, khan, kalantar and ilkhani.

Each tribe had its own winter and summer pastures, and the khans' major function was allocation
of usufruct rights to their associated sub-tribes,
through the sub-tribal headman, who in turn allocated pasture rights to member households. Co-
ordination of the migration was not a major function
of any Qashqai leader, except when political circumstances warranted it, and then their roles were
essential. The khans, often through their headmen,
handled general tribal affairs: designation of local
leaders, administration of tribal law and justice,
resolution of intra-tribal and inter-tribal disputes,
conduct of relations with sedentary authorities,
tax collection, and certain kinds of economic redistribution. They organised defensive and offensive activities, and attempted to prevent their affiliated groups from raiding when it was not

politically advisable. The state and foreign powers
often judged the strength of tribal leaders by their
ability to control raiding by their followers.[39]
Khans were in charge of diplomatic relations with
the ilkhani, with other tribes, and with sedentary
and state authorities. Given the political and
strategic setting and the many external pressures, a
centralised, co-ordinated and effective leadership
was essential if the Qashqai were to maintain control of their territory and compete successfully
against their neighbours and intruding forces.
     The ability of the Qashqai to act as a quasi-
independent political entity, as a state within a
state, was due to the co-ordinating and mediating
efforts of the confederacy leader, the ilkhani.
While he served as khan to his Amaleh supporters,
his main functions related to external powers and to
the administration of the confederacy. An ilbegi,
usually his brother, often served as his lieutenant,
and other close relatives also performed leadership
functions, which were informally divided out according to personal skills and interests. Under Ismail
Khan Soulat al-Douleh (ilkhani from 1902-33) the
Qashqai had some of the main attributes of sovereignty - 'an independent army, an independent economy and independent foreign policy'.[40] While the
'independence' of these entities can be questioned,
the ilkhani did function as the head of a political
group which was often beyond the state's control.
He depended on the support and loyalty of the tribal
khans, and they depended on and profited from his
wider leadership functions. That he could and occasionally did act without their consent or knowledge
was due to his many external political contacts, his
mediatory position, and his membership in the local
and national political elite. One of his bases was
Shiraz, where he conducted affairs like the non-
tribal elite. What differentiated him from the
latter, however, was that he could use the tribal
support behind him and could call upon his fellow
khans and followers. His presence in Shiraz and
other cities and settled areas stimulated interaction with powers external to the tribe; his position as tribal co-ordinator was a major factor in
the degree of interaction that occurred.
     There were limits, however, on the activity of
the confederacy and the power of the ilkhani. First,
tribal leaders were restricted by the fact that
their political activity had consequences for, and
generated reactions from, other political powers.
As part of the state, the Qashqai were always vul-

nerable to its instabilities and power struggles.
Also, their leaders lacked an adequate understanding
of the aims of foreign powers concerning them, and
were frequently deceived. Second, the confederacy
never functioned as a single, unified entity. The
most concerted military effort by 'the Qashqai'
involved, at most, 5,000 horsemen (at a time when
their total population approached 500,000). Third,
tribal khans could act independently, and some directly opposed the ilkhani; this sometimes included
members of the ilkhani's family. And fourth, some
tribal activities were always separate from the
workings of ilkhani leadership, and many continued
uninterrupted when the ilkhani was removed from the
scene. (Sometimes a de facto ilkhani acted as leader when the official ilkhani was on trips, under
house arrest, removed from office, or weak.)

Membership of tribe and confederacy often
benefited the Qashqai population,[41] and leaders
rarely needed to rule by coercion. Through allegiance and loyalty to tribal leaders, the Qashqai
gained relatively secure and protected access to
pastureland, which facilitated pastoral and agricultural production and market relations. They
profited economically from raids and other actions
co-ordinated or supported by their leaders. They
were economically assisted by those who were in a
position to extract the surplus of others. Relations with external powers were mediated for them.
In individual interactions with non-Qashqai they
had the advantage of the superior political position
and reputation of the Qashqai in the region.

As members of tribe and confederacy, Qashqai
households and sub-tribes had certain obligations.
An animal tithe of one to three per cent of household herds was collected occasionally by the khans
to support their expenses and life-style. When the
central government was able to collect taxes from
the Qashqai, and when the ilkhani needed revenue for
warfare or other reasons, he demanded a tithe of one
to three per cent of herds to be collected and transferred to him by the khans and the ilbegi. Tribesmen fought in the khans' and ilkhanis' battles;
this was handled through a summons to the headmen,
who were each to supply a certain number of warriors,
mounted and armed. With the possibility of booty,
this was often a privilege rather than a burden.
The Amaleh tribe was the ilkhani's standing army,
as were the Amaleh sections of the component Qashqai
tribes for their respective khans. The khans and
ilkhani occasionally relied on additional support

from their associated sections. Tribespeople also
owed labour and gift offerings to the khans and
ilkhani on special occasions.
     The extraction of surplus from the Qashqai mas-
ses by tribal leaders seems not to have been exploit-
ative. The tithe occasionally collected was not
burdensome and at any rate was a small proportion
of household property. Household economies (based
on pastoralism, agriculture, weaving) were not controlled by tribal politics, except that access to
pastureland derived from tribal ties and obligations.
Matters of animal and land ownership, allocation of
labour, production, and exchange were solely in the
hands of individual households. The khans and ilkhani were hospitable and generous to their supporters. Poverty-stricken Qashqai were exempt from the
tithe, and those in serious economic difficulty
could expect some help from tribal leaders. Also
exempt from the tithe were those who performed regular services for tribal leaders, such as headmen,
tax-collectors, overseers, mediators, and gunmen,
as well as descendants of warriors killed in khans'
battles. The actions and demands of leaders were
checked by the ability of dissatisfied followers to
sever their ties. Leaders dissatisfied with tribal
followers were also, however, in a position to apply
sanctions and punishments. Denial of access to
pasture was the strongest sanction, although those
removed by one leader could seek land with another
who was anxious to increase his following. Allocation of poor pastures and the temporary imposition
of high taxes were other sanctions. Khans were supported by mediators, scribes, tax-collectors, overseers and gunmen who enforced tribal law and the
policy of the leaders. The khans and ilkhanis did
not use government forces against tribal members to
enforce their rule, as has been the case elsewhere
in Iran.[42]
     The wealth of the khans and ilkhani did not
derive primarily from their tribal supporters. Other
sources were more profitable and kept the leaders
from making heavy extractions of wealth from the
tribe itself, which would have undermined and weakened its support. (It is true, however, that the
khans retained the best pastures and garden locations for themselves.) The ilkhani and some khans
were given governorships of territories, which
allowed them to acquire private property and to
collect government taxes, some of which they held
back. Most khans were wealthy landowners, acquiring
land from government service, investment of income

from other economic activities, and confiscation.
They extracted part of the yearly production of
their share-croppers and tenants, who were usually
Persians or Lurs. Khans who organised or sanctioned
raids received a share of the booty. Finally, khans
who engaged in mediatory functions, especially those
who held formal positions and titles, derived additional income from their association with external
powers. The ilkhani received large cash and land
payments from the state for his administrative
functions and for arming and supporting a tribal
army. Foreign powers also paid him and other khans
to engage in such activities as the protection of
trade routes and military aggression against other
tribes.

The ilkhani and the khans used their various
political positions in their own class and personal
interests, in ways that prevented them from being
economically dependent on tribal followers. Their
political and economic strength was drawn primarily
from domains beyond the tribe, but they were able to
use the threat of tribal action in these external
domains to buttress their regional and national
positions.[43] Both these features help to explain
the enduring political power of the Qashqai confederacy.

NOTES

1. I am indebted to Houman Qashqai for his special
insights on historical and contemporary Qashqai leadership.
In addition John Perry offered many helpful suggestions on
earlier drafts of this chapter. The chapter does not present
a chronological history of the Qashqai confederacy: this is
available in P. Oberling, *The Qashqā'i Nomads of Fārs* (Mouton,
The Hague, 1974). Anthropological field research among the
Qashqai was conducted in 1969-71 and 1977, and a brief visit
was possible in 1979. For an account of the Qashqai since
1962, see L. Beck, 'Economic transformations among Qashqa'i
nomads, 1962-1978', in *MIDCC,* pp. 99-122. The chapter's
discussion was greatly assisted by a number of sources, in
particular documents in the India Office Library, London, and
the following: P. Oberling, *Qashqa'i Nomads;* id., 'British
tribal policy in southern Persia 1906-11', *Journal of Asian
History,* 4 (1970), pp. 50-79; F. Barth, *Nomads of South Persia*
(Allen and Unwin, London, 1961); R. Cottam, *Nationalism in
Iran* (Pittsburgh University Press, 1964); Hasan Fasā'ī,
History of Persia under Qājār Rule (Fārsnāmeh-i Nāsirī), tr.
H. Busse (Columbia University Press, New York, 1972); O.
Garrod, 'The nomadic tribes of Persia today', *JRCAS,* 33 (1946),

pp. 32-46; id., 'The Qashqa'i tribe of Fars', *JRCAS*, 33 (1946),
pp. 293-306; G. Garthwaite, chapter 10 below; A.K.S. Lambton,
Landlord and Peasant in Persia (Oxford University Press, 1953);
ead., 'Īlāt', *EI*, 2nd ed., 3, pp. 1095-1110; R. Tapper, 'The
tribes in eighteenth and nineteenth century Iran', forthcoming in P. Avery and G. Hambly (eds.), *The Afshars, Zands
and Qajars*, vol. 7 of the Cambridge History of Iran (Cambridge
University Press).

    2. W. Irons, 'Political stratification among pastoral
nomads' in *PPS*, pp. 362, 372.

    3. Tapper, 'The tribes'; Garthwaite, chapter 10 below.

    4. L. Helfgott, 'Tribalism as a socioeconomic formation
in Iranian history', *IS*, 10 (1977), pp. 54-5.

    5. Lambton, 'Ilat', p. 1098; J. Aubin, 'Références pour
Lar médiévale', *Journal Asiatique*, 218 (1955), p. 504;
Oberling, *Qashqa'i Nomads*, p. 35 and *passim*.

    6. Oberling, *Qashqa'i Nomads*; Garrod, 'Qashqa'i', p.
296; G.R. Fazel, 'Economic Organization and Change among the
Boir Ahmad: a Nomadic Pastoral Tribe of Southwest Iran', unpublished PhD dissertation, University of California,
Berkeley, 1971, p. 31 (Fazel states that a Boyr Ahmadi was
appointed supreme chief of the major Kuhgiluyeh tribes during
the reign of Karim Khan Zand; however, the date he gives for
this - ca.1796 - comes some years after Karim Khan's death);
A.K.S. Lambton, 'The tribal resurgence and the decline of
the bureaucracy in eighteenth century Persia', in T. Naff and
R. Owen (eds.), *Studies in Eighteenth-Century Islamic History*
(Southern Illinois University Press, Carbondale, 1977), p.
111; Fasai, *History of Persia*, p. 160; Malik Mansur Khan, personal interview, 28 Aug. 1979, Tehran; Muhammad Huseyn Khan,
personal interview, 29 July 1979, London.

    7. P. Oberling, 'The Turkic Peoples of Southern Iran',
PhD dissertation, Columbia University, 1960, p. 211; see also
J. Perry, *Karim Khan Zand* (University of Chicago Press,
1979); Lambton, 'Tribal resurgence'.

    8. D. Brooks, chapter 12 below.

    9. Oberling, *Qashqa'i Nomads*, pp. 31, 35; id., 'Turkic
Peoples', p. 202.

    10. For discussion of this period, see my 'Tribe and
state in revolutionary Iran: the return of the Qashqa'i khans',
in F. Kazemi (ed.), *Iranian Revolution in Perspective, IS*,
13 (1980), pp. 215-55.

    11. X. de Planhol, 'Geography of settlement', in W.B.
Fisher (ed.), *The Land of Iran*, vol. 1 of the Cambridge
History of Iran (Cambridge University Press, 1968), pp. 409-
10.

    12. Barth, *Nomads*, pp. 127-30.

    13. L. Beck, 'Herd owners and hired shepherds: the
Qashqa'i of Iran', *Ethnology*, 19 (1980), pp. 327-51.

    14. Control of urban centres and international trade
routes was a key factor in the development of the Aqqoyunlu

confederacy: J. Woods, *The Aqquyunlu: Clan, Confederacy, Empire* (Bibliotheca Islamica, Minneapolis and Chicago, 1976), p. 43.

15. See W. Irons, 'Nomadism as a political adaptation', *AE*, 1 (1974), pp. 635-58.

16. J. Perry, 'Forced migration in Iran during the seventeenth and eighteenth centuries', *IS,* 8 (1975), pp. 199-215.

17. See chapters 4 (above) and 13 (below).

18. Oberling, *Qashqa'i Nomads,* p. 218.

19. Beck, 'Tribe and state'.

20. Cf. Irons, 'Nomadism'.

21. F. Barth, 'The land use pattern of migratory tribes of South Persia', *Norsk Geografisk Tidsskrift,* 17 (1959), pp. 1-11; id., *Nomads*.

22. For discussion of the amalgamating process, see Garthwaite, chapter 10 below.

23. Oberling, *Qashqa'i Nomads,* p. 39; also Perry, *Karim Khan,* pp. 225, 255-6.

24. Lambton, 'Tribal resurgence', p. 111; Garrod, 'Qashqa'i', p. 296.

25. Fasai, *History,* pp. 208-16.

26. H. Field, *Contributions to the Anthropology of Iran* (Field Museum of Natural History, Chicago, 1939), p. 217.

27. Oberling, *Qashqa'i Nomads,* p. 66.

28. Ibid., p. 101.

29. Ibid., p. 140.

30. See B. Schulze-Holthus, *Daybreak in Iran: a Story of the German Intelligence Services* (Staples Press, London, 1954); Oberling, *Qashqa'i Nomads,* pp. 183-6.

31. Beck, 'Economic transformations'.

32. Barth, *Nomads,* p. 130.

33. P. Oberling, 'The Turkic tribes of southwestern Persia', *Ural-Altaische Jahrbücher,* 35 (1964), p. 178.

34. One explanation often given for the lack of political development among Lur tribes is strife (feuds and fratricides) among tribal leaders, which, in turn, is explained by polygyny. The complex phenomenon of tribal leadership is not adequately explained by either strife or polygyny. The converse - that the reason for harmonious rule and succession to office among Qashqai khans was the absence of polygyny - is also inadequate.

35. Oberling, *Qashqa'i Nomads,* pp. 186, 188.

36. Beck, 'Tribe and state'.

37. Beck, 'Herd owners'.

38. See R. Tapper, review of Oberling's *Qashqa'i Nomads,* *BSOAS*, 40 (1977), pp. 165-6; L. Beck, review of the same, *IS,* 10 (1977), pp. 116-19.

39. E.g. D. Austin Lane, 'Hajji Mirza Hasan-i-Shirazi on the nomad tribes of Fars in the Fars-Nameh-i-Nasiri', *Journal of the Royal Asiatic Society,* 2 (1923), pp. 213, 217.

40. Oberling, *Qashqa'i Nomads*, p. 195.

41. Cf. F. Barth, *Principles of Social Organization in Southern Kurdistan* (Jørgensen, Oslo, 1953), pp. 42-3.

42. See P.C. Salzman, 'Inequality and oppression in nomadic society', in *PPS*, pp. 429-46.

43. Helfgott, 'Tribalism', p. 53, makes a similar judgement:

> While the Qajar khans collected personal income and property as provincial governors, there is no evidence to indicate that they obtained any significant income from the surplus of tribal wealth. On the contrary, because the Qajar khans relied on their tribe for military support both locally and to pursue their broader political and military aims, they maintained and attempted to strengthen tribal ties.

Chapter 10
TRIBES, CONFEDERATION AND THE STATE: AN HISTORICAL OVERVIEW OF THE BAKHTIARI AND IRAN

Gene R. Garthwaite

Introduction

Bakhtiari history, stretching back to the fourteenth
century, tantalises the social historian of Iran.
There is a great temptation to assume that the
extraordinary continuity in that name can also be
found in Bakhtiari political, economic and social
organisation. The historian is frustrated further
because a narrative of Bakhtiari political history
cannot be reconstructed from primary sources until
the late nineteenth century, and even then major
parts of it are still fragmentary. The social
scientist is likewise thwarted in attempting to
obtain a detailed account of Bakhtiari social structure. Basic institutions, relationships and values
are obscured by the very nature of complex societies, by differences between internal and external
perceptions of the Bakhtiari, and by the lack of
sources. The basic problem continues to be the
absence of detailed information from which generalisations may be drawn - generalisations which, in
turn, may prove to be of little value except in
specific, concrete instances and which, consequently,
risk the charge of being either commonplace or self-
evident. Whether the approach is synchronic or
diachronic, major analytical problems arise - which
should not discourage the attempt.
   This chapter explores heuristically a hypothesis, and, using the Bakhtiari and their relationship to the state as illustration, sets out to demonstrate aspects of it. This hypothesis may be
useful in looking at other tribal groups in the
Zagros and beyond. The hypothesis is: the potential
for tribal confederation is directly proportional to
the strength of an external stimulus.[1]
   The nature of tribal socio-economic organisa-

The Bakhtiari and Iran

tion - in this case, that of the Bakhtiari - militates against a <u>sui generis</u> formation of tribal confederation. In tribal areas not under the control
of an organised state, or when no state structure
exists, confederations form only in response to an
external stimulus - typically, a need for common
defence or an opportunity for expansion or conquest.
The confederation's strength is proportional to the
strength of the stimulus, and the confederation does
not long outlast the existence of the stimulus.

In tribal areas under the control of an organised state - the imposed control of a bureaucracy
and army with a supporting ideology - the state
itself is the 'external' stimulus. Tribes form confederations to defend and expand interests <u>vis-à-vis</u>
the state. The traditional, relatively decentralised state government may seek to utilise the power
of tribal confederations for its own purposes by
reinforcing internal processes by recognising the
confederation or by creating one. As such governments, however, become more centralised, they
increasingly regard the existence of tribal confederations as antithetical to their interests. When
centralised bureaucracies become strong, they
attempt to limit the confederations' power and,
because of the state's control of greater resources
and its superior organisation, typically succeed in
doing so. A corollary of the hypothesis would be:
within a modern organised state the potential for
tribal confederation is inversely proportional to
the degree of bureaucratic organisation.

Periods when a Bakhtiari confederation (or confederations, for example the Haft Lang and Chahar
Lang moieties of the eighteenth century) may have
existed earlier within a strong traditional state,
would include the reigns of Shah Abbas I (1587-1629)
and Shah Abbas II (1642-66); documentation supports
the hypothesis in that circumstance for the periods
of Nadir Shah (1736-47), Karim Khan Zand (1751-79)
and Nasir al-Din Shah (1848-96). Periods characterised by weak state structures, or their absence altogether - when smaller competing segments characterised the Bakhtiari - would possibly include pre-
and late Safavid times, and can be supported by
sources for the years preceding Karim Khan Zand's
consolidation of his power, the reigns of the early
Qajars, and the decade of World War I. (Ali Mardan
Khan's attempt to unite the Bakhtiari in the mid-
eighteenth century in order to rule Iran perhaps
constitutes a variation of confederation formation
for the purpose of expansion.) An example of the

Bakhtiari under a centralised state - again, with
the break-up into lesser units but in this instance
initiated by the state - is dramatically illustrated
by Riza Shah's destruction of the Bakhtiari confederational structure in the early 1930s.

'Tribe'

'Tribe', 'confederation', and 'state' are protean
notions, encompassing a whole matrix of alliances
and, as analytical categories, resist agreed defini-
tions. As heuristic models each may be conceived as
a continuum.
    The Bakhtiari tribal continuum begins with the
family and ends with the taifeh (tribe) - the family's ultimate extension - which defines the limits
of primary economic, social and political activity,
organisation and identity.[2] The form of the taifeh
has been more persistent than the confederation and
less affected by external developments, for their
function derives from basic pastoral and agricultural structures.
    The family unit takes on the key and enduring
ideological role, forming the basis for everyday
activity and giving rise to most demands and conflicts. In addition, the family provides the
conceptual basis for the process of group formation
at all levels. The nuclear family, which owns the
flocks and works together in the agricultural cycle,
constitutes the key economic unit. The yield of the
flocks and of the land is largely utilised for
family consumption; similarly, marketing is a family
concern.
    Extended or related families come together as
an oulad, or tash, approximating a descent group,
which functions as a camp (mal) of from three to
twelve tents and shares common herding, migration
and defence interests. At this level of segmentation, decisions are reached by heads of family.
    The tireh, roughly 'sub-tribe', forms the next
level, constitutes the maximum group of related
camps, and functions primarily during the migration.
A tireh is represented by a kadkhuda. Tireh come
together to form a taifeh (numbering up to 25,000
individuals), headed by a kalantar appointed from
among the group by the khans. Pasture rights derive
from membership in the taifeh, which exists as a
named group with its own identity and, probably, as
an endogamous unit. Even though it may not always
act as an entity, the taifeh, indeed even the

Bakhtiari confederation, provides a conceptual
framework for organising people politically and
attaching them to leaders.

Continuing with the segmentary pyramid, every
taifeh belongs to one of eight bab; each bab has a
dominant lineage from which khans are chosen. The
babs are grouped into the two moieties (il) of the
Haft Lang or Chahar Lang, and finally the confederation (also il) of the Bakhtiari after 1867. Today,
five babs are found in the Haft Lang (the Duraki,
Babadi, Bakhtiarvand (or Bahdarvand), Dinarani, and
Janiki) and four in the Chahar Lang (Mamivand,
Mamsaleh, Mugui and Kianursi).

The larger the group, the weaker the commitment
and the identification with the family level of
organisation. The taifeh, composed of autonomous
segments, hence a microcosm of the Bakhtiari confederation, constitutes the terminal unit of the
'family's' functional limits, in which internal factors such as herding of flocks, pastures, water, and
migration assume primary importance in group formation.

'Confederation'

The confederation of the Bakhtiari (usually il, but
also taifeh, buluk or bakhsh[3] in colloquial and
oral usage) begins with the taifeh and terminates in
either the moieties or the whole of the Bakhtiari.
The difference between taifeh and confederation is
primarily one of function; size and organisation,
which may appear as additional variables, derive
from function. The confederation has unified taifehs
for defence and resolution of internal disputes and
for administrative purposes in the state system.
The confederation especially rallies the taifehs
for defence and expansion against the state, neighbouring tribes, and settled communities, and, on an
ideological level, integrates them into the greater
cultural system. The confederation is less binding
on its members, in terms of economic, social and
political activity, loyalty and identity, than even
the taifeh, and may even be perceived as exploita-
tive or as a structure whose goals are in basic
conflict with those of the taifeh or the lesser
units.

The confederational function is set off from
the tribal one (which helps to account for the
tribes' negative perceptions of the confederation)
by the factors of power base, leadership roles,

317

potential conflict of interest between the tribes and the confederation, and exacerbation of internal competition for limited resources. Kalantars and khans depend primarily upon internal support as their power base, while confederation leaders, khavanin-i buzurg (the Great Khans), possess an internal base but draw support from the government, from land, and from leaders and groups external to the Bakhtiari.

The khans were usually selected from those born into the chiefly families of the bab. Although one khan was regarded as paramount by his bab, or even others, multiple candidates competed for that position: brothers, cousins (father's brother's sons), and uncles (father's brothers). The two dominant rivalries found among the khans were those of half-brothers (same father) and of nephew against paternal uncle; these particular antagonisms should not be surprising given polygyny and the notion, contradicted in inheritance practice,[4] of the equality of all sons. Positions of power among Bakhtiari khans were insecure, at least from late Safavid times to the mid-nineteenth century and again from 1882-1936, for there were always rival claimants who acted as an important check against the potential for absolutism by allowing babs and taifehs to transfer support and allegiance to a rival khan.

The khans' power was both personal and vested in their chiefly office: it was based on the benefits they were able to dispense, the respect they may have commanded because of their lineage, and the coercive capabilities within the tribe or confederation provided by armed retainers. Their chiefly functions included maintenance of order and adjudication of disputes; co-ordination of internal tribal affairs such as migration, assignment of pastures, appointment of headmen and agents; collection of tribal levies, taxes and dues; and co-ordination of external relations, including representation of the tribe.

The Great Khans, leaders of the Bakhtiari confederation in the late nineteenth century and after, were members of the ruling Haft Lang lineage of the Duraki from which the ilkhani paramount khans were chosen by the Shah after 1867. They possessed major land holdings in Chahar Mahall; functioned as government officials and military leaders there, in the Bakhtiari, and on campaigns; and represented major Bakhtiari components and after 1867 the whole of them. These Great Khans were part of a tribal/pastoral/nomadic world as well as a non-tribal/agricultural/sedentary one.

They were set apart from the khans of the other babs by differences in degree of wealth, power and function that were compounded by their involvement in state affairs as major landlords, government officials, and representatives of the confederation, and by the support given them by the state. To maintain their many positions they sought ties with Qajar factions, Qashqai khans, the Qavams in Shiraz, Arab sheykhs in Khuzistan, the ulama and the British. Such a range of ties is reflected not only in political alliances and rivalries but in marraige bonds as well.[5] In the confederation, the Great Khans held executive power, and retained the largest military units within it. Despite military superiority and government support, their power was far from absolute, for it was limited by the internal rivalry among the Duraki khans, and by the ability of the various segments of the Bakhtiari to withhold support or transfer it to a rival within the Duraki lineage or even outside it. Similarly the state could recognise a rival and thus manipulate Bakhtiari politics.[6]

During the late nineteenth and early twentieth centuries, Bakhtiari confederation leaders, the Great Khans, could have been removed only by a combination of the tribes and the state, thus limiting the tribes' independent action and power. The leaders of the confederation acted as government surrogates in their role as administrators in the collection of taxes and conscripts, and the maintenance of order. This resulted in one form of conflict of interest but, in addition, the tribes were exploited by confederation leaders who sought a broader, external role in the state. Those leaders who sought to form a state from the confederation base had to maintain its cohesion, but also had to appeal to those outside the confederation through an acceptable ideology reinforced by the expectation of meeting economic, social and political wants. Finally, the confederation leaders' external support and internal domination gave them, at times, a monopoly of power so that they could reward and punish individuals or whole taifehs and, despite internal opposition, award pastures, land, or exemptions to external groups in return for their support.

The great confederations commonly associated with Iran today probably date from the nineteenth century (scholars are of course aware of earlier ones such as the Qara-qoyunlu, Qizilbash and Shahsevan) when the Qajars, who were possibly reviving a much earlier practice, invested leaders with the title and office of ilkhani (or its equivalent) which gave its holders authority and power to act on behalf of the central government as official administrators of what were thus formally created and recognised by Tehran as autonomous administrative units. This occurred in 1818 for the Qashqai and 1867 for the Bakhtiari.[7] The Khamseh confederation came into existence during Nasir al-Din Shah's reign, and even though its head never held the title ilkhani he functioned as such. The dates for the first appointment of an ilkhani for the Qajar confederation (possibly early nineteenth century and of special status given its relationship to the ruling dynasty) and the Zafaranlu of Quchan are not yet known. None of the other Kurdish leaders possessed the title nor did the Arab sheykhs who held like office as administrators for their respective areas.

The great confederations in Iran came about as the result of designation, amalgamation, or a combination of these two processes. In designation, the central government possibly sought to centralise or to limit tribal autonomy, when it would select a leader, not necessarily from within the group, as the one responsible for order, taxes and conscripts. The Khamseh, formed by order of the Qajars and directed by the Qavams, a Shiraz merchant-landlord family, are an example of this type.

Confederations also emerged through a process of amalgamation, when a leader forged successively larger and more effective units, relying on a variety of leadership skills and symbols and manipulating the basic kin structures to achieve goals beyond those associated with smaller groups. Over a period of time corporate interests would be identified with the confederation, but would be weaker in comparison with the corporate interests of the smaller units. The Qashqai provide but one successful illustration for this variation; they constitute a Turkic-speaking minority and their migrations take them through thickly-settled agricultural regions close to urban areas; minority status is thus a stimulus factor.

Although this second model was often attempted in Iranian history, most tribal leaders failed because of internal and external rivalries and opposition, especially in times of strong central government. Even with the Qashqai, Shahs elevated and deposed ilkhanis in attempts, however ineffective, to control the confederation. Examples of failure to form such confederations are common in Bakhtiari history up to the mid-nineteenth century. Huseyn

Quli Khan Ilkhani, who succeeded, exemplifies the
third process, a combination of designation and
amalgamation, in which the central government capi-
talised on a khan who was in the process of forming
a confederation, and, by assisting him with resources
and thus retaining a degree of control over him,
turned a potential threat to its own advantage.

'State'

The state continuum, to return to the last of our
models, starts with a fragmented polity and terminates with a centralised state maintained by a
bureaucracy and a standing army, thus claiming a
monopoly of power: the modern state in the Weberian
sense. Conveniently, this continuum accords roughly
with Iranian historical reality.
     The eighteenth century (the first period for
which a greater number of documents relating to the
Bakhtiari may be found) saw the final disintegration
of the Safavid state, a resurgence of tribalism, but
short-lived confederations, the emergence of other
local and provincial groups, and a breakdown of state
functions. At the other end of the continuum are
the Pahlavis with a centralised state. The Qajars
of the nineteenth century are sandwiched in between.
(The Zand decades, for the Bakhtiari at least,
approximated conditions under the Qajars.[8])
     Pahlavi centralisation contrasts with eighteenth
century fragmentation and Qajar decentralisation. The
Qajars tolerated and created confederations as autonomous administrative entities, rather than take on
the expense and challenge of a standing army and
centralised bureaucracy.[9] Furthermore, an Irano-
Shii ideology persisted throughout these three centuries for these three states in the continuum. The
Pahlavis, in addition, however, attempted to stress
Iran's pre-Islamic and future glory as justification
for their centralising policy and as an assurance of
loyalty to the dynasty.

Historical Survey

Between the fourteenth century, when the term
'Bakhtiari' (denoting a taifeh that had entered Iran
from Syria along with some thirty other such groups
in the thirteenth century[10]) first appears in
sources, and the mid-eighteenth century, the historical record provides only a narrow base for analy-

sis. In summary, the term designates a taifeh of
indeterminate size and organisation and a geographic
and administrative unit of Luristan. Safavid chronicles identify individuals who functioned as military leaders and civil administrators of Bakhtiari
and adjacent regions, and who were, perhaps, Bakhtiari themselves.[11]   If Chardin's description is
assumed to include the Bakhtiari as a Lur component,
they may be further identified as pastoral nomads
with an economy based on flocks traded in the nearby
capital of Isfahan.[12] Iskandar Munshi, in addition,
implies that Bakhtiari are not peasants: he refers
to rayat (peasants) and Bakhtiari.[13] Chardin suggests a political structure when he mentions the
autonomy of the Lurs, and that they were governed by
appointees who functioned as sub-governors, chosen
from among themselves by the central government.

Negatively, the few references to the Bakhtiari
in the Safavid period suggest that they were (at
least as a large Bakhtiari unit until the seventeenth
century) outside the major political rivalry network
of the Turkic tribes and the Safavids. The Bakhtiari occupied the midpoint of the Safavid power axis
in the Zagros, as it extended from Georgia to the
Gulf;[14] furthermore, they were strategically located
in relation to the capital at Isfahan. Had the
Bakhtiari constituted a major confederation, this
would have at least been noted in the chronicles.
More probably they organised themselves in small
groups and tribes, which seldom, except in unusual
circumstances, coalesced into larger ones. These
small units were administered by Safavid governors
through local leaders, who were not necessarily
Bakhtiari.

By the end of the seventeenth century, the era
when Safavid rule became increasingly decentralised,
the Bakhtiari had emerged as an important administrative post. The Tadhkirat al-Muluk (1725),
listing the ranks and honours given to Persian amirs,
notes that the governor of Bakhtiari follows immediately after the four valis of Arabistan, Luristan-
Feyli, Georgia, and Kurdistan. 'After him [i.e. the
vali of Kurdistan] comes the ruler of the Bakhtiari
il who in former days enjoyed great esteem and
respect.'[15] In this same period both Persian and
European sources note the Bakhtiari moieties of the
Haft Lang and Chahar Lang for the first time,[16] and
mid-eighteenth-century sources record the great
antipathy between them. The Haft Lang and Chahar
Lang may both have constituted confederations that
emerged as bureaucratic devices under the decentral-

ised government of the late seventeenth century. The
Afghan offensive at the end of the first quarter of
the eighteenth century may have temporarily stimulated Bakhtiari unification and even a confederation;
the historical record notes the unity of the Haft
Lang and Chahar Lang in the ill-fated defence of
Isfahan in 1722.[17]

In the subsequent Afshar era, the Bakhtiari
were peripheral to Nadir Shah's major concerns,
except as a threat to his southern flank; consequently he sought to utilise Bakhtiari military
units in his eastern campaigns and to resettle large
numbers of them in Khurasan. In both instances he
worked within the moiety framework of the Haft Lang
and Chahar Lang. During this period, with the continued decentralisation of the state and the absence
of Haft Lang leaders, the Bakhtiari region too would
appear to have been fragmented and taifeh leaders
challenged both Nadir Shah and the Haft Lang leadership.

Increased fragmentation - 'tribalism' - persisted in the Bakhtiari until Karim Khan Zand re-
established central authority in south-central Iran,
when he asserted suzerainty over the Haft Lang
through its own leaders, the khans of the Duraki
taifeh. Before Karim could succeed, however, he
had to establish his own power and destroy that of
his Bakhtiari rival, Ali Mardan Chahar Lang. The
two of them had established rule in the name of a
Safavid pretender, Ismail III. Ali Mardan Khan is
one of the infrequent examples of expansion as 'stimulus' in Bakhtiari history - others occurring chiefly in the 1870s and the Constitutional period of the
early twentieth century. Ali Mardan, about whom
little is known other than his membership in the
Kianursi taifeh of the Haft Lang, may have emerged
as a leader in the tumultuous period of Nadir Shah.
Possibly the Chahar Lang had constituted a confederation, but there was no single Bakhtiari confederation, for Ali Mardan, in a letter to Haft Lang
leaders acknowledging the need for unity, indicated
contemporary fragmentation in the Bakhtiari and
alluded to an earlier, presumably Safavid, harmony
and unity.[18]

Official Zand documents, corroborating traditional Bakhtiari genealogies and histories, clearly
indicate that the Haft Lang was treated as an administrative unit. In the firmans and raqams awarding
tuyuls, governorships, exemptions, and admonitions
to eighteenth-century Duraki notables, they possessed the titles of sardar, beg, aqa, rish-safid, zabit,

and <u>hakim</u>.[19] These documents suggest only the relationship between these Haft Lang leaders and their
taifehs, and add little to our knowledge about
Bakhtiari commoners, except their organisation into
small groups headed by kadkhudas and kalantars, with
an interdependence between them and the Duraki khans,
who are responsible for good administration. On an
ideological basis, these same documents indicate
that the Bakhtiari shared the prevailing Irano-Shii
ethos. The Bakhtiari supported various Safavid pre-
tenders, or those who upheld Safavid legitimacy,
throughout the eighteenth century. They often de-
fied the rulers of the Afshar and Zand eras, including Ali Mardan Khan, but never challenged existing
political and religious ideas and institutions by
offering new ones.

Few early Qajar documents relating to the
Bakhtiari are extant, until about 1840; possibly
others have been lost, or their absence indicates
that the Duraki khans and the Haft Lang were fragmented and no longer dominant, or even that the
Bakhtiari were peripheral to Qajar concerns. The
far more numerous documents from between 1840 and
1880, however, reveal a significant number of khans
competing among the taifehs and at the level of what
was to become the confederation of the whole of the
Bakhtiari.

Order, with reassertion of central authority,
came about in the mid-nineteenth-century Bakhtiari
and adjacent areas to the south (notably the northern edge of Fars and the borders with Kuhgiluyeh and
Arabistan) through an alliance between the governors
of Isfahan, the central government in Tehran, and
Huseyn Quli Khan. Huseyn Quli had been one of the
contending Duraki khans, and to outsiders appeared
to be a rather unlikely victor. His signal success
was due to various factors: his lineage, that of the
khans of the largest and certainly the most powerful
Haft Lang taifeh; his seniority by age; his political and military skills which enabled him to defeat
his most powerful Haft Lang and Chahar Lang rivals;
the collaboration and support of his three brothers;
his increasingly broad network of social, political
and economic ties, including ulama and great merchants; and his vast land holdings in Chahar Mahall to
the east and in Arabistan to the south-west. Government support increased and was demonstrated by
additional land grants and exemptions, appointments
and titles - including <u>nazim</u> of the Bakhtiari in
1864 and then ilkhani of the whole of the Bakhtiari
in 1867.[20] The general result was good order and

such an increase in his power that he was feared by
elements within his own family and by the provincial
and central governments. Nasir al-Din Shah ordered
his death, which was brought about by Zill al-Sultan,
governor of Isfahan, in 1882.[21]
    Although the expected and feared general up-
rising of the Bakhtiari did not result, the tribes
were characterised for the next twelve years by
fragmentation, exacerbated by the Zill al-Sultan's
fall from power. Three factions emerged: Ilkhani
(Huseyn Quli's sons); Hajji Ilkhani (Huseyn Quli's
brother's sons); and Ilbegi (Huseyn Quli's half-
brother's sons), who formed various combinations in
attempts to gain pre-eminence. There was no question
but that the office of ilkhani would be filled by
candidates from one of these three groups. During
Huseyn Quli Khan Ilkhani's rule of some 20-25 years,
authority had become even more firmly identified
with his descent group; and their wealth had so
increased that none of the khans from other lineages
could hope to compete. In addition, Ilkhani, Hajji
Ilkhani and Ilbegi ties within the Bakhtiari and
with all factions of the Qajars were so encompassing
that all other Bakhtiari leaders were removed from
contention, unless the government imprisoned the
Great Khans and confiscated their estates - which did
occur in the 1930s under Riza Shah, but which Nasir
al-Din Shah shrank from out of fear of Bakhtiari
power and because of the inadequacy of his army.
    In 1894 an agreement was reached by the Ilkhani
and Hajji Ilkhani khans which excluded the Ilbegi
khans from power and determined that the positions
of ilkhani and ilbegi would be confined to those two
factions and would be based on seniority of age.[21]
Within this general framework, tribal, confederational
and family disputes (over matters such as the Bakhtiari road (1897), oil agreements (pre-World War I)
and the division of government positions following
the Constitutional Revolution[23]) have continued to
be resolved.
    Increasingly throughout the nineteenth century
the British played a role analagous to the traditional decentralised Qajar state: their various commercial and strategic interests required stability,
but they lacked the resources to ensure this directly
and sought to obtain order by reinforcing traditional
leaders and institutions. The Tehran/Isfahan/Ilkhani
and Hajji Ilkhani nexus was reinforced by the London/
Government of India/Arabistan/Ilkhani and Hajji
Ilkhani connection. (British support was also extended to Sheykh Khazal and, less successfully, to the

Qavams.)

Just as Huseyn Quli Khan Ilkhani had failed to
expand Bakhtiari power in the 1870s, so too (although
for different reasons) did his sons and nephews fail
in the Constitutional period, when the taifehs and
Bakhtiari leaders were temporarily united. Both
internal divisions and external opposition developed
once Muhammad Ali Shah had been removed and Ahmad
Shah was installed; the decline of central authority
stimulated internal rivalries and ambitions. Moreover, Bakhtiari leaders, for example Hajji Ali Quli
Khan Sardar Asad II, lost external support as they
became identified with traditional values and came
to be regarded as anti-nationalist and anti-
constitutionalist; they had no alternative and acceptable ideology to offer to widen their Bakhtiari
power, and that base was suspect.

The decade of World War I saw a resurgence of
tribalism and fragmentation in the Bakhtiari as the
authority and power of the central government collapsed. The British presence too was greatly undermined until the war's end. Furthermore, the senior
Ilkhani and Hajji Ilkhani khans had moved to Tehran,
leaving affairs in the hands of their sons and grandsons, who constituted a sizable group that not only
lacked authority but competed for the same limited
resources to maintain themselves and their bastagan
(armed and mounted retainers). Order came only with
the restoration of power and authority at the centre.

Changes in the traditional Iranian system and
the structure of the state began with Riza Shah and
were continued by Muhammad Riza Shah. These included
a centralisation of power and authority, the emergence of the nation-state, and an expanded role for
the state, calling for economic and social progress.
Even before the Sardar Sipah was crowned as Riza
Shah, the Great Khans (especially Khusrou Khan Sardar
Zafar) perceived him and his policies as a threat to
their autonomy and power. Their challenge to him
failed, however, because it followed essentially
traditional lines while he utilised the methods of
both the traditional Iranian system and the new
nation-state. Tehran successfully identified the
'feudal' Bakhtiari leadership with the decadent past
and foreign domination. The new nation-state of Iran
need not share authority and power; it had its own
army and bureaucracy, and enforced policies that
integrated Iranians into the national economy and
promoted an 'Iranian' identity through education and
new national symbols.

Riza Shah's actual campaign against the Bakhtiari

was initiated in June 1922 with the 'Shalil Incident', in which the Bakhtiari were provoked into attacking a small Iranian force that was being sent by Riza Khan through the Bakhtiari to Khuzistan. This attack aroused nationalist sentiment in Tehran and enabled Riza Khan to impose an economically crushing indemnity on the Bakhtiari, one which could not be evaded by traditional means.[24] In 1921 and 1922 the khans had lost their governorships of Kirman, Yazd and Isfahan. In 1923 Riza Khan withdrew their right to be accompanied by military retainers[25] and removed the Chahar Lang from the authority of the ilkhani.[26] This was followed by the appointment of non-Bakhtiari governors for the Bakhtiari area itself.[27] In 1928 the Anglo-Persian Oil Company was instructed to lease land through the governor of Khuzistan and not from the khans.[28] This was an attempt to separate the Bakhtiari from British influence, both economic and political, and to strengthen the position of the central government, which insisted henceforth on its sovereign powers. A delayed revolt occurred in 1929 at Safid Dasht in the eastern Bakhtiari, and following a Bakhtiari defeat three khans were executed.[29] In 1933 the positions of ilkhani and ilbegi were abolished; however, Murtaza Quli Khan, the ilkhani at the time, was appointed governor.[30] The next year, three important khans were executed, including Jafar Quli Khan Sardar Asad III, Riza Shah's minister of war,[31] and a number of others were imprisoned.[32] In 1937 Bakhtiari territory was divided and placed in two separate administrative districts, Isfahan and Khuzistan, under central government administrators.[33] And in 1938-39, Riza Shah exacted his last due from the khans by forcing them to turn their villages and their oil shares over to the central government. Such policies effectively destroyed the power of the Great Khans, some of whose descendants have continued to play national roles until recently, but decreasingly as Bakhtiari leaders. The actual tribal role of the Duraki khans came to an end after some 200 years.
     Despite Pahlavi centralisation, the form and function of the taifeh and levels below have persisted, and have been less affected by external developments, for they derive from basic pastoral and agricultural structures. Some 500,000 Bakhtiari still follow traditional social and economic patterns including the migration.[34] Even today the taifeh structure continues to provide the framework for traditional internal, socio-political activities, because the symbolic role of the Great Khans contin-

ues. Despite the state's assumption of their juri-
dical and administrative functions, the taifehs
continue to align themselves into one of the Great
Khan moieties of either the Ilkhani or the Hajji
Ilkhani.[35] Pahlavi tribal policy of continuing to
treat the Bakhtiari as an administrative unit has
possibly resulted in a more precise delineation of
internal and external social and physical boundaries,
which may have strengthened both Bakhtiari identity
as a social unit with a given territory, and the
Ilkhani-Hajji Ilkhani framework for social, economic
and political interaction.

The state's general economic and political
policies, especially over the past decade, have
probably had an accelerating impact on change in the
Bakhtiari, particularly with the attraction of the
oil fields and new industrial centres adjacent to
the region, but the impact has probably been less
far-reaching than among the Qashqai,[36] given the
relative isolation of the Bakhtiari. In spite of
centralisation and modernisation under the Pahlavis,
then, those within the Bakhtiari family-taifeh
structure have continued to enjoy a degree of autonomy, because they have been largely peripheral to
the nation-state and its economy; those who have
left the region permanently, however, have become
integrated into contemporary Iran. Even if the new
Islamic Republic of Iran were to reverse Pahlavi
centralisation, there is little likelihood of the
re-emergence of a Bakhtiari confederation. A single
confederation would be unlikely if there were a long
period of political turmoil and uncertainty, for the
taifehs would compete among themselves - at least if
this chapter's bypothesis is correct.

NOTES

1. My thanks to my Dartmouth colleague, John Major, for
his assistance in focusing and phrasing this hypothesis, and
to Lois Beck and Jean-Pierre Digard for comments on an early
draft of this chapter.

2. Late-nineteenth-century sources corroborate the
essential classification and terminology of Digard's fieldwork; see J.-P. Digard, 'De la nécessité et des inconvénients,
pour un Baxtyâri, d'être Baxtyâri. Communauté, territoire et
inégalité chez des pasteurs nomades d'Iran', in *PPS*, pp. 128-9.

3. *Buluk* and *bakhsh* are not found in nineteenth and
early twentieth-century sources, and their use today possibly
stems from administrative policies established by Tehran in
the 1920s and 1930s.

4. G.R. Garthwaite, 'Two Persian wills of Ḥājj ʿAlī Qulī Khān Sardār Asʿad', *Journal of the American Oriental Society*, 114, 4 (1974), pp. 645-50).

5. G.R. Garthwaite, 'Rivalry and alliances: kinship and the Bakhtiyari Khans', paper presented at MESA meeting, Louisville, November 1975.

6. G.R. Garthwaite, 'The Bakhtiyâri Khans, the government of Iran, and the British, 1846-1915', *IJMES*, 3 (1972), pp. 24-44; id., 'The Bakhtiyārī Īlkhānī: an illusion of unity', *IJMES*, 8 (1977), pp. 145-60.

7. Fasai records:

> In that year (1234) [1818] by mediation of Ḥaji Mirzā Rezā Qoli Navā'i, vizier of Fārs, the title 'Ilkhāni' was bestowed upon Jāni Khān-e Qashqā'i, ilbegi of Fārs. His son Moḥammad ʿAli he appointed ilbegi. Up to that year nobody in Fārs had been called by the title 'Ilkhani'. The head of the tribes in Khorasan used to be called 'Ilkhani'.

Hasan Fasā'ī, *History of Persia under Qājār Rule (Fārsnāmeh-i Nāṣirī)*, tr. H. Busse (Columbia University Press, New York, 1972), p. 160. Cf. firman of Nāṣir al-Dīn Shāh, Tehran, Shaʿban 1284/December 1867.

8. J.R. Perry, *Karim Khan Zand* (Chicago University Press, 1979).

9. N. Keddie, 'The Iranian power structure and social change 1800-1969: an overview', *IJMES*, 2 (1971), pp. 3-20.

10. Hamdullah Mustoufī Qazvīnī, *Tārīkh-i Guzīdeh*, ed. ʿAbd al-Ḥuseyn Navā'ī (Tehran, 1339/1961), p. 540.

11. Amīr Sharaf Khān Bidlisī, *Sharafnāmeh: Tārīkh-i Mufassal-i Kurdistān*, ed. M. ʿAbbāsī (Ilmi, Tehran, 1343/1965); J. Chardin, *Travels, etc.* (London, 1686); Iskandar Beg Munshī, *Tārīkh-i ʿAlam-Ārā-yi ʿAbbāsī*, ed. Ī. Afshār (Amir Kabir, Tehran, 1350/1971); Anon, *Tadhkirat al-Mulūk*, ed. V. Minorsky (Luzac, London, 1943).

12. Chardin, *Travels*, p. 147.

13. Iskandar Beg, *Tarikh*, p. 503.

14. J.R. Perry, 'Forced migration in Iran during the seventeenth and eighteenth centuries', *IS*, 8 (1975), p. 212.

15. *Tadhkirat al-Muluk*, p. 44.

16. Jonas Hanway, *The Revolutions of Persia* (London, 1754), p. 238; Father Krusinski, *The History of the Late Revolutions of Persia* (London, 1740), vol. 1, p. 97.

17. Hanway, *Revolutions*, p. 238.

18. G.R. Garthwaite, *Khāns and Shahs: a Documentary Analysis of the Bakhtiyāri in Iran* (Cambridge University Press, forthcoming).

19. Ibid.

20. Nāṣir al-Dīn Shāh, firman, Tehran, Shaʿban 1284/December 1867; also, G.R. Garthwaite, 'The Bakhtiyārī Khans as Landlords and Governors', paper presented at MESA meeting, Boston, 1974.

21. I'timād al-Saltaneh, *Rūznāmeh-i Khāṭirāt-i I'timād al-Saltaneh,* ed. Ī. Afshār (Amir Kabir, Tehran, 1345/1967), p. 197.

22. Garthwaite, 'The Bakhtiyari Khans'...'

23. Ibid.

24. IOL: Loraine to Curzon, no. 200 of 10 May 1923, LPS/ 20/32.

25. Great Britain, Gault Report, 1944.

26. Loraine to Curzon, no. 130 of 20 Sept. 1923, FO 416/ 73.

27. Anglo-Persian Oil Co. Ltd., 'Confidential Newsletter' no. N2/193, Greenhouse to General Manager Abadan, 25 Aug. 1928.

28. Anglo-Perisan Oil Co. Ltd., 'Confidential Letter', Jacks to Director in London, 29 Aug. 1928.

29. Gault Report.

30. IOL: 'Persia: Ahwaz Diaries, no. 10 of 1933', Dec. 1933, LPS/28/6.

31. IOL: Hoare to Simon, no. 175 of 7 Apr. 1934, LPS/28/ 9.

32. Hoare to Simon, no. 581 of 16 Dec. 1933, FO 416/92.

33. IOL: 'Persia: Ahwaz Diaries, no. 3 of 1937', March 1937, LPS/28/6.

34. Digard, 'De la nécessité'.

35. Digard, personal communication.

36. L. Beck, 'Economic transformations among Qashqa'i nomads, 1962-1978', in *MIDCC,* pp. 99-122.

Chapter 11
ON THE BAKHTIARI: COMMENTS ON 'TRIBES, CONFEDERATION AND THE STATE'

Jean-Pierre Digard

As other activities prevented me from participating in the conference and presenting a paper, I am glad of this opportunity to offer some observations on some of the problems that were raised.[1] Although these observations have mostly been suggested by long and most interesting discussions with Gene Garthwaite and by reading his chapter on the Bakhtiari (whom I too am studying), they seem to me to be relevant to the theoretical concerns that have emerged from several other papers as well as the discussions to which they gave place.
   On the strictly historical part of Garthwaite's work I will say nothing - the author's competence in this respect is too well known for me to risk questioning it in any way! What poses a problem for me as an anthropologist is rather the interpretation Garthwaite gives to this history. Of course it is almost inevitable that the materials on which we are reflecting - for him, texts from last century concerning the chiefs, for me, contemporary data collected in the field from 'simple' nomads - impel us willy-nilly to orient our research on different lines; but the fact that we belong to disciplines that are traditionally distinct should not in theory lead us to divergent interpretations of the same general social processes. In fact, as will become clear and as Garthwaite has himself stressed, our respective analyses are far from contradictory.

The External ... The opposition between external and internal factors (or stimuli) has, in my view, a value which is much more didactic than heuristic; but let us retain it, since Garthwaite uses it and so as not to complicate the debate from the start. Among the factors in the formation of a Bakhtiari confederation, Garthwaite stresses the 'external

stimulus' (in this case the central state, to whose
role we shall return). The importance of such a
stimulus is evident, and Garthwaite rightly under-
lines it; but in so doing he tends to forget or to
neglect the 'internal factors' (differences between
pastoral and agricultural productivity, division of
labour, inequality of access to natural resources,
etc.) in the evolution of Bakhtiari tribal society,
notably towards forms of class organisation.[2]

... and the internal. In particular, Garthwaite
seems to me to be on quite the wrong track when he
justifies putting the emphasis on this external stimulus by the fact that, according to him, Bakhtiari
social organisation is inherently constrained from
forming a proper confederation, that is (for him), a
tribal structure endowed with a more or less centralised and hierarchical political apparatus. I
showed several years ago, along with many others,
that this was not the case and that we must abandon
the myth, which has been decidedly tenacious since
The Nuer, that segmentary systems are necessarily
acephalous.[3] Several other participants in the conference (see, among others, chapter 8) agree with me
on this point.
    Moreover, how can it be maintained that a seg-
mentary structure is inherently contradictory with a
class structure, when, as a matter of fact, these
two forms of organisation coexist and 'function'
simultaneously in several societies, including the
Bakhtiari? Thus, among the latter, the khavanin-i
buzurg (Great Khans) would often make use of the
lineage structure of tribal society so as to make it
serve the interests of the dominant class which they
represented (see, for example, the organisation of
the Ilkhani and Hajji-Ilkhani basteh). I would go
further: it is because they were able to define
themselves in relation to this structure (they belonged to the Ahmad-Khusrowi, of the Zarrasvand
taifeh, Duraki il, Haft Lang) that the khans could
socially legitimate their domination of the other
Bakhtiari, whatever the means of coercion they may
also have used (i.e., mainly an authentic tribal
state, or - as Brooks would say - 'mini-state' apparatus), and whatever the resistance that they often
faced within the tribe, expressing a veritable class
struggle.

Tribe or Confederation? That said, the presence
among the Bakhtiari of a strong dominant class and
of the centralised and hierarchical political appa-

ratus that is its emanation, seems to me inadequate
to explain the formation and infer the existence of
a confederation. Without of course dismissing the
thesis of the unifying action of such socio-political
structures, there are however at least two reasons
not to be content with the type of explanation this
can suggest. The first is that an analogous power,
with some differences, existed for example in Luristan (the Vali of Khurramabad) without having similar effects: Luristan remains divided into different
Lur tribes which have no political unity. The
second reason lies in the fact that Bakhtiari political and territorial unity has survived, and sur-
vives today, the progressive elimination, begun in
the 1930s by the Pahlavis, of the khans and of their
corresponding political apparatus. The non-
partitioning and inalienability of Bakhtiari territory, the very existence of a circle of social
membership as large as that of the tribe (il) - of
which all Bakhtiari, despite their other divisions
(and contrary to what Brooks says) are very vividly
conscious - are the result 'in the last instance' of
the constraints of a communal management of natural
resources, adapted to the practice of pastoral
nomadism in conditions of demographic saturation of
a particular mountain environment in the central
Zagros. They would in fact appear, in this precise
context, as the best guarantees of a system of pasture exploitation at once uniform and flexible,
particularly in obtaining, for the small semi-
autonomous social units on the lower levels of segmentation (oulad, tash, tireh) the scope for manoeuvre that is indispensable for the spatial readjust-
ments necessitated periodically by variations in the
size of flocks and in the state of the vegetation.[4]
    In the end, what is at issue here is the very
notion and definition of 'confederation'. Iran provides the purest example of a tribal confederation:
that of the Khamseh, formed from five tribes - Arab
(Arabic-speaking), Aynalu/Inallu, Baharlu and Nafar
(all Turkic-speaking) and Basiri (Persian-speaking)
- that would have almost no connection if they had
not been united, 'federated' to be precise, in the
last century by a powerful family of Shiraz merchants, the Qavams, who assumed leadership of the
whole group.[5] From the point of view that interests
us here, the Khamseh offers the following features:
First, the federated elements are each organised on
their own lineage bases as tribes, and independent
of each other in terms of descent, real or fictive.
Secondly, the unification, at least in the beginning,

was of a strictly political nature, and was instigated, 'from above' one could say, by a dominant group external to the tribes in question, and for reasons that were equally foreign to them.

Far from being so simple, the Bakhtiari case differs from that of the Khamseh in at least three fundamental ways: First, the large social units (taifeh, bab, il, according to place and circumstance) that constitute the Bakhtiari tribe (il), are not so independent from each other in terms of descent as are the five units that form the Khamseh. In the absence of proof of the existence (or the non-existence) of real descent ties linking all members of the Bakhtiari tribe, one finds fictive genealogies that reveal at least an anxiety to translate political affiliation, a posteriori, into terms of descent; further, there exist among the Bakhtiari other institutions (the Ilkhani and Hajji-Ilkhani basteh) that make use of and cut vertically across the lineage segmentation and should be interpreted, not as divisive factors, but on the contrary, in my view, as factors in the unity of the tribe.[6]

Secondly, the constitution of a Bakhtiari tribe and its persistence today - on which I insist - reflect constraints, and give rise to processes, that are different in nature (political, social, economic, etc.) and impossible to separate.

Thirdly, the Bakhtiari political apparatus, even if its role in the formation of the tribe in the present or the recent past has not been negligible, would rather appear to be the result of these constraints and processes; and even if its elaboration has been favoured by external instances or factors, it is unquestionably an emanation of the tribe, which it probably served before dominating;[7] besides, just as it has outlived the political apparatus of the khans, the Bakhtiari tribe already existed well before it was centralised in the hands of an ilkhani from 1867 ...

Finally, in my view there is no continuum from tribe to confederation. These two terms refer rather to two different but complementary processes of formation of the same corporate groups, the one stressing descent, the other affiliation on political grounds. These two types of process most often act simultaneously in the genesis of the groups that interest us here, whatever their size or the level of segmentation at which they are situated: even if it is not the most widely found case, the former (descent) can intervene on the scale of the largest units (il, taifeh), and the latter (affiliation) on

the most restricted scale (tash and oulad, even
families, through an intermediate type of process:
adoption). It matters little after all whether one
then uses the term 'tribe' or the term 'confederation' to designate, on the largest scale, the integrated result of these two processes; it will,
however, be understood that for the Bakhtiari case
my own preference is clearly for the term 'tribe',
which is more widely accepted and carries fewer misleading connotations.

The External ... again: Tribe and State. When zones
of tribal population are under the control of a
central state, Garthwaite writes again, it is this
state that plays the role of external stimulus; but
the tendency to confederation is then inversely proportional to the degree of bureaucratic centralisation of the state. I believe that this degree of
centralisation can constitute a useful index for
evaluating the number or the intensity of interactions between tribes and the state; but I strongly
doubt the value of this notion for explaining the
transformations that result from these interactions,
as much for the tribes as for the state. For these
transformations depend on quite another logic: i.e.
on the movement of the dominant relations of production and the fundamental nature of the state that
is their expression, whose eventual bureaucratic
centralisation is only an effect, or, one might also
say, a means. Thus, for example, it is clear that
if the Pahlavi bureaucracy worked unceasingly at
destroying pastoral nomadism and the tribes, it was
not because it was strongly centralised but because
the dominant system of production, whose instrument
it was (system of production tied mainly to oil revenues and only secondarily to landed revenues), was
in contradiction with the traditional system of production of the nomad tribes. Inversely, if the
tendency for great tribal concentrations endowed
with strongly structured political apparatus was
reinforced in the Qajar period, it was not because
the state was weakly centralised but because its
politics evidently served the interests of the class
from which it came itself, that is the tribal arist-
ocracies.[8] In such conditions, is it really reasonable to relegate the central state to the rank of
'external stimulus'?
     These are some of the main questions that
Garthwaite's chapter, among others, seems to me to
raise. I do not pretend to have resolved them.
Garthwaite has at least the merit of having posed

them and having inspired me as an anthropologist to reflect on them, giving proof once more of the necessity if not always the fruitfulness (a reservation that applies only to me) of a dialogue between history and anthropology.

NOTES

1. Translated by the editor.

2. See my 'Histoire et anthropologie des sociétés nomades: le cas d'une tribu d'Iran', *Annales*, 28, 6 (1973), pp. 1423-35; and my 'La dynamique sociale et les facteurs de changement chez les pasteurs nomades', *Production Pastorale et Société*, 3 (1978), pp. 2-9; and chapter 12 below.

3. E. Evans-Pritchard, *The Nuer* (Clarendon, Oxford, 1940). See my 'Histoire et anthropologie'; J. Black, 'Tyranny as a strategy for survival in an "egalitarian" society: Luri facts versus an anthropological mystique', *Man (NS)*, 7 (1972), pp. 614-34; T. Asad, 'Equality in nomadic social systems? Notes towards the dissolution of an anthropological category', *Critique of Anthropology*, 11 (1978), pp. 57-66; *PPS*.

4. See my 'De la nécessité et des inconvénients, pour un Baxtyâri, d'être Baxtyâri. Communauté, territoire et inégalité chez des pasteurs nomades d'Iran', in *PPS*, pp. 127-39.

5. F. Barth, *Nomads of South Persia* (Allen and Unwin, London, 1961).

6. Cf. G. Garthwaite, 'The Bakhtiyārī Īlkhānī: an illusion of unity', *IJMES*, 8 (1977), pp. 145-60. There is no space here to demonstrate my argument, but I am preparing a work on the question which I hope will not be too long in appearing.

7. On this point, see my 'Histoire et anthropologie', pp. 1431-2, as well as the very suggestive ideas of M. Godelier, 'Infrastructures, sociétés, histoire', *Dialectiques*, 21 (1977), pp. 41-53, esp. pp. 50-2.

8. See my 'Les nomades et l'état central en Iran: quelques enseignements d'un long passé d'"hostilité réglementée"', *Peuples Mediterranéens/Mediterranean Peoples*, 7 (1979), pp. 37-53.

Chapter 12
THE ENEMY WITHIN: LIMITATIONS ON LEADERSHIP IN THE BAKHTIARI

David Brooks

> Then his soul prompted him to slay his brother,
> and he slew him, and became one of the losers
> (Kuran, Sura V, The Table: 30).
>
> I have slain a man to the wounding of myself
> (Genesis, 5: 23).

Nomads, Tribes and the State

The many tribal groups of the Zagros mountain region
in western Iran have exhibited a wide range of political forms throughout their long but only partially
retrievable history. Not only do these tribal
groups differ from each other in the specifics of
their political structures, but internally they
reveal variations of political form. Some tribal
groups have undergone considerable transformations
over the past several hundred years, others have not.
The emergence and dissolution of tribal emirates,
federations and confederations, the decay and dis-
appearance of powerful tribes, the rise and resilience of others, have been familiar features of
Iranian history for centuries. Fragmented and scattered remnants of once-dominant groups are still
found in the region, reduced now to impoverished
echoes of a former power, adding to the social and
ethnic complexity of a region better known for
larger, still powerful tribal groups such as the
Kurds, Lurs, Bakhtiari and Qashqai.
    The turbulent dynamism of the tribal history of
the Zagros mountains is the product of the continuously variable interplay of complex and often
conflicting ecological, economic, political, social
and cultural forces. These forces emanate not only
from within tribal territory, from the necessarily

flexible adaptations to the mountainous terrain, but
from a wider spatial and temporal context. The differential development, the continuous evolution and
devolution of political forms among these mountain
tribes, can be fully understood only when appreciated
as unfolding through time and located in a space
which is but part of the wider and more differentiated context of Iran. The tribes have always been
a part of, as well as being in varying degrees apart
from, the Iranian state. The presence of the Iranian state has always been, as it still is, a problem
for the tribal populations of Iran. The specific
nature of this 'state presence' differs markedly for
different tribal groups and moreover is itself
variable historically. Each tribe has its own unique
experience of the state, its own history of interaction.

In its turn, the state has also constantly been
forced to contend with the presence of these tribes
as a permanent feature of its own political life,
and likewise this 'tribal presence' has been historically varied in its significance for the state. At
times dormant, more often highly volatile, on frequent occasions during the past two hundred years
this tribal presence has offered a real or perceived
threat to the stability, security or even the continuity of the state. Neither has ever been able
to ignore the other with impunity, each has had to
interact with and react to the other. Forced to coexist uneasily, the one rarely able to dominate the
other completely, the interaction and mutual reaction
between 'tribe' and 'state' has always been problematic for both and each has developed distinctive
characteristics arising directly out of the history
of this interaction. Hostility, suspicion, fear,
and mutually reinforcing misperceptions of each
other have tended to dominate tribe-state interactions for centuries.

In their varied attempts to harness, contain,
control or crush tribal power, successive dynasties
have pursued many different strategies as determined
by the political necessities current at the time.
The political arena relevant at state level is of
course wider and more complex than the political
arena of the tribe, and different tribal groups,
particularly those close to international borders,
have often been embroiled in conflicts emanating
from border disagreements with Turkey, Russia, or
Iraq. The state has encouraged tribal dissidence in
border areas as a strategy of temporary convenience
for discouraging aggressive neighbours. Moreover,

until the establishment of a modern state army under
the Pahlavis in the twentieth century, the armed
forces of Iran were primarily made up of tribal
levies, under their own tribal commanders. Tribal
contingents were not expected to fight against their
own tribal groups, but were often used to control
other tribal groups, thereby exacerbating inter-
tribal conflict, another strategy often employed by
the state to weaken the tribal power-base within its
own borders. Other strategies used in the constant
struggle against the threat of tribal power included
the forced removal of large numbers of tribesmen and
their families to other parts of Iran, the taking of
hostages from leading tribal families, the imprisonment and murder of chiefs and the instigation of
internal rivalries. Such strategies varied with the
political importance of different tribes, but when
carried out always had considerable effects on
internal power struggles and consequently on leadership roles in the affected tribes. State involvement and interference had the effect of intensifying
internal conflict through the selective rewarding
and support of particular chiefs against potential
rivals.

The rewards the state could confer on tribal
chiefs in return for their support were considerable.
Tax reliefs, land grants, trade concessions and, in
the south particularly, local governorships and tax
farming agreements, were only some of the benefits
that involvement or co-operation with the state could
bring. However, as is common in all forms of interaction between tribe and state in Iran, these one-
time supporters and beneficiaries of the state can
soon become perceived as a potential threat, and
alternative strategies follow, quite logically leading to the elimination of this threat. Viewed from
a historical perspective, apparently contrary state
policies towards the tribes dissolve into two aspects
of a single but flexible policy of control. Enemies
transform into friends and allies, and back to enemies, in a social system that to be effective requires to be janus-faced. Tribe-state relations in
Iran, from the perspective of both, are necessarily
ambiguous. The ambiguity inherent in these relationships allows for room to manoeuvre so long as
neither side has the power completely to dominate
the other.

Modern Variation on a Traditional Theme

For the tribes, the significance of the state took
on a less ambiguous quality with the rise to power
of the Pahlavis, and the establishment of a specific
'tribal policy' aimed at the complete control of the
tribal groups in Iran and the final elimination of
their role in the politics of the state. The nomadic movement of animals and people in the Zagros was
to be forcibly stopped, and the economic basis of
tribal life, pastoral nomadism, destroyed. Tribal
power was to be crushed once and for all, bringing
the nomadic sections finally under the control of
government. What marks the Pahlavi period (1925-79)
as apparently different from the Qajar period of the
nineteenth and early twentieth century is the application of a single determined policy of ruthless
control over the tribes by an increasingly monolithic
and centralised state apparatus set on a path of
national integration and modernisation under a strong
ruler. The social fabric of the state itself was
changing, with no place for politically semi-
autonomous and self-governing tribal groups. The
rule of government was to be applied uniformly
throughout the kingdom. The densely textured and
ambiguous relations between tribe and state were
reduced, clarified into an unambiguous and deter-
minedly anti-tribal policy whose political nature
alone was paramount. The effects on the tribes were
devastating.
    In 1923, the British Military Attaché in Iran
commented informatively on the historical background
to the state's perception of the perennial tribal
problem and on the Minister of War's new policy:

> [Historically] the different tribes have been
> allowed semi-autonomous privileges, the extent
> of which has fluctuated in inverse ratio to
> the powers of the Central Government ... On
> the whole the tribes have played their part
> pretty well in Persia's chequered career and
> the system [of tribal levies] has had immense
> advantages for the Central regime in reducing
> expenditure on regular forces to a very low
> figure. The new policy ... declared by the
> Central Government being put into practice by
> the War Minister with the help of the regular
> army, is a complete break with the traditional
> policy of the past, and is to establish com-
> plete political and military control over all
> parts of Persia and to effect the disarmament

of the entire civil population. <u>The tribal
system of the country forms the greatest
obstacle to the fulfillment of this policy</u>.[1]

Elaborating on the last observation, he continued:

Many tribes are powerful, both in numbers and
armaments and are not always obedient to the
orders of the Central Government; they often
evade their taxes, are apt to exact tolls from
travellers passing through their territory and
obey orders of their chiefs alone. Added to
this is the fact that most tribal territories
are mostly mountainous and devoid of good
communications, rendering military operations
by regular troops difficult and prolonged in
the face of serious tribal opposition.[2]

The Minister of War concerned was Riza Khan,
who two years later was to crown himself Riza Shah
Pahlavi. The political perception which formed the
basis of Riza Shah's tribal policy, aptly summarised
in these observations, was incorporated within the
new regime's broader political and economic aims,
of forcibly transforming Iran into a modern state.
Parochial ethnic and tribal cultural identities and
loyalties were attacked, as was the power of the
religious establishment. Such measures as forbidding
the veil for women and violating national religious
sanctuaries provoked intense opposition to Riza Shah
on a national level. As far as the tribes were concerned, the ban on tribal dress and military attacks
on local religious shrines induced considerable
resentment and hatred of the Pahlavi regime. Military conscription was enforced, military and later
civil administrators replaced traditional tribal
rulers, the tax system was reorganised to increase
the revenue due to the state, and tax concessions
granted to tribal leaders by previous dynasties were
revoked. In some cases enormous claims for unpaid
taxes due to the state were enforced, notably against
the powerful Bakhtiari leaders in the south. A concerted drive to disarm the tribes was also undertaken, with only partial success.
Resistance to such measures was particularly
strong among the very powerful and politically centralised tribes of the southern Zagros, whose leaders Riza Shah was determined to break. Many of the
khans were imprisoned, some were murdered and their
land holdings removed from them, tribal titles of
leadership were abolished, and military rule was

established in the attempt to destroy the tribal
political structure. While the power and wealth of
these tribal leaders was diminished, and the state
penetrated tribal society to an extent not previously
encountered, the Pahlavi tribal policy failed to
achieve its aim. The tribal system of the country
was not successfully broken, although other aspects
of the policy, in particular the enforced settlement,
had disastrous economic consequences for the bulk of
the tribesmen.

Nomadic Responses to State Policies

Throughout the length of the Zagros various and
flexible combinations of pastoral nomadism and agriculture have been continuously practised, giving
rise to a range of complex and subtly responsive
ecological adaptations to a mountainous environment
exploitable in its higher slopes primarily by animals, but capable of sustaining dry and irrigated
cultivation in the foothills. The variations found
range from tribes that are solely pastoral nomadic,
with no cultivation at all, though this is in fact
rare, to many tribes who are solely cultivators. By
no means have all the tribes of the Zagros been
exclusively pastoral in orientation, although it is
probably accurate to say that their economic basis
has been nomadism with their wealth and livelihood
dependent on animals, predominantly herds of sheep
and goats. It is possible to maintain larger herds
of animals by moving to higher and cooler slopes in
the summer months, and returning to warmer and lower
pastures in the winter when the snows of the upper
slopes make grazing impossible. Climatic conditions
- changes in temperature rather than just lack of
water - underlie the movement between delimited
summer and winter pastures along equally delimited
migration routes. Such migrations, in spring and
back in the autumn, involving thousands of tribesmen
and their flocks, are found everywhere in the Zagros.
Migration routes differ in length and difficulty,
some being a matter of only a few days' travel, a
type of transhumance, while others, particularly in
the high mountains of the south, require many weeks'
travel over several hundred kilometers between summer and winter quarters. Long-range nomadism,
transhumance and, for many, forms of semi-nomadic
movement between settled villages where they farm,
are all found.
    Dependence on nomadism thus varies, and the

enforced settlement programme carried out by Riza Shah, like so much of state interference, had variable effects: economic disaster and ruin for some, a necessary shift towards agriculture for others. The policy was enforced by the army, in the case of the Qashqai in the south and the Lur tribes of Luristan; among the Bakhtiari, tribal leaders mitigated the disaster by directing the settlement to areas best capable of sustaining a settled population, either in winter or summer quarters. Everywhere, however, animal stocks were considerably depleted, and effective utilisation of the entire region was radically disrupted. Resistance to this direct attack on their livelihood was surprisingly small in most tribal areas, many ordinary tribesmen proving vulnerable to the growing might of the army, but, particularly in the more distant and less accessible mountain regions, active opposition continued throughout Riza Shah's reign. In 1941, however, with his enforced abdication and the political weakening of the state, the tribes literally rose, destroyed their settlements and took to the mountains again in large numbers.

Under the increasingly dictatorial rule of Riza Shah's son Muhammad Riza Pahlavi, a wide range of policies was implemented discriminating against the nomadic tribes in particular, especially during the 1960s under the general land reforms. The nationalisation of forests and pastures, the distribution of land, and more general economic and social inducements to settle, such as the building of roads, the provision of social services and agricultural loans, and the bureaucratic penetration of tribal territories, have produced a major swing away from traditional forms of animal husbandry. Major disruption of the tribal modes of ecological adaptation and semi-annual migrations have eroded pastures considerably since the economic boom of the period from 1973, which saw the take-off of the Shah's modernisation and industrialisation programme. The removal of tribal groups from areas to be flooded by huge dams to provide sufficient water for the rapidly expanding cities may well have done irreversible damage to the rich habitat of parts of the Zagros.

The radical changes in the state under both Pahlavi rulers has however failed to destroy the tribal basis of society in the region totally, as was witnessed in 1941 and more recently in the tribal resurgence since the fall of the late Shah in 1979. There have since been demands for tribal autonomy, by the Kurds in particular, and by the Turkmens and

343

Baluches in the east, and a return to nomadism in the southern Zagros has also been reported.

Structural Resilience

The increasing involvement and interference of the modernizing Iranian state, and a multiplicity of bureaucratic organs of government opening up tribal areas to state control, have by no means had uniform effects. Complex social, economic, cultural, as well as political tribal forces continue to respond with a variety of strategies and a resilience due to the institutionalisation of social forms developed during centuries of constant interaction with an antagonistic state. While (as commented by the Military Attaché quoted earlier) the regime may have thought it was formulating a radically new policy, from the perspective of the tribes this policy was merely more extreme than before, was less ambiguous, and allowed them less room to manoeuvre or manipulate the state to their own advantage. Although the upper levels of tribal leadership were removed, and the political links with their own tribesmen were broken or attenuated, at local levels clear signs of processes of 're-tribalisation' can be observed. Progressive attempts to eliminate and replace traditional local tribal leadership roles were only partially effective. In many places they were circumvented and this form of state interference resulted in the shoring up and politicisation of already decaying lineage leadership roles. The impact of the state on different tribes was as varied in its effects under the Pahlavis as it was under previous dynasties, although of course the context had altered considerably and the nature of the state itself had changed.

Tribal social forms in Iran would appear to be remarkably resilient, capable of responding to external state intrusions in flexible ways while retaining continuity throughout economic and political transformations. This continuity of basic form within tribal organisation itself is precisely one of the features of tribal society that requires explanation. For this a diachronic perspective is essential. Tribal structures exist not only in time, but through the passage of time, the differentiating effects of which, while everywhere inescapable, are at least partially annulled by the dynamic inherent in tribal organisation, its lineage-based structure.

To illustrate these general remarks about
tribe-state relations I shall deal specifically with
one tribal group, the Bakhtiari. Bakhtiari political organisation carries the imprint of a long and
particularly complex history of interaction with the
state, during which they developed a hierarchy of
centralised, institutionalised leadership under a
paramount leader, the ilkhani; this was destroyed to
a great extent under the Pahlavis, but they retain a
strong tribal identity grounded on long-range nomadism, migrating over some of the highest reaches of
the Zagros mountain range. This process of centralisation of power in the late nineteenth century in
the hands of autocratic tribal chiefs, and the subsequent dismantling during the Pahlavi period of the
political and administrative structure developed by
the Bakhtiari khans to rule their own tribesmen,
have produced marked political and economic differentiation within the Bakhtiari polity. The political environment of the numerous Bakhtiari tribes,
dominated by their own autocratic khans in the
recent past, took on aspects of a 'tribal state'
within the nation-state. The impact of the Iranian
state on the Bakhtiari tribes thus was not only
direct, but to a great extent indirect, mediated
through the 'tribal-state-like' administration of
the dominant Bakhtiari khans, whom even the Pahlavi
shahs maintained in control. This 'mediation' was
unusually beneficial during the notorious period of
enforced settlement, when the Bakhtiari khans themselves directed the settlement according to the
carrying capacity of land suitable for permanent
settlement, thus saving their followers from the
ravages brought by military enforcement on the Lur
tribes to the north of Bakhtiari territory. Some
groups were settled in their summer quarters, others
in winter areas. In this case, the tribal administration alleviated the impact of the Shah's policy.
The tribesmen affected of course viewed the role
played by their khans rather differently, as collusion with government, a tribal perception to which I
shall refer in more detail below.

The Bakhtiari and the State

Shifting Centres of state Power. Historically the
Bakhtiari tribes have had an intense and continuous
but varied involvement with the state. During the
past 250 years the centre of power in Iran shifted
from Isfahan, the Safavid capital until 1722 when it

was sacked by the invading Afghans, briefly to
Mashhad in the eastern province of Khurasan under
Nadir Afshar, then to Shiraz in the southern province of Fars under the Zand dynasty until the 1780s,
and finally north under the Qajar dynasty to Tehran,
where it has stayed to the present day. Throughout
these shifts of central government, the strategic
central location of Bakhtiari territory, close to
Isfahan, has been a significant element in the evolution of Bakhtiari tribal organisation.

During the exceptional period of Nadir Shah's
rule, when the centre of power shifted from the
north-south axis to Khurasan, thousands of Bakhtiari
families had been forcibly removed from their territory following a revolt instigated and led by one
Ali Murad of the major Chahar Lang branch of the
Bakhtiari. Along with these thousands of Bakhtiari
in Khurasan, Bakhtiari tribal contingents fought
with distinction in Nadir Shah's forces, particularly
in the taking of Kandahar. For his role in this
military adventure, and his undertaking to maintain
peace and control in Bakhtiari territory, one of
the Bakhtiari commanders, Ali Salih Beg of the Haft
Lang group of Bakhtiari tribes, the major opponents
of the Chahar Lang tribes, was rewarded with agricultural land in the rich district of Chahar Mahall
in Isfahan province on the edges of tribal territory,
and granted the title of khan, the first recorded
khan of the Bakhtiari.[3] Ali Salih's descendants
became the dominant khans of the nineteenth century.
In the political chaos following the murder of Nadir
Shah (1747) these armed forces and the many Bakhtiari
families exiled in Khurasan returned to their tribal
territory in the Zagros, under their leader Ali
Merdun Khan, also of the Chahar Lang, who made a bid
for the vacant throne. In this he was unsuccessful,
being killed by the forces of Karim Khan Zand, who
did succeed in establishing his own dynasty based on
Shiraz.

The theme of Bakhtiari fighting both for and
simultaneously against the state is one that continues to the present day. Under Karim Khan Zand,
again following a revolt of some sections of the
Bakhtiari, several thousand families were moved from
their tribal territory, some to the north near
Varamin, others to Fasa in the south where they remain to this day. Abdul, son of Ali Salih, was in
1754 appointed by firman as zabit of Chahar Mahall,
and in another document of 1780 he is described as
Governor of the Haft Lang Bakhtiari.[4] He also extended his land holdings in Chahar Mahall, further

consolidating the wealth and expanding power of this group of khans, the leaders of the Duraki tribes of the Haft Lang Bakhtiari.

In the continuing political chaos of the eighteenth century, as the Qajars emerged to dynastic success, they fought the Bakhtiari on two occasions. In 1785 a Bakhtiari force comprising tribesmen from both Haft Lang and Chahar Lang, led by Abdul Khan, routed the Qajars near Isfahan, but was later roundly defeated, Abdul Khan being captured. Shortly thereafter the capital was moved to Tehran.

The eighteenth century has been aptly characterised as one of tribal resurgence[5] as a result of the political situation at national level. The effects on the tribal populations of the central Zagros were particularly marked and reveal the ramifying effects of the wider political environment, itself highly unstable during this period, and therefore unpredictable. This period is crucial to consider, not only as the beginning of the rise to power of the Duraki khans, but as a time of major economic and ecological disruption in Bakhtiari territory, resulting from the political turbulence. The Safavid period, especially at its height during the reign of Shah Abbas, saw the deforestation of the Bakhtiari foothills to supply timber for Safavid building projects in Isfahan; the ecological effects of this deforestation later worsened on the invasion of the Afghans and of Nadir Shah deep into the Zagros, when there appears (the evidence is not conclusive) to have been large-scale destruction of agriculture and settlements, notably in the central Bazuft region of the Bakhtiari. Raids by Nadir's forces, the crushing of tribal revolts and the removal of thousands of families from the region made agriculture impossible. This appears to have been the period when the Bakhtiari turned increasingly to the long-range pastoral nomadism which has characterised them since. The labour-intensive requirements of agriculture could not be met with the reportedly large numbers of men away in the armies of Nadir, Ali Merdun and the Zands. To judge from the archaeological evidence, as well as the sheer number of ruined settlements dating from the eighteenth century, Bakhtiari territory has been exploited agriculturally everywhere, except in the very highest reaches of the Zagros. The recurrent depopulation of the eighteenth century made pastoral nomadism a more secure response, ecologically as well as politically. Meanwhile the Duraki leaders were expanding their agricultural holdings on the edges of tribal territory proper, and moving towards positions of provincial landownership in non-tribal areas. The distance grew between them and the bulk of the tribal population who were becoming more nomadic. This divergence of economic interest and widening social distance between khans and the tribesmen has since become a permanent feature of the Bakhtiari system. It arises out of interaction with the state, tribal leaders being drawn increasingly into a political arena dominated by more diversified and non-tribal issues. It is from the eighteenth century that the nomads began to perceive and experience the move of the khans in effect into the state itself, resulting in the typically negative relationship that developed between the dominating Duraki khans and the tribesmen.

Bakhtiari Ecology and the State. Continuous geographical proximity to the shifting centres of state authority thus inevitably embroiled the Bakhtiari directly in the political as well as economic life of the state, in different ways and with different implications for them under successive dynasties. At no time could any ruler have the luxury of ignoring the presence of the Bakhtiari, while for their part the Bakhtiari rarely avoided attracting the unwelcome, usually antagonistic attentions of the state. Each came to constitute for the other at best a perpetual irritant, at worst an implacable enemy.

Although almost always relatively close to the various capital cities, Bakhtiari territory, being almost entirely mountainous, was not easily accessible to invading government forces. This has prevented total control and domination by successive Iranian dynasties. Settlement makes for greater vulnerability, and the earliest settlements of powerful tribal chiefs in the eighteenth and nineteenth centuries were typically in almost impregnable fortresses (qaleh), which could withstand military bombardment as well as more common tribal raiding parties.

Bakhtiari territory comprises approximately 75,000 square kilometers of the central Zagros, roughly between the cities of Isfahan and Ahwaz. Six chains of mountains run the length of this region, rising to about 4,500 metres at Zardeh Kuh in the centre of Bakhtiari tribal territory. All except the very poorest Bakhtiari have during this century practised a dual economy, varied combinations of cultivation, usually of unirrigated wheat and barley,

with long-range nomadism, herding sheep and goats
between winter pastures on the western foothills of
the Zagros in Khuzistan and summer pastures in the
eastern slopes of the mountain chain in Isfahan province. The migrations of people and animals occur
in the spring and back along the same difficult
routes in the autumn. These periods of movement,
crossing rivers and climbing over snowfields and
mountain passes up to 3,500 metres, constitute for
the Bakhtiari the height of involvement with fellow-
tribesmen and with their nomadic roots, the dynamic
source of their cultural identity and of their
values and many of their distinctive tribal institutions. The strongly developed Bakhtiari sense of
unique identity, their tribal self-image, is rooted
in their ecological adaptation to this extremely
harsh mountain habitat.

The Bakhtiari number approximately 300,000
people. While proportions are difficult to establish
and vary through time, perhaps as much as one half
of the Bakhtiari population was to some degree
nomadic in the 1960s. The escalating modernisation
programme during the boom years of the 1970s undoubtedly produced a considerable increase in the numbers
of settled Baktiari. The foothills of the Zagros in
both winter and summer pasture areas are now heavily
populated, with Bakhtiari settled in hundreds of
small lineage-based hamlets of between three and
30 households, as well as many larger tribal villages with populations of several thousands, particularly in the fertile Fireydun and Chahar Mahal
regions in Isfahan province. Small market towns
have also developed in both winter and summer areas.

While circumstances vary a great deal, few
Bakhtiari nomads now live permanently in their goat-
hair tents, but rather move between settled villages,
practising some cultivation in summer and winter
villages and moving with their flocks and living in
tents only during migrations. Others have one area
of permanent settlement either in summer or winter
quarters and move and live in tents for only one
season. The Bakhtiari thus balance two economic
modes in different proportions, allowing for a
flexible and fluid ecological response to an environment in which animals die, climate is unpredictable,
and crop yields for all but the very wealthy are low
and also unpredictable.

The ecology of the Bakhtiari is such that their
migrations between pastures take place exclusively
within Bakhtiari-controlled territory, and keep them
at maximum ecological and social distance from gov-

ernment. Their nomadism was thus a way of evading
state interference and military invasions of their
territory. In this they differ from other groups
such as the powerful Qashqai to the south, whose
migrations brought them through areas not tribally
controlled and thus made them vulnerable to government forces, from which they suffered under Riza
Pahlavi. For the Bakhtiari, particularly this
century, state interference and administrative penetration have occurred in either summer or winter
quarters, when they are either settled in villages
or at least less mobile. An antagonistic state was
thus a factor in inducing Bakhtiari to adopt pastoral nomadism as a means of escaping state authority,
while for the Qashqai an antagonistic state could
prevent movement and attack the economic basis of
their society. This perhaps explains why it was the
Qashqai who fought the Pahlavi forces more bitterly.
The differing political response from these two
powerful groups to state pressure is a result of
ecological differences between them.

State Administrative Structure and the Bakhtiari.
Bakhtiari experience of the state has been particularly diverse as a consequence not only of the geographical location and ecology of their territory,
but of the administrative structure of Iran. Bakhtiari territory lies within four provinces: primarily
in the two important provinces of Khuzistan (formerly Arabistan) and Isfahan, more peripherally in Fars
and Luristan.

The summer pastures of the Bakhtiari lie
exclusively within Isfahan province. Here the bulk
of the animal products such as lambs, wool and ghee
are sold after completion of the spring migration.
The winter quarters of the tribes lie however in
Khuzistan province, where pastoral products are
also sold and winter provisions are bought. The
Bakhtiari are thus involved economically in two quite
different market systems, as well as two different
provincial administrations, at different times of
the year. The rhythms of their ecological adaptation necessarily bring them into contact with
strikingly different economies in the agriculturally
rich province of Isfahan in summer and in the more
arid, less fertile plains of Khuzistan in winter.
Different supply and demand mechanisms operated in
these provinces, affecting price structures of both
agricultural and pastoral produce. The effects of
this dual involvement in different market systems
were particularly important during Qajar rule in the

nineteenth century, where state power was markedly
different in the provinces concerned. Under the Pahlavis these differences were merged within a more
uniform centralised system, and more recently within
an economy increasingly dominated by the Shah's industrialisation and modernisation drive. The oil-
fields of Khuzistan have provided potential employment
for Bakhtiari labour since early this century, and in
the 1970s some Bakhtiari found jobs at the Russian-
built steel mill close to their summer quarters.

The northern part of Bakhtiari territory, inhabited by Chahar Lang tribes, was in the nineteenth
century under the administrative control of Luristan,
while the southernmost reaches of Bakhtiari country
paid taxes to the Governor of Fars.

The network of economic, political and social
ties of those Bakhtiari tribes whose territories
partially lay within the administrative control of
Luristan or Fars was different from those whose
summer quarters lay in Isfahan province and winter
quarters in Khuzistan. Thus different Bakhtiari
tribes had very different types of involvement with
the state, particularly at the provincial level.
Typically in the nineteenth century, when Isfahan
and Arabistan provinces were governed by powerful
Qajar princes, Bakhtiari leaders were on occasion
closely allied with one prince while locked in
deadly political struggle with the other. Frequent
changes in the personal political fortunes of the
Qajar provincial governors could be beneficial or
disastrous for Bakhtiari leaders, depending on the
nature of their involvement with these governors.
The political arena in which the Bakhtiari found
themselves was not only diverse but inherently unstable, subject as it was to political forces quite
outside the local tribal context, making the tribal
chiefs vulnerable to political power struggles ori-
ginating within the administration itself, and
logically compelling the Bakhtiari leaders towards
the source of these political forces, the capital,
as a political move necessary to curb these provincial intrusions on their own tribal power.

While subject to provincial instability, the
Bakhtiari themselves contributed considerably to it.
A provincial governor who was unable to control the
Bakhtiari when faced with tribal raiding or inter-
tribal conflict, or who had difficulty extracting
tribal taxes, soon found his position threatened
from the capital. The Bakhtiari in turn naturally
resisted attempts to destroy their independence,
and where possible avoided paying taxes to provincial

authorities not strong enough to enforce it.   Mutual
vulnerability characterised relations between tribal
chiefs and provincial governors, each manoeuvring to
take advantage of this.   The Bakhtiari and the state
were inextricably linked at the local provincial
level under the Qajars, in two provinces, forming
two diverse but connected local political universes
dominated by a continuously shifting and fluid balance of power involving each in the other's differently constituted arena.   Political survival at this
level, where interaction was at its most varied and
intense, impelled the Bakhtiari leaders increasingly out of the tribal context, the basis of their
power and onto the level of the state.   As mentioned
above in an economic context, again arising out of
involvement with state representatives, the Bakhtiari
leadership found itself becoming distanced from the
tribesmen.   Those who could not move out but retained close links to their tribal base were swallowed
up in this political escalation.   The most successful tribal leaders, the political survivors, were
the ones who most successfully interacted with
government, who entered the non-tribal political
arena, and who inevitably became increasingly identified with the state.

The Social Environment of the Bakhtiari.   The non-
Bakhtiari populations with whom the Bakhtiari regularly interact are as diverse as the other elements
which make up the Bakhtiari interaction with the
state.   This diversity marks out the Bakhtiari as
having rather different circumstances to confront
than do the other tribal groups of the Zagros.   The
configuration of elements making up the total environment, changing in their relative significance
throughout the last several hundred years, is the
basis of the variations of political form developed
within the Bakhtiari.
     In the rich and fertile province of Isfahan,
the non-Bakhtiari population consists of a non-
tribal Persian peasantry, with some Turkish-speaking
villagers and the scattered remnants of once sizable
Georgian and Armenian communities.   In the nineteenth century, with the centralisation of the
Bakhtiari polity under the successful and dominating
Duraki khans of the Haft Lang Bakhtiari, the leaders
came to acquire vast agricultural holdings, particularly in the Chahar Mahall region.   They became
major landlords in the region, which not only made
them immensely wealthy but brought them into direct
political conflict with the other major landlord of

the region, the powerful Qajar prince Zill al-Sultan, Governor of Isfahan, who was himself in conflict with his father, the Shah.

To the north of Bakhtiari tribal territory live the nomadic tribal Lurs, ethnically of the same group as the Bakhtiari. The Lurs never developed the centralised and hierarchical political structure which emerged in the Bakhtiari, and at no time ever threatened the Bakhtiari, although their raids troubled those sections of the Bakhtiari on their borders. The frontier with these decentralised Lurs was the scene, particularly during the nineteenth century, of much local inter-tribal fighting, in which the Bakhtiari became embroiled.

To the south, Bakhtiari territory borders on two different types of tribal groups. In the south-east, the summer pasture area of some of the Bakhtiari is bordered by the very powerful Turkish-speaking Qashqai confederation, the major tribal power in Fars. Mutual raiding and enmity have always existed in this area, causing the downfall of more than one Bakhtiari leader, and making agriculture relatively unsafe. Inter-tribal fighting here involved the Bakhtiari in the political problems of Fars, of which the Qajar governors of Fars complained in Tehran, often causing the regime concern over possible Bakhtiari expansion. In Bakhtiari winter quarters in the south-west, they have as neighbours another tribal group, the Kuhgilu Lurs, who had one of the worst reputations of all the tribes of the Zagros for lawlessness and ferocity. This border area, along which runs a major Bakhtiari migration route, has been the scene of constant and fierce inter-tribal conflict between the Kuhgilu and sections of the Bakhtiari. From the state point of view, however, what was important was the trade route between Khuzistan and Isfahan provinces that passes through this area, ostensibly under the control and protection of the Bakhtiari khans. The insecurity caused by inter-tribal fighting and the raiding of passing caravans, which on occasion in the late nineteenth and early twentieth century halted trade entirely, brought the Bakhtiari into real disfavour. This isolated border area in fact provided the location for a disastrous confrontation between Bakhtiari forces and a regiment of the Persian army in 1921, which brought on the Bakhtiari leaders the wrath of Riza Khan, then Minister of War, with demands for very large indemnities.

In the west, in Khuzistan, furthest from the capital, the bulk of the population was Arabic-

speaking and ethnically quite distinct. The powerful Sheykh of Muhammarah was the key figure in the
province, and was semi-autonomous in the nineteenth
century. Here too the dominant Duraki khans acquired considerable property, especially near the cities
of Dizful and Shushtar in the plains, as well as in
the foothills near the smaller town of Behbehan, an
administrative centre of the Kuhgilu. These property holdings lay outside Bakhtiari territory proper
and repeatedly brought the khans into military conflict with the Sheykh of Muhammarah and his Arab
tribesmen.

To summarise, the social environment of the
Bakhtiari comprised, on the northern and southern
borders, tribal groups, some with centralised power
structures, others with non-centralised lineage
systems under local leaders, producing endemic
inter-tribal rivalries. On the more settled western
and eastern borders, neighbouring groups were non-
tribal peasants of diverse ethnic composition, who
farmed land owned by nationally powerful figures,
and with whom the Bakhtiari traded in a symbiotic
relationship typical of all the pastoral economies
of the Zagros. The major provincial market centres
on which the Bakhtiari depended were Isfahan itself
for summer quarters and Dizful, Shushtar and Ahwaz
in the winter areas.

The Bakhtiari were thus drawn unavoidably into
a multiplicity of diverse economic and political
arenas, involving other tribal groups, non-tribal
groups, different ethnic divisions and powerful
provincial landowners and governors, with all the
competing economic and political interests that this
implies, cross-cutting the four major provinces of
south-west Iran. The Bakhtiari were quite literally
in the centre of nineteenth-century Iran's most
dissident and troublesome area. This unique central
position, with interaction on all fronts, kept them
in the attention of the regime, in one context or
another, more or less all the time. Not surprisingly, therefore, the Bakhtiari won a reputation at
national level as the most troublesome tribal group
in the realm, a reputation in which their tribal
power reached legendary proportions, and which the
Bakhtiari khans used to propel themselves into the
national arena, albeit for a brief period, during
the Constitutional revolution. Under the Pahlavis
they paid dearly for this reputation, the creation
of a history of interaction in which a tribal political strategy, necessary for survival in the
diverse contexts from which the Bakhtiari could not

escape, was to project an image of power, independence and tribal ferocity which was based on the mobility of pastoral nomadism. The show of aggression, the mythological manipulation of apparent power, has been part of Bakhtiari strategy for centuries, but with the exception of their reported role in the taking of Kandahar in 1738, they have rarely if ever taken on the armed forces of the state with the real success of other tribal groups such as the Qashqai and more particularly the Kurds in the north. The complex involvement of the Bakhtiari with the state would appear at least partially to have domesticated the Bakhtiari tribes politically, though failing to eliminate the pastoral nomadic economic bases of a still thriving tribal society.

European Powers and the Bakhtiari

Since the middle of the nineteenth century the Bakhtiari have had particularly close associations with the British, who had trade interests in the south of Iran and who financed an improved trade route through Bakhtiari territory from Khuzistan to Isfahan, building bridges and caravanserais on what became known as the Lynch road, after the British company which helped finance this route. This trade route brought considerable wealth to the Duraki khans, who rose to power under their leader Huseyn Quli Khan (appointed by the regime as ilkhani or paramount leader of all the Bakhtiari in 1867) and remained the dominant khans from that time. The economic and political importance of the Bakhtiari was transformed however by the discovery of oil in the Khuzistan foothills in 1908, and in fact, until the effective take-over by Riza Pahlavi, the Bakhtiari leaders interacted more directly with the British than with the Iranian state on many occasions. Tribal lands were ceded to the British for oil exploration and building, the khans receiving payment, though the tribes concerned were not compensated by them for the loss of their land. The Bakhtiari khans were share-holders in the first oil company formed. Henceforth the political arena in which the Bakhtiari leaders effectively found themselves was an international one in which the British and the Iranian states often had conflicting interests in the Bakhtiari area. While the British required political stability to make possible the effective exploitation of oil, such local stability did not suit the troubled Qajar regime, which could see a stable and united Bakhtiari only as a real threat to its own shaky security.

Of all the tribes of the south, the Bakhtiari have had the most intense and long-term interaction with the British. Anticipating what since the 1960s has become a world-wide issue, the Bakhtiari khans used oil as a political weapon against the British from the time of its discovery, threatening the Oil Companies with the disruption of their early exploitation, setting their tribes to attack the new pipelines, blowing up oil installations, escalating their financial demands as well as demanding political protection from the Iranian government. The Bakhtiari again became the focus of conflicting international political forces, which inevitably had ramifying effects on the leaders and indirectly on their relations with their own tribesmen, who received little economic benefit from oil and reaped all the political problems that the growing aspirations of their leaders brought them. The social worlds of khans and tribesmen were increasingly separated and their relations more tense, precisely at the time when control of these tribesmen became crucial to the British to maintain the flow of oil out of the region.

The British also found increased internal differences within the growing families of Bakhtiari khans, making them difficult to control, just as these internal conflicts within the body of khans fomented dissent within the Bakhtiari tribes, who were coming to see their relationship with the khans as one of oppression. The problem of controlling the Bakhtiari khans was the subject of a mistakenly optimistic memorandum sent in 1916 by Marling, then British Minister in Tehran, to the Foreign Office in London:

> Although by no means the largest tribe in Persia, the Bakhtiari are probably the most important tribal unit in the Empire, despite family quarrels they have been taught the value of unity by the considerable role they played in late years, and still play in Persian politics, thanks to our support.[6]

The notorious inability of the Bakhtiari khans to unite to overcome increasing internal differences, even when ruthlessly attacked, imprisoned and murdered during Riza Shah's reign, has been documented in detail.[7] Marling's miscalculation about the effects of British support for Bakhtiari stability is shown up by Major-General Frazer, serving in Iran

during the Second World War, when he states, with
perhaps ungenerous exasperation, 'I am getting to
the point of cursing Reza Shah for being such a soft
old mutt as to leave any Bakhtiari Khan alive. They
just can not stop quarrelling.'[8] As we have seen in
other contexts, such internal dissension is in fact
the consequence of the multi-faceted involvement with
'state' politics, a product of the growing differentiation of the khans' economic circumstances in
the twentieth century, with pastoral wealth and
tribal taxes, agricultural holdings, urban property,
governorships, income from the muleteer trade passing through their territory, and oil royalties, on
which they frequently raised loans from the British.
With the progression of the twentieth century the
khans became an integral, and occasionally a dominating part of the state itself.

        This last point is important from the perspect-
ive of the Bakhtiari tribesmen, who came to see
their own khans as oppressive representatives of
the state, and, except on a very selective and spor-
adic basis, saw none of the benefits of having their
own chiefs in positions of national power. Unusually for the tribes of the Zagros, the Bakhtiari in
the 1960s would repeatedly state their hatred for
their own khans, by whom they felt consistently used
and abused. They considered the khans, unlike those
of the Qashqai to the south, to be 'city people'
(shahri), no longer tribal or even Bakhtiari at all.
The modern khans were contrasted with those of the
nineteenth century as having betrayed their tribal
identity, no longer attempting to help their own
tribes as those in the past had done even when serving their own interests. This loathing of the
Bakhtiari for their khans has however been reported
by many observers this century. One of the many
political officers protecting British interests in
Bakhtiari territory, in a report on conditions within the Bakhtiari submitted to the British Embassy in
Tehran in 1921, quotes several of his British predecessors:

        In 1908, Col. Wilson wrote, 'The Khans are
        tolerated as a disagreeable necessity and
        feared and obeyed in proportion to their
        strength.' In 1911, the vice consul at Ahwaz
        wrote, 'While the personal loyalty of the
        tribesmen to their chiefs is despicable, it is
        still not for a moment to be assumed that they
        would in consequence, acquiesce with any out-
        side power, which by attempting to remove their

lightly esteemed chiefs, would threaten the
present form of independence enjoyed by the
tribe as a whole.' The most striking feature
[since 1917, four years previously] is the
increase in ill feeling to the Khans ... True
the ill feeling among the tribesmen towards
their chiefs is of such long standing as to be
characterized as symptomatic.[9]

The Internal Enemy

The chiefs to whom the above report refers are the
Duraki khans who rose to power over all the dozens
of different tribes of the Bakhtiari after considerable bloodshed. No Bakhtiari apart from the groups
making up the Duraki had particular love for the
emergence of the Duraki khans. What marks the particular type of hierarchical leadership of the
Bakhtiari tribes, is that to produce this centralised monopoly of power, the Duraki khans first had
to wipe out all internal opposition and bring the
leaders of each of the constituent tribes under
their control. They faced problems similar to those
experienced, on a larger scale, by government.
Under the nomadic conditions that primarily prevailed in the nineteenth century, Duraki central control
could only be partial, particularly over the tribal
groups whose territories lay high in the mountains,
most distant from Duraki territory, and particularly
as one of the prerequisites for the exercise of
power was to have a secure economic base, and that
only agriculture could bring. Animal wealth is
hazardous and precarious given the regional ecology.
    Tribal power in the hands of the Duraki, and
the elaborate administration they developed to
handle the problems of control from the middle of
the nineteenth century onwards, were based on the
agricultural land holdings acquired first during the
reign of Nadir Shah in the Chahar Mahall, and later
in the plains of Khuzistan. Just as the Bakhtiari
have faced shifting centres of state power, the
tribesmen within their own geographical area experienced the annual shift in Duraki centres of power
between summer and winter pastures.
    There have been marked variations therefore
within the Bakhtiari in the extent of control achieved by the Duraki khans. The Duraki groups were
ruled directly, but the other major tribal groups,
the Chahar Lang tribes, those of the Bakhtiarwand
Babadi Bab and Aurek Haft Lang,[10] were ruled in-

directly through their own local chiefs, who had
been defeated and were now partially and resentfully
under the control of the Duraki. The latter managed
to monopolise interaction with government and with
the British. The political sphere of the dominating
khans was the nation-state, that of the defeated
leaders of the other Bakhtiari groups a much more
parochial tribal or at most provincial arena.
     For most Bakhtiari, the Duraki khans, although
themselves fraught with internal dissension, thus
not only became identified with the state but were
in fact part of it. The increasing polarisation
between khans and tribes, and the internal divisions
among the khans, resulted in a necessary division of
political labour between those khans who were in the
end exclusively occupied with economic and political
affairs outside the tribal context, in particular as
city-based provincial governors during the last 15
years of the Qajar dynasty, and those usually junior
khans delegated by the ilkhani to administer the
extensive tribal region on his behalf. These junior
khans, in their more restricted local arena, were
more closely associated with the tribesmen, and used
this association as a basis from which to rebel and
intrigue against their own relatives. Inevitably
such internal divisions, intensified by the differentiating effects of time, were seized upon, not
only by the Pahlavi regime but by the tribesmen
themselves. A particularly interesting example of
this occurred in 1921, when a Bakhtiari Soviet was
formed by several younger discontented khans, who
had a published manifesto aimed at establishing
more socialist relations within the Bakhtiari and
curtailing the oppressive power of the Tehran-based
khans.[11] One of the founder-members of the short-
lived social experiment, later murdered by Riza
Shah, was the father of the recent Prime Minister,
Dr Shapur Bakhtiar, himself the victim in 1980 of an
assassination attempt by reputed representatives of
the new Islamic Republic.
     The state strategy of murdering tribal leaders
runs like a bloody thread throughout the history of
the Bakhtiari since at least the sixteenth century.
Such murders might be carried out directly by state
officials, or by rival Bakhtiari instigated either
from the centre in Tehran or through provincial
representatives of the state. This twin bloody
thread of Bakhtiari, allied with government, murder-
ing rival Bakhtiari, was one crucial and pernicious
effect of the intensity of Bakhtiari relations with
the state in the variety of circumstances and con-

texts elaborated earlier. Such internal violence at
all levels of Bakhtiari tribal organisation reached
a degree not found in other tribal groups, constituting an enemy within their own ranks more dangerous
and immediate than the distant external enemy, the
state. The Bakhtiari are as suspicious and cautious
in their relations with each other as they are with
outsiders.

The intensification of their interaction and
involvement in the national economic and political
arena, made it politically expedient for the dominant
Bakhtiari to operate within the 'state' taken in its
broadest sense. In the twentieth century there has
been a quite bewildering series of contexts and conflicting situations in which Bakhtiari are found to
be on all sides. The two World Wars saw some Bakhtiari co-operating with the Germans, others with the
British; in the 1920s there were pro-Russians and
anti-Russians; others worked with the Arabs of
Khuzistan against fellow-Bakhtiari. More important,
during the Pahlavi period many of the khans worked
within the state in government capacities, in a
period when the tensions between the Bakhtiari and
the Pahlavis saw the murder of several khans in
1934, including the already mentioned father of Dr
Shapur Bakhtiar and the Bakhtiari Minister of War,
and the imprisonment of many more, while the late
Shah took a Bakhtiari, Soraya, as his second wife,
and founded the infamous SAVAK under General Teymur
Bakhtiar, who was himself later exiled on the instigation of the Shah and murdered in 1970. The very
success of the dominant Bakhtiari khans in emerging
onto the national scene also led to disaster for
many individual khans, with imprisonment, torture,
exile and death the all-too-common fate. The Bakhtiari tribes also paid the penalty for this success
by leaders they saw as oppressive.

Their deeply ambivalent experience of the
state, and of their own 'state-like' leaders, is
evocatively expressed in popular Bakhtiari songs in
the region. Their rich oral culture sings not only
of the delights of the nomadic life, but of clashes
with the state, of tribal heroes killed in battles
caused by the khans against Iranian armed forces.
These songs provide the Bakhtiari with a continuously
articulated and culturally powerful memory of heroic
deaths in their struggles against the state and the
khans who betrayed the tribes. Through these songs
the history of Bakhtiari relations with the state,
their tribal and independent identity, are brought
provocatively into the present, energising the

present, only partially by nostalgia, with the shed
blood and glories of their past. Significantly, few
khans are remembered in this way, with the exception
of two renegade khans who, at least in their youth,
led the tribesmen against the military oppressions
of the Pahlavis and of their senior leaders co-
operating with the state, and thus provided the content for two of the best-loved Bakhtiari ballads.
These commemorate the activities of Ali Merdun Khan
of the Chahar Lang section, murdered in 1934 on the
Shah's orders, and Abul-Qasim Khan of the opposing
Haft Lang section, who on several different occasions
between 1942 and 1950 led tribal rebellions in the
style of the great nineteenth-century ilkhani
Huseyn Quli Khan, a style that shows signs of recur-
ring at local levels in the current Islamic Republic.
Local tribalism proves to be remarkably resilient,
surviving not only external enemies but, at least
for the Bakhtiari, the equally dangerous internal
enemy as well.

Conclusion

While this chapter has concentrated on an attempt to
unravel the widest relevant economic, social and
political relations in which the Bakhtiari participated, detailed discussion of their specific effects
on internal tribal political structure is required
and will be the subject of a later publication. What
is clear, however, is that for the Bakhtiari tribes,
relations with the nation-state have been monopolised
by the dominant Duraki khans since the middle of the
nineteenth century. In the bloody rise of the original ilkhan, and the subsequent consolidation of
centralised power by his descendants, these khans
became patrons to local-level leaders, the kalantars,
able to reward them with access to the wider political arena of a modernising state and a range of economic resources not available within the Bakhtiari
mountains. The khans allowed the kalantars selective access to the widest range of economic resources
in return for their support. For administrative
purposes such as maintaining peace and extracting
taxes on both agricultural and animal produce, the
khans worked through these kalantars in conjunction
with their own representatives, sent to each tribe
to ensure the collection of revenue. These representatives were members of the khan family, or members of the tribe from which the khans sprang, the
Zarraswand of the Haft Lang section. The khans main-

tained a treasury for administrative expenses, and themselves received state stipends as governors of the tribal area under their jurisdiction. This administration came to constitute a 'state within a state', albeit of a tribal nature. It was this Bakhtiari 'tribal state' with which most Bakhtiari interacted, rather than with the nation-state. Bakhtiari tribal leaders thus came to be seen as part of the nation-state's administrative apparatus, and in this sense were simultaneously part of the 'external stimulus' of the state.

An analytic distinction between external and internal factors, with the external factor being held to be primarily responsible for the development of centralised tribal systems of a confederative type, would appear to be of dubious value. The forces that produced this centralisation of power and hierarchical structure come from a single socio-economic universe for which the polarisation into 'tribe and state' or 'internal and external' is perhaps not the most useful framework for analysis. The Bakhtiari, within such analytic categories, become both 'tribe' and 'state', internal and external, which is not only confusing but makes problematic the choice of what is external or internal to what.

The dialogue between historians and anthropologists, with the different source material and theoretical orientations utilised by each, promises to be mutually beneficial in helping to develop more useful analytic categories. From my own reading of the historical sources, combined with anthropological fieldwork, I would characterise the Bakhtiari as less a confederation in structure than a 'failed state', limited by its own inability to overcome the tribal basis of its own administration. This now decayed 'failed state' within the nation-state produced the inequalities found within the Bakhtiari tribal structure, with the variations in political organisation and types of leadership still prevailing. Political history is carried into the present internal tensions, an understanding of which demands a diachronic analysis utilising all the historical documentation available.

NOTES

1. My emphasis. IOL: Persia: Printed Correspondence 1923-25: Encl. 1 in File 481 of 3 Oct. 1923, LPS/10/3151.
2. Ibid.

3. G. Garthwaite, 'The Bakhtiyārī Khans as Landlords and Governors', paper presented at MESA meeting, Boston, 1974, p. 4 and Doc. 1.

4. Ibid., p. 6 and Docs. 3 and 4.

5. A.K.S. Lambton, 'The tribal resurgence and the decline of the bureaucracy in eighteenth century Persia', in T. Naff and R. Owen (eds.), *Studies in Eighteenth Century Islamic History* (Southern Illinois University Press, Carbondale, 1977).

6. My emphasis. IOL: Persia Confidential Paper 10710: 1916; LPS/18, C. 154.

7. G. Garthwaite, 'The Bakhtiyārī Īlkhānī: an illusion of unity', *IJMES*, 8 (1977), pp. 145-60.

8. Fraser to Gault, Isfahan, 19 July 1944, FO 799/20, File 997/5/z/22.

9. Encl. Major Noel Report, Isfahan, 12 May 1921, FO 371/6405.

10. In chapter 10 above, Garthwaite gives a somewhat different discussion of the history of the Bakhtiari, including a schematic breakdown of tribal political divisions.

11. FO 248/1279, 1920. FO 371/6407, E. 13435/2/34, Oct. 1921 includes a manifesto of this group, which called itself the 'Bakhtiari Star'. FO 371/7805, E.4742/6/34, 1921.

Chapter 13
KURDISH TRIBES AND THE STATE OF IRAN: THE CASE OF SIMKO'S REVOLT

Martin van Bruinessen

> Their pretext is independence and their war
> cry is 'Ashirat', the Kurdish equivalent for
> Bolsheviki[1] (An American eye-witness on
> Simko's Kurds)

Introduction

Kurdish tribes (ashiret) have on several occasions
played important roles in Iran's politics, both
internal and foreign. The Kurds constitute one of
Iran's major ethnic groups, even though only a
minority of all Kurds (some 3.5 millions out of an
estimated 14 millions) live within the borders of
Iran.[2] During the past centuries the state of Iran
has dealt directly and overtly with only a small
fraction of the important Kurdish tribes. Covert
contact with Kurdish tribes across the political
border has, however, always been an ingredient of
Iran's foreign politics. The most recent and probably best-known instance of this was Iran's massive
support to the Kurdish insurgents in Iraq in the
late 1960s and early 1970s which ended so dramatically in 1975.
  Iran was, however, not the only state, nor the
most important one, to have an impact on the Kurdish
tribes and on the political process in Kurdistan.
Since the early sixteenth century most of Kurdistan
had been incorporated in the Ottoman Empire, while
during the past century and a half the impact of the
great Powers can hardly be overestimated. The social and political organisation of Kurdistan, the
very nature of the Kurdish tribes, underwent great
changes as a result of contacts with all these
states. The impact of the Kurdish tribes on these
states was less dramatic: the Kurds themselves have
always been quite marginal to their interests. The

main threat that the Kurds posed to the states in
which they lived was that of secession and/or collaboration with rival powers. (The term 'bolsheviki'
in the quotation at the beginning of this chapter,
although nonsensical, appealed to ever-present appre-
hensions). It was especially in connection with
Kurdish nationalism and aspirations for independence
that Kurdish tribes affected the state - in more
than one sense: the centralising and authoritarian
tendencies of Kemalist Turkey and Pahlavi Iran were
strengthened in reaction to Kurdish separatism.
    This chapter consists of two parts. In the
first some general observations are made on the evolution of the social and political organisation of
Kurdistan since 1800 under the impact of the states
mentioned. These general remarks are then illustrated by a more detailed study of a case where Kurdish
tribes challenged the Iranian state: the rebellion
led by Simko in the 1920s.

Kurdish Tribes between Powerful States

Kurdistan has for millennia been not just a frontier
area, but a buffer between two or more empires.
Unlike Afghanistan, however, it has never been politically distinct, but has been partitioned between
two empires, the Ottoman and the Iranian, for almost
five centuries. Nevertheless, the natural conditions are such that these, like previous conquerors,
could establish only a very tenuous suzerainty over
Kurdistan. Direct rule could only rarely be maintained, and usually some form of indirect rule
through local chieftains was practised, as it still
is in some parts. This contact with well-developed
states, stretching over many centuries, could not
but have profound effects on the social organisation
of Kurdistan.
    When the Ottomans incorporated most of Kurdistan
(c. 1515) there existed several emirates, state-like
units of varying size and organisational complexity,
some of which were quite ancient. Their political
system more or less resembled that of the Qaraqoyunlu
and Aqqoyunlu Turkman confederation-states, with
which they had been in relations of alliance and/or
vassalage. The Ottoman conquest did not result in
the destruction, but in the preservation of the
emirates and consolidation of the ruler (mir)'s position within each emirate. Around 1800 some of these
emirates still existed. Their internal organisation
by that time seems to have been much influenced by

MAP 7: *Sketch-map of Kurdistan and north-western Iran to show places mentioned in chapters 13 and 14*

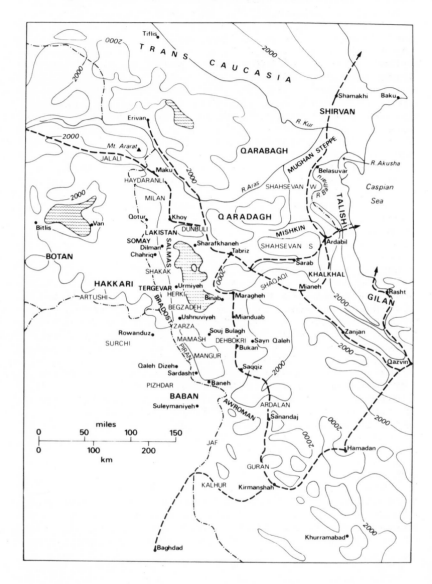

that of the Ottoman state.[3] The two emirates in
Iranian Kurdistan on which some information is available, Ardalan and Guran, both seem to have differed
considerably from those under Ottoman suzerainty:
for instance, the ruling stratum was largely non-
tribal. It is tempting to think that this represents
differences in organisation and policies of the
Ottoman and Iranian states. There are, however,
other factors at work that may be equally important:
natural conditions, population density, the ratio of
settled and nomadic population, etc.

The presence of more than one strong state in
the vicinity also had its specific effects on the
political process in Kurdistan. For instance, it
gave the local chieftains more leverage in dealing
with the suzerain state: they could threaten to
switch loyalties (or actually do so). Moreover, the
local rivals of these chieftains were not dependent
on popular support if they desired to replace them
but could attempt to invoke the aid of the rival
state. In several emirates, the ruling families were
thus split in 'pro-Turkish' and 'pro-Iranian'
branches.[4] The nineteenth century witnessed, for
obvious reasons, the emergence of 'pro-British' and
'pro-Russian' wings in Kurdistan's ruling circles.
By the second half of the century Russia and Britain
had become the most significant powers in the environment. The actions of the leading Kurds were
strongly influenced by their perception that those
states were stronger than the Ottoman and the Iranian, and that both intended to acquire control of
Kurdistan. Moreover, the emergence of Kurdish nationalism received a firm boost from the political
and military advances these powers made, and, of
course, from the news of Greek and Slav independence,
due to the powers' support. Most Kurdish nationalists of the period 1880-1930 envisaged an independent state, under British and/or Russian protection.
To this day, the nature of the Kurdish nationalist
movement is strongly influenced by the presence of
the successors of these rival powers, the USA and the
USSR, and the generally perceived need to enlist
their support.[5]

Emirate, Confederacy, Tribe

It is especially during the nineteenth and twentieth
centuries that great changes in the social and political organisation of Kurdistan took place, as central control by the Ottoman and Iranian states became

increasingly effective. The consequence of the
elaboration and refining of the administrative networks of the encompassing states was that the highly
complex indigenous forms of political organisation
(the emirates) gave way to simpler ones.
    The basic organisational pattern of the emirates
had been the same as that of many Middle Eastern
states - the most obvious parallels being the Turkman
confederation-states. The ruler belonged to a chiefly lineage that usually claimed prestigious descent
different from that of the powerful tribes of the
emirate. There was no set rule of succession, only
certain minimum requirements of descent (belonging
to the ruling lineage), intelligence, courage, etc.
The actual selection of a successor usually involved
fierce competition within the ruling lineage and
numerous intrigues by internal and external interested powers. The ruler was surrounded by a court consisting of leading military men (tribal chieftains)
and civilian officials and scholars. There was a
standing army or armed retinue drawn from different
tribes of the emirate as well as from outside. The
loyalty of this retinue was ideally to the ruler
alone, but they constituted only a small fraction of
the total military strength of the emirate. The
bulk of the army consisted of tribesmen, led by their
own chieftains, who could mobilise them in case of
need. The tribesmen, usually nomadic or semi-nomadic,
constituted in fact a military 'caste' that dominated a lower stratum of cultivators and artisans: non-
tribal Kurds, Christians, Jews. Not all tribes were
equally closely bound to the emirate. The permanent
core was organised in a number of confederacies,
typically two, each again under a chiefly lineage
unrelated to the component tribes. In none of the
cases that I studied more closely could I ascertain
whether these confederacies had already been in
existence prior to the emirate. Legend suggests so
for some,[6] but it seems to me that in at least several cases the emirate itself was the <u>raison</u> <u>d'être</u>
of the confederacies.
    It was the organisation of the tribes into con-
federacies more or less balancing each other that
made the mir's (divide and) rule possible. The
chieftains of these confederacies were the mir's
advisers and counsellors, and in many cases the real
makers of policy. Each of the component tribes also
had its own chieftain, but these appear to have been
of the <u>primus</u> <u>inter</u> <u>pares</u> type, and rarely played
important political roles.
    In emirates that had more than one urban centre

the mir kept the most important town as his own residence and capital, and appointed governors, usually
from among his close relatives, to the other towns
and surrounding districts. These governors took care
of military and financial affairs and the most important judicial cases; other affairs were left to the
chieftains of tribes or subtribes. As yet, I have
found few data about the division of revenue between
tribal chieftains, governors, the mir and the central government. Most probably this showed great
fluctuations, as the actual balance of power between
these authorities changed frequently.

Not all tribes belonged to one emirate or the
other. There were probably always (and certainly
around 1800) groups that managed to maintain a deli-
cate independence, by balancing emirates against each
other: nomadic tribes whose migration routes passed
through more than one emirate, semi-nomadic (transhumant) tribes living at the periphery of the emirates. These tribes belonged, as it were, to the
frontier of the emirates. The political processes
there replicated, on a lower, less complicated level,
those of the empires' frontiers, i.e. those in and
between the emirates.

The distinction made here between 'confederacy'
and 'tribe' is one of degree rather than of kind.
Kurdish usage does not make the same distinction:
both may be called ashiret or taifeh, and the same
terms may even be applied to sections of tribes.
The Kurdish tribes are political associations consisting of at least one descent group (but usually
several) with a number of other people who have
attached themselves to it. Quite different degrees
of complexity are possible and do or did in fact
occur in Kurdistan: tribes consisting of one or two
lineages, tribes consisting of a number of (named)
associations of lineages, tribes consisting of associations of associations of lineages, etc. Size and
degree of complexity form a continuum, and it is
largely a matter of choice where one finds the term
'confederacy' more appropriate than 'tribe'. A confederacy, as I use the term, is a large-scale association, less integrated than a tribe, and with less
clearly defined boundaries. It is a political association of tribes that previously had an independent
existence and that retain a separate identity. Individual persons are referred to by the name of their
tribe rather than that of their confederacy. When
there is a tendency to invent a common ancestor this
suggests increasing integration and I would use the
term 'tribe' rather than 'confederacy'.

369

In confederacies and tribes there are chieftains at several levels of segmentation: confederacy, tribe, lineage, extended family, household - there may be one or more intermediate levels between the tribe and the maximal lineage: I shall speak of 'sub-tribes'. In confederacies and large tribes the chieftains generally belonged to separate chiefly lineages not closely related to the commoners and had an armed retinue ('praetorian guard') to enforce their rule, whereas in smaller tribes the chieftain was (is) usually related to the commoners and ruled by consent rather than by coercion. In different historical periods it was chieftains of different levels of segmentation that played the most significant political parts. In recent times, for instance, several former confederacies have continued to exist, if only in name. The paramount chieftain enjoys respect but has no political functions any more. Real political power is in the hands of the chiefs of tribes or, frequently, sub-tribes - who were much less important two centuries ago. This change is connected less with economic changes than with changes in the political environment, i.e. the central state, as will be discussed below.

Kurdish Tribes and the Ottoman State

In the first half of the nineteenth century the Ottoman and Iranian governments, in their drive for administrative reform, abolished the remaining Kurdish emirates. These reforms were the result of European pressure, as the Kurds realised only too well. The destruction of the last great emirate, Botan, and the capture of its ruler Bedir Khan Beg (1847), was the immediate result of British intervention with the Porte - Bedir Khan Beg was responsible for the massacre of some of his Nestorian subjects, and the British demanded his punishment.[7]
The dissolution of the emirates resulted in chaos and lawlessness. Tribal conflicts, no longer checked by the emirs, proliferated. Not only the emirates as such, also most of the tribal confederations fell apart. Ambitious chieftains attempted to usurp as much as possible of the power formerly belonging to the emirs - which involved a lot of raiding, feuding and warfare. Many leaders of the 'chief' type had to cede to 'brigands'.[8] Contemporary reports all mention the absence of physical security. The state was as yet too weak to restore law and order. The most that provincial governors

could do was to send punitive raids, or support one
chieftain against others and occasionally back him
with military support. They did not have the authority to negotiate or impose a solution in the many
tribal conflicts.

In this Hobbesian situation there remained one
type of 'traditional' authority who could restore
some kind of order: the sheykh. Sheykhs are 'holy
men', usually associated with a sufi or dervish
order. Many have reputations for piety, wisdom and
miraculous powers that earn them wide respect. Many
people had (and have) a special relationship with a
particular sheykh whom they visit(ed) periodically -
sometimes just a courtesy visit, but more often with
the intention of receiving a protective amulet, a
cure for barrenness or disease, advice in spiritual
or worldly matters, mediation in a conflict. Sheykhs
are generally not associated with any particular
tribe (although an entire tribe may consider themselves the followers of one and the same sheykh),
so that they are not party to any conflicts between
tribes. This and the wide respect some of them enjoyed made them the only persons remaining that could
resolve such conflicts - as go-betweens, counsellors,
mediators, notaries and guarantors of the agreements
reached. The successful resolution of tribal conflicts in turn increased their prestige and political
influence. Gradually some sheykhs took over a part
of the role of the former emirs. After a few decades of chaos and insecurity, from ca. 1860 we find
sheykhs as the most influential political leaders all
over Kurdistan. It is not accidental that most of
the Kurdish national revolts (until, say, 1950) were
led by sheykhs: these were virtually the only leaders that could make a number of tribes act in con-
cert. Another factor that contributed to the increasing political influence of these primarily religious
leaders was European missionary activity, which resulted in anti-Christian feeling and a stressing of
the Muslim identity of the Kurds. Sheykhs not only
resolved conflicts: precisely because their political power derived from their ability to do so, they
also needed conflicts if they wished to increase
their power. Some ambitious sheykhs therefore even
provoked conflicts.[9]

Gradually, and not without reversals, the
Ottoman state and its twentieth-century successors
brought Kurdistan under closer central control,
breaking the power of the great tribal chieftains
and sheykhs. This process is usually assumed to be
one of detribalisation. This assumption should how-

ever be qualified; in some respects one might even speak of re-tribalisation. It was not simply that indirect rule (through Kurdish chieftains) was replaced with direct rule (through appointed, generally non-Kurdish, officials). Rather, the delegation of power and authority that is implicit in indirect rule took place on ever lower levels of (tribal) organisation, and accordingly less power was delegated. Two centuries ago provincial governors dealt with the Kurds largely through the mirs and interfered but little in the internal affairs of the emirates. Later the administrative network was refined, and governors at the sub-provincial level dealt with the chieftains of large tribes or confederations, or with sheykhs. Further refining of the administrative network was accompanied by the breaking of many big tribal chieftains' power and the splitting up of large tribes. It is now the chieftains of lower levels that can consolidate their position and derive some power from the lower-rank officials who deal with the Kurdish population through them.

The tribes did not disappear, but changed character. Emirates, confederacies and large, complex tribes gradually gave way to smaller and simpler tribes, ever more closely resembling descent groups. The chieftains tend to be kinsmen of their fellow-tribesmen and to have less despotic powers. Because there remain only a few sheykhs and widely respected chieftains who might contain feuding, tribal conflicts are many. Blood feuds are endemic, especially in Turkish Kurdistan, where many sheykhs and great chieftains were forcibly removed. In some respects Kurdish social organisation seems to have become more tribal: segmentary opposition and alliance are more in evidence, and the same may be true for kinship ideology. As a result of state interference, the Kurdish tribes have experienced a development that resembles the evolutionary sequence that is often assumed[10] but in reverse order!

This is not to deny that real de-tribalisation occurs, both autonomously and as a consequence of deliberate policies of the state. Deportations, labour migration, education, land reform, alienating chieftains from their tribes, introduction of mechanised agriculture, etc.: the processes are well-known. I wish only to stress here that state intervention does not necessarily mean de-tribalisation, and that tribal organisation such as is now found (especially in Turkish Kurdistan) owes much to the indirect rule that is still informally practised.

372

This general trend of 'devolution' of the tribes was sometimes reversed if only for a short time. The years around the First World War were such a period. The Ottoman Empire collapsed, as did the Qajar dynasty, and it took some years before new central regimes were sufficiently well-organised to reassert strong central control. In this period several Kurdish confederacies regained their former unity and even drew neighbouring tribes into their orbit. It is the most recent period in Kurdish history in which a process of confederation took place, and probably the only period for which it is relatively well-documented. Several of the reviving confederacies even reached the newspaper headlines, mainly for their association with Kurdish nationalism: the Heverkan (east of Mardin, Turkey), the Jalali (around Mt. Ararat), the Pizhdar (east of Qaleh Dizeh, Iraq) and the Shakak, who are the subject of the case-study below.

In this period the organisation of the Heverkan and the Shakak confederacies, and probably also of the Jalali, differed at a few points from the usual pattern as sketched above (and as illustrated by Barth's somewhat idealised description of the Jaf confederacy[11]). There was not one but several chiefly lineages competing for paramount leadership, and each of them was associated with a specific component tribe of the confederacy. This seems to me an indication of the recent (re-)constitution of the confederacies. Their growth and integration went together with the victory of one of the chiefly lineages.

The component tribes maintained their own identity. Each inhabited a well-defined territory and owned or had rights in well-defined pasturelands. Leadership in these tribes seems more permanent than in the confederacies. They were by and large marriage isolates - though not the minimal ones, given the strong preference for father's brother's daughter marriage. These component tribes could be quite heterogeneous, as in the case of the Heverkan where some were Muslim, some Yezidi, and where even militant Christians were considered on a par with the Kurdish tribes. Not all of these tribes had equal political status within the confederacy: there were 'central' tribes, which dominated the confederacy, politically and militarily, and more marginal 'client' or 'vassal' tribes that had joined it because of its success or had been subjected by it. The latter were the first to break away in times of adversity.

In periods of relative quiet it was virtually
impossible for ambitious chieftains to rise to or
maintain a position of effective paramount leadership of such large confederacies, unless supported
by a strong central state. Prestigious descent,
lavish hospitality, wisdom, readiness to help his
subjects (characteristics of the 'chief' type of
chieftain) might be necessary to make a chieftain
respected, but were rarely sufficient to guarantee
him general recognition as a paramount ruler. In
such periods there were several competitors for paramount leadership over the confederacy, each recognised by some of the tribesmen only. Within the
component tribes there were also several aspirant
chieftains, each of whom allied himself with one of
the competitors at the confederate level. Thus
resulted a factional system of the 'chequer-board'
type, in which the relevant units were sections of
the component tribes.

At times of weak government, however, such as
the period 1915-1930, the rival chieftains could in-
dulge in the kind of military activities that increased their hold over the tribes - the 'brigand'
aspect of the chieftain. These included raiding
caravans or towns, or villages of neighbouring
tribes - an excellent means of reinforcing the unity
of one's own tribe; but apparently raids against
villages or camp groups of one's own tribe were
equally important. These raids were directed mainly
against the 'non-tribal' subjects of a rival chieftain and the client (sub-)tribes that recognised his
authority. There was usually little killing and
destruction in these raids; only the animals were
driven away and movable property taken, and both
might later be partially restored. These raids were
carried out by the chieftain's retinue, tough warriors of diverse origins (sometimes even including
non-Kurds), who had cut all previous social ties
('they were ready to kill their own parents if the
chieftain ordered them to'); they lived with and at
the expense of the chieftain, to whom alone they were
loyal. In more peaceful times these retainers performed the related task of collecting the tithe for
the chieftain and of enforcing the labour corvée
from the 'non-tribal' subjects. If a number of raids
were successful, villages and tribal sections would
switch their loyalties to the raiding chieftain both
out of fear and because the most courageous and cun-
ning chieftain is thought to be the best.[12]

'Brigand' and 'chief' are not necessarily different <u>types</u> of chieftains; they are rather comple-

mentary aspects of the ideal chieftain. Scions of
old, established tribal dynasties may act as brigands
as well as any parvenu that challenges them. It is
largely external political factors that determine
which aspect will prevail.

It should be stressed, however, that even the
most successful 'brigand' chieftains did not rise to
power by the above means alone. They supplemented
them with the method employed by chieftains of all
types and in all periods: political alliances with
outside powers. These outside powers might include
other tribes or confederacies (it is significant
that the great chieftains of the Shakak and the
Heverkan acquired a large following among other
tribes before they completely dominated the 'central'
tribes of their own confederations), as well as
urban merchants, but the most significant powers were
of course the states. Even when the state had no
effective control a chieftain might derive much
power from it - as long as it was not entirely absent
and could in theory apply the ultimate sanction of
violence. The state might recognise a chieftain as
the one and only paramount leader of his tribe or
confederation in exchange for promises of 'loyalty'.
If the Ottoman Sultan (who was also widely accepted
as the Caliph) recognised a chieftain, this in itself was already effective. Frequently, however,
recognition by the state was substantiated with
significant gifts and by increasing the coercive
powers of the recognised chieftain.

Two examples may serve to illustrate this.
First, in 1891 Sultan Abdülhamid established tribal
militias (the Hamidiye) in the eastern provinces of
the Ottoman Empire. He appointed tribal chieftains
as commanders of cavalry regiments, 800-1,000 strong,
recruited from their own tribes. These Hamidiye
were armed by the state, enjoyed tax exemption, and
received salaries when on active duty. However much
they raided the civil population, they were never
punished. The appointed commanders achieved despotic powers over their tribes. After the Young
Turk coup d'état, the Hamidiye units were disbanded,
but later the Young Turks reconstituted tribal militias along the same lines, that were to take part
actively in the Great War.

Secondly, the British in Iraq delegated extraordinary powers, if only for a short time, to those
chieftains whom they recognised as paramount. Some
of them were appointed as district governors, with
authority over locally recruited gendarmes. Understandably, the latter were often used as a private

retine.

The rivals of the chosen chieftains were thus
forced into the position of 'bandits' or 'collabor-
ators' with a rival state. This was often sufficient
reason for the government to send troops to assist
in their elimination.

From the last decades of the nineteenth century
on, many chieftains thought it useful to establish
contacts with Russia and/or Britain. These powers,
though despised, were seen as more powerful (and
therefore more useful allies) than the Sultan or the
Shah. The British seem to have remained non-committal
until the Great War, but Russia several times invited
leading Kurds, made them many promises and distributed much money and other presents among chieftains,[13]
which strengthened the latters' positions.

Tribes and Non-Tribal Population

It should not be assumed that at any period in the
past all Kurds were 'tribal'. There have always
been large numbers of Kurdish 'non-tribal' cultivators (variously called kurmanj, guran, rayat, misken),
with no autonomous social organisation beyond shal-
low lineages. The tribesmen that dominate(d) and
exploit(ed) them superimpose(d) their own organisational structure on theirs. Thus a kurmanj living
on land controlled by the Shakak confederacy might
identify himself with a particular tribe or sub-
tribe of that confederacy, and even feel antagonism
towards kurmanj living with rival Shakak sections.
They might play a part, though mainly as victims, in
feuds between sub-tribes, but no one would consider
them Shakak proper. The tribesmen were a military
elite, usually (but not necessarily) nomadic or
transhumant pastoralists. The term ashir or ashiret
is often used not to denote any particular tribe, but
the tribesmen as a sort of military caste. Several
nineteenth-century travellers[14] observed that the
terms ashiret and sipahi - the latter referred to
the traditional Ottoman military class, the feudal
cavalry - were used interchangeably in Kurdistan.

Since many nomadic tribesmen have settled and
taken up agriculture the difference between tribal
and 'non-tribal' Kurds has become less obvious. It
is however still recognised by the Kurds themselves,
and is frequently reflected in the control of land.
Tribesmen generally own some land; informants from
several Kurdish tribes in Iran claimed not to know
of any fellow-tribesman who is not at least a

<u>khurdeh-malik</u> (small landowner). 'Non-tribal' Kurds,
on the other hand, were usually tenants, share-
croppers or landless agricultural labourers. Rayats
who received title to land under the Iranian Land
Reform have not, as yet, been accepted as equal to
the tribesmen, in spite of the fact that they differ
very little from the sedentary tribesmen.

Although within any one tribe a rather strict
caste-like division was maintained between the tribesmen and their non-tribal subjects, there appears at
times to have been a significant mobility between the
two strata. The rapid growth shown by some tribes at
times of prosperity (increased by 200 per cent within
a five to ten year period are not rare) was only possible by the incorporation of 'non-tribal' elements
from elsewhere. The reverse process, detribalisation,
could result from conquest by another tribe, or from
impoverishment followed by settlement.

Until quite recently, the Kurds (tribal and non-
tribal) were not the only inhabitants of these lands,
but they shared them with other ethnic groups, Christians (Armenians and Syriac-speaking Jacobites and Nestorians) and Jews. Most craftsmen and many urban merchants belonged to these ethnic groups. The majority
of the Christians were, however, cultivators, often
more prosperous than the non-tribal Kurds because they
possessed a more sophisticated technology. At most
places they were dominated politically and exploited
economically by the Kurdish tribesmen, though not everywhere. In the Hakkari district of central Kurdistan
there were large communities of Nestorians that were
called 'tribal (the term referred to their militancy
and independence rather than to their social organisation) and dominated the local 'non-tribal' Kurds.

The nature of the relations between the Kurds
and the local Christians and Jews varied widely from
time to time and from place to place. There was,
however, a marked deterioration during the nineteenth
century as the European powers increased their missionary efforts among the Christians of Kurdistan.
Both Christians and Kurds perceived the activity of
the missionaries as a preparation for more direct
interference by the Powers. The Christians, feeling
they had powerful protectors, began to resist the
traditional exploitation and oppression by Kurdish
chieftains. Many Kurds, understandably, felt threatened by the growing control of the European powers
over the Ottoman and Iranian governments, by the
increasing missionary activity in Kurdistan, and
by the resulting militancy of the local Christians;
they directed their anger against the latter. This

increasing antagonism was to make the Kurds receptive to the pan-Islamist propaganda of Sultan Abdülhamid (1876-1908), and to lead to several massacres of Christians.[15]

Pan-Islamism and Kurdish Nationalism

The loyalties of Kurdish tribesmen are embedded in a system of segmentary alliance and opposition. In the period under consideration, however, there appeared two important ideologies that appealed to wider loyalties than the tribal ones: pan-Islamism and Kurdish nationalism. There is a certain similarity between the pan-Islamic and Kurdish nationalist movements on the one hand and the states on the other, in their relations with the Kurdish tribes and chieftains. For the chieftains these movements offered the same ideological and material sources of power as the state. The movements, on the other hand, needed the tribes to give them military strength, but they found them as unstable a basis as the states did. This is especially true of the nationalist movement: tribal division has always been its main weakness.

The pan-Islamic movement was closely linked to the Ottoman state or more precisely to the Sultan-Caliph. It became influential in Kurdistan for at least three reasons: first, the European powers and their perceived support for the Christians in Kurdistan excited Kurdish anxieties. The 'Christian threat' made Muslim solidarity appear necessary for defensive reasons. Moreover, pan-Islamism was to give the Kurdish tribesmen a licence to loot Christian property. Secondly, it was in the interest of the sheykhs, the most influential leaders in Kurdistan, to strengthen Islamic sentiment (legitimation!). They were its most fervent propagandists. Thirdly, Sultan Abdülhamid, the initiator of the movement, was perceived by the Kurdish chieftains as their protector against the state bureaucracy that desired to break their powers. The pan-Islamic propaganda was so effective that in 1914-15 almost all Kurds (including those of Iran) responded to the call for jihad - including many of those who had received money from the Russians.[16]

Kurdish nationalism developed partly as a reaction to and imitation of Armenian nationalism and (later) the Young Turk movement. Both the British and the Russians stimulated this nationalism, which they intended to use against the Ottoman state.

Kurdish Tribes and Simko's Revolt

The first serious attempt to establish an independent
Kurdish state was made in 1880 by Ubeydullah, a
sheykh of great influence in the districts south-east
of Lake Van. With an army recruited from the many
tribes under his influence, he invaded Iranian Azarbayjan, where many of the local tribes joined him.[17]
The sheykh had the tacit support of Sultan Abdülhamid
who approved of the idea of a Kurdish vassal state on
formerly Iranian territory, and intended to use the
sheykh against the Armenian revolutionaries. Not
deeming the Sultan's support sufficient, Ubeydullah
also wrote letters to the British government to inform them of his intentions.[18] He failed, but the
ideal of an independent Kurdish state remained. It
was embraced by many chieftains, if only because it
seemed to promise them more personal freedom and
power.
        During the Great War, pan-Islamic sentiment
proved stronger than Kurdish national feeling,[19] and
there were no serious attempts to separate Kurdish
territory from the Ottoman Empire. After the Ottoman defeat, however, nationalism spread very rapidly
all across Kurdistan. There was a general awareness
of president Wilson's 'fourteen points' (which included the principle of self-determination; Lenin's
and Stalin's ideas on the same subject were as yet
not influential) and of British plans for a Kurdish
buffer-state between Turkey and Mesopotamia. As an
independent Kurdish state became feasible, many
sheykhs and tribal chieftains suddenly became nationalists and revolted. The difference between
such national rebellions and the more traditional
type of a chieftain's yaghigiri was not a sharp one,
as may be shown by the case of Simko's rebellion,
the most important of the type to occur in Iranian
Kurdistan.

Simko and the Shakak Confederacy

Simko rose to paramount leadership of the Shakak,
the second largest Kurdish confederacy in Iran -
only the Kalhur, living west of Kirmanshah, exceed
them in numbers. The Shakak inhabit(ed) the mountainous districts of Somay and Bradost, west of
Salmas and Urmiyeh. Around 1920 they numbered some
2000 households, non-tribal subjects not included.
        There are no statistics on the neighbouring
tribes for that period, but figures from the late
1960s give an indication of the relative strengths
of the tribes as they may have been in Simko's

time:[20]

Shakak	4400 households	Mamash	950
Milan	2030	Zarza	750
Mangur	1500	Piran	650
Herki	1350	Begzadeh	500
Jalali	1135	Haydaranli	300

It should be noted, however, that most of these tribes have sections living across the border which are not included in these figures. Notably the Herki and the Haydaranli are stronger than these figures suggest.

By 1920 those Shakak who remained fully nomadic were already a minority. They used khaliseh (crown lands) summer-pastures in the Tergevar and Dasht-i Bil districts, and spent the winters in the plains of Salmas and Urmiyeh. Most were transhumant, spending the winter in mountain villages. The Shakak dominated a kurmanj population ('non-tribal' Kurdish cultivators) three times more numerous than themselves and had a similar parasitic/symbiotic relationship with the Christians in their midst. Many of the latter were quite rich; they were not only cultivators and craftsmen but also pastoralists, several of them each owning something like 1000 sheep and 40 horse. These went together with the Shakak flocks in summer to the yaylaq, accompanied by one or more members of the family, while the other men remained in the village to cultivate.[21] Additional income was generated by raiding: the Shakak had one of the worst reputations as robbers and raiders (now: as smugglers). Some authors even claimed that this, and not animal husbandry, was their chief occupation. It seems that their raids were directed not so much at trading caravans as against the settled population of the plains and valleys: Christian Assyrians (Nestorians or converts to one of the European or American churches) and Shiite Azaris. They did not take loot indiscriminately, however; Nikitine found, in fact, that the poor population of the plains had a rather favourable opinion of Jafar Agha (Simko's elder brother, responsible for much of the bad reputation of his tribe), for 'souvent, après avoir dépouillé un richard, il distribuait une partie du butin aux miséreux'.[22]

The Shakak consist of numerous tribes of quite unequal size and status: the lists I found add up to 25, of which nine occur in most.[23] Three of these are generally mentioned as the central, politically

dominant tribes: Avdovi, Mamedi (or Mamdoi) and
Kardar. The others appear more peripheral, joining
the tribes mentioned when these were led by a great
chieftain, but otherwise keeping a low profile.
Some were apparently in a dependent position as
'client' tribes. Thus Ghilan wrote about the strong
Henareh sub-tribe:

> tribu...dans une espèce de vassalité à l'égard
> des Chéqqaq, car leur chef doit être accepté
> par l'Agha de ces derniers..... Ils n'aiment
> pas la guerre, sont surtout marchands et
> éleveurs de bétail; mais les Chéqqaq les
> poussent dans leurs guerres, et occasionnent
> d'ailleurs contre eux des représailles des
> tribus qu'ils lésaient.[24]

When Blau visited the area in 1857, the Henareh were
still considered a fully separate tribe, neighbour
to the Shakak; in all recent lists they are mentioned as a component tribe of the Shakak with no
apparent lower status. Similarly the Mamedi, who
were a leading Shakak tribe by the turn of the century, were in 1857 an independent nomadic tribe.[25]
This means that the Shakak grew into the present
confederation in the second half of the nineteenth
century, a period when many other confederations
were in decay.
   One factor that made this growth possible and
contributed to the rise of powerful chieftains here
is immediately apparent from a study of local history: frontier warfare. Somay used to be administered by a Kurdish dynasty on behalf of the Ottomans,
and it was the Iranian government that actively
encouraged the Shakak (who then lived further south)
to conquer these districts, which took them from
1841 to 1893.[26] As a reward, and later also in vain
attempts to restrain the Shakak from raiding Iranian
territory, the Iranian government appointed Shakak
chieftains as governors of the frontier districts.
   There are two chiefly lineages (called Pisaqa)
among the Shakak, associated with the Avdovi and
Kardar tribes respectively. The former family
claimed descent from Kurdish chieftains who had
participated in Saladin's military campaigns.[27] Between these two families there was always competition
for leadership of the entire confederation. Most of
the time each controlled only part of the Shakak.
   In order to put the events into their proper
context a few short remarks on political developments in the area during Simko's time should be made.

In 1906 Ottoman troops invaded Iranian Azarbayjan
and occupied a significant part of the Kurdish-
inhabited districts of that province. They remained
present, though not in full control, until 1911,
when they were expelled by the Russians. The latter
had in 1909 invaded the province and occupied Tabriz
which was then, together with Rasht, the last bastion
of the Constitutionalists. They stationed infantry
and cossacks in Tabriz, Khoy, Dilman and Urmiyeh.
Until the outbreak of the Great War these managed to
keep a measure of law and order. During the war,
Azarbayjan was occupied in turn by the Turks (January
1915), the Russians (1916-17) and the Turks again
(1918). In late 1914 the Nestorians of Hakkari,
fearing genocide, fled to Urmiyeh and Salmas, seeking
Russian protection. Many of them were to help the
Russians as advance scouts when these invaded central
Kurdistan and often took private revenge on the
Muslim population. Christian-Muslim relations deteriorated badly during the war.[28]

After the 1918 armistice Britain was in control
of present Iraq with the exception of its mountainous north-east. The Kemalists (Turkish nationalist
followers of Mustafa Kemal, the future Atatürk) were
soon active all over Turkey. They had important
centres at Rowanduz (which the British considered
theirs) and at Van, and attempted to mobilise the
Kurds against the British. The latter did the same:
they made many promises with respect to the establishment of an independent Kurdistan, which was to
serve as a buffer between Turkey and Iraq.

Meanwhile Iran's post-war government was very
weak and torn by internal struggles among the political elite and by secessionist movements in Gilan
and Azarbayjan. The Anglo-Iranian treaty signed by
the Tehran government in 1919 provoked a wave of
popular protest. In 1920 the middle classes of
Tabriz revolted. Some other Azarbayjani towns followed suit, and for several months an independent
republic (Azadistan) existed there.[29] It was Riza
Khan who, after his coup d'etát of 1921, succeeded
in eliminating all centrifugal tendencies (including
that of the Kurds) and in reintegrating Iran. By
1923, Kemalist Turkey was also internationally
accepted. The possibility of an independent Kurdistan seemed lost, or at least receded into an unclear and probably distant future.

Around the turn of the century at least three
chieftains were competing for paramount leadership
of the Shakak. The strongest was probably Ali Agha
of the Avdovi Pisaqas; his sons (or grandsons? the

sources are contradictory) Jafar Agha and Ismail
Agha, nicknamed Simko, made themselves quite a reputation as daring warriors and bold raiders. The
second chieftain was Umar Agha, who led the Mamedi
tribe (according to some sources he was an uncle of
Simko, but there is much confusion), and the third
was Mustafa Agha (later succeeded by his brother
Ismail) of the Kardar Pisaqas who had also some
other tribes and sub-tribes under his control. There
was a high turnover of chieftains during those years.
Another section of Avdovi Pisaqas, led by Ali's
brother Yusuf, living further south, was dispersed
when Ali rose to power at Yusuf's expense, and many
of them were subsequently killed by the rival
Kardars. Umar Agha of the Mamedi was killed by
Iranian officials in 1902, and Mustafa Agha by his
Avdovi rivals in 1906. Around the same time Jafar
Agha, who had held official titles but continued to
irritate the government of Azarbayjan by his raids
on Urmiyeh, Salmas and Khoy, was invited to Tabriz
by the Iranian heir apparent and treacherously
killed.[30]
     Maybe it was this disappearance of most other
experienced chieftains that made Simko's rapid rise
possible. However, he was a clever and opportunist
politician who knew with whom to ally himself and
when. As a young man he had assisted his brother
Jafar in his raids, and he was to continue raiding
throughout his career, thus attracting many roughs
into his retinue. In the Constitutional Revolution
Simko turned against the Constitutionalists (urban
Azaris) and, without being invited, took 300 horsemen to join the forces of Iqbal al-Saltaneh, governor of Maku, against the anjuman of Khoy. As a
reward Simko was made sub-governor of Qotur district.
In spite of his continuing raids the central government confirmed the appointment.[31]
     Neither the Turks nor the Russians occupied the
Shakak lands before the Great War; Simko's contacts
with both were mainly indirect. Prior to 1913 he
appears to have co-operated with pro-Ottoman, anti-
Russian Azarbayjanis, but in 1913 he delivered one
of these, who had sought refuge with him, to the
Russians in an attempt to gain their goodwill.[32] He
was apparently successful, for in that same year a
Russian observer noticed that two chieftains who had
previously been clients of Ismail Agha of the Kardar
Pisaqas (Simko's main rival) swore, under Russian
pressure, fidelity to him.[33] By that time Simko was
in regular contact with Kurdish nationalist circles.
Nationalist and private ambitions went together in

him and cannot be separated. He had married a sister of Sheykh Sayyid Taha, grandson and successor of the famous Sheykh Ubeydullah.[34] This was a convenient marriage, for the sayyid was the most influential man across the border, besides being a leading nationalist. Simko and Sayyid Taha were to cooperate much in the following decade. Another of Simko's contacts was Abd al-Razzaq Bedirkhan of the famous nationalist family descending from the mirs of Botan. Sayyid Taha, Abd al-Razzaq and Simko's brother Jafar had previously been invited to Russia, whence they had returned with 'generous gifts and encouraging messages that stimulated their imaginations and ambitions'.[35] Abd al-Razzaq started publishing a monthly Kurdish newspaper in Urmiyeh in 1912. After some time, however, the Russians banished him from Urmiyeh, and according to one historian it was Simko who took over the responsibility for the paper until it stopped publication in 1914.[36]

During the war Simko stood aloof from the real fighting, trying to keep all doors open, while expanding his control of the frontier districts. The Russians once arrested him and sent him to prison in Tiflis but, expecting to achieve more with the carrot than the stick, they let him return to Azarbayjan on the condition that he lived in the town of Khoy and remained 'loyal'.[37] When the troops of the Russian general Baratoff were called back from central Kurdistan after the Revolution, Simko managed to capture many of their arms, including fieldguns. From other parts of Kurdistan too arms started flowing towards Simko, who had by then already a wide reputation as a nationalist leader. These arms were either left behind by departing Russians or had belonged to the Kurdish militias that had fought on the Turkish side.

Simko was not the only one to arm himself, however. The Nestorian Assyrians (the local ones, but especially the refugees from Hakkari, who were more militant) were quite well-armed too, and they were reinforced by equally well-armed Armenians from Anatolia. The departing Russians, unable to protect them any longer, left many arms behind and stimulated them to organise in fighting units. According to Arfa[38] a French military mission had also brought arms for the Assyrians to defend themselves against the Turks. The Assyrians had desires similar to Simko's: the establishment of an independent state, in Urmiyeh and Salmas. The local Muslim population (Azaris in the plains and Kurds in the mountains) were hardly pleased, and the Iranian government even less so. Famine and mutual depredations, in which the departing Russians had no small share, led to increased bitterness between Christians and Muslims. It was especially the Azaris and the 'non-tribal' Kurds that suffered, for the Christians were better armed. During riots in Urmiyeh (February 1918) the Christians got the upper hand and took control of the entire town. The Iranian government was incapable of restoring order. The governor of Tabriz, Mukht-i Shams, then approached Simko. At his instigation Simko invited Mar Shimun, the religious and secular leader of the Nestorians, for talks on a proposed alliance, and had him treacherously killed (March 1918).[39]

Simko's men took no part, however, in the subsequent fighting between the invading Turkish armies and the Armenians and Nestorians, whom the British then attempted to mould into a force capable of stopping the Turkish advance. Only when most of the Nestorians - lacking strong leadership after the death of their leader - fled in panic from Urmiyeh did his men join Turkish soldiers in their pursuit, killing many (June or July 1918). Turkish soldiers and irregular bands of Kurds (sent, some claim, by Simko and Sayyid Taha) entered the town and plundered what was left.[40]

The Armistice brought an end to the Turkish presence in Azarbayjan, and no strong government was left. The Iranian government appointed new governors at Tabriz and Urmiyeh, but these did not succeed in establishing control of western Azarbayjan. The only authority with a strong power base was Simko, whose private retinue had been reinforced with several hundred Ottoman soldiers, many of them Kurds, either simply deserters or people with nationalist motivations; others, mercenaries attracted by the high pay (!) and the fact that Simko gave them wives. With their field-guns (some of them taken from the Russians) and machine-guns, they were to prove more than a match for the ill-trained government troops of Azarbayjan.

The government had for some time no way of subjecting Simko, who continued more boldly than ever to raid the plains. The governor of Urmiyeh, Sardar-i Fatih, visited Simko in his stronghold at Chahriq (south-west of Dilman) and attempted to win him over by peaceful means, but Simko apparently saw this as further proof of weakness, and even expanded the areas where he took the tribute ('loot' in the Iranian perception, 'taxation' in his own) necessary to maintain his army. Some time later the

governor of Tabriz, Mukarram al-Mulk, had recourse
to modern technology and sent Simko a bomb-parcel
that had been made to look like a box of sweets. Its
explosion killed a younger brother of Simko and several of his retainers but failed to hurt the person
for whom it was intended.[41]

Simko's Rebellion against the Central Government

Meanwhile Simko was busily preparing for the establishment of independence. In February 1919 there
was a meeting of most important chieftains of Iranian Kurdistan, at which the proposal for an open
insurrection against the Iranian government was discussed. It was decided to postpone the rising until
it had become clear what the attitude of the Powers
was going to be.[42] Sayyid Taha, who had joined
Simko and closely co-operated with him (without however forgetting his own private interests) visited
Baghdad in May 1919 in order to obtain British support for an independent Kurdish state. Simko himself addressed the Civil Commissioner (A.T. Wilson)
by letter with similar requests. Neither received
a definite commitment. According to Armenian
sources[43] Simko and Sayyid Taha were at the same
time in touch with the Turkish nationalists at Van,
who wished to employ them for resisting the proposed
repatriation of Armenians to eastern Anatolia and
therefore promised help. In the following years the
two Kurdish chieftains were to remain in contact
with both the British and the Turkish nationalists.
    Without waiting for the other chieftains to
declare themselves in open rebellion, Simko took
the town of Dilman, looted Khoy, laid siege to
Urmiyeh and massacred part of the (Azari) population
of the Lakistan district (north-west of Dilman) that
refused to recognise his authority and pay taxes.
Those who escaped were pursued as far as Sharafkhaneh
on the northern shore of Lake Urmiyeh. During the
autumn of 1919 then Simko's Kurds kept these districts north of the lake under occupation.[44] Tabriz
had however a new military commander, Intisar, who
efficiently mobilised and co-ordinated whatever
troops he could find (gendarmerie, cossacks, irregular Azari cavalry). Led by Filipov, a Russian cossack
officer who had just arrived from Tehran, these
troops managed to repel Simko's Kurds and to inflict
heavy losses upon them. Simko was forced to take
refuge in his mountain stronghold at Chahriq; many
of his partisans deserted him (including several of

the former Ottoman soldiers). For reasons which are unclear,[45] however, instead of following up their initial success and forcing Simko to surrender unconditionally, Filipov and Intisar entered negotiations with him. As a result of the negotiations, Simko promised to return the loot taken from Lakistan, to send off his Turkish soldiers and to surrender all his arms to the state.

None of these promises was fully executed, and the whole affair ultimately strengthened Simko's standing among the Kurds: he could apparently act against the state with impunity. During 1920 he re-established his control of the plains of Urmiyeh and Salmas and the southern part of Khoy district. In Urmiyeh he appointed men of his own choice as governors: at first Arshad al-Mulk, a local man, later Teymur Agha, a Kurdish chieftain from Kuhneh-shahr. His men raided a vast area, mainly to acquire firearms and finance his future exploits. One day they took thousands of the inhabitants of Urmiyeh, people of all walks of life, hostage in a garden near the city, demanding 40,000 rifles and a similar quantity of gold liras for their release.[46] The villages were similarly 'taxed'. Gendarmerie troops sent from Tabriz to relieve the area were defeated by the Kurds and pushed back behind Sharafkhaneh (March 1921). Simko proved the strongest again, and thereby attracted many new followers.

Other victories over government troops during that year resulted in further increases. In March 1921 his forces were still described as '1000 horse and 500 foot, with a Turkish flag'; in a summer campaign they were already estimated at 4000, in the autumn of 1921 at 7000, while in his last great campaign, in the summer of 1922, 10,000 men are said to have participated.[47] Each of these estimates is rather rough and - except the last - includes only a part of what Simko could mobilise. The increase is nevertheless clear. Simko's authority was recognised by a growing number of tribes.

Early in 1920 there had been several meetings of a 'Council of Kurdish chiefs' presided over by Simko, which were attended not only by chieftains of some of the biggest tribes of Azarbayjan (Herki, Begzadeh, Haydaranli, Shakak), but also by chieftains of the Artushi confederacy and other tribes of Hakkari. It was said that in 1921 Simko appointed a certain Ahmad Khan as the paramount chieftain of the Herki, and that this was generally accepted by this powerful tribe.[48]

By the middle of 1921 the area under Simko's

authority included all Iranian territory west of
Lake Urmiyeh and from there south as far as Baneh
and Sardasht, as well as the north-western districts
of Iraq, where the British and the Kemalists were
still competing for control. Besides the entire
Shakak confederacy and the Herki tribe, also the
Mamash, Mangur, Dehbokri, Piran, Zarza, Gewrik,
Feyzullabegi, Pizhdar and the minor tribes around
Baneh had joined Simko.[49] In October 1921 Simko's
troops entered the town of Souj Bulagh (Mahabad),
which had until that date been held by government
troops. 200 of the gendarmarie garrison were
killed, another 150 wounded. It may be illustrative
of the motivation and attitude of many of Simko's
men that they sacked the town upon capturing it - in
spite of the fact that the inhabitants of Souj
Bulagh, unlike those of Urmiyeh and Dilman, were
mainly Kurds.
     Other Kurdish nationalists later severely
rebuked Simko for this pillage. Why sow discord
among the Kurds and thus serve the interests of
their enemies? In answer to such accusations from
a Kurdish notable from Suleymaniyeh Simko said that
first, the gendarmarie had forced him to offer battle inside the town, and thereafter he had not been
able to restrain his men who were used to follow up
battle with plunder; and that secondly, he had his
doubts about the attitude towards himself of the
Dehbokri and the Mangur tribes that lived immediately
around Souj Bulagh.[50]
     Souj Bulagh naturally became the capital.
Simko did not take residence there himself, however,
but appointed a loyal chieftain, Hamzeh Agha of the
Mamash, as governor. The Azari towns of Mianduab,
Maragheh and Binab sent letters of submission to
Souj Bulagh.[51]
     Further military successes against government
troops that year added to Simko's standing among the
Kurds, and swelled the number of his followers. By
July 1922 his territory reached its greatest extension: it stretched as far east and south as Sain
Qaleh (Shahin Dezh) and Saqqiz. Moreover, Simko was
in permanent communication with tribes further
south: he had influence in Mariwan and Awroman, and
even tribes as far south as Luristan were to rise in
support of his revolt.[52] Similarly, many Kurdish
chieftains in Turkey and Iraq had established friendly relations with him. There were no concrete
plans for united action, but it could never harm to
have relations with a climber such as Simko. Rumours
started to circulate that the Iranian government was

going to grant the Kurds autonomy because it could not subdue them.[53]

Those rumours were to prove unfounded, however. Since the coup d'état of February 1921 Riza Khan had devoted his energies to the building of a modern, disciplined, coherent national army. His efforts were soon to bear fruit. During 1921 and even in early 1922 Simko had been able to inflict repeated defeats on the motley troops (irregulars, cossacks, gendarmerie) sent against him, capturing many of their arms. In August 1922 however, a well-co-ordinated campaign by the reorganised army brought him to heel.[54] His followers dispersed, leaving him nothing but a small band of loyal men. He had to escape into Turkey, and from there to Iraq. Edmonds, who interviewed him on his arrival in Iraq, observed that he was especially bitter against the Turks and the British. The former had always promised him assistance but they too had now turned their armies against him, and the latter had passively allowed him to be crushed in spite of his usefulness to them.[55]

As a refugee in Iraq, Simko did not remain idle but immediately started attempting to strengthen old ties and establish new ones with Kurdish chieftains there, in preparation for return to Iran. He appro-ached his old ally Sayyid Taha (who was now used by the British to get the Turks out of Rowanduz and had lost interest in further adventures in Iran), and also Sheykh Mahmud of Suleymaniyeh (the most influen-tial nationalist leader of southern Kurdistan who showed equally little interest in Simko's problems), and many others. He even tried to appease the Assyrian refugees, who had been brought to Iraq by the British, and who still thought of return to Urmiyeh and Salmas. He was shown much respect wherever he went, but no one was ready to help him. In 1923 he went to Turkey, to solicit Turkish sup-port - but equally in vain. In 1924 Riza Khan par-doned him, and he returned to Iran. In 1926 he made a last abortive attempt to regain the virtual inde-pendence he had once held, and besieged the town of Dilman, assisted by sections of the Herki and Begzadeh tribes. Again he had to flee to Iraq. In 1929 the Iranian government invited him back again, offering him the governorship of Ushnuviyeh. A few days after his arrival he was killed in an ambush set up by the same government.[56]

The Organisation of Simko's Forces

The most serious weakness of Simko's movement was the absence of any kind of formal organisation. There was just the network of Simko's private relations, no party to organise the followers, no formal government or war council. The major towns, Urmiyeh and Souj Bulagh, were administered by governors appointed by Simko who were both tribal chieftains unrelated to the inhabitants of the towns and simply took over the offices of the previous Tabriz-appointed governors. There was no systematic and equitable taxation; Simko's treasury was filled by indiscriminate looting, although the latter aspect may be severely exaggerated in the sources, most of which are inimical to him.

The army always fluctuated in size, as tribal armies do. The more or less permanent nucleus consisted of the chieftains' retinues, more precisely those of Simko himself and of Amr Khan, head of the Kardar section of the Shakak. In 1918 Simko's retinue included several hundred former soldiers of the Ottoman army, well-armed and trained by German instructors. In 1921-22 Simko was said to have a large Turkish contingent which, so the Iranians and British suspected, had been put at his disposal by the Ankara government,[57] though proof of these suspicions was never found. Most probably there were Kurdish nationalists from Turkish Kurdistan among his retinue too: among the Kurds of Turkey I heard many accounts of local men who had gone east to join Simko. Even this central core, however, was not really permanent. Many of the Ottoman soldiers with Simko had surrendered when they were promised amnesty during the 1919 campaign by Intisar and Filipov. Other retainers also came and went according to Simko's fortunes, motivated more by pay and loot than by nationalist sentiment or personal loyalty. Whereas by July 1922 consistent success had swollen his forces to some 10,000, after the first reverses they dwindled, and within a few days no more than a thousand loyal followers remained.[58]

A strong retinue appears to be a necessary condition for any chieftain who embarks upon an expansive political career. Once his strength is perceived, many others may join who are not, and do not become retainers. They are not fed by the chieftain, and it is well nigh unavoidable that they compensate themselves for their military services by plunder. This is not to say that retainers do not engage in pillage but rather that the chieftain has the other tribesmen even less under control.

In Simko's raids and battles against government troops not only his retainers but many other tribesmen took part. These were primarily Shakak, and especially from the Avdovi, Mamedi and Kardar component tribes. At times of Simko's good fortune, chieftains of other tribes also joined, with their retainers and with common tribesmen. It was especially the Herki tribe that contributed many men: the Herki and the Mamash proved to be Simko's most loyal allies. Others joined later and deserted earlier. At times of adversity even the closest allies left Simko. Thus Amr Khan, the head of the Kardar Pisaqas and therefore Simko's main potential rival among the Shakak, who had on many occasions acted as Simko's plenipotentiary, in 1922 attempted to desert him. He contacted the government through a local sheykh as intermediary and demanded amnesty, in exchange for which he promised obedience to the government and willingness to fight against Simko.[59]

Even though after his defeat Simko lost his actual power, the capacity to mobilise large numbers of men, he continued to enjoy wide respect among the tribes. Immediately upon his last return to Iran many chieftains of the Shakak confederacy and the Herki, Surchi, and other tribes came to pay him their respects, accompanied by large retinues.[60]

Simko not only sought support among the tribes; he also attempted to ally himself with foreign powers. Repeatedly he tried to elicit British support, usually through chieftains who had better relations with the British than he had himself: Sayyid Taha, or Babakr Agha of the Pizhdar.[61] He had little if any success. At the same time he was in communication with the Soviet authorities in the Caucasus and with the Kemalists at Van. Some of his letters to the former were apparently intercepted,[62] while British and Iranian authorities were convinced that the Kemalists had put troops at his disposal, as already mentioned. None of these foreign powers came to his support when he most needed it. In early phases of his career, however, his association with state authorities (the Iranians, who made him a governor of Qotur; the Russians and Ottomans who recognised him during the occupation) had strengthened his position among the Kurds. Such relations with neighbouring states have - it has been said before - always been present in the politics of Kurdistan, and they continued to influence Kurdish nationalism in its later phases as well. They may well be considered part and parcel of Kurdish tribal politics.

The large confederacy of tribes that was Simko's movement continued to exist as long as the tribes were kept mobilised. One of the factors that did mobilise them was nationalism. The rapidity with which Simko's support dwindled in times of adversity, however, suggests that for the majority of his followers nationalism was at best an additional motive. As usual among tribes, mobilisation should have some more concrete and immediate object and there should be reasonable chances of attaining it, be it a military victory (over a rival tribe or government troops) or simply plunder. The frequent raiding associated with Simko's rebellion, which many contemporary and later nationalists held against him, was not simply accidental to it: it probably was a necessary condition for keeping the tribes mobilised and thus together. When mobilisation ended - in this case because most tribesmen judged the chances of further success very small and therefore gave up - the unity immediately broke down.

I would guess that the same happened to many large confederacies in the past: a combination of internal and external factors mobilised the tribes and made them confederate themselves. When these stimuli disappeared or when the costs of confederating became too high, the confederacy fell apart, and little remained beyond its name and sometimes a respected (but not obeyed) chiefly lineage. Mobilisation cannot be sustained indefinitely. Maintaining the unity once achieved requires some definite form of organisation, which is, however, beyond tribal politics. In the past the emirates to some extent provided such an organisational structure, while at the same time institutionalising a measure of mobilisation of the tribes through their division into rival confederacies. In later phases of Kurdish history the nationalist movement, usually in the form of political parties, provided a more lasting organisational framework. The nationalist movement continued however to rely heavily on tribal support, and often tribal chieftains came partially to dominate it, thus making it into an extension of tribal politics. This was a serious weakness that contributed to the rapid collapse of several movements in spite of the party framework.

The Kurdish republic of Mahabad, which existed for almost a year in 1946, is a case in point. It was led by a political party, the Democratic Party of Kurdistan (DPK), but the tribes had the decisive power. (In fact, the DPK was born when an earlier nationalist organisation, the Society for Kurdish

Revival (<u>Komala-i</u> <u>Zhianewe-i</u> <u>Kurd</u>, or Komala), consisting of young urban middle class, broadened its
base to include the tribes. Most founding members
of the DPK belonged to the tribal ruling families.)
The Shakak again played a significant part, under
the leadership of the above-mentioned Amr Khan who,
some time after Simko's death, had become the paramount chieftain. The government of the republic
never took any important decision without first con-
ferring with Amr Khan. It made him one of the three
generals of the republic's army, which consisted
mainly of tribal irregulars. When the tide turned,
however, and the central government seemed willing
and capable of bringing the semi-independent Kurdish
republic back under central control, Amr Khan sought
contact with it and pledged his loyalty, virtually
deserting the Mahabad republic.[63] Several other
tribal chieftains actively turned against the DPK
and the Mahabad government, which they perceived as
more serious threats to their traditional powers
than the central government. Tribalism contributed
as much as the campaign by the Iranian army to the
fall of the Mahabad republic. Nationalist leaders
are, of course, aware of the unstable basis tribal
support gives them. They are as yet, however,
unable to do without it.

Postscript

The recent revolution in Iran has once again brought
the Kurds to the front pages of the newspapers.
During the turbulent year of 1978 the situation in
Kurdistan was not much different from that in other
parts of Iran. In 1979, however, strong demands for
autonomy were put forward and it soon became evident
that these demands were supported by almost all segments of Kurdish society. As the gendarmerie and
the police had well-nigh disappeared, and the army -
reduced in numbers as a result of desertion - had
withdrawn to the major bases, central control was
weak and for some time a situation of virtual autonomy existed. Traditional leaders (mainly tribal
chieftains) and local or regional political organisations (revolutionary city councils, parties,
associations of workers, peasant unions) took over
the role of the central authorities.
      The role of the tribes is less in evidence
than in the past; the Kurdish protagonists are the
DPK, its more radical rival the Komala and the
charismatic urban mullah Izz al-Din Huseyni. The

latter plays a part similar to the peace-making and
unifying role sheykhs used to play in tribal society,
but he can hardly be considered a representative of
the traditional order. He enjoys the confidence of
most of the rural population including many tribesmen, but his particular blend of nationalism with
socialism and Islam endears him to the radical leftists in Komala as well.

Tribal chieftains did and do attempt to regain
the power and influence they lost during the preceding decades, but the effects of urbanisation, education and land reform cannot easily be undone, and
they have succeeded partially and temporarily at
best.

The Shakak changed less than most other tribes;
they are among the staunchest upholders of tribal
values. After Amr Khan's death Simko's son Tahir
Khan succeeded in climbing to paramount position
within the confederacy, and in the spring and summer
of 1979 his father's days seemed revived; he reigned
as an independent lord. In July however, trouble
arose when the central government remanned gendarmerie posts near the Turkish border. Tribesmen
(Shakak, Herki and other local tribes) laid siege to
one gendarmerie base and occupied several posts,
upon which army units were sent into the area. In
the ensuing fights the tribes found themselves
obliged to ask support from the DPK, which had by
then built up a standing, well-trained guerrilla
army. With united forces they beat off the army,
forcing some units even to take refuge on Turkish
territory. The whole affair (as DPK secretary-
general Qasimlu claimed[64]) elevated the standing of
the DPK among the tribesmen at the expense of the
traditional chiefs, convincing them of the superiority of party organisation over the tribal one. However that may be, later in the year Tahir Khan and
other tribal chieftains were to turn away from the
DPK, several even actively against it. On the other
hand, a young leading member of Mamedi (a component
tribe of the Shakak) is a member of the central committee of the DPK. Many young Shakak - not only
from the Mamedi - seem to be taking sides with the
DPK rather than with Tahir Khan.

In several parts of Kurdistan, tribal chieftains, like former landlords all over Iran, attempted
to take back by force the land they had lost in the
Shah's land reform to usually non-tribal peasants.
Leftist groups, consisting of village teachers,
engineers, young mullahs and students, organised the
non-tribal peasants in peasant unions, which in

several places successfully beat off the landlords'
first offensive. These peasant unions, together
with groups of urban leftists, united to form the
Komala.

The other important political organisation, the
DPK (Iran), which was established in 1945 and played
a central role in the Mahabad republic of 1946, has
since the late 1960s left its purely nationalist
stand and moved towards the left. Its programme not
only poses the demand for national and cultural
rights, including autonomy, but also contains anti-
'feudal' points, the principle of fully equal rights
for men and women, and separation of state and religion. It calls for a policy of economic development
resembling the state socialist model of, for instance, Iraq. The DPK is by far the strongest political organisation of Kurdistan. It enjoys mass
support in towns as well as villages, especially in
the areas of Mahabad, Bukan, Baneh.

The DPK's relation with the tribes is more
ambiguous than the Komala's. It is reluctant to
alienate the tribes; it wishes to reduce the chieftain's powers further but at the same time still
feels it cannot afford an all-out confrontation and
even needs the tribes' support. As a result of this
reluctant attitude, in some places the traditional
authorities have managed to bring the local party
branch under their control. In the Central Committee
too, some members still either belong to or have
close relations with the tribal 'milieu'. Nevertheless, during summer 1979 when chieftains around
Mahabad started to collect traditional dues (dahudo,
'two out of ten') from the mainly non-tribal peasantry, the party intervened. In the increasing number
of conflicts between (ex-)landlords and peasantry,
the former sought - and found - support with central
authorities (army, revolutionary guards) and turned,
with these, against the Komala and the DPK. The
Kurdish national cause and the cause of the peasantry against their oppressors became closely associated.

As early as March (1979) the first fights broke
out between Kurdish nationalists and representatives
of the new Islamic Republic (in this case the military at Sanandaj). Long and troublesome negotiations
led to an uneasy truce. Similar events followed
each other almost monthly. In August another incident provided the immediate cause for large-scale
military operations against the Kurds. The army
took all towns of Kurdistan, not without bloodshed.
The Kurds did not put up a serious defence of the

towns but took to the mountains. The DPK had several thousand well-armed guerrilla-fighters, whom they had trained in the previous months. Komala and the followers of Izz al-Din Huseyni were less well-armed (unlike the DPK, they had not been able to lay hands on army arsenals), but in the mountains they too were a force to be reckoned with. After two months these guerrilla forces, having established a united command, were able to force the government back to the negotiating table. The negotiations have been interrupted several times as the truce was broken or the umpteenth deadlock was reached. Sometimes quite serious fights occurred again. It appears that 'feudal' elements, who would rather not see autonomy reached under the leadership of the anti-'feudal' organisations, actively attempt to sabotage the negotiations by provoking fights. To all appearances, it will take a long time before a solution to the Kurdish problem is reached that will be satisfactory to a majority of those concerned.

NOTES

1. Augusta Gudhart, 'The blood of the martyrs', *Atlantic Monthly,* 130 (1922), p. 116. *Ashiret* is the term most commonly used for 'tribe'.

2. In the Iranian census of 1956, 5.6% of the respondents gave Kurdish as their native tongue, and this figure has been quoted ever since. A large number of speakers of dialects classified as 'Luri and Bakhtiari' (the Laki dialects), however, consider themselves Kurds and sympathise with Kurdish national aspirations, which is why I include them among the Kurds.

3. Two Kurdish emirates under Ottoman suzerainty, Bitlis (around 1650 AD) and Baban (as of 1820) are described in detail and analysed in my *Agha, Shaikh and State. On the Social and Political Organization of Kurdistan* (PhD dissertation, Utrecht, 1978), pp. 194-215.

4. For the Baban emirate this is nicely illustrated in C.J. Rich's diary, *Narrative of a Residence in Koordistan ...* (Duncan, London, 1836), vol. 1, passim. Some time after Rich's visit in 1820 the ruling Mir, Mahmud Pasha, an unwilling vassal of Baghdad, did in fact switch loyalties and submit to the Iranian Heir Apparent Abbas Mirza, thereby precipitating a war between the two empires.

5. Mullah Mustafa Barzani, who among recent contemporary Kurdish leaders was the one most representative of the tribal milieu, was in contact with both powers as early as 1946. He spent 11 years (1947-58) in exile in USSR, and in the Kurdish war in Iraq in spite of all vicissitudes remained in contact

and received Soviet support until 1972, when he received
definite promises of substantial aid from America. Before that
date he had on many occasions attempted to elicit American
support, even declaring his willingness to join the USA as the
51st state.

6. For instance, the Bilbasi confederacy in the emirate
of Bitlis had, according to the Sharafnameh, come from the
Hakkari district before the emirate was established; Amīr
Sharaf Khān Bidlisī, *Sharafnāmeh: Tārīkh-i Mufassal-i Kurdistān*, ed. M. ʿAbbāsī (Ilmi, Tehran, (1957) 1343/1965).

7. For these events and the situation in Botan after
the collapse of the emirate, see van Bruinessen, *Agha*, pp.222-
8. Missionary activity in central Kurdistan is excellently
described in J. Joseph, *The Nestorians and their Muslim Neighbours* (Princeton University Press, 1961).

8. See chapter 1 above.

9. The tale of Suto and Tato is a highly amusing but
true account of how a shrewd sheykh manipulated conflict between two rival chieftains and thereby appropriated part of
their power as well as their property, B. Nikitine and E.B.
Soane, 'The tale of Suto and Tato. Kurdish text with translation and notes', *BSOAS*, 3, 1 (1923), pp. 69-106. For an
extensive discussion of the political role of sheykhs in
Kurdistan, see van Bruinessen, *Agha*, pp. 277-96, 313-37.

10. E.g. M. Sahlins, *Tribesmen* (Prentice Hall, Englewood
Cliffs, 1966).

11. F. Barth, *Principles of Social Organization in
Southern Kurdistan* (Jørgensen, Oslo, 1953).

12. The career of a chieftain who applied these methods
with great success, Hajo of the Heverkan confederacy (flor.
ca. 1920-30) is described in some detail in van Bruinessen,
Agha, pp. 110-16.

13. B. Nikitine, *Īrānī ki man shinākhtam* (tr. from
French) (Maʿrifat, Tehran, 1329/1951), p. 229; W. Eagleton,
Jr., *The Kurdish Republic of 1946* (Oxford University Press,
1963), p. 7.

14. E.g. Rich, *Narrative*, p. 88; C. Sandreczki, *Reise
nach Mosul und durch Kurdistan nach Urmia* (Steinkopf, Stutt-
gart, 1857), vol. 2, p. 263.

15. In 1843 and 1846, Nestorians of central Kurdistan;
in 1895-6, Armenians; in 1915, Armenians, followed by all
Christian groups.

16. Nikitine, *Irani*, pp. 229-36; id., *Les Kurdes, Etude
Sociologique et Historique* (Klincksieck, Paris, 1956), pp.
216-23.

17. Joseph, *Nestorians*, pp. 107-13; W. Jwaideh, 'The
Kurdish Nationalist Movement: its Origins and Development',
unpublished PhD dissertation, Syracuse University, 1960, pp.
212-39; van Bruinessen, *Agha*, pp. 328-9.

18. Joseph, *Nestorians*, p. 109f.

19. A telling passage in the memoirs of the Kurdish

Kurdish Tribes and Simko's Revolt

nationalist Zinar Silopi (pseudonym of Cemilpaşazade Qadri Beg) relates to his failure to find willing ears for his propaganda among Kurdish officers, due to the prevailing pan-Islamic feeling; Z. Silopi, *Doza Kürdüstan* (Stewr, Beyrouth, 1969), pp. 38-39; partially translated in van Bruinessen, *Agha*, p. 360.

20. H. Arfa, *The Kurds. An Historical and Political Study* (Oxford University Press, 1966), p. 48; M.J. Mashkūr, *Naẓarī bi tārīkh-i Āzarbāyjān va āsār-i bāstānī van jamʿīat-shināsī-yi ān* (Anjuman-i Asar-i Milli, Tehran,1349/1971), p. 190: A. Dihqān, *Sarzamīn-i Zardasht. Ouẓāʿ-i tabīʿī, sīāsī, iqtiṣādī, farhangī, ijtimāʿī va tārīkhī-yi Riẓāʾīyeh* (Ibn Sina, Tehran, 1348/1969), p. 60.

21. Ghilan, 'Les Kurdes persans et l'invasion ottomane', *Revue du Monde Musulman,* 5 (1908), pp. 7, 10, 14.

22. Nikitine, *Les Kurdes,* p. 79.

23. Lists in Ghilan, 'Les Kurdes', *passim*; Mashkur, *Nazari,* p. 190; Dihqan, *Sarzamin,* p. 60; V. Minorsky, 'Shakak' *EI,* 1st ed., 4, 1, p. 290; *Central Asian Review* 7 (1959), p. 179 (after Sovremenniy Iran); and in Prof. Wolfgang Rudolph's fieldnotes, which he kindly showed me.

24. Ghilan, 'Les Kurdes', p. 14.

25. O. Blau, 'Die Stämme des nordostlichen Kurdistan', *Zeitschrift der Deutschen Morgenländischen Gesellschaft,* 12 (1858), p. 593.

26. V. Minorsky, 'Somai', *EI,* 1st ed., 4, 2, p. 482; Ghilan, 'Les Kurdes', p. 10-13.

27. A. Sharifi, *Ashāyir-i Shakāk va sharh-i zindigī-yi ānhā bi rahbarī-yi Ismāʿil Āghā Simko* (Sayyidyan, Mahabad, 1348/1970), pp. 10-11.

28. A.C. Wratislaw, *A Consul in the East* (Blackwoods, Edinburgh and London, 1924), pp. 213-14, 229-32; W.E.D. Allen and P. Muratoff, *Caucasian Battlefields. A History of the Wars on the Turco-Caucasian Border 1818-1921* (Cambridge University Press, 1953); A. Kasravi, *Tārīkh-i hijdah sāleh-yi Āzarbāyjān* (Amir Kabir, Tehran, 4th impression, 1346/1968); Joseph, *Nestorians.*

29. Kasravi, *Tarikh;* Y.P. Benab, 'Tabriz in perspective: a historical analysis of the current struggle of Iranian peoples', *RIPEH/Review of Iranian Political Economy & History,* 2, 2 (1978), pp. 1-42.

30. Ghilan, 'Les Kurdes', pp. 7-9, 14; other accounts of Jafar Agha's killing in Wratislaw, *Consul,* pp. 207-9; Nikitine, *Les Kurdes,* p. 79; Sharifi, *Ashayir,* p. 12.

31. Ghilan, 'Les Kurdes', pp. 7, 9n.; M. Aghasi, *Tārīkh-i Khoy* (Faculty of Arts, Tabriz, 1350/1971), pp. 312-3. A possible reason why Simko may have attacked the Constitution-alists voluntarily is the fact that the latter saw the Turkish invasion of 1906, in which many Kurds took part, as directed against themselves and in support of the Shah. 'Anti-Kurdish sentiment flared, and there was rioting against members of the

Sunni sect', R. Cottam, *Nationalism in Iran* (University of
Pittsburgh Press, 1964), pp. 68-9.
    32. Kasravi, *Tarikh*, pp. 454-5.
    33. These were Teymur Jang and Muhammad Sharif Agha of
the village of Somay. See L.W. Adamec (comp.), *Historical
Gazetteer of Iran, Part I. Tehran and Northwestern Iran*
(Akademische Druck und Verlaganstalt, Graz, 1976), entry
'Somay', quoting Voyenni Sbornik.
    34. Sharifi, *Ashayir*, p. 17.
    35. Eagleston, *Republic*, p. 7.
    36. J. Khaznadar, *Rūznāmeh-nigārī dar Kurdistān*, tr.
(from Kurdish) by A. Sharifi (privately published, Mahabad,
1357/1978), p. 5. This was not Simko's only involvement in
Kurdish publishing. Later in his career, in 1921, he had a
bilingual newspaper of a Kurdish nationalist nature published
in Urmiyeh: this was called *Kurd dar sāl-i 1340,* and was edited by Mullah Muhammad Tarjani of Mahabad, see M. Tamaddun,
Tārīkh-i Riẕā'īyeh (Islamiyeh, Tehran, 1350/1971), p. 371,
quoted in A. Sharifi, *Shūrishhā-yi Kurdān-i Mukrī dar dourān-i
salṭanat-i dūdmān-i Pahlavī* (Shafaq, Tabriz, 1357/1978), p. 6.
Oriente Moderno, 1, 9 (15 February 1922), p. 548, mentions a
paper *Il Kurdistan indipendente,* published in Souj Bulagh,
which is probably the same paper.
    37. Kasravi, *Tarikh*, p. 829; Aghasi, *Tarikh*, pp. 352-3;
Sharifi, *Ashayir*, pp. 18-19.
    38. H. Arfa, *Under Five Shahs* (Murray, London, 1964), p.
122.
    39. Kasravi, *Tarikh*, p. 734-50, 829; Arfa, *Kurds,* pp.
50-54; Joseph, *Nestorians,* pp. 138-44; Aghasi, *Tarikh,* pp.
384-8; F.G. Coan, *Yesterdays in Persia and Kurdistan* (Saunders,
Claremont, Col., 1939), pp. 264-70.
    40. ibid., pp. 270-2.
    41. Kasravi, *Tarikh*, pp. 830-2; Sharifi, *Ashayir*, pp.
19-20, 30-6; M. Bambad, *Sharḥ-i ḥāl-i rijāl-i Īrān* (Zawar,
Tehran, 1347/1968), vol. 1, p. 136; Jwaideh, 'Nationalist
Movement', pp. 401-2.
    42. *Précis of Affairs in Southern Kurdistan during the
Great War* (Government Press, Baghdad, 1919), p. 14; Jwaideh,
'Nationalist Movement', p. 403.
    43. FO 371/1919; No. 58/89585/512. A later denial of this
by Simko himself (in a letter to the British Consul-General
at Tabriz) is enclosed in FO 371/1919: W 34/88614/7972. For
the rumours about the repatriation of the Nestorians and their
effects, see also Jwaideh, 'Nationalist Movement', pp. 413-15.
    44. Kasravi, *Tarikh*, pp. 839-41, 851-2; Arfa, *Kurds,*
p. 57.
    45. See Kasravi's rather unsatisfactory explanation
(old-fashioned and corrupt politics on the part of Azarbayjan's
Governor, Eyn al-Douleh), *Tarikh,* pp. 854f.; the similar one in Aghasi
(implicating Prime Minister Vusuq al-Douleh), *Tarikh*, pp. 440-
4; and Sharifi's suggestion of British pressure, *Ashayir*,

pp. 47–8.

46. Dihqan, *Sarzamin*, pp. 574–6.

47. These estimates are given in FO 371/1921: E 6185/100/93; Arfa, *Kurds*, p. 58; FO 371/1921: E 13470/100/93; and Arfa, *Shahs*, p. 136, respectively.

48. FO 371/1920: E 15670/11/44; 1921: E 13470/100/93.

49. Arfa, *Kurds*, p. 59.

50. FO 371/1922: E 2402/96/65.

51. FO 371/1921: E 13470/100/93.

52. FO 371/1922: E 8437/6/34; A.J. Toynbee, *Survey of International Affairs 1925, Part I, The Islamic World since the Peace Settlement,* (Oxford University Press, 1927) p. 539; Jwaideh, 'Nationalist Movement', p. 410.

53. Toynbee, *Survey*, pp. 538–9.

54. The military campaigns of 1921 and 1922 are described in detail in Arfa, *Shahs*, pp. 118–41; id., *Kurds*, pp. 58–63; Dihqan, *Sarzamin*, pp. 585–94; and in the report by the British military attaché at Tehran enclosed in FO 371/1922: E 12242/1076/34.

55. C.J. Edmonds, *Kurds, Turks, and Arabs. Politics, Travel and Research in North-Eastern Iraq 1919–1925* (Oxford University Press, 1957) pp. 305–7.

56. On Simko's last years, see Jwaideh, 'Nationalist Movement', pp. 410–13; Arfa, *Kurds*, p. 63. On his killing, A.M. Hamilton, *Road Through Kurdistan* (Faber and Faber, London, 1937), pp. 162–4; Sharifi, *Ashayir*, pp. 64–71.

57. FO 371/1922: E 8437/6/34.

58. Arfa, *Shahs*, p. 141.

59. Aghasi, *Tarikh*, pp. 457–8. Simko was, however, informed and put Amr Khan under surveillance at Chahriq. After Simko's defeat the government arrested Amr Khan and imprisoned him for several years.

60. Sharifi, *Ashayir*, pp. 64–5.

61. The following is an excerpt from a letter sent by Simko to Babakr Agha, in which he asks him to demand British support on his behalf: 'I am aware that my reputation is one of treachery and deceit in dealing with Governments and I therefore address you who have a standing credit in the eyes of the British Government upon the following matter: my recent actions and all my actions have no hostile intention with respect to the British Government. On the contrary, I have a sincere desire to be on friendly terms with that Government on my behalf for the purpose of arranging some mutual understanding' (enclosed in FO 371/1921: E 11773/43/93).

62. Claimed by Aghasi, *Tarikh* p. 458, and, in a different version, by Sharifi, *Ashayir*, p. 59. I have found no further confirmation of these claims.

63. Eagleton, *Republic,* pp. 109–10.

64. Personal interview, 8 Aug. 1979. Unfortunately I have not been able to check this information with the Shakak themselves.

Chapter 14
NOMADS AND COMMISSARS IN THE MUGHAN STEPPE: THE SHAHSEVAN TRIBES IN THE GREAT GAME

Richard Tapper

Introduction

The substance of this chapter is a discussion of the role of a particular group of tribes in the Great Game, the policies pursued by the states concerned, and the effects of those policies on the social organisation of the tribes.[1]
   Russia's Caucasian frontier with Iran was in many ways as important an arena of the nineteenth-century Great Game as British India's frontier with Afghanistan. Both were of considerable strategic importance and crossed by major Asian trade routes. The main differences were in the nature of the terrain and the population. While the mountain ranges of the North West Frontier of India were of marginal agricultural value, rugged, remote and defensible, Transcaucasia included some of the most fertile agricultural lands of the area and for this reason, as well as its comparative accessibility, could not provide so remote and defensible a refuge where tribal populations could remain politically autonomous from competing states and empires.
   The frontier established by Russia with Iran in the early nineteenth century cut most of the Shahsevan nomad tribes of Iran off from their winter pastures. For some time they were permitted limited access to these pastures, but they failed to observe the limitations. Shahsevan disorder during the latter part of the century was used by both Iran and Russia to political advantage, and was an important factor in Great Power rivalry in Iran. Iranian government policy to the tribes varied from virtual abdication of authority to predatory expeditions and an attempt in 1860 at wholesale settlement - perhaps the first such case in Iran. This typically twentieth-century measure provoked one British con-

sular official to an illuminating and surprisingly
modern assessment of the role of nomad tribes within
the state.

Russian policy led inevitably to complete closure of the frontier to the nomads in the 1880s, and
a subsequent redistribution of pastures within Iran.
From this period dates the complex system of grazing
rights that distinguishes Shahsevan social organisation today. Also over the period, marked as it was
by escalating economic and political pressures on
the nomads, descent as a source of political legitimacy gave ground to more material factors: wealth
and manpower.

The Russian Annexation of Mughan

Eastern Transcaucasia has always offered a highly
favourable environment for both pastoral and agricultural activities. High mountains, with abundant
summer pasturages, command the vast and fertile
Shirvan, Qarabagh and Mughan plains of the lower
Aras and Kur rivers, which at once provide correspondingly extensive winter grazing and invite the
construction of large-scale irrigation works. These
plains were a favourite wintering place of conquerors, while not surprisingly the whole area was long
the object of intense struggle between powerful
nations. The Safavids gained control at the beginning of the sixteenth century, but had difficulty
keeping it from the Russians and various Caucasian
powers, and when the dynasty crumbled in the early
eighteenth century the area was divided briefly
between Ottomans and Russians. After a further
eighty years of Iranian hegemony, during which two
further conquerors had themselves crowned in Mughan
(Nadir Afshar in 1736 and Aqa Muhammad Qajar in
1796), it was Russia that managed to annex most of
the area for good.

The area is also a natural cross-roads, and
trade and travel between Russia and Iran and between
Anatolia and Central Asia passed through or close by.
From Safavid times, travellers and merchants from
Europe commonly journeyed overland through Russia,
took ship on the Caspian and landed at Shirvan to
halt awhile at the growing trade centre of Shamakhi
before crossing the Kur to pass via Mughan and
Ardabil into central Iran and beyond to India.

In the early eighteenth century, under the last
Safavid monarchs, the tribal population of Mughan
was heterogeneous: there were comparatively indige-

nous groups of Kurdish origins (Shaqaqi and Mughanlu) and more or less recently arrived immigrants from various of the Turkman Qizilbash tribes: groups of Afshar, Takalu, and particularly sections of the great composite Qizilbash confederacy of Shamlu (Ajirlu, Inanlu, Begdilu). Many of these groups were now known by the additional name of 'Shahsevan', but there was not yet any single unified tribe of this name; the traditional story, of the creation of a Shahsevan tribe a century earlier by Shah Abbas the Great, is a fiction for which Sir John Malcolm must bear the blame.[2]

These tribes underwent drastic upheavals in the years 1725-30, when their territory was occupied and divided between the Ottomans and Russians. The Shaqaqi, Afshar and Inanlu tribes remained in the area controlled by the Ottomans, while other Shahsevan and Mughanlu groups fled north and submitted to the Russians. When Tahmasp Quli Beg Afshar, later to become Nadir Shah, restored Iranian hegemony in Azarbayjan in 1730, he removed to Khurasan those tribes that had supported the Ottomans. The Shahsevan and Mughanlu remained subject to the Russians until the latter withdrew from the area in 1732. Soon after, Nadir Shah appears to have united the Shahsevan, the Mughanlu and other remaining tribes of Mughan and Ardabil, into a confederation with the name of Shahsevan, under the leadership of Badr Khan Sarikhanbeglu, one of his captains and probably of Afshar origins himself.

During the next fifty years or so, Badr Khan and his family consolidated their control of the tribes in this corner of Azarbayjan, though quarrels broke out among Badr Khan's descendants, who divided the tribes and the territory into two: the Ardabil division was the more powerful, having control of the town of Ardabil, where Shahsevan khans were governors until 1808, while many of their tribesmen began to settle in villages near the town; their opponents in the Mishkin division remained nomadic. Both branches, through their chiefs, became involved in the complex network of alliance, hostility and intrigue that characterised the khanates of Azarbayjan and Transcaucasia in the later eighteenth century. At this period, and during the two Russo-Iranian wars of the early nineteenth century, the Ardabil Shahsevan were among the firm supporters of the Qajars, while the Shahsevan chiefs of Mishkin, largely through traditional opposition to their cousins at Ardabil, ultimately sided with the Russians.

By the Treaty of Gulistan in 1813, the Russians acquired (among other territories) the greater and better part of the Mughan steppe and the neighbouring khanate of Talish, under whose jurisdiction much of the steppe remained. Iranian tribes of north-east Azarbayjan were permitted to cross the new Russian frontier to continue wintering in their traditional quarters, on two conditions: that they continue payment of pasture-dues to the Talish khan, and that nomadic Russian subjects from Talish be permitted to enter Iran during the summer months as they had done before. After the second Russian war, however, the situation altered. The Treaty of Turkmanchay (1828) confirmed the transfer of Mughan and Talish to the Russians, who set about consolidating their fertile territorial gains in Transcaucasia. Settlers were brought in, particularly groups of rich sectarians and various emigrant Polish and German communities. Many Russian nomadic groups were settled in Mughan along the banks of the Aras, Kur and Akusha; others remained semi-nomadic but were given settled bases, while, to reduce their dependance on mountain pastures in Iran, their pastoralism was converted from ovine to bovine, and they were encouraged to exploit the Mughan steppe pasturages more intensively.[3]

Most tribes indigenous to Iranian Azarbayjan had co-operated with the Russians during Count Paskevich's occupation of the province in 1827-28. Article 15 of the Turkmanchay Treaty granted them an amnesty and allowed them one year in which to migrate, if they chose, to Russian territory to settle there as Russian subjects. Numerous groups, from various parts of the province, did move north over the frontier, and several villages in districts bordering Russian Mughan were completely or partly settled by Shahsevan tribesmen at this time.[4]

After the Turkmanchay Treaty was signed, the Iranian government asked the Russian Administration of the Caucasus to permit the Shahsevan nomads to continue their migrations to Mughan as before, offering the annual sum of 2,000 silver roubles (700 toman or £350), formerly paid as pasture-dues to the Talish khans. In 1831 a preliminary contract concerning this was drawn up at Tiflis between Paskevich and an Iranian envoy, specifying conditions by which the migration should proceed and the pasture-dues be paid. One article laid down that the Shahsevan nomads should use only that part of the steppe which had formerly belonged to the Talish khanate, specifically excluding the part attached to Shirvan; the latter, comprising much of the territory along the

southern banks of the Aras and Kur rivers, was reserved for the use of the Russian nomads and village-
based flocks. A copy of this contract was sent to
Tehran for ratification, pending which the Shahsevan
were allowed to pasture their flocks in Mughan free
of charge. It seems, however, that the first instal-
ment of the pasture-dues was not paid until 1847.[5]
   Meanwhile Russian colonisation of the steppe
proceeded apace. From the beginning, however, the
new agricultural efforts suffered from raiding by
the Shahsevan, who destroyed crops, stole animals
and plundered villages. Some of the Iranian nomads
had been used to crossing the Kur and Aras and wintering in the Qarabagh and Shirvan steppes, and many
of them now continued to do so, but they fell foul
of the local nomads for whom these pastures had been
set aside by the Russian authorities, and both there
and on the southern banks of the rivers there was
continual bloodshed. In the course of time, the
division of Mughan into the Shirvan and Talish sectors lapsed, and the whole territory south of the
Kur and Aras was abandoned to the Shahsevan in
winter.[6]
   Such was the situation in Russian Mughan in
the middle of the last century. Before relating
measures taken by both Russian and Iranian authorities to deal with it, something must be said of
affairs in Iranian Azarbayjan, and of the social
organisation of the Shahsevan tribes at the time.

Azarbayjan and the Shahsevan in the Mid-nineteenth Century

After the Treaty of Turkmanchay, Azarbayjan continued to be, politically at least, the most important
province of Iran. It was the chief recruiting
ground for the Qajar armies, if not also the chief
supplier of agricultural produce, and Tabriz, second
city of the country and usually the seat of the Heir
Apparent, was the main emporium of the rapidly
expanding trade from Russia and the West. Russia
was naturally the paramount foreign influence in
the political and economic affairs of the province,
though the British often managed to exert some pressure through their consular officials in Tabriz.
   'The picture of the land revenue system and
administration of the early Qajars is one of decay,
maladministration, oppression and insecurity.'[7]
These proliferated in Azarbayjan throughout the nineteenth century, when the resources of the province

were steadily drained away by a succession of officials of all ranks who came simply to make their
fortunes. Their salaries were commonly paid by
revenue drafts, whether on Crown Land or privately
owned land, and much of the Crown Land was sold to
the officials and others such as wealthy merchants
and thus became private land. The landowning classes thus increasingly included government officials,
merchants and tribal chiefs, who squeezed the cultivating peasants for what they could contribute. The
tribal chiefs, at least among the Shahsevan, also
leased their pastures at steeply rising rentals. The
burden of taxation and other dues was passed on, in
the case of the nomads, by the chiefs and tax-
collectors, who as a rule demanded cash payments
from the ordinary tribesmen. Members of the chiefly
families had no employment other than occasional
military service, and raiding expeditions were their
characteristic preoccupation. The basic husbandry
practised by the ordinary nomad herdsman was much as
in the present century, and much the same kind of
production rate could be maintained, but higher
costs and heavy impositions probably meant a much
lower standard of consumption. Social relations
generally were characterised by widening gulfs between the landowning (non-productive) chiefs and the
hard-pressed pastoralists, between predatory officials and their victims, between nomads and villagers.

While the Russians colonised and settled their
new Transcaucasian territories, they were not interested in the annexation of Iranian Azarbayjan. They
put pressure on the Iranians to settle their frontier tribes, but in fact both sides had much to gain
from keeping groups like the Shahsevan nomadic. Iran
relied on the nomads' pastoral produce, and on their
role as frontier guards, while the Russians not only
gained considerably themselves from the Shahsevan
contribution to the economy of the Mughan settlers,
but were also able to put to good political use
their tally of the settlers' complaints of Shahsevan
raiding. The officials and diplomats concerned were
well aware of these factors in the situation. The
Russians pressed for settlement of the nomads, knowing the Iranians would not be keen, while British
agents were advising against such a policy. So the
officials took half-measures, and often succeeded
only in lining their pockets and further antagonis-
ing the nomads.

Shahsevan territory in north-east Azarbayjan
covered the districts of Mishkin and Ardabil and

others, all under the Governor resident at Ardabil.
Travellers who passed through the region in the
1830s and 1840s commented on the fertility and comparative prosperity of the Mishkin district, which
was well-cultivated and populous though it contained
no town of any size. The district of Ardabil itself,
on the other hand, was in a wretched condition, depopulated and depressed not only through plague and
cholera, but also through the exactions of the officials who were based there.[8]

These differences were also reflected in a comparison of the two Shahsevan tribal confederations.
After their chief Nazar Ali Khan was deposed from
the governorship of Ardabil in 1808, the power of
the Ardabil tribes declined, many of them settled
and others appear to have joined the Mishkin tribes,
who now, despite the disloyalty of their chiefs in
the Russian wars, had become the more numerous and
wealthy.

In the period 1828-84, the Shahsevan nomad population probably ranged between six and twelve thousand families. The leaders of the two confederations
(el) were officially constituted as elbegi (paramount chief) in 1839 following Russian complaints
about the tribes. Each of the forty-odd tribes
(taifa) had its own chief (beg); elbegis and begs
were appointed by and responsible to the Governor at
Ardabil, usually a Qajar prince. Elbegis had almost
unlimited powers over the tribesmen: they collected
taxes and military levies, they held court and could
sentence offenders to fines, corporal punishment,
imprisonment, confiscation of property and even
death; they profited substantially when deciding
cases of theft, and no appeal against their judge-
ments was possible. The chiefs of individual tribes
had lesser duties and kept order within their own
tribes, assisted by elected elders (aq-saqal) of
camp communities (oba). The cash collected annually
from the nomads was said to total two or three times
the official amount which reached the Treasury.
Governors, chiefs and tax-collectors all took their
legitimate percentages, while the elbegis also extorted a whole range of customary and irregular dues,
such as tribute in camels, sheep, felt, butter, and
cash for household 'expenses' and for 'presents' for
government officials. The pasture-due for Mughan
continued to be collected by the elbegis long after
the Russians had ceased receiving it.

Members of the elbegi dynasties and those half-
dozen tribes which could claim common descent with
them from Badr Khan's ancestor Yunsur Pasha, were

classed as 'nobles' (begzada), the rest were 'commoners' (rayat, hampa). To judge from the earliest
records mentioning individual tribes, the nobles'
dominance over the commoner tribes at this time
depended partly on their descent claims and partly
on the delegation of authority to them by the elbegi,
though probably they also had some degree of control
over the pastures. Each noble tribe consisted of
two 'classes': the ruling lineage with their small
suite of attendants (noukar) constituted the begzada,
who did no work, paid no tax, held rights in land,
and in many tribes amounted to over half the population; the rest of the tribe were hampa, a retinue of
'workers' and peasants, who had no control over pasture or farmland, but tended the flocks, paid the
taxes, and cultivated the farmlands owned by the
begzada. In addition, each commoner tribe was sub-
ordinated to one of the noble chiefs, and its own
chief or members of his family joined the latter's
suite, to be counted as begzada. There is little
information on the nature of political and territorial organisation within these tribal groups, but
it was probably echoed in that of the dominant
tribes later in the century, described below.

Certain important differences of organisation
distinguished the noble tribes from the commoners.
Each noble lineage formed the nucleus of its own
tribe, which it dominated not only by delegated
authority and by control of pasture, but also through
its superior descent - the name of each noble tribe
was that of the chiefly lineage's ancestor. None of
the workers or the commoner tribes, however strong,
could take over the leadership of a noble tribe:
they were bound by moral ties to the chiefly lineage
but not to individual chiefs. There was no formal
rule of chiefly succession other than patrilineal
descent from a former chief, and commoners would
follow whichever candidate offered greater economic
and political advantage. The noble lineages could
and did experience fission, and when this occurred
the worker and commoner following divided accordingly, each new noble tribe continuing to be dominated
by a noble lineage.

The chiefly lineages in the commoner tribes had
no such moral claims to legitimacy. Very few commoner tribes bore an ancestral name or even had an
ideology of common descent. All lineages of the
tribe could identify with the tribal name equally,
and were equally eligible to lead. The authority
of the chiefly lineage thus depended largely on the
support of the nobles and the elbegi, and it could

not afford to be weakened by fission, which might allow another lineage to take over the whole tribe.

This account of Shahsevan social organisation in the mid-nineteenth century is based mainly on reports by two Russian officials who had dealings with the tribes. I.A. Ogranovich, who was first appointed Frontier Commissar for the Shahsevan at Belasuvar in 1869, wrote various articles on them, while E. Krebel, Russian Consul-General in Tabriz from 1877, wrote a report which was used extensively in the studies of Gustav Radde, German naturalist, and Vl. Markov, Russian official, both of whom visited the Shahsevan themselves in the 1880s and collected further information.[9] They give considerable detail on domestic and economic activities, making clear the extent to which the nomads were involved in market exchange in Russian territory.[10]

In its general features, Shahsevan pastoral life probably changed little before the mid-nineteenth century. However, the Russian observers, while praising the tribesmen for their courage and hospitality and the high 'moral standards' of their women, inveigh against their overriding preoccupation with raiding and lawlessness. They make no attempt to assess how far Shahsevan behaviour and institutions in the latter half of the century were affected directly or indirectly by the Russian presence in Mughan.

The old hierarchy of groups and authority was already breaking down, and a new structure emerging, partly as a result of internal contradictions and partly as a response to the series of drastic changes in the economic and political environment which began with the Russian advent in Mughan. In particular, there was a radical change in economic conditions - in the availability of pasturage and markets.

Though there is no information on the nature of pasture ownership before the Russian acquisition of Mughan, it is clear that this event, and its immediate consequences in restricting Shahsevan winter pastures, brought about violent changes in patterns of economic and political organisation. Briefly, the available pastures fell into the hands of the chiefs of individual tribes (noble or commoner) who leased them at rapidly increasing rentals to their followers, over whom they thus gained an unprecedented degree of power. As the pastures become more and more restricted, so the division widened between owners and tenants. The elbegis lost the monopoly of authority. The Ardabil branch of the dynasty was

already assimilated to the administration and urban
life, and had lost touch with the tribes, while the
Mishkin elbegis either could not or would not control
the most recalcitrant brigands and were unacceptable
to the Russians. The noble tribes meanwhile were
weakened through rivalries within the chiefly lineages, and though they continued to control their own
workers, many of them were now diminished in numbers
and had lost their following of commoner tribes. One
noble tribe in each division, however, continued to
dominate the rest: Polatlu in Ardabil, Qojabeglu in
Mishkin. The half dozen or so larger and wealthier
commoner tribes now declared their independence of
the nobles and collected their own followings of
weaker tribes. The weaker commoner (and noble)
chiefs, if only to secure their control of their own
workers, sought the support of a dominant tribe. By
the time of the frontier closure in 1884, the original stratification of the tribes into nobles and
commoners had broken down, and a new one was emerging, based no longer on descent claims but rather on
size, material resources and territorial and transactional relations.

Troubles Begin

To try to keep the Shahsevan nomads away from the
settled colonists and the Russian nomads in Mughan,
in 1849 the Russian authorities took steps to give
precise definition to the tract which the Iranian
nomads were to be allowed to use. A distance of up
to 7 km. was left between the nomadic tract and the
banks of the Aras, Kur, Akusha and Balharu, and this
riverside strip was reserved for the use of the settlers there and their cattle. In addition the Shahsevan were shown places on the rivers at which their
flocks might drink, and tracks along which they
should lead them there.[11] These last provisions
were absolutely necessary because, although Mughan
had been widely irrigated centuries before, now
there was no surface water at all within the central
part of the steppe, other than a number of salt
lakes. The provisions were not, however, enough to
satisfy the Shahsevan, who had been accustomed to
camping by the rivers and to using pastures within
easy reach of the banks, and did not regard the
waterless central part of the steppe as usable grazing. They crossed the newly marked boundaries as
before, with the result that in late 1849 and again
the following year Russian authorities attempted to

prevent them from wintering in Mughan at all, and
the nomads lost large numbers of their animals.[12]
    In any case, the 1849 measures had little per-
manent effect. According to Ogranovich, the Shahsevan chiefs quickly divided the tract into pastures
(qishlaq), marking off the boundaries, and then
leased these pastures to their followers and others.
The distribution of pastures by written permits took
place before the annual migration to Mughan, and the
chiefs made sure that no unauthorised persons used
them. Poorer nomads, unable to afford the chiefs'
fees, came and rented pastures from Russian subjects,
nomad and settled; some joined the Russian nomads,
contracting marriages or serving as shepherds or
servants, in return for access to pasture. The
Russians complained that the Shahsevan would lease
all their pastures, then cross the boundary and
seize the lands of Russian subjects on the river
banks, which they would then lease out also, both to
Russian subjects and to Iranian nomads brought in
from as far as Urmiyeh, Khoy and Hamadan. In the
latter half of the century, over two million head of
animals (camels, horses, sheep and goats) were
brought to Mughan annually. As the pastures became
more crowded, so the rents rose, from between five
and ten toman initially to about 40 toman by 1860.[13]
    Meanwhile forceful measures were also being
taken by the Iranian authorities. For a year or so
after Muhammad Shah's death in September 1848, lawlessness reigned in north-east Azarbayjan as elsewhere in the province. His young successor Nasir
al-Din Shah sent Abbas Quli Javanshir to govern the
districts of Ardabil, Mishkin and Qaradagh, with
particular instructions to free the frontiers of his
province from robbers and highwaymen. He left the
capital in summer 1849, and on his way met Hamzeh
Mirza Hishmat al-Douleh, who was going to Tabriz to
take up his appointment as Governor-General of Azarbayjan. In Zanjan they were warned that the Hajjikhojalu and Damirchilu tribes, both of the Mishkin
division of the Shahsevan, had been fighting and
that several people had been killed, so, as they
approached north-east Azarbayjan, they sent to various Shahsevan and Qaradaghi chiefs, bidding them
collect forces and bring the Hajjikhojalu in submission; which they apparently did successfully. The
Governors proceeded together to Tabriz, and then
towards the end of the year Abbas Quli Khan left for
Qaradagh and Mishkin, where he took several Shahsevan chiefs prisoner. It was reported that his
severe but necessary punishments had 'produced a

salutary effect' in those districts, which were now
in a 'tolerably quiet state'.[14] In fact, the Shahsevan, who had just been prevented from crossing the
Russian frontier into Mughan, and were now experiencing an unusually severe winter, were no doubt
shocked into submission by this unprecedented threefold attack.

In spring 1851, after the second winter in
which the Russians tried to stop the Shahsevan from
wintering in Mughan, Nasir al-Din Shah's great
Minister, Mirza Taqi Khan the Amir Kabir, was reported to be contemplating removal of the Shahsevan
southwards out of Azarbayjan. Hamzeh Mirza was sent
to Ardabil and Mishkin in the summer, to adopt
'measures for preventing the Shahsevan tribes from
wintering on the Russian side of Mughan'. All he in
fact achieved, it seems, was to trick a number of
important Shahsevan chiefs into visiting him, whereupon he threw them into chains and sent them to jail
in Tabriz. In 1852, however, a Commissar was appointed over the Shahsevan, to deal with the Russians
and introduce order on the frontier - though the
Russians complained that he had neither the power
nor the authority necessary for satisfying their
claims against the tribesmen.[15]

During this time Iran continued to pay the
pasture-due of 2,000 roubles. Soon the Russians
became involved in a war with Turkey, and through
their envoy in Tehran endeavoured to win Iranian
support. In 1853 the Amir Kabir's successor as
Prime Minister, Mirza Aqa Khan Nuri, who was anxious
to rid Iran of foreign political influences, took
advantage of the Russian predicament to refuse payment of the Mughan dues, claiming on behalf of the
Shahsevan that the grass had been burnt by Russian
subjects before the nomads' arrival, while the
Russians claimed that the Shahsevan had themselves
fired the pastures. Later Mirza Aqa Khan swung back
to a pro-Russian position, and in 1856 the Iranian
Government paid the outstanding pasture-dues - but
after that year the payments ceased for good.[16]

Meanwhile Mirza Aqa Khan was intriguing against
the British, who in December 1855 withdrew their
Mission from Tehran. During the following year
Russian complaints of Shahsevan depredations in
Mughan and Talish increased rapidly, but Russo-
Iranian diplomatic relations were so cordial that
nothing was done about investigating them.[17]

In 1856-57 Iran sent a military expedition to
capture Herat, in defiance of treaty undertakings
to the British in India, whereupon the British

invaded Iranian territory in the Gulf area. After
the Treaty of Paris, ratified in spring 1857, the
British envoy returned to Iran; Nasir al-Din Shah
dismissed Mirza Aqa Khan and took over direct control
of the Government and foreign affairs. Relations
with the British were now favoured, principally since
they appeared more able to supply the financial aid
of which Iran was increasingly in need, while relations with Russia entered a decidedly cooler phase.

An Attempt at Settlement

On the Azarbayjan frontier the Russians now began to
demand satisfaction of the claims which they had to
date merely stored up. Between 1857 and 1860 both
sides sent a series of delegates to negotiate with
each other, to investigate and settle the claims -
which included Iranian counter-claims of inroads by
plunderers from the Russian side of the frontier.
The Russians complained, however, that their counterparts were not properly equipped for their duties,
while the Iranians for their part reported that the
Russian delegates were late in arriving at the ren-
dezvous, and when they did arrive, acted in a per-
emptory and overbearing manner, refused to listen
to reason or compromise, and in fact were not interested so much in satisfying claims as in embarrassing the Iranian Government.[18]
 As relations between Iran and Britain further
improved at the end of the 1850s, the Russians adopted a harder line, particularly concerning Shahsevan
affairs. In early 1860 the Governor of Azarbayjan,
Sardar Aziz Khan, Sardar-i Kull, himself went to
Ardabil to be in closer contact with his Commissar
for the Shahsevan, and to hasten settlement of
Russian claims. No Russian officer had yet appeared
by the time the tribes left Mughan in May, but a
mixed Commission met in the summer and settled some
important claims. The Sardar-i Kull remained at
Ardabil until July, being occupied in providing for
the settlement of large numbers of Shahsevan nomads,
in that district and in Mishkin, to keep them from
causing trouble on the frontier. He planned to prevent them from wintering in either Russian or Iranian Mughan, arrested several Shahsevan chiefs on
charges of theft and murder, and disposed of them
with utmost cruelty. In addition he accumulated a
great deal of the nomads' wealth in extortions and
confiscations. The Shahsevan cannot have retained
much, for the winter of 1859 had been one of the

severest known, 'when there was snow in Mughan for
over a month and the river Kur was frozen, and all
their property was lost'.[19]   Meanwhile, Sardar Aziz
Khan and other officials in Azarbayjan were reported
to be indulging in such speculations that food
prices had risen in mid-1860 to five or more times
their 1857 levels, and much of the population was
starving.   The British Consul-General Keith Abbott
remonstrated with the Sardar, with the result that
by the end of the year the former close British-
Iranian relations in Tabriz were completely reversed,
and Abbott was virtually ostracised.[20]

  The events of 1860, marking a significant point
in Shahsevan history, are not mentioned in Russian
accounts of frontier incidents; presumably because
the Sardar's measures to settle the Shahsevan were
undertaken at Russian instigation.   However, Abbott's
reports to Tehran, this year and in 1861, are highly
illuminating and deserve to be quoted at some length.

  On 13 June 1860, Abbott commented that the
Sardar's settlement policy,

> supposing it to be successfully carried out, is
> questionable, for although the Tribe may possi-
> bly be induced through fear to relinquish their
> nomadic habits and in time to turn their atten-
> tion to agriculture, so great and sudden a
> change in their circumstances would occasion
> much distress among them - their usefulness as
> a pastoral tribe would cease and their old
> haunts in Persian Moghan becoming deserted
> would probably fall into the hands of that
> division of the community which belongs to
> Russia - an event which would hardly fail to
> become a source of disquiet to the Persian
> Government.

Abbott did not believe any such change would last
long; the nomads would return as soon as possible
to their former way of life.[21]

  When the Sardar returned to Tabriz in July, he
boasted of having settled 15,000 families of nomads.
Abbott was thoroughly sceptical both of the numbers
and of the permanence of the supposed 'establishment
in villages'.   'Indeed', he wrote,

> [the nomads] appear to have demanded certain
> conditions of the Persian Government in return
> for their acquiescence in the scheme and it is
> not yet known whether these will be agreed to
> at Tehran.   The Shah had however consented to

a remission of one year's taxation amounting
to Ten or Twelve Thousand Tomans as some compensation for the loss and inconvenience to
which they would undoubtedly be put by the
contemplated change in their condition. It is
proposed by the Sardar to restrict the whole
of the Tribe from resorting to winter quarters
in Moghan the greater part of which is held by
Russia - and here I believe consists the main
difficulty to the execution of the scheme of
settling this people in villages. The Tribe
is rich in flocks, camels and cattle, to
abandon which would be ruinous to them, and
to maintain them, they require to resort to
the rich pasture lands of Moghan in winter.

According to Abbott's information, the Shahsevan
nomads residing south of the Aras amounted to no
more than 12,000 families, of which some 5,000 already had village bases in the Ardabil and Mishkin
districts, while the rest, mainly of the Mishkin
division, were nomadic tent-dwellers. It was to the
latter 7,000 families that the settlement plan ref-
erred.22

In November, following his fall from the
Sardar's favour, Abbot elaborated on a number of
the points already mentioned, particularly on the
value to the economy of the province of the nomads'
contribution, which would be lost if they were sedentarised. The Sardar's severity at Ardabil, and
his measures to settle the Shahsevan, he wrote,

have rendered this Tribe more discontented and
greater enemies of the Government than ever, so
that for some time to come it will probably
prove a scourge rather than an advantage to
the province ... there is no doubt the Tribe
has been the cause of pretty constant annoyance
to the Russian frontier Authorities and their
petty depredations have been the subject of
unceasing complaint - but the remedy for all
this will scarcely be found, I think, in the
measures taken to make them a stationary
people, at least for some years to come, and
for the present matters are rendered worse than
before by the Tribe pillaging far and near in
revenge for the treatment they have experienced.
A regiment and two guns have been posted in the
vicinity of Mooghan to cut off their access to
those plains and some trifling resistance has
been offered by the Tribe which no doubt finds

itself in a great measure ruined by the change
it is being compelled to make in it's habits
and mode of life.
I think it impolitic in the Persian Government
to seek to render it's great nomad Tribes a
stationary people. Persia is differently cir-
cumstanced to most other countries, and the
nature of it's climate, it's natural features
and the general habits of the people require
that it should possess a population which can
adapt itself to variations of mountain and
plain and draw from that condition of life
resources which are in a great measure denied
the fixed inhabitants. It is on these great
pastoral communities that the population of
the cities and plains nearly depend for their
supplies of animal food - for the flocks - for
the butter, cheese, and other preparations from
Milk which are so largely consumed in Persia
and for many coarse but useful articles of
woolen and other manufacture for which the
produce of the fields and cities is exchanged.
The Tribes are a further advantage to the
country in consequence of their wealth in
camels which afford a cheap means of conveyance
for merchandise to the most distant parts; but
these advantages are in great measure lost to
the country when the tribes are compelled to
renounce their nomadic condition to become
cultivators of the soil - and the State in
authorizing these changes lessens it's resources in a military point of view - for
whereas the Young men of the nomad Tribe are to
a great extent available for military service,
the duties and labour of the community being
chiefly performed by the females, the labour of
cultivating the soil must fall principally on
the males - and no doubt also the hardiest
races in Persia and the most valuable for military duties are the men of the wandering
Tribes.[23]

These observations on the nature of nomadic
pastoralism in Iran are perhaps surprisingly modern
in tone, and would have held good until quite recently as an assessment of the value of the nomad tribes
and of the valid arguments against a policy of enforced settlement such as was carried out by Riza
Shah in the 1930s.
Early in March 1861 Sardar Aziz Khan was in
Tehran, where he was interviewed concerning the

state of Azarbayjan by the British envoy Alison, who
sent a memorandum of the interview to Abbott in
Tabriz for comment. The Sardar claimed that, thanks
to his attention, the frontier was at present tranquil;

> A fruitful source of dispute between Persia
> and Russia had arisen from the depredations of
> the nomadic tribes who, during the winter
> months, frequented the plain of Moghan. Persian
> tribes committed depredations on Russian terri-
> tory, and Russian Tribes on Persian. The only
> remedy was to oblige them to renounce their
> nomadic habits. This was no easy matter, con-
> sidering that one of the Persian Tribes - the
> Shahseven - counted upwards of 12,000 families,
> and would strenuously resist any attempt to
> deprive them of a privilege which they and their
> ancestors had enjoyed for centuries. To have
> transferred them to another province would have
> been to deprive an important frontier of a
> strong barrier. The Serdar, therefore, pro-
> ceeded in person to Ardebil, and finding its
> neighbourhood a suitable locality, summoned the
> tribe and by a due mixture of fair proposals
> and threats induced about 9,000 families to
> build houses and settle. The remainder, he
> expects, will soon follow their example. By
> this means the chance of a War with Russia has,
> he hopes, been averted; the annual payment to
> that Power of 5,000 Tomans to permit the tribe
> to pasture their flocks on the other side of
> the Arras, will be saved, and should the neces-
> sity ever unfortunately arise, the tribe will
> henceforth for the protection of their own
> homes, be compelled the more efficiently to
> defend the frontier. The settlers have already
> contributed 500 horse to the Persian Army, and
> the Serdar hopes the number will next year be
> increased to 1,000. The Russian Authorities,
> he added, have expressed their intention to
> take similar measures with regard to their own
> frontier tribes, in which case a source of con-
> tinual ill-feeling and irritation between the
> two countries will be radically removed.[24]

Abbott commented at length, reiterating most of
his former points. He agreed that the Mughan frontier was now tranquil, though the province in general
was in an appalling state of insecurity. The Shahsevan had at first acquiesced 'under fear and with a

bad grace' in their sedentarisation, but the scheme
was as yet far from a success. A large part of the
tribe had broken through the inadequate force stationed in Mughan, which appeared to have confined its
activities to 'plundering of all its wealth one respectable division of the tribe on it proving refrac-
tory'. Abbott's objections to the policy still held:

> there is still every cause to apprehend the
> downfall and ruin of that great and flourishing
> pastoral community, for should they be forced
> to abandon their nomad habits it will be at a
> sacrifice of much which at present constitutes
> a source to them of wealth and prosperity - and
> should they continue refractory the Government
> may make this a pretext for plundering them as
> it is reputed has already happened to one divi-
> sion. Any such change in the condition of the
> Tribe as was contemplated by the Serdar will be
> attended likewise with injurious effects to the
> country generally - the prices of meat and of
> other articles of animal food which this people
> usually furnish, produce of their flocks and
> herds, will be greatly increased - indeed there
> is already every appearance of this having al-
> ready happened through the unsettled state of
> the Tribes, in the present high prices of
> Animal Food in Azerbaijan.

Abbott was further sceptical about the Sardar's
estimation of the seriousness of Shahsevan raids on
the frontier: there was no real danger of war there.
The Russian Shahsevan tribes were equally responsible
for raiding activities, but their Iranian cousins
'being the most numerous were better able to protect
their own property and they retaliated severely on
those who molested them'. The figure of 5,000 toman
for the pasture-dues was exaggerated: only 750 tomans
used to be paid. Abbott believed that the nomads did
not cross the Aras but kept themselves to the Mughan
plain south of the river. On the increase of the
long-established levy of 500 horsemen, Abbott commented, 'The Tribes generally are ready enough to
furnish horsemen to the State when their services are
remunerated,' and the Shahsevan could afford to contribute 1,000 men - but not if they were sedentarised.
He had no information on Russian intentions to settle
their own tribes - though Russian sources indicate
that this settlement was in fact proceeding.
     In conclusion, Abbott noted that the removal of
the Shahsevan from the frontier would undoubtedly

improve the situation there, but the trouble would
only move to the new locality, 'and the Persian districts would be exposed more than before to the
depredations of a people who whether stationary or
erratic is not likely to abandon all at once it's
ingrained and inherent propensity for appropriating
the property of it's neighbours.' Abbott's association of pastoral nomadism with kleptomania is perhaps the only jarring note in an otherwise perceptive analysis of the Shahsevan situation at the time.
He refrains from explicitly suggesting alternative
and more effective measures for dealing with the
problem, implying only that given better government
in Azarbayjan and less extortion on the part of
officials, the Shahsevan might be persuaded to restrict their lawless activities.[25]
    In the following years the Azarbayjan govern-
ment did not improve and, as Abbott predicted, Shahsevan disorder increased, until in 1867 even the
appointment as Governor of Ardabil of Muhammad Rahim
Mirza Zia al-Douleh, a man with a reputation for
justice and integrity, could do little to alleviate
the situation.

The Russians Increase the Pressure

The reports of the British Consul-General at Tabriz
are the main source for the preceding events, yet
British agents were apparently not aware of the
Shahsevan again for another twenty years. Meanwhile
the Russian accounts, having remained silent on the
settlement attempt of 1860-1, describe the next
phase of the story in detail. Presumably under the
influence of the new 'forward policy' prescribed by
the Gorchakov memorandum of 1864 on Central Asia
(see chapter 2 above), the Russians determined to
set in train a solution of affairs on their Mughan
frontier too. In 1869 for the first time they appointed a permanent Frontier Commissar: Colonel
Ogranovich, the source of much information on the
Shahsevan tribes in the nineteenth century. Iran
had had Commissars since 1859, but they had so far
dealt with temporary officials from the Baku Government, and with local chiefs and their assistants.
Now both Commissars were supposed to be present at
Belasuvar from October to April, throughout the Shahsevan residence in Mughan. Ogranovich complained
that his counterparts did not arrive until February,
leaving only one month in which disputes could be
settled; there was nothing to check Shahsevan law-

lessness earlier in the season, when complaints could
have been dealt with on the spot and satisfaction
rendered. Actually, if the Iranian Commissars were
late, it would have been understandable in view of
their previous experience of the unpunctuality of
Russian officials.

The rules according to which crimes and disputes
were dealt with were, first of all, those of local
customary law (adat): presentation of the case by
both sides with witnesses; if this did not solve the
case, mediators were called; if they could not agree,
the matter was referred to a court of mullahs, who
decided it according to the sharia, by means of
oaths and 'public expediency' (maslahat). These procedures were complicated for Ogranovich by certain
'unofficial' Iranian and Shahsevan practices: for
example, plaintiffs tended to demand twice or three
times what they expected by way of compensation, so
as to be able to afford the fees of 'informants' or
'detectives' (mushtulukchi). There was also a form
of self-help, whereby the victim of theft could
seize property from the suspected thief - or anyone
else - as a guarantee (girou) not to be returned
until his own property had been restored. If the
thief happened to be a chief or one of his henchmen
(noukar), the 'detectives' were easily bribed to
drop their investigations, and if the victim himself
appeared he might well be beaten until he swore he
had secured reparation. Finally, Iranians recognised
no distinction between criminal and civil law:
thieves were not punished but had only to restore the
stolen property if caught; the same was true of
homicide, for which Russian law demanded the death
penalty, while Iranian law allowed reconciliation and
compensation. Ogranovich was clearly much frustrated
by a lack of precision in his instructions as to how
to deal with this situation. Many disputes were
solved, however, law and order improved, and new settlements were formed in Mughan, even on the Iranian
side.[26]

The summer of 1870 was one of unprecedented
drought, followed as in the rest of Iran by a terrible
famine, and by cholera and two harsh winters. According to Ogranovich the Shahsevan nomad population was
literally halved, and two-thirds of their flocks died.
Destitute families, where they survived the famine
and cholera, scattered into the settlements of eastern Transcaucasia to find food.[27]

Reports of frontier incidents in the 1870s mostly concern the Qojabeglu of Mishkin, now emerging as
the most powerful and lawless of the Shahsevan nomad

tribes. The winter of 1879-80 was again one of terrible famine in Azarbayjan, and Ardabil was among the
worst hit districts, though reports from the Shahsevan indicate that they were surviving these disasters well, largely through the success of their
raiding activities. In late summer 1883, the Heir
Apparent visited Ardabil to collect huge sums of
money as 'presents' from the Shahsevan chiefs, and
thoroughly alienated the tribes, but the troops and
artillery which he brought with him persuaded them
of the inadvisability of revolt, and the Prince succeeded in taking three of the most notorious chiefs
hostage. He was said to be as surprised as his subordinates at the manner in which his expedition had
escaped serious opposition and returned safely to
Tabriz.[28]

This autumn, 1883, the Russians put into effect
measures which led to a 'final solution' of their
Shahsevan problem, which they had been planning for
some years. Internal troubles and failures of policy
at St Petersburg, in addition to recent British successes in Afghanistan, had moved the Tsar to more
aggressive policy on his eastern frontiers, particularly in Central Asia.[29] In 1876 the Caucasian
Government entrusted E. Krebel with the Shahsevan
question, and he was instructed, on becoming Russian
Consul-General in Tabriz the following year, to go
to Mughan, report on the state of affairs, and advise
on Russian policy. Krebel visited Mughan in autumn
1878; on his return he reported that in the Shahsevan
affair there were two policies open to the Russian
authorities: either the nomads must be brought under
their complete control while they were in Mughan,
and all interference by Iranian officials or the
Shahsevan elbegis must cease; or the Shahsevan must
be prevented from coming to Mughan at all. At this
stage the Caucasian Government would not favour the
latter solution, as it would lead to loss of the
nomads' herds and to consequent further disorder and
intensified raiding, and moreover the Mughan settlers
would lose the nomads' pastoral produce on which they
depended; so the former policy was adopted.[30]

The Caucasian authorities drew up a list of
regulations to cover the administration of the Shahsevan, which was approved by the Tsar at the end of
1882. The main provisions were that the Shahsevan
should be subject to the Belasuvar Commissar during
their stay in Russian territory; the Commissar would
deal with the chiefs of individual tribes and not
with the elbegis, who must not interfere in the
nomads' affairs while in Russia; the Commissar might

grant or refuse admission to specific tribes at his own discretion; those admitted were to be shown their allotted grazing grounds and handed documents defining their boundaries; the Commissar, responsible to Baku and assisted by the tribal chiefs and by two police officers and a special detachment of 100 Cossacks (apart from the regular frontier garrisons), would hear and judge minor complaints and disputes, and would investigate more serious cases which became subject to martial law; persistent Shahsevan offenders must be deported to Iran. Trouble was anticipated, since no more than 6,000 families of the Shahsevan were expected to cross the frontier, while the same number customarily remained in Iran under the authority of the elbegis and Iranian officials, just the other side of a thin cordon of Cossacks.

During 1883 the Iranian Government was informed of these measures. Their request that they be permitted to send an official to co-operate with the Russian Commissar was refused, as it would have been contrary to the main purpose of the regulations. A further request for an Iranian vice-consul in Mughan was also turned down, as there was already a vice-consul in Baku who was free to visit Mughan as an observer. Having given the Iranian authorities time to warn the nomads of their new position, and also hoping that 'this new measure might persuade the Persian Government to try to end the migration of the Persian Shahsevan onto our territory, to which end it might set aside winter quarters for the Shahsevan within Persia', the Caucasian Command put their new policy into effect in autumn 1883.

As the nomads crossed the frontier, the Commissar officially informed them of the new system. The chiefs claimed they had not been warned, that the Governor of Ardabil had in fact told them to continue to obey their elbegis in everything. According to Markov, the Commissar met with no co-operation from the chiefs, and raiding and other crimes rose to their previous levels. The Commissar received claims from Russian subjects against the Shahsevan, for the 1883-4 winter season, amounting to some 35,500 roubles. The new system had failed; the Caucasian Administration decided the time had come for a 'final solution': the Shahsevan must be banned from Mughan, whatever the consequences.[31]

The Closure of the Frontier

The Russians had always regarded this ban as inevitable if not desirable, but hoped they would be able, by diplomatic means, to get the Iranians to initiate it. Russian nomads had now been banned from Iran, so the Iranians could no longer insist on the Shahsevan right of reciprocity.

In March 1884 the Heir Apparent was ordered, in response to the new system in Mughan,

> to proceed to the spot and make arrangements for the localization of such portion of these tribes as can settle down to a sedentary life. With regard to those whose circumstances render it impossible for them to do so, some place within the Persian borders is to be fixed for their annual migration.[32]

Presumably less than eager to face the Shahsevan again after his narrow escape of the previous year, The Prince asked his father for 100,000 tomans as expenses for the journey to Mughan; the Shah refused, so the Heir Apparent did not go. Instead, Muhammad Sadiq Khan Qajar, Amin Nizam, was appointed to this mission, and left Tabriz in May for Mishkin and Mughan to carry it out.[33] In the autumn, when the Russian envoy Melnikov raised the matter with the Iranian Government, he was assured that the Governor of Ardabil (Amin Nizam) had been commissioned to examine the question of settling the Shahsevan within Iran.

Finally in early November the Iranian Foreign Minister sent Melnikov the Note for which he had been waiting, stating that the Government could not accept the regulations which the Tsar had approved in 1882;

> Despite the fact that the prohibition of the nomad tribes from migration to their customary wintering places presents great difficulties and occasions these nomads a considerable loss, nevertheless the Iranian Government has forbidden them to return to that part of Mughan which is Russian territory and to remain in winter quarters there. It has been decreed that on no account are the Shahsevan to migrate to Mughan, nor to remain there in winter quarters. The necessary instructions have already been sent to the Azarbayjan authorities and to the Governor of Ardabil and Mishkin, concerning the

measures to be taken to prevent the Shahsevan
from returning to Mughan, and the implementation
of the present order. The Azarbayjan authorities have already, specially and seriously,
taken the necessary steps to carry out the
Imperial Decree, but as it may happen that several of the Shahsevan secretly escape to Mughan,
which would clearly be against the orders of
their Government, and as the Russian Government
is obliged by Treaty to return such fugitives,
Your Excellency will not neglect to instruct
the Russian frontier authorities in good time
not to allow those tribes to remain in Russian
territory. On their side the Iranian authorities will show the utmost diligence in preventing the Qojabeglu, Joruġhlu and other Shahsevan
tribes from crossing to Mughan, and in carrying
out the stated decrees.[34]

Meanwhile the Shahsevan prepared to cross the
frontier as usual, in spite of Iranian attempts to
stop them. It seemed likely that if they crossed,
the Russians would not let them return the following
spring, and so the Heir Apparent, with instructions
to stop the migration at all costs, left Tabriz for
Mughan in early November, since he had no alternative
but to present himself personally so as to prevent
the crossing of the Polatlu tribe, the nearest to
the frontier, whose moves would be followed by all
the others. He would not hesitate to use force if
necessary, and was considering the sedentarisation
of the nomads, in spite of the failure of such a
policy 24 years before.[35]

When he reached the Mughan frontier, he was met
by the Amin Nizam and Colonel Ogranovich. The latter, according to Markov, informed the Heir Apparent
'of the real state of affairs and of the oppressions
which the Shahsevan suffered from their self-
interested rulers'. The Prince told the Amin Nizam
that he hoped such excesses would cease. He stayed
on the frontier until early March 1885, and while
there was reported to have settled almost all the
Shahsevan tribes on the lands put aside for them.
The Shahsevan remained peaceful throughout the winter
and made no attempt to cross the frontier.[36]

The British Consul-General in Tabriz, William
Abbott, did not mention the Shahsevan during 1885,
the year when he wrote: 'Azerbaijan - bound hand and
foot by Russia, her trade crippled, her army in rags,
without a single carriageable road, corruption per-
meating every pore';[37] and the year when Hasan Ali

Khan Garusi, the Amir Nizam, became the Heir
Apparent's Minister (pishkar), took over the governorship of the province with a firm hand, and began
to clear up the mess.

In the autumn, however, on their return to winter quarters, the Shahsevan were desperate. On 25
November (Russian calendar) over 700 families broke
through the insufficient Iranian and Russian frontier guards, and were quickly followed by thousands
more, some of whom declared it their wish to escape
harassment by the Iranian authorities and to take
Russian citizenship or death rather than return. The
Russian authorities could not allow this, not least
since the Shahsevan were hardly desirable as immigrants, but also since Iranian permission would properly be required. They took hasty measures, sending
500 Cossacks as reinforcements to Mughan, and had
their envoy in Tehran request the Iranian Government
to prevent the incursions and to remove the Shahsevan
from the frontier. Meanwhile the Governor of Baku,
accompanied by the Commissar, went round the Shahsevan pastures in early December, trying to persuade
the nomads to return; when they refused, they were
granted two days' grace before they were driven out
by force. On 10 December the 500 Cossacks arrived
and set off in the direction of areas where nomads
were said to be encamped. The first day they came
across scattered camps, who packed up their tents
and possessions on the arrival of the troops and
headed back towards the frontier, promising they
would not stop until they had crossed back into
Iran; and they sent word to the elders of two other
tribes, the Nouruzalibeglu and the Jahankhanumlu, to
move on by the following day. Then reports arrived
that a mass of nomads was encamped in the centre of
the steppe, known as Aji, so an official was sent
to find out more, and to tell the camps to return to
Iran. On the second day the Jahankhanumlu camps
were found to be on the move as instructed, and the
troops quickly cleared their pastures and proceeded
towards Belasuvar, which they reached two days later
without coming across any further nomads. Meanwhile
their agent had returned with the information that
up to 1,500 nomad families were indeed encamped at
Aji; he was accompanied by several chiefs, who asked
for a few more days' grace, since their animals were
exhausted from the snow and from lack of fodder.
They were allowed four more days, until the 16th, in
which to leave Mughan.

On the 15th the Mughanlu, a large but peaceful
tribe, numbering perhaps 750 families, broke through

425

the cordon into Russian Mughan. Shots were exchanged, both sides suffering casualties, but the rest of
the nomads escaped into the centre of the steppe,
leaving many of their animals and possessions in
the hands of the Cossacks. The Russian Commander
took 200 men in pursuit, caught the Mughanlu after
35 kilometres, and surrounded them. Even though
exhausted, the nomads turned back and crossed the
frontier again by evening, having lost more of their
animals, including all their new-born lambs. They
claimed they had come over because of oppressions
suffered at the hands of the more warlike Polatlu
and Qojabeglu tribes, and because they had heard
that they would be allowed to stay until spring.
Several wretched groups of women and children and
6,000 of their sheep were captured; the former were
allowed to return to their camps, but the animals
were taken eventually to Belasuvar.

On the 18th it was learnt that the Aji camps
had not yet moved, and now wanted a further week's
grace. The Commander sent a detachment to clear
them out at once. By the evening of the 21st all
the camps were rounded up and led eventually across
the frontier. Large numbers of nomads were known to
have hidden among camps and villages in the Russian
border districts, so energetic measures were at once
put in train to find them and return them with all
their property to the Iranian authorities. Markov
claims that within five days all Iranian subjects
had been found and sent back, and that by 27
December Russian Mughan was clear of the Shahsevan
nomads.[38]

The Aftermath of the Closure

There remained the question of the confiscated property, which had now been sold. According to Markov,
the Governor of Baku and the Frontier Commissar
brought the matter to the attention of the Caucasian
Government, who asked the Russian Ministry of Finance
for money compensation to pay the nomads, but this
was refused on the grounds that the property was
contraband and had been legally sold, and that the
Shahsevan would learn a salutary lesson from their
loss. The Amir Nizam wrote to the Shah in 1886:

> Most of the Shahsevan tribes which had gone to
> Mughan have now returned, through either Russian
> measures or the diligence of our own officials
> ... As I have already reported, however, the

Russian officials have behaved most immoderately towards all those tribes which crossed over, and have not only confiscated their goods and baggage but have also seized over 20,000 of their sheep and caused them great loss. Although I have ... telegraphed to the Mir Panj [the Governor of Ardabil] strictly enjoining him to request Russian border officials to restore the property and flocks of the Shahsevan, and have also written a full account and sent it to [our consul] at Tiflis, there has been no sign from the Caucasian Government that the Shahsevan property and flocks are to be restored... a large section of the Shahsevan has been ruined.[39]

The Iranian Government pressed their request for compensation, saying the nomads might be forced to take up brigandage if they were left without their pastoral resources. Finally the Tsar was informed of the matter, and in May 1886 agreed to allow compensatory payment to the Shahsevan; although there is no record of this having been made, Markov writes that with it 'there ended the direct relations of Russia with the Persian nomads. From 1885 to the present [1889] the Shahsevan have continued to conduct themselves peaceably and have made no more attempts to cross our frontier.'[40] These complacent remarks were premature, to say the least, though the Shahsevan did remain within Iran that winter (1885-6), which was one of heavy snowfalls.
On Russian recommendation, Mustafa Quli Khan, the Mir Panj, Governor of Ardabil, had been sent to the frontier at the beginning of 1886 to take all possible measures in co-operation with the Russian authorities to restore order and to remove the most lawless groups far from the frontier. In the same letter quoted earlier, the Amir Nizam complained that the Mir Panj merely plundered two of the worst tribes, the Polatlu and the Qojabeglu.[41] In autumn the Amir Nizam, seen by all sides as a Russophile, and now 'alive to the importance of Persia scrupulously fulfilling her part of the agreement with Russia concerning the Shahsevans', decided to send the Mir Panj to Mughan again, with a large force, to prevent any further border infringements.[42]
The Mir Panj died during the winter, and was replaced as Governor of Ardabil by another Russian nominee, Asadullah Khan Vakil al-Mulk, who was persuaded to resign his post as Iranian Minister at St Petersburg. He found further drastic measures

against the Shahsevan to be necessary, and began by
arresting and blowing from the cannon's mouth two
chiefs, and imprisoning ten or twelve other Shahsevan notables at Ardabil, all of whom were said to
have raided extensively in both Russia and Iran.
Abbott reported gloomily in July 1887:

> If what I hear be correct, the Russian frontier
> officials are unable to prevent or rather now
> wink at the Shahsevends proceeding periodically
> to the Moghan - within the Russian border - to
> pasture their flocks, because the villagers in
> the Moghan have represented to the Russian
> commissary that they depend for their living
> upon the annual visits of these nomads. It is
> quite impossible on frontiers situated and cir-
> cumstanced as are those of Ardebil and the
> Moghan to put a permanent stop to brigandage
> and other excesses - Russia and Persia both
> suffer from these causes; but the result must
> eventually be that the weaker of the two coter-
> minous states will go to the wall, when Russia
> will annex the Shahsevend districts including
> Ardebil and convert these tribes into valuable
> irregular cavalry, utilizing them as she has
> the Turkoman tribes.

Order was for the moment maintained to the satisfaction of the Russian authorities, who attributed the
prevention of conflicts to the Vakil al-Mulk's
energy and tact; but the Shahsevan question was
seething, 'though dormant not dead, and at Russia's
signal may crop up at any moment.'[43]
If Abbott was right in his suspicions that
Shahsevan nomads were still being allowed to enter
Russian Mughan, it can only have occurred on a small
scale at this time. The Russians for their part
soon began to 'open up' the steppe for cultivation.
Markov, writing in 1889, summarises his justifica-
tions for the Tsarist Government's action in finally
excluding the Iranian nomads from Mughan, and discusses the immense development potential of the
steppe, concluding:

> the fact that the Shahsevan were forbidden
> to pasture in Mughan augurs well for this
> extensive part of the Baku Province; with the
> improvement of communications up to the out-
> skirts of Mughan itself, it will be cultivated
> all over and covered by tilled fields and
> cotton plantations ... Thus, at the present

> time, when the Persian nomads have been removed
> once and for all from our territory, Russia
> has the prospect of reaping the benefit of its
> territorial gain by the Treaty of Turkmanchay
> with Persia, and with this aim she must turn
> special attention to the canals scattered
> throughout Mughan and with the aid of irriga-
> tion turn this almost waterless plain into one
> of the richest granaries of the Transcaucasian
> region.[44]

A later writer noted that now 'the face of the
steppe began to change under the cultivation and
filled with settlers',[45] and the Shahsevan nomads
did not try to use Russian Mughan for pasturage
again until the year of the Bolshevik Revolution -
though their raids on the Russian settlers increased
in the years after the frontier closure.

Until the early years of the twentieth century
no major political disturbances brought the Shahsevan to the attention of the Iranian Government -
or that of the representatives of the two imperial
Powers who had been previously interested in their
activities. At this time, however, north-east Azarbayjan, and the Shahsevan tribes confined there,
were undergoing drastic social and economic upheavals, which were to erupt into political activity in
a few years, and whose causes were to be found not
simply in the frontier closure but also in the increased oppression perpetrated by the officials of
the Qajar administration. A detailed and depressing
picture of this upheaval and its immediate causes
was given by two further Russian officials - who did
not apparently appreciate the degree to which
Russian imperialism and rivalry with Britain in the
nineteenth century were largely responsible for both
the frontier closure and the abuses of the Iranian
administration. Markov, concerned only to justify
Russian action in closing the frontier and its benefits to the inhabitants of Russian Mughan, did not
consider its effects on the Iranian side. L.
Artamonov, however, who visited the region in
November 1889, a year after Markov, was shocked at
the poverty and oppression of the peasantry and the
obvious distress and disorder suffered by the nomads
as a result of the closure. Fourteen years later
Colonel L. Tigranov of the Russian General Staff
carried out an investigation of the region, and published an informative and perceptive account of the
economic and social conditions of the Ardabil province and of the nomad and settled Shahsevan

tribes.[46]

In effect, for almost forty years after the closure, the Shahsevan were in sustained rebellion against all external authority. The half dozen or so chiefs who had emerged by 1900 as the most effective leaders divided the pastures and village lands of the region between them and sent their armed henchmen to raid widely in neighbouring regions of Russia and Iran. These chiefs led not only their own tribes but clusters of smaller and weaker neighbours, who sent mounted warriors to serve as henchmen in return for protection of their pastures and flocks. The chiefs' suites were swollen by these tribal levies, by refugees from other tribes, and by villagers who found settled agricultural pursuits increasingly difficult in prevailing conditions.

In 1909 most of the Shahsevan joined a coalition of local tribes in revolt against the Constitutionalist Government, and their plunder of the city of Ardabil received wide coverage in the European press. These and other exploits gave Russia an excuse for sending troops to subdue the tribesmen, but neither they nor various Iranian military expeditions had lasting success, being more often subjected to severe loss. The Shahsevan tribesmen retained control of the region until 1923, when they were finally defeated and disarmed by the troops of the War Minister Riza Khan, later Riza Shah Pahlavi.[47]

With the Shahsevan disarmed and many of their chiefs captured or executed, the region enjoyed a decade of unprecedented security. Agriculture revived, land ownership became more profitable, and the nomads too grazed their flocks in unusual tranquillity. Though by now the Ardabil tribes were almost all settled and administered in villages, most of the Mishkin groups remained nomadic and continued to winter in Iranian Mughan. An Army officer was appointed as elbegi over the nomads and made responsible for political security. Individual tribes were now recognised as independent fiscal and political units, with their chiefs as representatives expected to deal with officials of the administration. The former tribal clusters did not disappear, however, but reformed on a new basis. Both the authorities and the smaller tribes found it expedient to deal with each other through the more powerful chiefs. Their power in the new situation depended no longer on military force, but on material resources and their ability and willingness to use these to the advantage of followers in new ways, mainly as middlemen.

Further reforms of the Riza Shah period affected the nomads more directly. The young men were
subjected to conscription and men's traditional
dress was banned in favour of 'European' suits and
hats. Far more drastic, however, were the outlawing
in the 1930s of the Shahsevan tents and the ban on
migrations, measures which were brutally enforced.
The nomads were told to build houses and start cultivation. The results were catastrophic for them and
their flocks. By 1941, with the fall of Riza Shah
and the Allied invasion of Iran, the Shahsevan along
with other nomads reverted to their former way of
life, which they pursued unchecked throughout the
Soviet occupation of Azarbayjan (1941-6). The tribal clusters regained some of their military importance, under those chiefs who had acquired or consolidated their economic resources in the two previous
decades.

After the return to Iranian administration in
1946, there was a steady reduction in the chiefs'
power. Economic and political security and communications all improved, and in 1960 the chiefs were
deposed from recognised positions of authority. In
the 1960s the 30 to 40 Shahsevan tribes of the region formed a loose confederation under the effective
administration of the Central Government, with the
Army, the Gendarmerie, and the Court system as ultimate sanctions for the maintenance of order. Individual chiefs still wielded considerable local influence and played an important political role in
Shahsevan affairs, but the last foundations of their
power were being undermined as a result of Land
Reform, and the significance of the tribe as a political unit was declining.

Since the last war, intensive efforts have been
made to develop the Iranian part of Mughan. A
Government-sponsored irrigation scheme was initiated
in 1951, and commenced functioning a few years later.
Private schemes also began farming elsewhere in
Mughan, both irrigated and rain-fed crops, mainly of
wheat and cotton. The dry-farming at least expanded
unwarrantedly, but surveys have declared the region
to be potentially one of the most productive in Iran
and urged the intensive development of the pastoral
sector, given the nation's growing demand for livestock products and particularly meat. In the 1970s
a further scheme, involving Soviet co-operation with
dam construction on the Aras, expanded the irrigation network in Mughan to over 70,000 hectares. In
1972 it was announced that Mughan was to be the
centre of an agro-industrial complex and the Shah-

sevan people were to continue exploiting the region's
rangelands from settled bases and with modernised
technology. It would appear, however, that the Shahsevan were largely left out of consideration in the
eventual implementation of these plans, and were
rather subjected to increasing oppression in Mughan
by officials and entrepreneurs from outside the
region, while their pastures were nationalised and
pastoralism generally declined. This writer has
heard little of their situation since the Khumeyni
revolution. In spring 1979, 400 camp leaders from
30 Shahsevan tribes apparently went to Qum to present
the Ayatullahs Khumeyni and Shariat-madari with a
list of requests for the removal of oppressive
officials, the improvement of their conditions of
production and the provision of health and education
facilities.[48] As elsewhere, they probably will have
reclaimed their pastures and restored the pasture
tenure system of the 1960s, which had its origins
in the events described in this chapter.[49]

NOTES

1. This chapter is based on chapter 8 of my 'The Shahsavan of Azarbaijan: a study of economic and political change
in a Middle Eastern tribal society', unpublished PhD thesis,
University of London, 1972. I am most grateful to Leslie
Collins, Caroline Humphrey and Michael Cook for translations
from Russian sources, and to Ann Lambton, Sandy Morton and
Nancy Tapper for helpful comments on early drafts.
2. The origins and early history of the Shahsevan are
traced in my 'Shahsevan in Ṣafavid Persia', *BSOAS*, 37, 2
(1974), pp. 321-54. Another paper on the Shahsevan in the
eighteenth century is in preparation, based like the former
on chapters from my 'The Shahsavan of Azarbaijan'.
3. F.B. Rostopchin, 'Zametki o Shakhsevenakh', *Sovetskaya
Etnografiya*, 3/4 (1933), p. 98; G. Radde, *Reisen an der
persisch-russischen Grenze. Talysch und seine Bewohner*
(Brockhaus, Leipzig, 1886), p. 428; V. Markov, 'Shakhseveni na
Mugani. Istoriko-etnograficheskiy ocherk', *ZKORGO*, 19, 1
(1890), p. 25; Abbott to Sheil, no. 17 of 27 Mar. 1847, FO
248/125.
4. N. von Seidlitz, 'Etnograficheskiy ocherk Bakinskoy
gubernii', *Kavkazskiy Kalendar na 1871 god* (Tiflis, 1870),
part 2, pp. 1-67.
5. Markov, 'Shakhseveni', pp. 23-4.
6. On the position of nomads in Russian territory at
this time, see the most informative article, based on extensive study of contemporary official records, by D.I. Ismail-
zade, 'Iz istorii kochevogo khozyaystva Azerbaydzhana pervoy

polovini XIX v.', *Istoricheskie Zapiski*, 66 (1960), pp. 96-136.

7. A.K.S. Lambton, *Landlord and Peasant in Persia* (Oxford University Press, 1953), p. 150.

8. For example, E. d'Arcy Todd, 'Itinerary from Tabríz to Tehrán *via* Ahar, Mishkín, Ardabíl, Tálish, Gílán and Kazvín, in 1837', *JRGS*, 8 (1838), pp. 30-4; W.R. Holmes, *Sketches on the shores of the Caspian* (London, 1845); K.E. Abbott, 'Narrative of a Journey from Tabriz along the shores of the Caspian Sea, to Tehran', MS in FO 251/40.

9. I.A. Ogranovich, 'Svedeniya o Shakhsevenakh', *Kavkazskiy Kalendar na 1871 god* (Tiflis, 1870), part 1, pp. 68-84; id., 'Provintsii Persii Ardebilskaya i Serabskaya', *ZKORGO*, 10 (1876), pp. 141-235; Radde, *Reisen*, pp. 418-43; Markov, 'Shakhseveni'; cf. Tapper 'Shahsevan in Safavid Persia', p. 331.

10. Cf. J. Morier, 'Some account of the Íliyáts, or wandering tribes of Persia ...', *JRGS*, 7 (1837), pp. 239-41; Ismail-zade, 'Iz istorii', p. 111.

11. Radde, *Reisen*, p. 429; Markov, 'Shakhseveni', p. 25.

12. Stevens to Sheil, no. 3 of 13 Jan. 1850, FO 248/142; FO to Bloomfield, no. 25 of 29 Jan. 1850, FO 97/345; Bloomfield to Palmerston, no. 77 of 8 Mar. 1850, FO 65/376; same to same, no. 324 of 22 Oct. 1850, FO 65/380; Markov, 'Shakhseveni', p. 27.

13. I.A. Ogranovich, 'Shakhsevani na Muganskoy stepi', articles in various issues of *Kavkaz* (Tiflis), 1872, quoted in Rostopchin, 'Zametki', p. 101; also Radde, *Reisen*, pp. 429-30; Markov, 'Shakhseveni', p. 26; Ogranovich, 'Svedeniya', pp. 74-5.

14. Muḥammad Taqī Lisān al-Mulk Sipihr, *Tārīkh-i Qājāriyeh*, vol. 14 of *Nāsikh al-Tavārīkh*, ed. J. Qā'im-Maqāmī (Tehran, 1337/1958), part 3, pp. 76, 111f.; Stevens to Sheil, no. 3 of 13 Jan. 1850, FO 248/142.

15. Stevens to Sheil, no. 51 of 12 June 1851, no. 80 of 4 Sept. 1851, and no. 105 of 10 Dec. 1851, FO 248/145; also Sheil to FO, no. 19 of 26 June 1851, and no. 35 of 24 Sept. 1851, FO 60/166; Muhammad Taqi, *Tarikh*, p. 111; Markov, 'Shakhseveni', p. 27.

16. Markov, 'Shakhseveni, p. 24.

17. IOL: 'Papers relative to the Affairs of Persia, Jan.-Dec. 1856', LPS/20, A.7, 2, p. 237.

18. Markov, 'Shakhseveni', pp. 27-9; Abbott to Murray, no. 11 of 23 Feb. 1858, and no. 13 of 3 March 1858, FO 248/177; Murray to Malmesbury, no. 17 of 3 July 1858, FO 60/232; Dickson to Rawlinson, no. 3 of 22 Jan. 1860, FO 248/192.

19. Ogranovich, 'Provintsii', p. 201.

20. Abbott to Alison, no. 13 and no. 14 of 23 July 1860, and no. 38 of 29 Nov. 1860, FO 248/192.

21. Abbott to Pelly, no. 1 of 13 June 1860, ibid.

22. Abbott to Alison, no. 12 of 17 June 1860, ibid. Cf.

K.E. Abbott, 'Narrative'.

23. Abbott to Alison, no. 38 of 29 Nov. 1860, FO 248/192.

24. Alison to Abbott, no. 2 of 13 Mar. 1861, FO 248/201.

25. Abbott to Alison, no. 14 of 17 Apr. 1861, FO 248/199. Earlier, in 'Narrative', Abbott reported that the Shahsevan 'are not accused of marauding and pillaging on a large scale'; his more recent opinion coincided with that of the Russians, e.g. Radde, *Reisen,* pp. 423-4, Markov, 'Shakhseveni', p. 21.

26. Markov, 'Shakhseveni', pp. 33f; Radde, *Reisen,* pp. 435-6.

27. Ogranovich, 'Provintsii', p. 201; cf. id., 'Shakh-sevani', as quoted by Rostopchin, p. 104; Baron M. von Thielmann, *Journey in the Caucasus, etc.,* tr. C. Heneage (Murray, London, 1875), vol. 2, p. 29.

28. Bernay to Thomson, enclosed in Thomson to Granville, 2 Oct. 1883, FO 248/400. (The French Consul, M. Bernay, was acting for British Consul-General W. Abbott, on leave.)

29. Cf. F. Kazemzadeh, *Russia and Britain in Persia, 1864-1914* (Yale University Press, New Haven, 1968), pp. 57f.

30. Markov, 'Shakhseveni', pp. 37f.; Abbott to Thomson, no. 55 of 21 Oct. 1878, FO 450/8.

31. Markov, 'Shakhseveni', pp. 41f.

32. Thomson to FO, no. 57 of 5 Apr. 1884, FO 60/460.

33. Bernay to Thompson, letters of 6 May, 17 July and 31 Aug. 1884, FO 248/413.

34. Quoted in Markov, 'Shakhseveni', pp. 49-50.

35. Bernay, in Thompson to FO, no. 173 of 27 Nov. 1884, FO 60/461. W. Abbott sent Thompson a long review of the situation when he returned in December: no. 6 of 28 Dec. 1884, FO 60/464, also in FO 450/8 and FO 248/413.

36. Markov, 'Shakhseveni', pp. 50f.

37. Abbott to Thompson, no. 25 of 21 Sept. 1885, FO 248/425.

38. Markov, 'Shakhseveni', pp. 51-7. Unfortunately Markov, the sole source for the events of autumn 1885, was a Tsarist agent whose main purpose was clearly to justify Russian actions and presumably to cover up their errors and injustices; I have extracted the more circumstantial data from his account, but they still need to be treated with reserve.

39. Ḥasan ʿAlī Khan Amīr Niẓām Garusī, *Munshaʿat-i Amīr Niẓām,* ed. M. Mahdī (Tabriz, 1328/1910), p. 182.

40. Markov, 'Shakhseveni', p. 57.

41. Hasan Ali Khan, *Munshaʿat,* p. 182; but in another letter, ibid., pp. 94-6, he is more complimentary, and notes the arrest of the elbegi of the Ardabil Shahsevan.

42. Abbott to Nicolson, 29 Aug. 1886, FO 248/438.

43. Same to same, no. 6 of 16 July and no. 8 of 27 July 1887, FO 248/449. Abbott's fear that the Shahsevan would be recruited by the Russians as irregular cavalry was shared by the American envoy, S.W.G. Benjamin, *Persia and the Persians* (Murray, London, 1887), pp. 479-80.

44. Markov, 'Shakhseveni', pp. 58-62.

45. M. Avdeev, *Mugan i Salyanskaya Step* (Baku, 1927), p. 15.

46. L.K. Artamonov, *Severniy Azerbaydzhan. Voyenno-geogr. ocherk* (Tiflis 1890); L.F. Tigranov, *Iz obshchestvenno-ekonomicheskikh etnosheniy v Persii* (St Petersburg, 1909).

47. The role of the Shahsevan in the years up to and including the Constitutional Revolution is discussed in my 'Raiding, reaction and rivalry: the Shahsevan tribes in the Constitutional period', forthcoming in M. Bayat (ed.), *The Constitutional Revolution in Iran*.

48. S. Taymāz, *Seh maqāleh dar bāreh-yi Turkmān-ṣaḥrā, Dasht-i Mughān, va rūstāhā-yi dīgar* (Ilm, Tehran, 1979). I am indebted to Martin van Bruinessen for bringing this to my notice.

49. See L. Beck, 'Revolutionary Iran and its tribal peoples', *MERIP Reports,* no. 87 (May 1980).

Chapter 15
THE TRIBAL SOCIETY AND ITS ENEMIES

Ernest Gellner

The notion of the tribe has a variety of meanings: a
'primitive' tribe is sometimes conceived as an island
unto itself, morally and conceptually. The tribal
ancestor may in such cases be seen as the first man
as such, and the inclusion of non-members of the
tribe in humanity itself may be ambiguous. Such a
'closed' tribe then may or may not be a political
unit, but it certainly is a cultural one. The
limits of the society are the limits of a culture,
and the limits of the culture are the limits of the
world, and vice versa.
    This, I think, is the ideal type of <u>the tribe
as a Closed Society</u>. Whether and to what extent
such a concept has much application, may for the
time being be left to those who deal with such communities, or communities which look, prima facie, as
if they might fit this model. What however is beyond any doubt whatever is that the model has no
application to the communities customarily called
tribes in the Middle East (or rather, such as are
generically described, in the local languages, by
terms conventionally translated as 'tribe'). In
fact, one might well invert the characterisation of
the primitive closed society: these tribes may or
may not be cultural units, but they certainly are
political ones. Their political role may perhaps
not exhaust their essence, but it is a central part
of it. By contrast, their cultural role and differentiation, though it exists, is not very marked. The
tribe does not fill out the world, but defines itself in terms borrowed from a wider civilisation.
You can identify a woman's tribal allegiance by her
cloak, head-dress or jewellery, you may tell a man's
membership of a community by his accent; but the
amount of cultural equipment shared by diverse
tribes outweighs the part which is used to indicate

436

distinctiveness. In brief: in the Middle East and
culturally similar adjoining areas, tribes may be
distinct politically, but they are not separated
culturally or economically from a wider surrounding
world, which comprises both other tribes and non-
tribal populations.

These tribes exist in a cultural continuum.
This continuum has, for a millenium and a half, been
dominated by Islam. 'Muslim civilisation' is an
appropriate name for this shared culture of the arid
zone, notwithstanding the presence in it of non-
Muslim minorities and enclaves. It is probably fair
to say of most or all of these that they share the
cultural styles and assumptions of the Muslim majority, even if they do not formally endorse their supposed theological premisses. A more important qual-
ification arises from the plurality of cultural
layers present in Muslim civilisation itself. The
shared culture within which local communities articulate themselves is not necessarily identical in
its tacit assumptions (however these may be identified) with that which a formally trained and widely
recognised Muslim scholar would class as proper,
orthodox Islam. Islam is, so to speak, a normative
culture: it contains as part of itself procedures
for determining what is and is not part of itself -
criteria such as conformity to scriptural authority,
to well-attested Traditions concerning the life of
the Prophet and his Companions, communal consensus,
or valid argument from analogy. These criteria and
their applications are themselves sometimes contested: Islam is, to use Bryce Gallie's valuable philo-
sophical phrase-slogan,[1] an Essentially Contested
Concept (even though it may think of itself as an
Essentially Fixed or Immutable one). This is part
and parcel of its life, and the sociological observer must note it, even though it is none of his business to adjudicate in these disputes. But it is
highly relevant to the present subject: the culture
which these tribesmen share is Muslim, but not
necessarily, nor generally, altogether in conformity
with what the schoolmen would approve, though it is
continuous with it.

There is a certain danger here for anthropologists. Eager to avoid the normative stance of theo-
logians and of some orientalists, anthropologists
sometimes fall over themselves to insist that the
superstitions of the most 'ignorant' old woman are
as good a social fact, as much a part of the local
culture (more so, probably), as the ruling of a local
learned scholar. I remember distinguished experts

on Middle Eastern societies using this point on me
with insistence and anxiety, evidently suspecting
any attempt to isolate conceptually purer and less
pure variants of the faith as some kind of irrelevant, extraneously imposed, interfering, ethnocent-
ric censoriousness. Not so. The superstitions of
the ignorant are social facts as much as (or more
so than) the learning of the scholars; but the fact
that the scholars are deferred to, that the culture
itself stratifies its own practices into lower and
higher ones (even if it persists with the lower),
and in favourable circumstances tries to impose the
higher and eliminate the lower, is itself one
further social fact. In our time, which favours, in
the Muslim world, self-purification and revival
movements, it happens to be a supremely important
one. To neglect it, in the name of a misguided
Wertfreiheit, is disastrous. It is not for us to
judge what is or is not pure, in the societies we
study; but it is for us to note that the locals
themselves are preoccupied with the distinction, and
whilst admittedly they often sin against it, they
are also on occasion powerfully influenced by it.

   So much by way of preliminary about the cultural background of the political communities of the
Muslim arid zone. It is their politics which primarily concern us, but the cultural idiom in which
they are expressed cannot be ignored.

   What, then, are these 'tribes'?

   The definition I would propose would run something as follows:

   A tribe is a local mutual-aid association,
whose members jointly help maintain order internally
and defend the unit externally. This assumption of
peace-keeping and collective defence responsibility,
which thus defines the tribe, is contrasted with a
situation in which the maintenance of order, and
defence, is assured by the central state and its
specialised agencies (courts, nominated officials,
police forces, army).

   It follows from this definition (as is intended) that the contrast between centrally governed and
tribal areas is one which allows of gradation and
continuity. If all peace-keeping and defence responsibilities are permanently taken over by the
central state, we can no longer speak of tribes at
all (though named communities with shared sentiments
might conceivably survive); but there often is a
sharing of these responsibilities. A tribe may retain all or some of these responsibilities (though
if it retains none, it will cease to be a tribe).

A very characteristic situation is of course one in
which a leader with a tribal power-base is also confirmed as an agent of the state and granted a bureaucratic title. One may then ask whether he is
imposing the central order on the tribe, or defending the tribe against the state. A clear answer to
such a question probably belongs either to depth
psychology or to metaphysics (or indeed both): at
the level of visible social reality, it is precisely
the ambiguity of his status which is of the essence
of the situation.

These units may but need not be defined in
terms of kinship. In the area which concerns us,
they are generally patrilineal (the Tuareg of the
central Sahara are the only significant exception to
this within arid-zone Islam), but they invariably
possess devices for incorporating individuals and
groups without the benefit of the appropriate ancestry, and on occasion groups are defined by other
(notably territorial) criteria, in defiance of the
alleged predilection of such communities for the
genealogical principle.

The most significant trait of these groups is
the simultaneous coexistence of diverse groups at
different levels of size. This is a familiar, but
none the less extremely important theme in the discussion of 'segmentary' societies: the tribe resembles the tribal 'confederation' of which it is a
part, but it also resembles the 'clans' into which
it is divided, and so forth. This concept of segmentation derives of course from the classical work
of Evans-Pritchard on the Nuer and on the bedouin of
Cyrenaica, and his adaptation of Durkheim's concept
of segmentarity, by his stress on the vertical similarity of nested groups, as well as the lateral
resemblance of co-ordinate groups stressed by
Durkheim. (Durkheim was in fact perfectly familiar
with the existence of vertical similarity, from his
knowledge of Algerian material, but treated it as a
special highly-developed form of segmentation, without apparently understanding its full significance.
If segmentation is treated as the most important way
of achieving cohesion and the maintenance of order,
then, given the fact that conflict is liable to
arise at diverse levels, segmentation and balanced
opposition must likewise be present at diverse
levels.)

One may put the matter in this way: arid-zone
tribalism is a technique of order-maintenance which
dispenses with the specialised enforcement agencies
that are associated with the state (and, in a way,

439

are the state). They dispense with political specialisation internally as well as externally. They
not merely prevent the police of the central state
from imposing its will, they also refrain from having any internal police force of their own. Internally, they use the same technique as they do externally: order inside the tribe is maintained by
mutually-policing sub-tribes (clans, if you wish),
whose mutual opposition forces each of them to restrain its own members; and so on.

The characteristic form of social stratification in such societies is one in which the large
majority of adult males are formally equal, and
qualified to participate in politics and violence,
entitled and obliged to share the risks of feud and
the benefits of blood money. This is quite unlike
feudalism, in which a fairly small warrior stratum
monopolises politics and violence. Below the broad
tribesman stratum, subject minorities of slaves,
oasis cultivators and petty artisans are to be found,
with whom tribesmen ideally do not intermarry; above
them, there is a sometimes ambivalently viewed religious aristocracy (as Tocqueville already noted,
contrasting it with the noblesse d'épée of Europe),
which however enjoys the effective advantages of its
special status only when effective leadership is
conjoined with attribution of appropriate birth.
Within the dominant middle stratum, Big Men and
chiefly lineages often emerge, but their position
seems precarious and they do not seem to engender
any deep and permanent stratification. The ethos
characteristic of this large central stratum seems
to express the organisational principles of such
'mechanically solidary' society: it contains a marked disapproval of specialism, political and economic
(which does not prevent members of this stratum from
taking to specialist trade when opportunities are
favourable, or aspiring to political pre-eminence
when the situation is ripe). Only religious specialism is tolerated traditionally, and even that with
occasional ambivalence. Under modern conditions of
centralisation, all this seems to become inverted:
political and economic specialisation becomes possible and is favoured, whilst religious inequality,
pretension to differential access to the divine, is
subjected to severe criticism from Reform movements.
It seems to me that Dale Eickelman is in error in
his interesting Moroccan Islam,[2] when he suggests
that dyadic, asymmetrical relations between men are
reflected by similar relations in the spiritual
sphere; it seems to me that the relationship is

inverse, and a symmetrical society favoured asymmetrical patronage in religion, whilst a centralising patronage-ridden society veers towards an enthusiasm for the equality of believers. The Other world does not always mirror, but sometimes inverts, the relations of this world. But we are here concerned with the old world of the tribes, which is still vigorous in many places.

It is overwhelmingly tempting to say that the ecological basis of this form of tribalism is pastoralism, though it would be rash and probably wrong to say that extensive pastoralism necessarily imposes this form of organisation. Pastoralism, which implies a form of wealth which is mobile, on the hoof, makes political domination much harder than is the case in agrarian societies tied to the land. It is hard to oppress shepherds, for they can run away and, above all, can run away with much of their wealth intact. Moreover, a shepherd is primarily a guardian of flocks, against wild animals and, most of all, other shepherds. His defensive vigilance develops skills which are just as usable in aggressive as in defensive violence, and he will of course, given the opportunity, use them in order to raid, as much as to ward off being raided. But his only hope of security lies in being a member of a mutual-insurance group, which jointly announces to the world that it will avenge the death of any one of its members, indiscriminately, on any member of the group from which the aggressor was drawn or is supposed to have come. This implicit announcement provides the other and rival group with an incentive to restrain its own members, unless it is willing to face vengeance directed against the group as a whole. The argument applies to groups of groups as much as to groups of individuals, and results in that characteristic pattern of 'nested' groups, generally found in this area and adjoining ones. One should add that whilst this pattern is most characteristic of pastoralism, it tends to be emulated by neighbouring sedentary groups if they have the opportunity. The mountains offer as good a protection from the state as does the savannah, and a similar form of organisation is as characteristic of mountain populations of this zone as it is of mobile pastoralists.

The characteristic form of ownership in this kind of society, as the Russian anthropologist and historian A.M. Khazanov pointed out,[3] is private ownership of cattle and tribal ownership of pasture. Pasture can only be defended collectively, whilst flocks and herds are surveyed by much smaller groups, though these may still cluster together in camp units for greater security.

This tribalism, then, is a political solution to a political problem. It is an alternative to the state. Everything stated so far, though perhaps not uncontentious, has hardly been original. But it raises questions which, when properly answered on the basis of material such as that assembled in this volume, will constitute a significant advance in our understanding of human society.

The interesting thing about the tribal solution to the political problem of order-maintenance, is that it is a solution which consists of combining political autonomy with cultural and economic dependence. These tribal societies are accustomed to a level of technology, in their agricultural, pastoral, military and domestic equipment, which seems to presuppose centres of artisan production and trade, in other words towns, and this in turn presupposes protection of towns by a specialised agency (towns in this part of the world seem rarely capable of looking after their own defence), in other words, the state. Likewise, the religious ecology, so to speak, of these tribesmen presupposes not only the sanctity or holiness easily found in their own midst, incarnated in special lineages, but also centres of scholarship, perpetuating and affirming the literate theology of a scripturalist religion. Thus religion too seems to reinforce and/or symbolise the economico-cultural dependency of politically autonomous tribes.

In the social organisation of pastoral or partly pastoral tribes, we find a kind of spectrum. At one end, there are pastoralists with minimal organisation, where the neat pyramid favoured by the theorists of segmentation is largely absent. In the middle, we find the neat, aesthetically-pleasing, 'nested' groups; and at the other extreme, we find tribal tyrannies with dominant individuals or lineages. What causes this variety? It is tempting to seek the answer in the relationship to the central state. The anomic absence of clearly-defined groups may be the consequence both of a strong and a weak state: a strong state may have destroyed them, a very weak one, rendered them redundant. The absence of such groups (exemplified by some pastoralists and nomads from other parts of the world) may be due to lack of pressure from other groups and from the state (which may be wholly absent). One is tempted by the supposition that the cohesive nested groupings

which continue, probably correctly, to be the main
stereotype of Middle Eastern tribalism, arise as a
reaction of population pressure on resources, reinforced by pressure from the state itself as one of
the contestants.

Another issue which arises is the nature of the
economico-cultural dependency of these otherwise
proudly independent tribesmen. Is it inherent in
their economy? Is it so essentially non-autarchic
that it needs artisans and tradesmen, come what may,
simply for survival? Or does the existence of pastoral tribalism elsewhere (e.g. in East Africa),
where it did not seem to have such an intimate relationship to political/urban centres, prove that the
dependency is only engendered by the habituation to
a certain cultural standard?

Paradoxically, if the tribe is an alternative
to the state, it is also often a mini-state in itself, and, on the other hand, often also aspires to
capturing the state and becoming its centre. One
criticism of the segmentary model sometimes encountered insists that the model overrates the equality
and power-diffusion within such tribes, mistaking
ideology or wish for reality. No doubt: power does
often crystallise within such groups. The 'balancing' mechanisms are indeed precarious. The balance
often topples over, one side prevails under personal
leadership, and the leader becomes, for a time, a
possessor of great power, which can then stay in his
lineage for generations. A tribe may also need
strong leadership for all kinds of reasons, such as
for instance ensuring, by mixture of diplomacy and
violence, access to a pass crucial for its migrations. Leadership or group union may even be crystallised from urban centres by urban suppliers of arms,
and not always by the state.

There is again an entire spectrum, ranging from
rather small Big Men to really effective and powerful tribal Big Men. As Raymond Jamous has shown,[4]
the customary law of certain northern Moroccan tribes
actually drew the distinction between a situation in
which there was a Big Man in the segment, and one in
which there was not. The Urf called for a different
situation according to which of these alternatives
applied. Jamous' work constitutes an important cor-
rective to the extremely valuable and unjustly for-
gotten pioneering work of Robert Montagne,[5] who was
the first to draw attention forcefully to the tendency of such tribal societies to oscillate between
the 'republican' oligarchy of household heads, and
ephemeral personal tyrannies. Montagne's preoccupa-

tion with the very big Grand Caids gave the impression, which he may not have intended, that the oscillation had to be extremely polar, so to speak: that
there was either a very big robber chief, or the
assembly, the jemaa. In fact, there is room on the
spectrum and in reality for quite small Big Men. But
their existence does not destroy the usefulness of
the segmentary model which, in fact, is required to
explain why and how they emerge and why they do not
last. The tribal state of this kind is essentially
reversible: it does not seem to modify the conditions
which have engendered it.

This instability, and the variety of forms it
can engender, should I think be incorporated in segmentary theory, rather than be allowed to count as
its refutation. It shows that the over-idealised,
idyllic picture of symmetrical diffusion of power,
often, very often, does not apply. But it does not
destroy it, for a variety of reasons. The segmentary
diffusion of power remains a kind of baseline from
which this game started and, significantly, to which
it often reverts. Political centralisation in this
kind of society has a fragile, reversible character,
which distinguishes it from easily-dominated agrarian zones. Moreover, even when it loses its symmetrical character, it still has, to use S. Andreski's
useful phrase, a very high Military Participation
Ratio - even when, temporarily, the Political
Participation Ratio is drastically reduced.[6]

The question about whether we should see the
religious and cultural continuity of this society as
essential or accidental, as reflecting an ecological
dependency or, on the contrary, as historically contingent, also relates to the issue of the role of
religious personnel, both in keeping the tribal
system going by oiling its joints, and in suspending
it by facilitating the emergence of wider enthusiasms
and more effective centralisation. A fair amount has
been written on this question, but it is unlikely to
be fully settled for a long time.

The tribes sometimes engenders an internal
mini-state, and sometimes captures the larger maxi-
state. How central is or was religion to this process, permitting the fusion of urban enthusiasm and
tribal greed, providing the ideological joker card
which can trump the mutually neutralising ambitions
of the locally-tied sacred of the dervishes and the
marabout? To what extent can the state save itself
from tribal aggression by purchasing (or tax-
collecting) its own elite on the Mamluk, devshirme
and janissary principles, securing its members from

Tribal Society and its Enemies

rude environments and training them in isolation
from the temptations and pressures of kin connections, which otherwise seemed to be the only basis
and training for politico-military effectiveness?
Given the importance and longevity of the Ottoman
Empire, and of the Mamluk system within it, can it
be treated as atypical? In the tribal-central relations, did the flow of subsidies to supposedly loyal
chiefs exceed the payments extorted in taxation, or
was it the other way round?
     So, to sum up the situation: the tribe is an
alternative to the state. Is it engendered in part
by the threat of the state? Is it destroyed when a
strong state no longer tolerates it, or even when a
weak one makes it redundant? Is it above all the
relationship to the central state which, by providing an opportunity for ambition, turns the tribe
itself into a mini-state internally? When does it
itself capture the state? The tribal mechanisms
which evolve to evade the arm of the state seem
paradoxically also to fit the populations involved
in it to create a new state, and sometimes to build
a micro-state of their own.
     The view of Middle Eastern tribalism which I
have sketched out places it firmly in a certain context: tribalism emerges as pastoral and rural self-
administration, partial or complete, with many
nuances and intermediate forms and oscillations, but
presupposing an economic and cultural interdependence
with non-tribal units, notably towns, and often
brought into being as a reaction to non-tribal political forces, notably the state. The state differs
from the tribe in having a much more developed division of labour: it has full-time warriors and officials, sustained by the labour of peasants, artisans
and traders.
     In other words, this picture of Middle Eastern
tribalism is tied to an overall picture of Middle
Eastern society. This view, and hence the picture
of tribalism which it incorporates, has of late encountered various criticisms. The most prominent
critics can be placed in various groups. These
groups are not mutually exclusive: a man may certainly belong to more than one of them. They are defined
by the underlying intellectual motive or counter-idea
which inspires them. The groups I have in mind are
nationalists, Marxists, and followers of Clifford
Geertz. Nationalists and Marxists both dislike the
stability (perjoratively: stagnation) which the model
seems to attribute to Middle Eastern society as a
whole, notwithstanding its internal political turbu-

lence. Nationalists in addition dislike the stress on tribal units and the distinctive culture associated with Muslim tribalism, notably its religious aspect, which they prefer to see as a corrupt rather than an authentic version of local life (sometimes as one artificially encouraged by colonialism). Marxists combine a distaste for the overall stability of the system (notwithstanding the fact that Friedrich Engels endorsed this view in so many words) with a scepticism concerning the partial egalitarianism attributed to tribal society, and the inadequate concern with class conflict. The theme running through the work of anthropologists of Geertzian persuasion seems to be scepticism about the categories in terms of which the model is articulated, notably segmentation and the sharp opposition of government to tribal dissidence.[7] Like the nationalists, though presumably for other reasons, they suspect these notions of being projections of colonial anthropology or those influenced by it. Both individual manipulation and a shared culture are more prominent in their analyses, within which these two as it were corrosive agents (from my viewpoint) dissolve the unduly neat units (in their view) in terms of which the model is articulated.

No doubt it is a good thing that these questions should remain open and be explored further. For the time being, however, I must confess that I am less than convinced by the critics. Compared with the cataclysmic transformation wrought by the diffusion of industrialism (of which colonialism was merely the outward political expression), most traditional or agrarian societies must seem 'stable'. I do not think the attribution of stability should be seen as pejorative. Many past societies have valued stability and many of us rue its loss. The question concerning whether this or that society had an overall stability should be investigated without any spirit of attributing merit. Similarly, the existence of a tribal Little Culture, which does not meet the standards of an old Great Tradition, should not be denied for the past simply because it no longer satisfies the needs of a more urbanised, centralised, literate society which has replaced it. As for the third set of criticisms, one can only answer that a wide range of well-attested institutions - the feud, collective oath, a legal system relying heavily on arbitration, marriage patterns, pasture use - only makes sense on the assumptions of something like the model propounded. Both ethnography and history seem to me to support the model. But, no doubt, it will benefit

from criticism. One salient fact which seems to me
to emerge from the present collection of papers is
that we must heed Robert Montagne as much as Edward
Evans-Pritchard: tribal reality is more unstable and
volatile in its political forms than one would suppose if one took the segmentary idea in an excessive-
ly simple and literal way. Ephemeral crystallisat-
ions of power are endemic in it; but they are ephemeral, or were so until the modern world intervened.
   This varied range of relationship and variant
forms needs to be fully explored. It is only relatively recently that anthropologists have shifted
from cultural-island tribes to these kinds of marginal or peripheral tribes, whose peripheral but ultimate involvement with a wider economy and culture
and, turbulently, a wider polity strong enough to
threaten them but not strong enough to dominate and
replace them, is of their very essence rather than
something extraneous. The strong modern state tends
to destroy them, though it has not yet done so every-
where.8 I suspect they form a distinct species,
though this is something yet to be established and
discussed. The tribe is the anti-state, politically
unspecialised or very mildly specialised, and state-
resistant; it may also be the fruit of state pressure; it may be the seed of future states; and it
may crystallise mini-states internally. It can be
both agent and enemy and victim of the state. It is
the home of religious ignorance, and the sword-arm
of orthodox revivalism. These forms and relationships are multiple, complex and volatile - but not
devoid of pattern, and the pattern is beginning to
emerge in these studies. The material assembled in
the present symposium constitutes an extremely rich
and varied collection of clues and testimonies,
which when properly digested should do much to help
identify the answers.

NOTES

   1. W.B. Gallie, *Philosophy and the Historical Understanding* (Chatto and Windus, London, 1964).
   2. D.F. Eickelman, *Moroccan Islam* (University of Texas
Press, Austin, 1976).
   3. See his forthcoming comparative study of pastoral
nomadism in general, Cambridge University Press.
   4. R. Jamous, *Honneur et Baraka: Les Structures Sociales
Traditionelles dans le Rif* (Maison des Sciences de l'Homme,
Paris / Cambridge University Press, 1981).

5. R. Montagne, *Les Berberes et le Makhzen dans le Sud du Maroc* (Felix Alcan, Paris, 1930).

6. Cf. S. Andreski, *Military Organization and Society* (Routledge and Kegan Paul, London, 1954).

7. Cf. C. Geertz, H. Geertz & L. Rosen, *Meaning and Order in Moroccan Society* (Cambridge University Press, 1979); C. Geertz, 'In search of North Africa', *New York Review of Books*, 22 Apr. 1971.

8. For instance, tribalism in the Yemen has actually been strengthened, at the expense of the central state, in this century: see forthcoming work by M. Mundy, C. Myntti, S. Weir.

Chapter 16
TRIBE AND STATE: SOME CONCLUDING REMARKS

Andrew Strathern

The chapters in this volume closely reflect two dominant trends in contemporary social anthropology: the
fusion of anthropological and historical interests,
and the stress on studies of process rather than the
building of structural models. Both trends indicate
divergence from an earlier concern with typological
description and classification, best exemplified
perhaps in Fortes and Evans-Pritchard's work on
African political systems. Nowadays authors explicitly locate their descriptions in historical time,
look for interrelations between units as much as for
cohesion within them, and are determined to recognise
the essential complexity of their subject matter by
portraying such varying relations as dialectical,
existing at numerous levels, and determined by combinations of political and economic factors. Instead,
therefore, of separate accounts of 'stateless' and
'state-based' societies, we are presented with a
kaleidoscopic picture of the historical interaction
between tribal and state entities, culminating in the
most recent historical events within Iran and Afghanistan: collapse of a dynasty in one case and the
creation of a new puppet regime in the other. It is a
field ripe for further productive generalisations,
yet the very recognition of complexity makes such a
task considerably harder.

Throughout the conference two things struck me:
one was the ease with which social anthropologists
and historians accepted each other's participation.
It was encouraging to realise that such collaboration
is now a part of 'normal science', and does not have
to be commented on. The other was that despite this
ease of communication, signalled largely by a realistic adoption of the historical approach on the part
of all contributors, it was unclear whether much
theoretical advance was within our grasp. An explicit

focus on mechanisms of transformation might have
yielded at least a set of empirical generalisations
which could then be further refined, especially
since so many of the papers concentrated on Pashtun
society. What we do have is an extremely rich set
of accounts of how tribal populations have opposed
state control, have used state forces in their own
battles, have been absorbed into states, have merged
to form confederacies and quasi-states, have split
these, have toppled dynasties, have given them
crucial support: practically every process logically
imaginable is shown in ethnographic form here. Again,
it is a measure of the overall progress of our subject that so much can be added, and so forcefully,
to Fredrik Barth's early analysis of Swat Pathan
politics; yet it is also interesting that from all
this we do not gain a clear set of models, which
could supersede those of Barth. Barth's account was
most deficient where the contemporary studies are
strong: in analysis of how tribal alliances may
emerge into, or be capped by, state organisation.
Yet the perusal of history does not seem to have led
in a straight line to the creation of models replacing that of the segmentary lineage and the transformations of this effected in Barth's own analysis.
    One of the reasons for this is pin-pointed most
clearly, I believe, by Jon Anderson (chapter 3) when
he notes that

> considerable confusion and ambiguity obtain
> on the ground in 'tribe-and-state' relations
> in Afghanistan ... the more successful khans
> who survive the contradictory pulls of tribal
> and national associations, trade on the contra-
> dictions and flourish in the ambiguities that
> allow them to play more than one game at a
> time.

The same kind of process is alluded to by David
Brooks (chapter 12) when he writes that in some
sense Bakhtiari are their own enemies, for there is
always someone who will collaborate with an outside
power in order to secure the downfall of his rivals,
even if it should also mean some loss of his own
autonomy. Correlatively, there is bound also to be
bitter resistance to the outcome of such manoeuvres.
The terms of the game are set by segmentary competition, and the play is decided by network moves followed by resistance in blocs to the advantages gained
by those who have manipulated the networks. Such a
process probably occurs at numerous structural levels,

and seems to be at work at the level of the state of
Afghanistan itself at present. Of course, colonial
officials, as well as tribal leaders, have been well
aware of these processes for a long time, as Yapp
(chapter 4) and Ahmed (chapter 5) among others demonstrate: they are not an anthropological discovery but
a part of practical politics.

One chapter which does, however, illuminate the
problems to do with transformation, development, and
cyclical processes in this part of the world is that
by Salzman (chapter 8). He shows clearly how ecological factors do influence political structure, if
only in terms of limitations. The same kinds of in-
sight emerge in the sustained historical analyses of
Glatzer and the Tappers (chapters 6, 7 and 14), and
the general question of the relationship between
'nomadism' and 'tribalism' is also posed with ele-
gant force by Ernest Gellner (chapter 15). Brooks,
again, shows how the requirements of nomadic migration have influenced the Bakhtiari to create numerous
networks which run across and beyond formal segmentary structures. It is the combination of small
productive units and large areas of communal resources which produces the apparently contradictory
features of independence and interdependence which
are the hallmark of nomadic tribal populations, including peoples such as the Nuer, who inspired the
original creation of the segmentary model by Evans-
Pritchard. In Salzman's analysis chiefship is created by external political needs and limited by internal ecological circumstances, and it is a matter of
preference whether we regard the resulting structure
as an 'adaptation', a 'dialectic', or a 'contingency'.
What is clear is that there is an economic background
to the creation of states: but the states themselves
are not absolute transformations, but reminiscent
rather of the 'segmentary states' described by anthropologists such as Fallers and Southall who worked
in East Africa. The advantage which scholars who
are working on Middle Eastern materials have, however, is their access to a greater historical depth
of information and also the sheer volatility of political events and processes themselves.

For someone such as myself, who is not an expert on the area, a final interest lies in the potentials for extrapolation and comparison. As I have
earlier remarked, the greater the richness of historical specificity in the accounts with which one is
faced, the harder it is to tell whether an account
of, say, Pakhtun politics will provide analogies to
what is happening in Melanesia, for example, my own

field of study. Historical circumstances are quite different. Melanesia has neither the development of hierarchy nor the intermingling of tribes and states which shows so strongly in Afghanistan and Iran. Yet the same analytical problems of transformation and differentiation of systems from egalitarian bases certainly are set in Melanesia. It is noticeable that from time to time authors here have specified conditions under which 'big-man' politics become dominant: for the khans certainly are big-men, albeit with a hereditary position and depending on a stratification of society at large into nobles and commoners. They note also that big-manship is an open-ended continuum; it is almost by definition a 'transitional type' of leadership which can issue in more than one direction depending on historical factors. Here, then, would be another sphere for comparison and generalisation, analogous to that attempted much earlier by Sahlins for Melanesia in relation to Polynesia. One factor of great, if crude, importance is the technology of destruction, alluded to astutely in another context by Hager at the end of his powerfully argued chapter (2). Guns make war more deadly than arrows, as Melanesians found to their cost when they opposed colonial penetration. It has always seemed to me that the great urgency and emphasis on mustering forces in the Pathan system as described by Barth had to do not only with the intense material competition for land and its immaterial counterpart of prestige, but also with the physical dangers of warfare once begun. In Melanesia, arrows are sometimes shot deliberately to miss, or for fun. Guns, I think, lend themselves less to that kind of subtlety.

The concept of tribal dissidence interested me also from another viewpoint. In Melanesia numerous secessionist movements have arisen at or around the times of Independence from former colonial powers, either mirroring earlier opposition to colonialism or as an artefact of new struggles for power (or reflecting both of these). Such movements are the clear equivalent of the dissenting 'tribe', and although they usually have an overtly local or regional basis their ideology may be very similar to that of the tribes discussed in this book. Harder to place in context, however, is the phenomenon of clear violence between groups which are already constituted as descent groups, such as those of the New Guinea Highlanders, among whom violence over political and economic issues has been quite marked since just before self-government came in 1973. Here, the

colonial period was remarkably short, lasting no
more than forty years or slightly more than a single
generation, so that there is an obvious continuity
with pre-colonial patterns of conflict. Yet there
is a faint articulation of conflict with the emerging national state as well, in that the New Guinea
Highlanders have not readily given up the sanction
of force as an ultimate means of controlling one
another. Leaders whom I know well have sometimes
wondered why their government will not let them be,
to fight out an issue on their own, thus asserting
their sovereignty to do so. Hence fighting itself
comes to be a statement of independence within the
new Independent State. The condition for the transformation of such a pattern into one more directly
like that now being enacted in Afghanistan would
clearly be the use by the national government of
some outside force to control their Highlands populations.

In conclusion, then, it does seem to me that
the great richness of materials and the diversity of
insights displayed in these essays both lend themselves potentially to further comparisons and
reflections; but that to achieve this further step
we need to combine the background use of the segmentary model, as Ernest Gellner has argued, with the
development of further models of process which are
not limited either to tribal or to state politics
but can apply to either, and to their interconnect-
ions. This volume, therefore, points the way to
such a possibility.

INDEX

Index

Index

457

Index